Purchasing Power Parities and the Real Size of World Economies

Purchasing Power Parities and the Real Size of World Economies

A COMPREHENSIVE REPORT OF
THE 2011 INTERNATIONAL
COMPARISON PROGRAM

WORLD BANK GROUP

ISBN (paper): 978-1-4648-0329-1
ISBN (electronic): 978-1-4648-0330-7
DOI: 10.1596/978-1-4648-0329-1

Cover design: Jomo Tariku/World Bank Group.

Library of Congress Cataloging-in-Publication Data has been requested.

Contents

Boxes

Figures

Tables

Foreword

The International Comparison Program (ICP) is a worldwide statistical initiative—the largest in geographical scope, in implementation time frame, and in institutional partnership. It estimates purchasing power parities (PPPs) for use as currency converters to compare the size and price levels of economies around the world. The previous round of the program, for reference year 2005, covered 146 economies. The 2011 ICP round covered 199 economies from eight regions, seven of them geographical: Africa, Asia and the Pacific, Commonwealth of Independent States, Latin America, the Caribbean, Western Asia, and the Pacific Islands. The eighth region comprised the economies participating in the regular PPP program managed by the Statistical Office of the European Communities (Eurostat) and the Organisation for Economic Co-operation and Development (OECD).

On behalf of the ICP Executive Board and the World Bank, we would like to thank all those who contributed to the success of the 2011 ICP program: the national coordinating agencies that collected the necessary data in each economy; the regional coordinating agencies that supported country activities, compiled the results, and produced regional estimates—the African Development Bank, Asian Development Bank, Interstate Statistical Committee of the Commonwealth of Independent States, United Nations Economic Commission for Latin America and the Caribbean, United Nations Economic and Social Commission for Western Asia, Australian Bureau of Statistics, OECD, and Eurostat; and the ICP Global Office, which coordinated and managed the work at the global level. The office is hosted by the Development Data Group at the World Bank Group.

Although the responsibility for oversight rested with the ICP Executive Board established under the overall auspices of the United Nations Statistical Commission, the program would not have been such a success without the invaluable theoretical, conceptual, and methodological advice of the ICP Technical Advisory Group of renowned experts.

Thanks to the relentless efforts of all those participating in this federated governance structure, the work of ICP 2011 was carried out according to a schedule that, by and large, has remained unchanged since the inception of the round in the fourth quarter of 2009—an achievement in itself in view of the complexity of such an undertaking. All this testifies to the effectiveness of the system that was rolled out to manage the program and implement related statistical operations. Indeed, an economy cannot by itself produce a PPP with other economies. Likewise, a region cannot by itself generate interregional PPPs with other regions. Therefore, there is no other statistical program that requires as much cooperation and trust across economies and between regions as the ICP.

Methodological improvements covering four major areas were introduced in the 2011 round of the ICP, leveraging the very strong base provided by ICP 2005. First, the survey frameworks were further aligned with the ICP conceptual framework to ensure that related data collection would yield the most reliable average prices possible, and instruments for price surveys were enhanced accordingly. Second, an ICP national accounts framework was developed to ensure that expenditure values were compiled in compliance with the System of National Accounts, while also ensuring consistency with the prices collected and generating the relevant metadata documentation. Third, the Ring approach used in 2005 to link the regions and the Eurostat-OECD PPPs to the global results was changed to a global core list approach in which all participating economies were asked to include a common set of items in the regional list of products they surveyed. Fourth, more broadly, a research agenda was established and then implemented by the Technical Advisory Group and other experts to advise the Global Office on the price survey, expenditure compilation, data validation, and computation processes to be applied at the country, regional, and global levels.

In other developments, all major knowledge items related to the most recent ICP rounds were consolidated in a book entitled *Measuring the Real Size of the World Economy: The Framework, Methodology, and Results of the International Comparison Program (ICP)* (World Bank 2013). The items are also available on the ICP website (http://icp.worldbank.org), which was revamped to better serve as a repository of ICP knowledge resources and data. Meanwhile, a comprehensive ICP quality assurance framework was developed to ensure that major ICP principles were being met at the country, regional, and global levels. The aim of the framework was to introduce rigor, structure, and common criteria for assessment of the quality of the input data and the results produced. As part of the quality and transparency objective, at the global level parallel and independent processes were established for the validation of input data, computation of PPPs, and review of the final results. Finally, the limitations of the data and methods were identified,

and they are explicitly described in this report. Because of the many important changes in economic and price structures since 2005 and a number of methodological improvements, users of the data are urged to be cautious when comparing the ICP 2011 results with those for ICP 2005.

We believe the ICP 2011 results represent the most comprehensive price data and gross domestic product (GDP) expenditure values, using the best methods that have ever been developed. We are also very pleased to see that ICP-related activities have played a fruitful role in the regions, serving as capacity-building platforms in the areas of prices and national accounts statistics.

We trust that users of the ICP 2011 results will find this report useful and that those results will form a crucial information base for research in comparative analysis and policy making. We hope that in the future, more regular data collection and compilation will support a more frequent PPP exercise at the global level.

Once again, we wish to express our sincere thanks to all those involved in this very gratifying undertaking.

Martine Durand
OECD Chief Statistician
Chair, ICP Executive Board

Haishan Fu
Director
Development Data Group, World Bank

Acknowledgments

The International Comparison Program (ICP) is the largest worldwide statistical operation. The 2011 round of the ICP was a complex exercise, conceptually and organizationally, and the Global Office is pleased that, thanks to the strong engagement of the 199 participating economies in the entire process, we succeeded in bringing it to fruition.

The 2011 ICP round saw changes on several fronts by leveraging the successful implementation of the 2005 round: the scope of the exercise was broadened; quality assessment processes were streamlined; and statistical capacity-building activities were carried out with a specific focus on price statistics and implementation of the System of National Accounts. In addition, several improvements were introduced: preparation and implementation of an ICP data quality assurance framework; development of a national accounts framework for the ICP that was implemented using specifically defined guidelines for activities; development of a global core list of goods and services that were priced by all the participating economies in addition to their regional lists; introduction of a new method for construction and civil engineering; and improvements in the approach to computing global purchasing power parities (PPPs).

All these achievements were made possible by the financial support of donors who contributed to specifically established trust funds. Special thanks go to the United Kingdom's Department for International Development (DFID), Australian Agency for International Development (Aus-AID), International Monetary Fund (IMF), Islamic Development Bank, Norway's Ministry of Foreign Affairs, and the World Bank.

The ICP Global Office is hosted by the World Bank's Development Data Group (DECDG), whose directors during this ICP round were Shaida Badiee and then Haishan Fu and whose managers were Misha Belkindas and then Grant James Cameron. The World Bank equipped the Global Office with all the necessary workplace resources and provided support for various organs of the program's governance structure.

As the decision-making and strategic body of ICP governance, the ICP 2011 Executive Board provided leadership and ensured strict adherence to the program's objectives and strategic lines. Its successive chairs are hereby thanked for their leadership: Oystein Olsen, Enrico Giovannini, and Martine Durand. Thanks are also extended to the institutions represented on the board: African Development Bank, Asian Development Bank, Australian Bureau of Statistics, Brazilian Institute of Geography and Statistics, China's National Bureau of Statistics, Interstate Statistical Committee of the Commonwealth of Independent States, Eurostat, Statistics Department of the IMF, India's Ministry of Statistics and Programme Implementation, France's National Institute for Statistics and Economic Studies, Italy's National Institute for Statistics, Mexico's National Institute for Statistics and Geography, Organisation for Economic Co-operation and Development (OECD), Russian Federation Federal State Statistics Service, Saudi Arabia Central Department of Statistics and Information, Senegal National Agency for Statistics and Demography, Statistics Canada, Statistics Norway, Statistics South Africa, Uganda Bureau of Statistics, United Nations Economic Commission for Latin America and the Caribbean, United Nations Economic and Social Commission for Western Asia, United Nations Statistics Division, U.S. Office of Management and Budget, and the World Bank's Development Data Group.

The Technical Advisory Group deserves special acknowledgment. Under the chairmanship of Erwin Diewert and then the co-chairmanship of Paul McCarthy and Frederic Vogel, technical issues linked to the conceptual integrity and methodological adequacy of the program were addressed by the group's experts: Luigi Biggeri, Angus Deaton, Yuri Dikhanov, Qiu Dong, Louis Marc Ducharme, Alan Heston, Robert Hill, Youri Ivanov, Francette Koechlin, Paulus Konijn, Vasily Kouznetsov, Tom Andersen Langer, Julian May, Prasada Rao, Sergey Sergeev, Mick Silver, Jim Thomas, Marcel Timmer, and Kim Zieschang. The Technical Advisory Group was assisted by various experts on some topics, including Derek Blades, Richard Dibley, Jim Meikle, and David Roberts.

The results of ICP 2011 were calculated by the group of experts forming the PPP Computation Task Force: Bettina Aten, Yuri Dikhanov, Alan Heston, Robert Hill, Francette Koechlin, Paulus Konijn, and Sergey Sergeev. The results underwent the quality review of the experts forming the Results Review Group: Angus Deaton, Erwin Diewert, Alan Heston, Paul McCarthy, Prasada Rao, and Frederic Vogel.

Our achievement was made possible by the relentless work of the regional coordinators: Oliver Chinganya (Africa), Chellam Palanyandy (Asia and the Pacific), Andrey Kosarev (Commonwealth of Independent States), David Roberts and Derek Blades (Georgia-Armenia bilateral), Giovanni Savio (Latin America and the Caribbean), Athol Maritz (Pacific Islands), and Majed Skaini (Western Asia), as well as the great cooperation of Francette Koechlin and Paulus Konijn, who were leading the Eurostat-OECD PPP program. This testifies to the effective partnership between the Global Office and the regional agencies that assumed coordination of the ICP in their various regions: African Development Bank, Asian Development Bank, Australian Bureau of Statistics, Interstate Statistical Committee of the Commonwealth of Independent States, United Nations Economic Commission for Latin America and the Caribbean, and United Nations Economic and Social Commission for Western Asia, as well as Eurostat and OECD.

Although the Global Office and the regional coordinators play a crucial role in implementing the ICP, the cornerstone of the program is the national coordinating agencies, which are responsible for the bulk of ICP activities, from price data collection to the compilation of the national accounts expenditure data. The 2011 participating economies demonstrated complete commitment and dedication to the ICP. We truly owe them utmost respect and appreciation for the amazing job they did in carrying out the rigorous ICP activities over the last few years.

The Global Office also recognizes the technical advice provided by various experts, including the Academy for Educational Development, Roger Akers, Eric Peter Bruggeman, Richard Dibley, Gylliane Gervais, Simon Humphries, Robert Inklaar, Albert Keidel, Troy Michael Martin, Joseph McCormack, Jim Meikle, William Vigil Oliver, Ehraz Refayet, Gary Reid, Michael Scholz, Ruben Suarez, Michael Thomas, and Dennis Trewin. Nicole El-Hajj, Rouba Romanos, and Rachel Wilkins provided the ICP with valuable translation services. The consulting firms TATA and Prognoz helped to develop the software tools that supported implementation of the program.

This report was drafted by the Global Office and David Roberts with input from Paul McCarthy, Prasada Rao, and Frederic Vogel. It was edited by Sabra Bissette Ledent. The cover was designed by Jomo Tariku.

The Global Office team responsible for the day-to-day work was Morgan Brannon, Yuri Dikhanov, Biokou Mathieu Djayeola, Federico Escaler, Christelle Signo Kouame, Marko Olavi Rissanen, Virginia Romand, and Mizuki Yamanaka. Recognition for their efforts is also given to former Global Office members Miglena Abels, Olga Akcadag, Claude Djekadom Walendom, Imededdine Jerbi, Min Ji Lee, Kyung Sam Min, Inyoung Song, Seong Heon Song, and Estela Zamora. Several colleagues from other DECDG units provided valuable support to the Global Office: Awatif H. Abuzeid, Azita Amjadi, Colleen Burke, Lisa Burke, Ying Chi, Shelley Fu, Omar Hadi, Hulda Hunter, Elysee Kiti, Vilas Mandlekar, Maurice Nsabimana, Parastoo Oloumi, Beatriz Prieto-Oramas, William Prince, and Premi Rathan Raj. I was privileged to lead the Global Office with the outstanding collaboration of Nada Hamadeh, the current ICP team leader, who acted as de facto deputy global manager.

As a team, we are grateful to all the dedicated experts and international and regional institutions that contributed their knowledge, expertise, time, and resources to this daunting effort. We particularly recognize the major role played by the national implementing agencies in all the 199 participating economies. We all share the credit for the production of this unique public good.

Michel Mouyelo-Katoula
ICP 2011 Global Manager

Abbreviations

AIC	actual individual consumption
CAR	country aggregation with redistribution (procedure)
CEP	consumption expenditure of the population
CIS	Commonwealth of Independent States
COFOG	Classification of the Function of Government
COICOP	Classification of Individual Consumption according to Purpose
COMECON	Council for Mutual Economic Assistance
CPD	country product dummy (method)
CPD-W	country product dummy-weighted (method)
CPRD	country product representative dummy (method)
Eurostat	Statistical Office of the European Union
FISIM	financial intermediation services indirectly measured
f.o.b.	free on board
GDP	gross domestic product
GEKS	Gini-Èltetö-Köves-Szulc (method)
GNI	gross national income
ICP	International Comparison Program (Project prior to 1989)
ILO	International Labour Organization
IMF	International Monetary Fund
MORES	Model Report on Expenditure Statistics
NBS	National Bureau of Statistics (China)
NCA	national coordinating agency
n.e.c.	not elsewhere classified
NPISH	nonprofit institution serving households
OECD	Organisation for Economic Co-operation and Development
PISA	Programme for International Student Assessment
PLI	price level index
PPP	purchasing power parity
RCA	regional coordinating agency
SAR	special administrative region
SNA	System of National Accounts
SPD	structured product description
TAG	Technical Advisory Group (ICP)
TFP	total factor productivity
UN	United Nations
UNESCO	United Nations Educational, Scientific, and Cultural Organization

UNSC	United Nations Statistical Commission
UNSD	United Nations Statistics Division
UNSO	United Nations Statistics Office
VAT	value added tax
XR	exchange rate

All dollar amounts are U.S. dollars unless otherwise indicated.

Overview

The International Comparison Program (ICP) is a large and highly complex worldwide statistical program conducted under the charter of the United Nations Statistical Commission (UNSC). The ICP is designed to provide globally comparable economic aggregates in national accounts that can be used by individual researchers, analysts, and policy makers at the national and international levels and by international organizations such as the European Union, International Monetary Fund, Organisation for Economic Co-operation and Development (OECD), United Nations, and World Bank. Over its lifetime, the ICP has become the principal source of data on the purchasing power parities (PPPs) of currencies, measures of real per capita income, and measures of real gross domestic product (GDP) and its main components from the expenditure side, including private consumption, government expenditures, and gross fixed capital formation. Indeed, since its inception in 1970, successive rounds of the ICP have produced valuable data for international economic analyses of economic growth and the catch-up and convergence of incomes among nations; productivity levels and trends; analyses of systematic patterns in national price levels and trends; construction of the Human Development Index by the United Nations; measures of

regional and global inequality in incomes and consumption; and estimates of the incidence of absolute poverty using World Bank–developed yardsticks such as the US$1 a day and $2 a day poverty lines.[1]

ICP 2011, the latest round of the ICP, is the eighth phase of the program. The first phase in 1970 saw very limited program coverage, only 10 economies. By contrast, the 2011 round has achieved, for the first time, truly global coverage by including 199 economies from all regions of the world. The seven geographic regions covered by ICP 2011 were Africa, Asia and the Pacific, Commonwealth of Independent States (CIS), Latin America, the Caribbean, Western Asia, and the Pacific Islands. The eighth region comprised the economies that were participating in the PPP program run by Eurostat, the statistical arm of the European Union, and the OECD. This comprehensive report on ICP 2011 provides readers with details of the conceptual framework and the methodology employed by the ICP, along with detailed results of the 2011 round and a brief analysis of those results. This overview highlights the distinguishing features of ICP 2011 that make it a significant improvement over ICP 2005.

---

[1] All dollar amounts in this report are U.S. dollars unless otherwise indicated.

GOVERNANCE OF ICP 2011

The governance structure of ICP 2011 was designed to ensure the delivery of accurate, reliable, and timely estimates of the PPPs of currencies and real GDP and its components. At the apex of the structure was the *UNSC,* which provided overall supervision, ensuring that the ICP strictly adhered to accepted guiding principles for the production of official statistics and international standards for national accounts data. At the next level, the *Executive Board,* composed of internationally renowned chief statisticians, provided the ICP with leadership and played an important role in setting the strategic direction and ensuring progress in and attainment of the various milestones set for the program.

The governance and implementation of ICP 2011 were characterized by a strong bottom-up approach in which the participating economies were encouraged to actively participate in the program and assume ownership of the data and the final results. At the country level, the *national coordinating agencies* and the *national coordinators* assumed responsibility for the collection and validation of the information requested for analysis and the transmittal of that information to the respective *regional coordinating agencies*. The activities of the economies in any given region were coordinated by the regional coordinating agencies, and the *regional coordinators* were responsible for the development of product lists, coordination of data collection, and validation within the region. The regional coordinating agencies were responsible for compiling and disseminating the PPPs and real expenditures for the respective regions. Those agencies for the seven ICP 2011 regions were the African Development Bank, Asian Development Bank, Interstate Statistical Committee of the Commonwealth of Independent States, United Nations Economic Commission for Latin America and the Caribbean, United Nations Economic and Social Commission for Western Asia, and Australian Bureau of Statistics, which assumed responsibility for the Pacific Islands economies. The activities of the eighth region were organized by Eurostat and the OECD.

The overall coordination of ICP 2011 at the global level was entrusted to the *Global Office,* hosted by the World Bank. The Global Office was responsible for implementing the work program of the ICP. The preparation of regular reports for the Executive Board and the UNSC was also entrusted to the Global Office. It was responsible for compiling the global core list of products for household consumption, housing, government compensation, machinery and equipment, and construction. The Global Office was also responsible for linking regional comparisons in order to provide global comparisons of PPPs and real incomes, preparing and disseminating the global results, and publishing the ICP 2011 reports.

The Global Office was assisted by the *Technical Advisory Group, PPP Computation Task Force, Validation Expert Group,* and *Results Review Group*. Significantly, a major innovation of ICP 2011 was introduction of the PPP Computation Task Force. The main purpose of the task force was to ensure the accuracy of the ICP results and to guarantee their reproducibility. The task force was composed of four computational experts, each of whom calculated the global results, using his or her preferred software, to ensure convergence of the results in full accordance with the recommendations of the Technical Advisory Group.

REGIONAL AND COUNTRY COVERAGE

ICP 2011 achieved the first truly global coverage in the history of the ICP. Building on the impressive participation of 146 economies in ICP 2005, the 2011 round covered 199 economies, representing more than 90 percent of the world's economies. The 199 economies account for roughly 97 percent of the world's population and some 99 percent of the world nominal GDP (in U.S. dollars using exchange rates). Table O.1 shows the distribution of the economies covered, by region.

In addition to this impressive coverage, a number of features distinguish this ICP round from the previous rounds:

- For the first time in the history of the ICP, China fully participated in ICP 2011, following all the prescribed procedures and methods. In ICP 2005, China provided price data

Table 0.1 Number of Participating Economies, by ICP Region, ICP 2011

Africa	50
Asia and the Pacific	23
Commonwealth of Independent States	9
Eurostat-OECD	47
Latin America	17
Caribbean	22
Western Asia	12
Pacific Islands	21
Singletons[a]	2
Total (less four dual participants[b])	199

Source: ICP, http://icp.worldbank.org/.
a. Georgia and the Islamic Republic of Iran.
b. The Arab Republic of Egypt, Fiji, the Russian Federation, and Sudan.

collected only from 11 cities or provinces. By contrast, for ICP 2011 China conducted nationwide surveys covering both rural and urban outlets in all provinces of the country.

- India and Indonesia, the two other populous economies in the Asia and the Pacific region, also achieved coverage of both rural and urban areas in their collection of prices for consumption goods and services.

- The Latin America region consisted of 17 economies in ICP 2011 in contrast to only 10 economies in ICP 2005.

- The Caribbean region with its participation of 22 economies is a special feature of ICP 2011.

- Another achievement of ICP 2011 is its inclusion of 21 Pacific Island economies, even though their participation was limited to individual household consumption. The participation of these island economies was facilitated by the coordination and support of the Australian Bureau of Statistics. Participation in the ICP has helped these island economies improve the coverage and reliability of their price statistics and national accounts. Although this aspect of statistical capacity building is amply demonstrated by the benefits received by the Pacific Island economies, their limited participation in ICP 2011 ruled out the inclusion of their results in the main tables in this report.

Because of the global coverage of ICP 2011, there was little need for the extrapolation of PPPs and real incomes for nonparticipating economies, as undertaken in the earlier ICP rounds. However, the extrapolated results for the few nonparticipating economies are presented in this report.

METHODOLOGY AND INNOVATIONS

The ICP is a complex international statistical project, and its methodology has evolved over several decades. Challenging measurement and index number problems have been encountered in implementation of the ICP. The ICP 2005 methodological approach represented a major step forward from the less satisfactory round in 1993. Along with improved governance, considerable progress was made in establishing procedures for price surveys; data editing and validation; and methods for dealing with comparison-resistant sectors such as housing, the government expenditure on health and education, machinery and equipment, and construction. In ICP 2005, the statistical methodology for linking was based on data collected for a set of Ring countries and on the estimation of linking factors to link regional comparisons in order to yield global comparisons.

Learning from the invaluable experience gained through implementation of ICP 2005, the Technical Advisory Group recommended improved procedures in a number of areas for ICP 2011. As a result of these improvements and methodological innovations, ICP 2011 was significantly better than its 2005 predecessor. A few of these methodological innovations follow:

- *Coverage of rural and urban outlets.* Because of the importance of achieving national coverage for price surveys, particular care was taken by the large economies to ensure adequate coverage of rural and urban outlets when collecting the prices of individual household consumption items. Efforts were made to reduce urban bias, thereby leading to reliable national annual average prices for use in the computation of PPPs both at the basic heading level and for higher-level aggregates.

- *National accounts data.* Recognizing the importance of obtaining reliable national accounts data, the regional coordinating agencies conducted special workshops focusing on national accounts statistics and their validation. The Global Office provided the participating economies with manuals for the collection and validation of national accounts data. As a result, the weights used in aggregating price data in ICP 2011 were more reliable than in the earlier rounds.

- *Use of importance indicators.* In view of the competing requirements of *comparability* and *representativity* in the prices of goods and services in the participating economies, the Technical Advisory Group recommended use of an importance indicator and 3:1 weights for products considered important in the estimation of PPPs at the basic heading level.

- *Data editing and validation.* In addition to the standard methods of validation based on the Quaranta and Dikhanov tables, a new method of validation was developed and implemented. This method compares observed price movements in the participating economies, measured by domestic consumer price indexes and deflators, with a measure of price change over the period 2005 to 2011 implicit in the ICP price data provided by the participating economies over these two benchmarks. This method was used in the Asia and the Pacific region in identifying sources of major errors and deviations.

- *Construction.* The basket of construction components (BOCC) method used in ICP 2005 was replaced by a simple approach based on the prices of basic construction materials, different types of labor, and the hire of machinery and equipment. The new approach eliminated the requirement to provide the various types of weights needed in implementation of the BOCC. Instead, the new method relied on the cost shares of the materials, labor, and equipment that are needed for different types of construction and that were readily available from the participating economies.

- *Productivity adjustment for government compensation.* Because of the significant disparities in wages and salaries received for specific occupational categories across economies in a given region, and across regions, ICP 2011 implemented productivity adjustments for all of the participating economies in linking the regions (in ICP 2005 only three regions—Africa, Asia and the Pacific, and Western Asia—implemented productivity adjustments). The resulting parities for government compensation were thus more reliable than those used in ICP 2005.

- *Procedures for global linking.* The ex post assessment of ICP 2005 revealed several weaknesses in the linking procedures. The reliance on a set of 18 Ring countries for linking meant that the quality of the linking factors and global results critically depended on the quality of the price data supplied by these Ring countries. In addition, the product list used in the 2005 ICP Ring comparisons was found to contain numerous items that were not representative in a number of regions, including Africa and Asia and the Pacific. Finally, the methodology for linking at the higher levels of aggregation was found to be deficient in that it was not invariant to the choice of the reference or numéraire country. Consequently, major innovations were introduced to the linking procedures for ICP 2011:

  - The practice of using a small set of selected Ring countries was discontinued and replaced by the new approach in which the price data from all the economies of all the regions were used in the linking procedure. This approach resulted in robust estimates of linking factors that were minimally affected by deficient data from some of the participating economies.

  - The linking was based on price data collected for a global core list (GCL) of products. The Global Office developed a GCL for household consumption, housing, government compensation, machinery and equipment, and construction. The GCL for household consumption included 618 products representative of consumption in all ICP regions. The participating economies integrated the GCL products into their regional product lists—for example, 610 GCL items were added to the regional list in Africa, 412 in Asia and the Pacific, 394 in Eurostat-OECD, 489 in Latin America and the Caribbean, and 606 in Western Asia. The extent of this integration resulted in more reliable linking factors.

- The weighted country product dummy method was used on prices collected for all global core list items weighted by their importance to provide linking factors at the basic heading level.

- The aggregation at the GDP level and other aggregates such as household consumption, government expenditure, and gross fixed capital formation were based on the country aggregation with redistribution (CAR)–volume procedure.

- As for 2005 ICP, fixity of the regional-level relativities was ensured by the new methodology implemented for linking regions.

ICP 2011 VERSUS ICP 2005

The methodology for ICP 2011 and its implementation by regions and the Global Office marked a significant improvement over ICP 2005. Some of the deficiencies in the methodology used in ICP 2005, including the Ring country approach for linking, were addressed by incorporating new methods designed to provide more reliable and robust estimates of PPPs and real GDP and its components. Some of the major innovations, just listed and discussed in more detail, were (1) the use of a global core list of products for linking at the basic heading level; (2) the use of the CAR-volume method for linking above the basic heading level; (3) increased attention to the validation of national accounts data; (4) new procedures for data validation and editing; (5) improved coverage of price surveys in large economies, including China, India, and Indonesia; (6) implementation of productivity adjustments for all the participating economies instead of a subset of economies, as was the case in 2005; (7) a simplified approach to construction; and (8) the establishment of a PPP Computation Task Force to ensure the accuracy and replicability of the ICP results irrespective of

the software used in the computations. In view of these methodological improvements and innovations, the ICP 2011 results can be considered more reliable than those for ICP 2005, especially when taking into account the inconsistencies between the ICP 2011 benchmark results and extrapolations from ICP 2005. Thus it is recommended that greater reliance be placed on the ICP 2011 results.

THE ICP 2011 RESULTS: AN OVERVIEW

This report presents results from ICP 2011 for the 199 participating economies (the Pacific Islands economies, however, covered only individual household consumption). The results presented include estimates of the purchasing power parities of currencies, real expenditures derived using PPPs, nominal expenditures based on exchange rates, and price levels expressed relative to the world average. These results are available for GDP and its 25 subaggregates. Selected highlights from these results follow.

Size of the world economy. In 2011 the size of the world economy, as measured by world GDP, covered by the 177 participating economies,[2] was $90,647 billion in PPP terms. Measured by exchange rates, the size was $70,295 billion. In the ICP 2005 final report, world GDP was reported to be $54,976 billion in PPP terms and $44,309 billion in exchange rate terms.

Distribution of world GDP. In 2011, shares of world GDP in PPP terms accruing to the high-income economies were 50.3 percent (67.3 percent in exchange rate terms); middle-income economies, 48.2 percent (32.0 percent); and low-income economies, 1.5 percent (0.7 percent). The poorest 83.2 percent of the population received 49.7 percent of world real GDP. According to the results from ICP 2005, the poorest 83.6 percent of the global population received only 39.4 percent of world GDP in real terms. The regional shares of world GDP were 53.2 percent, Eurostat-OECD; 30 percent, Asia and the Pacific; 5.5 percent, Latin America;

---

[2] Because of comparability issues, world total GDP does not include two participating economies—Cuba and Bonaire—or the Pacific Islands.

4.8 percent, CIS; 4.5 percent, Africa and Western Asia; and 0.1 percent, the Caribbean.

Ranking of economies by size. ICP 2011 resulted in some significant changes in the rankings of economies determined by their share of world GDP. The United States retained top ranking with 17.1 percent of world GDP, followed by China with 14.9 percent and India with 6.4 percent. Of particular note was the performance of China with its GDP in 2011 of 86.9 percent of U.S. GDP compared with only 43.1 percent in 2005. The ranking of India rose from fifth in 2005 to third in 2011, and Indonesia became one of the top 10 world economies. In 2011 the top 12 economies accounted for two-thirds of world GDP in real terms.

Ranking of economies by real per capita GDP. For the purpose of assessing standards of living, it is more appropriate to rank economies by real per capita GDP. In 2011 Qatar and Macao SAR, China, were the highest-ranked economies, with $146,521 and $115,441 in real per capita GDP, respectively. They were followed by Luxembourg, Kuwait, Brunei Darussalam, Singapore, the United Arab Emirates, Bermuda, and Switzerland. The United States ranked 12th. China, Indonesia, and India ranked 99th, 107th, and 127th, respectively. The poorest economy was Liberia with $535, followed by the Comoros with $610 and the Democratic Republic of Congo with $655. Burundi, Niger, the Central African Republic, Mozambique, Malawi, Ethiopia, and Guinea were in the bottom 10 ranked economies.

Ranking of economies by actual individual consumption (AIC). In assessing the welfare of people in different economies, a more informative measure is real per capita actual individual consumption, which is the sum of individual consumption by households and individual consumption by government. A slightly different picture emerges when real per capita AIC is used in ranking economies. In 2011, Bermuda, the United States, and the Cayman Islands were the top-ranked economies with real per capita AIC of $37,924, $37,390, and $34,020, respectively. Qatar, which was top-ranked according to real per capita GDP, was now ranked 35th according to real per capita AIC. Indonesia, with a ranking of 118th, was placed above China and India, which ranked 121st and 134th,

respectively. The Democratic Republic of Congo, Liberia, and the Comoros were the lowest-ranked economies, according to real actual individual consumption.

Price level index. The price level index (PLI) is the ratio of the PPP of a currency in a given economy and the corresponding exchange rates. The PLI is usually expressed relative to the world average price level set at 100. According to ICP 2011, economies with the highest price level index for GDP were Switzerland, Norway, Bermuda, Australia, and Denmark, with indexes ranging from 210 to 185. The United States was ranked 25th in the world, according to PLI. Low-income economies usually had PLIs below 100. Twenty-three economies had PLIs of 50 or below, and the Arab Republic of Egypt, Pakistan, Myanmar, Ethiopia and the Lao People's Democratic Republic were identified as the least expensive economies.

Intereconomy inequality in incomes. It is possible to obtain a measure of intereconomy inequality using real per capita GDP estimates from ICP 2011. The population-weighted Gini measure of intereconomy inequality in real per capita income in PPP terms was 0.49, which indicated a sharp fall from the level of 0.57 for ICP 2005. A similar sharp decline from 0.71 to 0.64 in the Gini measure of inequality was observed when exchange rate–converted or nominal per capita incomes were used. Such a sharp fall in inequality would have significant implications for the estimates of poverty incidence in the world. Similar trends in intereconomy inequality were also evident when per capita household consumption or per capita actual individual consumption was used.

ORGANIZATION OF THIS REPORT

This final report on ICP 2011 contains a wealth of information on the compilation of PPPs, and it presents detailed results for major economic aggregates of GDP, including individual consumption, government expenditure, and investment. The report is divided into four chapters. Chapter 1 provides a general background of the ICP, including the concept and uses of PPPs. Chapter 2 is the core of the report, presenting and analyzing the 2011 results on PPPs, real expenditures, and price levels for GDP and its subaggregates. The salient features of the results of the 2011 round are discussed, and the PPPs from 2011 are compared and contrasted with the PPP extrapolations from ICP 2005. Chapters 3 and 4 focus on the methodology that underpinned ICP 2011. Chapter 3 describes the conceptual framework and the survey and data editing methods used. Chapter 4 provides details on the special approaches developed for household consumption as well as for the comparison-resistant aggregates: housing, government compensation, machinery and equipment, and construction. The methodology used in linking regional comparisons in 2011 ICP is also described. The appendixes provide additional information on the history and governance of the ICP (appendixes A and B); the Eurostat–OECD comparison (appendix C); the expenditure classification used in the ICP (appendix D); the estimation and compilation of national accounts (appendix E); the changes in methodology between ICP 2005 and ICP 2011 (appendix F); reference PPPs (appendix G); the updated set of 2005 results incorporating all the data revisions that have taken place since publication of the ICP 2005 report in 2008 (appendix H); comparison of the ICP 2011 results with the 2011 results extrapolated from ICP 2005 (appendix I); the ICP data access and archiving policy (appendix J); and the ICP revision policy (appendix K). The appendixes are followed by an extensive glossary.

Chapter 1

Background

The International Comparison Program (ICP) was established in the late 1960s on the recommendation of the United Nations Statistical Commission (UNSC). It began as a research project carried out jointly by the United Nations Statistical Office (UNSO) and the University of Pennsylvania. Comparisons were carried out in 1970 for 10 economies, in 1973 for 16 economies, and in 1975 for 34 economies. After the 1975 comparison, the ICP shifted from being a research project to being a regular operational part of the UNSO work program. It was also regionalized; comparisons were organized by region and then combined to obtain a global comparison. Comparisons were carried out in 1980 for 60 economies, in 1985 for 64 economies, and in 1993 for 83 economies.

The 1993 regional comparisons could not be combined to produce a global comparison. In response, the UNSC commissioned a thorough review of the ICP before further comparisons were attempted. Subsequently, the UNSC asked the World Bank to draw up an action plan that would address the issues raised by the review. This request resulted in the establishment of the ICP Global Office within the Bank to coordinate and combine the regional comparisons and the formation of a multi-tiered governance structure headed by the UNSC to oversee and assist the Global Office. The first global comparison made under the new arrangements was ICP 2005 involving 146 economies. The second was

ICP 2011 in which 199 economies participated. The results of the 2011 comparison are presented in this report. A history of the ICP appears in appendix A and a description of the governance structure of ICP 2011 in appendix B.

Since its beginning, the purpose of the ICP has been to compare the gross domestic products (GDPs) of economies with a view toward determining their relative size, productivity, and material well-being. More specifically, the ICP's objective is to compile on a timely and regular basis internationally comparable price and volume measures with which to compare the price and real expenditure levels of GDP and its component expenditures across participating economies. The GDPs and their component expenditures of the economies are valued at national price levels and expressed in national currencies. But to be compared, they must be valued at a common price level and expressed in a common currency. The ICP uses purchasing power parities (PPPs) to effect this double conversion. PPPs are price indexes that serve as spatial price deflators. They make it possible to compare the GDPs and component expenditures of economies in real terms by removing the price level differences between them. This approach closely parallels that for GDP comparisons over time for a single economy where it is necessary to remove the price changes between the periods being compared in order to assess the change in underlying volumes.

To calculate PPPs for its comparisons, the ICP holds worldwide surveys at regular intervals—currently every six years—to collect comparable price and expenditure data for the whole range of final goods and services that make up the final expenditure on GDP: consumer goods and services, government services, and capital goods. The surveys are organized by region and are coordinated by an agency located in the region. The intention is to produce regional comparisons that can be combined in a single global comparison for a given reference year. The main reasons for conducting the surveys on a regional basis are that the products to be priced tend to be more homogeneous within regions, expenditure patterns are likely to be similar, and language differences are reduced. In addition, there are operational advantages in having the ICP carried out by agencies that are in relatively close proximity to the economies they are coordinating.

ORGANIZATION OF ICP 2011

ICP 2011 covered eight regions. Seven of the eight were ICP regions (geographical) overseen by the Global Office: Africa, Asia and the Pacific, Commonwealth of Independent States (CIS), Latin America, the Caribbean, Western Asia, and the Pacific Islands. The eighth region was neither an ICP region nor a geographical entity. It comprised the economies that were participating in the PPP program run by Eurostat, the statistical arm of the European Union, and the Organisation for Economic Co-operation and Development (OECD). The economies were mainly European, but they included some from regions outside Europe as well. Even so, the economies were treated as though they were an autonomous region for the purpose of incorporating them in the global comparison. The agenda and timetable of the Eurostat-OECD PPP Programme differ from those of the ICP, but it employs a similar methodology, as described in appendix C. Eurostat and the OECD worked closely with the Global Office to ensure that their economies could be included with the economies of the seven ICP regions in the 2011 global comparison.

The regional agencies responsible for the comparisons within the seven ICP regions were the African Development Bank, Asian Development Bank, Interstate Statistical Committee of the Commonwealth of Independent States, United Nations Economic Commission for Latin America and the Caribbean, United Nations Economic and Social Commission for Western Asia, and Australian Bureau of Statistics. The responsibility was shared with the national agencies coordinating the comparison. The national agencies carried out data collection and data validation within their respective economies. The regional agencies provided the national agencies with methodological and operational guidance, and they coordinated and supervised data collection and data validation within the region in line with the global timetable. They also computed and finalized the regional comparisons and published the results. The ICP Global Office was responsible for ensuring that the seven regional comparisons and the Eurostat-OECD comparison could be combined in the global comparison and then actually combining them. The compilation, validation, and publication of the global results were also responsibilities of the Global Office.

The global results presented in chapter 2 of this volume include two singleton economies—Georgia and the Islamic Republic of Iran—that did not participate in any of the regional comparisons. They were each linked to the global comparison through a bilateral comparison with an economy participating in a regional comparison. The bilateral comparison provided a bridge to the regional comparison, and the regional comparison provided a bridge to the other regions in the global comparison. Georgia was linked to the CIS comparison through a bilateral comparison with Armenia, and the Islamic Republic of Iran was linked to the Eurostat-OECD comparison through a bilateral comparison with Turkey. The bilateral comparisons were organized and coordinated by the Global Office.

The global results also cover four economies that participated in two regional comparisons. The dual participants were the Arab Republic of Egypt and Sudan, which participated in the Africa and Western Asia comparisons; the Russian Federation, which participated in the CIS and Eurostat-OECD comparisons; and Fiji, which participated in the Asia and the Pacific and the Pacific Islands comparisons. In the presentation of the global results, these dual participants appear under both regions, but they are included only once in the world totals. Dual participation required additional coordination between the regional agencies responsible for the regional comparisons affected because each of the economies had to price products specified in each region's product lists. And they had to ensure that the price, expenditure, population, and other data common to both comparisons were the same.

Throughout all stages of the 2011 comparison, the activities of the Global Office were overseen by the ICP Executive Board, which reported in turn to the UNSC. The board provided strategic leadership, set priorities and standards, and determined the Global Office's overall work program. The objective was to ensure that the global comparison was completed on time and within budget and that it produced price and real expenditure measures of high quality. To this end, the board appointed a Technical Advisory Group of international experts to assist the Global Office with the conceptual, methodological, and technical questions that would arise during the comparison. In addition, three task forces were formed: the Validation Expert Group to oversee validation of the data provided for the global comparison; the PPP Computation Task Force (a group of computation experts) to calculate the global results independently from each other and ensure their convergence; and the Results Review Group to review the global results in terms of their plausibility and adherence to agreed-on methodologies and procedures. Details on the various tiers of governance for ICP 2011 appear in appendix B.

THE ICP APPROACH TO GDP COMPARISONS

ICP comparisons of GDP are based on the value of an individual product equaling the product of its price and quantity (that is, the identity of value = price × quantity). Once more than one product is involved, the identity can no longer be expressed in terms of price × quantity. Therefore, in ICP terms it becomes value = price × volume.

GDP is a measure of production, and it is commonly estimated as the sum of the value of the outputs from production less the cost of the goods and services used in their production (the so-called production approach). It also can be estimated as the sum of the final expenditures on goods and services plus exports less imports of goods and services, which is known as the expenditure side of national accounts and is the approach used by the ICP. Yet another alternative is to estimate GDP as the sum of the incomes arising from production (wages, profits, etc.), which is referred to as the income approach. In theory, the three approaches yield the same result. However, whereas values estimated from the production side and the expenditure side can be split into meaningful price and volume components, values estimated from the income side cannot. In other words, price and volume comparisons of GDP can be made from the production side and from the expenditure side, but not from the income side. ICP comparisons are made from the expenditure side. This approach allows comparison of the levels of the principal elements of final demand—consumption and investment. It also avoids the difficulties encountered in organizing comparisons from the production side, which requires data for both intermediate consumption and gross output in order to effect double deflation. The disadvantage of the expenditure approach is that, unlike the production approach, it does not identify individual industries, and so productivity comparisons can be made only at the level of the whole economy. On the other hand, a major advantage is that the estimates of final demand can be used in many different types of economic analysis, including forecasting and poverty analysis.

Economies estimate their expenditures on GDP at national price levels and in national currencies. But before the estimates can be used to compare the volumes of goods and services produced by economies, differences in national price levels have to be eliminated and national currencies have to be converted to a common currency. Differences in price levels between economies can be removed either by observing the volumes directly as the sum of their underlying quantities or by deriving them indirectly using a measure of relative prices to place the expenditures of all economies on the same price level. Prices are easier to observe than quantities, and direct measures of relative prices usually have a smaller variability than direct measures of relative quantities. In ICP comparisons, volumes (referred to as real expenditures) are mostly estimated indirectly using direct measures of relative prices—PPPs— to deflate nominal expenditures. In addition to being spatial price deflators, PPPs are currency converters. Thus PPP-deflated expenditures are expressed in a common currency unit and are also valued at the same price level.

EXCHANGE RATES

Before PPPs became widely available, exchange rates were used to make international comparisons of GDP. Exchange rates, however, only convert GDPs to a common currency. They do not provide GDPs valued at a common price level because exchange rates do not reflect the relative purchasing power of currencies in their national markets. For them to do so, all goods and services would have to be traded internationally, and the supply and demand for currencies would have to be driven predominantly, if not solely, by the currency requirements of international trade. But this is not the case. Many goods and services such as buildings, government services, and most household market services are not traded internationally, and the supply and demand for currencies are influenced primarily by factors such as currency speculation, interest rates, government intervention, and capital flows between economies. Consequently, as equation (1.2) in box 1.1 indicates, GDPs converted to a common currency using exchange rates remain valued at national price levels. The differences between the levels of GDP in two or more economies reflect both differences in the volumes of goods and services produced by the economies and differences in the price levels of the economies. On the other hand, as equation (1.4) in box 1.1 shows, GDPs converted with PPPs reflect only differences in the volumes produced by the economies.

BOX **1.1**

Using Exchange Rates and PPPs to Convert to a Common Currency

1. The ratio of the gross domestic products (GDPs) of two economies when both GDPs are valued at national price levels and expressed in national currencies has three component ratios:

$$\text{GDP ratio} = \text{price level ratio} \times \text{volume ratio} \times \text{currency ratio}. \qquad (1.1)$$

2. When converting the GDP ratio in (1.1) to a common currency using the exchange rate, the resulting GDP_{XR} ratio has two component ratios:

$$\text{GDP}_{\text{XR}} \text{ ratio} = \text{price level ratio} \times \text{volume ratio}. \qquad (1.2)$$

The GDP ratio in (1.2) is expressed in a common currency, but it reflects both the price level differences and the volume differences between the two economies.

3. A purchasing power parity (PPP) is defined as a spatial price deflator and currency converter. It is composed of two component ratios:

$$\text{PPP} = \text{price level ratio} \times \text{currency ratio}. \qquad (1.3)$$

4. When a PPP is used, the GDP ratio in (1.1) is divided by (1.3), and the resulting GDP_{PPP} ratio has only one component ratio:

$$\text{GDP}_{\text{PPP}} \text{ ratio} = \text{volume ratio}. \qquad (1.4)$$

The GDP ratio in (1.4) is expressed in a common currency, is valued at a common price level, and reflects only volume differences between the two economies.

Exchange rate–converted GDPs can be highly misleading on the relative sizes of economies and levels of material well-being. Price levels are normally higher in high-income economies than they are in low-income economies, and, as a result, differences in price levels between high-income economies and low-income economies are greater for nontraded products than they are for traded products. Before the addition of tariffs, subsidies, and trade costs, the prices of traded products are basically determined globally by the law of one price, whereas the prices of nontraded products are determined by local circumstances, in particular by wages and salaries, which are generally higher in high-income economies. If the larger price level differences for nontraded products are not taken into account when converting GDPs to a common currency, the size of high-income economies with high price levels will be overstated and the size of low-income economies with low price levels will be understated. This is known as the Penn effect. No distinction is made between traded products and nontraded products when exchange rates are used to convert GDPs to a common currency—the rate is the same for all products. PPP-converted GDPs do not have this bias because, as explained shortly, PPPs are calculated first for individual products. They thus take into account the different price levels for traded products and nontraded products.

ICP PPPs are designed specifically for international comparisons of GDP. They are not designed to compare monetary flows or trade flows. International comparisons of flows—such as development aid, foreign direct investment, migrants' remittances, or imports and exports of goods and services—should be made with exchange rates, not with PPPs.

PURCHASING POWER PARITIES

PPPs are price relatives that show the ratio of the prices in national currencies of the same good or service in different economies. For example, if the price of a hamburger is €4.80 in France and $4.00 in the United States, the PPP for hamburgers between the two economies is $0.83 to the euro from the French perspective (4.00/4.80) and €1.20 to the dollar from the U.S. perspective

(4.80/4.00). In other words, for every euro spent on hamburgers in France, $0.83 would have to be spent in the United States to obtain the same quantity and quality—that is, the same volume—of hamburgers. Conversely, for every dollar spent on hamburgers in the United States, €1.20 would have to be spent in France to obtain the same volume of hamburgers. To compare the volumes of hamburgers purchased in the two economies, either the expenditure on hamburgers in France can be expressed in dollars by dividing by 1.20 or the expenditure on hamburgers in the United States can be expressed in euros by dividing by 0.83.

PPPs are calculated in stages: first for individual goods and services, then for groups of products, and finally for each of the various levels of aggregation up to GDP. PPPs continue to be price relatives whether they refer to a product group, to an aggregation level, or to GDP. As one moves up the aggregation hierarchy, the price relatives refer to increasingly complex assortments of goods and services. Therefore, if the PPP for GDP between France and the United States is €0.95 to the dollar, it can be inferred that for every dollar spent on GDP in the United States, €0.95 would have to be spent in France to purchase the same volume of goods and services. Purchasing the same volume of goods and services does not mean that the baskets of goods and services purchased in both economies will be identical. The composition of the baskets will vary between economies and reflect differences in taste, culture, climate, price structure, product availability, and income level, but both baskets will, in principle, provide equivalent satisfaction or utility.

PRICE LEVEL INDEXES

PPPs are spatial price indexes. They show—with reference to a base economy (or region)—the price of a given basket of goods and services in each of the economies being compared. This index is similar to a temporal price index, which shows with reference to a base period the price of a given basket of goods and services at different points in time. However, unlike the temporal price index in which the indexes at the different points in time are expressed in the same currency unit so that price changes over time are readily identifiable, the PPP index for each economy is expressed in the economy's national currency. It is thus not possible to say whether one economy is more expensive or less expensive than another. For this type of comparison, one would have to standardize the indexes by expressing them in a common unit of currency. The common currency used for the global comparison is the U.S. dollar, and so each economy's PPP has been standardized by dividing it by that economy's dollar exchange rate. The standardized indexes so obtained are called price level indexes (PLIs).

Economies with PLIs greater than 100 have price levels that are higher than that of the base economy. Economies with PLIs less than 100 have price levels that are lower than that of the base economy. So, returning to the hamburger example, if the exchange rate is $1.00 to €0.79, the PLI for a hamburger with the United States as the base economy is 152 (1.20/0.79 × 100). From this, it can be inferred that, given the relative purchasing power of the dollar and the euro, hamburgers cost 52 percent more in France than they do in the United States. In addition to products, PLIs can be calculated for product groups, aggregates, and GDP. At the level of GDP, PLIs provide a measure of the differences in the general price levels of economies. Thus, if the PPP for GDP between France and the United States is €0.95 to the dollar, the PLI for GDP based on the United States is 120 (0.95/0.79 × 100), indicating that the general price level of France is 20 percent higher than that of the United States. The PLIs of economies can be compared directly. For example, if the PLI of one economy is 120 while that of another economy is 80 (both with the United States as base), then it is valid to infer that the price level in the former is 50 percent (that is, 120/80) higher than in the latter.

It is worth remembering that PPPs evolve slowly, whereas exchange rates can change quickly. Sudden changes in PLIs are usually the result of fluctuations in exchange rates. When exchange rates change rapidly, a PLI for an economy could change rapidly as well, reflecting the fact that an economy that was relatively cheap has now become relatively expensive compared with the base economy. The volatility of exchange rates is another reason they should not be used to compare the size of economies. Fluctuations in exchange rates can make economies appear suddenly larger or smaller even though there has been little or no change in the relative volume of goods and services produced.

REAL EXPENDITURES

Economies report nominal expenditures on GDP and its constituent aggregates and product groups. Nominal expenditures are expenditures that are valued at national price levels. They can be expressed in national currencies or, when converted with exchange rates, in a common currency. In the latter, the converted expenditures remain nominal because, as explained earlier, exchange rates do not correct for differences in price levels between economies, and so the expenditures are still valued at national price levels. For the ICP, economies report their nominal expenditures in national currencies.

PPPs are used to convert these nominal expenditures to real expenditures. Real expenditures are expenditures that are valued at a common price level. They reflect real or actual differences in the volumes purchased in economies and provide the measures required for international volume comparisons: indexes of real expenditure and indexes of real expenditure per capita. At the level of GDP, indexes of real expenditure are widely used to compare the size of economies, and indexes of real expenditure per capita are frequently used to compare the material well-being of their resident populations. Although the indexes of real expenditure and real expenditure per capita for GDP are the most well known, indexes of real expenditure and real expenditure per capita for aggregates and product groups are also important, allowing an in-depth analysis of comparison results.

ACTUAL INDIVIDUAL CONSUMPTION

One aggregate below the level of GDP that has particular significance in ICP comparisons is actual individual consumption (AIC). On a per capita basis, it is a better measure of material well-being than either GDP or the household final consumption expenditure when material well-being is defined in terms of the goods and services consumed by households to satisfy their individual needs. Such goods and services are referred to as individual goods and services, and the expenditure on individual goods and services is referred to as the individual consumption expenditure.

GDP covers the individual goods and services consumed by resident households. But it also includes collective services—such as defense, police, and environment protection—that general government produces to meet the collective needs of the community, as well as gross fixed capital formation and net exports, which do not constitute final consumption. The household final consumption expenditure, on the other hand, covers only the individual goods and services that households purchase. It does not take into account the individual services—such as health, education, and social protection—that general government and nonprofit institutions serving households (NPISHs) provide to households individually. The provision of such services, particularly health and education, can vary considerably from economy to economy. If only the household expenditure is compared, economies in which households purchase health and education services themselves will appear to consume more than economies in which these services are provided to households by general government or NPISHs.

Actual individual consumption comprises only the goods and services that households consume to meet their individual needs. It covers all such goods and services whether they are purchased by households or are provided by general government and NPISHs. AIC is defined as the sum of the individual consumption expenditures of households, general government, and NPISHs. The concept of actual individual consumption dates back to the earliest years of the ICP, when it was called the consumption expenditure of the population. Initially, the individual consumption expenditure by NPISHs was not included. Later, however, the concept was expanded to include the consumption expenditure of NPISHs, and it was adopted by national accountants in the System of National Accounts 1993 or SNA93 (Commission of the European Communities et al. 1993).

USES OF PPPs AND REAL EXPENDITURES

PPPs and the PLIs and indexes of real expenditure to which they give rise are used for research and analysis, for statistical compilation, and for administrative purposes. The principal users are international bodies such as the World Bank, the International Monetary Fund (IMF), the United Nations and its affiliates, the OECD, and the European Commission. Improvements in the timeliness, frequency, and coverage of ICP comparisons, however, have sparked a growing demand for PPP-based measures from a variety of national users—in particular, government agencies, universities, and research institutes.

At the same time, there has been a switch in user focus. The ICP was established to compare the GDPs of economies in real terms, and PPPs were seen primarily as a means of converting nominal expenditures to real expenditures. Comparisons of real expenditure are still the ICP's primary purpose. But now international users and national users are showing a growing interest in PPPs as measures of the relative prices between economies at all levels of aggregation and in the national annual average prices underlying them. As a result of this interest, the Global Office has had to establish a set of rules governing access to unpublished results and basic data.

Researchers and policy makers at both the international and national levels use PPPs as inputs into economic research and policy analysis that involve comparisons of economies. In this context, PPPs are employed either to generate measures of real expenditure with which to compare the size of economies and their levels of material well-being, consumption, investment, government expenditure, and overall productivity, or to generate price measures with which to compare price levels, price structures, price convergence, and competitiveness. PPP-converted GDP is used to standardize other economic variables such as carbon emissions per unit of GDP, energy use per unit of GDP, GDP per employee, or GDP per hour worked. Multinational corporations, for example, use PPPs to evaluate the cost of investment in different economies.

One major use of PPPs is poverty assessment using the World Bank's international poverty threshold of $1.25 per day per person. National poverty assessments differ because the purchasing power of national currencies differs from one economy to another. Therefore, establishing an international poverty line requires equalizing purchasing power over economies. The international poverty line of $1.25 per day is converted to national price levels by using the PPPs for the individual consumption expenditures by households. Data from household income and expenditure surveys are then used to determine the number of people whose consumption per capita is below this poverty line. The international poverty line itself has typically been calculated as the average of the national poverty lines of the world's poorest economies, converted to international dollars using consumption PPPs. The PPPs thus enter the calculation at two stages—first, in establishing the poverty line and, second, in calculating the number of people below it in each economy.

Eradication of hunger and poverty is the first United Nations Millennium Development Goal. Other goals are in the areas of health care, particularly that of mothers and children, and primary education. The World Health Organization uses PPPs when comparing expenditures per capita on health care across economies. Similarly, the United Nations Educational, Scientific and Cultural Organization (UNESCO) uses PPPs when assessing the expenditures per capita of different economies on education. A related use is the estimation of the United Nations Human Development Index. PPP-converted gross national income per capita is one of the three variables that constitute the index.

PPPs are also used for statistical compilation. International organizations use PPPs to obtain totals and averages for a group of economies such as an ICP region. Real GDP and its components are aggregated across the economies in a group to obtain totals for the group. The shares of economies in these totals are used as weights when economic indicators, such as price indexes or growth rates, are combined to obtain averages for the group. Both the IMF and the OECD use PPP-based GDP and GDP aggregates to provide estimates of regional and world output and growth in their respective publications *World Economic Outlook* and *Economic Outlook*.

Finally, PPPs are employed for administrative purposes by the European Commission and the IMF. The European Commission uses the PPPs of its member states when allocating the structural funds intended to reduce economic disparities between and within member states. The principal indicator influencing the allocation is PPP-deflated intra-economy regional GDP per capita. The IMF uses PPP-based GDP from the *World Economic Outlook* in its current quota formula. In the past, that measure often helped guide increases in members' quotas. Quota subscriptions determine the maximum financial resources that member economies are obliged to provide the IMF, the amount of financing that members can obtain from the IMF, their share in a general allocation of special drawing rights, and their voting power in IMF decisions. PPP-based GDP has a weight of 20 percent in the current quota formula.

The uses of PPPs and related data are continuing to expand as the limitations of the main alternative method of adjusting values to a common currency—using exchange rates—become more widely recognized and as the number of economies included in the ICP continues to increase. The main issue that needs to be addressed now is the availability of more timely PPP data sets. The World Bank is investigating ways in which PPPs can be estimated more frequently.

Chapter 2

Presentation and Analysis of Results

The results presented here are based exclusively on the price and national accounts data provided by all economies participating in the global comparison undertaken in the 2011 round of the International Comparison Program (ICP). Purchasing power parities (PPPs) and real expenditures were compiled in accordance with established ICP principles and procedures recommended by the Technical Advisory Group for ICP 2011. Users of ICP results are reminded to recognize that the ICP is a complex major statistical exercise whose methodology is constantly being refined and improved.

The National Bureau of Statistics (NBS) of China expressed reservations about some aspects of the methodology employed in ICP 2011 and did not agree to publish the headline results for China. Those results were estimated by the 2011 ICP Regional Office in the Asian Development Bank and the 2011 ICP Global Office hosted by the World Bank. However, the NBS of China does not endorse these results as official statistics.

In addition to providing the ICP 2011 results and analysis, this chapter addresses the reliability and limitations of PPPs and real expenditures, the differences between the 2005 and 2011 comparisons, and the differences between 2011 PPPs extrapolated from ICP 2005 and ICP 2011 benchmark PPPs.

PRESENTATION OF RESULTS

Eleven tables of ICP 2011 results and two supplementary tables appear at the end of this section, preceded by a detailed description of their various components. The tables are as follows:

- Table 2.1 Summary Results and Reference Data

- Table 2.2 Nominal Expenditures in National Currency Units

- Table 2.3 Shares of Nominal Expenditures (GDP = 100)

- Table 2.4 Purchasing Power Parities (U.S. Dollar = 1.00)

- Table 2.5 Real Expenditures in U.S. Dollars

- Table 2.6 Shares of World Real Expenditures (World = 100)

- Table 2.7 Real Expenditures Per Capita in U.S. Dollars

- Table 2.8 Indexes of Real Expenditures Per Capita (World = 100)

- Table 2.9 Price Level Indexes (World = 100)

- Table 2.10 Nominal Expenditures in U.S. Dollars

- Table 2.11 Nominal Expenditures Per Capita in U.S. Dollars

- Supplementary Table 2.12 Main Results and Reference Data, Pacific Islands

- Supplementary Table 2.13 Estimated Results and Reference Data, Nonbenchmark Economies

In all tables, results are presented by economy and by region and include regional totals and averages as well as world totals and averages. The world is defined as all economies covered by the tables with the exception of Cuba and Bonaire, which do not have a full set of results and are not included in either the regional or world totals. Afghanistan, Argentina, Lebanon, Libya, South Sudan, and the Syrian Arab Republic are the only large economies that did not take part in ICP 2011, and so they are not included in the world totals. They are included in supplementary table 2.13, which shows the estimated real gross domestic product (GDP) per capita for economies that did not participate in ICP 2011.

Eight regions participated in ICP 2011: Africa, Asia and the Pacific, Commonwealth of Independent States (CIS), Eurostat–Organisation for Economic Co-operation and Development (OECD), Latin America, the Caribbean, Western Asia, and the Pacific Islands. All are geographical regions except the Eurostat-OECD group of economies, which, though predominantly European, include a worldwide spread of non-European economies as well. Thus the regional classification used to present the results differs from the regional classifications used by other international statistical programs. Of the eight regions listed, only the first seven are covered in the tables. The comparison for the eighth region—the Pacific Islands—was limited to household consumption, and so its results are shown in supplementary table 2.12 and not in the tables that cover all GDP.

Two economies, Georgia and the Islamic Republic of Iran, did not participate in a regional comparison. Instead, they were linked to the global comparison through a bilateral comparison with an economy participating in a regional comparison: Armenia and the CIS comparison in the case of Georgia; Turkey and the Eurostat-OECD comparison in the case of the Islamic Republic of Iran. The linking took place after the global comparison was calculated, and so their inclusion does not influence either the global or regional relativity between economies. The two economies are listed at the end of each table as singletons and are included in world totals and averages.

Four economies—the Arab Republic of Egypt, Sudan, the Russian Federation, and Fiji—participated in two regional comparisons, but only the dual participation of Egypt, Sudan, and Russia is of concern here because the dual participation of Fiji involved the Pacific Islands comparison covered in supplementary table 2.12. Egypt and Sudan participated in the Africa comparison and the Western Asia comparison, and Russia participated in the CIS comparison and the Eurostat-OECD comparison. In the tables, they appear under both regions and are included in the totals and averages of both regions. They are included only once in the world totals and averages.

Summary results: table 2.1 and supplementary tables 2.12 and 2.13

Table 2.1 provides the summary results for ICP 2011 broken down into the following indicators:

- Column (01): GDP based on PPPs in U.S. dollars

- Column (02): GDP based on exchange rates in U.S. dollars

- Column (03): GDP per capita based on PPPs in U.S. dollars

- Column (04): GDP per capita based on exchange rates in U.S. dollars

- Column (05): Price level index for GDP with the world equal to 100

- Column (06): GDP per capita index based on PPPs with the world equal to 100

- Column (07): GDP per capita index based on exchange rates with the world equal to 100

- Column (08): GDP per capita index based on PPPs with the United States equal to 100

- Column (09): GDP per capita index based on exchange rates with the United States equal to 100

- Column (10): Share of PPP-based world GDP

- Column (11): Share of exchange rate–based world GDP

- Column (12): Share of world population

- Column (13): PPP for GDP with the U.S. dollar equal to 1.000

- Column (14): Exchange rate with the U.S. dollar equal to 1.000

- Column (15): Resident population

- Column (16): Nominal GDP in national currency unit

Supplementary tables 2.12 and 2.13 provide the same information but for a limited set of indicators.

Column (01) shows the real expenditures of economies and regions on GDP in U.S. dollars. The expenditures reflect only volume differences between economies and regions. They were obtained by dividing the nominal expenditures on GDP in column (16) by the PPPs for GDP in column (13). The GDP per capita in column (03), the GDP per capita indexes in columns (06) and (08), and the shares of world GDP in column (10) are all based on the real expenditures in column (01).

Column (02) shows the nominal expenditures of economies and regions on GDP in U.S. dollars. The expenditures reflect both price differences and volume differences between economies and regions (see box 2.1). They were derived by dividing the nominal expenditures on GDP in column (16) by the exchange rates in column (14). The GDP per capita in column (04), the GDP per capita indexes in columns (07) and (09), and the shares of world GDP in column (11) are all based on the nominal expenditures in column (02).

Users are reminded that, as explained in chapter 1, exchange rate–converted GDPs are not reliable measures of either the size of economies or the material well-being of their populations. They are included in the summary table and in the supplementary tables for reference only.

Detailed results: tables 2.2–2.11

Tables 2.2–2.11 present the results for ICP 2011 broken down into 26 analytical categories. These categories, which cover GDP and a selection of component final expenditures, are listed and defined in box 2.1. Their codes in the ICP expenditure classification in appendix D are also

---

BOX **2.1**

Analytical Categories: Tables 2.2–2.11 and Supplementary Tables 2.12 and 2.13

Column (01) Gross domestic product: Actual individual consumption at purchasers' prices *plus* collective consumption expenditure by government at purchasers' prices *plus* gross capital formation at purchasers' prices *plus* the f.o.b. (free on board) value of exports of goods and services *less* the f.o.b. value of imports of goods and services. *Code in ICP expenditure classification, appendix D: 100000*

Column (02) Actual individual consumption: The total value of the individual consumption expenditures of households, nonprofit institutions serving households (NPISHs), and general government at purchasers' prices. *Code in ICP expenditure classification, appendix D: not identified in classification; sum of 110000 + 120000 + 130000*

Column (03) Food and nonalcoholic beverages: Household expenditure on food products and nonalcoholic beverages purchased for consumption at home (excludes food products and nonalcoholic beverages sold for immediate consumption away from home by hotels, restaurants, cafés, bars, kiosks, street vendors, automatic vending machines, etc.; cooked dishes prepared by restaurants for consumption off their premises; cooked dishes prepared by catering contractors whether collected by the customer or delivered to the customer's home; and products sold specifically as pet foods). *Code in ICP expenditure classification, appendix D: 110100*

(continued)

BOX **2.1**   *(Continued)*

Column (04) Alcoholic beverages, tobacco, and narcotics: Household expenditure on alcoholic beverages purchased for consumption at home (includes low or nonalcoholic beverages that are generally alcoholic such as nonalcoholic beer, and excludes alcoholic beverages sold for immediate consumption away from the home by hotels, restaurants, cafés, bars, kiosks, street vendors, automatic vending machines, etc.) and household expenditure on tobacco (covers all purchases of tobacco, including purchases of tobacco in cafés, bars, restaurants, and service stations). *Code in ICP expenditure classification, appendix D: 110200*

Column (05) Clothing and footwear: Household expenditure on clothing materials; garments for men, women, children, and infants; other articles of clothing and clothing accessories; cleaning, repair, and hire of clothing; all footwear for men, women, children, and infants; and repair and hire of footwear. *Code in ICP expenditure classification, appendix D: 110300*

Column (06) Housing, water, electricity, gas, and other fuels: Household expenditure on actual and imputed rentals for housing; maintenance and repair of the dwelling; water supply and services related to the dwelling; and electricity, gas, and other fuels *plus* expenditure by NPISHs on housing *plus* general government expenditure on housing services provided to individuals. *Codes in ICP expenditure classification, appendix D: 110400 + (120000) + 130100*

Column (07) Furnishings, household equipment, and maintenance: Household expenditure on furniture and furnishings; carpets and other floor coverings; household textiles; household appliances; glassware, tableware, and household utensils; tools and equipment for house and garden; and goods and services for routine household maintenance. *Code in ICP expenditure classification, appendix D: 110500*

Column (08) Health: Household expenditure on pharmaceuticals; medical products, appliances, and equipment; outpatient services; and hospital services *plus* expenditure of NPISHs on health *plus* general government expenditure on health benefits and reimbursements, and the production of health services. *Codes in ICP expenditure classification, appendix D: 110600 + (120000) + 130200*

Column (09) Transport: Household expenditure on purchase of vehicles, operation of personal transport equipment, and transport services. *Code in ICP expenditure classification, appendix D: 110700*

Column (10) Communication: Household expenditure on postal services, telephone and telefax equipment, and telephone and telefax services. *Code in ICP expenditure classification, appendix D: 110800*

Column (11) Recreation and culture: Household expenditure on audiovisual, photographic, and information processing equipment; other major durables for recreation and culture; other recreational items and equipment; gardens and pets; recreational and cultural services; newspapers, books, and stationery; and package holidays *plus* expenditure by NPISHs on recreation and culture *plus* general government expenditure on recreation and culture. *Codes in ICP expenditure classification, appendix D: 110900 + (120000) + 130300*

Column (12) Education: Household expenditure on pre-primary, primary, secondary, postsecondary, and tertiary education *plus* expenditure of NPISHs on education *plus* general government expenditure on education benefits and reimbursements and the production of education services. *Codes in ICP expenditure classification, appendix D: 111000 + (120000) + 130400*

Column (13) Restaurants and hotels: Household expenditure on food products and beverages sold for immediate consumption away from the home by hotels, restaurants, cafés, bars, kiosks, street vendors, automatic vending machines, etc. (includes cooked dishes prepared by restaurants for consumption off their premises and cooked dishes prepared by catering contractors, whether collected by the customer or delivered to the customer's home) and household expenditure on accommodation services provided by hotels and similar establishments. *Code in ICP expenditure classification, appendix D: 111100*

BOX **2.1**   *(Continued)*

Column (14) Miscellaneous goods and service: Household expenditure on personal care, personal effects, social protection, insurance, and financial and other services *plus* expenditure by NPISHs on social protection and other services *plus* general government expenditure on social protection. *Codes in ICP expenditure classification, appendix D: 111200 + (120000) + 130500*

Column (15) Net purchases abroad: Purchases by resident households outside the economic territory of the economy *less* purchases by nonresident households in the economic territory of the economy. *Code in ICP expenditure classification, appendix D: 111300*

Column (16) Individual consumption expenditure by households: The total value of actual and imputed final consumption expenditures incurred by households on individual goods and services. It also includes expenditures on individual goods and services sold at prices that are not economically significant. *Code in ICP expenditure classification, appendix D: 110000*

Column (17) Individual consumption expenditure by government: The total value of actual and imputed final consumption expenditures incurred by general government on individual goods and services. *Code in ICP expenditure classification, appendix D: 130000*

Column (18) Collective consumption expenditure by government: The final consumption expenditure of general government on collective services. *Code in ICP expenditure classification, appendix D: 140000*

Column (19) Gross fixed capital formation: The total value of acquisitions *less* disposals of fixed assets by resident institutional units during the accounting period *plus* the additions to the value of nonproduced assets realized by the productive activity of resident institutional units. *Code in ICP expenditure classification, appendix D: 150000*

Column (20) Machinery and equipment: Capital expenditure on fabricated metal products, general-purpose machinery, special-purpose machinery, electrical and optical equipment, transport equipment, and other manufactured goods. *Code in ICP expenditure classification, appendix D: 150100*

Column (21) Construction: Capital expenditure on the construction of new structures and renovation of existing structures. Structures include residential buildings, nonresidential buildings, and civil engineering works. *Code in ICP expenditure classification, appendix D: 150200*

Column (22) Other products: Capital expenditure on plantation, orchard, and vineyard development; change in stocks of breeding stock, draft animals, dairy cattle, animals raised for wool clippings, etc.; computer software that a producer expects to use in production for more than one year; land improvement, including dams and dikes that are part of flood control and irrigation projects; mineral exploration; acquisition of entertainment, literary, or artistic originals; and other intangible fixed assets. *Code in ICP expenditure classification, appendix D: 150300*

Column (23) Changes in inventories and valuables: The acquisition *less* disposals of stocks of raw materials, semi-finished goods, and finished goods that are held by producer units prior to being further processed or sold or otherwise used; and the acquisition *less* disposals of valuables (produced assets that are not used primarily for production or consumption but purchased and held as stores of value). *Code in ICP expenditure classification, appendix D: 160000*

Column (24) Balance of exports and imports: The f.o.b. value of exports of goods and services *less* the f.o.b. value of imports of goods and services. *Code in ICP expenditure classification, appendix D: 170000*

(continued)

Column (25) Domestic absorption: Actual individual consumption at purchasers' prices *plus* collective consumption expenditure by government at purchasers' prices *plus* gross capital formation at purchasers' prices. *Code in ICP expenditure classification, appendix D: not identified in the classification; sum of 110000 + 120000 + 130000 + 140000 + 150000 + 160000*

Column (26) Individual consumption expenditure by households, excluding housing: Individual consumption expenditure by households in column (16) without the actual and imputed rentals included in column (06). *Codes in ICP expenditure classification, appendix D: 110000–110410*

given to show the correspondence between the tables and the classification.

In the classification, consumption expenditures are structured by who pays: households, nonprofit institutions serving households (NPISHs), or general government. But in tables 2.2–2.9 and the supplementary tables, consumption expenditures are structured by who consumes: households, under actual individual consumption in column (02), or general government, under collective consumption expenditure by government in column (18). The analytical categories affected by the change in structure—which entails adding the expenditures on individual services by NPISHs and general government to the expenditure on individual services by households—are those covering individual household consumption in column (02), housing in column (6), health in column (08), recreation and culture in column (11), education in column (12), and social protection in column (14). These categories are shaded in blue in box 2.1.

In the tables, actual individual consumption in column (02) is broken down by the analytical categories covering the expenditure on consumer goods and services in columns (03) to (15). The expenditure includes the individual consumption expenditures of NPISHs and general government as well as the individual consumption expenditure of households. Because *actual individual consumption* is defined as the sum of the individual consumption expenditures of households, NPISHs, and general government, the tables also show the individual consumption expenditure by households in column (16) and the individual consumption expenditure by government in column (17) as

memorandum items. The individual consumption expenditure by households includes the individual consumption expenditure by NPISHs. Two other memorandum items that appear in the tables are domestic absorption, column (25), and individual consumption expenditure, excluding housing, column (26).

Table 2.2 shows the nominal expenditures in the analytical categories reported by the economies. The expenditures are valued at national price levels and expressed in national currency units. They are converted to real expenditures in table 2.5 by deflating them by the PPPs in table 2.4. The nominal expenditures at the more detailed basic heading level (not shown) are the weights used to calculate PPPs for the analytical categories. The nominal expenditures are additive, and tables 2.2, 2.3, 2.10, and 2.11 contain four additional analytical categories for completeness: net purchases abroad, column (15); other products, column (22); changes in inventories and valuables, column (23); and balance of exports and imports, column (24).

Table 2.3 contains each economy's nominal expenditures in the analytical categories in table 2.2 as a percentage of its GDP.

Table 2.4 presents the PPPs for the analytical categories. The final PPPs were calculated by the Global Office. The Gini-Èltetö-Köves-Szulc (GEKS) method and country aggregation with redistribution (CAR) procedure described in chapter 4 were used to provide PPPs and real expenditures with the following properties:

- They are *commensurate*, meaning they do not change when the units of quantity to which their prices refer are changed—for example, when the price of petrol is quoted per gallon rather than per liter.

- They are *transitive*, meaning that every indirect multilateral PPP between a pair of economies calculated via a third economy equals the direct multilateral PPP between the economies.

- They are *base economy–invariant*, meaning that the relativities between economies are the same whichever economy or region is taken as base.

- They provide real expenditures that are free of the *Gerschenkron effect*, which is the bias resulting when high-income economies receive more weight in the estimation process, resulting in overestimates of the real size of low-income economies.

- Their real expenditures are not *additive*, meaning that the real expenditures at higher levels of aggregation are not equal to the sum of the real expenditures of their components. (Many users consider additivity to be an important feature of real expenditures. However, in practice it is not possible to maintain the additivity of the component aggregates within real GDP without having real expenditures for GDP that are significantly biased between low- and high-income economies (that is, the Gerschenkron effect).

- Moreover, the PPPs and real expenditures respect *fixity*, meaning that the relativities established between economies in a regional comparison remain the same when the economies are included in the global comparison.

For the PPPs in table 2.4, the United States serves as the base and the U.S. dollar as numéraire. But, being base economy–invariant, they can be rebased on another economy or on a region by dividing them by the PPP for the economy or region selected as the new base. For example, they can be rebased on the United Kingdom with the pound sterling as numéraire by dividing them by the PPP for the United Kingdom.

Table 2.5 gives the real expenditures in the analytical categories. They were derived by dividing the nominal expenditures in table 2.2 by the PPPs in table 2.4. The real expenditures

are in U.S. dollars, they are free of the Gerschenkron effect, and they respect fixity, but they are not additive. They reflect only volume differences between economies.

Table 2.6 shows for economies and regions their real expenditures in each analytical category as a percentage share of the world real expenditure in the analytical category. The percentage shares are based on the real expenditures in table 2.5. At the level of GDP, they measure the relative size of the economies covered in the table.

Table 2.7 presents the real expenditures per capita in the analytical categories. The expenditures are in U.S. dollars. They were obtained by dividing the real expenditures in table 2.5 by the population totals in column (15) of table 2.1.

Table 2.8 provides the indexes of real expenditures per capita in the analytical categories with the world equal to 100. They are based on the real expenditures per capita in table 2.7. The indexes are base economy–invariant and can be rebased on an economy or on a region. At the level of actual individual consumption, they measure the relative material well-being of the resident populations of the economies included in the table.

Table 2.9 gives the price level indexes (PLIs) for the analytical categories relative to the world average. A value above 100 indicates that the economy's price level for the analytical category in question is higher than the world average; a value below 100 indicates that the economy's price level for the analytical category is lower than the world average. The PLIs are base country–invariant and can be rebased on an economy or on a region. For example, the PLIs in the table were first calculated with the United States as base by dividing the PPPs in table 2.4 by the exchange rates in table 2.1. They were subsequently rebased on the world.

Table 2.10 presents the nominal expenditures in table 2.3 in U.S. dollars. The expenditures were converted using the exchange rates in column (14) of table 2.1.

Table 2.11 gives the nominal expenditures per capita on the analytical categories in U.S. dollars. They were derived by dividing the nominal expenditures in table 2.10 by the population totals in column (15) of table 2.1.

Table 2.1 Summary Results and Reference Data, ICP 2011

GROSS DOMESTIC PRODUCT	Expenditure (US$, billions)		Expenditure per capita (US$)		Price level index	Expenditure per capita index World = 100.0		US = 100.0		Share (world = 100.0) Expenditure		Popula-tion	PPP	Reference data Exchange rate	Popula-tion	Expendi-ture in national currency unit
Economy	Based on PPPs	Based on XRs	Based on PPPs	Based on XRs	(world = 100.0)	Based on PPPs	Based on XRs	Based on PPPs	Based on XRs	Based on PPPs	Based on XRs		(US$ = 1.000)	(US$ = 1.000)	(millions)	(billions)
(00)	(01)	(02)	(03)	(04)	(05)	(06)	(07)	(08)	(09)	(10)[a]	(11)[a]	(12)[a]	(13)[b]	(14)[b]	(15)	(16)
AFRICA																
Algeria	474.8	198.5	13,195	5,518	53.9	98.0	52.9	26.5	11.1	0.5	0.3	0.5	30.502	72.938	35.98	14,481.0
Angola	143.0	104.2	7,288	5,311	94.0	54.1	50.9	14.6	10.7	0.2	0.1	0.3	68.315	93.741	19.62	9,767.6
Benin	16.1	7.3	1,766	801	58.5	13.1	7.7	3.5	1.6	0.0	0.0	0.1	214.035	471.866	9.10	3,439.8
Botswana	27.2	15.0	13,409	7,381	71.0	99.6	70.7	26.9	14.8	0.0	0.0	0.0	3.764	6.838	2.03	102.5
Burkina Faso	22.8	10.3	1,343	608	58.4	10.0	5.8	2.7	1.2	0.0	0.0	0.3	213.659	471.866	16.97	4,868.5
Burundi	6.1	2.1	712	240	43.5	5.3	2.3	1.4	0.5	0.0	0.0	0.1	425.768	1,261.074	8.58	2,599.9
Cameroon	55.2	26.6	2,757	1,327	62.1	20.5	12.7	5.5	2.7	0.1	0.0	0.3	227.212	471.866	20.03	12,545.7
Cape Verde	3.1	1.9	6,126	3,773	79.4	45.5	36.1	12.3	7.6	0.0	0.0	0.0	48.592	78.886	0.50	149.0
Central African Republic	4.0	2.2	897	486	69.9	6.7	4.7	1.8	1.0	0.0	0.0	0.1	255.862	471.866	4.49	1,029.7
Chad	22.9	12.1	1,984	1,053	68.4	14.7	10.1	4.0	2.1	0.0	0.0	0.2	250.443	471.866	11.53	5,725.3
Comoros	0.5	0.3	610	358	75.6	4.5	3.4	1.2	0.7	0.0	0.0	0.0	207.584	353.900	0.75	95.4
Congo, Rep.	24.1	14.8	5,830	3,575	79.1	43.3	34.2	11.7	7.2	0.0	0.0	0.1	289.299	471.866	4.14	6,982.5
Congo, Dem. Rep.	44.4	25.2	655	372	73.2	4.9	3.6	1.3	0.7	0.0	0.0	1.0	521.870	919.491	67.76	23,146.1
Côte d'Ivoire	53.8	26.0	2,669	1,291	62.4	19.8	12.4	5.4	2.6	0.1	0.0	0.3	228.228	471.866	20.15	12,275.5
Djibouti	2.2	1.2	2,412	1,276	68.2	17.9	12.2	4.8	2.6	0.0	0.0	0.0	94.003	177.721	0.91	205.3
Egypt, Arab Rep.[c]	843.8	229.9	10,599	2,888	35.1	78.7	27.7	21.3	5.8	0.9	0.3	1.2	1.625	5.964	79.62	1,371.1
Equatorial Guinea	28.4	17.7	39,440	24,621	80.5	293.0	235.9	79.2	49.5	0.0	0.0	0.0	294.572	471.866	0.72	8,367.3
Ethiopia	102.9	29.9	1,214	353	37.5	9.0	3.4	2.4	0.7	0.1	0.0	1.3	4.919	16.899	84.73	506.1
Gabon	25.3	17.1	16,483	11,114	86.9	122.5	106.5	33.1	22.3	0.0	0.0	0.0	318.156	471.866	1.53	8,046.1
Gambia, The	2.7	0.9	1,507	508	43.5	11.2	4.9	3.0	1.0	0.0	0.0	0.0	9.939	29.462	1.78	26.6
Ghana	85.5	39.6	3,426	1,585	59.7	25.5	15.2	6.9	3.2	0.1	0.1	0.4	0.699	1.512	24.97	59.8
Guinea	13.2	5.0	1,287	490	49.0	9.6	4.7	2.6	1.0	0.0	0.0	0.2	2,518.386	6,620.841	10.22	33,128.3
Guinea-Bissau	2.1	1.0	1,365	637	60.1	10.1	6.1	2.7	1.3	0.0	0.0	0.0	220.085	471.866	1.55	464.7
Kenya	88.9	34.3	2,136	825	49.8	15.9	7.9	4.3	1.7	0.1	0.0	0.6	34.298	88.811	41.61	3,048.9
Lesotho	4.7	2.5	2,130	1,151	69.7	15.8	11.0	4.3	2.3	0.0	0.0	0.0	3.923	7.261	2.19	18.3
Liberia	2.2	1.1	537	278	66.7	4.0	2.7	1.1	0.6	0.0	0.0	0.1	0.517	1.000	4.13	1.1
Madagascar	30.1	10.0	1,412	470	42.9	10.5	4.5	2.8	0.9	0.0	0.0	0.3	673.730	2,025.118	21.32	20,276.4
Malawi	15.0	7.3	973	476	63.1	7.2	4.6	2.0	1.0	0.0	0.0	0.2	76.259	155.776	15.38	1,140.8
Mali	23.9	10.6	1,509	672	57.4	11.2	6.4	3.0	1.4	0.0	0.0	0.2	210.193	471.866	15.84	5,024.5
Mauritania	11.3	4.6	3,191	1,295	52.3	23.7	12.4	6.4	2.6	0.0	0.0	0.1	115.855	285.470	3.54	1,309.4
Mauritius	20.3	11.3	15,506	8,611	71.6	115.2	82.5	31.1	17.3	0.0	0.0	0.0	15.941	28.706	1.31	323.0
Morocco	218.3	99.2	6,764	3,074	58.6	50.2	29.5	13.6	6.2	0.2	0.1	0.5	3.677	8.090	32.27	802.6
Mozambique	22.8	12.5	951	524	71.1	7.1	5.0	1.9	1.1	0.0	0.0	0.4	16.030	29.068	23.93	364.7
Namibia	19.4	12.5	8,360	5,369	82.8	62.1	51.4	16.8	10.8	0.0	0.0	0.0	4.663	7.261	2.32	90.6
Niger	13.7	6.4	852	399	60.4	6.3	3.8	1.7	0.8	0.0	0.0	0.2	221.087	471.866	16.07	3,025.5
Nigeria	511.1	247.0	3,146	1,520	62.3	23.4	14.6	6.3	3.1	0.6	0.4	2.4	74.378	153.903	162.47	38,017.0
Rwanda	14.6	6.3	1,337	579	55.9	9.9	5.5	2.7	1.2	0.0	0.0	0.2	260.751	601.833	10.94	3,814.4

Table 2.1 (Continued)

GROSS DOMESTIC PRODUCT	Expenditure (US$, billions)		Expenditure per capita (US$)		Price level index	Expenditure per capita index				Share (world = 100.0)			PPP	Reference data		
						World = 100.0		US = 100.0		Expenditure		Popula-tion		Exchange rate	Popula-tion	Expendi-ture in national currency unit
Economy	Based on PPPs	Based on XRs	Based on PPPs	Based on XRs	(world = 100.0)	Based on PPPs	Based on XRs	Based on PPPs	Based on XRs	Based on PPPs	Based on XRs		(US$ = 1.000)	(US$ = 1.000)	(millions)	(billions)
(00)	(01)	(02)	(03)	(04)	(05)	(06)	(07)	(08)	(09)	(10)[a]	(11)[a]	(12)[a]	(13)[b]	(14)[b]	(15)	(16)
São Tomé and Príncipe	0.5	0.2	3,045	1,473	62.4	22.6	14.1	6.1	3.0	0.0	0.0	0.0	8,527.157	17,622.933	0.17	4,375.5
Senegal	28.6	14.3	2,243	1,123	64.6	16.7	10.8	4.5	2.3	0.0	0.0	0.2	236.287	471.866	12.77	6,766.8
Seychelles	2.0	1.1	22,569	12,196	69.7	167.7	116.8	45.3	24.5	0.0	0.0	0.0	6.690	12.381	0.09	13.1
Sierra Leone	8.2	2.9	1,369	490	46.2	10.2	4.7	2.8	1.0	0.0	0.0	0.1	1,553.139	4,336.129	6.00	12,754.9
South Africa	611.1	401.8	12,111	7,963	84.8	90.0	76.3	24.3	16.0	0.7	0.6	0.7	4.774	7.261	50.46	2,917.5
Sudan[d]	152.4	70.0	3,608	1,656	59.2	26.8	15.9	7.2	3.3	0.2	0.1	0.6	1.224	2.667	42.25	186.6
Swaziland	7.6	4.1	6,328	3,399	69.3	47.0	32.6	12.7	6.8	0.0	0.0	0.0	3.900	7.261	1.20	29.7
Tanzania	71.8	23.9	1,554	517	42.9	11.5	4.9	3.1	1.0	0.1	0.0	0.7	522.483	1,572.115	46.22	37,533.0
Togo	8.1	3.7	1,314	599	58.8	9.8	5.7	2.6	1.2	0.0	0.0	0.1	215.060	471.866	6.15	1,739.2
Tunisia	109.3	46.0	10,319	4,340	54.2	76.7	41.6	20.7	8.7	0.1	0.1	0.2	0.592	1.408	10.59	64.7
Uganda	55.1	18.2	1,597	528	42.6	11.9	5.1	3.2	1.1	0.1	0.0	0.5	833.540	2,522.747	34.51	45,944.1
Zambia	42.5	20.8	3,155	1,544	63.1	23.4	14.8	6.3	3.1	0.0	0.0	0.2	2,378.380	4,860.667	13.47	101,104.8
Zimbabwe	17.6	8.9	1,378	695	65.0	10.2	6.7	2.8	1.4	0.0	0.0	0.0	0.504	1.000	12.75	8.9
Total (50)	**4,115.1**	**1,870.4**	**4,044**	**1,838**	**58.6**	**30.0**	**17.6**	**8.1**	**3.7**	**4.5**	**2.7**	**15.1**	**n.a.**	**n.a.**	**1,017.60**	**n.a.**
ASIA AND THE PACIFIC																
Bangladesh	419.2	130.9	2,800	874	40.3	20.8	8.4	5.6	1.8	0.5	0.2	2.2	23.145	74.152	149.70	9,702.9
Bhutan	5.1	1.8	7,199	2,600	46.6	53.5	24.9	14.5	5.2	0.0	0.0	0.0	16.856	46.670	0.71	85.9
Brunei Darussalam	29.3	16.7	74,397	42,432	73.5	552.7	406.5	149.4	85.2	0.0	0.0	0.0	0.717	1.258	0.39	21.0
Cambodia	38.7	12.8	2,717	902	42.8	20.2	8.6	5.5	1.8	0.0	0.0	0.2	1,347.115	4,058.500	14.23	52,068.7
China[e]	13,495.9	7,321.9	10,057	5,456	70.0	74.7	52.3	20.2	11.0	14.9	10.4	19.9	3.506	6.461	1,341.98	47,310.4
Fiji	6.5	3.8	7,558	4,393	75.0	56.1	42.1	15.2	8.8	0.0	0.0	0.0	1.042	1.793	0.85	6.7
Hong Kong SAR, China	354.5	248.7	50,129	35,173	90.5	372.4	337.0	100.7	70.7	0.4	0.4	0.1	5.462	7.784	7.07	1,936.1
India	5,757.5	1,864.0	4,735	1,533	41.7	35.2	14.7	9.5	3.1	6.4	2.7	18.1	15.109	46.670	1,215.96	86,993.1
Indonesia	2,058.1	846.3	8,539	3,511	53.0	63.4	33.6	17.2	7.1	2.3	1.2	3.6	3,606.566	8,770.433	241.04	7,422,781.2
Lao PDR	26.2	8.1	4,108	1,262	39.6	30.5	12.1	8.3	2.5	0.0	0.0	0.1	2,467.753	8,030.055	6.39	64,727.1
Macao SAR, China	64.3	36.8	115,441	66,063	73.8	857.6	632.9	231.9	132.7	0.1	0.1	0.0	4.589	8.018	0.56	295.0
Malaysia	606.1	289.0	20,926	9,979	61.5	155.5	95.6	42.0	20.0	0.7	0.4	0.4	1.459	3.060	28.96	884.5
Maldives	3.7	2.2	11,392	6,653	75.3	84.6	63.7	22.9	13.4	0.0	0.0	0.0	8.527	14.602	0.33	31.6
Mongolia	23.4	9.9	8,719	3,701	54.7	64.8	35.5	17.5	7.4	0.0	0.0	0.0	537.127	1,265.516	2.68	12,546.8
Myanmar	192.1	55.2	3,181	914	37.0	23.6	8.8	6.4	1.8	0.2	0.1	0.9	234.974	817.917	60.38	45,128.0
Nepal	58.9	19.6	2,221	739	42.9	16.5	7.1	4.5	1.5	0.1	0.0	0.4	24.628	74.020	26.49	1,449.5
Pakistan	788.1	222.2	4,450	1,255	36.4	33.1	12.0	8.9	2.5	0.9	0.3	2.6	24.346	86.343	177.11	19,187.9
Philippines	543.7	224.1	5,772	2,379	53.2	42.9	22.8	11.6	4.8	0.6	0.3	1.4	17.854	43.313	94.19	9,706.3
Singapore	374.8	265.6	72,296	51,242	91.4	537.1	490.9	145.2	102.9	0.4	0.4	0.1	0.891	1.258	5.18	334.1
Sri Lanka	169.3	59.2	8,111	2,836	45.1	60.3	27.2	16.3	5.7	0.2	0.1	0.3	38.654	110.565	20.87	6,542.7
Taiwan, China	907.1	465.2	39,059	20,030	66.1	290.2	191.9	78.5	40.2	1.0	0.7	0.3	15.112	29.469	23.22	13,709.1
Thailand	899.0	364.7	13,299	5,395	52.3	98.8	51.7	26.7	10.8	1.0	0.5	1.0	12.370	30.492	67.60	11,120.5
Vietnam	414.3	135.5	4,717	1,543	42.2	35.0	14.8	9.5	3.1	0.5	0.2	1.3	6,709.192	20,509.750	87.84	2,779,880.2
Total (23)	**27,235.6**	**12,604.3**	**7,621**	**3,527**	**59.7**	**56.6**	**33.8**	**15.3**	**7.1**	**30.0**	**17.9**	**53.1**	**n.a.**	**n.a.**	**3,573.72**	**n.a.**

Table 2.1 (Continued)

GROSS DOMESTIC PRODUCT	Expenditure (US$, billions)		Expenditure per capita (US$)		Price level index	Expenditure per capita index				Share (world = 100.0)			PPP	Reference data		
						World = 100.0		US = 100.0		Expenditure		Popula-tion		Exchange rate	Popula-tion	Expendi-ture in national currency unit
Economy	Based on PPPs	Based on XRs	Based on PPPs	Based on XRs	(world = 100.0)	Based on PPPs	Based on XRs	Based on PPPs	Based on XRs	Based on PPPs	Based on XRs		(US$ = 1.000)	(US$ = 1.000)	(millions)	(billions)
(00)	(01)	(02)	(03)	(04)	(05)	(06)	(07)	(08)	(09)	(10)ᵃ	(11)ᵃ	(12)ᵃ	(13)ᵇ	(14)ᵇ	(15)	(16)
COMMONWEALTH OF INDEPENDENT STATES																
Armenia	20.2	10.1	6,696	3,363	64.8	49.7	32.2	13.5	6.8	0.0	0.0	0.0	187.095	372.501	3.02	3,777.9
Azerbaijan	144.5	66.0	15,963	7,285	58.8	118.6	69.8	32.1	14.6	0.2	0.1	0.1	0.360	0.790	9.05	52.1
Belarus	157.3	53.0	16,603	5,596	43.5	123.3	53.6	33.4	11.2	0.2	0.1	0.1	1,889.308	5,605.840	9.47	297,157.7
Kazakhstan	343.9	188.0	20,772	11,358	70.5	154.3	108.8	41.7	22.8	0.4	0.3	0.2	80.171	146.620	16.56	27,571.9
Kyrgyz Republic	16.1	6.2	3,062	1,178	49.6	22.7	11.3	6.2	2.4	0.0	0.0	0.1	17.757	46.144	5.26	286.0
Moldova	14.9	7.0	4,179	1,971	60.8	31.0	18.9	8.4	4.0	0.0	0.0	0.1	5.535	11.739	3.56	82.3
Russian Federationᶠ	3,216.9	1,901.0	22,502	13,298	76.2	167.2	127.4	45.2	26.7	3.5	2.7	2.1	17.346	29.352	142.96	55,799.6
Tajikistan	17.3	6.5	2,243	846	48.7	16.7	8.1	4.5	1.7	0.0	0.0	0.1	1.740	4.610	7.71	30.1
Ukraine	379.1	163.4	8,295	3,575	55.6	61.6	34.3	16.7	7.2	0.4	0.2	0.7	3.434	7.968	45.71	1,302.1
Total (9)	**4,310.3**	**2,401.3**	**17,716**	**9,870**	**71.8**	**131.6**	**94.6**	**35.6**	**19.8**	**4.8**	**3.4**	**3.6**	**n.a.**	**n.a.**	**243.29**	**n.a.**
EUROSTAT-OECD																
Albania	28.2	12.6	9,963	4,467	57.8	74.0	42.8	20.0	9.0	0.0	0.0	0.0	45.452	101.372	2.83	1,282.3
Australia	956.0	1,490.0	42,000	65,464	201.0	312.0	627.2	84.4	131.5	1.1	2.1	0.3	1.511	0.969	22.76	1,444.5
Austria	360.5	416.0	42,978	49,590	148.8	319.3	475.1	86.3	99.6	0.4	0.6	0.1	0.830	0.719	8.39	299.2
Belgium	440.1	513.3	40,093	46,759	150.4	297.9	448.0	80.5	93.9	0.5	0.7	0.2	0.839	0.719	10.98	369.3
Bosnia and Herzegovina	37.0	19.0	9,629	4,957	66.4	71.5	47.5	19.3	10.0	0.0	0.0	0.1	0.724	1.407	3.84	26.8
Bulgaria	114.1	53.5	15,522	7,284	60.5	115.3	69.8	31.2	14.6	0.1	0.1	0.1	0.660	1.407	7.35	75.3
Canada	1,416.2	1,778.3	41,069	51,572	161.9	305.1	494.1	82.5	103.6	1.6	2.5	0.5	1.243	0.990	34.48	1,759.7
Chile	349.1	251.2	20,216	14,546	92.8	150.2	139.4	40.6	29.2	0.4	0.4	0.3	348.017	483.668	17.27	121,492.7
Croatia	86.8	61.7	20,308	14,429	91.6	150.9	138.2	40.8	29.0	0.1	0.1	0.1	3.802	5.351	4.28	330.2
Cyprus	26.6	24.9	31,229	29,208	120.6	232.0	279.8	62.7	58.7	0.0	0.0	0.0	0.673	0.719	0.85	17.9
Czech Republic	283.9	216.1	27,045	20,592	98.2	200.9	197.3	54.3	41.4	0.3	0.3	0.2	13.468	17.689	10.50	3,823.4
Denmark	233.0	334.3	41,843	60,030	185.0	310.9	575.1	84.1	120.6	0.3	0.5	0.1	7.689	5.360	5.57	1,791.8
Estonia	30.9	22.5	23,088	16,821	93.9	171.5	161.1	46.4	33.8	0.0	0.0	0.0	0.524	0.719	1.34	16.2
Finland	208.0	262.3	38,611	48,686	162.6	286.8	466.4	77.6	97.8	0.2	0.4	0.1	0.907	0.719	5.39	188.7
France	2,369.6	2,782.2	36,391	42,728	151.4	270.4	409.3	73.1	85.8	2.6	4.0	1.0	0.845	0.719	65.11	2,001.4
Germany	3,352.1	3,628.1	40,990	44,365	139.6	304.5	425.0	82.3	89.1	3.7	5.2	1.2	0.779	0.719	81.78	2,609.9
Greece	300.8	289.9	26,622	25,654	124.3	197.8	245.8	53.5	51.5	0.3	0.4	0.2	0.693	0.719	11.30	208.5
Hungary	223.5	137.5	22,413	13,790	79.3	166.5	132.1	45.0	27.7	0.2	0.2	0.1	123.650	200.966	9.97	27,635.4
Iceland	12.2	14.0	38,226	43,969	148.3	284.0	421.2	76.8	88.3	0.0	0.0	0.0	133.563	116.118	0.32	1,628.7
Ireland	196.6	226.0	42,942	49,383	148.3	319.0	473.1	86.3	99.2	0.2	0.3	0.1	0.827	0.719	4.58	162.6
Israel	234.2	258.2	30,168	33,259	142.2	224.1	318.6	60.6	66.8	0.3	0.4	0.1	3.945	3.578	7.76	923.9
Italy	2,056.7	2,197.0	33,870	36,180	137.7	251.6	346.6	68.0	72.7	2.3	3.1	0.9	0.768	0.719	60.72	1,580.4
Japan	4,379.8	5,897.0	34,262	46,131	173.6	254.5	441.9	68.8	92.7	4.8	8.4	1.9	107.454	79.807	127.83	470,623.2
Korea, Rep.	1,445.3	1,114.5	29,035	22,388	99.4	215.7	214.5	58.3	45.0	1.6	1.6	0.7	854.586	1,108.290	49.78	1,235,160.5
Latvia	41.1	28.1	19,994	13,658	88.1	148.5	130.8	40.2	27.4	0.0	0.0	0.0	0.347	0.508	2.06	14.3
Lithuania	68.2	43.0	22,521	14,212	81.4	167.3	136.2	45.2	28.5	0.1	0.1	0.0	1.567	2.484	3.03	106.9
Luxembourg	46.1	58.0	88,670	111,689	162.4	658.8	1070.0	178.1	224.4	0.1	0.1	0.0	0.906	0.719	0.52	41.7

Table 2.1 *(Continued)*

GROSS DOMESTIC PRODUCT	Expenditure (US$, billions)		Expenditure per capita (US$)		Price level index	Expenditure per capita index				Share (world = 100.0)			PPP	Reference data		
						World = 100.0		US = 100.0		Expenditure		Popula-tion		Exchange rate	Popula-tion	Expendi-ture in national currency unit
Economy	Based on PPPs	Based on XRs	Based on PPPs	Based on XRs	(world = 100.0)	Based on PPPs	Based on XRs	Based on PPPs	Based on XRs	Based on PPPs	Based on XRs		(US$ = 1.000)	(US$ = 1.000)	(millions)	(billions)
(00)	(01)	(02)	(03)	(04)	(05)	(06)	(07)	(08)	(09)	(10)a	(11)a	(12)a	(13)b	(14)b	(15)	(16)
Macedonia, FYR	24.6	10.4	11,957	5,050	54.5	88.8	48.4	24.0	10.1	0.0	0.0	0.0	18.680	44.226	2.06	459.8
Malta	11.9	9.2	28,608	22,201	100.1	212.5	212.7	57.5	44.6	0.0	0.0	0.0	0.558	0.719	0.41	6.6
Mexico	1,894.6	1,170.1	16,377	10,115	79.6	121.7	96.9	32.9	20.3	2.1	1.7	1.7	7.673	12.423	115.68	14,536.9
Montenegro	8.8	4.5	14,128	7,244	66.1	105.0	69.4	28.4	14.6	0.0	0.0	0.0	0.369	0.719	0.62	3.2
Netherlands	720.3	832.8	43,150	49,888	149.1	320.6	477.9	86.7	100.2	0.8	1.2	0.2	0.832	0.719	16.69	599.0
New Zealand	137.6	161.5	31,172	36,591	151.4	231.6	350.5	62.6	73.5	0.2	0.2	0.1	1.486	1.266	4.41	204.5
Norway	306.5	490.5	61,879	99,035	206.4	459.7	948.8	124.3	198.9	0.3	0.7	0.1	8.973	5.606	4.95	2,750.0
Poland	838.0	515.5	21,753	13,382	79.3	161.6	128.2	43.7	26.9	0.9	0.7	0.6	1.823	2.964	38.53	1,528.1
Portugal	272.7	237.9	25,672	22,396	112.5	190.7	214.6	51.6	45.0	0.3	0.3	0.2	0.628	0.719	10.62	171.1
Romania	344.8	182.6	16,146	8,549	68.3	119.9	81.9	32.4	17.2	0.4	0.3	0.3	1.615	3.049	21.35	556.7
Russian Federationf	3,216.9	1,901.0	22,502	13,298	76.2	167.2	127.4	45.2	26.7	3.5	2.7	2.1	17.346	29.352	142.96	55,799.6
Serbia	86.1	43.8	11,854	6,027	65.6	88.1	57.7	23.8	12.1	0.1	0.1	0.1	37.288	73.338	7.26	3,208.6
Slovak Republic	135.7	95.9	25,130	17,762	91.1	186.7	170.2	50.5	35.7	0.1	0.1	0.1	0.508	0.719	5.40	69.0
Slovenia	57.8	50.3	28,156	24,480	112.1	209.2	234.5	56.6	49.2	0.1	0.1	0.0	0.625	0.719	2.05	36.1
Spain	1,483.2	1,454.5	32,156	31,534	126.5	238.9	302.1	64.6	63.3	1.6	2.1	0.7	0.705	0.719	46.13	1,046.3
Sweden	394.6	535.8	41,761	56,704	175.1	310.3	543.2	83.9	113.9	0.4	0.8	0.1	8.820	6.496	9.45	3,480.5
Switzerland	405.9	659.9	51,582	83,854	209.6	383.2	803.3	103.6	168.4	0.4	0.9	0.1	1.441	0.887	7.87	585.1
Turkey	1,314.9	771.7	17,781	10,435	75.7	132.1	100.0	35.7	21.0	1.5	1.1	1.1	0.987	1.682	73.95	1,297.7
United Kingdom	2,201.4	2,461.8	35,091	39,241	144.2	260.7	375.9	70.5	78.8	2.4	3.5	0.9	0.698	0.624	62.74	1,536.9
United States	15,533.8	15,533.8	49,782	49,782	129.0	369.8	476.9	100.0	100.0	17.1	22.1	4.6	1.000	1.000	312.04	15,533.8
Total (47)	**48,686.6**	**49,253.0**	**33,675**	**34,067**	**130.5**	**250.2**	**326.4**	**67.6**	**68.4**	**53.7**	**70.1**	**21.5**	**n.a.**	**n.a.**	**1,445.76**	**n.a.**
LATIN AMERICA																
Bolivia	56.4	23.9	5,557	2,360	54.8	41.3	22.6	11.2	4.7	0.1	0.0	0.2	2.946	6.937	10.15	166.1
Brazil	2,816.3	2,476.6	14,639	12,874	113.4	108.8	123.3	29.4	25.9	3.1	3.5	2.9	1.471	1.673	192.38	4,143.0
Colombia	535.0	336.3	11,360	7,142	81.5	84.4	68.4	22.8	14.3	0.6	0.5	0.7	1,161.910	1,848.139	47.09	621,615.0
Costa Rica	59.8	41.0	13,030	8,935	88.4	96.8	85.6	26.2	17.9	0.1	0.1	0.1	345.738	505.664	4.59	20,748.0
Cubag	…	…	…	…	41.5	…	…	…	…	…	…	…	0.322	1.000	11.17	…
Dominican Republic	109.0	55.6	10,858	5,541	65.8	80.7	53.1	21.8	11.1	0.1	0.1	0.1	13.449	38.109	10.04	2,119.3
Ecuador	151.6	79.8	9,932	5,226	67.9	73.8	50.1	20.0	10.5	0.2	0.1	0.2	0.526	1.000	15.27	79.8
El Salvador	46.0	23.1	7,357	3,701	64.9	54.7	35.5	14.8	7.4	0.1	0.0	0.1	0.503	1.000	6.25	23.1
Guatemala	102.4	47.7	6,971	3,247	60.1	51.8	31.1	14.0	6.5	0.1	0.1	0.2	3.626	7.785	14.69	371.3
Haiti	15.6	7.3	1,557	734	60.8	11.6	7.0	3.1	1.5	0.0	0.0	0.1	19.108	40.523	10.01	297.7
Honduras	33.8	17.7	4,349	2,282	67.7	32.3	21.9	8.7	4.6	0.0	0.0	0.1	9.915	18.895	7.77	335.0
Nicaragua	24.2	9.6	4,111	1,635	51.3	30.5	15.7	8.3	3.3	0.0	0.0	0.1	8.919	22.424	5.89	216.1
Panama	57.2	31.3	15,369	8,411	70.6	114.2	80.6	30.9	16.9	0.1	0.0	0.1	0.547	1.000	3.72	31.3
Paraguay	47.2	25.2	7,193	3,836	68.8	53.4	36.8	14.4	7.7	0.1	0.0	0.1	2,227.340	4,176.066	6.57	105,203.2
Peru	327.2	180.7	10,981	6,066	71.2	81.6	58.1	22.1	12.2	0.4	0.3	0.4	1.521	2.754	29.80	497.8
Uruguay	58.7	46.4	17,343	13,722	102.0	128.8	131.5	34.8	27.6	0.1	0.1	0.1	15.282	19.314	3.38	896.8

Table 2.1 (Continued)

GROSS DOMESTIC PRODUCT	Expenditure (US$, billions)		Expenditure per capita (US$)		Price level index	Expenditure per capita index				Share (world = 100.0)			PPP	Reference data		
						World = 100.0		US = 100.0		Expenditure		Popula-tion		Exchange rate	Popula-tion	Expendi-ture in national currency unit
Economy	Based on PPPs	Based on XRs	Based on PPPs	Based on XRs	(world = 100.0)	Based on PPPs	Based on XRs	Based on PPPs	Based on XRs	Based on PPPs	Based on XRs		(US$ = 1.000)	(US$ = 1.000)	(millions)	(billions)
(00)	(01)	(02)	(03)	(04)	(05)	(06)	(07)	(08)	(09)	(10)[a]	(11)[a]	(12)[a]	(13)[b]	(14)[b]	(15)	(16)
Venezuela, RB	500.3	316.5	16,965	10,731	81.6	126.0	102.8	34.1	21.6	0.6	0.5	0.4	2.713	4.289	29.49	1,357.5
Total (17)	**4,940.8**	**3,719.1**	**12,443**	**9,366**	**97.1**	**92.4**	**89.7**	**25.0**	**18.8**	**5.5**	**5.3**	**5.9**	**n.a.**	**n.a.**	**397.09**	**n.a.**
CARIBBEAN																
Anguilla	0.4	0.3	27,274	20,982	99.2	202.6	201.0	54.8	42.1	0.0	0.0	0.0	2.077	2.700	0.01	0.8
Antigua and Barbuda	1.8	1.1	20,540	13,172	82.7	152.6	126.2	41.3	26.5	0.0	0.0	0.0	1.731	2.700	0.09	3.0
Aruba	3.7	2.6	36,017	25,355	90.8	267.6	242.9	72.3	50.9	0.0	0.0	0.0	1.260	1.790	0.10	4.6
Bahamas, The	8.3	7.9	22,639	21,490	122.4	168.2	205.9	45.5	43.2	0.0	0.0	0.0	0.949	1.000	0.37	7.9
Barbados	4.3	4.4	15,354	15,483	130.0	114.1	148.3	30.8	31.1	0.0	0.0	0.0	2.017	2.000	0.28	8.7
Belize	2.6	1.5	8,212	4,721	74.1	61.0	45.2	16.5	9.5	0.0	0.0	0.0	1.150	2.000	0.32	3.0
Bermuda	3.6	5.6	54,899	85,839	201.6	407.9	822.4	110.3	172.4	0.0	0.0	0.0	1.564	1.000	0.06	5.6
Bonaire[h]	...	...	...	...	...	...	...	...	...	...	...	...	...	1.000	0.02	...
Cayman Islands	2.8	3.2	49,686	56,883	147.6	369.1	544.9	99.8	114.3	0.0	0.0	0.0	0.959	0.838	0.06	2.7
Curaçao	4.2	3.0	27,781	20,055	93.1	206.4	192.1	55.8	40.3	0.0	0.0	0.0	1.292	1.790	0.15	5.4
Dominica	0.7	0.5	9,983	6,881	88.9	74.2	65.9	20.1	13.8	0.0	0.0	0.0	1.861	2.700	0.07	1.3
Grenada	1.2	0.8	11,221	7,410	85.2	83.4	71.0	22.5	14.9	0.0	0.0	0.0	1.783	2.700	0.11	2.1
Jamaica	22.9	14.5	8,329	5,248	81.3	61.9	50.3	16.7	10.5	0.0	0.0	0.0	54.122	85.892	2.75	1,241.8
Montserrat	0.1	0.1	15,762	11,343	92.8	117.1	108.7	31.7	22.8	0.0	0.0	0.0	1.943	2.700	0.01	0.2
St. Kitts and Nevis	1.1	0.7	20,582	13,744	86.1	152.9	131.7	41.3	27.6	0.0	0.0	0.0	1.803	2.700	0.05	2.0
St. Lucia	1.8	1.2	9,893	6,755	88.1	73.5	64.7	19.9	13.6	0.0	0.0	0.0	1.844	2.700	0.18	3.3
St. Vincent and the Grenadines	1.1	0.7	9,883	6,191	80.8	73.4	59.3	19.9	12.4	0.0	0.0	0.0	1.691	2.700	0.11	1.8
Sint Maarten	1.2	1.0	32,972	25,402	99.3	245.0	243.4	66.2	51.0	0.0	0.0	0.0	1.379	1.790	0.04	1.7
Suriname	7.8	4.4	14,463	8,082	72.1	107.4	77.4	29.1	16.2	0.0	0.0	0.0	1.826	3.268	0.54	14.3
Trinidad and Tobago	38.3	23.5	28,743	17,660	79.2	213.5	169.2	57.7	35.5	0.0	0.0	0.0	3.938	6.409	1.33	150.9
Turks and Caicos Islands	0.7	0.7	20,878	22,971	141.9	155.1	220.1	41.9	46.1	0.0	0.0	0.0	1.100	1.000	0.03	0.7
Virgin Islands, British	0.9	0.9	30,290	32,580	138.7	225.0	312.1	60.8	65.4	0.0	0.0	0.0	1.076	1.000	0.03	0.9
Total (22)	**109.3**	**78.4**	**16,351**	**11,732**	**92.5**	**121.5**	**112.4**	**32.8**	**23.6**	**0.1**	**0.1**	**0.1**	**n.a.**	**n.a.**	**6.69**	**n.a.**
WESTERN ASIA																
Bahrain	51.8	28.9	43,360	24,200	72.0	322.1	231.8	87.1	48.6	0.1	0.0	0.0	0.211	0.378	1.20	10.9
Egypt, Arab Rep.[c]	843.8	229.9	10,599	2,888	35.1	78.7	27.7	21.3	5.8	0.9	0.3	1.2	1.625	5.964	79.62	1,371.1
Iraq	371.0	159.8	11,130	4,794	55.5	82.7	45.9	22.4	9.6	0.4	0.2	0.5	516.521	1,199.200	33.34	191,652.9
Jordan	69.8	28.8	11,169	4,615	53.3	83.0	44.2	22.4	9.3	0.1	0.0	0.1	0.293	0.710	6.25	20.5
Kuwait	257.7	160.6	84,058	52,379	80.4	624.5	501.8	168.9	105.2	0.3	0.2	0.0	0.172	0.276	3.07	44.3
Oman	140.4	70.0	42,619	21,234	64.2	316.6	203.4	85.6	42.7	0.2	0.1	0.0	0.192	0.385	3.30	26.9
Qatar	258.1	171.0	146,521	97,091	85.4	1,088.5	930.1	294.3	195.0	0.3	0.2	0.0	2.419	3.650	1.76	624.2
Saudi Arabia	1,366.7	669.5	48,163	23,594	63.2	357.8	226.0	96.7	47.4	1.5	1.0	0.4	1.837	3.750	28.38	2,510.6
Sudan[d]	152.4	70.0	3,608	1,656	59.2	26.8	15.9	7.2	3.3	0.2	0.1	0.6	1.224	2.667	42.25	186.6
United Arab Emirates	503.2	348.6	60,886	42,182	89.3	452.3	404.1	122.3	84.7	0.6	0.5	0.1	2.544	3.673	8.26	1,280.2

Table 2.1 (Continued)

GROSS DOMESTIC PRODUCT	Expenditure (US$, billions)		Expenditure per capita (US$)		Price level index	Expenditure per capita index				Share (world = 100.0)			PPP	Reference data		
						World = 100.0		US = 100.0		Expenditure		Popula-tion		Exchange rate	Popula-tion	Expendi-ture in national currency unit
Economy	Based on PPPs	Based on XRs	Based on PPPs	Based on XRs	(world = 100.0)	Based on PPPs	Based on XRs	Based on PPPs	Based on XRs	Based on PPPs	Based on XRs		(US$ = 1.000)	(US$ = 1.000)	(millions)	(billions)
(00)	(01)	(02)	(03)	(04)	(05)	(06)	(07)	(08)	(09)	(10)[a]	(11)[a]	(12)[a]	(13)[b]	(14)[b]	(15)	(16)
West Bank and Gaza	16.0	9.8	3,833	2,345	78.9	28.5	22.5	7.7	4.7	0.0	0.0	0.1	2.189	3.578	4.17	35.0
Yemen, Rep.	88.6	31.4	3,716	1,318	45.7	27.6	12.6	7.5	2.6	0.1	0.0	0.4	75.818	213.800	23.83	6,714.9
Total (12)	**4,119.5**	**1,978.3**	**17,499**	**8,403**	**61.9**	**130.0**	**80.5**	**35.2**	**16.9**	**4.5**	**2.8**	**3.5**	**n.a.**	**n.a.**	**235.41**	**n.a.**
SINGLETONS																
Georgia	28.3	14.4	6,343	3,231	65.7	47.1	31.0	12.7	6.5	0.0	0.0	0.1	0.859	1.686	4.47	24.3
Iran, Islamic Rep.	1,314.2	576.3	17,488	7,669	56.5	129.9	73.5	35.1	15.4	1.4	0.8	1.1	4,657.463	10,621.000	75.15	6,121,004.0
Total (2)	**1,342.6**	**590.7**	**16,863**	**7,420**	**56.7**	**125.3**	**71.1**	**33.9**	**14.9**	**1.5**	**0.8**	**1.2**	**n.a.**	**n.a.**	**79.62**	**n.a.**
WORLD[i] (179)	**90,646.6**	**70,294.6**	**13,460**	**10,438**	**100.0**	**100.0**	**100.0**	**27.0**	**21.0**	**100.0**	**100.0**	**100.0**	**n.a.**	**n.a.**	**6,734.36**	**n.a.**

Source: ICP, http://icp.worldbank.org/.

Note: n.a. = not applicable; PPP = purchasing power parity; XR = exchange rate; … = data suppressed because of incompleteness.

a. All shares are rounded to one decimal place. More precision can be found in the Excel version of the table, which can be downloaded from the ICP website.

b. All exchange rates and PPPs are rounded to three decimal places. More precision can be found in the Excel version of the table, which can be downloaded from the ICP website.

c. The Arab Republic of Egypt participated in both the Africa and Western Asia regions. The regional results for Egypt were averaged by taking the geometric mean of the regional PPPs, allowing Egypt to have the same global results in each region.

d. Sudan participated in both the Africa and Western Asia regions. The regional results for Sudan were averaged by taking the geometric mean of the regional PPPs, allowing Sudan to have the same global results in each region.

e. The results presented in the tables are based on data supplied by all the participating economies and compiled in accordance with ICP principles and the procedures recommended by the 2011 ICP Technical Advisory Group. The results for China were estimated by the 2011 ICP Asia and the Pacific Regional Office and the Global Office. The National Bureau of Statistics of China does not recognize these results as official statistics.

f. The Russian Federation participated in both the CIS and Eurostat-OECD comparisons. The PPPs for Russia are based on the Eurostat-OECD comparison. They were the basis for linking the CIS comparison to the ICP.

g. The official GDP of Cuba for reference year 2011 is 68,990.15 million in national currency. However, this number and its breakdown into main aggregates are not shown in the tables because of methodological comparability issues. Therefore, Cuba's results are provided only for the PPP and price level index. In addition, Cuba's figures are not included in the Latin America and world totals.

h. Bonaire's results are provided only for the individual consumption expenditure by households. Therefore, to ensure consistency across the tables, Bonaire is not included in the Caribbean or the world total.

i. This table does not include the Pacific Islands and does not double count the dual participation economies: the Arab Republic of Egypt, Sudan, and the Russian Federation.

Table 2.2 Nominal Expenditures in National Currency Units, ICP 2011

EXPENDITURES (national currency units, billions) Economy	Gross domestic product	Actual individual consumption	Food and nonalcoholic beverages	Alcoholic beverages, tobacco, and narcotics	Clothing and footwear	Housing, water, electricity, gas, and other fuels	Furnishings, household equipment and maintenance	Health	Transport	Communication	Recreation and culture	Education
(00)	(01)	(02)	(03)	(04)	(05)	(06)	(07)	(08)	(09)	(10)	(11)	(12)
AFRICA												
Algeria	14,481.0	6,515.4	1,955.5	111.9	190.1	318.1	161.5	460.8	787.3	369.0	165.7	623.0
Angola	9,767.6	5,929.1	2,433.6	257.3	299.5	622.3	330.8	311.4	318.2	61.1	126.8	289.8
Benin	3,439.8	2,779.0	1,339.9	80.4	117.9	283.0	75.1	94.7	202.0	84.1	41.8	142.6
Botswana	102.5	56.0	10.0	4.2	3.4	6.2	3.3	2.9	9.0	1.4	1.5	7.1
Burkina Faso	4,868.5	3,294.3	1,686.5	211.1	68.9	364.0	143.5	122.9	212.9	108.7	76.9	97.5
Burundi	2,599.9	2,424.1	1,058.2	334.0	23.5	374.3	21.6	67.9	158.9	27.4	25.2	134.1
Cameroon	12,545.7	9,829.0	4,521.7	259.2	811.5	897.1	903.8	149.7	798.9	149.1	151.4	224.0
Cape Verde	149.0	105.3	36.6	5.0	2.9	20.8	7.5	5.7	7.3	3.6	1.0	8.6
Central African Republic	1,029.7	951.6	545.3	86.6	68.4	46.7	49.1	14.5	34.2	8.2	16.1	28.1
Chad	5,725.3	3,931.6	1,890.1	182.3	88.4	369.8	263.3	276.1	367.7	148.2	90.6	55.7
Comoros	95.4	94.2	48.4	0.3	2.9	29.3	3.6	0.8	1.9	0.5	1.0	2.3
Congo, Rep.	6,982.5	1,729.3	634.4	71.1	46.3	227.2	59.6	135.7	141.0	89.9	47.2	129.4
Congo, Dem. Rep.	23,146.1	14,896.2	8,177.3	429.9	696.0	1,778.8	517.8	666.2	386.1	169.1	193.8	635.2
Côte d'Ivoire	12,275.5	8,766.0	3,727.4	276.3	304.3	857.7	724.1	372.1	957.3	251.7	304.4	375.2
Djibouti	205.3	146.7	44.2	11.5	4.3	45.9	8.2	4.7	9.1	0.4	1.7	9.5
Egypt, Arab Rep.[a]	1,371.1	1,090.5	457.0	35.4	65.9	142.3	52.7	99.5	64.4	27.8	32.4	72.2
Equatorial Guinea	8,367.3	1,076.8	408.2	24.5	32.5	152.4	40.9	101.0	86.3	40.4	19.9	52.6
Ethiopia	506.1	409.2	151.9	10.0	21.0	66.9	39.2	33.5	6.7	1.6	1.9	14.0
Gabon	8,046.1	3,066.5	921.4	173.3	155.1	439.6	139.5	210.5	257.1	136.4	69.8	160.4
Gambia, The	26.6	21.2	9.0	0.6	1.5	1.5	0.5	3.2	0.6	0.5	0.7	1.8
Ghana	59.8	40.0	14.9	0.6	5.7	4.0	2.8	1.4	2.6	0.6	0.4	5.5
Guinea	33,128.3	18,673.4	10,798.4	273.7	1,286.3	1,491.0	724.8	1,360.6	1,024.3	30.3	152.1	594.4
Guinea-Bissau	464.7	318.1	162.3	5.3	25.6	43.7	22.5	7.8	22.6	1.7	13.8	6.0
Kenya	3,048.9	2,669.6	913.5	129.9	65.9	208.1	120.5	193.7	271.0	81.5	90.9	385.2
Lesotho	18.3	20.2	5.2	0.5	2.5	2.1	1.8	0.9	0.7	0.6	0.7	1.9
Liberia	1.1	1.3	0.3	0.0	0.2	0.3	0.1	0.0	0.0	0.0	0.0	0.2
Madagascar	20,276.4	18,408.8	8,046.8	559.3	1,188.1	1,133.5	2,458.7	324.7	2,376.6	160.2	773.7	649.6
Malawi	1,140.8	1,125.8	549.7	54.4	29.3	122.9	114.3	44.5	87.5	18.9	26.3	56.7
Mali	5,024.5	3,352.6	1,559.4	47.3	193.2	326.5	199.5	132.8	444.4	74.7	133.3	146.6
Mauritania	1,309.4	766.3	461.7	7.3	25.7	72.9	21.6	30.6	33.2	29.6	7.4	57.1
Mauritius	323.0	255.2	73.8	21.3	14.9	39.4	20.4	12.6	34.4	7.8	16.6	20.4
Morocco	802.6	536.6	182.9	17.1	21.8	74.3	24.7	33.2	47.8	32.8	23.6	61.3
Mozambique	364.7	313.2	161.5	13.6	15.1	22.8	8.8	8.9	26.3	3.8	8.2	21.6
Namibia	90.6	64.8	13.0	2.6	3.1	12.4	4.6	7.2	2.6	0.5	2.6	9.1
Niger	3,025.5	2,427.9	1,013.4	54.2	187.3	245.0	117.2	98.6	184.0	56.5	133.1	79.4
Nigeria	38,017.0	24,474.5	9,243.1	345.1	3,537.5	2,504.4	1,727.1	777.3	1,628.3	381.1	262.9	3,122.0
Rwanda	3,814.4	3,313.2	1,586.9	111.0	109.7	546.5	107.1	86.5	213.4	40.1	55.0	173.3

Restaurants and hotels	Miscella-neous goods and services	Net purchases abroad	Individual consumption expenditure by households	Individual consumption expenditure by government	Collective consumption expenditure by government	Gross fixed capital formation	Machinery and equipment	Construc-tion	Other products	Changes in inventories and valuables	Balance of exports and imports	Domestic absorption	Individual consumption expenditure by households without housing
(13)	(14)	(15)	(16)	(17)	(18)	(19)	(20)	(21)	(22)	(23)	(24)	(25)	(26)
153.6	1,218.9	0.0	4,552.7	1,962.7	1,337.8	4,617.7	1,952.7	2,403.6	261.5	494.2	1,515.9	12,965.1	4,430.2
174.3	704.1	0.0	4,957.5	971.5	2,560.1	1,669.2	519.1	1,073.7	76.4	27.0	−417.8	10,185.4	4,815.0
258.9	85.4	−26.9	2,631.4	147.6	252.4	712.9	244.9	460.0	8.0	29.5	−334.1	3,773.8	2,453.1
2.2	4.7	0.0	48.6	7.4	12.0	33.6	13.9	19.4	0.4	6.9	−6.0	108.5	45.4
109.6	93.2	−1.3	3,169.0	125.4	741.4	802.6	329.6	407.8	65.2	375.8	−345.7	5,214.2	2,986.8
100.2	57.4	41.4	2,244.6	179.5	333.2	492.3	215.5	249.5	27.3	18.3	−667.9	3,267.9	1,906.9
658.6	223.3	80.9	9,519.1	309.8	1,147.4	2,582.6	1,202.8	1,319.5	60.4	1.0	−1,014.3	13,560.0	8,963.4
12.9	6.6	−13.1	93.0	12.3	15.1	69.8	25.2	41.8	2.8	1.4	−42.6	191.6	81.2
18.4	36.0	0.0	925.6	26.1	46.7	157.7	45.2	85.4	27.1	0.0	−126.4	1,156.1	917.7
29.5	86.2	83.8	3,811.5	120.2	249.1	1,637.9	661.2	788.0	188.7	68.2	−161.5	5,886.9	3,535.2
0.0	3.0	0.3	93.6	0.6	21.9	12.8	5.7	6.4	0.6	3.6	−37.1	132.6	70.4
129.9	51.4	−33.8	1,552.7	176.6	335.4	2,406.5	390.8	1,993.4	22.3	0.0	2,511.4	4,471.1	1,445.3
898.9	347.2	0.0	14,337.3	558.8	2,675.7	5,460.5	2,002.8	3,258.6	199.0	21.2	92.6	23,053.5	13,418.0
125.7	395.8	94.1	8,294.8	471.3	966.1	1,373.7	487.4	820.0	66.3	−804.8	1,974.4	10,301.1	7,735.9
1.4	3.4	2.3	136.0	10.5	40.7	54.1	17.9	36.0	0.3	9.1	−45.3	250.6	110.4
34.3	77.2	−70.7	1,036.1	54.4	102.6	229.1	106.5	116.4	6.2	5.4	−56.5	1,427.6	940.1
36.9	59.0	22.2	1,004.4	72.3	152.2	2,765.0	1,416.0	902.8	446.2	0.0	4,373.3	3,994.0	922.7
19.3	43.2	0.0	397.6	11.6	32.0	131.0	48.6	59.3	23.0	10.4	−76.5	582.6	363.7
141.2	99.1	163.1	2,813.0	253.5	762.2	1,528.4	447.1	450.5	630.8	3.1	2,686.0	5,360.1	2,527.0
0.2	1.0	0.0	20.2	1.0	1.9	7.1	4.5	2.2	0.4	0.0	−3.6	30.2	19.7
0.0	1.5	0.0	36.8	3.3	6.7	15.3	8.7	5.7	0.9	1.1	−3.3	63.2	36.2
264.3	466.8	206.4	18,424.7	248.7	1,518.1	7,899.0	5,023.5	2,604.4	271.1	641.7	4,396.2	28,732.2	17,419.2
1.5	5.3	0.0	311.0	7.1	81.9	59.7	26.4	31.0	2.3	5.0	0.0	464.7	299.8
165.7	185.9	−142.2	2,304.9	364.7	256.2	610.8	335.3	273.7	1.8	16.2	−503.9	3,552.8	2,195.8
0.3	1.2	1.9	17.8	2.4	3.9	4.9	1.3	3.4	0.2	0.2	−10.8	29.2	16.3
0.0	0.1	0.0	1.3	0.0	0.1	0.1	0.1	0.0	0.0	0.1	−0.5	1.7	1.1
603.0	289.2	−154.6	17,830.7	578.0	1,463.3	3,527.8	1,567.2	1,791.9	168.7	0.0	−3,123.5	23,399.8	17,644.3
28.1	26.0	−32.8	1,062.3	63.5	78.4	189.6	140.2	37.7	11.7	−37.4	−215.6	1,356.4	985.0
61.1	85.3	−51.6	3,180.8	171.8	604.3	1,114.2	479.6	583.7	51.0	43.8	−90.5	5,115.0	2,959.0
5.2	13.9	0.1	678.7	87.6	199.3	752.1	370.1	315.6	66.4	−313.4	−94.8	1,404.2	634.2
8.8	16.0	−31.1	237.2	18.0	25.7	77.6	23.3	50.7	3.6	6.3	−41.8	364.7	219.8
31.0	35.1	−48.8	472.9	63.7	82.6	246.4	105.7	127.2	13.4	42.2	−105.2	907.8	427.7
2.9	15.8	3.8	290.6	22.6	26.3	64.9	21.9	42.8	0.2	7.7	−47.5	412.2	276.4
3.9	5.7	−2.5	55.9	8.9	14.0	19.3	7.1	11.6	0.7	−1.1	−6.4	97.0	47.8
119.8	143.0	−3.6	2,342.3	85.6	301.9	1,120.9	493.0	601.7	26.3	2.0	−827.3	3,852.8	2,223.2
10.9	924.8	9.9	22,840.8	1,633.7	3,346.2	3,908.3	2,215.4	1,454.7	238.2	2.3	6,285.6	31,731.3	22,468.3
102.9	118.8	61.8	3,181.4	131.8	346.0	817.9	178.6	601.8	37.5	0.0	−662.7	4,477.1	2,828.1

(continued)

Table 2.2 *(Continued)*

EXPENDITURES (national currency units, billions) Economy	Gross domestic product	Actual individual consump- tion	Food and nonalcoholic beverages	Alcoholic beverages, tobacco, and narcotics	Clothing and footwear	Housing, water, electricity, gas, and other fuels	Furnishings, household equipment and mainte- nance	Health	Transport	Communi- cation	Recreation and culture	Education
(00)	(01)	(02)	(03)	(04)	(05)	(06)	(07)	(08)	(09)	(10)	(11)	(12)
São Tomé and Príncipe	4,375.5	5,117.2	2,793.7	230.9	201.0	483.0	172.9	202.0	500.8	65.0	74.4	198.1
Senegal	6,766.8	5,601.0	2,744.5	72.6	194.7	1,075.5	316.1	162.9	275.1	274.1	72.2	297.2
Seychelles	13.1	8.0	3.2	0.2	0.3	1.4	0.3	0.5	0.5	0.2	0.2	0.8
Sierra Leone	12,754.9	11,448.2	4,530.5	353.6	915.9	858.6	324.4	1,826.7	351.7	324.5	396.4	871.9
South Africa	2,917.5	1,992.4	353.1	87.6	86.0	271.4	122.0	220.7	257.5	51.3	81.3	213.0
Sudan[b]	186.6	130.9	67.7	0.9	5.8	19.2	8.5	1.7	10.7	2.1	3.0	4.3
Swaziland	29.7	26.8	12.2	0.2	1.5	3.6	2.8	1.7	2.1	0.3	1.1	2.2
Tanzania	37,533.0	25,647.6	16,914.0	171.1	1,708.1	1,822.3	1,115.7	899.9	989.0	17.9	274.6	1,230.2
Togo	1,739.2	1,539.4	667.2	36.1	76.5	119.8	69.3	100.2	86.0	36.1	19.8	103.2
Tunisia	64.7	48.2	10.6	1.5	3.3	6.8	2.9	3.4	6.9	1.7	1.6	3.8
Uganda	45,944.1	41,649.9	13,863.6	2,427.8	1,204.2	7,473.0	2,346.3	1,150.3	2,480.8	766.8	2,506.2	4,477.0
Zambia	101,104.8	55,896.0	32,622.8	449.3	3,508.4	6,652.1	851.2	2,876.9	760.9	1,443.9	387.2	3,471.5
Zimbabwe	8.9	8.5	4.7	0.3	0.5	0.5	0.2	0.2	0.6	0.0	0.2	0.6
Total (50)	**n.a.**	**n.a.**	**n.a.**	**n.a.**	**n.a.**	**n.a.**	**n.a.**	**n.a.**	**n.a.**	**n.a.**	**n.a.**	**n.a.**
ASIA AND THE PACIFIC												
Bangladesh	9,702.9	7,299.2	3,715.3	151.8	437.2	1,255.4	236.1	266.7	305.6	35.0	52.9	394.6
Bhutan	85.9	44.4	13.0	1.1	3.3	7.8	0.8	5.0	4.2	1.1	2.7	3.9
Brunei Darussalam	21.0	5.0	0.9	0.0	0.2	0.6	0.2	0.3	0.7	0.3	0.4	0.8
Cambodia	52,068.7	43,880.6	20,093.0	1,664.1	837.5	6,511.2	797.6	3,096.9	3,281.9	108.9	1,218.0	2,967.4
China[c]	47,310.4	20,301.3	3,814.9	437.2	1,403.2	2,813.9	990.3	3,045.5	1,186.4	689.1	1,103.2	2,042.4
Fiji	6.7	5.2	1.5	0.2	0.1	1.3	0.5	0.3	0.4	0.0	0.2	0.3
Hong Kong SAR, China	1,936.1	1,289.9	139.8	13.7	56.3	244.9	71.4	108.3	90.2	27.8	144.4	45.4
India	86,993.1	51,479.1	14,485.2	1,541.0	3,621.4	6,619.7	1,920.3	2,395.6	7,737.4	533.9	773.7	2,306.2
Indonesia	7,422,781.2	4,321,509.5	1,635,156.2	74,477.8	161,475.9	879,768.0	116,939.2	144,792.2	295,717.5	83,173.0	83,913.8	319,157.1
Lao PDR	64,727.1	37,958.6	19,378.0	1,935.0	592.6	4,857.2	1,002.5	857.5	4,010.0	466.0	1,003.5	1,582.0
Macao SAR, China	295.0	69.0	6.6	0.5	4.2	10.5	1.4	4.9	6.0	1.9	7.1	5.0
Malaysia	884.5	474.5	80.7	7.0	8.7	70.1	20.8	27.9	62.5	28.5	18.7	49.8
Maldives	31.6	12.0	2.3	0.5	0.2	4.7	0.5	0.7	0.5	0.2	0.2	1.6
Mongolia	12,546.8	7,613.9	2,176.4	543.7	381.3	1,092.5	112.5	357.3	1,196.3	222.8	217.1	767.8
Myanmar	45,128.0	31,485.5	16,452.6	643.0	971.6	4,169.9	427.8	1,948.8	1,033.0	482.4	360.6	2,619.1
Nepal	1,449.5	1,164.0	652.5	38.2	30.4	150.7	21.3	48.9	36.7	16.4	29.3	66.0
Pakistan	19,187.9	16,296.8	7,200.2	154.4	757.4	3,159.5	534.4	1,014.2	1,044.8	271.1	181.1	775.2
Philippines	9,706.3	7,468.0	3,053.3	91.8	100.9	885.0	291.9	236.2	770.4	225.4	129.6	532.2
Singapore	334.1	143.2	8.9	2.6	3.8	26.1	7.2	12.1	17.9	2.7	15.5	13.3
Sri Lanka	6,542.7	5,025.1	2,126.6	374.1	149.6	682.7	122.6	259.9	390.0	95.2	69.9	276.8
Taiwan, China	13,709.1	8,835.7	1,040.6	175.7	375.4	1,461.2	391.6	842.5	918.4	314.1	842.1	768.9
Thailand	11,120.5	6,890.0	1,765.5	242.9	231.9	625.9	280.5	522.7	964.3	143.0	320.6	604.6
Vietnam	2,779,880.2	1,762,838.5	455,802.1	49,429.5	72,689.9	402,769.2	101,638.7	128,338.8	176,330.7	13,025.9	69,843.1	151,555.0
Total (23)	**n.a.**	**n.a.**	**n.a.**	**n.a.**	**n.a.**	**n.a.**	**n.a.**	**n.a.**	**n.a.**	**n.a.**	**n.a.**	**n.a.**

Restaurants and hotels	Miscella-neous goods and services	Net purchases abroad	Individual consumption expenditure by households	Individual consumption expenditure by government	Collective consumption expenditure by government	Gross fixed capital formation	Machinery and equipment	Construc-tion	Other products	Changes in inventories and valuables	Balance of exports and imports	Domestic absorption	Individual consumption expenditure by households without housing
(13)	(14)	(15)	(16)	(17)	(18)	(19)	(20)	(21)	(22)	(23)	(24)	(25)	(26)
65.1	96.0	34.4	4,919.9	197.2	336.7	861.5	647.0	153.6	61.0	6.7	−1,946.6	6,322.1	4,650.4
50.6	215.2	−149.7	5,312.1	288.9	670.8	1,611.4	615.0	981.5	14.9	98.0	−1,214.5	7,981.3	4,740.3
0.1	0.2	0.0	6.9	1.0	2.7	4.5	1.8	2.4	0.2	0.8	−2.7	15.8	6.0
140.9	553.0	0.0	11,163.1	285.1	1,004.1	5,315.9	3,776.8	1,477.3	61.8	50.0	−5,063.2	17,818.1	10,839.6
41.4	226.9	−19.8	1,731.7	260.7	374.3	553.3	253.0	265.0	25.3	15.6	−18.0	2,935.6	1,545.7
2.9	3.4	0.7	129.9	1.0	11.7	41.6	21.7	19.9	0.0	4.9	−2.5	189.1	117.2
0.2	0.4	−1.7	25.1	1.7	2.8	2.8	1.1	1.3	0.4	0.0	−2.6	32.3	22.3
3.5	501.4	0.0	24,815.7	832.0	5,313.7	13,534.1	5,821.4	7,409.9	302.8	228.0	−7,190.4	44,723.4	24,741.9
125.6	164.3	−64.7	1,474.2	65.2	141.0	307.7	93.6	200.0	14.1	30.8	−279.7	2,018.9	1,417.7
4.6	3.0	−2.0	42.5	5.7	6.2	14.0	4.6	8.9	0.5	1.1	−4.8	69.5	37.2
1,187.7	1,766.1	0.0	37,758.9	3,891.0	756.4	11,341.5	3,291.1	7,541.0	519.4	144.4	−7,948.2	53,892.2	34,447.2
149.7	2,722.2	0.0	52,484.7	3,411.2	15,796.5	21,902.2	6,629.6	14,269.7	1,003.0	1,435.9	6,074.3	95,030.6	49,188.8
0.1	0.4	0.1	7.8	0.7	0.8	1.0	0.3	0.7	0.0	0.4	−1.8	10.6	7.5
n.a.	n.a.	n.a.	n.a.	n.a.	n.a.	n.a.	n.a.	n.a.	n.a.	n.a.	n.a.	n.a.	n.a.
165.8	282.8	0.0	7,154.3	144.9	359.8	2,748.6	652.8	2,059.8	36.0	53.1	−757.8	10,460.7	6,502.4
0.5	1.0	0.0	37.6	6.8	10.2	57.2	23.6	33.5	0.0	−0.3	−25.5	111.5	32.2
0.3	0.3	0.0	4.1	0.9	2.6	2.7	0.8	1.7	0.2	−0.1	10.7	10.3	3.6
2,101.9	1,202.0	0.0	41,431.0	2,449.5	1,931.4	6,035.3	2,966.8	3,002.6	65.9	277.9	−56.5	52,125.2	37,025.0
1,033.6	1,741.7	0.0	16,254.7	4,046.7	2,958.3	21,568.2	6,185.3	13,609.8	1,773.1	1,266.2	1,216.3	46,094.1	14,654.0
0.1	0.2	0.0	4.8	0.4	0.4	1.3	0.6	0.5	0.2	0.2	−0.3	7.1	3.8
129.6	218.1	0.0	1,224.8	65.0	103.5	455.0	200.6	214.0	40.5	11.7	76.0	1,860.1	1,017.4
1,283.5	8,261.0	0.0	48,648.2	2,830.9	7,196.2	26,908.2	10,274.4	15,618.4	1,015.4	6,344.1	−4,934.5	91,927.6	44,142.9
309,883.2	217,055.6	0.0	4,053,363.6	268,146.0	400,436.9	2,372,765.8	391,059.2	1,923,723.7	57,982.9	223,318.3	104,750.6	7,318,030.6	3,526,617.3
1,131.5	1,142.6	0.0	36,750.1	1,208.5	5,049.9	23,103.7	6,902.8	11,301.1	4,899.8	961.0	−2,346.2	67,073.2	34,671.0
13.1	7.8	0.0	60.5	8.5	12.4	36.6	8.5	27.8	0.3	4.2	172.8	122.2	52.2
39.1	60.7	0.0	418.3	56.3	58.8	197.2	71.3	98.3	27.6	8.7	145.3	739.2	379.2
0.2	0.3	0.0	10.2	1.8	5.6	15.9	6.1	9.8	0.0	0.0	−1.9	33.5	6.5
131.7	414.4	0.0	6,885.5	728.4	895.2	5,910.4	3,519.1	2,181.9	209.5	1,510.4	−3,383.2	15,930.0	5,949.8
1,417.3	959.3	0.0	28,760.0	2,725.5	1,895.4	12,061.2	5,872.0	5,231.0	958.1	5.7	−319.8	45,447.8	26,511.1
24.1	49.4	0.0	1,114.6	49.5	97.0	299.5	65.2	166.6	67.7	231.6	−342.6	1,792.1	993.5
166.3	1,038.1	0.0	15,712.2	584.6	1,356.4	2,481.8	796.6	1,186.4	498.8	307.0	−1,254.1	20,441.9	14,436.1
263.7	887.5	0.0	7,132.6	335.4	606.4	1,817.2	698.7	904.5	213.9	168.7	−354.0	10,060.3	6,521.9
14.8	18.2	0.0	130.2	13.0	21.6	79.4	29.6	46.7	3.1	−4.0	93.9	240.2	107.8
191.8	286.1	0.0	4,568.4	456.8	511.0	1,772.5	542.1	1,118.6	111.8	186.3	−952.3	7,494.9	4,143.2
473.4	1,231.8	0.0	8,235.4	600.3	1,096.3	2,866.0	1,334.2	1,297.3	234.5	−6.9	918.0	12,791.0	7,019.7
538.7	649.6	0.0	6,076.1	813.9	1,004.7	2,973.5	1,992.8	935.1	45.6	62.1	190.2	10,930.3	5,645.2
76,959.6	64,456.3	0.0	1,638,345.5	124,493.0	164,322.9	827,032.2	214,706.0	564,516.5	47,809.7	140,574.1	−114,887.5	2,894,767.7	1,388,272.7
n.a.	n.a.	n.a.	n.a.	n.a.	n.a.	n.a.	n.a.	n.a.	n.a.	n.a.	n.a.	n.a.	n.a.

(continued)

Table 2.2 *(Continued)*

EXPENDITURES (national currency units, billions) Economy	Gross domestic product	Actual individual consump-tion	Food and nonalcoholic beverages	Alcoholic beverages, tobacco, and narcotics	Clothing and footwear	Housing, water, electricity, gas, and other fuels	Furnishings, household equipment and mainte-nance	Health	Transport	Communi-cation	Recreation and culture	Education
(00)	(01)	(02)	(03)	(04)	(05)	(06)	(07)	(08)	(09)	(10)	(11)	(12)
COMMONWEALTH OF INDEPENDENT STATES												
Armenia	3,777.9	3,356.4	1,830.7	151.9	116.7	270.7	46.1	205.4	173.2	178.6	76.7	149.6
Azerbaijan	52.1	21.4	7.9	0.5	2.0	1.7	1.1	0.9	2.2	1.2	0.7	1.6
Belarus	297,157.7	168,548.8	53,321.4	10,240.9	10,656.8	13,051.3	7,630.1	15,115.5	14,014.2	7,235.4	8,995.9	14,331.7
Kazakhstan	27,571.9	13,329.9	2,717.1	296.8	785.6	2,887.3	526.1	1,044.9	1,429.0	521.7	655.3	1,118.6
Kyrgyz Republic	286.0	267.8	101.3	12.2	19.2	19.8	9.4	13.7	28.1	17.3	11.3	21.6
Moldova	82.3	92.6	26.0	5.4	5.3	11.9	6.6	3.3	9.3	3.4	3.0	7.7
Russian Federation[d]	55,799.6	32,186.9	8,155.0	2,211.3	2,437.8	3,135.3	1,322.0	2,553.4	3,322.8	1,238.2	1,756.8	1,790.3
Tajikistan	30.1	34.6	15.3	0.1	3.0	2.1	1.2	1.6	2.7	2.1	0.7	1.4
Ukraine	1,302.1	1,030.6	337.7	59.6	54.8	110.8	37.7	90.5	106.9	21.3	42.3	91.5
Total (9)	n.a.	n.a.	n.a.	n.a.	n.a.	n.a.	n.a.	n.a.	n.a.	n.a.	n.a.	n.a.
EUROSTAT-OECD												
Albania	1,282.3	1,094.3	413.5	29.1	41.8	133.6	72.5	62.4	55.6	21.9	25.8	36.0
Australia	1,444.5	928.0	80.4	28.5	26.1	182.4	35.7	117.7	81.2	19.3	93.1	76.5
Austria	299.2	197.3	16.6	5.7	9.9	35.3	10.8	20.8	22.0	3.3	19.1	15.8
Belgium	369.3	252.4	25.2	6.5	9.4	44.7	10.7	36.7	23.1	4.0	18.7	23.3
Bosnia and Herzegovina	26.8	25.0	7.2	1.6	1.0	3.2	1.3	2.1	2.1	0.7	1.2	1.4
Bulgaria	75.3	52.9	9.9	3.5	1.5	8.4	3.7	5.1	8.2	2.9	4.3	2.7
Canada	1,759.7	1,202.8	89.2	33.1	39.7	231.7	53.0	152.9	142.0	23.6	96.2	94.3
Chile	121,492.7	83,595.3	12,027.6	2,269.6	4,147.8	12,147.6	5,304.3	7,976.6	9,472.7	2,942.5	5,741.0	7,064.1
Croatia	330.2	233.4	44.4	14.9	10.1	41.1	12.3	27.6	22.5	7.6	23.6	18.6
Cyprus	17.9	13.7	1.7	0.6	0.8	2.4	0.6	1.2	1.5	0.4	1.1	1.3
Czech Republic	3,823.4	2,347.3	294.3	184.1	61.1	534.9	105.6	277.4	186.0	60.5	215.6	163.6
Denmark	1,791.8	1,236.6	97.6	30.4	39.7	249.4	42.9	160.9	105.1	14.6	107.2	113.7
Estonia	16.2	9.9	1.6	0.7	0.5	1.8	0.3	0.9	1.1	0.3	0.8	0.8
Finland	188.7	136.2	12.4	5.0	5.0	26.9	5.4	16.4	11.4	2.1	13.1	11.1
France	2,001.4	1,475.7	150.9	35.8	47.8	296.0	65.2	185.1	160.1	31.0	117.9	107.8
Germany	2,609.9	1,818.0	162.9	45.8	69.1	343.3	89.0	230.3	197.7	37.3	142.3	106.5
Greece	208.5	170.3	26.0	7.0	6.0	38.1	6.4	16.9	18.9	4.7	9.2	11.3
Hungary	27,635.4	17,717.0	2,582.8	1,120.6	431.1	3,294.8	652.2	2,012.8	1,952.3	563.5	1,356.4	1,219.7
Iceland	1,628.7	1,117.2	118.5	34.5	34.0	183.8	56.4	139.5	120.8	18.7	111.4	113.7
Ireland	162.6	99.2	7.6	4.1	3.1	18.5	3.2	14.6	9.7	2.2	5.9	7.7
Israel	923.9	642.2	84.5	13.3	15.5	128.3	32.1	55.1	82.7	20.6	40.6	66.3
Italy	1,580.4	1,156.1	139.4	26.5	73.2	216.2	69.5	138.4	123.0	23.3	78.3	68.6
Japan	470,623.2	340,953.4	38,436.2	7,607.6	8,858.4	70,934.6	14,061.2	36,104.6	30,162.8	9,624.9	25,592.3	17,222.5
Korea, Rep.	1,235,160.5	739,451.4	82,192.5	14,325.5	32,153.0	103,510.6	21,124.2	81,457.7	74,796.7	27,242.4	51,734.8	81,382.4
Latvia	14.3	10.0	1.7	0.7	0.4	2.0	0.3	0.7	1.3	0.3	0.8	0.7
Lithuania	106.9	78.7	16.4	5.2	4.1	11.0	4.0	7.8	10.2	1.6	5.1	5.2
Luxembourg	41.7	17.5	1.3	1.4	0.7	3.9	1.0	1.9	3.1	0.3	1.4	1.8

Restaurants and hotels	Miscellaneous goods and services	Net purchases abroad	Individual consumption expenditure by households	Individual consumption expenditure by government	Collective consumption expenditure by government	Gross fixed capital formation	Machinery and equipment	Construction	Other products	Changes in inventories and valuables	Balance of exports and imports	Domestic absorption	Individual consumption expenditure by households without housing
(13)	(14)	(15)	(16)	(17)	(18)	(19)	(20)	(21)	(22)	(23)	(24)	(25)	(26)
39.7	105.2	11.8	3,161.0	195.4	293.0	982.7	163.5	793.3	25.9	37.3	−891.5	4,669.4	3,051.1
0.7	0.9	0.0	19.4	2.0	3.3	10.5	5.4	4.6	0.5	0.0	16.8	35.2	18.8
4,891.8	6,935.0	2,128.9	141,646.8	26,902.0	14,485.3	112,308.9	48,972.0	62,402.2	934.8	5,020.9	−3,206.2	300,363.9	136,878.2
459.5	885.8	2.1	11,791.9	1,538.0	1,403.9	5,771.6	1,662.2	3,757.3	352.1	1,176.7	5,889.8	21,682.1	9,779.0
10.4	11.2	−7.6	238.5	29.3	22.9	67.8	30.2	35.4	2.1	5.1	−77.5	363.5	234.0
1.4	8.0	1.3	79.5	13.0	3.5	19.2	6.1	11.6	1.5	0.7	−33.6	116.0	75.2
898.9	2,747.3	617.7	27,398.6	4,788.3	5,252.5	11,595.2	4,163.3	6,489.2	942.7	1,988.6	4,776.5	51,023.0	26,024.0
0.4	1.7	2.3	32.1	2.5	1.6	9.7	4.3	4.4	1.0	1.1	−17.0	47.0	31.6
22.7	55.9	−1.0	875.6	155.1	82.4	241.8	92.7	143.6	5.4	28.2	−80.9	1,383.0	821.4
n.a.	n.a.	n.a.	n.a.	n.a.	n.a.	n.a.	n.a.	n.a.	n.a.	n.a.	n.a.	n.a.	n.a.
27.6	61.3	113.0	1,029.6	64.7	70.6	423.8	89.2	325.1	9.6	−10.9	−295.7	1,578.0	947.0
54.2	136.3	−3.3	774.5	153.6	101.4	389.3	94.2	223.8	71.3	7.0	18.8	1,425.7	633.2
19.8	24.6	−6.3	163.9	33.5	23.3	63.5	24.3	33.0	6.3	6.1	9.0	290.3	141.7
11.5	35.7	2.9	194.7	57.7	32.6	76.5	29.6	41.0	6.9	4.7	3.1	366.2	164.5
1.6	2.3	−0.7	22.2	2.8	3.1	4.8	2.0	2.6	0.2	0.1	−6.3	33.0	20.7
3.2	3.3	−3.7	47.0	5.9	5.9	16.2	7.0	8.6	0.6	0.3	0.0	75.3	42.0
64.5	166.0	16.7	980.1	222.7	159.1	412.0	82.0	273.8	56.3	7.7	−21.9	1,781.6	789.9
3,510.0	11,215.6	−224.1	74,405.2	9,190.1	5,385.9	27,248.3	10,690.3	14,472.6	2,085.4	1,280.7	3,982.5	117,510.2	67,304.3
35.1	20.3	−44.6	197.8	35.5	29.8	63.3	20.5	37.9	4.9	4.0	−0.2	330.4	174.9
2.0	1.2	−1.1	12.1	1.6	2.0	3.0	0.9	2.0	0.1	0.0	−0.8	18.7	10.5
154.1	200.4	−90.2	1,935.2	412.2	380.4	922.6	409.5	462.0	51.1	14.5	158.6	3,664.8	1,613.8
44.7	228.4	2.0	872.4	364.2	144.0	310.9	108.9	157.3	44.7	6.3	93.9	1,697.8	700.3
0.6	0.9	−0.4	8.2	1.7	1.4	3.8	1.8	1.9	0.1	0.5	0.6	15.6	7.0
6.4	21.3	−0.3	105.2	31.0	15.2	36.6	8.8	24.6	3.2	2.0	−1.4	190.0	86.5
79.1	206.5	−7.5	1,155.3	320.5	169.5	400.0	108.2	248.8	42.9	15.5	−59.3	2,060.7	951.2
82.6	275.4	35.7	1,498.4	319.6	179.9	473.2	181.2	263.3	28.6	3.2	135.7	2,474.3	1,262.5
18.8	15.3	−8.2	155.6	14.7	21.5	31.6	12.8	16.6	2.2	2.0	−16.9	225.4	130.0
1,001.3	2,270.6	−741.1	14,725.9	2,991.1	2,824.3	4,950.0	2,073.6	2,579.8	296.6	359.3	1,784.8	25,850.6	12,890.9
69.6	117.6	−1.3	844.8	272.4	141.0	229.5	87.3	124.7	17.5	4.6	136.3	1,492.4	699.3
9.5	11.2	1.9	78.2	21.0	8.9	17.3	6.5	9.3	1.5	2.1	35.1	127.5	64.9
35.5	75.3	−7.6	529.2	113.0	99.8	188.8	60.5	91.3	37.0	−2.3	−4.6	928.5	428.7
97.8	116.5	−14.4	967.9	188.2	133.8	301.3	120.6	143.6	37.1	11.2	−22.1	1,602.5	818.5
18,231.3	61,586.4	2,530.5	284,784.3	56,169.1	40,034.2	96,872.1	37,812.0	45,646.5	13,413.6	−2,953.1	−4,283.4	474,906.7	225,972.2
51,650.2	107,940.1	9,941.3	655,386.6	84,064.8	105,486.9	340,101.0	120,249.7	192,753.0	27,098.3	25,181.4	24,939.8	1,210,220.7	583,407.8
0.4	0.7	0.0	8.9	1.1	1.4	3.0	1.3	1.7	0.1	0.5	−0.7	15.0	7.7
1.9	6.9	−0.6	67.1	11.6	8.4	19.3	6.3	11.3	1.6	3.4	−2.9	109.8	62.7
1.1	3.1	−3.3	13.3	4.3	2.7	7.7	2.9	4.4	0.5	1.1	12.7	29.1	10.3

(continued)

Table 2.2 *(Continued)*

EXPENDITURES (national currency units, billions) Economy	Gross domestic product	Actual individual consumption	Food and nonalcoholic beverages	Alcoholic beverages, tobacco, and narcotics	Clothing and footwear	Housing, water, electricity, gas, and other fuels	Furnishings, household equipment and maintenance	Health	Transport	Communication	Recreation and culture	Education
(00)	(01)	(02)	(03)	(04)	(05)	(06)	(07)	(08)	(09)	(10)	(11)	(12)
Macedonia, FYR	459.8	380.6	116.9	11.5	17.0	66.6	14.1	24.0	34.2	20.2	12.0	20.2
Malta	6.6	4.7	0.7	0.1	0.2	0.6	0.3	0.6	0.6	0.2	0.5	0.3
Mexico	14,536.9	10,539.2	2,246.1	253.0	287.9	1,985.4	547.3	661.7	1,801.4	358.2	443.5	547.2
Montenegro	3.2	3.0	1.0	0.1	0.1	0.4	0.3	0.2	0.4	0.2	0.1	0.1
Netherlands	599.0	374.0	31.5	8.3	14.3	66.2	15.8	46.8	34.1	11.1	30.8	30.3
New Zealand	204.5	146.7	17.6	6.4	5.5	28.5	6.0	18.0	14.5	3.9	13.5	11.8
Norway	2,750.0	1,519.8	137.6	44.3	55.3	224.8	59.2	202.8	155.7	27.2	152.5	116.1
Poland	1,528.1	1,092.1	174.2	59.5	40.7	226.2	41.7	105.1	92.9	27.2	83.2	81.6
Portugal	171.1	131.5	19.4	3.9	6.4	18.7	6.4	16.0	15.3	3.4	9.6	10.2
Romania	556.7	402.1	94.8	17.3	13.1	76.5	17.0	44.6	38.0	17.1	24.7	19.2
Russian Federation[d]	55,799.6	32,186.9	8,155.0	2,211.3	2,437.8	3,103.8	1,322.0	2,538.5	3,322.8	1,238.2	1,721.6	1,780.9
Serbia	3,208.6	2,879.5	681.7	137.3	93.3	567.0	95.4	300.2	334.2	111.9	147.1	149.9
Slovak Republic	69.0	45.7	7.0	1.8	1.6	10.2	2.4	4.3	3.1	1.5	4.2	2.9
Slovenia	36.1	25.2	3.3	1.2	1.2	4.3	1.3	2.9	3.3	0.7	2.2	2.2
Spain	1,046.3	741.8	88.7	18.6	33.6	132.5	30.2	85.7	72.9	17.6	61.4	54.2
Sweden	3,480.5	2,337.4	198.7	59.0	78.8	442.0	82.2	281.4	216.9	54.1	213.4	229.0
Switzerland	585.1	371.6	29.5	11.8	11.1	79.4	13.7	50.0	29.9	7.9	29.9	29.5
Turkey	1,297.7	1,022.7	222.9	32.6	52.0	186.3	75.9	78.4	159.9	27.9	42.9	50.8
United Kingdom	1,536.9	1,205.1	86.6	33.8	55.2	239.8	47.2	133.8	128.1	20.4	134.4	95.6
United States	15,533.8	11,667.0	698.4	207.6	366.0	1,962.8	429.5	2,300.0	1,079.1	246.7	996.1	930.9
Total (47)	**n.a.**	**n.a.**	**n.a.**	**n.a.**	**n.a.**	**n.a.**	**n.a.**	**n.a.**	**n.a.**	**n.a.**	**n.a.**	**n.a.**
LATIN AMERICA												
Bolivia	166.1	104.0	35.1	1.6	2.2	11.1	7.4	9.0	17.8	1.1	1.1	6.3
Brazil	4,143.0	2,833.3	408.8	51.0	118.9	379.7	190.4	316.7	383.8	91.0	132.4	242.4
Colombia	621,615.0	422,979.0	70,269.0	11,791.0	24,695.0	60,636.0	16,114.0	31,460.5	46,840.0	16,804.0	19,893.0	36,552.5
Costa Rica	20,748.0	16,078.7	3,223.3	145.7	701.5	1,008.7	935.6	1,961.6	2,863.4	375.6	1,563.8	1,638.3
Cuba[e]	...	...	...	...	...	...	...	...	...	...	...	...
Dominican Republic	2,119.3	1,883.9	457.0	111.5	61.2	279.2	67.4	117.5	243.3	79.7	40.8	83.4
Ecuador	79.8	53.5	10.8	1.3	2.2	7.3	3.8	4.4	6.0	2.9	2.7	5.5
El Salvador	23.1	22.8	5.8	0.4	1.2	3.8	2.2	1.8	2.0	0.8	1.0	1.1
Guatemala	371.3	334.1	129.4	5.4	17.5	42.0	18.4	22.5	23.9	24.2	10.2	13.9
Haiti	297.7	337.5	197.1	7.8	23.2	38.0	11.3	11.3	17.4	1.4	8.0	14.4
Honduras	335.0	287.9	85.2	9.1	12.6	35.5	11.6	28.1	27.4	9.1	10.8	25.0
Nicaragua	216.1	181.4	47.3	5.1	5.2	24.2	10.0	19.5	22.2	6.2	6.9	12.9
Panama	31.3	20.7	3.5	0.1	1.3	4.1	1.5	1.5	2.7	0.7	1.1	1.2
Paraguay	105,203.2	80,072.8	22,129.6	1,013.0	4,162.6	7,226.3	6,471.4	6,500.1	6,862.1	2,949.0	5,181.8	7,436.4
Peru	497.8	311.2	70.5	6.9	19.4	32.9	15.4	20.1	33.2	12.2	18.5	26.2
Uruguay	896.8	677.3	125.1	15.9	30.5	129.3	37.5	81.7	49.9	26.7	22.8	44.1

Restaurants and hotels	Miscellaneous goods and services	Net purchases abroad	Individual consumption expenditure by households	Individual consumption expenditure by government	Collective consumption expenditure by government	Gross fixed capital formation	Machinery and equipment	Construction	Other products	Changes in inventories and valuables	Balance of exports and imports	Domestic absorption	Individual consumption expenditure by households without housing
(13)	(14)	(15)	(16)	(17)	(18)	(19)	(20)	(21)	(22)	(23)	(24)	(25)	(26)
13.0	26.9	4.0	345.3	35.4	48.8	94.7	31.8	59.0	3.9	25.8	−90.2	550.0	305.1
0.8	0.6	−0.7	4.0	0.7	0.6	1.0	0.4	0.5	0.1	0.0	0.3	6.4	3.7
393.1	1,063.5	−48.9	9,640.8	898.4	794.4	3,165.0	974.6	2,125.7	64.8	221.2	−182.9	14,719.9	8,040.4
0.4	0.2	−0.6	2.7	0.3	0.4	0.6	0.2	0.4	0.0	0.0	−0.7	4.0	2.4
13.4	72.9	−1.5	271.8	102.2	65.1	106.9	33.0	60.4	13.4	1.7	51.4	547.6	228.6
8.6	15.4	−3.0	122.2	24.5	16.9	37.1	12.7	21.3	3.1	0.9	2.9	201.6	98.1
62.7	239.7	41.8	1,131.7	388.1	202.7	536.8	173.0	255.3	108.5	125.9	364.8	2,385.1	965.0
26.4	139.9	−6.5	933.9	158.2	116.5	308.7	116.0	173.5	19.2	28.4	−17.6	1,545.7	868.6
12.9	14.7	−5.3	113.0	18.5	15.5	30.8	9.2	18.9	2.7	0.8	−7.5	178.6	101.1
11.5	27.0	1.2	353.5	48.7	35.2	145.2	47.1	91.3	6.8	3.8	−29.6	586.3	305.6
898.9	2,838.3	617.7	27,398.6	4,788.3	5,252.5	11,595.2	4,153.3	6,489.2	942.7	1,988.6	4,776.5	51,023.0	26,055.5
57.2	241.8	−37.5	2,469.4	410.2	209.3	592.8	252.0	304.2	36.6	53.5	−526.5	3,735.1	2,134.7
2.0	4.8	0.0	39.7	6.0	6.4	16.0	5.3	7.2	3.5	0.5	0.4	68.6	36.1
1.5	2.5	−1.4	20.8	4.5	3.1	6.7	2.9	3.3	0.5	0.6	0.6	35.6	18.4
108.5	70.8	−33.0	612.8	128.9	93.8	216.7	63.0	111.0	42.7	5.1	−11.0	1,057.3	523.4
91.8	403.6	−13.6	1,671.2	666.2	257.9	650.8	241.2	316.9	92.7	40.4	194.0	3,286.5	1,348.9
22.3	56.6	0.0	335.4	36.2	28.3	120.3	52.7	54.5	13.0	4.2	60.7	524.4	268.9
60.0	75.0	−41.9	923.8	98.9	81.8	283.2	164.2	118.0	1.0	22.5	−112.5	1,410.2	786.4
79.4	144.4	6.3	992.3	212.8	124.4	220.7	44.9	126.3	49.5	10.0	−23.3	1,560.2	792.9
670.7	1,803.2	−23.8	10,711.8	955.2	1,570.9	2,828.2	1,014.6	1,295.0	518.6	36.4	−568.7	16,102.5	9,105.2
n.a.	n.a.	n.a.	n.a.	n.a.	n.a.	n.a.	n.a.	n.a.	n.a.	n.a.	n.a.	n.a.	n.a.
8.1	3.1	0.1	101.3	2.7	20.2	31.5	17.7	11.8	2.0	1.0	9.4	156.7	95.6
159.9	358.1	0.0	2,499.5	333.8	522.9	798.7	418.1	330.8	49.8	18.5	−30.4	4,173.4	2,240.1
44,222.0	43,621.0	81.0	381,323.0	41,656.0	56,385.0	146,522.0	50,778.0	90,288.0	5,456.0	1,094.0	−5,365.0	626,980.0	342,707.8
748.3	753.0	159.9	13,555.4	2,523.3	1,203.6	4,104.9	1,767.8	2,214.8	122.2	377.0	−1,016.3	21,764.2	13,120.1
…	…	…	…	…	…	…	…	…	…	…	…	…	…
153.4	199.8	−10.4	1,833.7	50.1	105.8	345.4	98.0	241.9	5.5	2.9	−218.7	2,338.0	1,648.0
2.2	4.9	−0.3	48.7	4.8	5.3	20.8	6.7	5.9	8.1	2.4	−2.2	82.0	43.3
1.5	1.3	−0.1	21.6	1.2	1.4	2.9	1.5	1.4	0.0	0.4	−4.3	27.5	19.3
19.4	13.7	−6.3	316.6	17.6	20.8	54.6	28.6	25.9	0.1	1.6	−39.8	411.1	284.2
0.7	7.0	0.0	334.0	3.5	0.3	86.3	2.2	84.0	0.0	0.0	−126.4	424.1	320.1
15.7	17.8	0.0	260.1	27.8	26.0	81.9	45.5	32.1	4.3	5.2	−66.0	401.0	241.4
10.9	13.7	−2.7	168.1	13.3	18.5	48.7	18.8	26.0	3.9	1.8	−34.2	250.3	152.6
1.1	1.9	0.0	18.9	1.8	2.0	8.2	3.7	4.5	0.0	0.3	0.1	31.2	15.9
3,829.4	6,311.0	0.0	73,739.5	6,333.3	4,822.9	17,231.6	7,333.3	8,529.5	1,368.9	401.1	2,674.8	102,528.4	71,754.5
27.6	28.3	0.0	296.0	15.2	30.6	129.3	46.5	78.7	4.1	5.3	21.4	476.4	273.6
46.9	53.7	13.1	609.2	68.1	50.1	170.4	54.2	105.5	10.7	3.4	−4.4	901.2	511.0

(continued)

Table 2.2 (Continued)

EXPENDITURES (national currency units, billions) Economy	Gross domestic product	Actual individual consumption	Food and nonalcoholic beverages	Alcoholic beverages, tobacco, and narcotics	Clothing and footwear	Housing, water, electricity, gas, and other fuels	Furnishings, household equipment and maintenance	Health	Transport	Communication	Recreation and culture	Education
(00)	(01)	(02)	(03)	(04)	(05)	(06)	(07)	(08)	(09)	(10)	(11)	(12)
Venezuela, RB	1,357.5	823.8	177.4	24.3	37.7	40.3	47.2	74.3	109.3	46.1	52.3	69.7
Total (17)	**n.a.**	**n.a.**	**n.a.**	**n.a.**	**n.a.**	**n.a.**	**n.a.**	**n.a.**	**n.a.**	**n.a.**	**n.a.**	**n.a.**
CARIBBEAN												
Anguilla	0.8	0.7	0.1	0.0	0.0	0.1	0.0	0.0	0.1	0.1	0.0	0.0
Antigua and Barbuda	3.0	2.1	0.3	0.0	0.0	0.6	0.1	0.2	0.2	0.1	0.1	0.1
Aruba	4.6	3.6	0.3	0.0	0.1	1.2	0.1	0.4	0.4	0.1	0.2	0.2
Bahamas, The	7.9	6.0	0.6	0.1	0.2	1.9	0.3	0.5	0.5	0.2	0.3	0.4
Barbados	8.7	7.8	1.1	0.1	0.1	4.1	0.2	0.4	0.5	0.3	0.3	0.4
Belize	3.0	2.3	0.4	0.0	0.2	0.6	0.1	0.2	0.3	0.1	0.1	0.1
Bermuda	5.6	4.3	0.4	0.1	0.1	1.2	0.2	0.4	0.3	0.1	0.2	0.3
Bonaire[f]	...	...	0.0	0.0	0.0	...	0.0	...	0.0	0.0	...	...
Cayman Islands	2.7	2.0	0.1	0.0	0.1	0.7	0.1	0.1	0.2	0.1	0.1	0.1
Curaçao	5.4	4.2	0.4	0.1	0.3	1.3	0.1	0.3	0.4	0.2	0.2	0.2
Dominica	1.3	1.2	0.2	0.0	0.1	0.3	0.1	0.1	0.2	0.0	0.0	0.1
Grenada	2.1	2.0	0.4	0.0	0.1	0.4	0.1	0.1	0.4	0.2	0.1	0.1
Jamaica	1,241.8	1,155.4	324.2	15.5	20.9	156.7	64.3	69.8	164.5	31.2	102.3	85.5
Montserrat	0.2	0.1	0.0	0.0	0.0	0.0	0.0	0.0	0.0	0.0	0.0	0.0
St. Kitts and Nevis	2.0	1.5	0.2	0.0	0.1	0.4	0.1	0.1	0.1	0.1	0.1	0.1
St. Lucia	3.3	2.6	0.5	0.0	0.2	0.6	0.1	0.1	0.2	0.1	0.1	0.2
St. Vincent and the Grenadines	1.8	1.7	0.3	0.1	0.0	0.5	0.1	0.1	0.3	0.1	0.1	0.1
Sint Maarten	1.7	1.1	0.1	0.0	0.1	0.5	0.0	0.0	0.1	0.1	0.0	0.0
Suriname	14.3	5.5	2.0	0.1	0.2	0.9	0.3	0.3	0.4	0.2	0.2	0.1
Trinidad and Tobago	150.9	87.7	18.5	0.9	1.2	10.7	3.7	6.8	9.4	1.8	5.7	9.3
Turks and Caicos Islands	0.7	0.3	0.0	0.0	0.0	0.0	0.0	0.0	0.1	0.0	0.0	0.0
Virgin Islands, British	0.9	0.4	0.1	0.0	0.0	0.1	0.0	0.0	0.0	0.0	0.0	0.0
Total (22)	**n.a.**	**n.a.**	**n.a.**	**n.a.**	**n.a.**	**n.a.**	**n.a.**	**n.a.**	**n.a.**	**n.a.**	**n.a.**	**n.a.**
WESTERN ASIA												
Bahrain	10.9	4.8	0.6	0.0	0.3	1.0	0.3	0.3	0.5	0.2	0.3	0.5
Egypt, Arab Rep.[a]	1,371.1	1,090.5	457.0	35.4	65.9	142.3	52.7	99.5	64.4	27.8	32.4	72.2
Iraq	191,652.9	90,152.8	27,607.4	510.1	5,363.9	23,449.2	4,234.5	6,461.7	6,537.8	1,278.2	1,048.7	9,982.6
Jordan	20.5	16.3	4.6	0.5	0.7	3.3	0.7	1.1	1.7	0.6	0.3	2.0
Kuwait	44.3	12.3	1.9	0.0	1.0	2.9	1.5	1.0	0.9	0.4	0.4	1.2
Oman	26.9	9.7	1.9	0.0	0.5	1.8	0.4	0.6	1.5	0.5	0.3	1.1
Qatar	624.2	103.3	11.0	0.3	3.6	23.2	4.2	7.5	8.9	2.2	7.6	15.8
Saudi Arabia	2,510.6	922.3	146.2	3.2	44.3	191.4	60.7	76.3	62.5	38.5	28.1	158.4
Sudan[b]	186.6	130.9	67.7	0.9	5.8	19.2	8.5	1.7	10.7	2.1	3.0	4.3
United Arab Emirates	1,280.2	675.8	79.2	1.2	83.4	224.0	23.9	10.4	108.7	39.5	18.4	31.5

Restaurants and hotels	Miscella-neous goods and services	Net purchases abroad	Individual consumption expenditure by households	Individual consumption expenditure by government	Collective consumption expenditure by government	Gross fixed capital formation	Machinery and equipment	Construc-tion	Other products	Changes in inventories and valuables	Balance of exports and imports	Domestic absorption	Individual consumption expenditure by households without housing
(13)	(14)	(15)	(16)	(17)	(18)	(19)	(20)	(21)	(22)	(23)	(24)	(25)	(26)
99.3	42.4	3.5	748.8	75.0	81.3	240.7	103.1	122.9	8.6	72.5	139.1	1,218.4	719.6
n.a.	n.a.	n.a.	n.a.	n.a.	n.a.	n.a.	n.a.	n.a.	n.a.	n.a.	n.a.	n.a.	n.a.
0.0	0.1	0.0	0.7	0.0	0.1	0.1	0.0	0.1	0.0	0.0	–0.1	0.9	0.6
0.1	0.3	0.0	1.8	0.2	0.3	0.6	0.1	0.5	0.0	0.0	0.0	3.0	1.5
0.1	0.3	0.0	2.9	0.7	0.4	1.2	0.3	0.9	0.0	0.1	–0.7	5.4	2.1
0.3	0.9	0.0	5.6	0.5	0.7	2.1	1.0	1.1	0.0	0.1	–1.1	9.0	4.3
1.4	0.6	–1.8	7.1	0.7	0.9	1.4	0.7	0.7	0.0	–0.1	–1.3	10.0	3.6
0.0	0.1	0.0	2.1	0.1	0.3	0.5	0.2	0.3	0.0	0.0	–0.1	3.1	1.6
0.5	0.6	0.0	3.7	0.6	0.5	1.1	0.6	0.5	0.0	0.1	–0.4	6.0	2.6
0.0	...	0.0	0.2	...	...	...	...	...	...	...	...	...	0.1
0.1	0.4	0.0	1.9	0.1	0.2	0.6	0.3	0.3	0.0	0.0	–0.2	2.9	1.4
0.1	0.9	–0.3	3.8	0.4	0.4	2.2	1.2	0.6	0.4	0.1	–1.4	6.8	3.0
0.0	0.1	0.0	1.1	0.1	0.2	0.3	0.1	0.2	0.0	–0.1	–0.2	1.5	0.9
0.0	0.1	0.0	1.9	0.2	0.2	0.4	0.2	0.3	0.0	0.0	–0.5	2.6	1.7
141.8	136.2	–157.5	1,063.5	91.9	106.6	258.0	124.6	128.6	4.8	6.0	–284.2	1,526.0	969.0
0.0	0.0	0.0	0.1	0.0	0.1	0.0	0.0	0.0	0.0	0.0	–0.1	0.2	0.1
0.1	0.1	0.0	1.3	0.1	0.2	0.6	0.2	0.4	0.0	0.0	–0.3	2.3	1.1
0.0	0.3	0.0	2.4	0.2	0.3	1.0	0.3	0.7	0.0	0.0	–0.7	3.9	2.1
0.1	0.1	–0.2	1.5	0.2	0.2	0.4	0.1	0.3	0.0	0.0	–0.5	2.3	1.2
0.0	0.1	0.0	1.0	0.1	0.2	0.3	0.2	0.1	0.0	0.0	0.1	1.6	0.7
0.1	0.7	0.0	5.3	0.1	1.6	5.3	4.3	0.8	0.1	1.0	0.9	13.4	5.0
8.1	11.9	0.0	69.1	18.6	2.5	22.6	11.2	11.0	0.5	0.0	38.0	112.9	62.5
0.0	0.0	0.0	0.3	0.0	0.1	0.1	0.0	0.1	0.0	0.0	0.2	0.5	0.2
0.0	0.0	0.0	0.3	0.0	0.0	0.2	0.1	0.1	0.0	0.0	0.3	0.6	0.3
n.a.	n.a.	n.a.	n.a.	n.a.	n.a.	n.a.	n.a.	n.a.	n.a.	n.a.	n.a.	n.a.	n.a.
0.2	0.3	0.1	4.2	0.5	1.0	1.7	0.5	1.2	0.0	0.1	3.4	7.5	3.4
34.3	77.2	–70.7	1,036.1	54.4	102.6	229.1	106.5	116.4	6.2	5.4	–56.5	1,427.6	940.1
862.2	2,816.5	0.0	76,260.3	13,892.5	28,862.4	37,255.3	14,402.2	22,694.1	159.0	–832.3	36,214.8	155,438.1	59,573.4
0.3	0.5	0.1	14.6	1.7	2.3	4.4	1.1	3.0	0.3	0.3	–2.8	23.3	12.5
0.4	0.8	0.0	10.3	2.0	4.6	7.0	2.8	3.5	0.7	0.3	20.1	24.2	7.8
0.3	0.7	0.1	8.1	1.6	3.0	7.1	2.8	3.5	0.7	–0.8	8.0	19.0	6.7
2.0	14.6	2.3	79.7	23.6	54.4	182.9	89.5	28.6	64.8	0.0	283.6	340.6	58.4
34.8	44.9	33.0	681.8	240.5	247.5	568.8	219.5	282.2	67.2	103.6	668.4	1,842.2	547.6
2.9	3.4	0.7	129.9	1.0	11.7	41.6	21.7	19.9	0.0	4.9	–2.5	189.1	117.2
25.0	30.5	0.0	661.8	14.0	79.6	281.7	111.9	140.6	29.1	12.2	230.9	1,049.3	469.1

(continued)

Table 2.2 *(Continued)*

EXPENDITURES (national currency units, billions) Economy	Gross domestic product	Actual individual consump-tion	Food and nonalcoholic beverages	Alcoholic beverages, tobacco, and narcotics	Clothing and footwear	Housing, water, electricity, gas, and other fuels	Furnishings, household equipment and mainte-nance	Health	Transport	Communi-cation	Recreation and culture	Education
(00)	(01)	(02)	(03)	(04)	(05)	(06)	(07)	(08)	(09)	(10)	(11)	(12)
West Bank and Gaza	35.0	37.8	12.0	1.5	2.2	4.1	2.0	2.8	3.6	1.1	0.9	3.2
Yemen, Rep.	6,714.9	4,904.7	2,216.2	236.3	214.9	700.1	146.2	471.0	281.1	52.7	18.8	344.4
Total (12)	n.a.	n.a.	n.a.	n.a.	n.a.	n.a.	n.a.	n.a.	n.a.	n.a.	n.a.	n.a.
SINGLETONS												
Georgia	24.3	19.1	6.0	1.0	0.5	2.2	0.7	2.0	1.7	0.6	1.3	1.3
Iran, Islamic Rep.	6,121,004.0	2,717,581.9	659,037.8	12,538.2	116,321.1	782,477.8	100,873.7	221,043.0	199,053.5	84,484.1	65,577.4	86,156.1
Total (2)	n.a.	n.a.	n.a.	n.a.	n.a.	n.a.	n.a.	n.a.	n.a.	n.a.	n.a.	n.a.
WORLD[g] (179)	n.a.	n.a.	n.a.	n.a.	n.a.	n.a.	n.a.	n.a.	n.a.	n.a.	n.a.	n.a.

Source: ICP, http://icp.worldbank.org/.

Note: n.a. = not applicable; … = data suppressed because of incompleteness.

a. The Arab Republic of Egypt participated in both the Africa and Western Asia regions. The regional results for Egypt were averaged by taking the geometric mean of the regional PPPs, allowing Egypt to have the same global results in each region.

b. Sudan participated in both the Africa and Western Asia regions. The regional results for Sudan were averaged by taking the geometric mean of the regional PPPs, allowing Sudan to have the same global results in each region.

c. The results presented in the tables are based on data supplied by all the participating economies and compiled in accordance with ICP principles and the procedures recommended by the 2011 ICP Technical Advisory Group. The results for China are estimated by the 2011 ICP Asia and the Pacific Regional Office and the Global Office. The National Bureau of Statistics of China does not recognize these results as official statistics.

d. The Russian Federation participated in both the CIS and Eurostat-OECD comparisons. The PPPs for Russia are based on the Eurostat-OECD comparison. They were the basis for linking the CIS comparison to the ICP.

e. The official GDP of Cuba for reference year 2011 is 68,990.15 million in national currency. However, this number and its breakdown into main aggregates are not shown in the tables because of methodological comparability issues. Therefore, Cuba's results are provided only for the PPP and price level index. In addition, Cuba's figures are not included in the Latin America and world totals.

f. Bonaire's results are provided only for the individual consumption expenditure by households. Therefore, to ensure consistency across the tables, Bonaire is not included in the Caribbean or the world total.

g. This table does not include the Pacific Islands and does not double count the dual participation economies: the Arab Republic of Egypt, Sudan, and the Russian Federation.

Restaurants and hotels	Miscellaneous goods and services	Net purchases abroad	Individual consumption expenditure by households	Individual consumption expenditure by government	Collective consumption expenditure by government	Gross fixed capital formation	Machinery and equipment	Construction	Other products	Changes in inventories and valuables	Balance of exports and imports	Domestic absorption	Individual consumption expenditure by households without housing
(13)	(14)	(15)	(16)	(17)	(18)	(19)	(20)	(21)	(22)	(23)	(24)	(25)	(26)
0.9	3.1	0.5	33.7	4.1	6.3	7.2	1.3	5.2	0.8	−1.2	−15.3	50.2	32.3
1.6	221.4	0.0	4,573.2	331.6	614.0	886.4	83.5	686.9	116.1	379.0	−69.2	6,784.1	4,203.0
n.a.	n.a.	n.a.	n.a.	n.a.	n.a.	n.a.	n.a.	n.a.	n.a.	n.a.	n.a.	n.a.	n.a.
0.6	1.1	0.0	18.0	1.1	3.4	5.5	2.0	2.6	0.8	0.9	−4.5	28.9	17.0
31,387.9	289,176.1	69,455.2	2,557,440.1	160,141.8	513,541.4	1,570,527.5	710,604.0	812,701.0	47,222.5	666,188.3	653,165.0	5,467,839.0	1,924,614.9
n.a.	n.a.	n.a.	n.a.	n.a.	n.a.	n.a.	n.a.	n.a.	n.a.	n.a.	n.a.	n.a.	n.a.
n.a.	n.a.	n.a.	n.a.	n.a.	n.a.	n.a.	n.a.	n.a.	n.a.	n.a.	n.a.	n.a.	n.a.

Table 2.3 Shares of Nominal Expenditures (GDP = 100), ICP 2011

NOMINAL EXPENDITURE SHARES (GDP = 100)[a] Economy	Gross domestic product	Actual individual consumption	Food and nonalcoholic beverages	Alcoholic beverages, tobacco, and narcotics	Clothing and footwear	Housing, water, electricity, gas, and other fuels	Furnishings, household equipment and maintenance	Health	Transport	Communication	Recreation and culture	Education
(00)	(01)	(02)	(03)	(04)	(05)	(06)	(07)	(08)	(09)	(10)	(11)	(12)
AFRICA												
Algeria	100.0	45.0	13.5	0.8	1.3	2.2	1.1	3.2	5.4	2.5	1.1	4.3
Angola	100.0	60.7	24.9	2.6	3.1	6.4	3.4	3.2	3.3	0.6	1.3	3.0
Benin	100.0	80.8	39.0	2.3	3.4	8.2	2.2	2.8	5.9	2.4	1.2	4.1
Botswana	100.0	54.6	9.7	4.1	3.4	6.1	3.2	2.8	8.8	1.3	1.5	6.9
Burkina Faso	100.0	67.7	34.6	4.3	1.4	7.5	2.9	2.5	4.4	2.2	1.6	2.0
Burundi	100.0	93.2	40.7	12.8	0.9	14.4	0.8	2.6	6.1	1.1	1.0	5.2
Cameroon	100.0	78.3	36.0	2.1	6.5	7.2	7.2	1.2	6.4	1.2	1.2	1.8
Cape Verde	100.0	70.7	24.5	3.3	1.9	14.0	5.0	3.9	4.9	2.4	0.7	5.8
Central African Republic	100.0	92.4	53.0	8.4	6.6	4.5	4.8	1.4	3.3	0.8	1.6	2.7
Chad	100.0	68.7	33.0	3.2	1.5	6.5	4.6	4.8	6.4	2.6	1.6	1.0
Comoros	100.0	98.7	50.7	0.3	3.0	30.7	3.8	0.8	2.0	0.6	1.0	2.4
Congo, Rep.	100.0	24.8	9.1	1.0	0.7	3.3	0.9	1.9	2.0	1.3	0.7	1.9
Congo, Dem. Rep.	100.0	64.4	35.3	1.9	3.0	7.7	2.2	2.9	1.7	0.7	0.8	2.7
Côte d'Ivoire	100.0	71.4	30.4	2.3	2.5	7.0	5.9	3.0	7.8	2.1	2.5	3.1
Djibouti	100.0	71.5	21.5	5.6	2.1	22.3	4.0	2.3	4.4	0.2	0.8	4.6
Egypt, Arab Rep.[b]	100.0	79.5	33.3	2.6	4.8	10.4	3.8	7.3	4.7	2.0	2.4	5.3
Equatorial Guinea	100.0	12.9	4.9	0.3	0.4	1.8	0.5	1.2	1.0	0.5	0.2	0.6
Ethiopia	100.0	80.9	30.0	2.0	4.2	13.2	7.7	6.6	1.3	0.3	0.4	2.8
Gabon	100.0	38.1	11.5	2.2	1.9	5.5	1.7	2.6	3.2	1.7	0.9	2.0
Gambia, The	100.0	79.6	33.9	2.2	5.8	5.5	2.0	12.0	2.1	2.1	2.5	6.9
Ghana	100.0	66.9	24.9	0.9	9.5	6.7	4.6	2.3	4.4	1.0	0.7	9.2
Guinea	100.0	56.4	32.6	0.8	3.9	4.5	2.2	4.1	3.1	0.1	0.5	1.8
Guinea-Bissau	100.0	68.5	34.9	1.2	5.5	9.4	4.9	1.7	4.9	0.4	3.0	1.3
Kenya	100.0	87.6	30.0	4.3	2.2	6.8	4.0	6.4	8.9	2.7	3.0	12.6
Lesotho	100.0	110.3	28.2	2.9	13.7	11.5	9.6	4.8	3.7	3.1	3.8	10.4
Liberia	100.0	113.2	30.4	3.8	14.5	25.4	6.1	2.1	2.8	4.2	2.0	13.2
Madagascar	100.0	90.8	39.7	2.8	5.9	5.6	12.1	1.6	11.7	0.8	3.8	3.2
Malawi	100.0	98.7	48.2	4.8	2.6	10.8	10.0	3.9	7.7	1.7	2.3	5.0
Mali	100.0	66.7	31.0	0.9	3.8	6.5	4.0	2.6	8.8	1.5	2.7	2.9
Mauritania	100.0	58.5	35.3	0.6	2.0	5.6	1.6	2.3	2.5	2.3	0.6	4.4
Mauritius	100.0	79.0	22.9	6.6	4.6	12.2	6.3	3.9	10.6	2.4	5.1	6.3
Morocco	100.0	66.9	22.8	2.1	2.7	9.3	3.1	4.1	6.0	4.1	2.9	7.6
Mozambique	100.0	85.9	44.3	3.7	4.2	6.2	2.4	2.5	7.2	1.1	2.3	5.9
Namibia	100.0	71.5	14.3	2.9	3.4	13.7	5.1	7.9	2.9	0.6	2.8	10.0
Niger	100.0	80.2	33.5	1.8	6.2	8.1	3.9	3.3	6.1	1.9	4.4	2.6
Nigeria	100.0	64.4	24.3	0.9	9.3	6.6	4.5	2.0	4.3	1.0	0.7	8.2
Rwanda	100.0	86.9	41.6	2.9	2.9	14.3	2.8	2.3	5.6	1.1	1.4	4.5
São Tomé and Príncipe	100.0	116.9	63.8	5.3	4.6	11.0	4.0	4.6	11.4	1.5	1.7	4.5

Restaurants and hotels	Miscellaneous goods and services	Net purchases abroad	Individual consumption expenditure by households	Individual consumption expenditure by government	Collective consumption expenditure by government	Gross fixed capital formation	Machinery and equipment	Construction	Other products	Changes in inventories and valuables	Balance of exports and imports	Domestic absorption	Individual consumption expenditure by households without housing
(13)	(14)	(15)	(16)	(17)	(18)	(19)	(20)	(21)	(22)	(23)	(24)	(25)	(26)
1.1	8.4	0.0	31.4	13.6	9.2	31.9	13.5	16.6	1.8	3.4	10.5	89.5	30.6
1.8	7.2	0.0	50.8	9.9	26.2	17.1	5.3	11.0	0.8	0.3	−4.3	104.3	49.3
7.5	2.5	−0.8	76.5	4.3	7.3	20.7	7.1	13.4	0.2	0.9	−9.7	109.7	71.3
2.2	4.6	0.0	47.4	7.2	11.7	32.8	13.5	18.9	0.4	6.7	−5.9	105.9	44.3
2.3	1.9	0.0	65.1	2.6	15.2	16.5	5.8	8.4	1.3	7.7	−7.1	107.1	61.3
3.9	2.2	1.6	86.3	6.9	12.8	18.9	3.3	9.6	1.0	0.7	−25.7	125.7	73.3
5.2	1.8	0.6	75.9	2.5	9.1	20.6	3.6	10.5	0.5	0.0	−8.1	108.1	71.4
8.7	4.4	−8.8	62.4	8.3	10.1	46.8	13.9	28.1	1.9	0.9	−28.6	128.6	54.5
1.8	3.5	0.0	89.9	2.5	4.5	15.3	4.4	8.3	2.6	0.0	−12.3	112.3	89.1
0.5	1.5	1.5	66.6	2.1	4.4	28.6	11.5	13.8	3.3	1.2	−2.8	102.8	61.7
0.0	3.1	0.3	98.1	0.6	23.0	13.4	6.0	6.7	0.7	3.8	−38.9	138.9	73.8
1.9	0.7	−0.5	22.2	2.5	4.8	34.5	5.6	28.5	0.3	0.0	36.0	64.0	20.7
3.9	1.5	0.0	61.9	2.4	11.6	23.6	8.7	14.1	0.9	0.1	0.4	99.6	58.0
1.0	3.2	0.8	67.6	3.8	7.9	11.2	4.0	6.7	0.5	−6.6	16.1	83.9	63.0
0.7	1.7	1.1	66.3	5.1	19.8	26.4	8.7	17.5	0.1	4.4	−22.0	122.0	53.8
2.5	5.6	−5.2	75.6	4.0	7.5	16.7	7.8	8.5	0.5	0.4	−4.1	104.1	68.6
0.4	0.7	0.3	12.0	0.9	1.8	33.0	16.9	10.8	5.3	0.0	52.3	47.7	11.0
3.8	8.5	0.0	78.6	2.3	6.3	25.9	9.6	11.7	4.5	2.1	−15.1	115.1	71.9
1.8	1.2	2.0	35.0	3.2	9.5	19.0	5.6	5.6	7.8	0.0	33.4	66.6	31.4
0.9	3.6	0.0	76.0	3.6	7.0	26.9	17.1	8.4	1.3	0.0	−13.5	113.5	73.9
0.0	2.5	0.0	61.4	5.5	11.2	25.6	14.5	9.5	1.6	1.9	−5.6	105.6	60.4
0.8	1.4	0.6	55.6	0.8	4.6	23.8	15.2	7.9	0.8	1.9	13.3	86.7	52.6
0.3	1.1	0.0	66.9	1.5	17.6	12.8	5.7	6.7	0.5	1.1	0.0	100.0	64.5
5.4	6.1	−4.7	75.6	12.0	8.4	20.0	11.0	9.0	0.1	0.5	−16.5	116.5	72.0
1.5	6.6	10.5	97.0	13.3	21.0	26.5	6.9	18.4	1.2	1.2	−59.1	159.1	89.0
0.8	7.9	0.0	112.6	0.6	12.3	12.8	11.3	1.5	0.0	6.5	−44.7	144.7	96.4
3.0	1.4	−0.8	87.9	2.9	7.2	17.4	7.7	8.8	0.8	0.0	−15.4	115.4	87.0
2.5	2.3	−2.9	93.1	5.6	6.9	16.6	12.3	3.3	1.0	−3.3	−18.9	118.9	86.3
1.2	1.7	−1.0	63.3	3.4	12.0	22.2	9.5	11.6	1.0	0.9	−1.8	101.8	58.9
0.4	1.1	0.0	51.8	6.7	15.2	57.4	28.3	24.1	5.1	−23.9	−7.2	107.2	48.4
2.7	5.0	−9.6	73.4	5.6	7.9	24.0	7.2	15.7	1.1	1.9	−12.9	112.9	68.1
3.9	4.4	−6.1	58.9	7.9	10.3	30.7	13.2	15.9	1.7	5.3	−13.1	113.1	53.3
0.8	4.3	1.0	79.7	6.2	7.2	17.8	6.0	11.7	0.0	2.1	−13.0	113.0	75.8
4.3	6.2	−2.7	61.7	9.8	15.5	21.3	7.8	12.8	0.7	−1.2	−7.1	107.1	52.8
4.0	4.7	−0.1	77.4	2.8	10.0	37.0	16.3	19.9	0.9	0.1	−27.3	127.3	73.5
0.0	2.4	0.0	60.1	4.3	8.8	10.3	5.8	3.8	0.6	0.0	16.5	83.5	59.1
2.7	3.1	1.6	83.4	3.5	9.1	21.4	4.7	15.8	1.0	0.0	−17.4	117.4	74.1
1.5	2.2	0.8	112.4	4.5	7.7	19.7	14.8	3.5	1.4	0.2	−44.5	144.5	106.3

(continued)

Table 2.3 (Continued)

NOMINAL EXPENDITURE SHARES (GDP = 100)[a] Economy	Gross domestic product	Actual individual consumption	Food and nonalcoholic beverages	Alcoholic beverages, tobacco, and narcotics	Clothing and footwear	Housing, water, electricity, gas, and other fuels	Furnishings, household equipment and maintenance	Health	Transport	Communication	Recreation and culture	Education
(00)	(01)	(02)	(03)	(04)	(05)	(06)	(07)	(08)	(09)	(10)	(11)	(12)
Senegal	100.0	82.8	40.6	1.1	2.9	15.9	4.7	2.4	4.1	4.1	1.1	4.4
Seychelles	100.0	60.7	24.1	1.7	2.6	10.8	2.6	4.0	3.7	1.1	1.5	6.4
Sierra Leone	100.0	89.8	35.5	2.8	7.2	6.7	2.5	14.3	2.8	2.5	3.1	6.8
South Africa	100.0	68.3	12.1	3.0	2.9	9.3	4.2	7.6	8.8	1.8	2.8	7.3
Sudan[c]	100.0	70.2	36.3	0.5	3.1	10.3	4.5	0.9	5.7	1.1	1.6	2.3
Swaziland	100.0	90.1	41.1	0.8	5.0	12.1	9.6	5.7	7.0	1.2	3.8	7.6
Tanzania	100.0	68.3	45.1	0.5	4.6	4.9	3.0	2.4	2.6	0.0	0.7	3.3
Togo	100.0	88.5	38.4	2.1	4.4	6.9	4.0	5.8	4.9	2.1	1.1	5.9
Tunisia	100.0	74.4	16.4	2.4	5.1	10.5	4.5	5.3	10.6	2.6	2.4	5.9
Uganda	100.0	90.7	30.2	5.3	2.6	16.3	5.1	2.5	5.4	1.7	5.5	9.7
Zambia	100.0	55.3	32.3	0.4	3.5	6.6	0.8	2.8	0.8	1.4	0.4	3.4
Zimbabwe	100.0	95.3	53.3	3.1	5.2	6.1	2.8	2.6	7.2	0.1	2.0	6.8
Total (50)	**100.0**	**66.9**	**23.3**	**2.1**	**4.1**	**7.9**	**3.8**	**4.5**	**5.9**	**1.7**	**1.9**	**5.8**
ASIA AND THE PACIFIC												
Bangladesh	100.0	75.2	38.3	1.6	4.5	12.9	2.4	2.7	3.1	0.4	0.5	4.1
Bhutan	100.0	51.6	15.1	1.3	3.8	9.1	0.9	5.8	4.9	1.3	3.2	4.6
Brunei Darussalam	100.0	23.9	4.3	0.1	1.0	2.9	1.0	1.3	3.6	1.3	1.8	3.9
Cambodia	100.0	84.3	38.6	3.2	1.6	12.5	1.5	5.9	6.3	0.2	2.3	5.7
China[d]	100.0	42.9	8.1	0.9	3.0	5.9	2.1	6.4	2.5	1.5	2.3	4.3
Fiji	100.0	76.7	22.6	2.6	1.9	18.9	6.7	3.9	5.9	0.3	3.7	4.5
Hong Kong SAR, China	100.0	66.6	7.2	0.7	2.9	12.6	3.7	5.6	4.7	1.4	7.5	2.3
India	100.0	59.2	16.7	1.8	4.2	7.6	2.2	2.8	8.9	0.6	0.9	2.7
Indonesia	100.0	58.2	22.0	1.0	2.2	11.9	1.6	2.0	4.0	1.1	1.1	4.3
Lao PDR	100.0	58.6	29.9	3.0	0.9	7.5	1.5	1.3	6.2	0.7	1.6	2.4
Macao SAR, China	100.0	23.4	2.2	0.2	1.4	3.6	0.5	1.7	2.0	0.7	2.4	1.7
Malaysia	100.0	53.7	9.1	0.8	1.0	7.9	2.4	3.2	7.1	3.2	2.1	5.6
Maldives	100.0	37.9	7.3	1.7	0.8	14.7	1.5	2.2	1.5	0.8	0.7	5.0
Mongolia	100.0	60.7	17.3	4.3	3.0	8.7	0.9	2.8	9.5	1.8	1.7	6.1
Myanmar	100.0	69.8	36.5	1.4	2.2	9.2	0.9	4.3	2.3	1.1	0.8	5.8
Nepal	100.0	80.3	45.0	2.6	2.1	10.4	1.5	3.4	2.5	1.1	2.0	4.6
Pakistan	100.0	84.9	37.5	0.8	3.9	16.5	2.8	5.3	5.4	1.4	0.9	4.0
Philippines	100.0	76.9	31.5	0.9	1.0	9.1	3.0	2.4	7.9	2.3	1.3	5.5
Singapore	100.0	42.9	2.7	0.8	1.1	7.8	2.2	3.6	5.4	0.8	4.6	4.0
Sri Lanka	100.0	76.8	32.5	5.7	2.3	10.4	1.9	4.0	6.0	1.5	1.1	4.2
Taiwan, China	100.0	64.5	7.6	1.3	2.7	10.7	2.9	6.1	6.7	2.3	6.1	5.6
Thailand	100.0	62.0	15.9	2.2	2.1	5.6	2.5	4.7	8.7	1.3	2.9	5.4
Vietnam	100.0	63.4	16.4	1.8	2.6	14.5	3.7	4.6	6.3	0.5	2.5	5.5
Total (23)	**100.0**	**50.6**	**12.0**	**1.1**	**2.9**	**7.4**	**2.2**	**5.2**	**4.3**	**1.3**	**2.3**	**4.2**

Restaurants and hotels	Miscel-laneous goods and services	Net purchases abroad	Individual consumption expenditure by households	Individual consumption expenditure by government	Collective consumption expenditure by government	Gross fixed capital formation	Machinery and equipment	Construction	Other products	Changes in inventories and valuables	Balance of exports and imports	Domestic absorption	Individual consumption expenditure by households without housing
(13)	(14)	(15)	(16)	(17)	(18)	(19)	(20)	(21)	(22)	(23)	(24)	(25)	(26)
0.7	3.2	−2.2	78.5	4.3	9.9	23.8	9.1	14.5	0.2	1.4	−17.9	117.9	70.1
0.4	1.9	0.0	52.8	7.9	20.3	33.9	14.0	18.5	1.4	5.8	−20.8	120.8	46.0
1.1	4.3	0.0	87.5	2.2	7.9	41.7	29.6	11.6	0.5	0.4	−39.7	139.7	85.0
1.4	7.8	−0.7	59.4	8.9	12.8	19.0	9.0	9.1	0.9	0.5	−0.6	100.6	53.0
1.6	1.8	0.4	69.6	0.5	6.3	22.3	11.7	10.6	0.0	2.6	−1.4	101.4	62.8
0.6	1.4	−5.8	84.5	5.6	9.3	9.3	3.6	4.3	1.4	0.0	−8.7	108.7	75.0
0.0	1.3	0.0	66.1	2.2	14.2	36.1	15.5	19.7	0.8	0.6	−19.2	119.2	65.9
7.2	9.4	−3.7	84.8	3.7	8.1	17.7	5.4	11.5	0.8	1.8	−16.1	116.1	81.5
7.1	4.7	−3.1	65.6	8.8	9.6	21.7	7.1	13.8	0.8	1.7	−7.4	107.4	57.5
2.6	3.8	0.0	82.2	8.5	1.6	24.7	7.1	16.4	1.1	0.3	−17.3	117.3	75.0
0.1	2.7	0.0	51.9	3.4	15.6	21.7	6.6	14.1	1.0	1.4	6.0	94.0	48.7
0.6	4.7	0.8	87.4	7.9	8.8	11.1	3.8	7.3	0.0	4.6	−19.9	119.9	84.0
1.8	**5.2**	**−1.3**	**60.1**	**6.8**	**10.7**	**20.9**	**9.2**	**10.6**	**1.1**	**1.1**	**0.5**	**99.5**	**55.8**
1.7	2.9	0.0	73.7	1.5	3.7	28.3	6.7	21.2	0.4	0.5	−7.8	107.8	67.0
0.6	1.1	0.0	43.7	7.9	11.9	66.5	27.5	39.0	0.0	−0.4	−29.7	129.7	37.5
1.2	1.3	0.0	19.5	4.4	12.6	13.1	3.9	8.3	0.9	−0.7	51.1	48.9	17.3
4.0	2.3	0.0	79.6	4.7	3.7	11.6	5.7	5.8	0.1	0.5	−0.1	100.1	71.1
2.2	3.7	0.0	34.4	8.6	6.3	45.6	13.1	28.8	3.7	2.7	2.6	97.4	31.0
2.0	3.6	0.0	71.2	5.5	6.0	19.4	9.3	7.3	2.8	3.0	−5.1	105.1	56.2
6.7	11.3	0.0	63.3	3.4	5.3	23.5	10.4	11.1	2.1	0.6	3.9	96.1	52.6
1.5	9.5	0.0	55.9	3.3	8.3	30.9	11.8	18.0	1.2	7.3	−5.7	105.7	50.7
4.2	2.9	0.0	54.6	3.6	5.4	32.0	5.3	25.9	0.8	3.0	1.4	98.6	47.5
1.7	1.8	0.0	56.8	1.9	7.8	35.7	10.7	17.5	7.6	1.5	−3.6	103.6	53.6
4.4	2.6	0.0	20.5	2.9	4.2	12.4	2.9	9.4	0.1	1.4	58.6	41.4	17.7
4.4	6.9	0.0	47.3	6.4	6.6	22.3	8.1	11.1	3.1	1.0	16.4	83.6	42.9
0.7	1.0	0.0	32.2	5.6	17.9	50.4	19.4	30.9	0.0	0.0	−6.1	106.1	20.4
1.0	3.3	0.0	54.9	5.8	7.1	47.1	28.0	17.4	1.7	12.0	−27.0	127.0	47.4
3.1	2.1	0.0	63.7	6.0	4.2	26.7	13.0	11.6	2.1	0.0	−0.7	100.7	58.7
1.7	3.4	0.0	76.9	3.4	6.7	20.7	4.5	11.5	4.7	16.0	−23.6	123.6	68.5
0.9	5.4	0.0	81.9	3.0	7.1	12.9	4.2	6.2	2.6	1.6	−6.5	106.5	75.2
2.7	9.1	0.0	73.5	3.5	6.2	18.7	7.2	9.3	2.2	1.7	−3.6	103.6	67.2
4.4	5.5	0.0	39.0	3.9	6.5	23.8	8.9	14.0	0.9	−1.2	28.1	71.9	32.3
2.9	4.4	0.0	69.8	7.0	7.8	27.1	8.3	17.1	1.7	2.8	−14.6	114.6	63.3
3.5	9.0	0.0	60.1	4.4	8.0	20.9	9.7	9.5	1.7	−0.1	6.7	93.3	51.2
4.8	5.8	0.0	54.6	7.3	9.0	26.7	17.9	8.4	0.4	0.6	1.7	98.3	50.8
2.8	2.3	0.0	58.9	4.5	5.9	29.8	7.7	20.3	1.7	5.1	−4.1	104.1	49.9
2.5	**5.1**	**0.0**	**44.0**	**6.6**	**6.6**	**37.8**	**11.7**	**23.4**	**2.8**	**3.0**	**1.9**	**98.1**	**39.4**

(continued)

Table 2.3 (Continued)

NOMINAL EXPENDITURE SHARES (GDP = 100)[a] Economy	Gross domestic product	Actual individual consumption	Food and nonalcoholic beverages	Alcoholic beverages, tobacco, and narcotics	Clothing and footwear	Housing, water, electricity, gas, and other fuels	Furnishings, household equipment and maintenance	Health	Transport	Communication	Recreation and culture	Education
(00)	(01)	(02)	(03)	(04)	(05)	(06)	(07)	(08)	(09)	(10)	(11)	(12)
COMMONWEALTH OF INDEPENDENT STATES												
Armenia	100.0	88.8	48.5	4.0	3.1	7.2	1.2	5.4	4.6	4.7	2.0	4.0
Azerbaijan	100.0	41.0	15.1	1.0	3.8	3.3	2.1	1.8	4.3	2.3	1.4	3.0
Belarus	100.0	56.7	17.9	3.4	3.6	4.4	2.6	5.1	4.7	2.4	3.0	4.8
Kazakhstan	100.0	48.3	9.9	1.1	2.8	10.5	1.9	3.8	5.2	1.9	2.4	4.1
Kyrgyz Republic	100.0	93.6	35.4	4.3	6.7	6.9	3.3	4.8	9.8	6.0	3.9	7.5
Moldova	100.0	112.4	31.6	6.5	6.5	14.5	8.0	4.0	11.3	4.1	3.6	9.4
Russian Federation[e]	100.0	57.7	14.6	4.0	4.4	5.6	2.4	4.6	6.0	2.2	3.1	3.2
Tajikistan	100.0	115.1	50.9	0.4	9.9	7.0	3.9	5.3	8.9	7.0	2.4	4.8
Ukraine	100.0	79.2	25.9	4.6	4.2	8.5	2.9	6.9	8.2	1.6	3.2	7.0
Total (9)	**100.0**	**58.5**	**15.4**	**3.7**	**4.2**	**6.1**	**2.4**	**4.6**	**6.0**	**2.2**	**3.0**	**3.6**
EUROSTAT–OECD												
Albania	100.0	85.3	32.3	2.3	3.3	10.4	5.7	4.9	4.3	1.7	2.0	2.8
Australia	100.0	64.2	5.6	2.0	1.8	12.6	2.5	8.1	5.6	1.3	6.4	5.3
Austria	100.0	65.9	5.5	1.9	3.3	11.8	3.6	6.9	7.4	1.1	6.4	5.3
Belgium	100.0	68.3	6.8	1.8	2.5	12.1	2.9	9.9	6.3	1.1	5.1	6.3
Bosnia and Herzegovina	100.0	93.4	27.0	6.0	3.7	11.8	4.9	8.0	7.9	2.6	4.6	5.3
Bulgaria	100.0	70.3	13.2	4.6	1.9	11.2	4.9	6.8	10.9	3.8	5.7	3.5
Canada	100.0	68.4	5.1	1.9	2.3	13.2	3.0	8.7	8.1	1.3	5.5	5.4
Chile	100.0	68.8	9.9	1.9	3.4	10.0	4.4	6.6	7.8	2.4	4.7	5.8
Croatia	100.0	70.7	13.4	4.5	3.0	12.5	3.7	8.4	6.8	2.3	7.2	5.6
Cyprus	100.0	76.5	9.3	3.2	4.3	13.4	3.6	6.6	8.2	2.4	6.2	7.5
Czech Republic	100.0	61.4	7.7	4.8	1.6	14.0	2.8	7.3	4.9	1.6	5.6	4.3
Denmark	100.0	69.0	5.4	1.7	2.2	13.9	2.4	9.0	5.9	0.8	6.0	6.3
Estonia	100.0	61.3	10.1	4.6	3.3	11.0	1.9	5.5	6.5	1.9	4.7	4.8
Finland	100.0	72.2	6.6	2.6	2.6	14.3	2.8	8.7	6.1	1.1	6.9	5.9
France	100.0	73.7	7.5	1.8	2.4	14.8	3.3	9.2	8.0	1.5	5.9	5.4
Germany	100.0	69.7	6.2	1.8	2.6	13.2	3.4	8.8	7.6	1.4	5.5	4.1
Greece	100.0	81.7	12.5	3.3	2.9	18.3	3.1	8.1	9.1	2.2	4.4	5.4
Hungary	100.0	64.1	9.3	4.1	1.6	11.9	2.4	7.3	7.1	2.0	4.9	4.4
Iceland	100.0	68.6	7.3	2.1	2.1	11.3	3.5	8.6	7.4	1.1	6.8	7.0
Ireland	100.0	61.0	4.6	2.5	1.9	11.4	2.0	9.0	6.0	1.4	3.6	4.8
Israel	100.0	69.5	9.1	1.4	1.7	13.9	3.5	6.0	8.9	2.2	4.4	7.2
Italy	100.0	73.2	8.8	1.7	4.6	13.7	4.4	8.8	7.8	1.5	5.0	4.3
Japan	100.0	72.4	8.2	1.6	1.9	15.1	3.0	7.7	6.4	2.0	5.4	3.7
Korea, Rep.	100.0	59.9	6.7	1.2	2.6	8.4	1.7	6.6	6.1	2.2	4.2	6.6
Latvia	100.0	70.1	12.0	4.6	3.0	14.4	2.4	5.0	8.9	1.9	5.6	4.7
Lithuania	100.0	73.7	15.3	4.8	3.8	10.3	3.8	7.3	9.5	1.5	4.7	4.9
Luxembourg	100.0	42.0	3.2	3.3	1.8	9.4	2.4	4.5	7.3	0.6	3.3	4.4

Restaurants and hotels	Miscel-laneous goods and services	Net purchases abroad	Individual consumption expenditure by households	Individual consumption expenditure by government	Collective consumption expenditure by government	Gross fixed capital formation	Machinery and equipment	Construction	Other products	Changes in inventories and valuables	Balance of exports and imports	Domestic absorption	Individual consumption expenditure by households without housing
(13)	(14)	(15)	(16)	(17)	(18)	(19)	(20)	(21)	(22)	(23)	(24)	(25)	(26)
1.1	2.8	0.3	83.7	5.2	7.8	26.0	4.3	21.0	0.7	1.0	−23.6	123.6	80.8
1.3	1.7	0.0	37.3	3.8	6.4	20.2	10.5	8.8	0.9	0.1	32.3	67.7	36.2
1.6	2.3	0.7	47.7	9.1	4.9	37.8	16.5	21.0	0.3	1.7	−1.1	101.1	46.1
1.7	3.2	0.0	42.8	5.6	5.1	20.9	6.0	13.6	1.3	4.3	21.4	78.6	35.5
3.6	3.9	−2.7	83.4	10.2	8.0	23.7	10.6	12.4	0.7	1.8	−27.1	127.1	81.8
1.7	9.7	1.6	96.5	15.8	4.3	23.3	7.4	14.1	1.9	0.9	−40.9	140.9	91.4
1.6	4.9	1.1	49.1	8.6	9.4	20.8	7.5	11.6	1.7	3.6	8.6	91.4	46.6
1.3	5.7	7.5	106.9	8.2	5.2	32.4	14.3	14.7	3.4	3.7	−56.4	156.4	105.2
1.7	4.3	−0.1	67.2	11.9	6.3	18.6	7.1	11.0	0.4	2.2	−6.2	106.2	63.1
1.6	**4.6**	**0.9**	**50.0**	**8.5**	**8.6**	**21.1**	**7.6**	**11.9**	**1.5**	**3.4**	**8.4**	**91.6**	**47.1**
2.2	4.8	8.8	80.3	5.0	5.5	33.1	7.0	25.4	0.7	−0.8	−23.1	123.1	73.9
3.7	9.4	−0.2	53.6	10.6	7.0	26.9	6.5	15.5	4.9	0.5	1.3	98.7	43.8
6.6	8.2	−2.1	54.8	11.2	7.8	21.2	8.1	11.0	2.1	2.1	3.0	97.0	47.4
3.1	9.7	0.8	52.7	15.6	8.8	20.7	7.7	11.1	1.9	1.3	0.8	99.2	44.6
5.9	8.4	−2.5	82.9	10.6	11.8	17.9	7.6	9.7	0.6	0.2	−23.3	123.3	77.4
4.3	4.3	−4.9	62.4	7.9	7.8	21.5	9.3	11.5	0.8	0.4	0.0	100.0	55.7
3.7	9.4	0.9	55.7	12.7	9.0	23.4	4.7	15.6	3.2	0.4	−1.2	101.2	44.9
2.9	9.2	−0.2	61.2	7.6	4.4	22.4	8.8	11.9	1.7	1.1	3.3	96.7	55.4
10.6	6.1	−13.5	59.9	10.8	9.0	19.2	6.2	11.5	1.5	1.2	−0.1	100.1	53.0
11.0	6.5	−6.0	67.7	8.8	11.3	16.6	4.8	11.1	0.8	−0.1	−4.4	104.4	59.0
4.0	5.2	−2.4	50.6	10.8	9.9	24.1	10.7	12.1	1.3	0.4	4.1	95.9	42.2
2.5	12.7	0.1	48.7	20.3	8.0	17.4	6.1	8.8	2.5	0.4	5.2	94.8	39.1
3.9	5.6	−2.6	50.6	10.7	8.5	23.6	10.9	11.9	0.8	2.9	3.7	96.3	43.2
3.4	11.3	−0.2	55.7	16.4	8.0	19.4	4.7	13.1	1.7	1.1	−0.7	100.7	45.8
4.0	10.3	−0.4	57.7	16.0	8.5	20.0	5.4	12.4	2.1	0.8	−3.0	103.0	47.5
3.2	10.6	1.4	57.4	12.2	6.9	18.1	5.9	10.1	1.1	0.1	5.2	94.8	48.4
9.0	7.4	−4.0	74.6	7.1	10.3	15.1	6.1	8.0	1.1	1.0	−8.1	108.1	62.3
3.6	8.2	−2.7	53.3	10.8	10.2	17.9	7.5	9.3	1.1	1.3	6.5	93.5	46.6
4.3	7.2	−0.1	51.9	16.7	8.7	14.1	5.4	7.7	1.1	0.3	8.4	91.6	42.9
5.8	6.9	1.1	48.1	12.9	5.5	10.6	4.0	5.7	0.9	1.3	21.6	78.4	39.9
3.8	8.1	−0.8	57.3	12.2	10.8	20.4	6.5	9.9	4.0	−0.2	−0.5	100.5	46.4
6.2	7.4	−0.9	61.2	11.9	8.5	19.1	7.6	9.1	2.3	0.7	−1.4	101.4	51.8
3.9	13.1	0.5	60.5	11.9	8.5	20.6	8.0	9.7	2.9	−0.6	−0.9	100.9	48.0
4.2	8.7	0.8	53.1	6.8	8.5	27.5	9.7	15.6	2.2	2.0	2.0	98.0	47.2
2.9	4.6	0.0	62.2	7.9	9.8	21.3	8.8	11.8	0.6	3.6	−4.8	104.8	53.8
1.8	6.4	−0.6	62.8	10.8	7.8	18.0	5.9	10.6	1.5	3.2	−2.7	102.7	58.7
2.5	7.3	−7.9	31.8	10.3	6.5	18.5	6.9	10.5	1.1	2.6	30.4	69.6	24.7

(continued)

Table 2.3 (Continued)

NOMINAL EXPENDITURE SHARES (GDP = 100)[a] Economy	Gross domestic product	Actual individual consumption	Food and nonalcoholic beverages	Alcoholic beverages, tobacco, and narcotics	Clothing and footwear	Housing, water, electricity, gas, and other fuels	Furnishings, household equipment and maintenance	Health	Transport	Communication	Recreation and culture	Education
(00)	(01)	(02)	(03)	(04)	(05)	(06)	(07)	(08)	(09)	(10)	(11)	(12)
Macedonia, FYR	100.0	82.8	25.4	2.5	3.7	14.5	3.1	5.2	7.4	4.4	2.6	4.4
Malta	100.0	71.6	10.7	2.1	2.9	8.5	4.8	8.5	8.9	2.6	7.6	5.1
Mexico	100.0	72.5	15.5	1.7	2.0	13.7	3.8	4.6	12.4	2.5	3.1	3.8
Montenegro	100.0	91.9	30.7	4.4	3.0	12.8	9.3	6.3	11.2	5.1	3.7	4.0
Netherlands	100.0	62.4	5.3	1.4	2.4	11.0	2.6	7.8	5.7	1.9	5.1	5.1
New Zealand	100.0	71.7	8.6	3.1	2.7	13.9	2.9	8.8	7.1	1.9	6.6	5.8
Norway	100.0	55.3	5.0	1.6	2.0	8.2	2.2	7.4	5.7	1.0	5.5	4.2
Poland	100.0	71.5	11.4	3.9	2.7	14.8	2.7	6.9	6.1	1.8	5.4	5.3
Portugal	100.0	76.9	11.3	2.3	3.7	10.9	3.7	9.4	8.9	2.0	5.6	5.9
Romania	100.0	72.2	17.0	3.1	2.4	13.7	3.1	8.0	6.8	3.1	4.4	3.5
Russian Federation[e]	100.0	57.7	14.6	4.0	4.4	5.6	2.4	4.5	6.0	2.2	3.1	3.2
Serbia	100.0	89.7	21.2	4.3	2.9	17.7	3.0	9.4	10.4	3.5	4.6	4.7
Slovak Republic	100.0	66.3	10.2	2.7	2.4	14.8	3.4	6.2	4.5	2.1	6.1	4.1
Slovenia	100.0	69.8	9.0	3.3	3.3	11.9	3.7	8.0	9.2	2.0	6.1	6.1
Spain	100.0	70.9	8.5	1.8	3.2	12.7	2.9	8.2	7.0	1.7	5.9	5.2
Sweden	100.0	67.2	5.7	1.7	2.3	12.7	2.4	8.1	6.2	1.6	6.1	6.6
Switzerland	100.0	63.5	5.0	2.0	1.9	13.6	2.3	8.5	5.1	1.4	5.1	5.0
Turkey	100.0	78.8	17.2	2.5	4.0	14.4	5.9	6.0	12.3	2.1	3.3	3.9
United Kingdom	100.0	78.4	5.6	2.2	3.6	15.6	3.1	8.7	8.3	1.3	8.7	6.2
United States	100.0	75.1	4.5	1.3	2.4	12.6	2.8	14.8	6.9	1.6	6.4	6.0
Total (47)	**100.0**	**71.5**	**7.0**	**1.8**	**2.6**	**13.0**	**3.0**	**10.1**	**7.2**	**1.7**	**5.7**	**5.1**
LATIN AMERICA												
Bolivia	100.0	62.6	21.1	1.0	1.3	6.7	4.5	5.4	10.7	0.7	0.6	3.8
Brazil	100.0	68.4	9.9	1.2	2.9	9.2	4.6	7.6	9.3	2.2	3.2	5.9
Colombia	100.0	68.0	11.3	1.9	4.0	9.8	2.6	5.1	7.5	2.7	3.2	5.9
Costa Rica	100.0	77.5	15.5	0.7	3.4	4.9	4.5	9.5	13.8	1.8	7.5	7.9
Cuba[f]	...	...	...	...	...	...	...	...	...	...	...	...
Dominican Republic	100.0	88.9	21.6	5.3	2.9	13.2	3.2	5.5	11.5	3.8	1.9	3.9
Ecuador	100.0	67.1	13.6	1.7	2.7	9.1	4.7	5.5	7.5	3.6	3.4	6.9
El Salvador	100.0	98.5	25.1	1.9	5.2	16.5	9.3	7.9	8.6	3.4	4.5	4.5
Guatemala	100.0	90.0	34.9	1.4	4.7	11.3	5.0	6.1	6.4	6.5	2.8	3.7
Haiti	100.0	113.4	66.2	2.6	7.8	12.8	3.8	3.8	5.9	0.5	2.7	4.8
Honduras	100.0	85.9	25.4	2.7	3.8	10.6	3.5	8.4	8.2	2.7	3.2	7.5
Nicaragua	100.0	83.9	21.9	2.3	2.4	11.2	4.6	9.0	10.3	2.9	3.2	6.0
Panama	100.0	66.0	11.2	0.4	4.1	13.0	4.8	4.7	8.6	2.3	3.5	3.8
Paraguay	100.0	76.1	21.0	1.0	4.0	6.9	6.2	6.2	6.5	2.8	4.9	7.1
Peru	100.0	62.5	14.2	1.4	3.9	6.6	3.1	4.0	6.7	2.4	3.7	5.3
Uruguay	100.0	75.5	14.0	1.8	3.4	14.4	4.2	9.1	5.6	3.0	2.5	4.9
Venezuela, RB	100.0	60.7	13.1	1.8	2.8	3.0	3.5	5.5	8.1	3.4	3.9	5.1
Total (17)	**100.0**	**68.6**	**11.6**	**1.4**	**3.1**	**8.7**	**4.3**	**6.9**	**8.8**	**2.5**	**3.3**	**5.7**

Restaurants and hotels	Miscellaneous goods and services	Net purchases abroad	Individual consumption expenditure by households	Individual consumption expenditure by government	Collective consumption expenditure by government	Gross fixed capital formation	Machinery and equipment	Construction	Other products	Changes in inventories and valuables	Balance of exports and imports	Domestic absorption	Individual consumption expenditure by households without housing
(13)	(14)	(15)	(16)	(17)	(18)	(19)	(20)	(21)	(22)	(23)	(24)	(25)	(26)
2.8	5.8	0.9	75.1	7.7	10.6	20.6	6.9	12.8	0.8	5.6	−19.6	119.6	66.4
11.6	9.2	−10.8	60.8	10.8	9.6	15.1	5.5	7.7	1.9	−0.2	3.9	96.1	55.2
2.7	7.3	−0.3	66.3	6.2	5.5	21.8	6.7	14.6	0.4	1.5	−1.3	101.3	55.3
13.6	6.2	−18.3	82.5	9.4	12.1	18.4	5.7	12.3	0.4	−0.3	−22.2	122.2	75.1
2.2	12.2	−0.3	45.4	17.1	10.9	17.8	5.5	10.1	2.2	0.3	8.6	91.4	38.2
4.2	7.5	−1.5	59.8	12.0	8.2	18.2	6.2	10.4	1.5	0.5	1.4	98.6	48.0
2.3	8.7	1.5	41.2	14.1	7.4	19.5	6.3	9.3	3.9	4.6	13.3	86.7	35.1
1.7	9.2	−0.4	61.1	10.4	7.6	20.2	7.6	11.4	1.3	1.9	−1.2	101.2	56.8
7.5	8.6	−3.1	66.0	10.8	9.1	18.0	5.4	11.0	1.6	0.4	−4.4	104.4	59.1
2.1	4.9	0.2	63.5	8.7	6.3	26.1	8.5	16.4	1.2	0.7	−5.3	105.3	54.9
1.6	5.1	1.1	49.1	8.6	9.4	20.8	7.5	11.6	1.7	3.6	8.6	91.4	46.7
1.8	7.5	−1.2	77.0	12.8	6.5	18.5	7.9	9.5	1.1	1.7	−16.4	116.4	66.5
2.9	6.9	0.0	57.6	8.7	9.3	23.1	7.7	10.4	5.0	0.7	0.5	99.5	52.3
4.1	7.0	−3.9	57.5	12.4	8.5	18.6	8.0	9.2	1.4	1.6	1.5	98.5	51.0
10.4	6.8	−3.2	58.6	12.3	9.0	20.7	6.0	10.6	4.1	0.5	−1.1	101.1	50.0
2.6	11.6	−0.4	48.0	19.1	7.4	18.7	6.9	9.1	2.7	1.2	5.6	94.4	38.8
3.8	9.7	0.0	57.3	6.2	4.8	20.6	9.0	9.3	2.2	0.7	10.4	89.6	46.0
4.6	5.8	−3.2	71.2	7.6	6.3	21.8	12.7	9.1	0.1	1.7	−8.7	108.7	60.6
5.2	9.4	0.4	64.6	13.8	8.1	14.4	2.9	8.2	3.2	0.6	−1.5	101.5	51.6
4.3	11.6	−0.2	69.0	6.1	10.1	18.2	6.5	8.3	3.3	0.2	−3.7	103.7	58.6
4.2	**10.2**	**−0.1**	**61.4**	**10.1**	**8.7**	**19.6**	**6.7**	**10.2**	**2.7**	**0.6**	**−0.4**	**100.4**	**51.6**
4.9	1.9	0.0	61.0	1.6	12.1	19.0	10.6	7.1	1.2	0.6	5.7	94.3	57.6
3.9	8.6	0.0	60.3	8.1	12.6	19.3	10.1	8.0	1.2	0.4	−0.7	100.7	54.1
7.1	7.0	0.0	61.3	6.7	9.1	23.6	8.2	14.5	0.9	0.2	−0.9	100.9	55.1
3.6	3.6	0.8	65.3	12.2	5.8	19.8	8.5	10.7	0.6	1.8	−4.9	104.9	63.2
…	…	…	…	…	…	…	…	…	…	…	…	…	…
7.2	9.4	−0.5	86.5	2.4	5.0	16.3	4.6	11.4	0.3	0.1	−10.3	110.3	77.8
2.7	6.1	−0.4	61.1	6.0	6.7	26.0	8.4	7.4	10.2	3.0	−2.8	102.8	54.2
6.6	5.5	−0.6	93.3	5.2	5.9	12.5	6.3	6.2	0.1	1.8	−18.7	118.7	83.3
5.2	3.7	−1.7	85.3	4.7	5.6	14.7	7.7	7.0	0.0	0.4	−10.7	110.7	76.5
0.2	2.4	0.0	112.2	1.2	0.1	29.0	0.7	28.2	0.0	0.0	−42.5	142.5	107.5
4.7	5.3	0.0	77.6	8.3	7.8	24.4	13.6	9.6	1.3	1.6	−19.7	119.7	72.0
5.0	6.3	−1.3	77.8	6.2	8.5	22.5	8.7	12.0	1.8	0.8	−15.8	115.8	70.6
3.4	6.2	0.0	60.2	5.8	6.5	26.1	11.8	14.3	0.0	1.1	0.2	99.8	50.6
3.6	6.0	0.0	70.1	6.0	4.6	16.4	7.0	8.1	1.3	0.4	2.5	97.5	68.2
5.6	5.7	0.0	59.5	3.1	6.2	26.0	9.3	15.8	0.8	1.1	4.3	95.7	55.0
5.2	6.0	1.5	67.9	7.6	5.6	19.0	6.0	11.8	1.2	0.4	−0.5	100.5	57.0
7.3	3.1	0.3	55.2	5.5	6.0	17.7	8.0	9.1	0.6	5.3	10.2	89.8	53.0
4.6	**7.6**	**0.0**	**61.3**	**7.2**	**10.7**	**20.0**	**9.5**	**9.2**	**1.2**	**1.0**	**−0.2**	**100.2**	**55.4**

(continued)

Table 2.3 *(Continued)*

NOMINAL EXPENDITURE SHARES (GDP = 100)[a] Economy	Gross domestic product	Actual individual consumption	Food and nonalcoholic beverages	Alcoholic beverages, tobacco, and narcotics	Clothing and footwear	Housing, water, electricity, gas, and other fuels	Furnishings, household equipment and maintenance	Health	Transport	Communication	Recreation and culture	Education
(00)	(01)	(02)	(03)	(04)	(05)	(06)	(07)	(08)	(09)	(10)	(11)	(12)
CARIBBEAN												
Anguilla	100.0	87.6	10.9	2.0	2.6	17.9	3.4	2.1	15.9	6.8	3.7	3.6
Antigua and Barbuda	100.0	68.1	10.5	1.1	1.6	18.7	2.9	6.1	7.1	3.5	2.2	3.8
Aruba	100.0	78.2	5.8	0.5	2.5	26.0	3.2	9.3	9.3	2.8	5.4	4.8
Bahamas, The	100.0	76.8	7.3	0.9	2.5	23.5	3.3	6.5	5.9	3.1	3.2	5.0
Barbados	100.0	89.1	12.3	1.4	1.6	46.5	2.4	4.1	6.2	3.7	3.3	4.4
Belize	100.0	76.0	13.8	1.2	6.0	19.0	5.0	5.6	9.8	2.4	5.0	4.0
Bermuda	100.0	78.2	6.8	1.3	1.6	21.7	3.7	6.4	4.8	2.1	4.5	5.7
Bonaire[g]	...	...	...	...	...	...	...	...	...	...	...	...
Cayman Islands	100.0	74.8	4.6	0.9	2.2	25.8	3.5	3.4	7.0	3.2	3.6	3.7
Curaçao	100.0	76.7	8.1	0.9	5.8	24.5	2.3	5.8	7.2	2.9	3.4	3.2
Dominica	100.0	89.7	15.4	0.7	4.3	20.3	4.5	5.8	17.1	3.4	3.4	5.7
Grenada	100.0	97.2	19.2	1.7	4.3	18.8	4.0	3.9	17.6	9.4	2.6	6.0
Jamaica	100.0	93.0	26.1	1.2	1.7	12.6	5.2	5.6	13.2	2.5	8.2	6.9
Montserrat	100.0	95.3	15.0	2.0	1.2	17.9	4.0	9.6	25.4	6.1	2.8	5.6
St. Kitts and Nevis	100.0	74.9	12.3	2.1	3.2	19.6	4.7	4.4	6.8	3.9	2.6	4.0
St. Lucia	100.0	80.5	16.1	1.4	4.8	18.4	4.5	4.3	7.5	4.4	1.5	6.7
St. Vincent and the Grenadines	100.0	92.6	18.3	5.2	1.9	24.8	3.9	5.8	16.1	6.2	5.7	5.5
Sint Maarten	100.0	64.3	5.4	0.2	3.2	26.7	2.8	2.1	7.4	3.2	2.5	2.0
Suriname	100.0	38.3	14.3	1.0	1.3	6.5	1.8	1.9	2.9	1.4	1.4	0.5
Trinidad and Tobago	100.0	58.1	12.2	0.6	0.8	7.1	2.4	4.5	6.2	1.2	3.8	6.1
Turks and Caicos Islands	100.0	39.4	5.6	0.7	1.4	4.2	1.5	3.7	9.1	0.7	2.0	4.5
Virgin Islands, British	100.0	38.4	6.5	0.8	3.6	8.0	4.8	2.1	3.6	1.2	1.5	2.1
Total (22)	**100.0**	**72.2**	**13.3**	**1.0**	**1.9**	**16.3**	**3.3**	**5.0**	**7.8**	**2.4**	**4.4**	**5.3**
WESTERN ASIA												
Bahrain	100.0	43.7	5.9	0.2	2.5	8.9	3.1	3.2	4.6	2.0	2.8	4.9
Egypt, Arab Rep.[b]	100.0	79.5	33.3	2.6	4.8	10.4	3.8	7.3	4.7	2.0	2.4	5.3
Iraq	100.0	47.0	14.4	0.3	2.8	12.2	2.2	3.4	3.4	0.7	0.5	5.2
Jordan	100.0	79.8	22.3	2.5	3.5	16.0	3.4	5.6	8.1	3.1	1.3	9.8
Kuwait	100.0	27.8	4.3	0.1	2.2	6.5	3.4	2.2	2.0	0.9	1.0	2.7
Oman	100.0	36.0	7.0	0.1	2.0	6.6	1.4	2.1	5.7	1.7	1.2	4.0
Qatar	100.0	16.6	1.8	0.0	0.6	3.7	0.7	1.2	1.4	0.4	1.2	2.5
Saudi Arabia	100.0	36.7	5.8	0.1	1.8	7.6	2.4	3.0	2.5	1.5	1.1	6.3
Sudan[c]	100.0	70.2	36.3	0.5	3.1	10.3	4.5	0.9	5.7	1.1	1.6	2.3
United Arab Emirates	100.0	52.8	6.2	0.1	6.5	17.5	1.9	0.8	8.5	3.1	1.4	2.5
West Bank and Gaza	100.0	108.2	34.2	4.3	6.3	11.8	5.6	7.9	10.2	3.3	2.6	9.1
Yemen, Rep.	100.0	73.0	33.0	3.5	3.2	10.4	2.2	7.0	4.2	0.8	0.3	5.1
Total (12)	**100.0**	**45.7**	**11.2**	**0.5**	**3.1**	**9.9**	**2.5**	**3.0**	**4.2**	**1.7**	**1.3**	**4.6**

Restaurants and hotels	Miscellaneous goods and services	Net purchases abroad	Individual consumption expenditure by households	Individual consumption expenditure by government	Collective consumption expenditure by government	Gross fixed capital formation	Machinery and equipment	Construction	Other products	Changes in inventories and valuables	Balance of exports and imports	Domestic absorption	Individual consumption expenditure by households without housing
(13)	(14)	(15)	(16)	(17)	(18)	(19)	(20)	(21)	(22)	(23)	(24)	(25)	(26)
3.4	15.3	0.0	84.2	3.4	12.5	17.5	4.6	12.6	0.3	−1.6	−16.1	116.1	73.6
2.2	8.4	0.0	60.0	8.1	10.3	20.9	4.4	16.2	0.4	0.6	0.0	100.0	48.6
1.8	6.6	0.0	62.1	16.1	9.5	26.4	6.5	19.9	0.0	1.6	−15.7	115.7	44.5
4.1	11.4	0.0	71.0	5.8	9.0	26.4	12.9	13.4	0.1	1.7	−13.9	113.9	54.4
16.4	7.3	−20.6	81.5	7.6	10.6	15.6	7.6	7.9	0.0	−0.9	−14.4	114.4	40.9
0.5	3.7	0.0	71.6	4.4	11.3	15.1	6.4	8.4	0.3	1.4	−3.8	103.8	54.3
9.1	10.5	0.0	67.2	11.1	8.2	20.2	10.5	9.7	0.0	1.1	−7.8	107.8	47.6
...	...	...	...	...	...	...	...	...	...	...	...	...	...
3.6	13.4	0.0	70.3	4.5	8.9	22.4	11.1	11.3	0.1	0.0	−6.1	106.1	50.6
2.4	15.9	−5.8	69.1	7.6	7.3	39.8	21.6	11.3	6.9	1.5	−25.3	125.3	55.1
2.5	6.8	0.0	81.8	7.9	13.6	23.0	11.1	11.5	0.4	−11.2	−15.2	115.2	68.4
1.7	7.0	1.0	89.9	7.3	8.4	20.4	8.0	12.1	0.4	−0.1	−25.9	125.9	79.4
11.4	11.0	−12.7	85.6	7.4	8.6	20.8	10.0	10.4	0.4	0.5	−22.9	122.9	78.0
0.3	10.2	−4.9	80.8	14.5	33.0	28.7	8.4	19.8	0.5	0.0	−57.0	157.0	71.3
4.3	7.0	0.0	68.5	6.4	10.7	30.9	7.7	22.7	0.6	0.0	−16.5	116.5	54.7
1.4	9.5	0.0	73.9	6.6	10.0	30.0	3.2	20.2	0.6	0.0	−20.5	120.5	62.9
2.9	7.8	−11.6	82.1	10.5	10.3	23.9	7.3	16.1	0.4	1.5	−28.2	128.2	67.6
1.1	7.7	0.0	60.4	3.8	12.7	16.8	3.1	4.8	2.9	0.0	6.2	93.8	40.3
0.5	4.7	0.0	37.4	0.9	11.4	37.0	31.4	5.9	0.7	6.9	6.3	93.7	35.2
5.3	7.9	0.0	45.8	12.3	1.7	15.0	7.4	7.3	0.3	0.0	25.2	74.8	41.4
1.5	4.6	0.0	35.8	3.6	19.0	14.5	5.1	9.4	0.0	0.1	27.0	73.0	33.5
2.1	2.3	0.0	35.1	3.3	5.2	23.9	10.6	12.6	0.7	−1.9	34.4	65.6	29.8
6.2	**9.1**	**−3.8**	**63.6**	**8.6**	**7.1**	**21.3**	**10.6**	**10.1**	**0.6**	**0.7**	**−1.3**	**101.3**	**52.0**
1.9	2.7	1.1	38.7	5.0	8.7	15.6	4.8	10.8	0.1	0.7	31.2	68.8	31.4
2.5	5.6	−5.2	75.6	4.0	7.5	16.7	7.8	8.5	0.5	0.4	−4.1	104.1	68.6
0.4	1.5	0.0	39.8	7.2	15.1	19.4	7.5	11.8	0.1	−0.4	18.9	81.1	31.1
1.6	2.3	0.3	71.4	8.3	11.1	21.4	5.6	14.5	1.3	1.6	−13.8	113.8	60.8
0.8	1.8	0.0	23.3	4.5	10.5	15.8	6.3	7.9	1.6	0.6	45.4	54.6	17.5
1.0	2.8	0.3	30.0	6.0	11.2	26.3	10.5	13.1	2.7	−3.1	29.6	70.4	25.0
0.3	2.3	0.4	12.8	3.8	8.7	29.3	14.3	4.6	10.4	0.0	45.4	54.6	9.4
1.4	1.8	1.3	27.2	9.6	9.9	22.7	8.7	11.2	2.7	4.1	26.6	73.4	21.8
1.6	1.8	0.4	69.6	0.5	6.3	22.3	11.7	10.6	0.0	2.6	−1.4	101.4	62.8
1.9	2.4	0.0	51.7	1.1	6.2	22.0	8.7	11.0	2.3	1.0	18.0	82.0	36.6
2.6	9.0	1.4	96.5	11.7	18.2	20.7	3.6	14.8	2.2	−3.4	−43.6	143.6	92.4
0.0	3.3	0.0	68.1	4.9	9.1	13.2	1.2	10.2	1.7	5.6	−1.0	101.0	62.6
1.4	**2.5**	**−0.1**	**40.0**	**5.7**	**9.3**	**21.4**	**8.7**	**10.2**	**2.6**	**1.7**	**21.9**	**78.1**	**32.5**

(continued)

Table 2.3 (Continued)

NOMINAL EXPENDITURE SHARES (GDP = 100)[a] Economy	Gross domestic product	Actual individual consumption	Food and nonalcoholic beverages	Alcoholic beverages, tobacco, and narcotics	Clothing and footwear	Housing, water, electricity, gas, and other fuels	Furnishings, household equipment and maintenance	Health	Transport	Communication	Recreation and culture	Education
(00)	(01)	(02)	(03)	(04)	(05)	(06)	(07)	(08)	(09)	(10)	(11)	(12)
SINGLETONS												
Georgia	100.0	78.3	24.6	4.1	2.0	8.9	2.9	8.2	7.2	2.3	5.5	5.4
Iran, Islamic Rep.	100.0	44.4	10.8	0.2	1.9	12.8	1.6	3.6	3.3	1.4	1.1	1.4
Total (2)	**100.0**	**45.2**	**11.1**	**0.3**	**1.9**	**12.7**	**1.7**	**3.7**	**3.3**	**1.4**	**1.2**	**1.5**
WORLD[h] (179)	**100.0**	**66.5**	**8.7**	**1.6**	**2.7**	**11.5**	**2.9**	**8.6**	**6.6**	**1.7**	**4.7**	**5.0**

Source: ICP, http://icp.worldbank.org/.

Note: ... = data suppressed because of incompleteness.

a. All shares are rounded to one decimal place. More precision can be found in the Excel version of the table, which can be downloaded from the ICP website.

b. The Arab Republic of Egypt participated in both the Africa and Western Asia regions. The regional results for Egypt were averaged by taking the geometric mean of the regional PPPs, allowing Egypt to have the same global results in each region.

c. Sudan participated in both the Africa and Western Asia regions. The regional results for Sudan were averaged by taking the geometric mean of the regional PPPs, allowing Sudan to have the same global results in each region.

d. The results presented in the tables are based on data supplied by all the participating economies and compiled in accordance with ICP principles and the procedures recommended by the 2011 ICP Technical Advisory Group. The results for China are estimated by the 2011 ICP Asia and the Pacific Regional Office and the Global Office. The National Bureau of Statistics of China does not recognize these results as official statistics.

e. The Russian Federation participated in both the CIS and Eurostat-OECD comparisons. The PPPs for Russia are based on the Eurostat-OECD comparison. They were the basis for linking the CIS comparison to the ICP.

f. The official GDP of Cuba for reference year 2011 is 68,990.15 million in national currency. However, this number and its breakdown into main aggregates are not shown in the tables because of methodological comparability issues. Therefore, Cuba's results are provided only for the PPP and price level index. In addition, Cuba's figures are not included in the Latin America and world totals.

g. Bonaire's results are provided only for the individual consumption expenditure by households. Therefore, to ensure consistency across the tables, Bonaire is not included in the Caribbean or the world total.

h. This table does not include the Pacific Islands and does not double count the dual participation economies: the Arab Republic of Egypt, Sudan, and the Russian Federation.

Restaurants and hotels	Miscel-laneous goods and services	Net purchases abroad	Individual consumption expenditure by households	Individual consumption expenditure by government	Collective consumption expenditure by government	Gross fixed capital formation	Machinery and equipment	Construction	Other products	Changes in inventories and valuables	Balance of exports and imports	Domestic absorption	Individual consumption expenditure by households without housing
(13)	(14)	(15)	(16)	(17)	(18)	(19)	20)	(21)	(22)	(23)	(24)	(25)	(26)
2.6	4.6	0.0	74.0	4.3	13.9	22.5	8.4	10.8	3.2	3.8	−18.5	118.5	69.7
0.5	4.7	1.1	41.8	2.6	8.4	25.7	1.6	13.3	0.8	10.9	10.7	89.3	31.4
0.6	**4.7**	**1.1**	**42.6**	**2.7**	**8.5**	**25.6**	**11.5**	**13.2**	**0.8**	**10.7**	**10.0**	**90.0**	**32.4**
3.7	**8.7**	**−0.1**	**57.4**	**9.1**	**8.5**	**23.0**	**7.9**	**12.6**	**2.5**	**1.2**	**0.8**	**99.2**	**48.9**

Table 2.4 Purchasing Power Parities (U.S. Dollar = 1.00), ICP 2011

PPPs (US$ = 1.00)[a] Economy	Gross domestic product	Actual individual consumption	Food and nonalcoholic beverages	Alcoholic beverages, tobacco, and narcotics	Clothing and footwear	Housing, water, electricity, gas, and other fuels	Furnishings, household equipment and maintenance	Health	Transport	Communication
(00)	(01)	(02)	(03)	(04)	(05)	(06)	(07)	(08)	(09)	(10)
AFRICA										
Algeria	30.502	28.880	50.736	45.390	41.983	24.135	40.767	13.000	33.258	35.940
Angola	68.315	69.973	118.137	45.559	84.022	54.741	106.349	48.788	85.333	87.875
Benin	214.035	207.312	370.582	195.942	204.200	183.014	306.313	121.413	261.628	244.766
Botswana	3.764	4.068	6.493	5.494	3.612	4.464	6.733	2.265	4.975	3.263
Burkina Faso	213.659	203.814	384.850	213.069	184.918	150.487	294.974	118.447	319.797	251.165
Burundi	425.768	436.019	811.292	734.215	411.072	245.866	719.055	172.356	1,009.766	809.509
Cameroon	227.212	213.640	352.218	238.073	270.966	152.184	372.608	156.911	327.774	373.135
Cape Verde	48.592	44.321	73.270	50.568	55.775	42.236	57.249	25.849	70.940	37.054
Central African Republic	255.862	243.981	490.055	270.572	221.472	126.380	398.509	125.804	367.859	408.955
Chad	250.443	231.089	405.506	273.297	223.693	206.605	366.992	122.505	344.546	362.389
Comoros	207.584	201.132	355.581	316.673	219.065	149.348	395.660	105.986	297.720	353.045
Congo, Rep.	289.299	276.070	544.905	268.940	299.812	161.770	396.022	144.276	436.562	418.054
Congo, Dem. Rep.	521.870	492.254	995.879	619.168	501.385	276.923	643.047	241.443	759.322	659.755
Côte d'Ivoire	228.228	219.769	384.924	239.408	266.556	157.061	300.325	108.338	340.632	341.438
Djibouti	94.003	94.223	152.682	102.279	99.873	75.699	127.879	65.130	139.712	86.983
Egypt, Arab Rep.[b]	1.625	1.606	3.436	2.808	2.059	0.711	3.145	0.830	2.298	1.909
Equatorial Guinea	294.572	304.097	589.322	232.061	298.294	220.223	512.584	165.533	420.726	307.635
Ethiopia	4.919	4.934	8.869	6.164	5.821	4.581	7.853	2.385	7.979	5.305
Gabon	318.156	334.429	655.855	224.212	349.681	272.532	418.056	200.389	366.084	491.042
Gambia, The	9.939	9.766	19.680	10.536	6.736	7.793	13.390	4.379	13.590	8.031
Ghana	0.699	0.715	1.570	0.845	0.685	0.463	0.985	0.284	0.763	0.723
Guinea	2,518.386	2,316.675	5,352.043	2,579.447	2,128.158	783.311	3,128.116	1,181.841	3,516.903	3,411.063
Guinea-Bissau	220.085	221.672	400.082	252.336	258.633	175.909	364.520	99.848	354.574	276.273
Kenya	34.298	33.121	57.162	45.543	29.655	21.796	46.101	17.176	64.245	26.523
Lesotho	3.923	3.652	5.909	4.687	3.692	2.630	5.867	2.029	5.537	4.292
Liberia	0.517	0.519	0.974	0.627	0.446	0.585	0.600	0.221	0.721	0.668
Madagascar	673.730	648.609	1168.502	780.876	527.001	611.475	878.136	294.532	1,282.158	1,130.163
Malawi	76.259	72.760	139.599	80.997	61.783	32.754	116.176	29.785	170.095	86.546
Mali	210.193	202.208	337.779	198.514	211.992	183.738	323.588	92.883	374.476	224.925
Mauritania	115.855	103.576	187.179	118.403	85.477	79.922	146.549	56.410	149.556	142.122
Mauritius	15.941	16.535	26.573	26.403	14.211	11.609	24.149	8.425	32.685	14.309
Morocco	3.677	3.859	6.745	7.936	4.290	2.058	5.494	2.953	5.624	5.306
Mozambique	16.030	14.714	25.956	15.548	14.057	9.035	24.847	9.500	21.892	18.716
Namibia	4.663	4.787	8.100	4.866	3.702	5.223	5.367	3.069	6.475	4.015
Niger	221.087	210.030	404.077	249.451	155.168	172.083	238.900	124.830	315.442	359.186
Nigeria	74.378	72.612	147.012	69.312	63.131	58.511	76.549	31.751	92.809	88.164
Rwanda	260.751	234.141	395.081	321.317	281.734	156.671	273.610	118.960	488.544	278.187

Recreation and culture	Education	Restaurants and hotels	Miscella-neous goods and services	Individual consumption expenditure by households	Individual consumption expenditure by government	Collective consumption expenditure by government	Gross fixed capital formation	Machinery and equipment	Construction	Domestic absorption	Individual consumption expenditure by households without housing
(11)	(12)	(13)	(14)	(16)	(17)	(18)	(19)	(20)	(21)	(25)	(26)
30.056	7.265	35.529	31.437	31.772	12.652	16.887	42.024	92.827	22.862	30.305	32.518
105.365	27.003	127.387	70.663	73.833	44.125	56.269	56.979	127.789	30.395	66.927	80.752
280.396	80.370	296.896	152.285	224.917	117.370	145.384	300.059	596.385	174.495	216.125	245.853
4.914	1.433	6.456	3.869	4.438	2.017	3.206	3.280	8.340	1.576	3.736	4.661
309.305	56.244	231.348	185.561	222.242	107.352	178.693	282.177	632.359	151.518	215.759	247.388
672.530	97.107	621.541	412.487	487.327	168.112	267.615	694.095	1,537.329	376.842	451.102	566.859
312.047	81.898	318.543	184.641	230.375	147.671	191.977	313.991	576.878	204.738	228.238	254.190
57.595	17.731	48.689	40.568	47.565	25.998	39.411	58.738	106.972	37.180	47.065	51.239
332.745	53.939	319.759	230.136	267.869	108.142	222.564	326.106	644.138	195.366	254.555	301.388
263.169	58.233	366.836	189.836	251.296	138.720	194.455	352.971	646.425	233.637	250.393	273.669
307.250	59.084	266.392	221.546	220.572	99.914	161.339	235.828	483.486	138.494	203.046	249.360
375.075	100.640	355.001	198.525	296.500	166.999	249.543	389.529	645.298	237.979	304.566	328.144
563.809	118.748	819.140	492.233	537.732	263.255	433.663	670.561	1,262.883	411.468	520.880	624.732
349.107	97.615	262.761	187.185	235.688	142.951	201.782	280.418	637.984	147.727	227.432	259.002
138.358	36.887	143.404	97.928	101.481	56.525	73.427	95.412	221.793	49.438	93.384	111.787
1.981	0.507	2.410	1.585	1.803	0.566	0.822	2.689	6.656	1.391	1.646	2.096
471.311	92.634	396.115	288.349	321.354	208.318	421.930	276.018	651.258	139.287	296.396	347.065
5.573	1.042	4.918	3.936	5.439	2.109	3.563	7.257	22.179	2.796	5.206	5.685
346.142	151.414	449.083	294.853	359.219	200.687	270.502	341.082	641.631	238.831	329.296	382.640
11.260	3.338	18.363	8.225	10.826	3.865	5.318	15.386	40.512	6.639	10.361	11.878
0.917	0.217	1.214	0.580	0.788	0.328	0.566	0.728	2.192	0.273	0.703	0.870
3,007.694	491.235	3,939.802	2,193.499	2,572.343	757.024	1,452.971	3,918.304	8,810.390	2,112.444	2,519.622	3,078.433
349.481	36.493	357.777	200.254	248.236	64.014	141.517	284.615	648.499	150.102	220.501	269.672
43.897	16.344	43.244	27.262	35.430	20.076	34.539	45.103	107.244	22.760	35.328	40.572
4.124	1.831	6.030	3.182	3.864	2.405	3.803	4.480	9.989	2.388	3.847	4.338
0.571	0.128	0.621	0.423	0.568	0.261	0.407	0.567	1.368	0.265	0.516	0.591
734.663	185.694	537.343	534.671	704.913	371.423	623.767	1,057.595	2,641.207	510.621	705.252	764.790
117.541	31.032	126.817	61.150	78.017	45.753	89.255	94.347	215.156	49.599	76.604	90.743
252.679	67.442	337.254	169.240	221.868	96.115	158.062	280.664	609.570	154.951	211.692	238.355
133.247	37.018	179.295	98.129	112.807	52.798	87.516	172.135	395.510	90.122	118.151	124.699
18.718	6.358	30.157	16.094	18.285	6.849	10.190	16.322	34.607	9.035	15.794	19.559
4.754	1.642	5.484	3.819	4.193	2.040	3.245	3.535	9.616	1.581	3.711	4.897
17.793	8.538	16.117	11.285	15.527	11.507	20.501	19.633	37.092	11.817	15.913	17.391
5.455	1.554	7.415	3.630	5.131	2.773	4.006	4.108	9.814	2.084	4.582	5.224
293.685	47.662	292.256	185.423	228.753	113.222	199.902	284.825	520.917	183.047	223.884	248.570
85.736	28.683	98.119	52.658	79.531	35.768	56.511	92.040	210.505	48.496	74.143	85.360
338.584	119.571	311.579	223.509	246.834	193.765	361.760	373.046	754.637	210.292	265.992	279.765

(continued)

Table 2.4 (Continued)

Economy	PPPs (US$ = 1.00)[a] Gross domestic product	Actual individual consumption	Food and nonalcoholic beverages	Alcoholic beverages, tobacco, and narcotics	Clothing and footwear	Housing, water, electricity, gas, and other fuels	Furnishings, household equipment and maintenance	Health	Transport	Communication
(00)	(01)	(02)	(03)	(04)	(05)	(06)	(07)	(08)	(09)	(10)
São Tomé and Príncipe	8,527.157	9,091.140	17,061.052	10,212.969	9,837.834	7,455.455	14,014.117	3,994.580	13,685.972	10,968.728
Senegal	236.287	228.085	404.663	266.125	208.121	177.926	282.251	126.884	371.307	295.559
Seychelles	6.690	6.987	11.970	16.058	8.474	4.449	10.917	3.122	12.145	7.362
Sierra Leone	1,553.139	1,599.223	3,310.580	1,580.447	1,178.052	905.604	2,156.711	706.823	2,833.988	2,697.819
South Africa	4.774	4.769	6.637	4.994	5.357	4.155	7.736	3.543	6.995	4.181
Sudan[c]	1.224	1.342	2.405	2.278	0.899	1.125	1.783	0.537	2.283	1.594
Swaziland	3.900	3.820	5.971	4.686	4.258	3.294	5.440	1.949	5.791	3.756
Tanzania	522.483	539.161	948.924	764.066	483.312	527.251	743.475	206.764	829.729	530.828
Togo	215.060	209.618	402.353	220.192	197.023	148.357	303.684	108.131	410.501	396.666
Tunisia	0.592	0.624	1.068	0.984	1.024	0.461	0.930	0.382	0.877	0.445
Uganda	833.540	868.234	1,419.160	1,165.303	948.693	793.013	1,309.352	455.930	1,617.989	1,011.713
Zambia	2,378.380	2,332.796	3,914.496	3,169.257	2,363.291	1,703.604	3,697.202	1,125.337	4,781.428	5,040.040
Zimbabwe	0.504	0.491	0.825	0.435	0.572	0.391	0.941	0.265	0.885	0.649
Total (50)	n.a.	n.a.	n.a.	n.a.	n.a.	n.a.	n.a.	n.a.	n.a.	n.a.
ASIA AND THE PACIFIC										
Bangladesh	23.145	22.805	39.209	19.099	25.936	16.181	31.291	10.646	48.795	7.472
Bhutan	16.856	15.675	24.439	29.060	14.995	13.340	26.101	8.943	24.846	10.654
Brunei Darussalam	0.717	0.812	1.070	2.071	0.986	0.646	1.838	0.546	0.870	1.268
Cambodia	1,347.115	1,354.578	2,331.001	1,429.182	1,184.241	1,406.818	1,884.477	515.098	2,543.614	1,419.612
China[d]	3.506	3.493	5.155	5.564	4.351	2.651	5.827	2.026	4.619	2.392
Fiji	1.042	1.119	1.504	1.367	0.950	1.397	1.560	0.631	1.643	1.321
Hong Kong SAR, China	5.462	5.580	7.468	7.232	4.228	6.020	7.233	5.110	8.125	2.693
India	15.109	14.006	20.873	22.195	12.156	10.160	24.448	5.227	28.738	10.855
Indonesia	3,606.566	3,730.983	6,157.657	6,622.350	4,903.733	3,042.564	4,933.488	2,483.411	5,679.080	3,875.469
Lao PDR	2,467.753	2,539.736	5,270.823	3,453.660	2,361.992	1,346.045	4,076.574	1,032.080	5,810.923	1,858.096
Macao SAR, China	4.589	5.236	7.697	4.822	5.646	4.933	8.539	3.958	7.174	3.209
Malaysia	1.459	1.478	2.275	2.670	1.809	1.013	2.515	0.923	2.293	1.803
Maldives	8.527	9.479	11.468	6.454	7.155	18.378	11.559	3.560	12.006	4.804
Mongolia	537.127	516.566	902.689	537.792	702.971	493.523	1,099.131	167.374	765.573	709.616
Myanmar	234.974	229.428	460.487	392.505	236.055	177.945	383.760	80.253	588.254	282.002
Nepal	24.628	23.781	38.433	34.457	21.491	19.036	33.316	8.878	67.859	24.708
Pakistan	24.346	23.438	41.794	27.343	26.862	14.690	42.664	8.637	46.456	20.388
Philippines	17.854	17.658	27.590	16.870	22.757	14.333	23.305	12.516	26.851	28.026
Singapore	0.891	1.117	1.364	2.558	0.909	1.345	1.446	0.818	1.662	0.889
Sri Lanka	38.654	37.663	68.447	43.560	35.854	26.225	67.631	15.615	73.151	29.822
Taiwan, China	15.112	15.140	24.167	19.640	13.367	14.974	25.063	7.608	21.955	8.605
Thailand	12.370	12.024	19.962	19.982	11.307	7.399	20.897	7.141	20.666	10.809
Vietnam	6,709.192	6,709.833	11,848.213	6,325.120	6,165.746	7,010.913	9,838.586	2,192.803	16,568.476	7,836.986
Total (23)	n.a.	n.a.	n.a.	n.a.	n.a.	n.a.	n.a.	n.a.	n.a.	n.a.

Recreation and culture	Education	Restaurants and hotels	Miscella- neous goods and services	Individual consumption expenditure by households	Individual consumption expenditure by government	Collective consumption expenditure by government	Gross fixed capital formation	Machinery and equipment	Construction	Domestic absorption	Individual consumption expenditure by households without housing
(11)	(12)	(13)	(14)	(16)	(17)	(18)	(19)	(20)	(21)	(25)	(26)
13,376.353	2,149.474	12,688.537	6,993.394	10,194.790	2,819.715	4,126.597	9,241.418	24,171.930	3,747.563	8,579.655	11,177.667
278.748	88.128	337.755	200.000	246.107	139.583	194.217	292.180	613.280	164.140	236.736	272.043
8.671	2.223	21.400	7.254	7.895	2.524	3.370	8.787	16.854	5.415	6.674	8.864
1,922.111	599.129	2,161.433	1,376.626	1,767.190	638.725	1,096.515	2,116.595	5,503.057	920.123	1,650.738	2,019.469
5.761	2.411	6.942	4.700	5.068	3.064	4.499	4.596	9.138	2.782	4.730	5.548
1.659	0.436	1.306	1.348	1.486	0.424	0.600	1.258	3.317	0.597	1.223	1.584
4.796	2.278	5.118	3.914	4.049	2.677	4.116	3.651	9.939	1.603	3.879	4.374
706.846	216.587	649.250	441.795	585.520	286.040	531.374	589.644	1,952.579	223.196	547.716	629.659
352.321	48.523	306.679	156.687	232.215	84.953	160.620	289.650	675.887	149.704	217.596	258.365
0.872	0.179	0.864	0.590	0.697	0.259	0.404	0.611	1.913	0.253	0.598	0.765
1,133.831	269.971	1,129.419	745.005	946.890	441.279	787.670	991.598	3,438.705	381.763	872.463	1,017.697
3,000.717	1,261.497	2,770.402	1,697.794	2,505.341	1,491.393	2,269.101	2,502.117	6,248.330	1,231.789	2,377.336	2,761.234
0.632	0.180	0.761	0.387	0.536	0.255	0.386	0.661	1.363	0.374	0.505	0.584
n.a.	n.a.	n.a.	n.a.	n.a.	n.a.	n.a.	n.a.	n.a.	n.a.	n.a.	n.a.
32.074	7.271	25.561	32.419	24.849	11.428	19.139	27.331	74.844	13.711	23.409	27.241
19.221	5.932	15.131	18.018	16.963	8.356	11.145	22.242	59.395	10.943	17.103	17.590
0.980	0.397	1.031	0.939	0.853	0.519	0.545	0.845	1.444	0.547	0.787	0.915
1,659.132	295.104	1,435.989	1,782.481	1,527.558	455.657	903.485	1,546.795	4,210.961	731.735	1,346.019	1,647.472
3.179	1.761	3.453	4.425	3.696	2.115	3.407	3.769	7.771	2.184	3.538	4.024
1.317	0.395	1.283	1.239	1.217	0.594	0.766	0.964	2.035	0.567	1.042	1.165
4.406	3.586	5.661	5.623	5.753	4.823	6.577	5.582	9.148	4.013	5.587	5.798
19.151	5.442	20.778	20.227	14.975	8.824	14.580	18.887	48.134	9.598	15.241	16.394
3,972.661	1,130.723	4,075.512	3,973.200	4,091.939	1,745.408	2,946.737	3,644.949	9,087.622	1,920.377	3,619.225	4,303.985
3,870.335	323.801	3,453.192	3,603.112	2,914.847	608.252	1,257.088	2,903.759	8,303.871	1,365.707	2,494.284	3,311.374
5.107	2.187	5.577	6.179	5.462	3.601	5.561	4.972	8.000	3.210	5.157	5.699
1.641	0.632	1.380	1.857	1.586	0.863	1.236	1.589	3.307	0.929	1.477	1.736
9.295	3.062	6.705	8.582	10.676	3.994	5.157	8.725	16.291	5.474	8.527	8.367
704.127	120.073	626.364	754.770	590.330	171.697	321.823	673.132	1,513.112	374.028	543.470	617.312
300.591	30.875	244.550	384.713	275.828	57.672	117.871	309.744	899.997	137.510	234.780	306.294
29.046	6.722	26.447	31.820	25.759	13.065	24.727	31.785	76.442	16.875	25.265	27.710
29.495	7.940	33.426	34.012	25.414	12.828	18.950	33.691	93.382	16.141	24.637	28.125
21.404	5.933	18.506	21.844	18.873	11.541	19.032	19.201	47.289	9.959	17.945	20.811
0.839	0.642	0.921	1.159	1.171	0.820	0.835	0.809	1.379	0.540	0.984	1.176
43.336	9.979	60.263	52.204	42.219	14.294	25.064	51.363	130.729	26.378	39.263	46.186
16.055	7.844	13.900	16.885	15.995	10.415	14.252	16.316	30.511	10.555	15.225	16.501
14.539	4.823	10.778	15.871	12.844	7.264	12.386	13.503	33.118	6.793	12.441	14.398
7,493.130	1,377.315	7,199.463	8,406.631	7,624.973	2,144.721	3,507.570	8,252.133	20,999.077	4,261.080	6,717.197	7,815.116
n.a.	n.a.	n.a.	n.a.	n.a.	n.a.	n.a.	n.a.	n.a.	n.a.	n.a.	n.a.

(continued)

Table 2.4 (Continued)

Economy	Gross domestic product	Actual individual consumption	Food and nonalcoholic beverages	Alcoholic beverages, tobacco, and narcotics	Clothing and footwear	Housing, water, electricity, gas, and other fuels	Furnishings, household equipment and maintenance	Health	Transport	Communication
(00)	(01)	(02)	(03)	(04)	(05)	(06)	(07)	(08)	(09)	(10)
COMMONWEALTH OF INDEPENDENT STATES										
Armenia	187.095	152.389	307.022	132.876	308.634	45.532	278.122	80.450	290.455	217.902
Azerbaijan	0.360	0.282	0.497	0.257	0.569	0.087	0.517	0.169	0.566	0.401
Belarus	1,889.308	1,536.970	2,787.022	1,364.111	3,467.556	434.660	3,374.569	849.825	3,506.415	1,346.222
Kazakhstan	80.171	70.553	105.203	49.216	110.002	56.286	108.395	36.826	116.329	72.795
Kyrgyz Republic	17.757	14.522	31.037	11.766	32.355	3.431	27.833	7.695	31.229	14.494
Moldova	5.535	4.599	7.769	3.431	9.327	2.425	8.296	2.495	9.834	5.055
Russian Federation[e]	17.346	14.837	25.517	12.136	24.282	6.688	22.300	10.901	28.071	13.292
Tajikistan	1.740	1.484	3.136	1.545	3.815	0.346	3.449	0.611	3.987	1.120
Ukraine	3.434	2.852	5.011	2.470	6.081	0.982	4.685	1.601	5.842	3.104
Total (9)	**n.a.**	**n.a.**	**n.a.**	**n.a.**	**n.a.**	**n.a.**	**n.a.**	**n.a.**	**n.a.**	**n.a.**
EUROSTAT-OECD										
Albania	45.452	47.617	78.529	40.445	81.406	39.923	87.079	25.013	108.431	89.749
Australia	1.511	1.505	1.632	1.786	1.482	1.822	1.414	1.550	1.526	1.080
Austria	0.830	0.850	0.980	0.621	0.809	0.766	0.940	0.748	1.180	0.676
Belgium	0.839	0.876	0.898	0.655	0.907	0.918	0.910	0.734	1.138	0.873
Bosnia and Herzegovina	0.724	0.770	1.217	0.632	1.702	0.443	1.090	0.594	1.583	1.139
Bulgaria	0.660	0.657	1.095	0.839	1.295	0.442	1.068	0.330	1.434	1.048
Canada	1.243	1.271	1.546	1.491	1.212	1.223	1.427	1.192	1.450	1.223
Chile	348.017	353.270	512.602	362.499	478.358	327.442	489.811	277.773	486.429	434.318
Croatia	3.802	3.972	5.673	3.982	6.245	2.914	5.270	2.600	6.832	4.244
Cyprus	0.673	0.700	0.915	0.644	0.798	0.558	0.805	0.559	0.953	0.427
Czech Republic	13.468	13.447	16.631	13.897	20.094	14.214	17.901	8.458	21.523	20.396
Denmark	7.689	8.447	8.668	6.177	7.748	9.315	7.773	6.947	11.447	5.222
Estonia	0.524	0.537	0.709	0.537	0.818	0.539	0.726	0.312	0.913	0.534
Finland	0.907	0.951	0.953	0.898	0.985	1.049	0.971	0.727	1.293	0.579
France	0.845	0.856	0.893	0.718	0.843	0.948	0.956	0.677	1.157	0.841
Germany	0.779	0.781	0.865	0.628	0.830	0.868	0.845	0.565	1.170	0.584
Greece	0.693	0.709	0.864	0.653	0.764	0.675	0.850	0.469	1.055	0.914
Hungary	123.650	121.164	187.217	113.616	184.804	103.710	168.273	65.679	260.871	217.219
Iceland	133.563	135.543	149.608	178.242	178.096	100.261	167.395	109.906	207.367	95.485
Ireland	0.827	0.941	0.991	1.212	0.843	0.935	0.905	0.930	1.174	0.845
Israel	3.945	4.038	5.053	3.904	4.223	3.863	4.211	3.205	5.480	4.638
Italy	0.768	0.797	0.917	0.672	0.865	0.801	0.918	0.666	1.060	0.745
Japan	107.454	109.100	165.984	85.476	107.457	116.322	125.188	79.655	132.992	99.387
Korea, Rep.	854.586	849.741	1,559.073	744.912	1,411.931	552.128	1,076.292	501.343	1,181.480	625.231
Latvia	0.347	0.354	0.504	0.411	0.614	0.303	0.479	0.183	0.623	0.408
Lithuania	1.567	1.572	2.214	1.726	2.876	1.203	2.289	0.875	3.048	1.437
Luxembourg	0.906	1.056	0.953	0.590	0.821	1.351	0.951	1.005	1.054	0.644

Recreation and culture	Education	Restaurants and hotels	Miscellaneous goods and services	Individual consumption expenditure by households	Individual consumption expenditure by government	Collective consumption expenditure by government	Gross fixed capital formation	Machinery and equipment	Construction	Domestic absorption	Individual consumption expenditure by households without housing
(11)	(12)	(13)	(14)	(16)	(17)	(18)	(19)	(20)	(21)	(25)	(26)
216.106	28.693	266.080	161.591	183.780	45.272	107.557	387.109	472.609	314.908	183.741	232.422
0.423	0.077	0.526	0.283	0.329	0.112	0.241	0.788	0.967	0.646	0.353	0.398
2,319.743	354.870	3,100.710	2,113.921	1,832.435	516.563	1,310.124	4,012.222	5,556.187	3,003.890	1,899.071	2,210.871
94.378	16.355	104.543	57.224	83.612	24.275	48.057	137.116	177.032	108.372	78.948	80.998
24.871	2.744	31.997	13.756	17.538	4.473	9.700	44.935	59.957	34.392	18.139	21.786
6.778	1.094	6.781	4.635	5.451	1.628	2.605	11.531	13.655	9.581	5.475	6.588
22.012	4.762	26.264	15.844	16.769	6.824	14.905	27.911	33.765	22.944	17.071	19.430
1.796	0.205	2.797	1.631	1.883	0.297	0.729	4.409	5.247	3.693	1.826	2.298
4.582	0.830	5.961	3.087	3.311	1.128	2.250	6.877	8.760	5.474	3.416	3.967
n.a.	n.a.	n.a.	n.a.	n.a.	n.a.	n.a.	n.a.	n.a.	n.a.	n.a.	n.a.
63.108	3.801	50.314	50.444	58.168	11.211	27.455	57.947	117.937	35.018	47.680	63.141
1.444	1.070	1.462	1.468	1.527	1.220	1.299	1.706	1.450	1.734	1.526	1.473
0.960	0.761	0.903	0.873	0.848	0.699	0.894	0.792	0.851	0.732	0.838	0.892
0.895	0.688	0.968	0.917	0.879	0.674	0.957	0.710	0.862	0.589	0.844	0.887
0.978	0.194	1.034	0.857	0.867	0.353	0.561	0.810	1.633	0.448	0.753	1.002
0.851	0.174	0.758	0.729	0.765	0.243	0.363	0.879	1.515	0.538	0.656	0.891
1.341	0.998	1.487	1.268	1.285	1.036	1.166	1.197	1.150	1.098	1.244	1.296
473.689	113.723	432.197	366.239	391.644	172.765	248.533	373.660	552.221	267.717	346.942	417.614
4.830	1.878	5.691	4.100	4.359	2.134	2.777	3.778	6.065	2.542	3.800	4.835
0.837	0.617	0.856	0.716	0.712	0.568	0.629	0.608	0.855	0.451	0.674	0.768
15.268	6.014	12.567	13.841	14.901	7.002	10.363	14.931	20.398	11.082	13.422	15.450
8.822	6.255	9.797	8.959	8.524	6.166	7.720	6.247	6.910	5.817	7.871	8.565
0.689	0.210	0.633	0.552	0.609	0.256	0.361	0.555	0.823	0.385	0.522	0.634
1.077	0.637	1.111	1.019	0.980	0.656	0.842	0.822	0.927	0.700	0.912	0.972
0.926	0.571	0.885	0.892	0.880	0.600	0.867	0.812	0.848	0.735	0.846	0.873
0.910	0.502	0.873	0.789	0.818	0.514	0.792	0.819	0.832	0.769	0.786	0.832
0.862	0.418	0.846	0.723	0.758	0.427	0.566	0.719	0.971	0.546	0.693	0.772
146.268	47.007	122.914	124.296	137.883	55.982	91.196	144.767	209.985	102.368	121.888	152.506
176.255	95.506	162.761	141.116	138.895	95.632	112.211	155.029	162.494	143.619	136.054	150.779
0.983	0.524	1.080	1.012	0.952	0.705	0.774	0.615	0.870	0.455	0.858	0.965
4.804	2.304	5.145	4.046	4.270	2.626	3.315	4.027	5.984	3.057	3.954	4.369
0.930	0.479	0.919	0.820	0.825	0.560	0.815	0.666	0.855	0.520	0.771	0.843
113.130	64.286	111.304	110.687	116.103	68.523	95.251	110.171	114.375	105.534	107.629	117.140
977.072	568.013	1,273.910	858.964	912.021	514.561	780.601	895.660	1,178.551	693.771	853.226	1,010.707
0.435	0.126	0.484	0.373	0.403	0.151	0.230	0.400	0.575	0.285	0.348	0.440
2.003	0.592	1.888	1.692	1.786	0.714	1.035	1.883	2.743	1.321	1.569	2.007
0.941	1.370	0.922	1.005	0.989	1.005	1.029	0.729	0.848	0.615	0.962	0.901

(continued)

Table 2.4 (Continued)

Economy	PPPs (US$ = 1.00)[a] Gross domestic product	Actual individual consumption	Food and nonalcoholic beverages	Alcoholic beverages, tobacco, and narcotics	Clothing and footwear	Housing, water, electricity, gas, and other fuels	Furnishings, household equipment and maintenance	Health	Transport	Communication
(00)	(01)	(02)	(03)	(04)	(05)	(06)	(07)	(08)	(09)	(10)
Macedonia, FYR	18.680	19.500	29.821	16.318	35.648	15.257	32.456	9.712	43.517	32.391
Malta	0.558	0.581	0.783	0.656	0.804	0.441	0.830	0.401	1.008	0.666
Mexico	7.673	7.692	9.640	7.834	8.380	10.247	9.821	6.304	11.754	10.184
Montenegro	0.369	0.389	0.614	0.341	0.796	0.288	0.595	0.238	0.772	0.527
Netherlands	0.832	0.862	0.798	0.699	0.885	0.943	0.880	0.766	1.212	0.874
New Zealand	1.486	1.477	1.804	1.972	1.399	1.726	1.609	1.069	1.840	1.728
Norway	8.973	9.894	11.661	13.756	9.758	8.612	8.905	9.188	13.170	5.389
Poland	1.823	1.738	2.095	2.060	3.329	1.395	2.323	0.995	3.206	2.027
Portugal	0.628	0.666	0.737	0.580	0.859	0.646	0.789	0.566	1.038	0.802
Romania	1.615	1.684	2.492	2.170	3.115	1.771	2.485	0.768	3.311	2.083
Russian Federation[e]	17.346	14.837	25.517	12.136	24.282	6.688	22.300	10.901	28.071	13.292
Serbia	37.288	39.247	62.369	33.470	85.242	30.511	67.090	23.635	81.372	40.554
Slovak Republic	0.508	0.502	0.704	0.543	0.770	0.427	0.715	0.263	0.845	0.885
Slovenia	0.625	0.651	0.786	0.535	0.807	0.588	0.801	0.480	0.944	0.636
Spain	0.705	0.749	0.770	0.580	0.731	0.811	0.850	0.634	1.050	1.070
Sweden	8.820	9.236	8.993	8.394	9.433	8.875	9.387	7.838	12.268	5.113
Switzerland	1.441	1.603	1.587	1.043	1.367	2.128	1.364	1.488	1.645	1.062
Turkey	0.987	1.007	1.592	1.444	1.239	0.772	1.363	0.684	1.964	1.364
United Kingdom	0.698	0.735	0.688	0.901	0.577	0.927	0.776	0.570	0.993	0.598
United States	1.000	1.000	1.000	1.000	1.000	1.000	1.000	1.000	1.000	1.000
Total (47)	**n.a.**	**n.a.**	**n.a.**	**n.a.**	**n.a.**	**n.a.**	**n.a.**	**n.a.**	**n.a.**	**n.a.**
LATIN AMERICA										
Bolivia	2.946	2.801	4.404	3.461	4.226	1.284	4.254	2.785	3.654	4.967
Brazil	1.471	1.487	1.661	1.180	3.242	1.444	1.935	0.882	2.429	2.914
Colombia	1,161.910	1,146.218	1,615.194	1,193.256	1,778.228	643.113	1,986.418	863.861	1,841.147	1,921.748
Costa Rica	346.738	341.808	514.970	353.478	526.617	185.558	498.447	408.384	453.671	258.014
Cuba[f]	0.322	0.295	0.474	0.507	0.395	0.105	0.594	0.204	0.503	0.562
Dominican Republic	19.449	19.309	28.007	26.262	27.477	14.506	31.610	14.872	34.231	22.016
Ecuador	0.526	0.519	0.789	0.557	0.847	0.331	0.885	0.385	0.580	0.746
El Salvador	0.503	0.500	0.795	0.669	0.892	0.297	0.847	0.414	0.578	0.526
Guatemala	3.626	3.656	5.839	5.430	5.478	2.487	4.207	3.162	5.087	5.464
Haiti	19.108	19.976	31.450	16.429	44.005	11.714	23.191	15.105	24.596	25.732
Honduras	9.915	9.887	14.240	9.866	18.779	6.220	14.585	9.080	14.162	17.783
Nicaragua	8.919	8.581	14.935	10.936	12.256	3.927	11.988	7.119	14.294	16.145
Panama	0.547	0.523	0.808	0.582	0.889	0.334	0.795	0.458	0.701	0.419
Paraguay	2,227.340	2,180.826	3,315.801	2,114.347	4,855.416	1,164.644	3,160.069	1,868.982	3,453.794	2,077.333
Peru	1.521	1.461	2.121	1.591	2.434	1.035	2.539	1.023	2.058	2.137
Uruguay	15.282	15.517	22.144	18.197	28.689	11.479	24.106	12.366	21.420	14.176
Venezuela, RB	2.713	2.722	5.856	4.876	8.807	0.904	7.627	2.078	2.270	2.818
Total (17)	**n.a.**	**n.a.**	**n.a.**	**n.a.**	**n.a.**	**n.a.**	**n.a.**	**n.a.**	**n.a.**	**n.a.**

Recreation and culture	Education	Restaurants and hotels	Miscellaneous goods and services	Individual consumption expenditure by households	Individual consumption expenditure by government	Collective consumption expenditure by government	Gross fixed capital formation	Machinery and equipment	Construction	Domestic absorption	Individual consumption expenditure by households without housing
(11)	(12)	(13)	(14)	(16)	(17)	(18)	(19)	(20)	(21)	(25)	(26)
25.840	4.257	21.757	20.816	22.936	6.633	1.650	24.827	48.894	14.528	19.497	25.546
0.683	0.320	0.666	0.574	0.629	0.335	0.402	0.573	0.893	0.387	0.557	0.692
9.837	1.347	8.934	8.024	8.940	2.757	4.878	9.264	14.729	6.448	7.688	8.670
0.570	0.079	0.548	0.394	0.449	0.147	0.233	0.496	0.812	0.328	0.383	0.494
0.895	0.581	0.904	0.901	0.869	0.640	0.829	0.802	0.920	0.690	0.847	0.871
1.638	0.746	1.486	1.511	1.589	0.879	1.308	1.687	1.825	1.662	1.494	1.577
10.921	7.436	12.558	11.174	9.797	7.792	9.484	8.602	8.710	8.155	9.529	10.270
2.112	0.795	2.690	1.887	1.936	0.864	1.418	2.416	3.285	1.804	1.821	2.152
0.836	0.335	0.676	0.678	0.704	0.427	0.538	0.551	0.906	0.366	0.629	0.738
1.901	0.379	1.824	1.698	2.001	0.593	0.927	1.811	3.491	1.073	1.625	2.055
22.012	4.762	26.264	15.844	16.769	6.824	14.905	27.911	33.765	22.944	17.071	19.430
52.662	9.736	49.547	38.602	45.370	15.892	22.028	45.487	84.416	26.168	38.394	49.595
0.633	0.198	0.609	0.538	0.567	0.230	0.342	0.633	0.901	0.450	0.508	0.629
0.806	0.450	0.753	0.666	0.681	0.439	0.495	0.615	0.793	0.482	0.626	0.719
0.858	0.462	0.809	0.728	0.777	0.519	0.622	0.623	0.845	0.472	0.707	0.783
9.973	8.352	11.374	9.742	9.105	7.273	7.921	8.946	8.415	9.255	9.008	9.386
1.543	1.475	1.658	1.556	1.613	1.432	1.526	1.282	1.332	1.304	1.513	1.503
1.329	0.182	1.414	1.140	1.164	0.379	0.733	1.116	1.858	0.689	0.999	1.300
0.770	0.554	0.785	0.699	0.756	0.521	0.615	0.628	0.668	0.546	0.701	0.717
1.000	1.000	1.000	1.000	1.000	1.000	1.000	1.000	1.000	1.000	1.000	1.000
n.a.	n.a.	n.a.	n.a.	n.a.	n.a.	n.a.	n.a.	n.a.	n.a.	n.a.	n.a.
4.471	1.402	3.660	2.777	2.906	2.700	3.100	3.624	7.274	2.203	2.978	3.300
2.083	0.647	1.866	1.502	1.659	0.683	1.650	1.306	2.823	0.722	1.469	1.761
1,318.597	537.119	1,585.522	1,090.827	1,196.955	896.440	907.599	1,395.264	2,528.150	883.720	1,169.408	1,351.984
430.513	187.950	423.759	283.873	343.786	349.561	289.663	395.883	798.305	233.246	346.902	385.230
0.286	0.176	0.343	0.354	0.292	0.218	0.263	0.543	1.110	0.315	0.319	0.321
25.063	5.659	19.915	17.560	20.741	9.795	13.201	25.431	51.125	14.840	19.791	22.491
0.711	0.244	0.724	0.542	0.547	0.365	0.482	0.611	1.458	0.309	0.532	0.591
0.626	0.167	0.916	0.501	0.531	0.331	0.425	0.635	1.258	0.381	0.515	0.595
4.656	1.341	4.116	3.095	3.873	2.450	2.995	4.302	8.768	2.494	3.714	4.324
23.340	8.546	32.674	17.038	20.706	15.782	24.118	21.163	49.656	11.493	20.133	23.762
11.649	4.409	11.451	8.463	10.080	9.996	10.177	11.288	22.845	6.678	10.117	11.309
13.808	2.499	11.844	8.026	9.160	5.288	6.764	14.345	28.246	8.511	9.305	10.928
0.666	0.205	0.758	0.546	0.553	0.359	0.428	0.732	1.376	0.459	0.553	0.607
3,473.908	862.251	2,924.159	1,937.258	2,309.430	1,473.418	2,173.686	2,663.075	6,091.921	1,425.662	2,251.650	2,624.223
1.824	0.624	2.084	1.262	1.569	0.800	1.261	1.956	3.978	1.135	1.535	1.733
20.879	7.504	18.290	14.448	16.424	10.667	12.534	15.732	27.773	10.074	15.299	17.925
5.402	0.843	4.471	3.588	2.915	1.571	1.915	2.846	7.388	1.351	2.712	3.303
n.a.	n.a.	n.a.	n.a.	n.a.	n.a.	n.a.	n.a.	n.a.	n.a.	n.a.	n.a.

(continued)

Table 2.4 (Continued)

Economy	PPPs (US$ = 1.00)[a] Gross domestic product	Actual individual consumption	Food and nonalcoholic beverages	Alcoholic beverages, tobacco, and narcotics	Clothing and footwear	Housing, water, electricity, gas, and other fuels	Furnishings, household equipment and maintenance	Health	Transport	Communication
(00)	(01)	(02)	(03)	(04)	(05)	(06)	(07)	(08)	(09)	(10)
CARIBBEAN										
Anguilla	2.077	2.350	3.943	2.453	2.506	1.924	3.191	1.628	2.719	2.319
Antigua and Barbuda	1.731	1.931	3.377	2.046	2.291	1.435	3.018	1.039	3.600	2.383
Aruba	1.260	1.478	2.066	2.090	1.717	1.174	2.702	0.813	2.022	1.746
Bahamas, The	0.949	1.060	1.360	0.951	1.285	0.883	1.880	0.759	1.331	1.196
Barbados	2.017	2.238	2.685	2.551	1.885	1.942	2.722	1.366	2.452	2.363
Belize	1.150	1.105	1.934	2.456	1.519	0.556	1.762	0.846	2.224	1.241
Bermuda	1.564	1.771	1.836	1.118	1.484	2.600	2.111	1.236	1.491	1.120
Bonaire[g]	...	...	1.328	0.941	0.661	...	1.307	...	1.264	1.201
Cayman Islands	0.959	1.048	1.332	1.244	1.047	0.963	1.597	0.906	1.192	1.031
Curaçao	1.292	1.330	1.872	1.582	2.070	0.963	2.201	0.862	1.851	1.930
Dominica	1.861	1.924	3.231	2.321	1.534	1.393	3.662	1.252	2.843	1.914
Grenada	1.783	1.905	3.333	2.413	2.763	1.286	3.441	1.220	3.039	2.070
Jamaica	54.122	57.926	102.779	83.799	60.249	39.431	85.601	39.970	91.181	46.085
Montserrat	1.943	2.144	3.960	2.767	2.462	1.289	4.318	1.535	3.603	1.789
St. Kitts and Nevis	1.803	1.923	3.772	2.379	2.102	1.264	4.773	0.952	3.514	2.903
St. Lucia	1.844	1.952	3.041	2.566	2.295	1.204	4.828	1.289	2.838	2.420
St. Vincent and the Grenadines	1.691	1.852	3.141	2.167	2.067	1.344	3.393	1.039	2.562	2.516
Sint Maarten	1.379	1.514	2.107	1.013	1.399	1.326	2.295	0.809	1.856	2.243
Suriname	1.826	1.712	3.317	2.372	1.858	0.873	3.314	0.955	3.429	2.149
Trinidad and Tobago	3.938	4.193	6.703	6.444	5.260	3.131	7.911	2.770	5.920	4.094
Turks and Caicos Islands	1.100	1.193	1.417	1.275	0.880	1.350	1.459	0.795	1.523	0.748
Virgin Islands, British	1.076	1.164	1.543	0.644	1.078	1.223	1.731	0.777	1.171	0.950
Total (22)	**n.a.**	**n.a.**	**n.a.**	**n.a.**	**n.a.**	**n.a.**	**n.a.**	**n.a.**	**n.a.**	**n.a.**
WESTERN ASIA										
Bahrain	0.211	0.214	0.301	0.228	0.267	0.187	0.311	0.216	0.172	0.182
Egypt, Arab Rep.[b]	1.625	1.606	3.436	2.808	2.059	0.711	3.145	0.830	2.298	1.909
Iraq	516.521	502.565	938.605	803.639	820.477	319.578	838.134	306.231	667.454	467.485
Jordan	0.293	0.295	0.566	0.367	0.302	0.170	0.435	0.171	0.439	0.345
Kuwait	0.172	0.183	0.234	0.192	0.235	0.119	0.273	0.196	0.142	0.240
Oman	0.192	0.194	0.307	0.210	0.221	0.164	0.253	0.141	0.186	0.231
Qatar	2.419	2.854	3.231	2.266	2.974	2.730	3.551	2.749	2.013	2.664
Saudi Arabia	1.837	1.826	2.984	2.065	2.089	1.081	2.532	1.575	1.753	2.240
Sudan[c]	1.224	1.342	2.405	2.278	0.899	1.125	1.783	0.537	2.283	1.594
United Arab Emirates	2.544	2.776	3.504	2.689	2.804	2.646	2.672	2.857	2.592	2.254
West Bank and Gaza	2.189	2.230	3.382	5.117	2.119	2.207	2.778	1.111	3.840	2.366
Yemen, Rep.	75.818	74.499	166.661	71.501	70.023	38.681	128.799	39.244	98.140	96.748
Total (12)	**n.a.**	**n.a.**	**n.a.**	**n.a.**	**n.a.**	**n.a.**	**n.a.**	**n.a.**	**n.a.**	**n.a.**

Recreation and culture	Education	Restaurants and hotels	Miscella-neous goods and services	Individual consumption expenditure by households	Individual consumption expenditure by government	Collective consumption expenditure by government	Gross fixed capital formation	Machinery and equipment	Construction	Domestic absorption	Individual consumption expenditure by households without housing
(11)	(12)	(13)	(14)	(16)	(17)	(18)	(19)	(20)	(21)	(25)	(26)
3.640	0.756	3.231	2.774	2.591	1.142	1.392	1.574	3.113	0.996	2.081	2.729
2.932	0.551	2.180	2.052	2.200	0.724	1.002	1.581	3.457	0.969	1.745	2.572
2.059	0.650	2.568	1.504	1.653	0.693	0.780	0.959	1.656	0.664	1.272	1.878
1.136	0.553	1.148	1.121	1.151	0.601	0.499	0.798	1.330	0.570	0.930	1.234
2.386	1.013	3.084	2.152	2.413	1.361	1.086	1.512	2.578	1.039	1.952	2.412
1.820	0.456	1.725	1.349	1.183	0.796	0.814	1.844	2.695	1.456	1.167	1.572
1.794	0.718	2.082	1.664	1.900	1.078	1.145	0.966	1.141	1.025	1.490	1.636
...	...	0.986	...	0.919	...	...	...	...	...	...	1.027
1.238	0.418	1.112	1.106	1.136	0.615	0.716	0.795	1.237	0.596	0.955	1.150
1.846	0.620	2.031	1.378	1.429	0.830	0.802	1.469	2.290	1.112	1.307	1.705
2.656	0.726	2.374	2.201	2.069	1.230	1.416	2.034	3.500	1.391	1.885	2.375
2.933	0.494	2.562	1.907	2.092	0.969	1.089	2.006	3.444	1.368	1.828	2.476
81.680	20.280	81.394	63.874	63.354	30.555	37.720	58.977	113.403	36.789	55.667	74.167
2.799	0.686	2.481	2.325	2.336	1.152	1.328	1.739	3.544	1.080	1.978	2.821
2.924	0.354	2.299	2.068	2.221	0.610	0.795	2.196	3.650	1.518	1.835	2.687
2.785	0.635	3.882	2.230	2.139	1.019	1.188	1.984	3.640	1.331	1.875	2.535
2.623	0.589	3.481	2.058	2.039	0.916	1.097	1.768	3.704	1.077	1.749	2.345
1.661	0.568	2.140	1.745	1.678	0.686	0.848	1.210	1.764	1.003	1.374	1.813
2.235	0.857	2.159	1.794	1.885	0.872	1.197	2.178	4.093	1.224	1.842	2.072
4.943	1.353	6.277	3.922	4.619	2.054	2.073	3.610	6.488	2.390	3.832	4.703
1.301	0.621	1.499	1.199	1.282	0.775	0.692	1.177	1.310	1.113	1.140	1.270
1.347	0.647	1.545	1.219	1.250	0.775	0.702	1.151	1.345	1.109	1.123	1.206
n.a.	n.a.	n.a.	n.a.	n.a.	n.a.	n.a.	n.a.	n.a.	n.a.	n.a.	n.a.
0.220	0.130	0.231	0.208	0.215	0.199	0.223	0.188	0.400	0.112	0.211	0.195
1.981	0.507	2.410	1.585	1.803	0.566	0.822	2.689	6.656	1.391	1.646	2.096
706.104	167.996	752.625	783.801	573.418	226.398	317.367	695.065	1134.199	492.284	502.704	655.873
0.371	0.124	0.463	0.330	0.319	0.159	0.196	0.373	0.710	0.238	0.294	0.371
0.229	0.135	0.296	0.259	0.180	0.185	0.217	0.153	0.290	0.102	0.181	0.174
0.236	0.107	0.266	0.194	0.200	0.147	0.179	0.172	0.385	0.093	0.187	0.194
3.190	2.303	3.709	2.979	2.640	3.218	3.547	1.737	3.527	0.922	2.546	2.373
2.274	1.212	2.327	1.936	1.785	1.674	1.914	1.538	3.279	0.876	1.781	1.855
1.659	0.436	1.306	1.348	1.486	0.424	0.600	1.258	3.317	0.597	1.223	1.584
3.306	1.908	3.694	2.939	2.718	3.257	3.627	1.811	3.276	1.187	2.622	2.580
2.528	0.793	3.527	2.530	2.523	1.011	1.421	2.458	4.098	1.665	2.122	2.720
89.965	27.016	70.912	83.048	82.094	33.258	42.454	103.215	198.265	72.003	74.395	92.814
n.a.	n.a.	n.a.	n.a.	n.a.	n.a.	n.a.	n.a.	n.a.	n.a.	n.a.	n.a.

(continued)

Table 2.4 (Continued)

PPPs (US$ = 1.00)[a] Economy	Gross domestic product	Actual individual consumption	Food and nonalcoholic beverages	Alcoholic beverages, tobacco, and narcotics	Clothing and footwear	Housing, water, electricity, gas, and other fuels	Furnishings, household equipment and maintenance	Health	Transport	Communication
(00)	(01)	(02)	(03)	(04)	(05)	(06)	(07)	(08)	(09)	(10)
SINGLETONS										
Georgia	0.859	0.705	1.392	0.734	1.430	0.237	1.252	0.402	1.351	0.637
Iran, Islamic Rep.	4,657.463	4,216.441	7,960.468	3,154.675	8,110.943	3,527.879	7,674.926	1,943.926	6,321.803	2,749.561
Total (2)	n.a.	n.a.	n.a.	n.a.	n.a.	n.a.	n.a.	n.a.	n.a.	n.a.
WORLD[h] (179)	n.a.	n.a.	n.a.	n.a.	n.a.	n.a.	n.a.	n.a.	n.a.	n.a.

Source: ICP, http://icp.worldbank.org/.

Note: n.a. = not applicable; PPP = purchasing power parity; ... = data suppressed because of incompleteness.

a. PPPs are rounded to three decimal places. More precision can be found in the Excel version of the table, which can be downloaded from the ICP website.

b. The Arab Republic of Egypt participated in both the Africa and Western Asia regions. The regional results for Egypt were averaged by taking the geometric mean of the regional PPPs, allowing Egypt to have the same global results in each region.

c. Sudan participated in both the Africa and Western Asia regions. The regional results for Sudan were averaged by taking the geometric mean of the regional PPPs, allowing Sudan to have the same global results in each region.

d. The results presented in the tables are based on data supplied by all the participating economies and compiled in accordance with ICP principles and the procedures recommended by the 2011 ICP Technical Advisory Group. The results for China are estimated by the 2011 ICP Asia and the Pacific Regional Office and the Global Office. The National Bureau of Statistics of China does not recognize these results as official statistics.

e. The Russian Federation participated in both the CIS and Eurostat-OECD comparisons. The PPPs for Russia are based on the Eurostat-OECD comparison. They were the basis for linking the CIS comparison to the ICP.

f. The official GDP of Cuba for reference year 2011 is 68,990.15 million in national currency. However, this number and its breakdown into main aggregates are not shown in the tables because of methodological comparability issues. Therefore, Cuba's results are provided only for the PPP and price level index. In addition, Cuba's figures are not included in the Latin America and world totals.

g. Bonaire's results are provided only for the individual consumption expenditure by households. Therefore, to ensure consistency across the tables, Bonaire is not included in the Caribbean or the world total.

h. This table does not include the Pacific Islands and does not double count the dual participation economies: the Arab Republic of Egypt, Sudan, and the Russian Federation.

Recreation and culture	Education	Restaurants and hotels	Miscella-neous goods and services	Individual consumption expenditure by households	Individual consumption expenditure by government	Collective consumption expenditure by government	Gross fixed capital formation	Machinery and equipment	Construction	Domestic absorption	Individual consumption expenditure by households without housing
(11)	(12)	(13)	(14)	(16)	(17)	(18)	(19)	(20)	(21)	(25)	(26)
0.927	0.157	1.214	0.671	0.842	0.243	0.539	1.651	1.789	1.365	0.841	1.047
5,177.313	474.430	7,247.766	5,662.554	5,001.363	1,161.991	2,431.785	7,137.243	14,891.530	3,470.697	4,677.234	5,062.124
n.a.	n.a.	n.a.	n.a.	n.a.	n.a.	n.a.	n.a.	n.a.	n.a.	n.a.	n.a.
n.a.	n.a.	n.a.	n.a.	n.a.	n.a.	n.a.	n.a.	n.a.	n.a.	n.a.	n.a.

Table 2.5 Real Expenditures in U.S. Dollars, ICP 2011

REAL EXPENDITURES (US$, billions) Economy	Gross domestic product	Actual individual consumption	Food and nonalcoholic beverages	Alcoholic beverages, tobacco, and narcotics	Clothing and footwear	Housing, water, electricity, gas, and other fuels	Furnishings, household equipment and maintenance	Health	Transport	Communication
(00)	(01)	(02)	(03)	(04)	(05)	(06)	(07)	(08)	(09)	(10)
AFRICA										
Algeria	474.8	225.6	38.5	2.5	4.5	13.2	4.0	35.4	23.7	10.3
Angola	143.0	84.7	20.6	5.6	3.6	11.4	3.1	6.4	3.7	0.7
Benin	16.1	13.4	3.6	0.4	0.6	1.5	0.2	0.8	0.8	0.3
Botswana	27.2	13.8	1.5	0.8	1.0	1.4	0.5	1.3	1.8	0.4
Burkina Faso	22.8	16.2	4.4	1.0	0.4	2.4	0.5	1.0	0.7	0.4
Burundi	6.1	5.6	1.3	0.5	0.1	1.5	0.0	0.4	0.2	0.0
Cameroon	55.2	46.0	12.8	1.1	3.0	5.9	2.4	1.0	2.4	0.4
Cape Verde	3.1	2.4	0.5	0.1	0.1	0.5	0.1	0.2	0.1	0.1
Central African Republic	4.0	3.9	1.1	0.3	0.3	0.4	0.1	0.1	0.1	0.0
Chad	22.9	17.0	4.7	0.7	0.4	1.8	0.7	2.3	1.1	0.4
Comoros	0.5	0.5	0.1	0.0	0.0	0.2	0.0	0.0	0.0	0.0
Congo, Rep.	24.1	6.3	1.2	0.3	0.2	1.4	0.2	0.9	0.3	0.2
Congo, Dem. Rep.	44.4	30.3	8.2	0.7	1.4	6.4	0.8	2.8	0.5	0.3
Côte d'Ivoire	53.8	39.9	9.7	1.2	1.1	5.5	2.4	3.4	2.8	0.7
Djibouti	2.2	1.6	0.3	0.1	0.0	0.6	0.1	0.1	0.1	0.0
Egypt, Arab Rep.[a]	843.8	679.1	133.0	12.6	32.0	200.1	16.8	119.8	28.0	14.6
Equatorial Guinea	28.4	3.5	0.7	0.1	0.1	0.7	0.1	0.6	0.2	0.1
Ethiopia	102.9	82.9	17.1	1.6	3.6	14.6	5.0	14.0	0.8	0.3
Gabon	25.3	9.2	1.4	0.8	0.4	1.6	0.3	1.1	0.7	0.3
Gambia, The	2.7	2.2	0.5	0.1	0.2	0.2	0.0	0.7	0.0	0.1
Ghana	85.5	56.0	9.5	0.7	8.3	8.7	2.8	4.8	3.4	0.8
Guinea	13.2	8.1	2.0	0.1	0.6	1.9	0.2	1.2	0.3	0.0
Guinea-Bissau	2.1	1.4	0.4	0.0	0.1	0.2	0.1	0.1	0.1	0.0
Kenya	88.9	80.6	16.0	2.9	2.2	9.5	2.6	11.3	4.2	3.1
Lesotho	4.7	5.5	0.9	0.1	0.7	0.8	0.3	0.4	0.1	0.1
Liberia	2.2	2.5	0.4	0.1	0.4	0.5	0.1	0.1	0.0	0.1
Madagascar	30.1	28.4	6.9	0.7	2.3	1.9	2.8	1.1	1.9	0.1
Malawi	15.0	15.5	3.9	0.7	0.5	3.8	1.0	1.5	0.5	0.2
Mali	23.9	16.6	4.6	0.2	0.9	1.8	0.6	1.4	1.2	0.3
Mauritania	11.3	7.4	2.5	0.1	0.3	0.9	0.1	0.5	0.2	0.2
Mauritius	20.3	15.4	2.8	0.8	1.0	3.4	0.8	1.5	1.1	0.5
Morocco	218.3	139.1	27.1	2.2	5.1	36.1	4.5	11.2	8.5	6.2
Mozambique	22.8	21.3	6.2	0.9	1.1	2.5	0.4	0.9	1.2	0.2
Namibia	19.4	13.5	1.6	0.5	0.8	2.4	0.9	2.3	0.4	0.1
Niger	13.7	11.6	2.5	0.2	1.2	1.4	0.5	0.8	0.6	0.2
Nigeria	511.1	337.1	62.9	5.0	56.0	42.8	22.6	24.5	17.5	4.3
Rwanda	14.6	14.2	4.0	0.3	0.4	3.5	0.4	0.7	0.4	0.1
São Tomé and Príncipe	0.5	0.6	0.2	0.0	0.0	0.1	0.0	0.1	0.0	0.0

Recreation and culture	Education	Restaurants and hotels	Miscella-neous goods and services	Individual consumption expenditure by households	Individual consumption expenditure by government	Collective consumption expenditure by government	Gross fixed capital formation	Machinery and equipment	Construction	Domestic absorption	Individual consumption expenditure by households without housing
(11)	(12)	(13)	(14)	(16)	(17)	(18)	(19)	(20)	(21)	(25)	(26)
5.5	85.8	4.3	38.8	143.3	155.1	79.2	109.9	21.0	105.1	427.8	136.2
1.2	10.7	1.4	10.0	67.1	22.0	45.5	29.3	4.1	35.3	152.2	59.6
0.1	1.8	0.9	0.6	11.7	1.3	1.7	2.4	0.4	2.6	17.5	10.0
0.3	5.0	0.3	1.2	11.0	3.7	3.8	10.3	1.7	12.3	29.1	9.7
0.2	1.7	0.5	0.5	14.3	1.2	4.1	2.8	0.5	2.7	24.2	12.1
0.0	1.4	0.2	0.1	4.6	1.1	1.2	0.7	0.1	0.7	7.2	3.4
0.5	2.7	2.1	1.2	41.3	2.1	6.0	8.2	2.1	6.4	59.4	35.3
0.0	0.5	0.3	0.2	2.0	0.5	0.4	1.2	0.2	1.1	4.1	1.6
0.0	0.5	0.1	0.2	3.5	0.2	0.2	0.5	0.1	0.4	4.5	3.0
0.3	1.0	0.1	0.5	15.2	0.9	1.3	4.6	1.0	3.4	23.5	12.9
0.0	0.0	0.0	0.0	0.4	0.0	0.1	0.1	0.0	0.0	0.7	0.3
0.1	1.3	0.4	0.3	5.2	1.1	1.3	6.2	0.6	8.4	14.7	4.4
0.3	5.3	1.1	0.7	26.7	2.1	6.2	8.1	1.6	7.9	44.3	21.5
0.9	3.8	0.5	2.1	35.2	3.3	4.8	4.9	0.8	5.6	45.3	29.9
0.0	0.3	0.0	0.2	1.3	0.2	0.5	0.6	0.1	0.7	2.7	1.0
16.3	142.5	14.2	48.7	574.7	96.0	124.8	85.2	16.0	83.7	867.2	448.5
0.0	0.6	0.1	0.2	3.1	0.3	0.4	10.0	2.2	6.5	13.5	2.7
0.3	13.5	3.9	11.0	73.1	5.5	9.0	18.0	2.2	21.2	111.9	64.0
0.2	1.1	0.3	0.3	7.8	1.3	2.8	4.5	0.7	1.9	16.3	6.6
0.1	0.6	0.0	0.1	1.9	0.2	0.3	0.5	0.1	0.3	2.9	1.7
0.5	25.4	0.0	2.6	46.6	9.9	˙1.8	21.0	4.0	20.9	89.9	41.6
0.1	1.2	0.1	0.2	7.2	0.3	1.0	2.0	0.6	1.2	11.4	5.7
0.0	0.2	0.0	0.0	1.3	0.1	0.6	0.2	0.0	0.2	2.1	1.1
2.1	23.6	3.8	6.8	65.1	18.2	7.4	13.5	3.1	12.0	100.6	54.1
0.2	1.0	0.0	0.4	4.6	1.0	1.0	1.1	0.1	1.4	7.6	3.8
0.0	1.2	0.0	0.2	2.3	0.0	0.3	0.3	0.1	0.1	3.2	1.9
1.1	3.5	1.1	0.5	25.3	1.6	2.3	3.3	0.6	3.5	33.2	23.1
0.2	1.8	0.2	0.4	13.6	1.4	0.9	2.0	0.7	0.8	17.7	10.9
0.5	2.2	0.2	0.5	14.3	1.8	3.8	4.0	0.8	3.8	24.2	12.4
0.1	1.5	0.0	0.1	6.0	1.7	2.3	4.4	0.9	3.5	11.9	5.1
0.9	3.2	0.3	1.0	13.0	2.6	2.5	4.8	0.7	5.6	23.1	11.2
5.0	37.3	5.6	9.2	112.8	31.2	25.5	69.7	11.0	80.5	244.6	87.3
0.5	2.5	0.2	1.4	18.7	2.0	1.3	3.3	0.6	3.6	25.9	15.9
0.5	5.9	0.5	1.6	10.9	3.2	3.5	4.7	0.7	5.5	21.2	9.2
0.5	1.7	0.4	0.8	10.2	0.8	1.5	3.9	0.9	3.3	17.2	8.9
3.1	108.8	0.1	17.6	287.2	45.7	59.2	42.5	10.5	30.0	428.0	263.2
0.2	1.4	0.3	0.5	12.9	0.7	1.0	2.2	0.2	2.9	16.8	10.1
0.0	0.1	0.0	0.0	0.5	0.1	0.1	0.1	0.0	0.0	0.7	0.4

(continued)

Table 2.5 (Continued)

REAL EXPENDITURES (US$, billions) Economy	Gross domestic product	Actual individual consumption	Food and nonalcoholic beverages	Alcoholic beverages, tobacco, and narcotics	Clothing and footwear	Housing, water, electricity, gas, and other fuels	Furnishings, household equipment and maintenance	Health	Transport	Communication
(00)	(01)	(02)	(03)	(04)	(05)	(06)	(07)	(08)	(09)	(10)
Senegal	28.6	24.6	6.8	0.3	0.9	6.0	1.1	1.3	0.7	0.9
Seychelles	2.0	1.1	0.3	0.0	0.0	0.3	0.0	0.2	0.0	0.0
Sierra Leone	8.2	7.2	1.4	0.2	0.8	0.9	0.2	2.6	0.1	0.1
South Africa	611.1	417.8	53.2	17.5	16.0	65.3	15.8	62.3	36.8	12.3
Sudan[b]	152.4	97.5	28.1	0.4	6.5	17.0	4.8	3.1	4.7	1.3
Swaziland	7.6	7.0	2.0	0.0	0.4	1.1	0.5	0.9	0.4	0.1
Tanzania	71.8	47.6	17.8	0.2	3.5	3.5	1.5	4.4	1.2	0.0
Togo	8.1	7.3	1.7	0.2	0.4	0.8	0.2	0.9	0.2	0.1
Tunisia	109.3	77.2	9.9	1.6	3.2	14.8	3.2	8.9	7.9	3.8
Uganda	55.1	48.0	9.8	2.1	1.3	9.4	1.8	2.5	1.5	0.8
Zambia	42.5	24.0	8.3	0.1	1.5	3.9	0.2	2.6	0.2	0.3
Zimbabwe	17.6	17.2	5.7	0.6	0.8	1.4	0.3	0.9	0.7	0.0
Total (50)	**4,115.1**	**2,834.9**	**560.6**	**69.1**	**170.3**	**517.9**	**107.6**	**347.3**	**164.2**	**66.1**
ASIA AND THE PACIFIC										
Bangladesh	419.2	320.1	94.8	7.9	16.9	77.6	7.5	25.1	6.3	4.7
Bhutan	5.1	2.8	0.5	0.0	0.2	0.6	0.0	0.6	0.2	0.1
Brunei Darussalam	29.3	6.2	0.8	0.0	0.2	0.9	0.1	0.5	0.9	0.2
Cambodia	38.7	32.4	8.6	1.2	0.7	4.6	0.4	6.0	1.3	0.1
China[c]	13,495.9	5,811.5	740.1	78.6	322.5	1,061.3	170.0	1,503.0	256.8	288.1
Fiji	6.5	4.6	1.0	0.1	0.1	0.9	0.3	0.4	0.2	0.0
Hong Kong SAR, China	354.5	231.2	18.7	1.9	13.3	40.7	9.9	21.2	11.1	10.3
India	5,757.5	3,675.4	694.0	69.4	297.9	651.5	78.5	458.3	269.2	49.2
Indonesia	2,058.1	1,158.3	265.5	11.2	32.9	289.2	23.7	58.3	52.1	21.5
Lao PDR	26.2	14.9	3.7	0.6	0.3	3.6	0.2	0.8	0.7	0.3
Macao SAR, China	64.3	13.2	0.9	0.1	0.8	2.1	0.2	1.2	0.8	0.6
Malaysia	606.1	321.0	35.5	2.6	4.8	69.2	8.3	30.2	27.2	15.8
Maldives	3.7	1.3	0.2	0.0	0.0	0.3	0.0	0.2	0.0	0.0
Mongolia	23.4	14.7	2.4	1.0	0.5	2.2	0.1	2.1	1.6	0.3
Myanmar	192.1	137.2	35.7	1.6	4.1	23.4	1.1	24.3	1.8	1.7
Nepal	58.9	48.9	17.0	1.1	1.4	7.9	0.6	5.5	0.5	0.7
Pakistan	788.1	695.3	172.3	5.6	28.2	215.1	12.5	117.4	22.5	13.3
Philippines	543.7	422.9	110.7	5.4	4.4	61.8	12.5	18.9	28.7	8.0
Singapore	374.8	128.2	6.5	1.0	4.2	19.4	5.0	14.8	10.8	3.0
Sri Lanka	169.3	133.4	31.1	8.6	4.2	26.0	1.8	16.6	5.3	3.2
Taiwan, China	907.1	583.6	43.1	8.9	28.1	97.6	15.6	110.7	41.8	36.5
Thailand	899.0	573.0	88.4	12.2	20.5	84.6	13.4	73.2	46.7	13.2
Vietnam	414.3	262.7	38.5	7.8	11.8	57.4	10.3	58.5	10.6	1.7
Total (23)	**27,235.6**	**14,593.0**	**2,410.0**	**227.2**	**798.1**	**2,797.9**	**372.3**	**2,547.9**	**797.2**	**472.5**

Recreation and culture	Education	Restaurants and hotels	Miscella-neous goods and services	Individual consumption expenditure by households	Individual consumption expenditure by government	Collective consumption expenditure by government	Gross fixed capital formation	Machinery and equipment	Construction	Domestic absorption	Individual consumption expenditure by households without housing
(11)	(12)	(13)	(14)	(16)	(17)	(18)	(19)	(20)	(21)	(25)	(26)
0.3	3.4	0.1	1.1	21.6	2.1	3.5	5.5	1.0	6.0	33.7	17.4
0.0	0.4	0.0	0.0	0.9	0.4	0.8	0.5	0.1	0.4	2.4	0.7
0.2	1.5	0.1	0.4	6.3	0.4	0.9	2.5	0.7	1.6	10.8	5.4
14.1	88.4	6.0	48.3	341.7	85.1	83.2	120.4	28.8	95.3	620.6	278.6
1.8	9.8	2.2	2.5	87.4	2.4	19.5	33.1	6.6	33.3	154.6	74.0
0.2	1.0	0.0	0.1	6.2	0.6	0.7	0.8	0.1	0.8	8.3	5.1
0.4	5.7	0.0	1.1	42.4	2.9	10.0	23.0	3.0	33.2	81.7	39.3
0.1	2.1	0.4	1.0	6.3	0.8	0.9	1.1	0.1	1.3	9.3	5.5
1.8	21.3	5.3	5.1	61.0	22.0	15.4	22.9	2.4	35.2	116.2	48.7
2.2	16.6	1.1	2.4	39.9	8.8	1.0	11.4	1.0	19.8	61.8	33.8
0.1	2.8	0.1	1.6	20.9	2.3	7.0	8.8	1.1	11.6	40.0	17.8
0.3	3.4	0.1	1.1	14.5	2.7	2.0	1.5	0.2	1.7	21.0	12.8
63.4	**658.7**	**58.9**	**225.2**	**2,344.9**	**550.8**	**564.5**	**722.3**	**136.1**	**725.3**	**4,108.5**	**1,969.1**
1.6	54.3	6.5	8.7	287.9	12.7	18.8	100.6	8.7	150.2	446.9	238.7
0.1	0.7	0.0	0.1	2.2	0.8	0.9	2.6	0.4	3.1	6.5	1.8
0.4	2.1	0.2	0.3	4.8	1.8	4.9	3.3	0.6	3.2	13.0	4.0
0.7	10.1	1.5	0.7	27.1	5.4	2.1	3.9	0.7	4.1	38.7	22.5
347.1	1,159.9	299.3	393.6	4,397.8	1,913.6	868.3	5,723.1	795.9	6,230.3	13,029.2	3,641.6
0.2	0.8	0.1	0.2	3.9	0.6	0.5	1.4	0.3	0.9	6.8	3.2
32.8	12.6	22.9	38.8	212.9	13.5	15.7	81.5	21.9	53.3	332.9	175.5
40.4	423.8	61.8	408.4	3,248.6	320.8	493.6	1,424.7	213.5	1,627.2	6,031.6	2,692.7
21.1	282.3	76.0	54.6	990.6	153.6	135.9	651.0	43.0	1,001.7	2,022.0	819.4
0.3	4.9	0.3	0.3	12.6	2.0	4.0	8.0	0.8	8.3	26.9	10.5
1.4	2.3	2.3	1.3	11.1	2.4	2.2	7.4	1.1	8.7	23.7	9.2
11.4	78.8	28.4	32.7	263.7	65.2	47.6	124.1	21.6	105.9	500.4	218.4
0.0	0.5	0.0	0.0	1.0	0.4	1.1	1.8	0.4	1.8	3.9	0.8
0.3	6.4	0.2	0.5	11.7	4.2	2.8	8.8	2.3	5.8	29.3	9.6
1.2	84.8	5.8	2.5	104.3	47.3	16.1	38.9	6.5	38.0	193.6	86.6
1.0	9.8	0.9	1.6	43.3	3.8	3.9	9.4	0.9	9.9	70.9	35.9
6.1	97.6	5.0	30.5	618.2	45.6	71.6	73.7	8.5	73.5	829.7	513.3
6.1	89.7	14.3	40.6	377.9	29.1	31.9	94.6	14.8	90.8	560.6	313.4
18.5	20.7	16.1	15.7	111.2	15.9	25.8	98.2	21.4	86.5	244.1	91.7
1.6	27.7	3.2	5.5	108.2	32.0	20.4	34.5	4.1	42.4	190.9	89.7
52.5	98.0	34.1	73.0	514.9	57.6	76.9	175.7	43.7	122.9	840.2	425.4
22.1	125.4	50.0	40.9	473.1	112.0	81.1	220.2	60.2	137.6	878.6	392.1
9.3	110.0	10.7	7.7	214.9	58.0	46.8	100.2	10.2	132.5	430.9	177.6
576.2	**2,703.1**	**639.5**	**1,158.2**	**12,041.7**	**2,898.2**	**1,973.0**	**8,987.4**	**1,281.6**	**9,938.7**	**26,751.5**	**9,973.3**

(continued)

Table 2.5 *(Continued)*

REAL EXPENDITURES (US$, billions) Economy	Gross domestic product	Actual individual consumption	Food and nonalcoholic beverages	Alcoholic beverages, tobacco, and narcotics	Clothing and footwear	Housing, water, electricity, gas, and other fuels	Furnishings, household equipment and maintenance	Health	Transport	Communication
(00)	(01)	(02)	(03)	(04)	(05)	(06)	(07)	(08)	(09)	(10)
COMMONWEALTH OF INDEPENDENT STATES										
Armenia	20.2	22.0	6.0	1.1	0.4	5.9	0.2	2.6	0.6	0.8
Azerbaijan	144.5	75.7	15.9	2.0	3.5	19.6	2.1	5.4	3.9	3.0
Belarus	157.3	109.7	19.1	7.5	3.1	30.0	2.3	17.8	4.0	5.4
Kazakhstan	343.9	188.9	25.8	6.0	7.1	51.3	4.9	28.4	12.3	7.2
Kyrgyz Republic	16.1	18.4	3.3	1.0	0.6	5.8	0.3	1.8	0.9	1.2
Moldova	14.9	20.1	3.3	1.6	0.6	4.9	0.8	1.3	0.9	0.7
Russian Federation[d]	3,216.9	2,169.4	319.6	182.2	100.4	468.8	59.3	234.2	118.4	93.2
Tajikistan	17.3	23.3	4.9	0.1	0.8	6.1	0.3	2.6	0.7	1.9
Ukraine	379.1	361.4	67.4	24.1	9.0	112.8	8.1	56.5	18.3	6.9
Total (9)	**4,310.3**	**2,989.1**	**465.3**	**225.7**	**125.4**	**705.3**	**78.1**	**350.6**	**160.0**	**120.1**
EUROSTAT-OECD										
Albania	28.2	23.0	5.3	0.7	0.5	3.3	0.8	2.5	0.5	0.2
Australia	956.0	616.6	49.3	16.0	17.6	100.1	25.3	75.9	53.2	17.9
Austria	360.5	232.2	16.9	9.1	12.2	46.2	11.4	27.8	18.7	4.8
Belgium	440.1	288.2	28.0	10.0	10.3	48.7	11.7	50.0	20.3	4.6
Bosnia and Herzegovina	37.0	32.5	5.9	2.5	0.6	7.2	1.2	3.6	1.3	0.6
Bulgaria	114.1	80.6	9.1	4.2	1.1	19.1	3.4	15.6	5.7	2.7
Canada	1,416.2	946.0	57.7	22.2	32.7	189.4	37.2	128.3	97.9	19.3
Chile	349.1	236.6	23.5	6.3	8.7	37.1	10.8	28.7	19.5	6.8
Croatia	86.8	58.8	7.8	3.7	1.6	14.1	2.3	10.6	3.3	1.8
Cyprus	26.6	19.5	1.8	0.9	1.0	4.3	0.8	2.1	1.5	1.0
Czech Republic	283.9	174.6	17.7	13.2	3.0	37.6	5.9	32.8	8.6	3.0
Denmark	233.0	146.4	11.3	4.9	5.1	26.8	5.5	23.2	9.2	2.8
Estonia	30.9	18.5	2.3	1.4	0.6	3.3	0.4	2.9	1.2	0.6
Finland	208.0	143.2	13.1	5.5	5.0	25.6	5.5	22.6	8.8	3.7
France	2,369.6	1,724.6	168.9	49.9	56.7	312.1	68.3	273.4	138.4	36.8
Germany	3,352.1	2,328.9	188.3	73.0	83.3	395.5	105.3	407.6	168.9	63.9
Greece	300.8	240.2	30.1	10.7	7.8	56.4	7.5	36.1	17.9	5.1
Hungary	223.5	146.2	13.8	9.9	2.3	31.8	3.9	30.6	7.5	2.6
Iceland	12.2	8.2	0.8	0.2	0.2	1.8	0.3	1.3	0.6	0.2
Ireland	196.6	105.5	7.6	3.4	3.7	19.7	3.6	15.7	8.3	2.6
Israel	234.2	159.0	16.7	3.4	3.7	33.2	7.6	17.2	15.1	4.4
Italy	2,056.7	1,449.8	152.1	39.4	84.6	269.8	75.7	207.8	116.0	31.3
Japan	4,379.8	3,125.1	231.6	89.0	82.4	609.8	112.3	453.3	226.8	96.8
Korea, Rep.	1,445.3	870.2	52.7	19.2	22.8	187.5	19.6	162.5	63.3	43.6
Latvia	41.1	28.3	3.4	1.6	0.7	6.8	0.7	3.9	2.0	0.7
Lithuania	68.2	50.1	7.4	3.0	1.4	9.2	1.8	8.9	3.3	1.1

Recreation and culture	Education	Restaurants and hotels	Miscellaneous goods and services	Individual consumption expenditure by households	Individual consumption expenditure by government	Collective consumption expenditure by government	Gross fixed capital formation	Machinery and equipment	Construction	Domestic absorption	Individual consumption expenditure by households without housing
(11)	(12)	(13)	(14)	(16)	(17)	(18)	(19)	(20)	(21)	(25)	(26)
0.4	5.2	0.1	0.7	17.2	4.3	2.7	2.5	0.3	2.5	25.4	13.1
1.7	20.5	1.3	3.1	58.9	17.5	13.7	13.3	5.6	7.1	99.8	47.3
3.9	40.4	1.6	3.3	77.3	52.1	11.1	28.0	8.8	20.8	158.2	61.9
6.9	68.4	4.4	15.5	141.0	63.4	29.2	42.1	9.4	34.7	274.6	120.7
0.5	7.9	0.3	0.8	13.6	6.5	2.4	1.5	0.5	1.0	20.0	10.7
0.4	7.0	0.2	1.7	14.6	8.0	1.4	1.7	0.4	1.2	21.2	11.4
79.8	375.9	34.2	173.4	1,633.9	701.7	352.4	415.4	123.3	282.8	2,988.9	1,339.3
0.4	7.0	0.1	1.1	17.1	8.3	2.2	2.2	0.8	1.2	25.7	13.8
9.2	110.3	3.8	18.1	264.4	137.5	56.6	35.2	10.6	26.2	404.9	207.1
103.3	**642.7**	**46.1**	**217.7**	**2,238.0**	**999.2**	**451.6**	**541.9**	**159.8**	**377.6**	**4,018.8**	**1,825.4**
0.4	9.5	0.5	1.2	17.7	5.8	2.6	7.3	0.8	9.3	33.1	15.0
64.4	71.5	37.1	92.8	507.3	125.8	78.1	228.2	65.0	129.0	934.2	429.8
19.9	20.7	21.9	28.2	193.3	47.9	26.1	80.1	28.5	45.0	346.5	158.9
20.9	33.8	11.9	38.9	221.5	85.6	34.0	107.7	33.2	69.6	433.7	185.6
1.2	7.3	1.5	2.6	25.6	8.0	5.6	5.9	1.2	5.8	43.8	20.7
5.1	15.3	4.3	4.5	61.4	24.5	16.2	18.5	4.6	16.0	114.9	47.1
71.7	94.5	43.4	130.8	763.0	214.9	136.4	344.3	71.3	249.4	1,432.3	609.7
12.1	62.1	8.1	30.6	190.0	53.2	21.7	72.9	19.4	54.1	338.7	161.2
4.9	9.9	6.2	4.9	45.4	16.6	0.7	16.8	3.4	14.9	86.9	36.2
1.3	2.2	2.3	1.6	17.0	2.8	3.2	4.9	1.0	4.4	27.7	13.7
14.1	27.2	12.3	14.5	129.9	58.9	36.7	61.8	20.1	41.7	273.0	104.5
12.2	18.2	4.6	25.5	102.4	59.1	18.7	49.8	15.8	27.0	215.7	81.8
1.1	3.7	1.0	1.7	13.5	6.8	3.8	6.9	2.1	5.0	29.9	11.0
12.1	17.4	5.8	20.9	107.3	47.3	18.0	44.6	9.5	35.2	208.5	89.0
127.3	188.7	89.3	231.5	1,313.2	534.1	195.5	492.4	127.6	338.4	2,437.1	1,089.5
156.4	212.3	94.6	348.9	1,831.7	621.9	227.2	577.8	217.9	342.6	3,147.4	1,517.6
10.7	27.0	22.2	21.2	205.2	34.5	38.1	44.0	13.1	30.5	325.2	168.4
9.3	25.9	8.1	18.3	106.8	53.4	31.0	34.2	9.9	25.2	212.1	84.5
0.6	1.2	0.4	0.8	6.1	2.8	1.3	1.5	0.5	0.9	11.0	4.6
6.0	14.8	8.8	11.1	82.2	29.8	11.5	28.1	7.5	20.4	148.5	67.2
8.5	28.8	6.9	18.6	123.9	43.0	30.1	46.9	10.1	29.9	234.8	98.1
84.1	143.4	106.3	142.0	1,172.7	336.0	154.1	452.4	141.1	276.4	2,078.7	970.7
226.2	267.9	163.8	556.4	2,452.9	819.7	420.3	879.3	330.6	432.5	4,412.4	1,929.1
52.9	143.3	40.5	125.7	718.6	163.4	135.1	379.7	102.0	277.8	1,418.4	577.2
1.8	5.4	0.9	1.8	22.0	7.5	6.1	7.6	2.2	5.9	42.9	17.5
2.5	8.8	1.0	4.1	37.6	16.2	8.1	10.2	2.3	8.6	70.0	31.3

(continued)

Table 2.5 (Continued)

REAL EXPENDITURES (US$, billions) Economy	Gross domestic product	Actual individual consumption	Food and nonalcoholic beverages	Alcoholic beverages, tobacco, and narcotics	Clothing and footwear	Housing, water, electricity, gas, and other fuels	Furnishings, household equipment and maintenance	Health	Transport	Communication
(00)	(01)	(02)	(03)	(04)	(05)	(06)	(07)	(08)	(09)	(10)
Luxembourg	46.1	16.6	1.4	2.3	0.9	2.9	1.1	1.9	2.9	0.4
Macedonia, FYR	24.6	19.5	3.9	0.7	0.5	4.4	0.4	2.5	0.8	0.6
Malta	11.9	8.2	0.9	0.2	0.2	1.3	0.4	1.4	0.6	0.3
Mexico	1,894.6	1,370.1	233.0	32.3	34.4	193.8	55.7	105.0	153.3	35.2
Montenegro	8.8	7.6	1.6	0.4	0.1	1.4	0.5	0.8	0.5	0.3
Netherlands	720.3	433.7	39.4	11.8	16.2	70.2	18.0	61.1	28.2	12.7
New Zealand	137.6	99.3	9.7	3.2	3.9	16.5	3.7	16.8	7.9	2.2
Norway	306.5	153.6	11.8	3.2	5.7	26.1	6.6	22.1	11.8	5.0
Poland	838.0	628.3	83.2	28.9	12.2	162.1	17.9	105.6	29.0	13.4
Portugal	272.7	197.4	26.3	6.7	7.5	28.9	8.1	28.4	14.7	4.2
Romania	344.8	238.8	38.0	8.0	4.2	43.2	6.8	58.1	11.5	8.2
Russian Federation[d]	3,216.9	2,169.4	319.6	182.2	100.4	464.1	59.3	232.9	118.4	93.2
Serbia	86.1	73.4	10.9	4.1	1.1	18.6	1.4	12.7	4.1	2.8
Slovak Republic	135.7	91.1	10.0	3.4	2.1	23.9	3.3	16.3	3.7	1.6
Slovenia	57.8	38.8	4.2	2.2	1.5	7.3	1.7	6.1	3.5	1.1
Spain	1,483.2	991.0	115.2	32.1	46.0	163.4	35.6	135.3	69.4	16.4
Sweden	394.6	253.1	22.1	7.0	8.4	49.8	8.8	35.9	17.7	10.6
Switzerland	405.9	231.9	18.6	11.4	8.1	37.3	10.1	33.6	18.2	7.5
Turkey	1,314.9	1,015.5	140.0	22.6	42.0	241.3	55.7	114.5	81.4	20.4
United Kingdom	2,201.4	1,640.3	125.9	37.5	95.6	258.6	60.9	234.9	129.0	34.2
United States	15,533.8	11,667.0	698.4	207.6	366.0	1,962.8	429.5	2,300.0	1,079.1	246.7
Total (47)	**48,686.6**	**34,597.3**	**3,037.0**	**1,011.3**	**1,206.8**	**6,274.2**	**1,314.4**	**5,570.6**	**2,803.6**	**876.1**
LATIN AMERICA										
Bolivia	56.4	37.1	8.0	0.5	0.5	8.6	1.7	3.2	4.9	0.2
Brazil	2,816.3	1,905.7	246.1	43.2	36.7	263.0	98.4	359.0	158.0	31.2
Colombia	535.0	369.0	43.5	9.9	13.9	94.3	8.1	36.4	25.4	8.7
Costa Rica	59.8	47.0	6.3	0.4	1.3	5.4	1.9	4.8	6.3	1.5
Cuba[e]	...	...	...	...	...	...	...	...	...	...
Dominican Republic	109.0	97.6	16.3	4.2	2.2	19.2	2.1	7.9	7.1	3.6
Ecuador	151.6	103.2	13.7	2.4	2.5	21.9	4.3	11.3	10.3	3.8
El Salvador	46.0	45.5	7.3	0.7	1.3	12.8	2.5	4.4	3.4	1.5
Guatemala	102.4	91.4	22.2	1.0	3.2	16.9	4.4	7.1	4.7	4.4
Haiti	15.6	16.9	6.3	0.5	0.5	3.2	0.5	0.7	0.7	0.1
Honduras	33.8	29.1	6.0	0.9	0.7	5.7	0.8	3.1	1.9	0.5
Nicaragua	24.2	21.1	3.2	0.5	0.4	6.2	0.8	2.7	1.6	0.4
Panama	57.2	39.5	4.3	0.2	1.4	12.2	1.9	3.2	3.8	1.7
Paraguay	47.2	36.7	6.7	0.5	0.9	6.2	2.0	3.5	2.0	1.4
Peru	327.2	213.0	33.2	4.3	8.0	31.7	6.1	19.6	16.1	5.7

Recreation and culture	Education	Restaurants and hotels	Miscella-neous goods and services	Individual consumption expenditure by households	Individual consumption expenditure by government	Collective consumption expenditure by government	Gross fixed capital formation	Machinery and equipment	Construction	Domestic absorption	Individual consumption expenditure by households without housing
(11)	(12)	(13)	(14)	(16)	(17)	(18)	(19)	(20)	(21)	(25)	(26)
1.4	1.3	1.2	3.0	13.4	4.3	2.6	10.6	3.4	7.1	30.2	11.4
0.5	4.8	0.6	1.3	15.1	5.3	4.2	3.8	0.7	4.1	28.2	11.9
0.7	1.1	1.2	1.1	6.4	2.1	1.6	1.7	0.4	1.3	11.4	5.3
45.1	406.2	44.0	132.5	1,078.4	325.8	162.9	341.6	66.2	329.7	1,914.6	927.3
0.2	1.6	0.8	0.5	5.9	2.1	1.7	1.2	0.2	1.2	10.3	4.9
34.4	52.1	14.9	80.9	312.7	159.8	78.5	133.2	35.8	87.6	646.7	262.5
8.2	15.8	5.8	10.2	76.9	27.8	12.9	22.0	7.0	12.8	134.9	62.2
14.0	15.6	5.0	21.4	115.5	49.8	21.4	62.4	19.9	31.3	250.3	94.0
39.4	102.7	9.8	74.2	482.3	183.1	82.2	127.8	35.3	96.2	848.9	403.6
11.5	30.4	19.0	21.7	160.5	43.4	28.9	55.9	10.1	51.6	283.9	137.1
13.0	50.8	6.3	15.9	176.7	82.0	38.0	80.2	13.5	85.1	360.8	148.7
78.2	374.0	34.2	179.1	1,633.9	701.7	352.4	415.4	123.3	282.8	2,988.9	1,341.0
2.8	15.4	1.2	6.3	54.4	25.8	9.5	13.0	3.0	11.6	97.3	43.0
6.6	14.4	3.2	8.9	70.1	26.1	18.8	25.2	5.9	16.0	135.1	57.4
2.7	4.9	1.9	3.8	30.5	10.2	6.2	10.9	3.6	6.9	56.8	25.6
71.6	117.5	134.0	97.2	788.8	248.5	150.9	347.8	74.5	235.1	1,494.6	668.8
21.4	27.4	8.1	41.4	183.6	91.6	32.6	72.7	28.7	34.2	364.8	143.7
19.4	20.0	13.5	36.3	207.9	25.3	18.5	93.9	39.6	41.8	346.6	179.0
32.3	279.3	42.5	65.7	793.4	260.6	111.7	253.8	88.4	171.3	1,411.3	604.7
174.4	172.6	101.1	206.6	1,311.9	408.7	202.1	351.5	67.1	231.4	2,227.0	1,105.6
996.1	930.9	670.7	1,803.2	10,711.8	955.2	1,570.9	2,828.2	1,014.6	1,295.0	16,102.5	9,105.2
2,501.7	**4,099.4**	**1,822.7**	**4,690.5**	**28,697.9**	**7,058.7**	**4,588.4**	**9,256.7**	**2,881.8**	**5,530.0**	**48,802.6**	**23,862.9**
0.2	4.5	2.2	1.1	34.9	1.0	6.5	8.7	2.4	5.4	52.6	29.0
63.6	374.8	85.7	238.4	1,506.8	488.8	316.9	611.4	148.1	458.2	2,840.5	1,272.4
15.1	68.1	27.9	40.0	318.6	46.5	62.1	105.0	20.1	102.2	536.2	253.5
3.6	8.7	1.8	2.7	39.4	7.2	4.2	10.4	2.2	9.5	62.7	34.1
...	...	...	...	...	...	...	...	...	...	...	...
1.6	14.7	7.7	11.4	88.4	5.1	8.0	13.6	1.9	16.3	118.1	73.3
3.8	22.5	3.0	9.0	89.0	13.1	11.0	34.0	4.6	19.1	154.0	73.2
1.6	6.3	1.7	2.5	40.7	3.6	3.2	4.6	1.2	3.7	53.4	32.4
2.2	10.3	4.7	4.4	81.7	7.2	6.9	12.7	3.3	10.4	110.7	65.7
0.3	1.7	0.0	0.4	16.1	0.2	0.0	4.1	0.0	7.3	21.1	13.5
0.9	5.7	1.4	2.1	25.8	2.8	2.6	7.3	2.0	4.8	39.6	21.3
0.5	5.1	0.9	1.7	18.3	2.5	2.7	3.4	0.7	3.1	26.9	14.0
1.7	5.8	1.4	3.5	34.1	5.1	4.8	11.2	2.7	9.7	56.5	26.1
1.5	8.6	1.3	3.3	31.9	4.3	2.2	6.5	1.2	6.0	45.5	27.3
10.1	42.0	13.3	22.4	188.7	19.0	24.3	66.1	11.7	69.3	310.3	157.8

(continued)

Table 2.5 (Continued)

REAL EXPENDITURES (US$, billions) Economy	Gross domestic product	Actual individual consumption	Food and nonalcoholic beverages	Alcoholic beverages, tobacco, and narcotics	Clothing and footwear	Housing, water, electricity, gas, and other fuels	Furnishings, household equipment and maintenance	Health	Transport	Communication
(00)	(01)	(02)	(03)	(04)	(05)	(06)	(07)	(08)	(09)	(10)
Uruguay	58.7	43.6	5.7	0.9	1.1	11.3	1.6	6.6	2.3	1.9
Venezuela, RB	500.3	302.7	30.3	5.0	4.3	44.6	6.2	35.7	48.2	16.4
Total (17)	**4,940.8**	**3,399.3**	**459.0**	**75.0**	**79.0**	**563.3**	**143.3**	**509.4**	**296.8**	**83.1**
CARIBBEAN										
Anguilla	0.4	0.3	0.0	0.0	0.0	0.1	0.0	0.0	0.0	0.0
Antigua and Barbuda	1.8	1.1	0.1	0.0	0.0	0.4	0.0	0.2	0.1	0.0
Aruba	3.7	2.4	0.1	0.0	0.1	1.0	0.1	0.5	0.2	0.1
Bahamas, The	8.3	5.7	0.4	0.1	0.2	2.1	0.1	0.7	0.4	0.2
Barbados	4.3	3.5	0.4	0.0	0.1	2.1	0.1	0.3	0.2	0.1
Belize	2.6	2.1	0.2	0.0	0.1	1.0	0.1	0.2	0.1	0.1
Bermuda	3.6	2.5	0.2	0.1	0.1	0.5	0.1	0.3	0.2	0.1
Bonaire[f]	...	...	0.0	0.0	0.0	...	0.0	...	0.0	0.0
Cayman Islands	2.8	1.9	0.1	0.0	0.1	0.7	0.1	0.1	0.2	0.1
Curaçao	4.2	3.1	0.2	0.0	0.2	1.4	0.1	0.4	0.2	0.1
Dominica	0.7	0.6	0.1	0.0	0.0	0.2	0.0	0.1	0.1	0.0
Grenada	1.2	1.1	0.1	0.0	0.0	0.3	0.0	0.1	0.1	0.1
Jamaica	22.9	19.9	3.2	0.2	0.3	4.0	0.8	1.7	1.8	0.7
Montserrat	0.1	0.1	0.0	0.0	0.0	0.0	0.0	0.0	0.0	0.0
St. Kitts and Nevis	1.1	0.8	0.1	0.0	0.0	0.3	0.0	0.1	0.1	0.0
St. Lucia	1.8	1.3	0.2	0.0	0.1	0.5	0.0	0.1	0.1	0.1
St. Vincent and the Grenadines	1.1	0.9	0.1	0.0	0.0	0.3	0.0	0.1	0.1	0.0
Sint Maarten	1.2	0.7	0.0	0.0	0.0	0.3	0.0	0.0	0.1	0.0
Suriname	7.8	3.2	0.6	0.1	0.1	1.1	0.1	0.3	0.1	0.1
Trinidad and Tobago	38.3	20.9	2.8	0.1	0.2	3.4	0.5	2.4	1.6	0.4
Turks and Caicos Islands	0.7	0.2	0.0	0.0	0.0	0.0	0.0	0.0	0.0	0.0
Virgin Islands, British	0.9	0.3	0.0	0.0	0.0	0.1	0.0	0.0	0.0	0.0
Total (22)	**109.3**	**72.7**	**9.0**	**0.8**	**1.7**	**19.8**	**2.1**	**7.6**	**5.7**	**2.3**
WESTERN ASIA										
Bahrain	51.8	22.3	2.1	0.1	1.0	5.2	1.1	1.6	2.9	1.2
Egypt, Arab Rep.[a]	843.8	679.1	133.0	12.6	32.0	200.1	16.8	119.8	28.0	14.6
Iraq	371.0	179.4	29.4	0.6	6.5	73.4	5.1	21.1	9.8	2.7
Jordan	69.8	55.4	8.0	1.4	2.4	19.2	1.6	6.7	3.8	1.9
Kuwait	257.7	67.1	8.1	0.1	4.1	24.2	5.5	4.9	6.3	1.7
Oman	140.4	50.0	6.1	0.1	2.5	10.8	1.5	4.0	8.3	2.0
Qatar	258.1	36.2	3.4	0.1	1.2	8.5	1.2	2.7	4.4	0.8
Saudi Arabia	1,366.7	505.0	49.0	1.5	21.2	177.0	24.0	48.4	35.6	17.2
Sudan[b]	152.4	97.5	28.1	0.4	6.5	17.0	4.8	3.1	4.7	1.3
United Arab Emirates	503.2	243.5	22.6	0.5	29.8	84.7	9.0	3.7	41.9	17.5

Recreation and culture	Education	Restaurants and hotels	Miscellaneous goods and services	Individual consumption expenditure by households	Individual consumption expenditure by government	Collective consumption expenditure by government	Gross fixed capital formation	Machinery and equipment	Construction	Domestic absorption	Individual consumption expenditure by households without housing
(11)	(12)	(13)	(14)	(16)	(17)	(18)	(19)	(20)	(21)	(25)	(26)
1.1	5.9	2.6	3.7	37.1	6.4	4.0	10.8	2.0	10.5	58.9	28.5
9.7	82.6	22.2	11.8	256.9	47.8	42.5	84.6	14.8	91.0	449.3	217.9
117.7	**667.3**	**177.7**	**358.6**	**2,808.5**	**660.6**	**501.9**	**994.2**	**218.8**	**826.4**	**4,936.4**	**2,339.9**
0.0	0.0	0.0	0.0	0.3	0.0	0.1	0.1	0.0	0.1	0.4	0.2
0.0	0.2	0.0	0.1	0.8	0.3	0.3	0.4	0.0	0.5	1.7	0.6
0.1	0.3	0.0	0.2	1.7	1.1	0.6	1.3	0.2	1.4	4.2	1.1
0.2	0.7	0.3	0.8	4.9	0.8	1.4	2.6	0.8	1.9	9.6	3.5
0.1	0.4	0.5	0.3	2.9	0.5	0.9	0.9	0.3	0.7	5.1	1.5
0.1	0.3	0.0	0.1	1.8	0.2	0.4	0.2	0.1	0.2	2.7	1.0
0.1	0.4	0.2	0.3	2.0	0.6	0.4	1.2	0.5	0.5	4.0	1.6
...	...	0.0	...	0.2	...	...	...	...	...	...	0.1
0.1	0.2	0.1	0.3	1.7	0.2	0.3	0.8	0.2	0.5	3.0	1.2
0.1	0.3	0.1	0.6	2.6	0.5	0.5	1.5	0.5	0.6	5.2	1.8
0.0	0.1	0.0	0.0	0.5	0.1	0.1	0.2	0.0	0.1	0.8	0.4
0.0	0.3	0.0	0.1	0.9	0.2	0.2	0.2	0.0	0.2	1.4	0.7
1.3	4.2	1.7	2.1	16.8	3.0	2.8	4.4	1.1	3.5	27.4	13.1
0.0	0.0	0.0	0.0	0.1	0.0	0.0	0.0	0.0	0.0	0.1	0.0
0.0	0.2	0.0	0.1	0.6	0.2	0.3	0.3	0.0	0.3	1.2	0.4
0.0	0.3	0.0	0.1	1.1	0.2	0.3	0.5	0.1	0.5	2.1	0.8
0.0	0.2	0.0	0.1	0.7	0.2	0.2	0.2	0.0	0.3	1.3	0.5
0.0	0.1	0.0	0.1	0.6	0.1	0.3	0.2	0.1	0.1	1.2	0.4
0.1	0.1	0.0	0.4	2.8	0.2	1.4	2.4	1.1	0.7	7.3	2.4
1.1	6.8	1.3	3.0	15.0	9.1	1.2	6.3	1.7	4.6	29.5	13.3
0.0	0.1	0.0	0.0	0.2	0.0	0.2	0.1	0.0	0.1	0.5	0.2
0.0	0.0	0.0	0.0	0.3	0.0	0.1	0.2	0.1	0.1	0.5	0.2
3.5	**15.3**	**4.4**	**8.9**	**58.3**	**17.4**	**11.8**	**23.9**	**6.9**	**16.7**	**109.4**	**44.8**
1.4	4.1	0.9	1.4	19.6	2.7	4.3	9.1	1.3	10.5	35.6	17.6
16.3	142.5	14.2	48.7	574.7	96.0	124.8	85.2	16.0	83.7	867.2	448.5
1.5	59.4	1.1	3.6	133.0	61.4	90.9	53.6	12.7	46.1	309.2	90.8
0.7	16.2	0.7	1.4	45.8	10.8	11.5	11.8	1.6	12.4	79.2	33.6
1.9	8.8	1.2	3.1	57.2	10.8	21.4	45.7	9.6	34.2	133.6	44.7
1.4	10.1	1.0	3.9	40.4	10.9	16.8	41.3	7.3	37.9	101.2	34.6
2.4	6.9	0.6	4.9	30.2	7.3	15.3	105.3	25.4	31.0	133.8	24.6
12.4	130.7	15.0	23.2	381.9	143.7	129.3	369.7	66.9	322.0	1,034.1	295.3
1.8	9.8	2.2	2.5	87.4	2.4	19.5	33.1	6.6	33.3	154.6	74.0
5.6	16.5	6.8	10.4	243.5	4.3	22.0	155.6	34.2	118.5	400.2	181.8

(continued)

Table 2.5 *(Continued)*

REAL EXPENDITURES (US$, billions) Economy	Gross domestic product	Actual individual consumption	Food and nonalcoholic beverages	Alcoholic beverages, tobacco, and narcotics	Clothing and footwear	Housing, water, electricity, gas, and other fuels	Furnishings, household equipment and maintenance	Health	Transport	Communication
(00)	(01)	(02)	(03)	(04)	(05)	(06)	(07)	(08)	(09)	(10)
West Bank and Gaza	16.0	17.0	3.5	0.3	1.0	1.9	0.7	2.5	0.9	0.5
Yemen, Rep.	88.6	65.8	13.3	3.3	3.1	18.1	1.1	12.0	2.9	0.5
Total (12)	**4,119.5**	**2,018.3**	**306.8**	**21.1**	**111.3**	**640.1**	**72.2**	**230.6**	**149.6**	**62.0**
SINGLETONS										
Georgia	28.3	27.1	4.3	1.4	0.3	9.1	0.6	5.0	1.3	0.9
Iran, Islamic Rep.	1,314.2	644.5	82.8	4.0	14.3	221.8	13.1	113.7	31.5	30.7
Total (2)	**1,342.6**	**671.6**	**87.1**	**5.3**	**14.7**	**230.9**	**13.7**	**118.7**	**32.8**	**31.6**
WORLD[g] (179)	**90,646.6**	**58,230.1**	**6,854.0**	**1,440.2**	**2,368.2**	**11,063.6**	**2,023.0**	**9,325.5**	**4,258.7**	**1,604.8**

Source: ICP, http://icp.worldbank.org/.

Note: n.a. = not applicable; ... = data suppressed because of incompleteness.

a. The Arab Republic of Egypt participated in both the Africa and Western Asia regions. The regional results for Egypt were averaged by taking the geometric mean of the regional PPPs, allowing Egypt to have the same global results in each region.

b. Sudan participated in both the Africa and Western Asia regions. The regional results for Sudan were averaged by taking the geometric mean of the regional PPPs, allowing Sudan to have the same global results in each region.

c. The results presented in the tables are based on data supplied by all the participating economies and compiled in accordance with ICP principles and the procedures recommended by the 2011 ICP Technical Advisory Group. The results for China are estimated by the 2011 ICP Asia and the Pacific Regional Office and the Global Office. The National Bureau of Statistics of China does not recognize these results as official statistics.

d. The Russian Federation participated in both the CIS and Eurostat-OECD comparisons. The PPPs for Russia are based on the Eurostat-OECD comparison. They were the basis for linking the CIS comparison to the ICP.

e. The official GDP of Cuba for reference year 2011 is 68,990.15 million in national currency. However, this number and its breakdown into main aggregates are not shown in the tables because of methodological comparability issues. Therefore, Cuba's results are provided only for the PPP and price level index. In addition, Cuba's figures are not included in the Latin America and world totals.

f. Bonaire's results are provided only for the individual consumption expenditure by households. Therefore, to ensure consistency across the tables, Bonaire is not included in the Caribbean or the world total.

g. This table does not include the Pacific Islands and does not double count the dual participation economies: the Arab Republic of Egypt, Sudan, and the Russian Federation.

Recreation and culture	Education	Restaurants and hotels	Miscella-neous goods and services	Individual consumption expenditure by households	Individual consumption expenditure by government	Collective consumption expenditure by government	Gross fixed capital formation	Machinery and equipment	Construction	Domestic absorption	Individual consumption expenditure by households without housing
(11)	(12)	(13)	(14)	(16)	(17)	(18)	(19)	(20)	(21)	(25)	(26)
0.4	4.0	0.3	1.2	13.4	4.1	4.5	2.9	0.3	3.1	23.7	11.9
0.2	12.7	0.0	2.7	55.7	10.0	14.5	8.6	0.4	9.5	91.2	45.3
45.9	**421.7**	**44.0**	**107.0**	**1,682.6**	**364.4**	**474.8**	**921.8**	**182.3**	**742.3**	**3,363.6**	**1,302.6**
1.4	8.4	0.5	1.7	21.4	4.3	6.3	3.3	1.1	1.9	34.3	16.2
12.7	181.6	4.3	51.1	511.3	137.8	208.6	220.0	47.7	234.2	1,169.0	380.2
14.1	**190.0**	**4.8**	**52.7**	**532.7**	**142.2**	**214.9**	**223.4**	**48.9**	**236.1**	**1,203.3**	**396.4**
3,327.8	**8,870.0**	**2,747.5**	**6,594.3**	**48,108.7**	**11,891.4**	**8,284.1**	**21,137.9**	**4,770.3**	**17,993.4**	**89,283.4**	**39,852.6**

Table 2.6 Shares of World Real Expenditures (World = 100), ICP 2011

REAL EXPENDITURES: COUNTRY AND REGIONAL SHARES (world = 100)[a] Economy	Gross domestic product	Actual individual consumption	Food and nonalcoholic beverages	Alcoholic beverages, tobacco, and narcotics	Clothing and footwear	Housing, water, electricity, gas, and other fuels	Furnishings, household equipment and maintenance	Health	Transport	Communication
(00)	(01)	(02)	(03)	(04)	(05)	(06)	(07)	(08)	(09)	(10)
AFRICA										
Algeria	0.50	0.40	0.60	0.20	0.20	0.10	0.20	0.40	0.60	0.60
Angola	0.20	0.10	0.30	0.40	0.20	0.10	0.20	0.10	0.10	0.00
Benin	0.00	0.00	0.10	0.00	0.00	0.00	0.00	0.00	0.00	0.00
Botswana	0.00	0.00	0.00	0.10	0.00	0.00	0.00	0.00	0.00	0.00
Burkina Faso	0.00	0.00	0.10	0.10	0.00	0.00	0.00	0.00	0.00	0.00
Burundi	0.00	0.00	0.00	0.00	0.00	0.00	0.00	0.00	0.00	0.00
Cameroon	0.10	0.10	0.20	0.10	0.10	0.10	0.10	0.00	0.10	0.00
Cape Verde	0.00	0.00	0.00	0.00	0.00	0.00	0.00	0.00	0.00	0.00
Central African Republic	0.00	0.00	0.00	0.00	0.00	0.00	0.00	0.00	0.00	0.00
Chad	0.00	0.00	0.10	0.00	0.00	0.00	0.00	0.00	0.00	0.00
Comoros	0.00	0.00	0.00	0.00	0.00	0.00	0.00	0.00	0.00	0.00
Congo, Rep.	0.00	0.00	0.00	0.00	0.00	0.00	0.00	0.00	0.00	0.00
Congo, Dem. Rep.	0.00	0.10	0.10	0.00	0.10	0.10	0.00	0.00	0.00	0.00
Côte d'Ivoire	0.10	0.10	0.10	0.00	0.00	0.00	0.10	0.00	0.10	0.00
Djibouti	0.00	0.00	0.00	0.00	0.00	0.00	0.00	0.00	0.00	0.00
Egypt, Arab Rep.[b]	0.90	1.20	1.90	0.90	1.40	1.80	0.80	1.30	0.70	0.90
Equatorial Guinea	0.00	0.00	0.00	0.00	0.00	0.00	0.00	0.00	0.00	0.00
Ethiopia	0.10	0.10	0.20	0.10	0.20	0.10	0.20	0.20	0.00	0.00
Gabon	0.00	0.00	0.00	0.10	0.00	0.00	0.00	0.00	0.00	0.00
Gambia, The	0.00	0.00	0.00	0.00	0.00	0.00	0.00	0.00	0.00	0.00
Ghana	0.10	0.10	0.10	0.00	0.40	0.10	0.10	0.10	0.10	0.10
Guinea	0.00	0.00	0.00	0.00	0.00	0.00	0.00	0.00	0.00	0.00
Guinea-Bissau	0.00	0.00	0.00	0.00	0.00	0.00	0.00	0.00	0.00	0.00
Kenya	0.10	0.10	0.20	0.20	0.10	0.10	0.10	0.10	0.10	0.20
Lesotho	0.00	0.00	0.00	0.00	0.00	0.00	0.00	0.00	0.00	0.00
Liberia	0.00	0.00	0.00	0.00	0.00	0.00	0.00	0.00	0.00	0.00
Madagascar	0.00	0.00	0.10	0.00	0.10	0.00	0.10	0.00	0.00	0.00
Malawi	0.00	0.00	0.10	0.00	0.00	0.00	0.00	0.00	0.00	0.00
Mali	0.00	0.00	0.10	0.00	0.00	0.00	0.00	0.00	0.00	0.00
Mauritania	0.00	0.00	0.00	0.00	0.00	0.00	0.00	0.00	0.00	0.00
Mauritius	0.00	0.00	0.00	0.10	0.00	0.00	0.00	0.00	0.00	0.00
Morocco	0.20	0.20	0.40	0.10	0.20	0.30	0.20	0.10	0.20	0.40
Mozambique	0.00	0.00	0.10	0.10	0.00	0.00	0.00	0.00	0.00	0.00
Namibia	0.00	0.00	0.00	0.00	0.00	0.00	0.00	0.00	0.00	0.00
Niger	0.00	0.00	0.00	0.00	0.10	0.00	0.00	0.00	0.00	0.00
Nigeria	0.60	0.60	0.90	0.30	2.40	0.40	1.10	0.30	0.40	0.30
Rwanda	0.00	0.00	0.10	0.00	0.00	0.00	0.00	0.00	0.00	0.00
São Tomé and Príncipe	0.00	0.00	0.00	0.00	0.00	0.00	0.00	0.00	0.00	0.00

Recreation and culture	Education	Restaurants and hotels	Miscella-neous goods and services	Individual consumption expenditure by households	Individual consumption expenditure by government	Collective consumption expenditure by government	Gross fixed capital formation	Machinery and equipment	Construction	Domestic absorption	Individual consumption expenditure by households without housing
(11)	(12)	(13)	(14)	(16)	(17)	(18)	(19)	(20)	(21)	(25)	(26)
0.20	1.00	0.20	0.60	0.30	1.30	1.00	0.50	0.40	0.60	0.50	0.30
0.00	0.10	0.00	0.20	0.10	0.20	0.50	0.10	0.10	0.20	0.20	0.10
0.00	0.00	0.00	0.00	0.00	0.00	0.00	0.00	0.00	0.00	0.00	0.00
0.00	0.10	0.00	0.00	0.00	0.00	0.00	0.00	0.00	0.10	0.00	0.00
0.00	0.00	0.00	0.00	0.00	0.00	0.10	0.00	0.00	0.00	0.00	0.00
0.00	0.00	0.00	0.00	0.00	0.00	0.00	0.00	0.00	0.00	0.00	0.00
0.00	0.00	0.10	0.00	0.10	0.00	0.00	0.00	0.00	0.00	0.10	0.10
0.00	0.00	0.00	0.00	0.00	0.00	0.00	0.00	0.00	0.00	0.00	0.00
0.00	0.00	0.00	0.00	0.00	0.00	0.00	0.00	0.00	0.00	0.00	0.00
0.00	0.00	0.00	0.00	0.00	0.00	0.00	0.00	0.00	0.00	0.00	0.00
0.00	0.00	0.00	0.00	0.00	0.00	0.00	0.00	0.00	0.00	0.00	0.00
0.00	0.00	0.00	0.00	0.00	0.00	0.00	0.00	0.00	0.00	0.00	0.00
0.00	0.10	0.00	0.00	0.10	0.00	0.10	0.00	0.00	0.00	0.00	0.10
0.00	0.00	0.00	0.00	0.10	0.00	0.10	0.00	0.00	0.00	0.10	0.10
0.00	0.00	0.00	0.00	0.00	0.00	0.00	0.00	0.00	0.00	0.00	0.00
0.50	1.60	0.50	0.70	1.20	0.80	1.50	0.40	0.30	0.50	1.00	1.10
0.00	0.00	0.00	0.00	0.00	0.00	0.00	0.00	0.00	0.00	0.00	0.00
0.00	0.20	0.10	0.20	0.20	0.00	0.10	0.10	0.00	0.10	0.10	0.20
0.00	0.00	0.00	0.00	0.00	0.00	0.00	0.00	0.00	0.00	0.00	0.00
0.00	0.00	0.00	0.00	0.00	0.00	0.00	0.00	0.00	0.00	0.00	0.00
0.00	0.30	0.00	0.00	0.10	0.10	0.10	0.10	0.10	0.10	0.10	0.10
0.00	0.00	0.00	0.00	0.00	0.00	0.00	0.00	0.00	0.00	0.00	0.00
0.00	0.00	0.00	0.00	0.00	0.00	0.00	0.00	0.00	0.00	0.00	0.00
0.10	0.30	0.10	0.10	0.10	0.20	0.10	0.10	0.10	0.10	0.10	0.10
0.00	0.00	0.00	0.00	0.00	0.00	0.00	0.00	0.00	0.00	0.00	0.00
0.00	0.00	0.00	0.00	0.00	0.00	0.00	0.00	0.00	0.00	0.00	0.00
0.00	0.00	0.00	0.00	0.10	0.00	0.00	0.00	0.00	0.00	0.00	0.10
0.00	0.00	0.00	0.00	0.00	0.00	0.00	0.00	0.00	0.00	0.00	0.00
0.00	0.00	0.00	0.00	0.00	0.00	0.00	0.00	0.00	0.00	0.00	0.00
0.00	0.00	0.00	0.00	0.00	0.00	0.00	0.00	0.00	0.00	0.00	0.00
0.00	0.00	0.00	0.00	0.00	0.00	0.00	0.00	0.00	0.00	0.00	0.00
0.10	0.40	0.20	0.10	0.20	0.30	0.30	0.30	0.20	0.40	0.30	0.20
0.00	0.00	0.00	0.00	0.00	0.00	0.00	0.00	0.00	0.00	0.00	0.00
0.00	0.10	0.00	0.00	0.00	0.00	0.00	0.00	0.00	0.00	0.00	0.00
0.00	0.00	0.00	0.00	0.00	0.00	0.00	0.00	0.00	0.00	0.00	0.00
0.10	1.20	0.00	0.30	0.60	0.40	0.70	0.20	0.20	0.20	0.50	0.70
0.00	0.00	0.00	0.00	0.00	0.00	0.00	0.00	0.00	0.00	0.00	0.00
0.00	0.00	0.00	0.00	0.00	0.00	0.00	0.00	0.00	0.00	0.00	0.00

(continued)

Table 2.6 *(Continued)*

REAL EXPENDITURES: COUNTRY AND REGIONAL SHARES (world = 100)[a] Economy	Gross domestic product	Actual individual consumption	Food and nonalcoholic beverages	Alcoholic beverages, tobacco, and narcotics	Clothing and footwear	Housing, water, electricity, gas, and other fuels	Furnishings, household equipment and maintenance	Health	Transport	Communication
(00)	(01)	(02)	(03)	(04)	(05)	(06)	(07)	(08)	(09)	(10)
Senegal	0.00	0.00	0.10	0.00	0.00	0.10	0.10	0.00	0.00	0.10
Seychelles	0.00	0.00	0.00	0.00	0.00	0.00	0.00	0.00	0.00	0.00
Sierra Leone	0.00	0.00	0.00	0.00	0.00	0.00	0.00	0.00	0.00	0.00
South Africa	0.70	0.70	0.80	1.20	0.70	0.60	0.80	0.70	0.90	0.80
Sudan[c]	0.20	0.20	0.40	0.00	0.30	0.20	0.20	0.00	0.10	0.10
Swaziland	0.00	0.00	0.00	0.00	0.00	0.00	0.00	0.00	0.00	0.00
Tanzania	0.10	0.10	0.30	0.00	0.10	0.00	0.10	0.00	0.00	0.00
Togo	0.00	0.00	0.00	0.00	0.00	0.00	0.00	0.00	0.00	0.00
Tunisia	0.10	0.10	0.10	0.10	0.10	0.10	0.20	0.10	0.20	0.20
Uganda	0.10	0.10	0.10	0.10	0.10	0.10	0.10	0.00	0.00	0.00
Zambia	0.00	0.00	0.10	0.00	0.10	0.00	0.00	0.00	0.00	0.00
Zimbabwe	0.00	0.00	0.10	0.00	0.00	0.00	0.00	0.00	0.00	0.00
Total (50)	**4.50**	**4.90**	**8.20**	**4.80**	**7.20**	**4.70**	**5.30**	**3.70**	**3.90**	**4.10**
ASIA AND THE PACIFIC										
Bangladesh	0.50	0.50	1.40	0.60	0.70	0.70	0.40	0.30	0.10	0.30
Bhutan	0.00	0.00	0.00	0.00	0.00	0.00	0.00	0.00	0.00	0.00
Brunei Darussalam	0.00	0.00	0.00	0.00	0.00	0.00	0.00	0.00	0.00	0.00
Cambodia	0.00	0.10	0.10	0.10	0.00	0.00	0.00	0.10	0.00	0.00
China[d]	14.90	10.00	10.80	5.50	13.60	9.60	8.40	16.10	6.00	18.00
Fiji	0.00	0.00	0.00	0.00	0.00	0.00	0.00	0.00	0.00	0.00
Hong Kong SAR, China	0.40	0.40	0.30	0.10	0.60	0.40	0.50	0.20	0.30	0.60
India	6.40	6.30	10.10	4.80	12.60	5.90	3.90	4.90	6.30	3.10
Indonesia	2.30	2.00	3.90	0.80	1.40	2.60	1.20	0.60	1.20	1.30
Lao PDR	0.00	0.00	0.10	0.00	0.00	0.00	0.00	0.00	0.00	0.00
Macao SAR, China	0.10	0.00	0.00	0.00	0.00	0.00	0.00	0.00	0.00	0.00
Malaysia	0.70	0.60	0.50	0.20	0.20	0.60	0.40	0.30	0.60	1.00
Maldives	0.00	0.00	0.00	0.00	0.00	0.00	0.00	0.00	0.00	0.00
Mongolia	0.00	0.00	0.00	0.10	0.00	0.00	0.00	0.00	0.00	0.00
Myanmar	0.20	0.20	0.50	0.10	0.20	0.20	0.10	0.30	0.00	0.10
Nepal	0.10	0.10	0.20	0.10	0.10	0.10	0.00	0.10	0.00	0.00
Pakistan	0.90	1.20	2.50	0.40	1.20	1.90	0.60	1.30	0.50	0.80
Philippines	0.60	0.70	1.60	0.40	0.20	0.60	0.60	0.20	0.70	0.50
Singapore	0.40	0.20	0.10	0.10	0.20	0.20	0.20	0.20	0.30	0.20
Sri Lanka	0.20	0.20	0.50	0.60	0.20	0.20	0.10	0.20	0.10	0.20
Taiwan, China	1.00	1.00	0.60	0.60	1.20	0.90	0.80	1.20	1.00	2.30
Thailand	1.00	1.00	1.30	0.80	0.90	0.80	0.70	0.80	1.10	0.80
Vietnam	0.50	0.50	0.60	0.50	0.50	0.50	0.50	0.60	0.20	0.10
Total (23)	**30.00**	**25.10**	**35.20**	**15.80**	**33.70**	**25.30**	**18.40**	**27.30**	**18.70**	**29.40**

Recreation and culture	Education	Restaurants and hotels	Miscellaneous goods and services	Individual consumption expenditure by households	Individual consumption expenditure by government	Collective consumption expenditure by government	Gross fixed capital formation	Machinery and equipment	Construction	Domestic absorption	Individual consumption expenditure by households without housing
(11)	(12)	(13)	(14)	(16)	(17)	(18)	(19)	(20)	(21)	(25)	(26)
0.00	0.00	0.00	0.00	0.00	0.00	0.00	0.00	0.00	0.00	0.00	0.00
0.00	0.00	0.00	0.00	0.00	0.00	0.00	0.00	0.00	0.00	0.00	0.00
0.00	0.00	0.00	0.00	0.00	0.00	0.00	0.00	0.00	0.00	0.00	0.00
0.40	1.00	0.20	0.70	0.70	0.70	1.00	0.60	0.60	0.50	0.70	0.70
0.10	0.10	0.10	0.00	0.20	0.00	0.20	0.20	0.10	0.20	0.20	0.20
0.00	0.00	0.00	0.00	0.00	0.00	0.00	0.00	0.00	0.00	0.00	0.00
0.00	0.10	0.00	0.00	0.10	0.00	0.10	0.10	0.10	0.20	0.10	0.10
0.00	0.00	0.00	0.00	0.00	0.00	0.00	0.00	0.00	0.00	0.00	0.00
0.10	0.20	0.20	0.10	0.10	0.20	0.20	0.10	0.10	0.20	0.10	0.10
0.10	0.20	0.00	0.00	0.10	0.10	0.00	0.10	0.00	0.10	0.10	0.10
0.00	0.00	0.00	0.00	0.00	0.00	0.10	0.00	0.00	0.10	0.00	0.00
0.00	0.00	0.00	0.00	0.00	0.00	0.00	0.00	0.00	0.00	0.00	0.00
1.90	**7.40**	**2.10**	**3.40**	**4.90**	**4.60**	**6.80**	**3.40**	**2.90**	**4.00**	**4.60**	**4.90**
0.00	0.60	0.20	0.10	0.60	0.10	0.20	0.50	0.20	0.80	0.50	0.60
0.00	0.00	0.00	0.00	0.00	0.00	0.00	0.00	0.00	0.00	0.00	0.00
0.00	0.00	0.00	0.00	0.00	0.00	0.10	0.00	0.00	0.00	0.00	0.00
0.00	0.10	0.10	0.00	0.00	0.00	0.00	0.00	0.00	0.00	0.00	0.10
10.40	13.10	10.90	6.00	9.10	16.10	10.50	27.10	16.70	34.60	14.60	9.10
0.00	0.00	0.00	0.00	0.00	0.00	0.00	0.00	0.00	0.00	0.00	0.00
1.00	0.10	0.80	0.60	0.40	0.10	0.20	0.40	0.50	0.30	0.40	0.40
1.20	4.80	2.20	6.20	6.80	2.70	6.00	6.70	4.50	9.00	6.80	6.80
0.60	3.20	2.80	0.80	2.10	1.30	1.60	3.10	0.90	5.60	2.30	2.10
0.00	0.10	0.00	0.00	0.00	0.00	0.00	0.00	0.00	0.00	0.00	0.00
0.00	0.00	0.10	0.00	0.00	0.00	0.00	0.00	0.00	0.00	0.00	0.00
0.30	0.90	1.00	0.50	0.50	0.50	0.60	0.60	0.50	0.60	0.60	0.50
0.00	0.00	0.00	0.00	0.00	0.00	0.00	0.00	0.00	0.00	0.00	0.00
0.00	0.10	0.00	0.00	0.00	0.00	0.00	0.00	0.00	0.00	0.00	0.00
0.00	1.00	0.20	0.00	0.20	0.40	0.20	0.20	0.10	0.20	0.20	0.20
0.00	0.10	0.00	0.00	0.10	0.00	0.00	0.00	0.00	0.10	0.10	0.10
0.20	1.10	0.20	0.50	1.30	0.40	0.90	0.30	0.20	0.40	0.90	1.30
0.20	1.00	0.50	0.60	0.80	0.20	0.40	0.40	0.30	0.50	0.60	0.80
0.60	0.20	0.60	0.20	0.20	0.10	0.30	0.50	0.40	0.50	0.30	0.20
0.00	0.30	0.10	0.10	0.20	0.30	0.20	0.20	0.10	0.20	0.20	0.20
1.60	1.10	1.20	1.10	1.10	0.50	0.90	0.80	0.90	0.70	0.90	1.10
0.70	1.40	1.80	0.60	1.00	0.90	1.00	1.00	1.30	0.80	1.00	1.00
0.30	1.20	0.40	0.10	0.40	0.50	0.60	0.50	0.20	0.70	0.50	0.40
17.30	**30.50**	**23.30**	**17.60**	**25.00**	**24.40**	**23.80**	**42.50**	**26.90**	**55.20**	**30.00**	**25.00**

(continued)

Table 2.6 *(Continued)*

REAL EXPENDITURES: COUNTRY AND REGIONAL SHARES (world = 100)[a] Economy	Gross domestic product	Actual individual consumption	Food and nonalcoholic beverages	Alcoholic beverages, tobacco, and narcotics	Clothing and footwear	Housing, water, electricity, gas, and other fuels	Furnishings, household equipment and maintenance	Health	Transport	Communication
(00)	(01)	(02)	(03)	(04)	(05)	(06)	(07)	(08)	(09)	(10)
COMMONWEALTH OF INDEPENDENT STATES										
Armenia	0.00	0.00	0.10	0.10	0.00	0.10	0.00	0.00	0.00	0.10
Azerbaijan	0.20	0.10	0.20	0.10	0.10	0.20	0.10	0.10	0.10	0.20
Belarus	0.20	0.20	0.30	0.50	0.10	0.30	0.10	0.20	0.10	0.30
Kazakhstan	0.40	0.30	0.40	0.40	0.30	0.50	0.20	0.30	0.30	0.40
Kyrgyz Republic	0.00	0.00	0.00	0.10	0.00	0.10	0.00	0.00	0.00	0.10
Moldova	0.00	0.00	0.00	0.10	0.00	0.00	0.00	0.00	0.00	0.00
Russian Federation[e]	3.50	3.70	4.70	12.70	4.20	4.20	2.90	2.50	2.80	5.80
Tajikistan	0.00	0.00	0.10	0.00	0.00	0.10	0.00	0.00	0.00	0.10
Ukraine	0.40	0.60	1.00	1.70	0.40	1.00	0.40	0.60	0.40	0.40
Total (9)	**4.80**	**5.10**	**6.80**	**15.70**	**5.30**	**6.40**	**3.90**	**3.80**	**3.80**	**7.50**
EUROSTAT-OECD										
Albania	0.00	0.00	0.10	0.10	0.00	0.00	0.00	0.00	0.00	0.00
Australia	1.10	1.10	0.70	1.10	0.70	0.90	1.20	0.80	1.20	1.10
Austria	0.40	0.40	0.20	0.60	0.50	0.40	0.60	0.30	0.40	0.30
Belgium	0.50	0.50	0.40	0.70	0.40	0.40	0.60	0.50	0.50	0.30
Bosnia and Herzegovina	0.00	0.10	0.10	0.20	0.00	0.10	0.10	0.00	0.00	0.00
Bulgaria	0.10	0.10	0.10	0.10	0.00	0.20	0.20	0.20	0.10	0.20
Canada	1.60	1.60	0.80	1.50	1.40	1.70	1.80	1.40	2.30	1.20
Chile	0.40	0.40	0.30	0.40	0.40	0.30	0.50	0.30	0.50	0.40
Croatia	0.10	0.10	0.10	0.30	0.10	0.10	0.10	0.10	0.10	0.10
Cyprus	0.00	0.00	0.00	0.10	0.00	0.00	0.00	0.00	0.00	0.10
Czech Republic	0.30	0.30	0.30	0.90	0.10	0.30	0.30	0.40	0.20	0.20
Denmark	0.30	0.30	0.20	0.30	0.20	0.20	0.30	0.20	0.20	0.20
Estonia	0.00	0.00	0.00	0.10	0.00	0.00	0.00	0.00	0.00	0.00
Finland	0.20	0.20	0.20	0.40	0.20	0.20	0.30	0.20	0.20	0.20
France	2.60	3.00	2.50	3.50	2.40	2.80	3.40	2.90	3.30	2.30
Germany	3.70	4.00	2.70	5.10	3.50	3.60	5.20	4.40	4.00	4.00
Greece	0.30	0.40	0.40	0.70	0.30	0.50	0.40	0.40	0.40	0.30
Hungary	0.20	0.30	0.20	0.70	0.10	0.30	0.20	0.30	0.20	0.20
Iceland	0.00	0.00	0.00	0.00	0.00	0.00	0.00	0.00	0.00	0.00
Ireland	0.20	0.20	0.10	0.20	0.20	0.20	0.20	0.20	0.20	0.20
Israel	0.30	0.30	0.20	0.20	0.20	0.30	0.40	0.20	0.40	0.30
Italy	2.30	2.50	2.20	2.70	3.60	2.40	3.70	2.20	2.70	2.00
Japan	4.80	5.40	3.40	6.20	3.50	5.50	5.60	4.90	5.30	6.00
Korea, Rep.	1.60	1.50	0.80	1.30	1.00	1.70	1.00	1.70	1.50	2.70
Latvia	0.00	0.00	0.00	0.10	0.00	0.10	0.00	0.00	0.00	0.00
Lithuania	0.10	0.10	0.10	0.20	0.10	0.10	0.10	0.10	0.10	0.10

Recreation and culture	Education	Restaurants and hotels	Miscella-neous goods and services	Individual consumption expenditure by households	Individual consumption expenditure by government	Collective consumption expenditure by government	Gross fixed capital formation	Machinery and equipment	Construction	Domestic absorption	Individual consumption expenditure by households without housing
(11)	(12)	(13)	(14)	(16)	(17)	(18)	(19)	(20)	(21)	(25)	(26)
0.00	0.10	0.00	0.00	0.00	0.00	0.00	0.00	0.00	0.00	0.00	0.00
0.10	0.20	0.00	0.00	0.10	0.10	0.20	0.10	0.10	0.00	0.10	0.10
0.10	0.50	0.10	0.00	0.20	0.40	0.10	0.10	0.20	0.10	0.20	0.20
0.20	0.80	0.20	0.20	0.30	0.50	0.40	0.20	0.20	0.20	0.30	0.30
0.00	0.10	0.00	0.00	0.00	0.10	0.00	0.00	0.00	0.00	0.00	0.00
0.00	0.10	0.00	0.00	0.00	0.10	0.00	0.00	0.00	0.00	0.00	0.00
2.40	4.20	1.20	2.60	3.40	5.90	4.30	2.00	2.60	1.60	3.30	3.40
0.00	0.10	0.00	0.00	0.00	0.10	0.00	0.00	0.00	0.00	0.00	0.00
0.30	1.20	0.10	0.30	0.50	1.20	0.40	0.20	0.20	0.10	0.50	0.50
3.10	**7.20**	**1.70**	**3.30**	**4.70**	**8.40**	**5.50**	**2.60**	**3.40**	**2.10**	**4.50**	**4.60**
0.00	0.10	0.00	0.00	0.00	0.00	0.00	0.00	0.00	0.10	0.00	0.00
1.90	0.80	1.30	1.40	1.10	1.10	0.90	1.10	1.40	0.70	1.00	1.10
0.60	0.20	0.80	0.40	0.40	0.40	0.30	0.40	0.60	0.30	0.40	0.40
0.60	0.40	0.40	0.60	0.50	0.70	0.40	0.50	0.70	0.40	0.50	0.50
0.00	0.10	0.10	0.00	0.10	0.10	0.10	0.00	0.00	0.00	0.00	0.10
0.20	0.20	0.20	0.10	0.10	0.20	0.20	0.10	0.10	0.10	0.10	0.10
2.20	1.10	1.60	2.00	1.60	1.80	1.60	1.60	1.50	1.40	1.60	1.50
0.40	0.70	0.30	0.50	0.40	0.40	0.30	0.30	0.40	0.30	0.40	0.40
0.10	0.10	0.20	0.10	0.10	0.10	0.10	0.10	0.10	0.10	0.10	0.10
0.00	0.00	0.10	0.00	0.00	0.00	0.00	0.00	0.00	0.00	0.00	0.00
0.40	0.30	0.40	0.20	0.30	0.50	0.40	0.30	0.40	0.20	0.30	0.30
0.40	0.20	0.20	0.40	0.20	0.50	0.20	0.20	0.30	0.20	0.20	0.20
0.00	0.00	0.00	0.00	0.00	0.10	0.00	0.00	0.00	0.00	0.00	0.00
0.40	0.20	0.20	0.30	0.20	0.40	0.20	0.20	0.20	0.20	0.20	0.20
3.80	2.10	3.30	3.50	2.70	4.50	2.40	2.30	2.70	1.90	2.70	2.70
4.70	2.40	3.40	5.30	3.80	5.20	2.70	2.70	4.60	1.90	3.50	3.80
0.30	0.30	0.80	0.30	0.40	0.30	0.50	0.20	0.30	0.20	0.40	0.40
0.30	0.30	0.30	0.30	0.20	0.40	0.40	0.20	0.20	0.10	0.20	0.20
0.00	0.00	0.00	0.00	0.00	0.00	0.00	0.00	0.00	0.00	0.00	0.00
0.20	0.20	0.30	0.20	0.20	0.30	0.10	0.10	0.20	0.10	0.20	0.20
0.30	0.30	0.30	0.30	0.30	0.40	0.40	0.20	0.20	0.20	0.30	0.20
2.50	1.60	3.90	2.20	2.40	2.80	2.00	2.10	3.00	1.50	2.30	2.40
6.80	3.00	6.00	8.40	5.10	6.90	5.10	4.20	6.90	2.40	4.90	4.80
1.60	1.60	1.50	1.90	1.50	1.40	1.60	1.80	2.10	1.50	1.60	1.40
0.10	0.10	0.00	0.00	0.00	0.10	0.10	0.00	0.00	0.00	0.00	0.00
0.10	0.10	0.00	0.10	0.10	0.10	0.10	0.00	0.00	0.00	0.10	0.10

(continued)

Table 2.6 *(Continued)*

REAL EXPENDITURES: COUNTRY AND REGIONAL SHARES (world = 100)[a] Economy	Gross domestic product	Actual individual consumption	Food and nonalcoholic beverages	Alcoholic beverages, tobacco, and narcotics	Clothing and footwear	Housing, water, electricity, gas, and other fuels	Furnishings, household equipment and maintenance	Health	Transport	Communication
(00)	(01)	(02)	(03)	(04)	(05)	(06)	(07)	(08)	(09)	(10)
Luxembourg	0.10	0.00	0.00	0.20	0.00	0.00	0.10	0.00	0.10	0.00
Macedonia, FYR	0.00	0.00	0.10	0.00	0.00	0.00	0.00	0.00	0.00	0.00
Malta	0.00	0.00	0.00	0.00	0.00	0.00	0.00	0.00	0.00	0.00
Mexico	2.10	2.40	3.40	2.20	1.50	1.80	2.80	1.10	3.60	2.20
Montenegro	0.00	0.00	0.00	0.00	0.00	0.00	0.00	0.00	0.00	0.00
Netherlands	0.80	0.70	0.60	0.80	0.70	0.60	0.90	0.70	0.70	0.80
New Zealand	0.20	0.20	0.10	0.20	0.20	0.10	0.20	0.20	0.20	0.10
Norway	0.30	0.30	0.20	0.20	0.20	0.20	0.30	0.20	0.30	0.30
Poland	0.90	1.10	1.20	2.00	0.50	1.50	0.90	1.10	0.70	0.80
Portugal	0.30	0.30	0.40	0.50	0.30	0.30	0.40	0.30	0.30	0.30
Romania	0.40	0.40	0.60	0.60	0.20	0.40	0.30	0.60	0.30	0.50
Russian Federation[e]	3.50	3.70	4.70	12.70	4.20	4.20	2.90	2.50	2.80	5.80
Serbia	0.10	0.10	0.20	0.30	0.00	0.20	0.10	0.10	0.10	0.20
Slovak Republic	0.10	0.20	0.10	0.20	0.10	0.20	0.20	0.20	0.10	0.10
Slovenia	0.10	0.10	0.10	0.20	0.10	0.10	0.10	0.10	0.10	0.10
Spain	1.60	1.70	1.70	2.20	1.90	1.50	1.80	1.50	1.60	1.00
Sweden	0.40	0.40	0.30	0.50	0.40	0.50	0.40	0.40	0.40	0.70
Switzerland	0.40	0.40	0.30	0.80	0.30	0.30	0.50	0.40	0.40	0.50
Turkey	1.50	1.70	2.00	1.60	1.80	2.20	2.80	1.20	1.90	1.30
United Kingdom	2.40	2.80	1.80	2.60	4.00	2.30	3.00	2.50	3.00	2.10
United States	17.10	20.00	10.20	14.40	15.50	17.70	21.20	24.70	25.30	15.40
Total (47)	**53.70**	**59.40**	**44.30**	**70.20**	**51.00**	**56.70**	**65.00**	**59.70**	**65.80**	**54.60**
LATIN AMERICA										
Bolivia	0.10	0.10	0.10	0.00	0.00	0.10	0.10	0.00	0.10	0.00
Brazil	3.10	3.30	3.60	3.00	1.50	2.40	4.90	3.80	3.70	1.90
Colombia	0.60	0.60	0.60	0.70	0.60	0.90	0.40	0.40	0.60	0.50
Costa Rica	0.10	0.10	0.10	0.00	0.10	0.00	0.10	0.10	0.10	0.10
Cuba[f]	...	...	...	...	...	...	...	...	...	...
Dominican Republic	0.10	0.20	0.20	0.30	0.10	0.20	0.10	0.10	0.20	0.20
Ecuador	0.20	0.20	0.20	0.20	0.10	0.20	0.20	0.10	0.20	0.20
El Salvador	0.10	0.10	0.10	0.00	0.10	0.10	0.10	0.00	0.10	0.10
Guatemala	0.10	0.20	0.30	0.10	0.10	0.20	0.20	0.10	0.10	0.30
Haiti	0.00	0.00	0.10	0.00	0.00	0.00	0.00	0.00	0.00	0.00
Honduras	0.00	0.10	0.10	0.10	0.00	0.10	0.00	0.00	0.00	0.00
Nicaragua	0.00	0.00	0.00	0.00	0.00	0.10	0.00	0.00	0.00	0.00
Panama	0.10	0.10	0.10	0.00	0.10	0.10	0.10	0.00	0.10	0.10
Paraguay	0.10	0.10	0.10	0.00	0.00	0.10	0.10	0.00	0.00	0.10
Peru	0.40	0.40	0.50	0.30	0.30	0.30	0.30	0.20	0.40	0.40

Recreation and culture	Education	Restaurants and hotels	Miscella-neous goods and services	Individual consumption expenditure by households	Individual consumption expenditure by government	Collective consumption expenditure by government	Gross fixed capital formation	Machinery and equipment	Construction	Domestic absorption	Individual consumption expenditure by households without housing
(11)	(12)	(13)	(14)	(16)	(17)	(18)	(19)	(20)	(21)	(25)	(26)
0.00	0.00	0.00	0.00	0.00	0.00	0.00	0.10	0.10	0.00	0.00	0.00
0.00	0.10	0.00	0.00	0.00	0.00	0.10	0.00	0.00	0.00	0.00	0.00
0.00	0.00	0.00	0.00	0.00	0.00	0.00	0.00	0.00	0.00	0.00	0.00
1.40	4.60	1.60	2.00	2.20	2.70	2.00	1.60	1.40	1.80	2.10	2.30
0.00	0.00	0.00	0.00	0.00	0.00	0.00	0.00	0.00	0.00	0.00	0.00
1.00	0.60	0.50	1.20	0.60	1.30	0.90	0.60	0.80	0.50	0.70	0.70
0.20	0.20	0.20	0.20	0.20	0.20	0.20	0.10	0.10	0.10	0.20	0.20
0.40	0.20	0.20	0.30	0.20	0.40	0.30	0.30	0.40	0.20	0.30	0.20
1.20	1.20	0.40	1.10	1.00	1.50	1.00	0.60	0.70	0.50	1.00	1.00
0.30	0.30	0.70	0.30	0.30	0.40	0.30	0.30	0.20	0.30	0.30	0.30
0.40	0.60	0.20	0.20	0.40	0.70	0.50	0.40	0.30	0.50	0.40	0.40
2.40	4.20	1.20	2.70	3.40	5.90	4.30	2.00	2.60	1.60	3.30	3.40
0.10	0.20	0.00	0.10	0.10	0.20	0.10	0.10	0.10	0.10	0.10	0.10
0.20	0.20	0.10	0.10	0.10	0.20	0.20	0.10	0.10	0.10	0.20	0.10
0.10	0.10	0.10	0.10	0.10	0.10	0.10	0.10	0.10	0.10	0.10	0.10
2.20	1.30	4.90	1.50	1.60	2.10	1.80	1.60	1.60	1.30	1.70	1.70
0.60	0.30	0.30	0.60	0.40	0.80	0.40	0.30	0.60	0.20	0.40	0.40
0.60	0.20	0.50	0.60	0.60	0.20	0.20	0.40	0.80	0.20	0.40	0.40
1.00	3.10	1.50	1.00	1.60	2.20	1.30	1.20	1.90	1.00	1.60	1.50
5.20	1.90	3.70	3.10	2.70	3.40	2.40	1.70	1.40	1.30	2.50	2.80
29.90	10.50	24.40	27.30	22.30	8.00	19.00	13.40	21.30	7.20	18.00	22.80
75.20	**46.20**	**66.30**	**71.10**	**59.70**	**59.40**	**55.40**	**43.80**	**60.40**	**30.70**	**54.70**	**59.90**
0.00	0.10	0.10	0.00	0.10	0.00	0.10	0.00	0.10	0.00	0.10	0.10
1.90	4.20	3.10	3.60	3.10	4.10	3.80	2.90	3.10	2.50	3.20	3.20
0.50	0.80	1.00	0.60	0.70	0.40	0.70	0.50	0.40	0.60	0.60	0.60
0.10	0.10	0.10	0.00	0.10	0.10	0.10	0.00	0.00	0.10	0.10	0.10
...	...	...	...	...	...	...	...	...	...	...	...
0.00	0.20	0.30	0.20	0.20	0.00	0.10	0.10	0.00	0.10	0.10	0.20
0.10	0.30	0.10	0.10	0.20	0.10	0.10	0.20	0.10	0.10	0.20	0.20
0.00	0.10	0.10	0.00	0.10	0.00	0.00	0.00	0.00	0.00	0.10	0.10
0.10	0.10	0.20	0.10	0.20	0.10	0.10	0.10	0.10	0.10	0.10	0.20
0.00	0.00	0.00	0.00	0.00	0.00	0.00	0.00	0.00	0.00	0.00	0.00
0.00	0.10	0.10	0.00	0.10	0.00	0.00	0.00	0.00	0.00	0.00	0.10
0.00	0.00	0.00	0.00	0.00	0.00	0.00	0.00	0.00	0.00	0.00	0.00
0.00	0.10	0.10	0.10	0.10	0.00	0.10	0.10	0.10	0.10	0.10	0.10
0.00	0.10	0.00	0.00	0.10	0.00	0.00	0.00	0.00	0.00	0.10	0.10
0.30	0.50	0.50	0.30	0.40	0.20	0.30	0.30	0.20	0.40	0.30	0.40

(continued)

Table 2.6 *(Continued)*

REAL EXPENDITURES: COUNTRY AND REGIONAL SHARES (world = 100)[a] Economy	Gross domestic product	Actual individual consumption	Food and nonalcoholic beverages	Alcoholic beverages, tobacco, and narcotics	Clothing and footwear	Housing, water, electricity, gas, and other fuels	Furnishings, household equipment and maintenance	Health	Transport	Communication
(00)	(01)	(02)	(03)	(04)	(05)	(06)	(07)	(08)	(09)	(10)
Uruguay	0.10	0.10	0.10	0.10	0.00	0.10	0.10	0.10	0.10	0.10
Venezuela, RB	0.60	0.50	0.40	0.30	0.20	0.40	0.30	0.40	1.10	1.00
Total (17)	**5.50**	**5.80**	**6.70**	**5.20**	**3.30**	**5.10**	**7.10**	**5.50**	**7.00**	**5.20**
CARIBBEAN										
Anguilla	0.00	0.00	0.00	0.00	0.00	0.00	0.00	0.00	0.00	0.00
Antigua and Barbuda	0.00	0.00	0.00	0.00	0.00	0.00	0.00	0.00	0.00	0.00
Aruba	0.00	0.00	0.00	0.00	0.00	0.00	0.00	0.00	0.00	0.00
Bahamas, The	0.00	0.00	0.00	0.00	0.00	0.00	0.00	0.00	0.00	0.00
Barbados	0.00	0.00	0.00	0.00	0.00	0.00	0.00	0.00	0.00	0.00
Belize	0.00	0.00	0.00	0.00	0.00	0.00	0.00	0.00	0.00	0.00
Bermuda	0.00	0.00	0.00	0.00	0.00	0.00	0.00	0.00	0.00	0.00
Bonaire[g]	...	...	...	...	...	...	...	...	...	...
Cayman Islands	0.00	0.00	0.00	0.00	0.00	0.00	0.00	0.00	0.00	0.00
Curaçao	0.00	0.00	0.00	0.00	0.00	0.00	0.00	0.00	0.00	0.00
Dominica	0.00	0.00	0.00	0.00	0.00	0.00	0.00	0.00	0.00	0.00
Grenada	0.00	0.00	0.00	0.00	0.00	0.00	0.00	0.00	0.00	0.00
Jamaica	0.00	0.00	0.00	0.00	0.00	0.00	0.00	0.00	0.00	0.00
Montserrat	0.00	0.00	0.00	0.00	0.00	0.00	0.00	0.00	0.00	0.00
St. Kitts and Nevis	0.00	0.00	0.00	0.00	0.00	0.00	0.00	0.00	0.00	0.00
St. Lucia	0.00	0.00	0.00	0.00	0.00	0.00	0.00	0.00	0.00	0.00
St. Vincent and the Grenadines	0.00	0.00	0.00	0.00	0.00	0.00	0.00	0.00	0.00	0.00
Sint Maarten	0.00	0.00	0.00	0.00	0.00	0.00	0.00	0.00	0.00	0.00
Suriname	0.00	0.00	0.00	0.00	0.00	0.00	0.00	0.00	0.00	0.00
Trinidad and Tobago	0.00	0.00	0.00	0.00	0.00	0.00	0.00	0.00	0.00	0.00
Turks and Caicos Islands	0.00	0.00	0.00	0.00	0.00	0.00	0.00	0.00	0.00	0.00
Virgin Islands, British	0.00	0.00	0.00	0.00	0.00	0.00	0.00	0.00	0.00	0.00
Total (22)	**0.10**	**0.10**	**0.10**	**0.10**	**0.10**	**0.20**	**0.10**	**0.10**	**0.10**	**0.10**
WESTERN ASIA										
Bahrain	0.10	0.00	0.00	0.00	0.00	0.10	0.00	0.10	0.10	
Egypt, Arab Rep.[b]	0.90	1.20	1.90	0.90	1.40	1.80	0.80	1.30	0.70	0.90
Iraq	0.40	0.30	0.40	0.00	0.30	0.70	0.20	0.20	0.20	0.20
Jordan	0.10	0.10	0.10	0.10	0.10	0.20	0.10	0.10	0.10	0.10
Kuwait	0.30	0.10	0.10	0.00	0.20	0.20	0.30	0.10	0.10	0.10
Oman	0.20	0.10	0.10	0.00	0.10	0.10	0.10	0.00	0.20	0.10
Qatar	0.30	0.10	0.10	0.00	0.10	0.10	0.10	0.00	0.10	0.10
Saudi Arabia	1.50	0.90	0.70	0.10	0.90	1.60	1.20	0.50	0.80	1.10
Sudan[c]	0.20	0.20	0.40	0.00	0.30	0.20	0.20	0.00	0.10	0.10
United Arab Emirates	0.60	0.40	0.30	0.00	1.30	0.80	0.40	0.00	1.00	1.10
West Bank and Gaza	0.00	0.00	0.10	0.00	0.00	0.00	0.00	0.00	0.00	0.00

Recreation and culture	Education	Restaurants and hotels	Miscellaneous goods and services	Individual consumption expenditure by households	Individual consumption expenditure by government	Collective consumption expenditure by government	Gross fixed capital formation	Machinery and equipment	Construction	Domestic absorption	Individual consumption expenditure by households without housing
(11)	(12)	(13)	(14)	(16)	(17)	(18)	(19)	(20)	(21)	(25)	(26)
0.00	0.10	0.10	0.10	0.10	0.10	0.00	0.10	0.00	0.10	0.10	0.10
0.30	0.90	0.80	0.20	0.50	0.40	0.50	0.40	0.30	0.50	0.50	0.50
3.50	**7.50**	**6.50**	**5.40**	**5.80**	**5.60**	**6.10**	**4.70**	**4.60**	**4.60**	**5.50**	**5.90**
0.00	0.00	0.00	0.00	0.00	0.00	0.00	0.00	0.00	0.00	0.00	0.00
0.00	0.00	0.00	0.00	0.00	0.00	0.00	0.00	0.00	0.00	0.00	0.00
0.00	0.00	0.00	0.00	0.00	0.00	0.00	0.00	0.00	0.00	0.00	0.00
0.00	0.00	0.00	0.00	0.00	0.00	0.00	0.00	0.00	0.00	0.00	0.00
0.00	0.00	0.00	0.00	0.00	0.00	0.00	0.00	0.00	0.00	0.00	0.00
0.00	0.00	0.00	0.00	0.00	0.00	0.00	0.00	0.00	0.00	0.00	0.00
0.00	0.00	0.00	0.00	0.00	0.00	0.00	0.00	0.00	0.00	0.00	0.00
...	...	...	...	...	...	...	...	...	...	...	...
0.00	0.00	0.00	0.00	0.00	0.00	0.00	0.00	0.00	0.00	0.00	0.00
0.00	0.00	0.00	0.00	0.00	0.00	0.00	0.00	0.00	0.00	0.00	0.00
0.00	0.00	0.00	0.00	0.00	0.00	0.00	0.00	0.00	0.00	0.00	0.00
0.00	0.00	0.00	0.00	0.00	0.00	0.00	0.00	0.00	0.00	0.00	0.00
0.00	0.00	0.10	0.00	0.00	0.00	0.00	0.00	0.00	0.00	0.00	0.00
0.00	0.00	0.00	0.00	0.00	0.00	0.00	0.00	0.00	0.00	0.00	0.00
0.00	0.00	0.00	0.00	0.00	0.00	0.00	0.00	0.00	0.00	0.00	0.00
0.00	0.00	0.00	0.00	0.00	0.00	0.00	0.00	0.00	0.00	0.00	0.00
0.00	0.00	0.00	0.00	0.00	0.00	0.00	0.00	0.00	0.00	0.00	0.00
0.00	0.00	0.00	0.00	0.00	0.00	0.00	0.00	0.00	0.00	0.00	0.00
0.00	0.00	0.00	0.00	0.00	0.00	0.00	0.00	0.00	0.00	0.00	0.00
0.00	0.10	0.00	0.00	0.00	0.10	0.00	0.00	0.00	0.00	0.00	0.00
0.00	0.00	0.00	0.00	0.00	0.00	0.00	0.00	0.00	0.00	0.00	0.00
0.00	0.00	0.00	0.00	0.00	0.00	0.00	0.00	0.00	0.00	0.00	0.00
0.10	**0.20**	**0.20**	**0.10**	**0.10**	**0.10**	**0.10**	**0.10**	**0.10**	**0.10**	**0.10**	**0.10**
0.00	0.00	0.00	0.00	0.00	0.00	0.10	0.00	0.00	0.10	0.00	0.00
0.50	1.60	0.50	0.70	1.20	0.80	1.50	0.40	0.30	0.50	1.00	1.10
0.00	0.70	0.00	0.10	0.30	0.50	1.10	0.30	0.30	0.30	0.30	0.20
0.00	0.20	0.00	0.00	0.10	0.10	0.10	0.10	0.00	0.10	0.10	0.10
0.10	0.10	0.00	0.00	0.10	0.10	0.30	0.20	0.20	0.20	0.10	0.10
0.00	0.10	0.00	0.10	0.10	0.10	0.20	0.20	0.20	0.20	0.10	0.10
0.10	0.10	0.00	0.10	0.10	0.10	0.20	0.50	0.50	0.20	0.10	0.10
0.40	1.50	0.50	0.40	0.80	1.20	1.60	1.70	1.40	1.80	1.20	0.70
0.10	0.10	0.10	0.00	0.20	0.00	0.20	0.20	0.10	0.20	0.20	0.20
0.20	0.20	0.20	0.20	0.50	0.00	0.30	0.70	0.70	0.70	0.40	0.50
0.00	0.00	0.00	0.00	0.00	0.00	0.10	0.00	0.00	0.00	0.00	0.00

(continued)

Table 2.6 *(Continued)*

REAL EXPENDITURES: COUNTRY AND REGIONAL SHARES (world = 100)[a] Economy	Gross domestic product	Actual individual consumption	Food and nonalcoholic beverages	Alcoholic beverages, tobacco, and narcotics	Clothing and footwear	Housing, water, electricity, gas, and other fuels	Furnishings, household equipment and maintenance	Health	Transport	Communication
(00)	(01)	(02)	(03)	(04)	(05)	(06)	(07)	(08)	(09)	(10)
Yemen, Rep.	0.10	0.10	0.20	0.20	0.10	0.20	0.10	0.10	0.10	0.00
Total (12)	**4.50**	**3.50**	**4.50**	**1.50**	**4.70**	**5.80**	**3.60**	**2.50**	**3.50**	**3.90**
SINGLETONS										
Georgia	0.00	0.00	0.10	0.10	0.00	0.10	0.00	0.10	0.00	0.10
Iran, Islamic Rep.	1.40	1.10	1.20	0.30	0.60	2.00	0.60	1.20	0.70	1.90
Total (2)	**1.50**	**1.20**	**1.30**	**0.40**	**0.60**	**2.10**	**0.70**	**1.30**	**0.80**	**2.00**
WORLD[h] (179)	**100.00**	**100.00**	**100.00**	**100.00**	**100.00**	**100.00**	**100.00**	**100.00**	**100.00**	**100.00**

Source: ICP, http://icp.worldbank.org/.

Note: n.a. = not applicable; ... = data suppressed because of incompleteness.

a. All shares are rounded to one decimal place. More precision can be found in the Excel version of the table, which can be downloaded from the ICP website.

b. The Arab Republic of Egypt participated in both the Africa and Western Asia regions. The regional results for Egypt were averaged by taking the geometric mean of the regional PPPs, allowing Egypt to have the same global results in each region.

c. Sudan participated in both the Africa and Western Asia regions. The regional results for Sudan were averaged by taking the geometric mean of the regional PPPs, allowing Sudan to have the same global results in each region.

d. The results presented in the tables are based on data supplied by all the participating economies and compiled in accordance with ICP principles and the procedures recommended by the 2011 ICP Technical Advisory Group. The results for China are estimated by the 2011 ICP Asia and the Pacific Regional Office and the Global Office. The National Bureau of Statistics of China does not recognize these results as official statistics.

e. The Russian Federation participated in both the CIS and Eurostat-OECD comparisons. The PPPs for Russia are based on the Eurostat-OECD comparison. They were the basis for linking the CIS comparison to the ICP.

f. The official GDP of Cuba for reference year 2011 is 68,990.15 million in national currency. However, this number and its breakdown into main aggregates are not shown in the tables because of methodological comparability issues. Therefore, Cuba's results are provided only for the PPP and price level index. In addition, Cuba's figures are not included in the Latin America and world totals.

g. Bonaire's results are provided only for the individual consumption expenditure by households. Therefore, to ensure consistency across the tables, Bonaire is not included in the Caribbean or the world total.

h. This table does not include the Pacific Islands and does not double count the dual participation economies: the Arab Republic of Egypt, Sudan, and the Russian Federation.

Recreation and culture	Education	Restaurants and hotels	Miscella-neous goods and services	Individual consumption expenditure by households	Individual consumption expenditure by government	Collective consumption expenditure by government	Gross fixed capital formation	Machinery and equipment	Construction	Domestic absorption	Individual consumption expenditure by households without housing
(11)	(12)	(13)	(14)	(16)	(17)	(18)	(19)	(20)	(21)	(25)	(26)
0.00	0.10	0.00	0.00	0.10	0.10	0.20	0.00	0.00	0.10	0.10	0.10
1.40	4.80	1.60	1.60	3.50	3.10	5.70	4.40	3.80	4.10	3.80	3.30
0.00	0.10	0.00	0.00	0.00	0.00	0.10	0.00	0.00	0.00	0.00	0.00
0.40	2.00	0.20	0.80	1.10	1.20	2.50	1.00	1.00	1.30	1.30	1.00
0.40	2.10	0.20	0.80	1.10	1.20	2.60	1.10	1.00	1.30	1.30	1.00
100.00	100.00	100.00	100.00	100.00	100.00	100.00	100.00	100.00	100.00	100.00	100.00

Table 2.7 Real Expenditures Per Capita in U.S. Dollars, ICP 2011

REAL EXPENDITURES PER CAPITA (US$) Economy	Gross domestic product	Actual individual consumption	Food and nonalcoholic beverages	Alcoholic beverages, tobacco, and narcotics	Clothing and footwear	Housing, water, electricity, gas, and other fuels	Furnishings, household equipment and maintenance	Health	Transport	Communication
(00)	(01)	(02)	(03)	(04)	(05)	(06)	(07)	(08)	(09)	(10)
AFRICA										
Algeria	13,195	6,270	1,071	69	126	366	110	985	658	285
Angola	7,288	4,319	1,050	288	182	579	159	325	190	35
Benin	1,766	1,473	397	45	63	170	27	86	85	38
Botswana	13,409	6,780	758	379	469	688	243	626	889	208
Burkina Faso	1,343	953	258	58	22	143	29	61	39	26
Burundi	712	648	152	53	7	178	4	46	18	4
Cameroon	2,757	2,297	641	54	150	294	121	48	122	20
Cape Verde	6,126	4,747	997	196	104	983	262	444	206	194
Central African Republic	897	869	248	71	69	82	27	26	21	4
Chad	1,984	1,476	404	58	34	155	62	196	93	35
Comoros	610	621	180	1	17	260	12	10	8	2
Congo, Rep.	5,830	1,513	281	64	37	339	36	227	78	52
Congo, Dem. Rep.	655	447	121	10	20	95	12	41	8	4
Côte d'Ivoire	2,669	1,979	480	57	57	271	120	170	139	37
Djibouti	2,412	1,719	319	124	48	669	71	80	72	6
Egypt, Arab Rep.[a]	10,599	8,529	1,670	159	402	2,514	210	1,505	352	183
Equatorial Guinea	39,440	4,916	962	147	151	961	111	847	285	182
Ethiopia	1,214	979	202	19	43	172	59	166	10	4
Gabon	16,483	5,976	916	504	289	1,051	217	685	458	181
Gambia, The	1,507	1,221	258	32	129	105	23	412	24	38
Ghana	3,426	2,242	380	26	333	349	113	192	138	34
Guinea	1,287	789	197	10	59	186	23	113	28	1
Guinea-Bissau	1,365	928	262	14	64	161	40	50	41	4
Kenya	2,136	1,937	384	69	53	229	63	271	101	74
Lesotho	2,130	2,524	399	52	310	366	136	197	55	60
Liberia	537	606	87	17	90	121	28	26	11	17
Madagascar	1,412	1,332	323	34	106	87	131	52	87	7
Malawi	973	1,006	256	44	31	244	64	97	33	14
Mali	1,509	1,047	291	15	58	112	39	90	75	18
Mauritania	3,191	2,089	697	17	85	258	42	153	63	59
Mauritius	15,506	11,812	2,127	616	802	2,597	646	1,148	805	416
Morocco	6,764	4,309	840	67	157	1,118	139	348	263	192
Mozambique	951	890	260	37	45	105	15	39	50	9
Namibia	8,360	5,827	690	231	362	1,021	372	1,004	175	56
Niger	852	719	156	14	75	89	31	49	36	10
Nigeria	3,146	2,075	387	31	345	263	139	151	108	27
Rwanda	1,337	1,293	367	32	36	319	36	66	40	13
São Tomé and Príncipe	3,045	3,340	972	134	121	384	73	300	217	35

Recreation and culture	Education	Restaurants and hotels	Miscellaneous goods and services	Individual consumption expenditure by households	Individual consumption expenditure by government	Collective consumption expenditure by government	Gross fixed capital formation	Machinery and equipment	Construction	Domestic absorption	Individual consumption expenditure by households without housing
(11)	(12)	(13)	(14)	(16)	(17)	(18)	(19)	(20)	(21)	(25)	(26)
153	2,383	120	1,078	3,983	4,311	2,202	3,054	585	2,922	11,890	3,787
61	547	70	508	3,423	1,122	2,319	1,493	207	1,800	7,757	3,039
16	195	96	62	1,286	138	191	261	45	290	1,919	1,096
152	2,447	170	596	5,396	1,801	1,848	5,051	819	6,049	14,305	4,794
15	102	28	30	840	69	245	168	31	159	1,424	712
4	161	19	16	537	125	145	83	16	77	845	392
24	137	103	60	2,063	105	298	411	104	322	2,966	1,760
35	967	529	324	3,907	945	766	2,374	471	2,246	8,133	3,164
11	116	13	35	770	54	47	108	16	97	1,012	679
30	83	7	39	1,316	75	111	403	89	293	2,040	1,121
4	52	0	18	563	8	180	72	16	62	866	375
30	311	88	63	1,265	256	325	1,492	146	2,023	3,546	1,064
5	79	16	10	393	31	91	120	23	117	653	317
43	191	24	105	1,746	164	238	243	38	275	2,247	1,482
14	284	11	39	1,482	206	566	626	89	804	2,963	1,091
205	1,789	179	612	7,218	1,206	1,568	1,070	201	1,051	10,892	5,633
59	788	129	284	4,340	482	497	13,909	3,019	9,000	18,710	3,692
4	159	46	129	863	65	106	213	26	250	1,321	755
131	691	205	219	5,104	823	1,836	2,921	454	1,229	10,609	4,304
33	311	7	66	1,051	141	167	261	63	190	1,640	932
18	1,017	1	104	1,868	398	474	843	159	837	3,601	1,665
5	118	7	21	701	32	102	197	56	121	1,116	554
25	106	3	17	810	72	374	136	26	133	1,362	719
50	566	92	164	1,563	437	178	325	75	289	2,417	1,301
77	476	20	173	2,098	462	462	495	57	645	3,456	1,714
10	287	3	52	551	6	84	63	23	16	779	453
49	164	53	25	1,187	73	110	156	28	165	1,557	1,082
15	119	14	28	885	90	57	131	42	49	1,151	706
33	137	11	32	905	113	241	251	50	238	1,525	784
16	435	8	40	1,699	469	643	1,234	264	989	3,356	1,436
679	2,453	223	762	9,927	2,015	1,928	3,637	515	4,298	17,674	8,603
154	1,157	175	285	3,495	967	789	2,160	341	2,493	7,580	2,706
19	106	8	58	782	82	54	138	25	151	1,082	664
202	2,519	227	670	4,689	1,382	1,506	2,021	310	2,387	9,109	3,939
28	104	25	48	637	47	94	245	59	205	1,071	557
19	670	1	108	1,768	281	364	261	65	185	2,634	1,620
15	132	30	49	1,178	62	87	200	22	262	1,538	924
33	547	30	81	2,864	415	484	553	159	243	4,372	2,469

(continued)

Table 2.7 (Continued)

REAL EXPENDITURES PER CAPITA (US$) Economy	Gross domestic product	Actual individual consumption	Food and nonalcoholic beverages	Alcoholic beverages, tobacco, and narcotics	Clothing and footwear	Housing, water, electricity, gas, and other fuels	Furnishings, household equipment and maintenance	Health	Transport	Communication
(00)	(01)	(02)	(03)	(04)	(05)	(06)	(07)	(08)	(09)	(10)
Senegal	2,243	1,923	531	21	73	473	88	101	58	73
Seychelles	22,569	13,113	3,040	158	462	3,668	358	1,936	455	235
Sierra Leone	1,369	1,194	228	37	130	158	25	431	21	20
South Africa	12,111	8,280	1,054	347	318	1,295	313	1,235	729	243
Sudan[b]	3,608	2,309	666	9	154	403	112	74	111	32
Swaziland	6,328	5,822	1,701	41	291	908	434	728	299	77
Tanzania	1,554	1,029	386	5	76	75	32	94	26	1
Togo	1,314	1,193	269	27	63	131	37	151	34	15
Tunisia	10,319	7,290	937	147	307	1,394	298	842	742	361
Uganda	1,597	1,390	283	60	37	273	52	73	44	22
Zambia	3,155	1,778	618	11	110	290	17	190	12	21
Zimbabwe	1,378	1,349	449	50	63	108	21	68	57	2
Total (50)	**4,044**	**2,786**	**551**	**68**	**167**	**509**	**106**	**341**	**161**	**65**
ASIA AND THE PACIFIC										
Bangladesh	2,800	2,138	633	53	113	518	50	167	42	31
Bhutan	7,199	3,998	751	55	307	826	43	785	240	142
Brunei Darussalam	74,397	15,683	2,160	32	564	2,374	300	1,288	2,187	544
Cambodia	2,717	2,277	606	22	50	325	30	423	91	5
China[c]	10,057	4,331	551	59	240	791	127	1,120	191	215
Fiji	7,558	5,397	1,186	148	154	1,063	339	491	285	20
Hong Kong SAR, China	50,129	32,690	2,648	267	1,884	5,752	1,396	2,996	1,570	1,458
India	4,735	3,023	571	57	245	536	65	377	221	40
Indonesia	8,539	4,805	1,102	47	137	1,200	98	242	216	89
Lao PDR	4,108	2,341	576	88	39	565	39	130	108	39
Macao SAR, China	115,441	23,649	1,538	176	1,351	3,831	291	2,230	1,496	1,082
Malaysia	20,926	11,082	1,225	91	165	2,388	286	1,044	940	546
Maldives	11,392	3,883	619	256	104	780	128	599	118	152
Mongolia	8,719	5,501	900	377	202	826	38	797	583	117
Myanmar	3,181	2,273	592	27	68	388	18	402	29	28
Nepal	2,221	1,848	641	42	53	299	24	208	20	25
Pakistan	4,450	3,926	973	32	159	1,214	71	663	127	75
Philippines	5,772	4,490	1,175	58	47	656	133	200	305	85
Singapore	72,296	24,725	1,263	197	805	3,748	964	2,846	2,079	582
Sri Lanka	8,111	6,393	1,489	412	200	1,247	87	797	255	153
Taiwan, China	39,059	25,129	1,854	385	1,209	4,202	673	4,768	1,801	1,572
Thailand	13,299	8,477	1,308	180	303	1,251	199	1,083	690	196
Vietnam	4,717	2,991	438	89	134	654	118	666	121	19
Total (23)	**7,621**	**4,083**	**674**	**64**	**223**	**783**	**104**	**713**	**223**	**132**

Recreation and culture	Education	Restaurants and hotels	Miscella-neous goods and services	Individual consumption expenditure by households	Individual consumption expenditure by government	Collective consumption expenditure by government	Gross fixed capital formation	Machinery and equipment	Construction	Domestic absorption	Individual consumption expenditure by households without housing
(11)	(12)	(13)	(14)	(16)	(17)	(18)	(19)	(20)	(21)	(25)	(26)
20	264	12	84	1,691	162	271	432	79	468	2,641	1,365
258	4,315	30	385	10,102	4,702	9,108	5,830	1,251	5,169	27,324	7,830
34	243	11	67	1,053	74	153	419	114	268	1,800	895
280	1,751	118	957	6,772	1,686	1,349	2,386	570	1,888	12,299	5,521
44	232	53	59	2,069	57	462	783	155	787	3,660	1,752
197	819	27	90	5,152	514	557	628	89	668	6,915	4,230
8	123	0	25	917	63	216	497	65	718	1,767	850
9	346	67	170	1,031	125	143	173	23	217	1,507	892
171	2,010	499	482	5,758	2,078	1,451	2,166	226	3,326	10,970	4,595
64	481	30	69	1,156	256	28	331	28	572	1,790	981
10	204	4	119	1,555	170	517	650	79	860	2,967	1,322
22	263	5	85	1,134	216	159	117	19	137	1,650	1,001
62	**647**	**58**	**221**	**2,304**	**541**	**555**	**710**	**134**	**713**	**4,037**	**1,935**
11	363	43	58	1,923	85	126	672	58	1,004	2,985	1,595
201	931	47	76	3,127	1,152	1,296	3,629	561	4,325	9,202	2,585
990	5,279	620	764	12,190	4,512	12,332	8,273	1,452	8,057	33,145	10,092
52	707	103	47	1,907	378	150	274	50	288	2,722	1,580
259	864	223	293	3,277	1,426	647	4,265	593	4,643	9,709	2,714
221	897	124	231	4,611	727	622	1,581	361	1,009	7,949	3,801
4,636	1,788	3,238	5,484	30,104	1,906	2,225	11,527	3,101	7,540	47,081	24,815
33	349	51	336	2,672	264	406	1,172	176	1,338	4,960	2,214
88	1,171	315	227	4,110	637	564	2,701	179	4,156	8,389	3,399
41	765	51	50	1,975	311	629	1,246	130	1,296	4,212	1,640
2,497	4,105	4,203	2,256	19,887	4,223	4,007	13,222	1,905	15,545	42,562	16,442
393	2,720	979	1,129	9,105	2,251	1,642	4,284	744	3,656	17,278	7,539
78	1,580	98	116	2,934	1,373	3,369	5,607	1,159	5,488	12,091	2,374
115	2,387	78	205	4,354	1,583	1,038	3,277	868	2,177	10,941	3,597
20	1,405	96	41	1,727	783	266	645	108	630	3,206	1,433
38	371	34	59	1,633	143	148	356	32	373	2,677	1,353
35	551	28	172	3,491	257	404	416	48	415	4,685	2,898
64	952	151	431	4,013	309	338	1,005	157	964	5,952	3,327
3,564	3,994	3,104	3,030	21,444	3,061	4,984	18,936	4,137	16,692	47,087	17,683
77	1,329	153	263	5,185	1,531	977	1,654	199	2,032	9,147	4,299
2,258	4,221	1,466	3,141	22,169	2,482	3,312	7,563	1,883	5,292	36,175	18,317
326	1,854	739	605	6,998	1,658	1,200	3,258	890	2,036	12,997	5,800
106	1,253	122	87	2,446	661	533	1,141	116	1,508	4,906	2,022
161	**756**	**179**	**324**	**3,370**	**811**	**552**	**2,515**	**359**	**2,781**	**7,486**	**2,791**

(continued)

Table 2.7 (Continued)

REAL EXPENDITURES PER CAPITA (US$) Economy	Gross domestic product	Actual individual consumption	Food and nonalcoholic beverages	Alcoholic beverages, tobacco, and narcotics	Clothing and footwear	Housing, water, electricity, gas, and other fuels	Furnishings, household equipment and maintenance	Health	Transport	Communication
(00)	(01)	(02)	(03)	(04)	(05)	(06)	(07)	(08)	(09)	(10)
COMMONWEALTH OF INDEPENDENT STATES										
Armenia	6,696	7,304	1,977	379	125	1,972	55	847	198	272
Azerbaijan	15,963	8,366	1,755	216	384	2,169	228	598	435	331
Belarus	16,603	11,576	2,020	792	324	3,170	239	1,878	422	567
Kazakhstan	20,772	11,411	1,560	364	431	3,098	293	1,714	742	433
Kyrgyz Republic	3,062	3,506	621	197	113	1,096	65	339	171	227
Moldova	4,179	5,653	940	441	161	1,381	222	369	265	188
Russian Federation[d]	22,502	15,175	2,236	1,275	702	3,279	415	1,638	828	652
Tajikistan	2,243	3,025	634	10	101	790	44	336	88	243
Ukraine	8,295	7,907	1,475	528	197	2,468	176	1,236	400	150
Total (9)	**17,716**	**12,286**	**1,913**	**928**	**515**	**2,899**	**321**	**1,441**	**658**	**494**
EUROSTAT-OECD										
Albania	9,963	8,116	1,860	254	181	1,182	294	880	181	86
Australia	42,000	27,089	2,164	702	773	4,398	1,110	3,336	2,338	786
Austria	42,978	27,677	2,017	1,091	1,454	5,504	1,363	3,308	2,225	577
Belgium	40,093	26,250	2,552	909	941	4,434	1,069	4,557	1,852	418
Bosnia and Herzegovina	9,629	8,468	1,546	657	151	1,864	312	936	348	160
Bulgaria	15,522	10,970	1,233	566	154	2,595	467	2,124	778	370
Canada	41,069	27,434	1,674	643	949	5,493	1,078	3,720	2,839	561
Chile	20,216	13,703	1,359	363	502	2,148	627	1,663	1,128	392
Croatia	20,308	13,740	1,830	873	377	3,300	545	2,481	771	419
Cyprus	31,229	22,957	2,141	1,057	1,140	5,061	947	2,473	1,813	1,194
Czech Republic	27,045	16,631	1,686	1,262	290	3,585	562	3,124	823	282
Denmark	41,843	26,288	2,021	882	920	4,807	992	4,160	1,648	504
Estonia	23,088	13,795	1,716	1,041	484	2,476	318	2,151	863	427
Finland	38,611	26,582	2,423	1,027	934	4,760	1,024	4,198	1,641	686
France	36,391	26,486	2,593	766	871	4,793	1,048	4,198	2,126	565
Germany	40,990	28,478	2,303	892	1,018	4,836	1,287	4,984	2,066	781
Greece	26,622	21,254	2,660	944	693	4,994	664	3,193	1,587	454
Hungary	22,413	14,664	1,383	989	234	3,186	389	3,073	751	260
Iceland	38,226	25,839	2,484	607	598	5,747	1,057	3,979	1,826	614
Ireland	42,942	23,043	1,666	745	805	4,313	781	3,439	1,811	570
Israel	30,168	20,483	2,153	440	471	4,278	983	2,213	1,943	572
Italy	33,870	23,875	2,504	649	1,394	4,442	1,246	3,421	1,910	516
Japan	34,262	24,447	1,811	696	645	4,770	879	3,546	1,774	758
Korea, Rep.	29,035	17,481	1,059	386	457	3,766	394	3,264	1,272	875
Latvia	19,994	13,734	1,653	784	340	3,282	350	1,898	987	328
Lithuania	22,521	16,537	2,440	991	472	3,022	578	2,951	1,101	377
Luxembourg	88,670	32,000	2,667	4,432	1,735	5,563	2,060	3,633	5,580	802

Recreation and culture	Education	Restaurants and hotels	Miscellaneous goods and services	Individual consumption expenditure by households	Individual consumption expenditure by government	Collective consumption expenditure by government	Gross fixed capital formation	Machinery and equipment	Construction	Domestic absorption	Individual consumption expenditure by households without housing
(11)	(12)	(13)	(14)	(16)	(17)	(18)	(19)	(20)	(21)	(25)	(26)
118	1,729	49	216	5,704	1,431	903	842	115	835	8,427	4,353
193	2,262	143	348	6,507	1,933	1,514	1,473	622	787	11,028	5,223
409	4,263	167	346	8,160	5,498	1,167	2,955	930	2,193	16,696	6,535
419	4,131	265	935	8,518	3,827	1,734	2,542	567	2,094	16,588	7,292
86	1,495	62	155	2,586	1,243	448	287	96	196	3,810	2,042
123	1,978	60	486	4,097	2,250	382	467	125	340	5,951	3,208
558	2,630	239	1,213	11,429	4,908	2,465	2,906	863	1,978	20,907	9,369
52	913	18	137	2,215	1,075	280	287	106	155	3,340	1,786
202	2,414	83	396	5,785	3,008	801	769	232	574	8,859	4,530
424	**2,642**	**190**	**895**	**9,199**	**4,107**	**1,856**	**2,228**	**657**	**1,552**	**16,518**	**7,503**
144	3,346	194	429	6,251	2,039	909	2,583	267	3,279	11,687	5,297
2,831	3,140	1,628	4,079	22,288	5,529	3,430	10,026	2,854	5,669	41,042	18,885
2,375	2,467	2,616	3,364	23,049	5,708	3,107	9,553	3,401	5,367	41,311	18,943
1,902	3,080	1,083	3,546	20,173	7,796	3,098	9,814	3,020	6,338	39,504	16,906
325	1,898	395	686	6,667	2,084	1,463	1,543	323	1,517	11,417	5,386
689	2,083	581	610	8,358	3,328	2,202	2,512	627	2,180	15,631	6,406
2,079	2,740	1,257	3,794	22,127	6,232	3,356	9,984	2,068	7,234	41,537	17,680
702	3,597	470	1,773	11,002	3,080	1,255	4,223	1,121	3,131	19,614	9,333
1,144	2,312	1,442	1,157	10,616	3,894	2,507	3,918	790	3,487	20,333	8,459
1,551	2,564	2,711	1,913	19,999	3,251	3,763	5,749	1,188	5,144	32,532	16,149
1,345	2,592	1,168	1,379	12,372	5,608	3,497	5,887	1,913	3,972	26,012	9,951
2,182	3,264	819	4,579	18,379	10,605	3,350	8,937	2,831	4,855	38,734	14,682
828	2,788	741	1,237	10,051	5,065	2,849	5,142	1,603	3,748	22,337	8,245
2,249	3,229	1,071	3,880	19,917	8,771	3,343	8,274	1,760	6,541	38,695	16,526
1,954	2,898	1,372	3,555	20,167	8,202	3,002	7,562	1,959	5,198	37,427	16,732
1,912	2,596	1,157	4,267	22,398	7,605	2,779	7,066	2,664	4,189	38,487	18,557
946	2,388	1,962	1,878	18,156	3,050	3,368	3,890	1,162	2,695	28,780	14,903
930	2,602	817	1,832	10,710	5,358	3,106	3,429	990	2,527	21,269	8,477
1,981	3,733	1,340	2,611	19,066	8,931	3,940	4,640	1,684	2,722	34,386	14,539
1,302	3,223	1,918	2,416	17,949	6,513	2,504	6,147	1,638	4,455	32,443	14,691
1,089	3,709	889	2,395	15,963	5,541	3,879	6,038	1,302	3,847	30,243	12,640
1,386	2,361	1,751	2,338	19,311	5,533	2,703	7,449	2,323	4,552	34,232	15,985
1,770	2,096	1,281	4,353	19,188	6,412	3,288	6,878	2,586	3,384	34,518	15,091
1,064	2,878	814	2,524	14,436	3,282	2,715	7,628	2,050	5,581	28,494	11,596
894	2,612	417	855	10,700	3,634	2,965	3,701	1,069	2,890	20,868	8,499
835	2,907	337	1,343	12,416	5,357	2,665	3,379	763	2,831	23,111	10,322
2,780	2,571	2,215	5,851	25,804	8,213	5,042	20,440	6,512	13,753	58,182	22,004

(continued)

Table 2.7 *(Continued)*

REAL EXPENDITURES PER CAPITA (US$) Economy	Gross domestic product	Actual individual consumption	Food and nonalcoholic beverages	Alcoholic beverages, tobacco, and narcotics	Clothing and footwear	Housing, water, electricity, gas, and other fuels	Furnishings, household equipment and maintenance	Health	Transport	Communication
(00)	(01)	(02)	(03)	(04)	(05)	(06)	(07)	(08)	(09)	(10)
Macedonia, FYR	11,957	9,482	1,905	343	232	2,120	211	1,202	382	303
Malta	28,608	19,701	2,173	509	566	3,079	921	3,394	1,406	633
Mexico	16,377	11,844	2,014	279	297	1,675	482	907	1,325	304
Montenegro	14,128	12,315	2,606	666	198	2,313	816	1,368	755	501
Netherlands	43,150	25,983	2,361	708	969	4,205	1,079	3,662	1,688	763
New Zealand	31,172	22,502	2,204	734	886	3,744	849	3,809	1,790	506
Norway	61,879	31,014	2,383	650	1,144	5,270	1,343	4,457	2,387	1,018
Poland	21,753	16,307	2,159	750	317	4,207	465	2,741	752	348
Portugal	25,672	18,584	2,477	632	703	2,719	760	2,670	1,388	399
Romania	16,146	11,184	1,781	373	197	2,023	320	2,721	538	385
Russian Federation[d]	22,502	15,175	2,236	1,275	702	3,246	415	1,629	828	652
Serbia	11,854	10,107	1,506	565	151	2,560	196	1,750	566	380
Slovak Republic	25,130	16,880	1,852	629	393	4,426	609	3,017	685	304
Slovenia	28,156	18,880	2,026	1,093	729	3,553	819	2,953	1,722	546
Spain	32,156	21,484	2,497	696	997	3,544	771	2,933	1,505	356
Sweden	41,761	26,781	2,338	744	885	5,271	927	3,800	1,871	1,120
Switzerland	51,582	29,465	2,364	1,443	1,030	4,740	1,281	4,266	2,308	948
Turkey	17,781	13,732	1,893	305	568	3,264	753	1,549	1,101	276
United Kingdom	35,091	26,146	2,006	599	1,525	4,122	970	3,745	2,057	545
United States	49,782	37,390	2,238	665	1,173	6,290	1,376	7,371	3,458	790
Total (47)	**33,675**	**23,930**	**2,101**	**699**	**835**	**4,340**	**909**	**3,853**	**1,939**	**606**
LATIN AMERICA										
Bolivia	5,557	3,661	786	46	52	851	172	319	481	22
Brazil	14,639	9,906	1,279	225	191	1,367	511	1,866	821	162
Colombia	11,360	7,836	924	210	295	2,002	172	773	540	186
Costa Rica	13,030	10,244	1,363	90	290	1,184	409	1,046	1,374	317
Cuba[e]	...	...	...	...	...	...	...	...	...	...
Dominican Republic	10,858	9,722	1,626	423	222	1,918	212	787	708	361
Ecuador	9,932	6,759	901	155	167	1,435	280	740	675	252
El Salvador	7,357	7,285	1,170	108	215	2,053	407	703	549	238
Guatemala	6,971	6,222	1,509	67	217	1,149	299	484	319	302
Haiti	1,557	1,688	626	47	53	324	49	74	71	5
Honduras	4,349	3,748	770	118	87	734	102	399	249	66
Nicaragua	4,111	3,587	538	79	72	1,045	141	464	263	66
Panama	15,369	10,618	1,166	54	385	3,267	510	871	1,033	467
Paraguay	7,193	5,591	1,016	73	131	945	312	530	303	216
Peru	10,981	7,148	1,115	146	267	1,066	204	659	542	191
Uruguay	17,343	12,899	1,670	258	314	3,328	460	1,951	689	557
Venezuela, RB	16,965	10,263	1,027	169	145	1,513	210	1,212	1,633	555
Total (17)	**12,443**	**8,561**	**1,156**	**189**	**199**	**1,419**	**361**	**1,283**	**747**	**209**

Recreation and culture	Education	Restaurants and hotels	Miscella-neous goods and services	Individual consumption expenditure by households	Individual consumption expenditure by government	Collective consumption expenditure by government	Gross fixed capital formation	Machinery and equipment	Construction	Domestic absorption	Individual consumption expenditure by households without housing
(11)	(12)	(13)	(14)	(16)	(17)	(18)	(19)	(20)	(21)	(25)	(26)
225	2,310	290	627	7,313	2,590	2,036	1,853	316	1,973	13,704	5,802
1,775	2,553	2,786	2,555	15,455	5,145	3,821	4,209	990	3,163	27,562	12,740
390	3,511	380	1,146	9,322	2,817	1,408	2,953	572	2,850	16,550	8,016
335	2,614	1,291	825	9,565	3,332	2,709	1,939	364	1,955	16,618	7,932
2,060	3,120	891	4,844	18,732	9,570	4,705	7,981	2,146	5,249	38,743	15,727
1,866	3,581	1,316	2,310	17,425	6,302	2,921	4,985	1,581	2,907	30,559	14,085
2,819	3,153	1,008	4,331	23,322	10,055	4,315	12,598	4,009	6,322	50,535	18,971
1,023	2,666	254	1,925	12,519	4,754	2,134	3,317	917	2,497	22,034	10,476
1,081	2,861	1,793	2,043	15,112	4,090	2,721	5,261	952	4,857	26,725	12,905
609	2,380	295	745	8,274	3,841	1,779	3,754	632	3,986	16,894	6,964
547	2,616	239	1,253	11,429	4,908	2,465	2,906	863	1,978	20,907	9,380
385	2,121	159	863	7,498	3,556	1,309	1,795	411	1,601	13,402	5,930
1,222	2,675	602	1,650	12,981	4,840	3,478	4,670	1,087	2,968	25,026	10,637
1,326	2,393	949	1,843	14,856	4,961	3,018	5,326	1,772	3,375	27,684	12,489
1,552	2,547	2,906	2,107	17,101	5,388	3,271	7,541	1,616	5,098	32,404	14,499
2,265	2,901	854	4,384	19,424	9,693	3,446	7,698	3,034	3,623	38,610	15,209
2,460	2,544	1,710	4,618	26,418	3,212	2,353	11,927	5,030	5,316	44,050	22,744
437	3,776	574	889	10,729	3,524	1,510	3,431	1,195	2,316	19,084	8,177
2,780	2,751	1,612	3,293	20,912	6,515	3,222	5,603	1,070	3,689	35,499	17,624
3,192	2,983	2,150	5,779	34,329	3,061	5,034	9,064	3,252	4,150	51,605	29,180
1,730	**2,835**	**1,261**	**3,244**	**19,850**	**4,882**	**3,174**	**6,403**	**1,993**	**3,825**	**33,756**	**16,505**
23	444	218	110	3,436	100	641	857	239	530	5,187	2,856
330	1,948	446	1,239	7,833	2,541	1,647	3,178	770	2,382	14,765	6,614
320	1,445	592	849	6,765	987	1,319	2,230	427	2,170	11,385	5,383
791	1,898	385	578	8,586	1,572	905	2,258	482	2,068	13,662	7,417
...	...	...	...	...	...	...	...	...	...	...	...
162	1,468	768	1,134	8,810	510	799	1,353	191	1,624	11,771	7,301
251	1,474	195	591	5,832	858	721	2,225	303	1,250	10,089	4,793
264	1,004	268	407	6,503	582	510	732	186	600	8,535	5,179
150	703	320	302	5,565	488	472	865	222	708	7,536	4,474
34	169	2	41	1,612	22	1	407	4	730	2,105	1,346
119	730	177	271	3,321	358	329	934	257	618	5,102	2,747
85	873	156	290	3,113	428	463	576	113	519	4,564	2,369
447	1,547	382	952	9,154	1,358	1,283	3,000	724	2,613	15,183	7,018
227	1,313	199	496	4,862	655	338	985	183	911	6,934	4,164
341	1,409	445	753	6,332	638	815	2,219	393	2,326	10,412	5,297
323	1,737	758	1,099	10,962	1,886	1,182	3,201	577	3,095	17,408	8,424
328	2,802	753	401	8,710	1,619	1,440	2,868	501	3,084	15,234	7,388
296	**1,681**	**448**	**903**	**7,073**	**1,664**	**1,264**	**2,504**	**551**	**2,081**	**12,432**	**5,893**

(continued)

Table 2.7 *(Continued)*

REAL EXPENDITURES PER CAPITA (US$) Economy (00)	Gross domestic product (01)	Actual individual consumption (02)	Food and nonalcoholic beverages (03)	Alcoholic beverages, tobacco, and narcotics (04)	Clothing and footwear (05)	Housing, water, electricity, gas, and other fuels (06)	Furnishings, household equipment and maintenance (07)	Health (08)	Transport (09)	Communication (10)
CARIBBEAN										
Anguilla	27,274	21,119	1,560	458	587	5,268	607	743	3,319	1,662
Antigua and Barbuda	20,540	12,549	1,108	192	242	4,634	345	2,084	704	522
Aruba	36,017	24,000	1,284	100	659	10,061	541	5,212	2,094	737
Bahamas, The	22,639	15,565	1,150	197	419	5,731	378	1,854	960	556
Barbados	15,354	12,326	1,422	166	268	7,405	277	934	780	489
Belize	8,212	6,492	672	46	370	3,233	267	628	414	183
Bermuda	54,899	37,924	3,168	1,034	898	7,160	1,507	4,468	2,756	1,624
Bonaire[f]	...	...	920	71	790	...	504	...	1,531	486
Cayman Islands	49,686	34,020	1,628	330	1,006	12,748	1,046	1,784	2,793	1,482
Curaçao	27,781	20,690	1,553	211	1,008	9,120	376	2,435	1,400	546
Dominica	9,983	8,664	885	53	524	2,709	226	856	1,119	327
Grenada	11,221	10,211	1,150	143	308	2,926	231	642	1,160	912
Jamaica	8,329	7,241	1,145	67	126	1,442	273	634	655	246
Montserrat	15,762	13,609	1,159	217	146	4,243	280	1,922	2,163	1,051
St. Kitts and Nevis	20,582	14,444	1,213	322	564	5,770	368	1,702	713	495
St. Lucia	9,893	7,520	964	97	386	2,783	170	612	481	333
St. Vincent and the Grenadines	9,883	8,356	973	402	154	3,086	193	935	1,053	410
Sint Maarten	32,972	19,298	1,171	86	1,036	9,144	550	1,176	1,816	642
Suriname	14,463	5,913	1,138	114	191	1,978	147	522	226	170
Trinidad and Tobago	28,743	15,691	2,066	103	170	2,555	347	1,831	1,187	325
Turks and Caicos Islands	20,878	7,593	902	125	357	716	240	1,082	1,365	206
Virgin Islands, British	30,290	10,753	1,367	380	1,074	2,119	895	898	1,012	395
Total (22)	**16,351**	**10,867**	**1,343**	**117**	**247**	**2,962**	**309**	**1,142**	**848**	**346**
WESTERN ASIA										
Bahrain	43,360	18,626	1,780	64	853	4,366	912	1,342	2,422	1,022
Egypt, Arab Rep.[a]	10,599	8,529	1,670	159	402	2,514	210	1,505	352	183
Iraq	11,130	5,381	882	19	196	2,201	152	633	294	82
Jordan	11,169	8,868	1,288	227	380	3,078	256	1,066	603	296
Kuwait	84,058	21,888	2,637	48	1,324	7,878	1,798	1,613	2,070	556
Oman	42,619	15,182	1,866	34	751	3,273	449	1,217	2,518	602
Qatar	146,521	20,552	1,927	73	689	4,830	675	1,552	2,497	479
Saudi Arabia	48,163	17,797	1,726	54	748	6,238	845	1,707	1,256	606
Sudan[b]	3,608	2,309	666	9	154	403	112	74	111	32
United Arab Emirates	60,886	29,463	2,735	56	3,600	10,245	1,084	442	5,073	2,119
West Bank and Gaza	3,833	4,070	849	71	248	447	169	596	222	116
Yemen, Rep.	3,716	2,762	558	139	129	759	48	504	120	23
Total (12)	**17,499**	**8,574**	**1,303**	**90**	**473**	**2,719**	**307**	**979**	**635**	**263**

Recreation and culture	Education	Restaurants and hotels	Miscellaneous goods and services	Individual consumption expenditure by households	Individual consumption expenditure by government	Collective consumption expenditure by government	Gross fixed capital formation	Machinery and equipment	Construction	Domestic absorption	Individual consumption expenditure by households without housing
(11)	(12)	(13)	(14)	(16)	(17)	(18)	(19)	(20)	(21)	(25)	(26)
571	2,721	601	3,116	18,416	1,672	5,101	6,306	830	7,185	31,600	15,282
268	2,475	357	1,453	9,708	3,976	3,663	4,708	451	5,934	20,385	6,716
1,181	3,375	316	2,001	17,040	10,539	5,540	12,498	1,786	13,584	41,264	10,759
606	1,943	761	2,185	13,249	2,077	3,837	7,109	2,086	5,056	26,314	9,477
426	1,339	1,648	1,053	10,453	1,733	3,034	3,187	917	2,357	18,143	5,247
259	838	28	262	5,718	517	1,315	774	224	548	8,401	3,265
2,146	6,872	3,753	5,405	30,343	8,804	6,194	17,994	7,875	8,146	62,109	24,960
...	...	800	...	12,119	...	...	...	...	...	...	9,142
1,395	4,253	1,545	5,755	29,497	3,474	5,921	13,439	4,262	9,036	52,931	20,953
662	1,830	418	4,140	17,354	3,282	3,257	9,733	3,383	3,658	34,418	11,601
237	1,446	192	575	7,347	1,193	1,784	2,102	590	1,531	11,351	5,346
176	2,437	133	736	8,603	1,503	1,542	2,036	462	1,767	13,786	6,419
455	1,530	632	774	6,094	1,091	1,026	1,588	399	1,269	9,951	4,743
311	2,518	37	1,344	10,589	3,858	7,609	5,059	723	5,621	24,308	7,745
336	4,240	687	1,249	11,441	3,896	5,015	5,225	780	5,544	23,565	7,556
100	1,920	65	776	6,299	1,180	1,537	2,757	462	2,769	11,720	4,525
363	1,560	140	637	6,727	1,917	1,563	2,258	330	2,504	12,255	4,818
692	1,608	225	2,017	16,375	2,553	6,319	6,307	2,344	2,165	31,031	10,118
163	154	59	697	5,239	285	2,513	4,487	1,961	1,277	13,430	4,484
862	5,137	965	2,282	11,225	6,791	917	4,703	1,290	3,450	22,097	9,973
362	1,652	223	888	6,421	1,058	6,320	2,830	888	1,947	14,711	6,058
371	1,075	438	604	9,147	1,394	2,395	6,768	2,561	3,701	19,018	8,055
530	**2,290**	**657**	**1,335**	**8,719**	**2,600**	**1,771**	**3,575**	**1,033**	**2,497**	**16,359**	**6,706**
1,165	3,402	762	1,201	16,419	2,300	3,584	7,584	1,097	8,791	29,822	14,704
205	1,789	179	612	7,218	1,206	1,568	1,070	201	1,051	10,892	5,633
45	1,782	34	108	3,989	1,841	2,728	1,608	381	1,383	9,275	2,724
114	2,585	115	229	7,328	1,724	1,844	1,882	259	1,991	12,671	5,371
608	2,881	390	1,013	18,653	3,507	6,971	14,911	3,129	11,158	43,562	14,587
428	3,069	314	1,171	12,252	3,319	5,100	12,529	2,217	11,495	30,713	10,485
1,344	3,906	313	2,785	17,140	4,163	8,707	59,793	14,413	17,614	75,947	13,981
435	4,605	527	818	13,457	5,064	4,556	13,029	2,359	11,349	36,443	10,405
44	232	53	59	2,069	57	462	783	155	787	3,660	1,752
675	2,000	818	1,254	29,459	522	2,656	18,824	4,134	14,341	48,431	22,000
86	964	63	298	3,209	973	1,072	706	75	747	5,678	2,851
9	535	1	112	2,337	418	607	360	18	400	3,826	1,900
195	**1,791**	**187**	**455**	**7,148**	**1,548**	**2,017**	**3,916**	**774**	**3,153**	**14,288**	**5,533**

(continued)

Table 2.7 *(Continued)*

REAL EXPENDITURES PER CAPITA (US$) Economy	Gross domestic product	Actual individual consumption	Food and nonalcoholic beverages	Alcoholic beverages, tobacco, and narcotics	Clothing and footwear	Housing, water, electricity, gas, and other fuels	Furnishings, household equipment and maintenance	Health	Transport	Communication
(00)	(01)	(02)	(03)	(04)	(05)	(06)	(07)	(08)	(09)	(10)
SINGLETONS										
Georgia	6,343	6,054	963	306	76	2,043	128	1,115	289	198
Iran, Islamic Rep.	17,488	8,576	1,102	53	191	2,951	175	1,513	419	409
Total (2)	**16,863**	**8,435**	**1,094**	**67**	**184**	**2,900**	**172**	**1,491**	**412**	**397**
WORLD[g] (179)	**13,460**	**8,647**	**1,018**	**214**	**352**	**1,643**	**300**	**1,385**	**632**	**238**

Source: ICP, http://icp.worldbank.org/.

Note: n.a. = not applicable; ... = data suppressed because of incompleteness.

a. The Arab Republic of Egypt participated in both the Africa and Western Asia regions. The regional results for Egypt were averaged by taking the geometric mean of the regional PPPs, allowing Egypt to have the same global results in each region.

b. Sudan participated in both the Africa and Western Asia regions. The regional results for Sudan were averaged by taking the geometric mean of the regional PPPs, allowing Sudan to have the same global results in each region.

c. The results presented in the tables are based on data supplied by all the participating economies and compiled in accordance with ICP principles and the procedures recommended by the 2011 ICP Technical Advisory Group. The results for China are estimated by the 2011 ICP Asia and the Pacific Regional Office and the Global Office. The National Bureau of Statistics of China does not recognize these results as official statistics.

d. The Russian Federation participated in both the CIS and Eurostat-OECD comparisons. The PPPs for Russia are based on the Eurostat-OECD comparison. They were the basis for linking the CIS comparison to the ICP.

e. The official GDP of Cuba for reference year 2011 is 68,990.15 million in national currency. However, this number and its breakdown into main aggregates are not shown in the tables because of methodological comparability issues. Therefore, Cuba's results are provided only for the PPP and price level index. In addition, Cuba's figures are not included in the Latin America and world totals.

f. Bonaire's results are provided only for the individual consumption expenditure by households. Therefore, to ensure consistency across the tables, Bonaire is not included in the Caribbean or the world total.

g. This table does not include the Pacific Islands and does not double count the dual participation economies: the Arab Republic of Egypt, Sudan, and the Russian Federation.

Recreation and culture	Education	Restaurants and hotels	Miscellaneous goods and services	Individual consumption expenditure by households	Individual consumption expenditure by government	Collective consumption expenditure by government	Gross fixed capital formation	Machinery and equipment	Construction	Domestic absorption	Individual consumption expenditure by households without housing
(11)	(12)	(13)	(14)	(16)	(17)	(18)	(19)	(20)	(21)	(25)	(26)
322	1,884	116	374	4,789	973	1,402	742	256	433	7,675	3,624
169	2,417	58	680	6,804	1,834	2,776	2,928	635	3,116	15,556	5,059
177	2,387	61	662	6,691	1,786	2,699	2,805	614	2,965	15,114	4,979
494	1,317	408	979	7,144	1,766	1,230	3,139	708	2,672	13,258	5,918

Table 2.8 Indexes of Real Expenditures Per Capita (World = 100), ICP 2011

INDEX OF REAL EXPENDITURES PER CAPITA (world = 100) Economy	Gross domestic product	Actual individual consumption	Food and nonalcoholic beverages	Alcoholic beverages, tobacco, and narcotics	Clothing and footwear	Housing, water, electricity, gas, and other fuels	Furnishings, household equipment and maintenance	Health	Transport	Communication
(00)	(01)	(02)	(03)	(04)	(05)	(06)	(07)	(08)	(09)	(10)
AFRICA										
Algeria	98.0	72.5	105.3	32.1	35.8	22.3	36.6	71.1	104.0	119.7
Angola	54.1	50.0	103.2	134.6	51.7	35.3	52.8	23.5	30.1	14.9
Benin	13.1	17.0	39.0	21.1	18.0	10.3	9.0	6.2	13.4	15.8
Botswana	99.6	78.4	74.4	177.3	133.4	41.9	80.8	45.2	140.6	87.3
Burkina Faso	10.0	11.0	25.4	27.3	6.2	8.7	9.5	4.4	6.2	10.7
Burundi	5.3	7.5	14.9	24.8	1.9	10.8	1.2	3.3	2.9	1.7
Cameroon	20.5	26.6	63.0	25.4	42.5	17.9	40.3	3.4	19.2	8.4
Cape Verde	45.5	54.9	98.0	91.7	29.5	59.9	87.1	32.1	32.6	81.3
Central African Republic	6.7	10.1	24.4	33.4	19.6	5.0	9.1	1.9	3.3	1.9
Chad	14.7	17.1	39.7	27.1	9.8	9.5	20.7	14.1	14.6	14.9
Comoros	4.5	7.2	17.7	0.5	4.9	15.8	4.0	0.7	1.3	0.9
Congo, Rep.	43.3	17.5	27.6	29.9	10.6	20.6	12.1	16.4	12.3	21.8
Congo, Dem. Rep.	4.9	5.2	11.9	4.8	5.8	5.8	4.0	2.9	1.2	1.6
Côte d'Ivoire	19.8	22.9	47.2	26.8	16.1	16.5	39.8	12.3	22.1	15.3
Djibouti	17.9	19.9	31.4	58.1	13.7	40.7	23.6	5.8	11.4	2.4
Egypt, Arab Rep.[a]	78.7	98.6	164.1	74.1	114.4	153.0	70.0	108.7	55.7	76.7
Equatorial Guinea	293.0	56.9	94.5	68.6	43.0	58.5	36.9	61.2	45.0	76.5
Ethiopia	9.0	11.3	19.9	8.9	12.1	10.5	19.6	12.0	1.6	1.5
Gabon	122.5	69.1	90.0	235.6	82.2	64.0	72.4	49.4	72.4	76.0
Gambia, The	11.2	14.1	25.4	14.9	36.6	6.4	7.6	29.7	3.7	16.0
Ghana	25.5	25.9	37.3	12.3	94.7	21.2	37.6	13.9	21.8	14.3
Guinea	9.6	9.1	19.4	4.9	16.8	11.3	7.5	8.1	4.5	0.4
Guinea-Bissau	10.1	10.7	25.8	6.4	18.2	9.8	13.3	3.6	6.5	1.6
Kenya	15.9	22.4	37.7	32.1	15.2	14.0	20.9	19.6	16.0	31.0
Lesotho	15.8	29.2	39.2	24.3	88.3	22.3	45.4	14.2	8.7	25.3
Liberia	4.0	7.0	8.5	8.0	25.6	7.4	9.4	1.9	1.7	7.3
Madagascar	10.5	15.4	31.7	15.7	30.1	5.3	43.7	3.7	13.8	2.8
Malawi	7.2	11.6	25.2	20.4	8.8	14.9	21.3	7.0	5.3	6.0
Mali	11.2	12.1	28.6	7.0	16.4	6.8	13.0	6.5	11.8	7.5
Mauritania	23.7	24.2	68.4	8.1	24.2	15.7	13.8	11.0	9.9	24.7
Mauritius	115.2	136.6	208.9	288.1	228.0	158.1	215.2	82.9	127.3	174.7
Morocco	50.2	49.8	82.6	31.2	44.7	68.1	46.3	25.2	41.6	80.4
Mozambique	7.1	10.3	25.5	17.1	12.8	6.4	4.9	2.8	7.9	3.6
Namibia	62.1	67.4	67.8	108.2	102.9	62.2	123.7	72.5	27.7	23.3
Niger	6.3	8.3	15.3	6.3	21.4	5.4	10.2	3.5	5.7	4.1
Nigeria	23.4	24.0	38.0	14.3	98.1	16.0	46.2	10.9	17.1	11.2
Rwanda	9.9	15.0	36.1	14.8	10.1	19.4	11.9	4.8	6.3	5.5
São Tomé and Príncipe	22.6	38.6	95.5	62.7	34.5	23.4	24.4	21.7	34.3	14.8

Recreation and culture	Education	Restaurants and hotels	Miscella-neous goods and services	Individual consumption expenditure by households	Individual consumption expenditure by government	Collective consumption expenditure by government	Gross fixed capital formation	Machinery and equipment	Construction	Domestic absorption	Individual consumption expenditure by households without housing
(11)	(12)	(13)	(14)	(16)	(17)	(18)	(19)	(20)	(21)	(25)	(26)
31.0	180.9	29.5	110.0	55.7	244.2	179.0	97.3	82.5	109.4	89.7	64.0
12.4	41.5	17.1	51.9	47.9	63.6	188.5	47.6	29.2	67.4	58.5	51.4
3.3	14.8	23.5	6.3	18.0	7.8	15.5	8.3	6.4	10.8	14.5	18.5
30.8	185.7	41.6	60.9	75.5	102.0	150.2	160.9	115.6	226.4	107.9	81.0
3.0	7.8	6.8	3.0	11.8	3.9	19.9	5.3	4.3	5.9	10.7	12.0
0.9	12.2	4.6	1.7	7.5	7.1	11.8	2.6	2.3	2.9	6.4	6.6
4.9	10.4	25.3	6.2	28.9	5.9	24.3	13.1	14.7	12.0	22.4	29.7
7.0	73.5	129.7	33.1	54.7	53.5	62.2	75.6	66.5	84.1	61.3	53.5
2.2	8.8	3.1	3.6	10.8	3.0	3.8	3.4	2.2	3.6	7.6	11.5
6.0	6.3	1.7	4.0	18.4	4.3	9.0	12.8	12.5	11.0	15.4	18.9
0.8	4.0	0.0	1.8	7.9	0.5	14.6	2.3	2.2	2.3	6.5	6.3
6.1	23.6	21.7	6.4	17.7	14.5	26.4	47.5	20.7	75.7	26.7	18.0
1.0	6.0	4.0	1.1	5.5	1.8	7.4	3.8	3.3	4.4	4.9	5.4
8.8	14.5	5.8	10.7	24.4	9.3	19.3	7.7	5.4	10.3	17.0	25.0
2.7	21.6	2.7	3.9	20.7	11.7	46.0	20.0	12.6	30.1	22.4	18.4
41.6	135.9	43.8	62.5	101.0	68.3	127.4	34.1	28.4	39.3	82.2	95.2
11.9	59.8	31.7	29.0	60.8	27.3	40.4	443.1	426.2	336.8	141.1	62.4
0.8	12.1	11.4	13.2	12.1	3.7	8.6	6.8	3.7	9.4	10.0	12.8
26.6	52.4	50.2	22.4	71.4	46.6	149.3	93.0	64.1	46.0	80.0	72.7
6.7	23.6	1.8	6.7	14.7	8.0	13.6	8.3	8.9	7.1	12.4	15.7
3.7	77.2	0.1	10.7	26.2	22.6	38.5	26.9	22.4	31.3	27.2	28.1
1.0	9.0	1.6	2.1	9.8	1.8	8.3	6.3	7.9	4.5	8.4	9.4
5.2	8.1	0.7	1.7	11.3	4.1	30.4	4.3	3.7	5.0	10.3	12.1
10.1	43.0	22.6	16.7	21.9	24.7	14.5	10.4	10.6	10.8	18.2	22.0
15.6	36.1	5.0	17.7	29.4	26.1	37.6	15.8	8.1	24.1	26.1	29.0
1.9	21.8	0.8	5.3	7.7	0.3	6.8	2.0	3.2	0.6	5.9	7.7
10.0	12.5	12.9	2.6	16.6	4.1	3.9	5.0	3.9	6.2	11.7	18.3
2.9	9.0	3.5	2.8	12.4	5.1	4.6	4.2	6.0	1.8	8.7	11.9
6.7	10.4	2.8	3.2	12.7	6.4	19.6	8.0	7.0	8.9	11.5	13.2
3.2	33.1	2.0	4.1	23.8	26.5	52.3	39.3	37.3	37.0	25.3	24.3
137.4	186.2	54.6	77.8	139.0	114.1	156.8	115.9	72.7	160.8	133.3	145.4
31.1	87.9	42.9	29.1	48.9	54.8	64.1	68.8	48.1	93.3	57.2	45.7
3.9	8.0	1.9	6.0	10.9	4.6	4.4	4.4	3.5	5.7	8.2	11.2
40.8	191.2	55.7	68.4	65.6	78.3	122.4	64.4	43.7	89.4	68.7	66.6
5.7	7.9	6.3	4.9	8.9	2.7	7.6	7.8	8.3	7.7	8.1	9.4
3.8	50.9	0.2	11.0	24.7	15.9	29.6	8.3	9.1	6.9	19.9	27.4
3.0	10.1	7.4	5.0	16.5	3.5	7.1	6.4	3.1	9.8	11.6	15.6
6.7	41.5	7.5	8.3	40.1	23.5	39.4	17.6	22.4	9.1	33.0	41.7

(continued)

Table 2.8 (Continued)

INDEX OF REAL EXPENDITURES PER CAPITA (world = 100) Economy	Gross domestic product	Actual individual consumption	Food and nonalcoholic beverages	Alcoholic beverages, tobacco, and narcotics	Clothing and footwear	Housing, water, electricity, gas, and other fuels	Furnishings, household equipment and maintenance	Health	Transport	Communication
(00)	(01)	(02)	(03)	(04)	(05)	(06)	(07)	(08)	(09)	(10)
Senegal	16.7	22.2	52.2	10.0	20.8	28.8	29.2	7.3	9.2	30.5
Seychelles	167.7	151.6	298.7	73.7	131.4	223.3	119.1	139.8	72.0	98.8
Sierra Leone	10.2	13.8	22.4	17.4	36.9	9.6	8.3	31.1	3.3	8.4
South Africa	90.0	95.8	103.6	162.5	90.4	78.8	104.1	89.2	115.3	102.0
Sudan[b]	26.8	26.7	65.5	4.3	43.7	24.5	37.4	5.3	17.6	13.3
Swaziland	47.0	67.3	167.1	19.3	82.8	55.2	144.3	52.6	47.3	32.3
Tanzania	11.5	11.9	37.9	2.3	21.7	4.6	10.8	6.8	4.1	0.3
Togo	9.8	13.8	26.5	12.5	17.9	8.0	12.3	10.9	5.4	6.2
Tunisia	76.7	84.3	92.1	68.8	87.2	84.8	99.3	60.8	117.4	151.3
Uganda	11.9	16.1	27.8	28.2	10.5	16.6	17.3	5.3	7.0	9.2
Zambia	23.4	20.6	60.8	4.9	31.3	17.6	5.7	13.7	1.9	8.9
Zimbabwe	10.2	15.6	44.1	23.5	18.0	6.6	6.8	4.9	9.0	0.6
Total (50)	**30.0**	**32.2**	**54.1**	**31.7**	**47.6**	**31.0**	**35.2**	**24.6**	**25.5**	**27.3**
ASIA AND THE PACIFIC										
Bangladesh	20.8	24.7	62.2	24.8	32.0	31.5	16.8	12.1	6.6	13.1
Bhutan	53.5	46.2	73.8	25.9	87.2	50.3	14.3	56.7	37.9	59.8
Brunei Darussalam	552.7	181.4	212.3	14.9	160.3	144.5	99.8	93.0	345.8	228.2
Cambodia	20.2	26.3	59.5	38.3	14.1	19.8	9.9	30.5	14.3	2.3
China[c]	74.7	50.1	54.2	27.4	68.3	48.1	42.2	80.9	30.3	90.1
Fiji	56.1	62.4	116.5	69.0	43.8	64.7	112.8	35.5	45.1	8.2
Hong Kong SAR, China	372.4	378.1	260.2	125.1	535.9	350.1	464.7	216.4	248.2	611.9
India	35.2	35.0	56.1	26.7	69.7	32.6	21.5	27.2	35.0	17.0
Indonesia	63.4	55.6	108.2	21.8	38.8	73.0	32.7	17.5	34.2	37.4
Lao PDR	30.5	27.1	56.6	41.0	11.2	34.4	12.8	9.4	17.1	16.5
Macao SAR, China	857.6	273.5	151.1	82.4	384.1	233.2	97.0	161.0	236.6	454.0
Malaysia	155.5	128.2	120.4	42.3	47.1	145.3	95.3	75.4	148.7	229.3
Maldives	84.6	44.9	60.9	119.8	29.6	47.5	42.7	43.3	18.6	63.7
Mongolia	64.8	63.6	88.4	176.4	57.6	50.3	12.7	57.5	92.2	49.2
Myanmar	23.6	26.3	58.1	12.7	19.4	23.6	6.1	29.0	4.6	11.9
Nepal	16.5	21.4	63.0	19.6	15.2	18.2	8.0	15.0	3.2	10.5
Pakistan	33.1	45.4	95.6	14.9	45.3	73.9	23.5	47.9	20.1	31.5
Philippines	42.9	51.9	115.5	27.0	13.4	39.9	44.3	14.5	48.2	35.8
Singapore	537.1	285.9	124.1	92.3	229.0	228.1	321.0	205.5	328.8	244.2
Sri Lanka	60.3	73.9	146.3	192.4	56.8	75.9	28.9	57.6	40.4	64.2
Taiwan, China	290.2	290.6	182.2	180.1	343.9	255.7	224.0	344.3	284.8	659.6
Thailand	98.8	98.0	128.6	84.1	86.3	76.2	66.1	78.2	109.2	82.1
Vietnam	35.0	34.6	43.0	41.6	38.2	39.8	39.2	48.1	19.2	7.9
Total (23)	**56.6**	**47.2**	**66.3**	**29.7**	**63.5**	**47.7**	**34.7**	**51.5**	**35.3**	**55.5**

Recreation and culture	Education	Restaurants and hotels	Miscellaneous goods and services	Individual consumption expenditure by households	Individual consumption expenditure by government	Collective consumption expenditure by government	Gross fixed capital formation	Machinery and equipment	Construction	Domestic absorption	Individual consumption expenditure by households without housing
(11)	(12)	(13)	(14)	(16)	(17)	(18)	(19)	(20)	(21)	(25)	(26)
4.1	20.1	2.9	8.6	23.7	9.2	22.0	13.8	11.1	17.5	19.9	23.1
52.2	327.6	7.3	39.4	141.4	266.3	740.4	185.7	176.5	193.5	206.1	132.3
7.0	18.4	2.7	6.8	14.7	4.2	12.4	13.3	16.2	10.0	13.6	15.1
56.6	132.9	28.9	97.7	94.8	95.5	134.0	76.0	80.5	70.7	92.8	93.3
8.8	17.6	12.9	6.1	29.0	3.2	37.6	24.9	21.9	29.5	27.6	29.6
39.9	62.2	6.7	9.2	72.1	29.1	45.3	20.0	12.6	25.0	52.2	71.5
1.7	9.3	0.0	2.5	12.8	3.6	17.6	15.8	9.1	26.9	13.3	14.4
1.8	26.2	16.3	17.4	14.4	7.1	11.6	5.5	3.2	8.1	11.4	15.1
34.7	152.6	122.4	49.3	80.6	117.7	118.0	69.0	31.9	124.5	82.7	77.6
13.0	36.5	7.5	7.0	16.2	14.5	2.3	10.6	3.9	21.4	13.5	16.6
1.9	15.5	1.0	12.2	21.8	9.6	42.0	20.7	11.1	32.2	22.4	22.3
4.5	20.0	1.3	8.7	15.9	12.2	12.9	3.7	2.7	5.1	12.4	16.9
12.6	**49.1**	**14.2**	**22.6**	**32.3**	**30.7**	**45.1**	**22.6**	**18.9**	**26.7**	**30.5**	**32.7**
2.2	27.5	10.6	6.0	26.9	4.8	13.2	21.4	8.2	37.6	22.5	26.9
40.8	70.7	11.6	7.8	43.8	65.3	105.3	115.6	79.3	161.9	69.4	43.7
200.3	400.8	151.9	78.0	170.6	255.5	1002.5	263.6	205.0	301.5	250.0	170.5
10.4	53.7	25.2	4.8	26.7	21.4	12.2	8.7	7.0	10.8	20.5	26.7
52.3	65.6	54.7	30.0	45.9	80.8	52.6	135.9	83.7	173.8	73.2	45.9
44.8	68.1	30.5	23.6	64.5	41.2	50.5	50.4	51.0	37.8	60.0	64.2
938.2	135.8	793.7	560.1	421.4	108.0	180.8	367.3	437.8	282.2	355.1	419.3
6.7	26.5	12.5	34.3	37.4	14.9	33.0	37.3	24.8	50.1	37.4	37.4
17.7	88.9	77.3	23.1	57.5	36.1	45.8	86.0	25.2	155.5	63.3	57.4
8.2	58.1	12.6	5.1	27.6	17.6	51.1	39.7	18.4	48.5	31.8	27.7
505.2	311.7	1030.1	230.4	278.4	239.1	325.8	421.2	268.9	581.8	321.0	277.8
79.6	206.5	240.0	115.3	127.4	127.5	133.5	136.5	105.1	136.8	130.3	127.4
15.8	119.9	24.1	11.9	41.1	77.8	273.8	178.6	163.6	205.4	91.2	40.1
23.3	181.2	19.2	20.9	60.9	89.7	84.4	104.4	122.5	81.5	82.5	60.8
4.0	106.7	23.5	4.2	24.2	44.3	21.6	20.5	15.3	23.6	24.2	24.2
7.7	28.2	8.4	6.0	22.9	8.1	12.0	11.3	4.5	13.9	20.2	22.9
7.0	41.9	6.9	17.6	48.9	14.6	32.9	13.3	6.8	15.5	35.3	49.0
13.0	72.3	37.1	44.1	56.2	17.5	27.5	32.0	22.1	36.1	44.9	56.2
721.3	303.2	760.7	309.5	300.2	173.3	405.2	603.3	584.0	624.7	355.2	298.8
15.6	100.9	37.4	26.8	72.6	86.7	79.4	52.7	28.1	76.1	69.0	72.6
457.0	320.4	359.4	320.8	310.3	140.5	269.2	241.0	265.8	198.1	272.9	309.5
66.0	140.8	181.2	61.8	98.0	93.9	97.5	103.8	125.7	76.2	98.0	98.0
21.5	95.1	29.8	8.9	34.2	37.4	43.4	36.3	16.4	56.4	37.0	34.2
32.6	**57.4**	**43.9**	**33.1**	**47.2**	**45.9**	**44.9**	**80.1**	**50.6**	**104.1**	**56.5**	**47.2**

(continued)

Table 2.8 (Continued)

INDEX OF REAL EXPENDITURES PER CAPITA (world = 100) Economy	Gross domestic product	Actual individual consumption	Food and nonalcoholic beverages	Alcoholic beverages, tobacco, and narcotics	Clothing and footwear	Housing, water, electricity, gas, and other fuels	Furnishings, household equipment and maintenance	Health	Transport	Communication
(00)	(01)	(02)	(03)	(04)	(05)	(06)	(07)	(08)	(09)	(10)
COMMONWEALTH OF INDEPENDENT STATES										
Armenia	49.7	84.5	194.3	177.2	35.7	120.0	18.3	61.1	31.3	114.1
Azerbaijan	118.6	96.8	172.4	101.2	109.2	132.0	75.9	43.2	68.8	139.0
Belarus	123.3	133.9	198.4	370.6	92.3	192.9	79.5	135.6	66.7	238.1
Kazakhstan	154.3	132.0	153.3	170.3	122.7	188.6	97.6	123.8	117.3	181.6
Kyrgyz Republic	22.7	40.5	61.0	92.0	32.1	66.7	21.5	24.5	27.0	95.2
Moldova	31.0	65.4	92.4	206.3	45.7	84.1	74.0	26.6	41.9	78.8
Russian Federation[d]	167.2	175.5	219.7	596.0	199.7	199.6	138.0	118.3	130.9	273.4
Tajikistan	16.7	35.0	62.3	4.7	28.7	48.1	14.6	24.2	13.8	102.2
Ukraine	61.6	91.4	144.9	247.1	56.0	150.2	58.7	89.3	63.3	63.0
Total (9)	**131.6**	**142.1**	**187.9**	**433.8**	**146.6**	**176.5**	**106.9**	**104.1**	**104.0**	**207.2**
EUROSTAT-OECD										
Albania	74.0	93.9	182.7	119.0	51.6	72.0	97.9	63.6	28.7	36.2
Australia	312.0	313.3	212.6	328.3	219.8	267.7	369.4	240.9	369.7	330.0
Austria	319.3	320.1	198.2	510.0	413.4	335.0	453.6	238.9	351.9	242.1
Belgium	297.9	303.6	250.8	424.9	267.7	269.9	355.7	329.1	292.8	175.5
Bosnia and Herzegovina	71.5	97.9	151.9	307.1	43.0	113.5	103.9	67.6	55.1	67.1
Bulgaria	115.3	126.9	121.2	264.7	43.8	158.0	155.5	153.4	123.1	155.3
Canada	305.1	317.3	164.5	300.8	269.9	334.4	358.8	268.7	448.9	235.3
Chile	150.2	158.5	133.5	169.5	142.8	130.8	208.8	120.1	178.3	164.6
Croatia	150.9	158.9	179.8	408.4	107.2	200.9	181.3	179.2	122.0	176.0
Cyprus	232.0	265.5	210.4	494.4	324.1	308.1	315.4	178.6	286.7	501.1
Czech Republic	200.9	192.3	165.6	590.2	82.4	218.2	187.0	225.6	130.2	118.5
Denmark	310.9	304.0	198.6	412.6	261.7	292.6	330.1	300.4	260.6	211.3
Estonia	171.5	159.5	168.6	486.8	137.6	150.7	105.9	155.3	136.5	179.4
Finland	286.8	307.4	238.1	480.3	265.6	289.7	340.8	303.1	259.5	288.0
France	270.4	306.3	254.8	358.0	247.8	291.7	348.9	303.2	336.2	237.2
Germany	304.5	329.4	226.3	417.2	289.5	294.4	428.6	359.9	326.7	327.8
Greece	197.8	245.8	261.3	441.6	197.1	304.0	221.0	230.6	251.0	190.3
Hungary	166.5	169.6	135.9	462.5	66.5	193.9	129.4	221.9	118.7	109.2
Iceland	284.0	298.8	244.1	283.7	170.0	349.8	351.9	287.3	288.8	257.5
Ireland	319.0	266.5	163.6	348.6	228.9	262.5	260.0	248.3	286.3	239.4
Israel	224.1	236.9	211.6	205.7	134.1	260.4	327.3	159.8	307.3	240.1
Italy	251.6	276.1	246.0	303.3	396.4	270.4	414.8	247.1	302.1	216.4
Japan	254.5	282.7	178.0	325.6	183.4	290.4	292.5	256.1	280.6	317.9
Korea, Rep.	215.7	202.2	104.1	180.7	130.1	229.2	131.3	235.7	201.1	367.3
Latvia	148.5	158.8	162.4	366.5	96.6	199.8	116.6	137.0	156.1	137.8
Lithuania	167.3	191.3	239.8	463.3	134.3	183.9	192.6	213.1	174.1	158.0
Luxembourg	658.8	370.1	262.1	2072.6	493.5	338.6	685.9	262.4	882.4	336.7

Recreation and culture	Education	Restaurants and hotels	Miscella-neous goods and services	Individual consumption expenditure by households	Individual consumption expenditure by government	Collective consumption expenditure by government	Gross fixed capital formation	Machinery and equipment	Construction	Domestic absorption	Individual consumption expenditure by households without housing
(11)	(12)	(13)	(14)	(16)	(17)	(18)	(19)	(20)	(21)	(25)	(26)
23.8	131.3	12.1	22.0	79.8	81.1	73.4	26.8	16.2	31.3	63.6	73.6
39.0	171.7	35.0	35.5	91.1	109.5	123.1	46.9	87.8	29.4	83.2	88.3
82.8	323.7	40.8	35.4	114.2	311.3	94.9	94.1	131.3	82.1	125.9	110.4
84.9	313.6	65.1	95.5	119.2	216.7	143.4	81.0	80.1	78.4	125.1	123.2
17.4	113.5	15.2	15.8	36.2	70.4	36.4	9.1	13.5	7.3	28.7	34.5
24.9	150.1	14.6	49.6	57.3	127.4	31.0	14.9	17.6	12.7	44.9	54.2
113.0	199.6	58.7	123.9	160.0	278.0	200.4	92.6	121.8	74.0	157.7	158.3
10.6	69.3	4.4	14.0	31.0	60.9	22.8	9.1	15.0	5.8	25.2	30.2
40.9	183.3	20.4	40.4	81.0	170.3	65.1	24.5	32.7	21.5	66.8	76.6
85.9	**200.6**	**46.5**	**91.4**	**128.8**	**232.6**	**150.9**	**71.0**	**92.7**	**58.1**	**124.6**	**126.8**
29.2	254.1	47.5	43.8	87.5	115.5	73.3	82.3	37.7	122.7	88.2	89.5
572.9	238.4	399.1	416.5	312.0	313.1	278.8	319.4	402.9	212.2	309.6	319.1
480.6	187.3	641.2	343.5	322.6	323.2	252.6	304.3	480.1	200.9	311.6	320.1
385.0	233.8	265.6	362.1	282.4	441.5	251.9	312.7	426.4	237.2	298.0	285.7
65.8	144.1	96.9	70.1	93.3	118.0	119.0	49.2	45.7	56.8	86.1	91.0
139.4	158.1	142.4	62.3	117.0	188.4	179.0	80.0	88.5	81.6	117.9	108.2
420.8	208.1	308.2	387.5	309.7	353.0	321.6	318.1	292.0	270.7	313.3	298.8
142.0	273.1	115.3	181.1	154.0	174.5	102.0	134.5	158.3	117.2	147.9	157.7
231.5	175.5	353.4	118.2	148.6	220.5	203.8	124.8	111.6	130.5	153.4	142.9
313.8	194.7	664.4	195.4	279.9	184.1	305.9	183.1	167.8	192.5	245.4	272.9
272.2	196.8	286.3	140.8	173.2	317.6	284.3	187.5	270.0	148.6	196.2	168.2
441.6	247.8	200.8	467.6	257.3	600.6	272.3	284.7	399.6	181.7	292.2	248.1
167.6	211.7	181.7	126.3	140.7	286.9	231.6	163.8	226.3	140.3	168.5	139.3
455.1	245.1	262.4	396.3	278.8	496.7	271.8	263.6	248.5	244.8	291.9	279.3
395.5	220.0	336.2	363.1	282.3	464.5	244.0	240.9	276.6	194.5	282.3	282.7
387.0	197.1	283.5	435.7	313.5	430.7	225.9	225.1	376.2	156.8	290.3	313.6
191.3	181.3	480.9	191.8	254.1	172.8	273.8	123.9	164.0	100.9	217.1	251.8
188.2	197.6	200.2	187.1	149.9	303.4	252.5	109.2	139.8	94.6	160.4	143.2
400.9	283.4	328.3	266.7	266.9	505.8	320.3	147.8	237.7	101.9	259.4	245.7
263.5	244.7	470.2	246.7	251.2	368.9	203.5	195.8	231.2	166.7	244.7	248.2
220.3	281.6	218.0	244.6	223.5	313.8	315.3	192.4	183.8	144.0	228.1	213.6
280.4	179.2	429.2	238.8	270.3	313.4	219.7	237.3	327.9	170.4	258.2	270.1
358.1	159.1	314.1	444.5	268.6	363.2	267.3	219.1	365.1	126.6	260.4	255.0
215.3	218.5	199.6	257.8	202.1	185.9	220.7	243.0	289.4	208.9	214.9	195.9
181.0	198.3	102.2	87.4	149.8	205.8	241.0	117.9	150.9	108.1	157.4	143.6
169.1	220.7	82.7	137.2	173.8	303.4	216.7	107.7	107.8	106.0	174.3	174.4
562.6	195.2	542.9	597.5	361.2	465.1	409.9	651.2	919.2	514.7	438.8	371.8

(continued)

Table 2.8 *(Continued)*

INDEX OF REAL EXPENDITURES PER CAPITA (world = 100) Economy	Gross domestic product	Actual individual consumption	Food and nonalcoholic beverages	Alcoholic beverages, tobacco, and narcotics	Clothing and footwear	Housing, water, electricity, gas, and other fuels	Furnishings, household equipment and maintenance	Health	Transport	Communication
(00)	(01)	(02)	(03)	(04)	(05)	(06)	(07)	(08)	(09)	(10)
Macedonia, FYR	88.8	109.7	187.1	160.5	65.8	129.0	70.3	86.8	60.4	127.1
Malta	212.5	227.8	213.5	238.1	160.9	187.4	306.6	245.1	222.4	265.8
Mexico	121.7	137.0	197.9	130.5	84.4	102.0	160.4	65.5	209.5	127.6
Montenegro	105.0	142.4	256.0	311.4	56.4	140.8	271.5	98.8	119.4	210.4
Netherlands	320.6	300.5	232.0	331.3	275.6	256.0	359.3	264.4	266.9	320.3
New Zealand	231.6	260.2	216.5	343.2	251.8	227.9	282.6	275.1	283.0	212.4
Norway	459.7	358.7	234.1	304.0	325.3	320.8	446.9	321.9	377.4	427.3
Poland	161.6	188.6	212.1	350.7	90.2	256.1	154.9	198.0	118.9	146.1
Portugal	190.7	214.9	243.4	295.5	200.0	165.5	253.0	192.8	219.5	167.5
Romania	119.9	129.3	175.0	174.7	56.0	123.2	106.5	196.5	85.0	161.4
Russian Federation[d]	167.2	175.5	219.7	596.0	199.7	197.6	138.0	117.6	130.9	273.4
Serbia	88.1	116.9	148.0	264.2	42.9	155.8	65.2	126.4	89.5	159.5
Slovak Republic	186.7	195.2	182.0	294.0	111.9	269.4	202.8	217.9	108.3	127.6
Slovenia	209.2	218.3	199.0	511.2	207.3	216.3	272.7	213.2	272.4	229.0
Spain	238.9	248.5	245.4	325.3	283.5	215.7	256.7	211.8	238.0	149.4
Sweden	310.3	309.7	229.7	347.9	251.5	320.8	308.5	274.4	295.9	469.9
Switzerland	383.2	340.8	232.3	674.6	292.9	288.5	426.4	308.0	365.0	397.7
Turkey	132.1	158.8	186.0	142.8	161.5	198.7	250.8	111.9	174.1	116.0
United Kingdom	260.7	302.4	197.1	279.9	433.6	250.9	323.0	270.4	325.3	228.5
United States	369.8	432.4	219.9	311.1	333.5	382.9	458.2	532.3	546.8	331.7
Total (47)	**250.2**	**276.8**	**206.4**	**327.1**	**237.4**	**264.2**	**302.6**	**278.2**	**306.6**	**254.3**
LATIN AMERICA										
Bolivia	41.3	42.3	77.2	21.4	14.8	51.8	57.2	23.0	76.0	9.1
Brazil	108.8	114.6	125.7	105.0	54.2	83.2	170.3	134.8	129.9	68.1
Colombia	84.4	90.6	90.8	98.1	83.9	121.9	57.3	55.8	85.4	77.9
Costa Rica	96.8	118.5	133.9	42.0	82.5	72.1	136.1	75.5	217.3	133.0
Cuba[e]	...	...	...	...	...	...	...	...	...	...
Dominican Republic	80.7	112.4	159.8	197.8	63.1	116.8	70.7	56.8	112.0	151.4
Ecuador	73.8	78.2	88.5	72.7	47.4	87.3	93.1	53.4	106.7	105.7
El Salvador	54.7	84.3	115.0	50.3	61.3	124.9	135.6	50.8	86.7	100.0
Guatemala	51.8	72.0	148.3	31.5	61.8	69.9	99.4	34.9	50.5	126.6
Haiti	11.6	19.5	61.5	22.1	15.0	19.7	16.2	5.4	11.2	2.2
Honduras	32.3	43.4	75.6	55.4	24.7	44.7	34.0	28.8	39.4	27.6
Nicaragua	30.5	41.5	52.8	36.8	20.6	63.6	47.0	33.5	41.6	27.5
Panama	114.2	122.8	114.5	25.1	109.3	198.9	169.7	62.9	163.3	195.8
Paraguay	53.4	64.7	99.9	34.1	37.1	57.5	103.8	38.2	47.8	90.7
Peru	81.6	82.7	109.5	68.2	76.0	64.9	67.9	47.6	85.6	80.2
Uruguay	128.8	149.2	164.1	120.6	89.3	202.6	153.0	140.9	108.9	233.9
Venezuela, RB	126.0	118.7	100.9	78.9	41.3	92.1	69.9	87.5	258.3	232.8
Total (17)	**92.4**	**99.0**	**113.6**	**88.3**	**56.6**	**86.4**	**120.2**	**92.6**	**118.2**	**87.8**

Recreation and culture	Education	Restaurants and hotels	Miscella-neous goods and services	Individual consumption expenditure by households	Individual consumption expenditure by government	Collective consumption expenditure by government	Gross fixed capital formation	Machinery and equipment	Construction	Domestic absorption	Individual consumption expenditure by households without housing
(11)	(12)	(13)	(14)	(16)	(17)	(18)	(19)	(20)	(21)	(25)	(26)
45.6	175.4	71.1	64.0	102.4	146.7	165.5	59.0	44.6	73.9	103.4	98.0
359.3	193.9	682.9	260.9	216.3	291.4	310.6	134.1	139.8	118.4	207.9	215.3
78.9	266.6	93.2	117.0	130.5	159.5	114.4	94.1	80.7	106.7	124.8	135.5
67.7	198.5	316.3	84.3	133.9	188.7	220.2	61.8	51.4	73.2	125.3	134.0
416.8	236.9	218.4	494.7	262.2	542.0	382.5	254.3	303.0	196.5	292.2	265.8
377.5	271.9	322.6	235.9	243.9	356.9	237.5	158.8	223.1	108.8	230.5	238.0
570.5	239.4	247.1	442.3	326.5	569.4	350.8	401.4	566.0	236.6	381.2	320.6
206.9	202.4	62.4	196.6	175.2	269.2	173.4	105.7	129.4	93.5	166.2	177.0
218.7	217.2	439.4	208.6	211.5	231.6	221.2	167.6	134.4	181.8	201.6	218.1
123.2	180.7	72.3	76.1	115.8	217.5	144.7	119.6	89.2	149.2	127.4	117.7
110.7	198.6	58.7	128.0	160.0	278.0	200.4	92.6	121.8	74.0	157.7	158.5
77.8	161.1	39.0	88.1	105.0	201.4	106.4	57.2	58.1	59.9	101.1	100.2
247.3	203.1	147.4	168.5	181.7	274.1	282.7	148.8	153.5	111.1	188.8	179.8
268.3	181.7	232.7	188.3	208.0	280.9	245.4	169.7	250.1	126.3	208.8	211.0
314.1	193.4	712.3	215.2	239.4	305.1	265.9	240.2	228.1	190.8	244.4	245.0
458.3	220.3	209.3	447.7	271.9	549.0	280.1	245.3	428.3	135.6	291.2	257.0
497.7	193.2	419.2	471.7	369.8	181.9	191.3	380.0	710.2	199.0	332.3	384.3
88.4	286.7	140.7	90.8	150.2	199.6	122.8	109.3	168.8	86.7	143.9	138.2
562.7	208.9	395.2	336.3	292.7	369.0	261.9	178.5	151.1	138.1	267.8	297.8
646.0	226.5	526.9	590.1	480.5	173.4	409.3	288.8	459.0	155.3	389.2	493.1
350.2	**215.3**	**309.0**	**331.3**	**277.9**	**276.5**	**258.0**	**204.0**	**281.4**	**143.2**	**254.6**	**278.9**
4.7	33.7	53.6	11.3	48.1	5.6	52.1	27.3	33.8	19.8	39.1	48.3
66.9	147.9	109.2	126.6	109.6	143.9	133.9	101.3	108.7	89.1	111.4	111.8
64.8	109.7	145.2	86.7	94.7	55.9	107.2	71.0	60.2	81.2	85.9	91.0
160.1	144.1	94.3	59.0	120.2	89.0	73.6	71.9	68.1	77.4	103.0	125.3
…	…	…	…	…	…	…	…	…	…	…	…
32.8	111.5	188.2	115.8	123.3	28.9	64.9	43.1	27.0	60.8	88.8	123.4
50.8	111.9	47.7	60.4	81.6	48.6	58.6	70.9	42.7	46.8	76.1	81.0
53.4	76.3	65.8	41.6	91.0	33.0	41.4	23.3	26.3	22.4	64.4	87.5
30.3	53.4	78.5	30.9	77.9	27.6	38.4	27.6	31.3	26.5	56.8	75.6
6.9	12.8	0.5	4.2	22.6	1.3	0.1	13.0	0.6	27.3	15.9	22.7
24.1	55.4	43.4	27.7	46.5	20.3	26.7	29.7	36.2	23.1	38.5	46.4
17.3	66.3	38.3	29.6	43.6	24.2	37.7	18.4	15.9	19.4	34.4	40.0
90.4	117.4	93.6	97.2	128.1	76.9	104.3	95.6	102.2	97.8	114.5	118.6
46.0	99.7	48.9	50.7	68.1	37.1	27.5	31.4	25.9	34.1	52.3	70.4
68.9	107.0	109.0	76.9	88.6	36.1	66.3	70.7	55.4	87.0	78.5	89.5
65.3	131.9	185.9	112.2	153.4	106.8	96.1	102.0	81.4	115.8	131.3	142.3
66.5	212.7	184.5	40.9	121.9	91.7	117.0	91.4	70.7	115.4	114.9	124.8
60.0	**127.6**	**109.7**	**92.2**	**99.0**	**94.2**	**102.7**	**79.8**	**77.8**	**77.9**	**93.8**	**99.6**

(continued)

Table 2.8 *(Continued)*

INDEX OF REAL EXPENDITURES PER CAPITA (world = 100) Economy	Gross domestic product	Actual individual consumption	Food and nonalcoholic beverages	Alcoholic beverages, tobacco, and narcotics	Clothing and footwear	Housing, water, electricity, gas, and other fuels	Furnishings, household equipment and maintenance	Health	Transport	Communication
(00)	(01)	(02)	(03)	(04)	(05)	(06)	(07)	(08)	(09)	(10)
CARIBBEAN										
Anguilla	202.6	244.2	153.3	214.1	167.0	320.7	202.1	53.6	524.8	697.4
Antigua and Barbuda	152.6	145.1	108.9	90.0	68.7	282.1	114.8	150.5	111.3	219.0
Aruba	267.6	277.6	126.2	46.6	187.4	612.4	180.2	376.3	331.2	309.4
Bahamas, The	168.2	180.0	113.0	91.9	119.2	348.9	125.7	133.9	151.8	233.1
Barbados	114.1	142.6	139.7	77.6	76.1	450.7	92.2	67.5	123.3	205.2
Belize	61.0	75.1	66.0	21.5	105.3	196.8	88.8	45.3	65.5	76.8
Bermuda	407.9	438.6	311.3	483.7	255.4	435.8	501.6	322.7	435.9	681.4
Bonaire[f]	...	...	90.4	33.2	224.6	...	167.7	...	242.1	204.0
Cayman Islands	369.1	393.4	160.0	154.1	286.1	776.0	348.2	128.8	441.7	621.7
Curaçao	206.4	239.3	152.6	98.8	286.7	555.1	125.3	175.9	221.4	229.2
Dominica	74.2	100.2	87.0	24.6	148.9	164.9	75.2	61.8	177.0	137.1
Grenada	83.4	118.1	113.0	66.7	87.5	178.1	77.0	46.4	183.4	382.8
Jamaica	61.9	83.7	112.5	31.4	35.8	87.8	90.8	45.8	103.6	103.1
Montserrat	117.1	157.4	113.8	101.6	41.5	258.3	93.3	138.8	342.0	441.0
St. Kitts and Nevis	152.9	167.0	119.2	150.4	160.4	351.2	122.4	122.9	112.8	207.7
St. Lucia	73.5	87.0	94.7	45.6	109.6	169.4	56.5	44.2	76.0	139.9
St. Vincent and the Grenadines	73.4	96.6	95.6	187.8	43.7	187.8	64.1	67.5	166.5	172.2
Sint Maarten	245.0	223.2	115.0	40.1	294.6	556.6	183.2	84.9	287.2	269.6
Suriname	107.4	68.4	111.8	53.4	54.4	120.4	48.8	37.7	35.7	71.3
Trinidad and Tobago	213.5	181.5	203.0	48.1	48.2	155.5	115.6	132.3	187.7	136.5
Turks and Caicos Islands	155.1	87.8	88.6	58.2	101.6	43.6	79.8	78.2	215.9	86.3
Virgin Islands, British	225.0	124.4	134.3	177.5	305.5	129.0	298.0	64.8	160.0	165.8
Total (22)	**121.5**	**125.7**	**132.0**	**54.8**	**70.3**	**180.3**	**102.9**	**82.5**	**134.1**	**145.2**
WESTERN ASIA										
Bahrain	322.1	215.4	174.9	30.1	242.4	265.8	303.6	96.9	383.0	429.0
Egypt, Arab Rep.[a]	78.7	98.6	164.1	74.1	114.4	153.0	70.0	108.7	55.7	76.7
Iraq	82.7	62.2	86.7	8.9	55.8	134.0	50.4	45.7	46.5	34.4
Jordan	83.0	102.6	126.5	106.0	107.9	187.4	85.1	77.0	95.4	124.3
Kuwait	624.5	253.1	259.1	22.3	376.4	479.5	598.6	116.5	327.3	233.2
Oman	316.6	175.6	183.3	16.1	213.4	199.3	149.3	87.9	398.2	252.8
Qatar	1088.5	237.7	189.4	34.0	195.8	294.0	224.8	112.0	394.9	200.9
Saudi Arabia	357.8	205.8	169.6	25.2	212.7	379.7	281.3	123.3	198.5	254.1
Sudan[b]	26.8	26.7	65.5	4.3	43.7	24.5	37.4	5.3	17.6	13.3
United Arab Emirates	452.3	340.7	268.7	26.1	1023.8	623.6	360.8	31.9	802.2	889.2
West Bank and Gaza	28.5	47.1	83.4	33.1	70.6	27.2	56.3	43.0	35.1	48.7
Yemen, Rep.	27.6	31.9	54.8	64.8	36.6	46.2	15.9	36.4	19.0	9.6
Total (12)	**130.0**	**99.2**	**128.0**	**42.0**	**134.4**	**165.5**	**102.1**	**70.7**	**100.5**	**110.4**

Recreation and culture	Education	Restaurants and hotels	Miscellaneous goods and services	Individual consumption expenditure by households	Individual consumption expenditure by government	Collective consumption expenditure by government	Gross fixed capital formation	Machinery and equipment	Construction	Domestic absorption	Individual consumption expenditure by households without housing
(11)	(12)	(13)	(14)	(16)	(17)	(18)	(19)	(20)	(21)	(25)	(26)
115.5	206.6	147.2	318.3	257.8	94.7	414.7	200.9	117.1	268.9	238.4	258.2
54.2	187.9	87.5	148.4	135.9	225.2	297.8	150.0	63.6	222.1	153.8	113.5
238.9	256.2	77.5	204.3	238.5	596.9	450.4	398.2	252.2	508.4	311.2	181.8
122.7	147.5	186.6	223.1	185.5	117.6	316.0	226.5	294.5	189.2	198.5	160.1
86.2	101.7	403.8	107.5	146.3	98.1	246.7	101.5	129.5	88.2	136.8	88.7
52.3	63.6	6.8	26.7	80.0	29.3	106.9	24.7	31.6	20.5	63.4	55.2
434.3	521.8	919.8	552.0	424.7	498.6	502.7	573.3	1111.7	304.9	468.5	421.8
...	...	196.1	...	169.6	...	...	...	...	...	...	154.5
282.3	322.9	378.6	587.7	412.9	196.7	481.3	428.2	601.7	338.2	399.2	354.1
133.9	138.9	102.4	422.8	242.9	185.9	264.3	310.1	477.6	136.9	259.6	196.0
48.0	109.8	47.1	58.7	102.8	67.6	145.0	67.0	83.3	57.3	85.6	90.3
35.7	185.0	32.6	75.2	120.4	85.1	125.4	64.9	65.3	66.1	104.0	108.5
92.0	116.2	155.0	79.1	85.3	61.8	83.4	50.6	56.3	47.5	75.1	80.1
63.0	191.1	8.9	137.2	148.2	218.5	618.6	161.2	102.0	210.4	183.3	130.9
67.9	321.9	168.4	127.6	160.2	220.6	407.6	166.5	110.2	207.5	177.7	127.7
20.3	145.8	15.9	79.2	88.2	66.9	124.9	87.8	65.3	103.6	88.4	76.5
73.5	118.5	34.3	65.1	94.2	108.6	127.1	71.9	46.6	93.7	92.4	81.4
140.1	122.0	55.1	206.0	229.2	144.6	554.3	200.9	331.0	81.0	234.1	171.0
32.9	11.7	14.4	71.2	73.3	16.2	204.3	143.0	276.9	47.8	101.3	75.8
174.4	390.0	236.4	233.1	157.1	384.6	74.6	149.8	182.1	129.1	166.7	168.5
73.2	125.4	54.6	90.7	89.9	59.9	513.7	90.1	125.4	72.9	111.0	102.4
75.1	81.6	107.3	61.7	128.0	79.0	194.7	215.6	361.5	138.5	143.4	136.1
107.2	**173.8**	**161.1**	**136.3**	**122.0**	**147.2**	**144.0**	**113.9**	**145.9**	**93.4**	**123.4**	**113.3**
235.7	258.3	186.7	122.7	229.8	130.2	291.4	241.6	154.9	329.0	224.9	248.5
41.6	135.9	43.8	62.5	101.0	68.3	127.4	34.1	28.4	39.3	82.2	95.2
9.0	135.3	8.4	11.0	55.8	104.2	221.8	51.2	53.8	51.8	70.0	46.0
23.1	196.3	28.2	23.4	102.6	97.6	143.9	59.9	36.6	74.5	95.6	90.8
123.0	218.7	95.6	103.5	261.1	198.6	566.7	475.1	441.7	417.6	328.6	246.5
86.6	233.0	77.1	119.5	171.5	188.0	414.6	399.2	313.0	430.2	231.7	177.2
272.1	296.6	76.8	284.5	239.9	235.7	707.8	1904.9	2034.7	659.2	572.8	236.2
88.1	349.6	129.2	83.5	188.4	286.8	370.4	415.1	333.0	424.8	274.9	175.8
8.8	17.6	12.9	6.1	29.0	3.2	37.6	24.9	21.9	29.5	27.6	29.6
136.6	151.8	200.4	128.1	412.4	29.6	215.9	599.7	583.6	536.7	365.3	371.8
17.4	73.2	15.3	30.5	44.9	55.1	87.1	22.5	10.5	27.9	42.8	48.2
1.8	40.6	0.2	11.4	32.7	23.7	49.3	11.5	2.5	15.0	28.9	32.1
39.5	**136.0**	**45.8**	**46.4**	**100.1**	**87.7**	**164.0**	**124.8**	**109.3**	**118.0**	**107.8**	**93.5**

(continued)

Table 2.8 *(Continued)*

INDEX OF REAL EXPENDITURES PER CAPITA (world = 100) Economy	Gross domestic product	Actual individual consumption	Food and nonalcoholic beverages	Alcoholic beverages, tobacco, and narcotics	Clothing and footwear	Housing, water, electricity, gas, and other fuels	Furnishings, household equipment and maintenance	Health	Transport	Communication
(00)	(01)	(02)	(03)	(04)	(05)	(06)	(07)	(08)	(09)	(10)
SINGLETONS										
Georgia	47.1	70.0	94.6	143.0	21.6	124.3	42.5	80.5	45.7	83.0
Iran, Islamic Rep.	129.9	99.2	108.2	24.7	54.3	179.7	58.2	109.3	66.3	171.6
Total (2)	**125.3**	**97.6**	**107.5**	**31.4**	**52.4**	**176.5**	**57.3**	**107.7**	**65.1**	**166.6**
WORLD[g] (179)	**100.0**	**100.0**	**100.0**	**100.0**	**100.0**	**100.0**	**100.0**	**100.0**	**100.0**	**100.0**

Source: ICP, http://icp.worldbank.org/.

Note: n.a. = not applicable; ... = data suppressed because of incompleteness.

a. The Arab Republic of Egypt participated in both the Africa and Western Asia regions. The regional results for Egypt were averaged by taking the geometric mean of the regional PPPs, allowing Egypt to have the same global results in each region.

b. Sudan participated in both the Africa and Western Asia regions. The regional results for Sudan were averaged by taking the geometric mean of the regional PPPs, allowing Sudan to have the same global results in each region.

c. The results presented in the tables are based on data supplied by all the participating economies and compiled in accordance with ICP principles and the procedures recommended by the 2011 ICP Technical Advisory Group. The results for China are estimated by the 2011 ICP Asia and the Pacific Regional Office and the Global Office. The National Bureau of Statistics of China does not recognize these results as official statistics.

d. The Russian Federation participated in both the CIS and Eurostat-OECD comparisons. The PPPs for Russia are based on the Eurostat-OECD comparison. They were the basis for linking the CIS comparison to the ICP.

e. The official GDP of Cuba for reference year 2011 is 68,990.15 million in national currency. However, this number and its breakdown into main aggregates are not shown in the tables because of methodological comparability issues. Therefore, Cuba's results are provided only for the PPP and price level index. In addition, Cuba's figures are not included in the Latin America and world totals.

f. Bonaire's results are provided only for the individual consumption expenditure by households. Therefore, to ensure consistency across the tables, Bonaire is not included in the Caribbean or the world total.

g. This table does not include the Pacific Islands and does not double count the dual participation economies: the Arab Republic of Egypt, Sudan, and the Russian Federation.

Recreation and culture	Education	Restaurants and hotels	Miscella-neous goods and services	Individual consumption expenditure by households	Individual consumption expenditure by government	Collective consumption expenditure by government	Gross fixed capital formation	Machinery and equipment	Construction	Domestic absorption	Individual consumption expenditure by households without housing
(11)	(12)	(13)	(14)	(16)	(17)	(18)	(19)	(20)	(21)	(25)	(26)
65.2	143.0	28.4	38.2	67.0	55.1	114.0	23.6	36.1	16.2	57.9	61.2
34.1	183.5	14.1	69.4	95.2	103.9	225.7	93.3	89.6	116.6	117.3	85.5
35.9	**181.2**	**14.9**	**67.6**	**93.7**	**101.1**	**219.4**	**89.4**	**86.6**	**111.0**	**114.0**	**84.1**
100.0	**100.0**	**100.0**	**100.0**	**100.0**	**100.0**	**100.0**	**100.0**	**100.0**	**100.0**	**100.0**	**100.0**

Table 2.9 Price Level Indexes (World = 100), ICP 2011

PRICE LEVEL INDEX (world = 100) Economy	Gross domestic product	Actual individual consumption	Food and nonalcoholic beverages	Alcoholic beverages, tobacco, and narcotics	Clothing and footwear	Housing, water, electricity, gas, and other fuels	Furnishings, household equipment and maintenance	Health	Transport	Communication
(00)	(01)	(02)	(03)	(04)	(05)	(06)	(07)	(08)	(09)	(10)
AFRICA										
Algeria	53.9	49.4	77.7	78.0	70.8	45.2	55.2	27.5	41.8	67.8
Angola	94.0	93.0	140.7	61.0	110.2	79.8	112.1	80.4	83.4	129.0
Benin	58.5	54.8	87.7	52.1	53.2	53.0	64.2	39.7	50.8	71.4
Botswana	71.0	74.1	106.0	100.8	65.0	89.2	97.3	51.2	66.7	65.6
Burkina Faso	58.4	53.8	91.1	56.6	48.2	43.6	61.8	38.8	62.1	73.2
Burundi	43.5	43.1	71.8	73.0	40.1	26.7	56.4	21.1	73.4	88.3
Cameroon	62.1	56.4	83.3	63.3	70.6	44.1	78.1	51.4	63.6	108.8
Cape Verde	79.4	70.0	103.7	80.4	86.9	73.2	71.7	50.6	82.4	64.6
Central African Republic	69.9	64.5	116.0	71.9	57.7	36.6	83.5	41.2	71.4	119.2
Chad	68.4	61.0	95.9	72.6	58.3	59.9	76.9	40.1	66.9	105.7
Comoros	75.6	70.8	112.2	112.2	76.1	57.7	110.5	46.3	77.1	137.2
Congo, Rep.	79.1	72.9	128.9	71.5	78.1	46.9	83.0	47.2	84.8	121.9
Congo, Dem. Rep.	73.2	66.7	120.9	84.5	67.0	41.2	69.1	40.6	75.7	98.7
Côte d'Ivoire	62.4	58.1	91.1	63.6	69.5	45.5	62.9	35.5	66.1	99.5
Djibouti	68.2	66.1	95.9	72.2	69.1	58.2	71.1	56.6	72.0	67.3
Egypt, Arab Rep.[a]	35.1	33.6	64.3	59.1	42.4	16.3	52.1	21.5	35.3	44.0
Equatorial Guinea	80.5	80.3	139.4	61.7	77.7	63.8	107.4	54.2	81.7	89.7
Ethiopia	37.5	36.4	58.6	45.7	42.3	37.1	45.9	21.8	43.3	43.2
Gabon	86.9	88.3	155.2	59.6	91.1	79.0	87.6	65.6	71.1	143.2
Gambia, The	43.5	41.3	74.6	44.8	28.1	36.2	44.9	23.0	42.3	37.5
Ghana	59.7	59.0	116.0	70.1	55.7	41.9	64.4	29.1	46.2	65.8
Guinea	49.0	43.6	90.3	48.9	39.5	16.2	46.7	27.6	48.7	70.9
Guinea-Bissau	60.1	58.6	94.7	67.1	67.4	51.0	76.4	32.7	68.8	80.5
Kenya	49.8	46.5	71.9	64.3	41.1	33.5	51.3	29.9	66.3	41.1
Lesotho	69.7	62.7	90.9	80.9	62.5	49.5	79.9	43.2	69.9	81.3
Liberia	66.7	64.7	108.8	78.6	54.8	80.0	59.3	34.2	66.1	92.0
Madagascar	42.9	39.9	64.4	48.4	32.0	41.3	42.9	22.5	58.0	76.8
Malawi	63.1	58.2	100.1	65.2	48.8	28.7	73.7	29.5	100.0	76.4
Mali	57.4	53.4	79.9	52.8	55.2	53.2	67.8	30.4	72.7	77.2
Mauritania	52.3	45.2	73.2	52.0	36.8	38.3	50.7	30.5	48.0	68.5
Mauritius	71.6	71.8	103.4	115.4	60.9	55.3	83.2	45.3	104.3	68.6
Morocco	58.6	59.5	93.1	123.0	65.2	34.8	67.1	56.4	63.7	90.2
Mozambique	71.1	63.1	99.7	67.1	59.5	42.5	84.5	50.5	69.0	88.6
Namibia	82.8	82.2	124.6	84.0	62.7	98.3	73.1	65.3	81.7	76.1
Niger	60.4	55.5	95.6	66.3	40.4	49.9	50.0	40.9	61.2	104.7
Nigeria	62.3	58.8	106.7	56.5	50.4	52.0	49.2	31.9	55.2	78.8
Rwanda	55.9	48.5	73.3	67.0	57.6	35.6	44.9	30.5	74.4	63.6
São Tomé and Príncipe	62.4	64.3	108.1	72.7	68.6	57.8	78.6	35.0	71.2	85.6

Recreation and culture	Education	Restaurants and hotels	Miscellaneous goods and services	Individual consumption expenditure by households	Individual consumption expenditure by government	Collective consumption expenditure by government	Gross fixed capital formation	Machinery and equipment	Construction	Domestic absorption	Individual consumption expenditure by households without housing
(11)	(12)	(13)	(14)	(16)	(17)	(18)	(19)	(20)	(21)	(25)	(26)
41.4	25.3	50.9	46.4	52.0	32.3	32.1	75.2	108.8	63.9	53.2	51.7
112.9	73.1	142.1	81.1	94.0	87.7	83.2	79.3	116.6	66.1	91.4	99.8
59.7	43.2	65.8	34.7	56.9	46.3	42.7	83.0	108.1	75.4	58.7	60.4
72.1	53.2	98.7	60.9	77.4	54.9	65.0	62.6	104.3	47.0	70.0	79.0
65.8	30.3	51.3	42.3	56.2	42.4	52.5	78.1	114.6	65.5	58.6	60.8
53.5	19.5	51.5	35.2	46.1	24.8	29.4	71.8	104.2	60.9	45.8	52.1
66.4	44.1	70.6	42.1	58.2	58.3	56.4	86.9	104.5	88.5	61.9	62.4
73.3	57.1	64.5	55.3	71.9	61.4	69.2	97.2	115.9	96.1	76.4	75.3
70.8	29.0	70.9	52.5	67.7	42.7	65.4	90.2	116.7	84.4	69.1	74.0
56.0	31.3	81.3	43.3	63.5	54.8	57.1	97.6	117.1	100.9	68.0	67.2
87.2	42.4	78.7	67.3	74.3	52.6	63.2	87.0	116.8	79.8	73.5	81.7
79.8	54.1	78.7	45.2	75.0	65.9	73.3	107.8	116.9	102.8	82.7	80.6
61.6	32.8	93.2	57.6	69.8	53.3	65.4	95.2	117.4	91.2	72.5	78.7
74.3	52.5	58.2	42.7	59.6	56.4	59.3	77.6	115.6	63.8	61.7	63.6
78.2	52.7	84.4	59.3	68.1	59.2	61.9	70.1	106.7	56.7	67.3	72.9
33.4	21.6	42.3	28.6	36.1	17.7	19.1	58.9	95.4	47.6	35.3	40.7
100.3	49.8	87.8	65.7	81.2	82.2	124.8	76.4	118.0	60.2	80.4	85.3
33.1	15.6	30.4	25.0	38.4	23.2	29.2	56.1	112.2	33.7	39.5	39.0
73.6	81.5	99.5	67.2	90.8	79.2	79.4	94.4	116.3	103.2	89.4	94.0
38.4	28.8	65.2	30.0	43.8	24.4	29.7	68.2	117.6	45.9	45.0	46.7
60.9	36.5	84.0	41.3	62.2	40.5	51.8	62.8	124.0	36.8	59.5	66.7
45.6	18.8	62.2	35.6	46.3	21.3	30.4	77.3	113.8	65.0	48.7	53.9
74.4	19.6	79.3	45.6	62.8	25.3	41.6	78.7	117.5	64.9	59.8	66.2
49.6	46.7	50.9	33.0	47.6	42.1	53.9	66.3	103.2	52.2	50.9	53.0
57.0	64.0	86.9	47.1	63.5	61.7	72.6	80.5	117.6	67.1	67.9	69.2
57.3	32.5	65.0	45.5	67.7	48.7	56.5	74.0	116.9	54.0	66.1	68.5
36.4	23.3	27.7	28.4	41.5	34.2	42.7	68.2	111.5	51.4	44.6	43.8
75.8	50.6	85.1	42.2	59.7	54.7	79.4	79.1	118.1	64.9	63.0	67.5
53.8	36.3	74.7	38.6	56.1	37.9	46.4	77.6	110.4	66.9	57.5	58.5
46.9	32.9	65.7	37.0	47.1	34.5	42.5	78.7	118.5	64.4	53.0	50.6
65.5	56.2	109.9	60.3	76.0	44.4	49.2	74.2	103.1	64.2	70.5	79.0
59.0	51.5	70.9	50.8	61.8	47.0	55.6	57.0	101.6	39.9	58.7	70.2
61.5	74.6	58.0	41.8	63.7	73.7	97.7	88.2	109.1	82.9	70.1	69.3
75.4	54.3	106.8	53.8	84.3	71.1	76.4	73.9	115.6	58.5	80.8	83.4
62.5	25.6	64.8	42.3	57.8	44.7	58.7	78.8	94.4	79.1	60.8	61.1
55.9	47.3	66.7	36.8	61.6	43.3	50.9	78.1	116.9	64.2	61.7	64.3
56.5	50.4	54.1	39.9	48.9	60.0	83.3	80.9	107.2	71.2	56.6	53.9
76.2	31.0	75.3	42.7	69.0	29.8	32.4	68.5	117.3	43.4	62.3	73.5

(continued)

Table 2.9 *(Continued)*

PRICE LEVEL INDEX (world = 100) Economy	Gross domestic product	Actual individual consumption	Food and nonalcoholic beverages	Alcoholic beverages, tobacco, and narcotics	Clothing and footwear	Housing, water, electricity, gas, and other fuels	Furnishings, household equipment and maintenance	Health	Transport	Communication
(00)	(01)	(02)	(03)	(04)	(05)	(06)	(07)	(08)	(09)	(10)
Senegal	64.6	60.3	95.7	70.7	54.2	51.5	59.1	41.5	72.1	86.2
Seychelles	69.7	70.3	107.9	162.7	84.2	49.1	87.2	38.9	89.9	81.8
Sierra Leone	46.2	46.0	85.2	45.7	33.4	28.6	49.2	25.2	59.9	85.6
South Africa	84.8	81.9	102.0	86.3	90.7	78.2	105.3	75.4	88.3	79.2
Sudan[b]	59.2	62.7	100.7	107.1	41.4	57.7	66.1	31.1	78.4	82.2
Swaziland	69.3	65.6	91.8	80.9	72.1	62.0	74.1	41.5	73.1	71.2
Tanzania	42.9	42.7	67.4	61.0	37.8	45.8	46.7	20.3	48.4	46.5
Togo	58.8	55.4	95.2	58.5	51.3	43.0	63.6	35.4	79.7	115.6
Tunisia	54.2	55.2	84.7	87.7	89.4	44.7	65.3	41.9	57.0	43.4
Uganda	42.6	42.9	62.8	57.9	46.2	43.0	51.3	27.9	58.8	55.2
Zambia	63.1	59.8	89.9	81.8	59.8	47.9	75.2	35.8	90.1	142.7
Zimbabwe	65.0	61.2	92.1	54.6	70.3	53.5	93.0	40.9	81.1	89.3
Total (50)	**58.6**	**55.0**	**86.9**	**71.7**	**56.0**	**39.1**	**65.4**	**37.8**	**61.1**	**68.0**
ASIA AND THE PACIFIC										
Bangladesh	40.3	38.3	59.0	32.3	43.0	29.8	41.7	22.2	60.3	13.9
Bhutan	46.6	41.9	58.5	78.1	39.5	39.1	55.3	29.6	48.8	31.4
Brunei Darussalam	73.5	80.5	95.0	206.5	96.4	70.2	144.5	67.0	63.3	138.7
Cambodia	42.8	41.6	64.1	44.2	35.9	47.4	45.9	19.6	57.4	48.1
China[c]	70.0	67.4	89.1	108.0	82.8	56.1	89.1	48.4	65.5	50.9
Fiji	75.0	77.8	93.7	95.6	65.1	106.5	86.0	54.4	83.9	101.4
Hong Kong SAR, China	90.5	89.4	107.1	116.5	66.8	105.7	91.9	101.4	95.6	47.6
India	41.7	37.4	49.9	59.6	32.0	29.8	51.8	17.3	56.4	32.0
Indonesia	53.0	53.0	78.4	94.7	68.7	47.4	55.6	43.7	59.3	60.8
Lao PDR	39.6	39.4	73.3	53.9	36.2	22.9	50.2	19.9	66.3	31.8
Macao SAR, China	73.8	81.4	107.2	75.4	86.6	84.1	105.3	76.2	82.0	55.1
Malaysia	61.5	60.2	83.0	109.4	72.7	45.3	81.2	46.6	68.7	81.1
Maldives	75.3	80.9	87.7	55.4	60.2	172.1	78.2	37.7	75.3	45.3
Mongolia	54.7	50.9	79.6	53.3	68.3	53.3	85.9	20.4	55.4	77.1
Myanmar	37.0	35.0	62.9	60.2	35.5	29.7	46.4	15.2	65.9	47.4
Nepal	42.9	40.0	58.0	58.4	35.7	35.2	44.5	18.5	84.0	45.9
Pakistan	36.4	33.8	54.0	39.7	38.3	23.3	48.8	15.5	49.3	32.5
Philippines	53.2	50.8	71.1	48.8	64.6	45.2	53.2	44.6	56.8	89.0
Singapore	91.4	110.7	121.1	255.0	88.9	146.1	113.6	100.5	121.1	97.3
Sri Lanka	45.1	42.5	69.1	49.4	39.9	32.4	60.5	21.8	60.6	37.1
Taiwan, China	66.1	64.0	91.6	83.6	55.8	69.5	84.1	39.9	68.3	40.2
Thailand	52.3	49.2	73.1	82.2	45.6	33.2	67.7	36.2	62.1	48.8
Vietnam	42.2	40.8	64.5	38.7	37.0	46.7	47.4	16.5	74.0	52.6
Total (23)	**59.7**	**54.5**	**70.3**	**79.3**	**57.2**	**45.7**	**73.3**	**39.5**	**62.5**	**49.4**

Recreation and culture	Education	Restaurants and hotels	Miscellaneous goods and services	Individual consumption expenditure by households	Individual consumption expenditure by government	Collective consumption expenditure by government	Gross fixed capital formation	Machinery and equipment	Construction	Domestic absorption	Individual consumption expenditure by households without housing
(11)	(12)	(13)	(14)	(16)	(17)	(18)	(19)	(20)	(21)	(25)	(26)
59.3	47.4	74.9	45.6	62.2	55.1	57.0	80.8	111.1	70.9	64.2	66.8
70.3	45.6	180.8	63.0	76.1	38.0	37.7	92.6	116.4	89.2	69.0	83.0
44.5	35.1	52.1	34.1	48.6	27.4	35.0	63.7	108.5	43.3	48.8	54.0
79.7	84.3	100.0	69.6	83.2	78.6	85.9	82.6	107.6	78.1	83.4	88.6
62.5	41.5	51.2	54.4	66.5	29.6	31.2	61.6	106.3	45.7	58.7	68.8
66.3	79.6	73.7	58.0	66.5	68.7	78.5	65.6	117.0	45.0	68.4	69.8
45.1	35.0	43.2	30.2	44.4	33.9	46.8	49.0	106.2	28.9	44.6	46.4
75.0	26.1	68.0	35.7	58.7	33.5	47.2	80.1	122.5	64.7	59.1	63.5
62.2	32.3	64.2	45.1	59.0	34.2	39.8	56.6	116.2	36.6	54.4	63.0
45.1	27.2	46.8	31.8	44.8	32.6	43.3	51.3	116.5	30.9	44.3	46.8
62.0	65.9	59.6	37.6	61.5	57.2	64.7	67.2	109.9	51.7	62.6	65.8
63.4	45.8	79.6	41.6	63.9	47.5	53.5	86.3	116.6	76.2	64.7	67.6
55.9	**42.0**	**61.3**	**46.7**	**57.2**	**43.0**	**48.9**	**70.5**	**108.1**	**55.8**	**58.0**	**61.4**
43.4	24.9	36.0	47.0	40.0	28.7	35.8	48.1	86.3	37.7	40.4	42.6
41.3	32.3	33.9	41.5	43.4	33.4	33.1	62.2	108.8	47.8	46.9	43.7
78.2	80.2	85.8	80.3	80.9	76.8	60.1	87.7	98.2	88.6	80.1	84.3
41.0	18.5	37.0	47.2	44.9	20.9	30.8	49.7	88.7	36.8	42.5	47.0
49.4	69.2	55.9	73.6	68.2	61.0	73.1	76.1	102.8	68.9	70.1	72.2
73.7	55.9	74.8	74.3	80.9	61.7	59.2	70.2	97.0	64.5	74.4	75.3
56.8	117.0	76.1	77.7	88.2	115.4	117.1	93.6	100.5	105.1	91.9	86.3
41.2	29.6	46.6	46.6	38.3	35.2	43.3	52.8	88.2	41.9	41.8	40.7
45.5	32.7	48.6	48.7	55.7	37.1	46.6	54.2	88.6	44.6	52.8	56.9
48.4	10.2	45.0	48.3	43.3	14.1	21.7	47.2	88.4	34.7	39.8	47.8
64.0	69.2	72.7	82.9	81.3	83.7	96.1	80.9	85.3	81.6	82.4	82.4
53.9	52.4	47.2	65.3	61.8	52.5	56.0	67.8	92.4	61.9	61.8	65.8
63.9	53.2	48.0	63.2	87.2	50.9	48.9	78.0	95.4	76.4	74.8	66.4
55.9	24.1	51.8	64.1	55.6	25.3	35.2	69.4	102.2	60.3	55.0	56.5
36.9	9.6	31.3	50.6	40.2	13.1	20.0	49.4	94.1	34.3	36.8	43.4
39.4	23.1	37.4	46.2	41.5	32.9	46.3	56.1	88.3	46.5	43.7	43.4
34.3	23.3	40.5	42.4	35.1	27.7	30.4	50.9	92.5	38.1	36.5	37.8
49.6	34.8	44.7	54.2	52.0	49.6	60.9	57.9	93.3	46.9	53.1	55.7
66.9	129.6	76.6	99.1	111.1	121.5	92.0	84.0	93.7	87.5	100.2	108.4
39.4	22.9	57.0	50.8	45.5	24.1	31.4	60.6	101.1	48.6	45.5	48.4
54.7	67.6	49.3	61.6	64.7	65.8	67.0	72.3	88.5	73.0	66.2	64.9
47.9	40.2	37.0	56.0	50.2	44.4	56.3	57.8	92.9	45.4	52.3	54.7
36.7	17.0	36.7	44.1	44.3	19.5	23.7	52.5	87.5	42.4	41.9	44.2
49.8	**49.2**	**52.0**	**59.7**	**54.9**	**53.7**	**58.6**	**69.2**	**98.1**	**60.5**	**59.2**	**57.7**

(continued)

Table 2.9 (Continued)

PRICE LEVEL INDEX (world = 100) Economy	Gross domestic product	Actual individual consumption	Food and nonalcoholic beverages	Alcoholic beverages, tobacco, and narcotics	Clothing and footwear	Housing, water, electricity, gas, and other fuels	Furnishings, household equipment and maintenance	Health	Transport	Communication
(00)	(01)	(02)	(03)	(04)	(05)	(06)	(07)	(08)	(09)	(10)
COMMONWEALTH OF INDEPENDENT STATES										
Armenia	64.8	51.0	92.0	44.7	101.9	16.7	73.8	33.4	71.4	80.5
Azerbaijan	58.8	44.5	70.2	40.7	88.5	15.0	64.8	33.1	65.6	69.9
Belarus	43.5	34.2	55.5	30.5	76.1	10.6	59.5	23.4	57.3	33.0
Kazakhstan	70.5	60.0	80.1	42.1	92.2	52.5	73.1	38.8	72.7	68.3
Kyrgyz Republic	49.6	39.2	75.1	32.0	86.2	10.2	59.6	25.8	62.0	43.2
Moldova	60.8	48.8	73.9	36.7	97.7	28.2	69.9	32.8	76.8	59.2
Russian Federation[d]	76.2	63.0	97.1	51.9	101.7	31.1	75.1	57.4	87.6	62.3
Tajikistan	48.7	40.1	75.9	42.0	101.8	10.3	74.0	20.5	79.2	33.4
Ukraine	55.6	44.6	70.2	38.9	93.8	16.8	58.1	31.0	67.2	53.6
Total (9)	**71.8**	**58.6**	**89.0**	**49.2**	**99.5**	**28.6**	**72.4**	**48.8**	**82.5**	**60.5**
EUROSTAT-OECD										
Albania	57.8	58.6	86.5	50.0	98.7	53.8	84.9	38.1	98.0	121.8
Australia	201.0	193.5	188.0	231.0	187.9	257.0	144.2	247.0	144.2	153.3
Austria	148.8	147.3	152.1	108.3	138.2	145.5	129.2	160.6	150.3	129.2
Belgium	150.4	151.8	139.3	114.2	155.1	174.5	125.0	157.6	144.9	166.9
Bosnia and Herzegovina	66.4	68.2	96.6	56.4	148.7	43.0	76.6	65.2	103.1	111.4
Bulgaria	60.5	58.2	86.9	74.7	113.2	42.9	75.0	36.2	93.4	102.5
Canada	161.9	160.2	174.4	188.9	150.7	169.0	142.6	186.0	134.3	170.0
Chile	92.8	91.0	118.3	94.0	121.6	92.5	100.1	88.7	92.1	123.5
Croatia	91.6	92.5	118.4	93.3	143.5	74.4	97.4	75.1	117.0	109.1
Cyprus	120.6	121.4	142.1	112.2	136.4	106.1	110.6	120.1	121.4	81.6
Czech Republic	98.2	94.8	105.0	98.5	139.7	109.8	100.0	73.9	111.5	158.6
Denmark	185.0	196.4	180.6	144.5	177.8	237.6	143.4	200.2	195.7	134.0
Estonia	93.9	93.1	110.1	93.6	139.8	102.4	99.8	66.9	116.3	102.2
Finland	162.6	164.8	147.9	156.6	168.4	199.3	133.4	156.2	164.6	110.7
France	151.4	148.3	138.7	125.2	144.1	180.2	131.3	145.4	147.3	160.9
Germany	139.6	135.3	134.3	109.4	141.9	165.0	116.1	121.3	149.0	111.6
Greece	124.3	122.9	134.2	113.9	130.5	128.3	116.7	100.7	134.4	174.8
Hungary	79.3	75.2	104.0	70.9	113.1	70.5	82.8	50.5	118.9	148.7
Iceland	148.3	145.5	143.9	192.5	188.6	118.0	142.5	146.2	163.6	113.1
Ireland	148.3	163.0	153.9	211.2	144.1	177.8	124.3	199.6	149.6	161.7
Israel	142.2	140.7	157.7	136.8	145.1	147.6	116.3	138.3	140.3	178.3
Italy	137.7	138.2	142.3	117.2	147.8	152.3	126.2	143.0	135.0	142.5
Japan	173.6	170.4	232.2	134.3	165.6	199.2	155.1	154.2	152.7	171.3
Korea, Rep.	99.4	95.6	157.1	84.3	156.6	68.1	96.0	69.9	97.7	77.6
Latvia	88.1	86.9	110.8	101.5	148.5	81.6	93.1	55.7	112.4	110.4
Lithuania	81.4	78.9	99.5	87.1	142.4	66.2	91.1	54.4	112.4	79.6
Luxembourg	162.4	182.9	147.9	102.8	140.3	256.7	130.6	215.7	134.2	123.1
Macedonia, FYR	54.5	55.0	75.3	46.3	99.1	47.2	72.5	33.9	90.1	100.8

Recreation and culture	Education	Restaurants and hotels	Miscellaneous goods and services	Individual consumption expenditure by households	Individual consumption expenditure by government	Collective consumption expenditure by government	Gross fixed capital formation	Machinery and equipment	Construction	Domestic absorption	Individual consumption expenditure by households without housing
(11)	(12)	(13)	(14)	(16)	(17)	(18)	(19)	(20)	(21)	(25)	(26)
58.2	19.6	74.7	46.7	58.9	22.6	40.0	135.7	108.5	172.3	63.2	72.3
53.8	24.7	69.6	38.5	49.8	26.5	42.4	130.3	104.6	166.8	57.2	58.5
41.5	16.1	57.8	40.6	39.0	17.2	32.4	93.4	84.7	109.2	43.4	45.7
64.6	28.3	74.6	42.0	68.0	30.8	45.4	122.1	103.2	150.7	69.0	64.0
54.1	15.1	72.5	32.1	45.3	18.1	29.1	127.1	111.1	151.9	50.3	54.7
58.0	23.7	60.4	42.5	55.4	25.8	30.7	128.2	99.4	166.4	59.7	65.0
75.3	41.2	93.6	58.1	68.1	43.3	70.4	124.1	98.4	159.4	74.5	76.7
39.1	11.3	63.5	38.1	48.7	12.0	21.9	124.9	97.3	163.3	50.7	57.8
57.7	26.4	78.2	41.7	49.6	26.4	39.1	112.7	94.0	140.1	54.9	57.7
71.0	**34.2**	**88.2**	**54.6**	**64.0**	**37.9**	**63.7**	**121.9**	**97.9**	**154.7**	**70.1**	**71.8**
62.5	9.5	51.9	53.5	68.4	20.6	37.5	74.6	99.5	70.4	60.2	72.2
149.5	280.2	157.7	162.8	187.8	234.5	185.7	229.7	127.9	364.7	201.6	176.1
134.0	268.7	131.3	130.5	140.5	181.0	172.3	143.8	101.1	207.5	149.1	143.7
124.9	242.9	140.8	137.0	145.8	174.6	184.4	128.8	102.5	167.0	150.3	142.8
69.8	35.0	76.9	65.5	73.5	46.8	55.2	75.2	99.2	64.9	68.6	82.5
60.7	31.4	56.3	55.7	64.9	32.2	35.8	81.6	92.1	78.0	59.7	73.4
136.1	256.1	157.1	137.9	154.9	195.0	163.3	157.9	99.3	226.1	161.0	151.8
98.3	59.7	93.5	81.4	96.6	66.5	71.2	100.8	97.6	112.8	91.9	100.1
90.6	89.1	111.2	82.4	97.2	74.3	71.9	92.1	96.9	96.8	90.9	104.7
116.8	217.7	124.5	107.0	118.0	147.1	121.2	110.3	101.6	127.9	120.0	123.7
86.7	86.3	74.3	84.2	100.5	73.7	81.2	110.2	98.6	127.7	97.2	101.2
165.3	296.2	191.2	179.8	189.7	214.3	199.6	152.1	110.2	221.3	188.1	185.2
96.2	74.1	92.0	82.6	100.9	66.3	69.6	100.7	97.8	109.0	92.9	102.2
150.4	224.8	161.6	152.4	162.5	170.0	162.2	149.1	110.1	198.2	162.3	156.5
129.3	201.7	128.7	133.4	145.9	155.4	167.1	147.4	100.8	208.4	150.5	140.7
127.0	177.1	127.0	118.0	135.6	133.1	152.5	148.6	98.8	217.9	139.9	134.0
120.4	147.5	123.0	108.1	125.7	110.5	109.0	130.4	115.5	154.8	123.4	124.4
73.1	59.4	64.0	66.5	81.8	51.9	62.9	94.0	89.3	103.8	77.7	88.0
152.4	208.8	146.6	130.7	142.7	153.4	133.9	174.3	119.6	252.1	150.0	150.5
137.2	185.1	157.1	151.3	157.8	182.6	149.1	111.5	103.5	128.9	152.8	155.5
134.8	163.5	150.4	121.6	142.4	136.7	128.4	146.9	143.0	174.2	141.5	141.5
129.9	169.0	133.7	122.6	136.9	145.1	157.1	120.9	101.6	147.2	137.2	135.9
142.3	204.5	145.9	149.2	173.5	159.9	165.4	180.2	122.5	269.6	172.7	170.1
88.5	130.1	120.2	83.4	98.2	86.5	97.6	105.5	90.9	127.6	98.6	105.7
85.9	63.0	99.6	79.0	94.7	55.4	62.8	102.7	96.7	114.2	87.8	100.3
81.0	60.5	79.5	73.3	85.8	53.6	57.7	99.0	94.4	108.4	80.9	93.7
131.4	483.6	134.1	150.2	164.1	260.2	198.3	132.3	100.8	174.3	171.2	145.1
58.7	24.4	51.4	50.6	61.9	27.9	36.5	73.3	94.5	67.0	56.5	66.9

(continued)

Table 2.9 *(Continued)*

PRICE LEVEL INDEX (world = 100) Economy	Gross domestic product	Actual individual consumption	Food and nonalcoholic beverages	Alcoholic beverages, tobacco, and narcotics	Clothing and footwear	Housing, water, electricity, gas, and other fuels	Furnishings, household equipment and maintenance	Health	Transport	Communication
(00)	(01)	(02)	(03)	(04)	(05)	(06)	(07)	(08)	(09)	(10)
Malta	100.1	100.6	121.6	114.4	137.5	83.8	114.1	86.0	128.4	127.3
Mexico	79.6	77.2	86.6	79.1	82.9	112.8	78.1	78.4	86.7	112.8
Montenegro	66.1	67.4	95.3	59.5	136.1	54.8	81.7	51.1	98.4	100.8
Netherlands	149.1	149.4	123.9	121.9	151.3	179.1	120.9	164.4	154.3	167.2
New Zealand	151.4	145.4	159.1	195.4	135.9	186.4	125.6	130.5	133.2	187.8
Norway	206.4	220.0	232.2	307.7	214.0	210.0	157.0	253.1	215.2	132.2
Poland	79.3	73.1	78.9	87.1	138.1	64.4	77.5	51.8	99.1	94.1
Portugal	112.5	115.5	114.3	101.2	146.8	122.8	108.4	121.5	132.2	153.3
Romania	68.3	68.8	91.2	89.2	125.6	79.4	80.6	38.9	99.5	94.0
Russian Federation[d]	76.2	63.0	97.1	51.9	101.7	31.1	75.1	57.4	87.6	62.3
Serbia	65.6	66.7	95.0	57.2	142.9	56.9	90.4	49.8	101.7	76.1
Slovak Republic	91.1	87.0	109.2	94.7	131.7	81.2	98.3	56.4	107.6	169.3
Slovenia	112.1	112.9	122.0	93.2	138.0	111.8	110.0	103.1	120.3	121.7
Spain	126.5	129.7	119.5	101.1	124.9	154.1	116.8	136.1	133.7	204.7
Sweden	175.1	177.2	154.6	162.1	178.5	186.8	142.8	186.4	173.0	108.3
Switzerland	209.6	225.3	199.8	147.5	189.5	328.1	152.1	259.2	170.0	164.7
Turkey	75.7	74.6	105.7	107.7	90.6	62.7	80.1	62.9	107.0	111.6
United Kingdom	144.2	146.7	123.1	180.9	113.7	203.0	122.8	140.9	145.7	131.7
United States	129.0	124.7	111.7	125.4	123.0	136.7	98.8	154.5	91.6	137.6
Total (47)	**130.5**	**126.9**	**127.3**	**110.7**	**130.7**	**139.3**	**111.3**	**137.3**	**115.8**	**129.3**
LATIN AMERICA										
Bolivia	54.8	50.3	70.9	62.6	74.9	25.3	60.6	62.0	48.3	98.5
Brazil	113.4	110.8	110.9	88.5	238.3	118.0	114.3	81.5	133.0	239.7
Colombia	81.1	77.3	97.6	81.0	118.3	47.6	106.2	72.2	91.3	143.1
Costa Rica	88.4	84.3	113.7	87.7	128.0	50.2	97.4	124.7	82.2	70.2
Cuba[e]	41.5	36.7	52.9	63.6	48.5	14.4	58.7	31.6	46.1	77.3
Dominican Republic	65.8	63.2	82.1	86.4	88.6	52.0	82.0	60.3	82.3	79.5
Ecuador	67.9	64.6	88.1	69.9	104.1	45.3	87.5	59.5	53.1	102.6
El Salvador	64.9	62.4	88.7	83.9	109.7	40.7	83.7	63.9	52.9	72.4
Guatemala	60.1	58.5	83.7	87.5	86.5	43.7	53.4	62.7	59.9	96.6
Haiti	60.8	61.4	86.7	50.8	133.5	39.5	56.6	57.6	55.6	87.4
Honduras	67.7	65.2	84.1	65.5	122.2	45.0	76.3	74.2	68.7	129.5
Nicaragua	51.3	47.7	74.4	61.2	67.2	23.9	52.8	49.0	58.4	99.1
Panama	70.6	65.2	90.2	73.0	109.3	45.7	78.6	70.7	64.2	57.6
Paraguay	68.8	65.1	88.7	63.5	143.0	38.1	74.8	69.1	75.8	68.4
Peru	71.2	66.1	86.0	72.5	108.7	51.4	91.1	57.4	68.5	106.8
Uruguay	102.0	100.1	128.0	118.2	182.6	81.2	123.4	98.9	101.6	101.0
Venezuela, RB	81.6	79.1	152.4	142.6	252.4	28.8	175.8	74.8	48.5	90.4
Total (17)	**97.1**	**93.5**	**105.3**	**88.7**	**178.3**	**78.8**	**109.3**	**78.3**	**101.2**	**152.4**

Recreation and culture	Education	Restaurants and hotels	Miscellaneous goods and services	Individual consumption expenditure by households	Individual consumption expenditure by government	Collective consumption expenditure by government	Gross fixed capital formation	Machinery and equipment	Construction	Domestic absorption	Individual consumption expenditure by households without housing
(11)	(12)	(13)	(14)	(16)	(17)	(18)	(19)	(20)	(21)	(25)	(26)
95.3	112.8	96.8	85.8	104.2	86.8	77.5	104.1	106.1	109.7	99.2	111.5
79.5	27.5	75.2	69.5	85.8	41.3	54.4	97.3	101.4	105.8	79.3	80.9
79.6	27.8	79.7	59.0	74.5	38.1	44.8	89.9	96.5	93.1	68.2	79.6
125.0	205.0	131.4	134.7	144.1	165.6	159.8	145.6	109.4	195.5	150.7	140.3
129.9	149.6	122.8	128.4	149.8	129.4	143.2	173.9	123.3	267.6	151.2	144.4
195.6	336.7	234.3	214.4	208.5	258.9	234.4	200.3	132.8	296.5	217.7	212.3
71.5	68.1	94.9	68.5	77.9	54.3	66.3	106.4	94.8	124.0	78.7	84.2
116.6	118.1	98.2	101.4	116.7	110.5	103.6	99.9	107.7	103.8	112.0	118.9
62.6	31.5	62.6	59.9	78.3	36.2	42.1	77.5	97.9	71.7	68.3	78.1
75.3	41.2	93.6	58.1	68.1	43.3	70.4	124.1	98.4	159.4	74.5	76.7
72.1	33.7	70.7	56.6	73.8	40.4	41.6	81.0	98.4	72.7	67.0	78.4
88.3	69.8	88.5	80.4	94.0	59.6	65.8	114.9	107.1	127.4	90.4	101.3
112.6	158.7	109.5	99.6	113.0	113.6	95.3	111.5	94.3	136.6	111.5	115.8
119.7	162.9	117.6	108.8	128.8	134.3	119.8	113.1	100.4	133.8	125.9	126.1
154.1	326.4	183.1	161.3	167.2	208.6	169.0	179.8	110.8	290.5	177.6	167.5
174.8	422.3	195.6	188.8	217.1	300.8	238.5	188.7	128.5	299.7	218.5	196.4
79.3	27.5	87.9	72.9	82.6	42.0	60.4	86.6	94.5	83.5	76.1	89.6
123.9	225.3	131.6	120.4	144.5	155.3	136.6	131.3	91.5	178.2	143.7	133.1
100.4	253.9	104.6	107.5	119.3	186.3	138.6	130.5	85.5	203.9	128.1	115.9
113.5	**156.8**	**118.5**	**115.2**	**125.7**	**131.6**	**129.9**	**136.0**	**98.5**	**184.6**	**129.8**	**123.4**
64.7	51.3	55.2	43.1	50.0	72.5	61.9	68.2	89.7	64.7	55.0	55.1
125.0	98.1	116.7	96.6	118.3	76.0	136.7	101.9	144.3	88.0	112.5	122.0
71.6	73.8	89.7	63.5	77.3	90.4	68.0	98.5	117.0	97.5	81.0	84.8
85.5	94.4	87.6	60.4	81.1	128.8	79.4	102.2	135.0	94.0	87.9	88.3
28.7	44.6	35.9	38.1	34.8	40.6	36.4	70.9	94.9	64.1	40.9	37.2
66.0	37.7	54.7	49.6	64.9	47.9	48.0	87.1	114.7	79.4	66.5	68.4
71.4	62.0	75.7	58.3	65.3	68.1	66.8	79.8	124.6	63.0	68.2	68.5
62.9	42.5	95.8	53.8	63.3	61.6	58.9	82.8	107.5	77.6	65.9	69.0
60.0	43.7	55.3	42.8	59.3	58.6	53.3	72.1	96.3	65.3	61.1	64.4
57.8	53.5	84.3	45.2	61.0	72.5	82.5	68.2	104.8	57.8	63.6	68.0
61.9	59.2	63.4	48.2	63.6	98.5	74.6	78.0	103.4	72.1	68.6	69.4
61.8	28.3	55.2	38.5	48.7	43.9	41.8	83.5	107.7	77.4	53.1	56.5
66.9	52.0	79.3	58.7	66.0	66.9	59.3	95.6	117.7	93.6	70.8	70.3
83.5	52.4	73.2	49.9	66.0	65.7	72.1	83.2	124.7	69.6	69.0	72.8
66.5	57.5	79.1	49.3	67.9	54.1	63.4	92.7	123.5	84.0	71.4	72.9
108.5	98.6	99.0	80.5	101.4	102.9	89.9	106.3	122.9	106.3	101.4	107.6
126.4	49.9	109.0	90.0	81.1	68.2	61.9	86.6	147.3	64.2	81.0	89.2
104.8	**80.9**	**100.8**	**84.2**	**96.9**	**75.9**	**110.0**	**97.4**	**137.5**	**84.8**	**96.7**	**102.1**

(continued)

Table 2.9 (Continued)

PRICE LEVEL INDEX (world = 100) Economy	Gross domestic product	Actual individual consumption	Food and nonalcoholic beverages	Alcoholic beverages, tobacco, and narcotics	Clothing and footwear	Housing, water, electricity, gas, and other fuels	Furnishings, household equipment and maintenance	Health	Transport	Communication
(00)	(01)	(02)	(03)	(04)	(05)	(06)	(07)	(08)	(09)	(10)
CARIBBEAN										
Anguilla	99.2	108.5	163.0	113.9	114.1	97.4	116.8	93.2	92.3	118.2
Antigua and Barbuda	82.7	89.2	139.6	95.1	104.3	72.6	110.5	59.4	122.2	121.4
Aruba	90.8	102.9	128.9	146.4	117.9	89.7	149.2	70.1	103.5	134.2
Bahamas, The	122.4	132.1	151.9	119.3	158.0	120.7	185.8	117.2	122.0	164.5
Barbados	130.0	139.5	149.9	160.0	115.9	132.8	134.5	105.5	112.3	162.5
Belize	74.1	68.9	107.9	154.0	93.4	38.0	87.1	65.3	101.9	85.4
Bermuda	201.6	220.7	205.0	140.2	182.5	355.4	208.7	191.0	136.6	154.1
Bonaire[f]	...	...	148.3	118.0	81.2	...	129.2	...	115.8	165.2
Cayman Islands	147.6	155.9	177.6	186.2	153.8	157.2	188.5	167.1	130.5	169.4
Curaçao	93.1	92.7	116.8	110.8	142.2	73.5	121.5	74.4	94.7	148.3
Dominica	88.9	88.8	133.6	107.8	69.9	70.5	134.1	71.6	96.5	97.5
Grenada	85.2	87.9	137.8	112.1	125.8	65.1	126.0	69.8	103.1	105.5
Jamaica	81.3	84.1	133.6	122.4	86.2	62.8	98.5	71.9	97.3	73.8
Montserrat	92.8	99.0	163.8	128.5	112.1	65.3	158.1	87.8	122.3	91.2
St. Kitts and Nevis	86.1	88.8	156.0	110.5	95.7	64.0	174.8	54.5	119.2	147.9
St. Lucia	88.1	90.1	125.7	119.2	104.5	61.0	176.7	73.7	96.3	123.3
St. Vincent and the Grenadines	80.8	85.5	129.9	100.7	94.1	68.0	124.2	59.4	86.9	128.2
Sint Maarten	99.3	105.4	131.4	71.0	96.1	101.3	126.7	69.8	95.0	172.4
Suriname	72.1	65.3	113.3	91.0	69.9	36.5	100.2	45.1	96.1	90.5
Trinidad and Tobago	79.2	81.5	116.8	126.1	100.9	66.8	122.0	66.8	84.6	87.9
Turks and Caicos Islands	141.9	148.7	158.2	160.0	108.2	184.5	144.2	122.7	139.5	102.9
Virgin Islands, British	138.7	145.1	172.3	80.8	132.5	167.1	171.1	120.1	107.3	130.6
Total (22)	**92.5**	**97.2**	**130.0**	**123.0**	**111.0**	**88.3**	**124.7**	**79.8**	**98.9**	**109.9**
WESTERN ASIA										
Bahrain	72.0	70.8	89.1	75.7	86.9	67.6	81.4	88.4	41.7	66.2
Egypt, Arab Rep.[a]	35.1	33.6	64.3	59.1	42.4	16.3	52.1	21.5	35.3	44.0
Iraq	55.5	52.2	87.4	84.0	84.1	36.4	69.1	39.4	51.0	53.6
Jordan	53.3	51.7	89.1	64.9	52.3	32.8	60.5	37.3	56.6	66.8
Kuwait	80.4	82.8	94.7	87.3	104.6	58.9	97.6	109.7	47.3	119.8
Oman	64.2	62.8	89.2	68.6	70.6	58.2	64.9	56.5	44.4	82.6
Qatar	85.4	97.5	98.8	77.9	100.2	102.2	96.2	116.3	50.5	100.4
Saudi Arabia	63.2	60.7	88.8	69.1	68.5	39.4	66.7	64.9	42.8	82.2
Sudan[b]	59.2	62.7	100.7	107.1	41.4	57.7	66.1	31.1	78.4	82.2
United Arab Emirates	89.3	94.2	106.5	91.8	93.9	98.5	71.9	120.2	64.7	84.4
West Bank and Gaza	78.9	77.7	105.5	179.4	72.8	84.3	76.8	47.9	98.3	91.0
Yemen, Rep.	45.7	43.4	87.0	41.9	40.3	24.7	59.5	28.4	42.1	62.3
Total (12)	**61.9**	**55.9**	**80.9**	**62.0**	**67.9**	**41.8**	**67.0**	**39.1**	**50.3**	**73.0**

Recreation and culture	Education	Restaurants and hotels	Miscellaneous goods and services	Individual consumption expenditure by households	Individual consumption expenditure by government	Collective consumption expenditure by government	Gross fixed capital formation	Machinery and equipment	Construction	Domestic absorption	Individual consumption expenditure by households without housing
(11)	(12)	(13)	(14)	(16)	(17)	(18)	(19)	(20)	(21)	(25)	(26)
135.4	71.1	125.1	110.5	114.5	78.8	71.4	76.1	98.6	75.2	98.7	117.2
109.0	51.8	84.4	81.7	97.2	49.9	51.4	76.5	109.5	73.1	82.8	110.4
115.5	92.2	150.0	90.4	110.1	72.2	60.4	69.9	79.1	75.6	91.0	121.6
114.0	140.5	120.0	120.6	137.3	111.9	69.2	104.1	113.7	116.1	119.1	143.0
119.8	128.6	161.2	115.7	143.9	126.7	75.2	98.7	110.2	106.0	125.0	139.8
91.4	57.9	90.2	72.5	70.5	74.1	56.4	120.3	115.2	148.4	74.7	91.1
180.1	182.3	217.7	179.0	226.7	200.8	158.6	126.1	97.6	209.0	190.8	189.6
...	...	103.1	...	109.7	...	...	...	...	...	...	119.0
148.5	126.6	138.9	142.0	161.8	136.8	118.4	123.9	126.3	145.1	146.1	159.1
103.5	88.0	118.6	82.8	95.2	86.4	62.1	107.1	109.4	126.7	93.5	110.4
98.8	68.3	91.9	87.7	91.4	84.9	72.7	98.3	110.8	105.1	89.4	102.0
109.1	46.4	99.2	76.0	92.4	66.8	55.9	97.0	109.1	103.3	86.7	106.3
95.5	59.9	99.1	80.0	88.0	66.3	60.9	89.6	112.9	87.3	83.0	100.1
104.1	64.5	96.1	92.6	103.2	79.5	68.1	84.1	112.2	81.6	93.8	121.1
108.7	33.3	89.0	82.4	98.1	42.1	40.8	106.2	115.6	114.6	87.0	115.4
103.6	59.7	150.3	88.8	94.5	70.3	61.0	95.9	115.3	100.5	88.9	108.8
97.5	55.4	134.8	82.0	90.1	63.2	56.3	85.5	117.3	81.3	83.0	100.7
93.2	80.6	125.0	104.8	111.8	71.4	65.7	88.3	84.3	114.2	98.3	117.4
68.7	66.6	69.1	59.0	68.8	49.7	50.8	87.0	107.1	76.3	72.2	73.5
77.4	53.6	102.4	65.8	86.0	59.7	44.8	73.5	86.6	76.0	76.6	85.1
130.6	157.5	156.8	129.0	153.0	144.3	95.9	153.6	112.0	226.8	146.0	147.2
135.3	164.1	161.5	131.1	149.1	144.4	97.3	150.2	115.0	226.1	143.8	139.8
96.9	**68.3**	**116.2**	**86.4**	**102.1**	**72.5**	**65.2**	**91.1**	**103.3**	**96.3**	**93.0**	**105.5**
58.6	87.6	63.9	59.3	68.0	98.3	81.7	65.1	90.6	60.4	71.5	59.9
33.4	21.6	42.3	28.6	36.1	17.7	19.1	58.9	95.4	47.6	35.3	40.7
59.1	35.6	65.6	70.3	57.0	35.2	36.7	75.7	80.9	83.7	53.7	63.4
52.4	44.4	68.2	49.9	53.7	41.6	38.3	68.6	85.5	68.4	53.1	60.6
83.5	123.9	112.2	100.7	78.0	124.6	109.0	72.4	89.8	75.4	84.1	72.9
61.5	70.4	72.3	54.2	62.1	71.4	64.6	58.2	85.6	49.5	62.4	58.6
87.7	160.2	106.3	87.8	86.3	164.2	134.7	62.1	82.6	51.5	89.3	75.3
60.9	82.1	64.9	55.5	56.8	83.2	70.7	53.6	74.8	47.6	60.8	57.3
62.5	41.5	51.2	54.4	66.5	29.6	31.2	61.6	106.3	45.7	58.7	68.8
90.4	131.9	105.2	86.1	88.3	165.2	136.8	64.4	76.3	65.9	91.4	81.4
70.9	56.3	103.1	76.1	84.1	52.6	55.0	89.7	97.9	94.8	76.0	88.1
42.2	32.1	34.7	41.8	45.8	29.0	27.5	63.0	79.3	68.7	44.6	50.3
56.8	**54.8**	**65.3**	**49.3**	**56.1**	**58.0**	**53.5**	**60.1**	**81.0**	**55.2**	**58.8**	**57.1**

(continued)

Table 2.9 *(Continued)*

PRICE LEVEL INDEX (world = 100) Economy	Gross domestic product	Actual individual consumption	Food and nonalcoholic beverages	Alcoholic beverages, tobacco, and narcotics	Clothing and footwear	Housing, water, electricity, gas, and other fuels	Furnishings, household equipment and maintenance	Health	Transport	Communication
(00)	(01)	(02)	(03)	(04)	(05)	(06)	(07)	(08)	(09)	(10)
SINGLETONS										
Georgia	65.7	52.1	92.2	54.6	104.3	19.2	73.4	36.8	73.4	52.0
Iran, Islamic Rep.	56.5	49.5	83.7	37.3	93.9	45.4	71.4	28.3	54.5	35.6
Total (2)	**56.7**	**49.6**	**84.1**	**41.7**	**94.1**	**44.4**	**71.5**	**28.6**	**55.3**	**36.1**
WORLD[g] (179)	**100.0**	**100.0**	**100.0**	**100.0**	**100.0**	**100.0**	**100.0**	**100.0**	**100.0**	**100.0**

Source: ICP, http://icp.worldbank.org/.

Note: n.a. = not applicable; ... = data suppressed because of incompleteness.

a. The Arab Republic of Egypt participated in both the Africa and Western Asia regions. The regional results for Egypt were averaged by taking the geometric mean of the regional PPPs, allowing Egypt to have the same global results in each region.

b. Sudan participated in both the Africa and Western Asia regions. The regional results for Sudan were averaged by taking the geometric mean of the regional PPPs, allowing Sudan to have the same global results in each region.

c. The results presented in the tables are based on data supplied by all the participating economies and compiled in accordance with ICP principles and the procedures recommended by the 2011 ICP Technical Advisory Group. The results for China are estimated by the 2011 ICP Asia and the Pacific Regional Office and the Global Office. The National Bureau of Statistics of China does not recognize these results as official statistics.

d. The Russian Federation participated in both the CIS and Eurostat-OECD comparisons. The PPPs for Russia are based on the Eurostat-OECD comparison. They were the basis for linking the CIS comparison to the ICP.

e. The official GDP of Cuba for reference year 2011 is 68,990.15 million in national currency. However, this number and its breakdown into main aggregates are not shown in the tables because of methodological comparability issues. Therefore, Cuba's results are provided only for the PPP and price level index. In addition, Cuba's figures are not included in the Latin America and world totals.

f. Bonaire's results are provided only for the individual consumption expenditure by households. Therefore, to ensure consistency across the tables, Bonaire is not included in the Caribbean or the world total.

g. This table does not include the Pacific Islands and does not double count the dual participation economies: the Arab Republic of Egypt, Sudan, and the Russian Federation.

Recreation and culture	Education	Restaurants and hotels	Miscellaneous goods and services	Individual consumption expenditure by households	Individual consumption expenditure by government	Collective consumption expenditure by government	Gross fixed capital formation	Machinery and equipment	Construction	Domestic absorption	Individual consumption expenditure by households without housing
(11)	(12)	(13)	(14)	(16)	(17)	(18)	(19)	(20)	(21)	(25)	(26)
55.2	23.6	75.3	42.8	59.6	26.8	44.3	127.8	90.7	165.0	63.9	72.0
48.9	11.3	71.4	57.3	56.2	20.4	32.1	87.7	119.9	66.6	56.4	55.2
49.6	**11.9**	**71.8**	**56.9**	**56.3**	**20.6**	**32.5**	**88.3**	**119.2**	**67.4**	**56.6**	**55.9**
100.0	**100.0**	**100.0**	**100.0**	**100.0**	**100.0**	**100.0**	**100.0**	**100.0**	**100.0**	**100.0**	**100.0**

Table 2.10 Nominal Expenditures in U.S. Dollars, ICP 2011

NOMINAL EXPENDITURES (US$, billions) Economy	Gross domestic product	Actual individual consumption	Food and nonalcoholic beverages	Alcoholic beverages, tobacco, and narcotics	Clothing and footwear	Housing, water, electricity, gas, and other fuels	Furnishings, household equipment and maintenance	Health	Transport	Commu- nication	Recreation and culture	Education
(00)	(01)	(02)	(03)	(04)	(05)	(06)	(07)	(08)	(09)	(10)	(11)	(12)
AFRICA												
Algeria	198.5	89.3	26.8	1.5	2.6	4.4	2.2	6.3	10.8	5.1	2.3	8.5
Angola	104.2	63.3	26.0	2.7	3.2	6.6	3.5	3.3	3.4	0.7	1.4	3.1
Benin	7.3	5.9	2.8	0.2	0.2	0.6	0.2	0.2	0.4	0.2	0.1	0.3
Botswana	15.0	8.2	1.5	0.6	0.5	0.9	0.5	0.4	1.3	0.2	0.2	1.0
Burkina Faso	10.3	7.0	3.6	0.4	0.1	0.8	0.3	0.3	0.5	0.2	0.2	0.4
Burundi	2.1	1.9	0.8	0.3	0.0	0.3	0.0	0.1	0.1	0.0	0.0	0.1
Cameroon	26.6	20.8	9.6	0.5	1.7	1.9	1.9	0.3	1.7	0.3	0.3	0.5
Cape Verde	1.9	1.3	0.5	0.1	0.0	0.3	0.1	0.1	0.1	0.0	0.0	0.1
Central African Republic	2.2	2.0	1.2	0.2	0.1	0.1	0.1	0.0	0.1	0.0	0.0	0.1
Chad	12.1	8.3	4.0	0.4	0.2	0.8	0.6	0.6	0.8	0.3	0.2	0.1
Comoros	0.3	0.3	0.1	0.0	0.0	0.1	0.0	0.0	0.0	0.0	0.0	0.0
Congo, Rep.	14.8	3.7	1.3	0.2	0.1	0.5	0.1	0.3	0.3	0.2	0.1	0.3
Congo, Dem. Rep.	25.2	16.2	8.9	0.5	0.8	1.9	0.6	0.7	0.4	0.2	0.2	0.7
Côte d'Ivoire	26.0	18.6	7.9	0.6	0.6	1.8	1.5	0.8	2.0	0.5	0.6	0.8
Djibouti	1.2	0.8	0.2	0.1	0.0	0.3	0.0	0.0	0.1	0.0	0.0	0.1
Egypt, Arab Rep.[a]	229.9	182.8	76.6	5.9	11.1	23.9	8.8	16.7	10.8	4.7	5.4	12.1
Equatorial Guinea	17.7	2.3	0.9	0.1	0.1	0.3	0.1	0.2	0.2	0.1	0.0	0.1
Ethiopia	29.9	24.2	9.0	0.6	1.2	4.0	2.3	2.0	0.4	0.1	0.1	0.8
Gabon	17.1	6.5	2.2	0.4	0.3	0.9	0.3	0.4	0.5	0.3	0.1	0.3
Gambia, The	0.9	0.7	0.3	0.0	0.1	0.0	0.0	0.1	0.0	0.0	0.0	0.1
Ghana	39.6	26.5	9.8	0.4	3.8	2.7	1.8	0.9	1.7	0.4	0.3	3.7
Guinea	5.0	2.8	1.6	0.0	0.2	0.2	0.1	0.2	0.2	0.0	0.0	0.1
Guinea-Bissau	1.0	0.7	0.3	0.0	0.1	0.1	0.0	0.0	0.0	0.0	0.0	0.0
Kenya	34.3	30.1	10.3	1.5	0.7	2.3	1.4	2.2	3.1	0.9	1.0	4.3
Lesotho	2.5	2.8	0.7	0.1	0.3	0.3	0.2	0.1	0.1	0.1	0.1	0.3
Liberia	1.1	1.3	0.3	0.0	0.2	0.3	0.0	0.0	0.0	0.0	0.0	0.2
Madagascar	10.0	9.1	4.0	0.3	0.6	0.6	1.2	0.2	1.2	0.1	0.4	0.3
Malawi	7.3	7.2	3.5	0.3	0.2	0.8	0.7	0.3	0.6	0.1	0.2	0.4
Mali	10.6	7.1	3.3	0.1	0.4	0.7	0.4	0.3	0.9	0.2	0.3	0.3
Mauritania	4.6	2.7	1.6	0.0	0.1	0.3	0.1	0.1	0.1	0.1	0.0	0.2
Mauritius	11.3	8.9	2.6	0.7	0.5	1.4	0.7	0.4	1.2	0.3	0.6	0.7
Morocco	99.2	66.3	22.6	2.1	2.7	9.2	3.0	4.1	5.9	4.1	2.9	7.6
Mozambique	12.5	10.8	5.6	0.5	0.5	0.8	0.3	0.3	0.9	0.1	0.3	0.7
Namibia	12.5	8.9	1.8	0.4	0.4	1.7	0.6	1.0	0.4	0.1	0.4	1.3
Niger	6.4	5.1	2.1	0.1	0.4	0.5	0.2	0.2	0.4	0.1	0.3	0.2
Nigeria	247.0	159.0	60.1	2.2	23.0	16.3	11.2	5.1	10.6	2.5	1.7	20.3
Rwanda	6.3	5.5	2.6	0.2	0.2	0.9	0.2	0.1	0.4	0.1	0.1	0.3
São Tomé and Príncipe	0.2	0.3	0.2	0.0	0.0	0.0	0.0	0.0	0.0	0.0	0.0	0.0

Restaurants and hotels	Miscella-neous goods and services	Net purchases abroad	Individual consumption expenditure by households	Individual consumption expenditure by government	Collective consumption expenditure by government	Gross fixed capital formation	Machinery and equipment	Construc-tion	Other products	Changes in inventories and valuables	Balance of exports and imports	Domestic absorption	Individual consumption expenditure by households without housing
(13)	(14)	(15)	(16)	(17)	(18)	(19)	(20)	(21)	(22)	(23)	(24)	(25)	(26)
2.1	16.7	0.0	62.4	26.9	18.3	63.3	26.8	33.0	3.6	6.8	20.8	177.8	60.7
1.9	7.5	0.0	52.9	10.4	27.3	17.8	5.5	11.5	0.8	0.3	−4.5	108.7	51.4
0.5	0.2	−0.1	5.6	0.3	0.5	1.5	0.5	1.0	0.0	0.1	−0.7	8.0	5.2
0.3	0.7	0.0	7.1	1.1	1.8	4.9	2.0	2.8	0.1	1.0	−0.9	15.9	6.6
0.2	0.2	0.0	6.7	0.3	1.6	1.7	0.7	0.9	0.1	0.8	−0.7	11.1	6.3
0.1	0.0	0.0	1.8	0.1	0.3	0.4	0.2	0.2	0.0	0.0	−0.5	2.6	1.5
1.4	0.5	0.2	20.2	0.7	2.4	5.5	2.5	2.8	0.1	0.0	−2.1	28.7	19.0
0.2	0.1	−0.2	1.2	0.2	0.2	0.9	0.3	0.5	0.0	0.0	−0.5	2.4	1.0
0.0	0.1	0.0	2.0	0.1	0.1	0.3	0.1	0.2	0.1	0.0	−0.3	2.5	1.9
0.1	0.2	0.2	8.1	0.3	0.5	3.5	1.4	1.7	0.4	0.1	−0.3	12.5	7.5
0.0	0.0	0.0	0.3	0.0	0.1	0.0	0.0	0.0	0.0	0.0	−0.1	0.4	0.2
0.3	0.1	−0.1	3.3	0.4	0.7	5.1	0.8	4.2	0.0	0.0	5.3	9.5	3.1
1.0	0.4	0.0	15.6	0.6	2.9	5.9	2.2	3.5	0.2	0.0	0.1	25.1	14.6
0.3	0.8	0.2	17.6	1.0	2.0	2.9	1.0	1.7	0.1	−1.7	4.2	21.8	16.4
0.0	0.0	0.0	0.8	0.1	0.2	0.3	0.1	0.2	0.0	0.1	−0.3	1.4	0.6
5.8	13.0	−11.9	173.7	9.1	17.2	38.4	17.9	19.5	1.0	0.9	−9.5	239.4	157.6
0.1	0.1	0.0	2.1	0.2	0.3	5.9	3.0	1.9	0.9	0.0	9.3	8.5	2.0
1.1	2.6	0.0	23.5	0.7	1.9	7.8	2.9	3.5	1.4	0.6	−4.5	34.5	21.5
0.3	0.2	0.3	6.0	0.5	1.6	3.2	0.9	1.0	1.3	0.0	5.7	11.4	5.4
0.0	0.0	0.0	0.7	0.0	0.1	0.2	0.2	0.1	0.0	0.0	−0.1	1.0	0.7
0.0	1.0	0.0	24.3	2.2	4.4	10.1	5.7	3.8	0.6	0.7	−2.2	41.8	23.9
0.0	0.1	0.0	2.8	0.0	0.2	1.2	0.8	0.4	0.0	0.1	0.7	4.3	2.6
0.0	0.0	0.0	0.7	0.0	0.2	0.1	0.1	0.1	0.0	0.0	1.0	1.0	0.6
1.9	2.1	−1.6	26.0	4.1	2.9	6.9	3.8	3.1	0.0	0.2	−5.7	40.0	24.7
0.0	0.2	0.3	2.4	0.3	0.5	0.7	0.2	0.5	0.0	0.0	−1.5	4.0	2.2
0.0	0.1	0.0	1.3	0.0	0.1	0.1	0.1	0.0	0.0	0.1	−0.5	1.7	1.1
0.3	0.1	−0.1	8.8	0.3	0.7	1.7	0.8	0.9	0.1	0.0	−1.5	11.6	8.7
0.2	0.2	−0.2	6.8	0.4	0.5	1.2	0.9	0.2	0.1	−0.2	−1.4	8.7	6.3
0.1	0.2	−0.1	6.7	0.4	1.3	2.4	1.0	1.2	0.1	0.1	−0.2	10.8	6.3
0.0	0.0	0.0	2.4	0.3	0.7	2.6	1.3	1.1	0.2	−1.1	−0.3	4.9	2.2
0.3	0.6	−1.1	8.3	0.6	0.9	2.7	0.8	1.8	0.1	0.2	−1.5	12.7	7.7
3.8	4.3	−6.0	58.5	7.9	10.2	30.5	13.1	15.7	1.7	5.2	−13.0	112.2	52.9
0.1	0.5	0.1	10.0	0.8	0.9	2.2	0.8	1.5	0.0	0.3	−1.6	14.2	9.5
0.5	0.8	−0.3	7.7	1.2	1.9	2.7	1.0	1.6	0.1	−0.2	−0.9	13.4	6.6
0.3	0.3	0.0	5.0	0.2	0.6	2.4	1.0	1.3	0.1	0.0	−1.8	8.2	4.7
0.1	6.0	0.1	148.4	10.6	21.7	25.4	14.4	9.5	1.5	0.0	40.8	206.2	146.0
0.2	0.2	0.1	5.3	0.2	0.6	1.4	0.3	1.0	0.1	0.0	−1.1	7.4	4.7
0.0	0.0	0.0	0.3	0.0	0.0	0.0	0.0	0.0	0.0	0.0	−0.1	0.4	0.3

(continued)

Table 2.10 *(Continued)*

NOMINAL EXPENDITURES (US$, billions) Economy	Gross domestic product	Actual individual consumption	Food and nonalcoholic beverages	Alcoholic beverages, tobacco, and narcotics	Clothing and footwear	Housing, water, electricity, gas, and other fuels	Furnishings, household equipment and maintenance	Health	Transport	Commu- nication	Recreation and culture	Education
(00)	(01)	(02)	(03)	(04)	(05)	(06)	(07)	(08)	(09)	(10)	(11)	(12)
Senegal	14.3	11.9	5.8	0.2	0.4	2.3	0.7	0.3	0.6	0.6	0.2	0.6
Seychelles	1.1	0.6	0.3	0.0	0.0	0.1	0.0	0.0	0.0	0.0	0.0	0.1
Sierra Leone	2.9	2.6	1.0	0.1	0.2	0.2	0.1	0.4	0.1	0.1	0.1	0.2
South Africa	401.8	274.4	48.6	12.1	11.8	37.4	16.8	30.4	35.5	7.1	11.2	29.3
Sudan[b]	70.0	49.1	25.4	0.3	2.2	7.2	3.2	0.6	4.0	0.8	1.1	1.6
Swaziland	4.1	3.7	1.7	0.0	0.2	0.5	0.4	0.2	0.3	0.0	0.2	0.3
Tanzania	23.9	16.3	10.8	0.1	1.1	1.2	0.7	0.6	0.6	0.0	0.2	0.8
Togo	3.7	3.3	1.4	0.1	0.2	0.3	0.1	0.2	0.2	0.1	0.0	0.2
Tunisia	46.0	34.2	7.5	1.1	2.4	4.8	2.1	2.4	4.9	1.2	1.1	2.7
Uganda	18.2	16.5	5.5	1.0	0.5	3.0	0.9	0.5	1.0	0.3	1.0	1.8
Zambia	20.8	11.5	6.7	0.1	0.7	1.4	0.2	0.6	0.2	0.3	0.1	0.7
Zimbabwe	8.9	8.5	4.7	0.3	0.5	0.5	0.2	0.2	0.6	0.0	0.2	0.6
Total (50)	**1,870.4**	**1,251.8**	**436.5**	**39.5**	**77.5**	**148.1**	**71.1**	**84.9**	**109.5**	**32.7**	**35.3**	**109.0**
ASIA AND THE PACIFIC												
Bangladesh	130.9	98.4	50.1	2.0	5.9	16.9	3.2	3.6	4.1	0.5	0.7	5.3
Bhutan	1.8	1.0	0.3	0.0	0.1	0.2	0.0	0.1	0.1	0.0	0.1	0.1
Brunei Darussalam	16.7	4.0	0.7	0.0	0.2	0.5	0.2	0.2	0.6	0.2	0.3	0.7
Cambodia	12.8	10.8	5.0	0.4	0.2	1.6	0.2	0.8	0.8	0.0	0.3	0.7
China[c]	7,321.9	3,141.9	590.4	67.7	217.2	435.5	153.3	471.3	183.6	106.7	170.7	316.1
Fiji	3.8	2.9	0.9	0.1	0.1	0.7	0.3	0.1	0.2	0.0	0.1	0.2
Hong Kong SAR, China	248.7	165.7	18.0	1.8	7.2	31.5	9.2	13.9	11.6	3.6	18.6	5.8
India	1,864.0	1,103.0	310.4	33.0	77.6	141.8	41.1	51.3	165.8	11.4	16.6	49.4
Indonesia	846.3	492.7	186.4	8.5	18.4	100.3	13.3	16.5	33.7	9.5	9.6	36.4
Lao PDR	8.1	4.7	2.4	0.2	0.1	0.6	0.1	0.1	0.5	0.1	0.1	0.2
Macao SAR, China	36.8	8.6	0.8	0.1	0.5	1.3	0.2	0.6	0.7	0.2	0.9	0.6
Malaysia	289.0	155.1	26.4	2.3	2.8	22.9	6.8	9.1	20.4	9.3	6.1	16.3
Maldives	2.2	0.8	0.2	0.0	0.0	0.3	0.0	0.0	0.0	0.0	0.0	0.1
Mongolia	9.9	6.0	1.7	0.4	0.3	0.9	0.1	0.3	0.9	0.2	0.2	0.6
Myanmar	55.2	38.5	20.1	0.8	1.2	5.1	0.5	2.4	1.3	0.6	0.4	3.2
Nepal	19.6	15.7	8.8	0.5	0.4	2.0	0.3	0.7	0.5	0.2	0.4	0.9
Pakistan	222.2	188.7	83.4	1.8	8.8	36.6	6.2	11.7	12.1	3.1	2.1	9.0
Philippines	224.1	172.4	70.5	2.1	2.3	20.4	6.7	5.5	17.8	5.2	3.0	12.3
Singapore	265.6	113.8	7.1	2.1	3.0	20.8	5.7	9.6	14.2	2.1	12.3	10.6
Sri Lanka	59.2	45.4	19.2	3.4	1.4	6.2	1.1	2.4	3.5	0.9	0.6	2.5
Taiwan, China	465.2	299.8	35.3	6.0	12.7	49.6	13.3	28.6	31.2	10.7	28.6	26.1
Thailand	364.7	226.0	57.9	8.0	7.6	20.5	9.2	17.1	31.6	4.7	10.5	19.8
Vietnam	135.5	86.0	22.2	2.4	3.5	19.6	5.0	6.3	8.6	0.6	3.4	7.4
Total (23)	**12,604.3**	**6,382.1**	**1,518.2**	**143.6**	**371.5**	**935.8**	**276.0**	**652.3**	**544.0**	**169.8**	**285.6**	**524.2**

Restaurants and hotels	Miscella-neous goods and services	Net purchases abroad	Individual consumption expenditure by households	Individual consumption expenditure by government	Collective consumption expenditure by government	Gross fixed capital formation	Machinery and equipment	Construc-tion	Other products	Changes in inventories and valuables	Balance of exports and imports	Domestic absorption	Individual consumption expenditure by households without housing
(13)	(14)	(15)	(16)	(17)	(18)	(19)	(20)	(21)	(22)	(23)	(24)	(25)	(26)
0.1	0.5	−0.3	11.3	0.6	1.4	3.4	1.3	2.1	0.0	0.2	−2.6	16.9	10.0
0.0	0.0	0.0	0.6	0.1	0.2	0.4	0.1	0.2	0.0	0.1	−0.2	1.3	0.5
0.0	0.1	0.0	2.6	0.1	0.2	1.2	0.9	0.3	0.0	0.0	−1.2	4.1	2.5
5.7	31.2	−2.7	238.5	35.9	51.6	76.2	36.2	36.5	3.5	2.1	−2.5	404.3	212.9
1.1	1.3	0.3	48.7	0.4	4.4	15.6	8.2	7.4	0.0	1.8	−0.9	70.9	43.9
0.0	0.1	−0.2	3.5	0.2	0.4	0.4	0.1	0.2	0.1	0.0	−0.4	4.4	3.1
0.0	0.3	0.0	15.8	0.5	3.4	8.6	3.7	4.7	0.2	0.1	−4.6	28.4	15.7
0.3	0.3	−0.1	3.1	0.1	0.3	0.7	0.2	0.4	0.0	0.1	−0.6	4.3	3.0
3.2	2.1	−1.4	30.2	4.0	4.4	10.0	3.3	6.3	0.4	0.8	−3.4	49.4	26.5
0.5	0.7	0.0	15.0	1.5	0.3	4.5	1.3	3.0	0.2	0.1	−3.2	21.4	13.7
0.0	0.6	0.0	10.8	0.7	3.2	4.5	1.4	2.9	0.2	0.3	1.2	19.6	10.1
0.1	0.4	0.1	7.8	0.7	0.8	1.0	0.3	0.7	0.0	0.4	−1.8	10.6	7.5
34.5	**97.7**	**−24.6**	**1,124.6**	**127.3**	**199.2**	**390.3**	**172.1**	**198.5**	**19.7**	**20.5**	**8.5**	**1,861.9**	**1,043.7**
2.2	3.8	0.0	96.5	2.0	4.9	37.1	8.8	27.8	0.5	0.7	−10.2	141.1	87.7
0.0	0.0	0.0	0.8	0.1	0.2	1.2	0.5	0.7	0.0	0.0	−0.5	2.4	0.7
0.2	0.2	0.0	3.3	0.7	2.1	2.2	0.7	1.4	0.2	−0.1	8.5	8.2	2.9
0.5	0.3	0.0	10.2	0.6	0.5	1.5	0.7	0.7	0.0	0.1	0.0	12.8	9.1
160.0	269.5	0.0	2,515.6	626.3	457.8	3,338.0	957.3	2,106.3	274.4	196.0	188.2	7,133.7	2,267.9
0.1	0.1	0.0	2.7	0.2	0.2	0.7	0.4	0.3	0.1	0.1	−0.2	3.9	2.1
16.7	28.0	0.0	157.4	8.4	13.3	58.5	25.8	27.5	5.2	1.5	9.8	239.0	130.7
27.5	177.0	0.0	1,042.4	60.7	154.2	576.6	220.1	334.7	21.8	135.9	−105.7	1,969.7	945.8
35.3	24.7	0.0	462.2	30.6	45.7	270.5	44.6	219.3	6.6	25.5	11.9	834.4	402.1
0.1	0.1	0.0	4.6	0.2	0.6	2.9	0.9	1.4	0.6	0.1	−0.3	8.4	4.3
1.6	1.0	0.0	7.5	1.1	1.5	4.6	1.1	3.5	0.0	0.5	21.6	15.2	6.5
12.8	19.8	0.0	136.7	18.4	19.2	64.4	23.3	32.1	9.0	2.8	47.5	241.6	123.9
0.0	0.0	0.0	0.7	0.1	0.4	1.1	0.4	0.7	0.0	0.0	−0.1	2.3	0.4
0.1	0.3	0.0	5.4	0.6	0.7	4.7	2.8	1.7	0.2	1.2	−2.7	12.6	4.7
1.7	1.2	0.0	35.2	3.3	2.3	14.7	7.2	6.4	1.2	0.0	−0.4	55.6	32.4
0.3	0.7	0.0	15.1	0.7	1.3	4.0	0.9	2.3	0.9	3.1	−4.6	24.2	13.4
1.9	12.0	0.0	182.0	6.8	15.7	28.7	9.2	13.7	5.8	3.6	−14.5	236.8	167.2
6.1	20.5	0.0	164.7	7.7	14.0	42.0	16.1	20.9	4.9	3.9	−8.2	232.3	150.6
11.8	14.5	0.0	103.5	10.3	17.2	63.1	23.5	37.2	2.5	−3.2	74.6	191.0	85.7
1.7	2.6	0.0	41.3	4.1	4.6	16.0	4.9	10.1	1.0	1.7	−8.6	67.8	37.5
16.1	41.8	0.0	279.5	20.4	37.2	97.3	45.3	44.0	8.0	−0.2	31.2	434.1	238.2
17.7	21.3	0.0	199.3	26.7	32.9	97.5	65.4	30.7	1.5	2.0	6.2	358.5	185.1
3.8	3.1	0.0	79.9	6.1	8.0	40.3	10.5	27.5	2.3	6.9	−5.6	141.1	67.7
318.2	**642.8**	**0.0**	**5,546.2**	**835.9**	**834.6**	**4,767.6**	**1,470.2**	**2,950.8**	**346.6**	**382.1**	**237.8**	**12,366.4**	**4,966.7**

(continued)

Table 2.10 (Continued)

NOMINAL EXPENDITURES (US$, billions) Economy	Gross domestic product	Actual individual consumption	Food and nonalcoholic beverages	Alcoholic beverages, tobacco, and narcotics	Clothing and footwear	Housing, water, electricity, gas, and other fuels	Furnishings, household equipment and maintenance	Health	Transport	Commu-nication	Recreation and culture	Education
(00)	(01)	(02)	(03)	(04)	(05)	(06)	(07)	(08)	(09)	(10)	(11)	(12)
COMMONWEALTH OF INDEPENDENT STATES												
Armenia	10.1	9.0	4.9	0.4	0.3	0.7	0.1	0.6	0.5	0.5	0.2	0.4
Azerbaijan	66.0	27.1	10.0	0.6	2.5	2.2	1.4	1.2	2.8	1.5	0.9	2.0
Belarus	53.0	30.1	9.5	1.8	1.9	2.3	1.4	2.7	2.5	1.3	1.6	2.6
Kazakhstan	188.0	90.9	18.5	2.0	5.4	19.7	3.6	7.1	9.7	3.6	4.5	7.6
Kyrgyz Republic	6.2	5.8	2.2	0.3	0.4	0.4	0.2	0.3	0.6	0.4	0.2	0.5
Moldova	7.0	7.9	2.2	0.5	0.5	1.0	0.6	0.3	0.8	0.3	0.3	0.7
Russian Federation[d]	1,901.0	1,096.6	277.8	75.3	83.1	106.8	45.0	87.0	113.2	42.2	59.9	61.0
Tajikistan	6.5	7.5	3.3	0.0	0.6	0.5	0.3	0.3	0.6	0.5	0.2	0.3
Ukraine	163.4	129.4	42.4	7.5	6.9	13.9	4.7	11.4	13.4	2.7	5.3	11.5
Total (9)	**2,401.3**	**1,404.2**	**370.9**	**88.5**	**101.5**	**147.5**	**57.2**	**110.8**	**144.1**	**52.8**	**73.0**	**86.5**
EUROSTAT-OECD												
Albania	12.6	10.8	4.1	0.3	0.4	1.3	0.7	0.6	0.5	0.2	0.3	0.4
Australia	1,490.0	957.3	82.9	29.4	26.9	188.2	36.8	121.4	83.7	19.9	96.0	78.9
Austria	416.0	274.3	23.0	7.9	13.7	49.1	14.9	28.9	30.6	4.5	26.6	21.9
Belgium	513.3	350.8	35.0	9.1	13.0	62.1	14.8	51.0	32.2	5.6	26.0	32.4
Bosnia and Herzegovina	19.0	17.8	5.1	1.1	0.7	2.3	0.9	1.5	1.5	0.5	0.9	1.0
Bulgaria	53.5	37.6	7.1	2.5	1.0	6.0	2.6	3.7	5.8	2.0	3.1	1.9
Canada	1,778.3	1,215.5	90.2	33.4	40.1	234.1	53.6	154.5	143.5	23.9	97.2	95.3
Chile	251.2	172.8	24.9	4.7	8.6	25.1	11.0	16.5	19.6	6.1	11.9	14.6
Croatia	61.7	43.6	8.3	2.8	1.9	7.7	2.3	5.2	4.2	1.4	4.4	3.5
Cyprus	24.9	19.0	2.3	0.8	1.1	3.3	0.9	1.6	2.0	0.6	1.5	1.9
Czech Republic	216.1	132.7	16.6	10.4	3.5	30.2	6.0	15.7	10.5	3.4	12.2	9.3
Denmark	334.3	230.7	18.2	5.7	7.4	46.5	8.0	30.0	19.6	2.7	20.0	21.2
Estonia	22.5	13.8	2.3	1.0	0.7	2.5	0.4	1.2	1.5	0.4	1.1	1.1
Finland	262.3	189.3	17.3	6.9	6.9	37.4	7.4	22.9	15.9	3.0	18.1	15.4
France	2,782.2	2,051.5	209.7	49.8	66.5	411.4	90.7	257.3	222.6	43.1	163.9	149.9
Germany	3,628.1	2,527.3	226.5	63.7	96.1	477.3	123.7	320.2	274.8	51.8	197.8	148.1
Greece	289.9	236.7	36.1	9.7	8.3	53.0	8.9	23.5	26.3	6.5	12.8	15.7
Hungary	137.5	88.2	12.9	5.6	2.1	16.4	3.2	10.0	9.7	2.8	6.7	6.1
Iceland	14.0	9.6	1.0	0.3	0.3	1.6	0.5	1.2	1.0	0.2	1.0	1.0
Ireland	226.0	137.9	10.5	5.7	4.3	25.7	4.5	20.3	13.5	3.1	8.1	10.8
Israel	258.2	179.5	23.6	3.7	4.3	35.8	9.0	15.4	23.1	5.8	11.3	18.5
Italy	2,197.0	1,607.2	193.8	36.8	101.8	300.5	96.6	192.4	170.9	32.4	108.8	95.4
Japan	5,897.0	4,272.2	481.6	95.3	111.0	888.8	176.2	452.4	377.9	120.6	320.7	215.8
Korea, Rep.	1,114.5	667.2	74.2	12.9	29.0	93.4	19.1	73.5	67.5	24.6	46.7	73.4
Latvia	28.1	19.7	3.4	1.3	0.8	4.0	0.7	1.4	2.5	0.5	1.6	1.3
Lithuania	43.0	31.7	6.6	2.1	1.7	4.4	1.6	3.1	4.1	0.7	2.0	2.1
Luxembourg	58.0	24.4	1.8	1.9	1.0	5.4	1.4	2.6	4.2	0.4	1.9	2.5

Restaurants and hotels	Miscellaneous goods and services	Net purchases abroad	Individual consumption expenditure by households	Individual consumption expenditure by government	Collective consumption expenditure by government	Gross fixed capital formation	Machinery and equipment	Construction	Other products	Changes in inventories and valuables	Balance of exports and imports	Domestic absorption	Individual consumption expenditure by households without housing
(13)	(14)	(15)	(16)	(17)	(18)	(19)	(20)	(21)	(22)	(23)	(24)	(25)	(26)
0.1	0.3	0.0	8.5	0.5	0.8	2.6	0.4	2.1	0.1	0.1	−2.4	12.5	8.2
0.9	1.1	0.0	24.6	2.5	4.2	13.3	6.9	5.8	0.6	0.1	21.3	44.6	23.9
0.9	1.2	0.4	25.3	4.8	2.6	20.0	8.7	11.1	0.2	0.9	−0.6	53.6	24.4
3.1	6.0	0.0	80.4	10.5	9.6	39.4	11.3	25.6	2.4	8.0	40.2	147.9	66.7
0.2	0.2	−0.2	5.2	0.6	0.5	1.5	0.7	0.8	0.0	0.1	−1.7	7.9	5.1
0.1	0.7	0.1	6.8	1.1	0.3	1.6	0.5	1.0	0.1	0.1	−2.9	9.9	6.4
30.6	93.6	21.0	933.4	163.1	178.9	395.0	141.8	221.1	32.1	67.7	162.7	1,738.3	886.6
0.1	0.4	0.5	7.0	0.5	0.3	2.1	0.9	1.0	0.2	0.2	−3.7	10.2	6.9
2.8	7.0	−0.1	109.9	19.5	10.3	30.3	11.6	18.0	0.7	3.5	−10.2	173.6	103.1
38.9	**110.6**	**21.8**	**1,201.0**	**203.2**	**207.6**	**505.9**	**183.0**	**286.5**	**36.4**	**80.8**	**202.9**	**2,198.5**	**1,131.2**
0.3	0.6	1.1	10.2	0.6	0.7	4.2	0.9	3.2	0.1	−0.1	−2.9	15.6	9.3
55.9	140.6	−3.4	798.9	158.4	104.6	401.5	97.2	230.8	73.6	7.2	19.4	1,470.6	653.2
27.5	34.2	−8.7	227.8	46.5	32.4	88.3	33.7	45.8	8.7	8.5	12.4	403.5	197.0
16.0	49.6	4.1	270.6	80.2	45.3	106.3	39.7	57.0	9.6	6.6	4.3	509.1	228.7
1.1	1.6	−0.5	15.8	2.0	2.2	3.4	1.4	1.9	0.1	0.0	−4.4	23.5	14.7
2.3	2.3	−2.6	33.4	4.2	4.2	11.5	5.0	6.1	0.4	0.2	0.0	53.5	29.8
65.1	167.7	16.9	990.5	225.0	160.8	416.4	82.8	276.7	56.9	7.7	−22.1	1,800.4	798.2
7.3	23.2	−0.5	153.8	19.0	11.1	56.3	22.1	29.9	4.3	2.6	8.2	243.0	139.2
6.6	3.8	−8.3	37.0	6.6	5.6	11.8	3.8	7.1	0.9	0.7	0.0	61.7	32.7
2.7	1.6	−1.5	16.8	2.2	2.8	4.1	1.2	2.7	0.2	0.0	−1.1	25.9	14.7
8.7	11.3	−5.1	109.4	23.3	21.5	52.2	23.2	26.1	2.9	0.8	9.0	207.2	91.2
8.3	42.6	0.4	162.8	67.9	26.9	58.0	20.3	29.3	8.3	1.2	17.5	316.8	130.7
0.9	1.3	−0.6	11.4	2.4	1.9	5.3	2.5	2.7	0.2	0.7	0.8	21.7	9.7
8.9	29.6	−0.4	146.2	43.1	21.1	50.9	12.2	34.3	4.4	2.8	−1.9	264.2	120.3
109.9	287.1	−10.4	1,606.0	445.5	235.6	556.0	150.4	345.9	59.7	21.6	−82.4	2,864.7	1,322.2
114.9	382.9	49.6	2,082.9	444.3	250.1	657.8	251.9	366.1	39.8	4.4	188.6	3,439.5	1,755.0
26.1	21.3	−11.5	216.3	20.5	29.9	43.9	17.7	23.1	3.1	2.8	−23.5	313.3	180.7
5.0	11.3	−3.7	73.3	14.9	14.1	24.6	10.3	12.8	1.5	1.8	8.9	128.6	64.1
0.6	1.0	0.0	7.3	2.3	1.2	2.0	0.8	1.1	0.2	0.0	1.2	12.9	6.0
13.2	15.6	2.6	108.7	29.2	12.3	24.0	9.1	12.9	2.1	2.9	48.8	177.2	90.2
9.9	21.0	−2.1	147.9	31.6	27.9	52.8	16.9	25.5	10.3	−0.6	−1.3	259.5	119.8
135.9	161.9	−20.0	1,345.5	261.7	186.0	418.9	167.7	199.6	51.6	15.6	−30.7	2,227.7	1,137.9
228.4	771.7	31.7	3,568.4	703.8	501.6	1,213.8	473.8	572.0	168.1	−37.0	−53.7	5,950.7	2,831.5
46.6	97.4	9.0	591.3	75.9	95.2	306.9	108.5	173.9	24.5	22.7	22.5	1,092.0	526.4
0.8	1.3	0.0	17.5	2.2	2.8	6.0	2.5	3.3	0.2	1.0	−1.3	29.4	15.1
0.8	2.8	−0.3	27.0	4.7	3.4	7.8	2.6	4.6	0.6	1.4	−1.2	44.2	25.3
1.5	4.2	−4.6	18.4	6.0	3.7	10.8	4.0	6.1	0.7	1.5	17.6	40.4	14.3

(continued)

Table 2.10 *(Continued)*

NOMINAL EXPENDITURES (US$, billions) Economy	Gross domestic product	Actual individual consumption	Food and nonalcoholic beverages	Alcoholic beverages, tobacco, and narcotics	Clothing and footwear	Housing, water, electricity, gas, and other fuels	Furnishings, household equipment and maintenance	Health	Transport	Commu-nication	Recreation and culture	Education
(00)	(01)	(02)	(03)	(04)	(05)	(06)	(07)	(08)	(09)	(10)	(11)	(12)
Macedonia, FYR	10.4	8.6	2.6	0.3	0.4	1.5	0.3	0.5	0.8	0.5	0.3	0.5
Malta	9.2	6.6	1.0	0.2	0.3	0.8	0.4	0.8	0.8	0.2	0.7	0.5
Mexico	1,170.1	848.3	180.8	20.4	23.2	159.8	44.1	53.3	145.0	28.8	35.7	44.0
Montenegro	4.5	4.1	1.4	0.2	0.1	0.6	0.4	0.3	0.5	0.2	0.2	0.2
Netherlands	832.8	519.8	43.7	11.5	19.9	92.0	22.0	65.1	47.5	15.5	42.8	42.1
New Zealand	161.5	115.9	13.9	5.0	4.3	22.5	4.8	14.2	11.5	3.1	10.7	9.3
Norway	490.5	271.1	24.5	7.9	9.9	40.1	10.6	36.2	27.8	4.8	27.2	20.7
Poland	515.5	368.4	58.8	20.1	13.7	76.3	14.1	35.5	31.3	9.2	28.1	27.5
Portugal	237.9	182.8	26.9	5.4	8.9	25.9	8.9	22.3	21.3	4.7	13.3	14.1
Romania	182.6	131.9	31.1	5.7	4.3	25.1	5.6	14.6	12.5	5.6	8.1	6.3
Russian Federation[d]	1,901.0	1,096.6	277.8	75.3	83.1	105.7	45.0	86.5	113.2	42.2	58.7	60.7
Serbia	43.8	39.3	9.3	1.9	1.3	7.7	1.3	4.1	4.6	1.5	2.0	2.0
Slovak Republic	95.9	63.6	9.8	2.6	2.3	14.2	3.3	6.0	4.3	2.0	5.8	4.0
Slovenia	50.3	35.1	4.5	1.7	1.7	6.0	1.9	4.0	4.6	1.0	3.1	3.1
Spain	1,454.5	1,031.1	123.3	25.9	46.7	184.3	42.0	119.2	101.3	24.4	85.4	75.4
Sweden	535.8	359.8	30.6	9.1	12.1	68.1	12.7	43.3	33.4	8.3	32.9	35.3
Switzerland	659.9	419.1	33.3	13.4	12.5	89.5	15.5	56.3	33.7	8.9	33.7	33.3
Turkey	771.7	608.1	132.6	19.4	30.9	110.8	45.2	46.6	95.1	16.6	25.5	30.2
United Kingdom	2,461.8	1,930.3	138.7	54.2	88.4	384.1	75.6	214.3	205.3	32.7	215.2	153.2
United States	15,533.8	11,667.0	698.4	207.6	366.0	1,962.8	429.5	2,300.0	1,079.1	246.7	996.1	930.9
Total (47)	**49,253.0**	**35,226.8**	**3,462.0**	**892.4**	**1,283.1**	**6,391.4**	**1,479.4**	**4,951.2**	**3,543.0**	**823.7**	**2,827.8**	**2,532.5**
LATIN AMERICA												
Bolivia	23.9	15.0	5.1	0.2	0.3	1.6	1.1	1.3	2.6	0.2	0.2	0.9
Brazil	2,476.6	1,693.7	244.4	30.5	71.1	227.0	113.8	189.3	229.4	54.4	79.1	144.9
Colombia	336.3	228.9	38.0	6.4	13.4	32.8	8.7	17.0	25.3	9.1	10.8	19.8
Costa Rica	41.0	31.8	6.4	0.3	1.4	2.0	1.9	3.9	5.7	0.7	3.1	3.2
Cuba[e]	…	…	…	…	…	…	…	…	…	…	…	…
Dominican Republic	55.6	49.4	12.0	2.9	1.6	7.3	1.8	3.1	6.4	2.1	1.1	2.2
Ecuador	79.8	53.5	10.8	1.3	2.2	7.3	3.8	4.4	6.0	2.9	2.7	5.5
El Salvador	23.1	22.8	5.8	0.4	1.2	3.8	2.2	1.8	2.0	1.0	1.0	1.1
Guatemala	47.7	42.9	16.6	0.7	2.2	5.4	2.4	2.9	3.1	3.1	1.3	1.8
Haiti	7.3	8.3	4.9	0.2	0.6	0.9	0.3	0.3	0.4	0.0	0.2	0.4
Honduras	17.7	15.2	4.5	0.5	0.7	1.9	0.6	1.5	1.5	0.5	0.6	1.3
Nicaragua	9.6	8.1	2.1	0.2	0.2	1.1	0.4	0.9	1.0	0.3	0.3	0.6
Panama	31.3	20.7	3.5	0.1	1.3	4.1	1.5	1.5	2.7	0.7	1.1	1.2
Paraguay	25.2	19.2	5.3	0.2	1.0	1.7	1.5	1.6	1.6	0.7	1.2	1.8
Peru	180.7	113.0	25.6	2.5	7.0	11.9	5.6	7.3	12.1	4.4	6.7	9.5
Uruguay	46.4	35.1	6.5	0.8	1.6	6.7	1.9	4.2	2.6	1.4	1.2	2.3
Venezuela, RB	316.5	192.1	41.4	5.7	8.8	9.4	11.0	17.3	25.5	10.7	12.2	16.2
Total (17)	**3,719.1**	**2,549.6**	**432.8**	**53.0**	**114.5**	**324.9**	**158.5**	**258.2**	**327.7**	**92.0**	**122.8**	**212.6**

Restaurants and hotels	Miscella-neous goods and services	Net purchases abroad	Individual consumption expenditure by households	Individual consumption expenditure by government	Collective consumption expenditure by government	Gross fixed capital formation	Machinery and equipment	Construc-tion	Other products	Changes in inventories and valuables	Balance of exports and imports	Domestic absorption	Individual consumption expenditure by households without housing
(13)	(14)	(15)	(16)	(17)	(18)	(19)	(20)	(21)	(22)	(23)	(24)	(25)	(26)
0.3	0.6	0.1	7.8	0.8	1.1	2.1	0.7	1.3	0.1	0.6	−2.0	12.4	6.9
1.1	0.8	−1.0	5.6	1.0	0.9	1.4	0.5	0.7	0.2	0.0	0.4	8.9	5.1
31.6	85.6	−3.9	776.0	72.3	63.9	254.8	78.4	171.1	5.2	17.8	−14.7	1,184.9	647.2
0.6	0.3	−0.8	3.7	0.4	0.5	0.8	0.3	0.6	0.0	0.0	−1.0	5.5	3.4
18.7	101.3	−2.1	377.8	142.1	90.6	148.6	45.8	84.0	18.7	2.3	71.5	761.3	317.7
6.8	12.2	−2.4	96.6	19.3	13.3	29.3	10.1	16.8	2.4	0.7	2.3	159.3	77.5
11.2	42.8	7.5	201.9	69.2	36.2	95.7	30.9	45.5	19.3	22.5	65.1	425.4	172.1
8.9	47.2	−2.2	315.1	53.4	39.3	104.1	39.1	58.5	6.5	9.6	−5.9	521.5	293.0
17.9	20.4	−7.3	157.1	25.8	21.6	42.8	12.7	26.3	3.8	1.1	−10.4	248.3	140.6
3.8	8.9	0.4	115.9	16.0	11.6	47.6	15.4	29.9	2.2	1.2	−9.7	192.3	100.2
30.6	96.7	21.0	933.4	163.1	178.9	395.0	141.8	221.1	32.1	67.7	162.7	1,738.3	887.7
0.8	3.3	−0.5	33.7	5.6	2.9	8.1	3.4	4.1	0.5	0.7	−7.2	50.9	29.1
2.7	6.7	0.0	55.2	8.4	8.9	22.2	7.4	10.0	4.8	0.7	0.5	95.4	50.2
2.0	3.5	−2.0	28.9	6.2	4.3	9.3	4.0	4.6	0.7	0.8	0.8	49.5	25.6
150.8	98.4	−45.8	851.9	179.2	130.4	301.2	87.5	154.3	59.4	7.1	−15.3	1,469.8	727.6
14.1	62.1	−2.1	257.3	102.6	39.7	100.2	37.1	48.8	14.3	6.2	29.9	506.0	207.7
25.2	63.8	0.0	378.3	40.8	31.9	135.7	59.5	61.5	14.7	4.7	68.5	591.4	303.3
35.7	44.6	−24.9	549.3	58.8	48.7	168.4	97.7	70.1	0.6	13.4	−66.9	838.6	467.6
127.3	231.3	10.0	1,589.5	340.8	199.2	353.5	71.9	202.3	79.4	16.0	−37.3	2,499.1	1,270.1
670.7	1,803.2	−23.8	10,711.8	955.2	1,570.9	2,828.2	1,014.6	1,295.0	518.6	36.4	−568.7	16,102.5	9,105.2
2,066.0	**5,023.2**	**−48.7**	**30,241.8**	**4,985.0**	**4,299.8**	**9,644.7**	**3,321.1**	**5,007.5**	**1,316.1**	**286.6**	**−204.9**	**49,457.9**	**25,395.7**
1.2	0.4	0.0	14.6	0.4	2.9	4.5	2.5	1.7	0.3	0.1	1.4	22.6	13.8
95.6	214.1	0.0	1,494.2	199.5	312.6	477.5	249.9	197.7	29.8	11.1	−18.2	2,494.8	1,339.1
23.9	23.6	0.0	206.3	22.5	30.5	79.3	27.5	48.9	3.0	0.6	−2.9	339.2	185.4
1.5	1.5	0.3	26.8	5.0	2.4	8.1	3.5	4.4	0.2	0.7	−2.0	43.0	25.9
...	...	...	...	...	...	...	...	...	...	...	...	...	...
4.0	5.2	−0.3	48.1	1.3	2.8	9.1	2.6	6.3	0.1	0.1	−5.7	61.3	43.2
2.2	4.9	−0.3	48.7	4.8	5.3	20.8	6.7	5.9	8.1	2.4	−2.2	82.0	43.3
1.5	1.3	−0.1	21.6	1.2	1.4	2.9	1.5	1.4	0.0	0.4	−4.3	27.5	19.3
2.5	1.8	−0.8	40.7	2.3	2.7	7.0	3.7	3.3	0.0	0.2	−5.1	52.8	36.5
0.0	0.2	0.0	8.2	0.1	0.0	2.1	0.1	2.1	0.0	0.0	−3.1	10.5	7.9
0.8	0.9	0.0	13.8	1.5	1.4	4.3	2.4	1.7	0.2	0.3	−3.5	21.2	12.8
0.5	0.6	−0.1	7.5	0.6	0.8	2.2	0.8	1.2	0.2	0.1	−1.5	11.2	6.8
1.1	1.9	0.0	18.9	1.8	2.0	8.2	3.7	4.5	0.0	0.3	0.1	31.2	15.9
0.9	1.5	0.0	17.7	1.5	1.2	4.1	1.8	2.0	0.3	0.1	0.6	24.6	17.2
10.0	10.3	0.0	107.5	5.5	11.1	47.0	16.9	28.6	1.5	1.9	7.8	173.0	99.3
2.4	2.8	0.7	31.5	3.5	2.6	8.8	2.8	5.5	0.6	0.2	−0.2	46.7	26.5
23.1	9.9	0.8	174.6	17.5	19.0	56.1	25.4	28.7	2.0	16.9	32.4	284.0	167.8
171.3	**280.9**	**0.2**	**2,280.6**	**269.0**	**398.5**	**742.0**	**351.8**	**343.8**	**46.4**	**35.4**	**−6.5**	**3,725.6**	**2,060.6**

(continued)

Table 2.10 (Continued)

NOMINAL EXPENDITURES (US$, billions) Economy	Gross domestic product	Actual individual consumption	Food and nonalcoholic beverages	Alcoholic beverages, tobacco, and narcotics	Clothing and footwear	Housing, water, electricity, gas, and other fuels	Furnishings, household equipment and maintenance	Health	Transport	Commu-nication	Recreation and culture	Education
(00)	(01)	(02)	(03)	(04)	(05)	(06)	(07)	(08)	(09)	(10)	(11)	(12)
CARIBBEAN												
Anguilla	0.3	0.3	0.0	0.0	0.0	0.1	0.0	0.0	0.0	0.0	0.0	0.0
Antigua and Barbuda	1.1	0.8	0.1	0.0	0.0	0.2	0.0	0.1	0.1	0.0	0.0	0.0
Aruba	2.6	2.0	0.2	0.0	0.1	0.7	0.1	0.2	0.2	0.1	0.1	0.1
Bahamas, The	7.9	6.0	0.6	0.1	0.2	1.9	0.3	0.5	0.5	0.2	0.3	0.4
Barbados	4.4	3.9	0.5	0.1	0.1	2.0	0.1	0.2	0.3	0.2	0.1	0.2
Belize	1.5	1.1	0.2	0.0	0.1	0.3	0.1	0.1	0.1	0.0	0.1	0.1
Bermuda	5.6	4.3	0.4	0.1	0.1	1.2	0.2	0.4	0.3	0.1	0.2	0.3
Bonaire[f]	...	...	0.0	0.0	0.0	...	0.0	...	0.0	0.0	...	...
Cayman Islands	3.2	2.4	0.1	0.0	0.1	0.8	0.1	0.1	0.2	0.1	0.1	0.1
Curaçao	3.0	2.3	0.2	0.0	0.2	0.7	0.1	0.2	0.2	0.1	0.1	0.1
Dominica	0.5	0.4	0.1	0.0	0.0	0.1	0.0	0.0	0.1	0.0	0.0	0.0
Grenada	0.8	0.8	0.1	0.0	0.0	0.1	0.0	0.0	0.1	0.1	0.0	0.0
Jamaica	14.5	13.5	3.8	0.2	0.2	1.8	0.7	0.8	1.9	0.4	1.2	1.0
Montserrat	0.1	0.1	0.0	0.0	0.0	0.0	0.0	0.0	0.0	0.0	0.0	0.0
St. Kitts and Nevis	0.7	0.5	0.1	0.0	0.0	0.1	0.0	0.0	0.0	0.0	0.0	0.0
St. Lucia	1.2	1.0	0.2	0.0	0.1	0.2	0.1	0.1	0.1	0.1	0.0	0.1
St. Vincent and the Grenadines	0.7	0.6	0.1	0.0	0.0	0.2	0.0	0.0	0.1	0.0	0.0	0.0
Sint Maarten	1.0	0.6	0.1	0.0	0.0	0.3	0.0	0.0	0.1	0.0	0.0	0.0
Suriname	4.4	1.7	0.6	0.0	0.1	0.3	0.1	0.1	0.1	0.1	0.1	0.0
Trinidad and Tobago	23.5	13.7	2.9	0.1	0.2	1.7	0.6	1.1	1.5	0.3	0.9	1.4
Turks and Caicos Islands	0.7	0.3	0.0	0.0	0.0	0.0	0.0	0.0	0.1	0.0	0.0	0.0
Virgin Islands, British	0.9	0.4	0.1	0.0	0.0	0.1	0.0	0.0	0.0	0.0	0.0	0.0
Total (22)	**78.4**	**56.7**	**10.5**	**0.8**	**1.5**	**12.8**	**2.6**	**3.9**	**6.1**	**1.8**	**3.4**	**4.1**
WESTERN ASIA												
Bahrain	28.9	12.6	1.7	0.0	0.7	2.6	0.9	0.9	1.3	0.6	0.8	1.4
Egypt, Arab Rep.[a]	229.9	182.8	76.6	5.9	11.1	23.9	8.8	16.7	10.8	4.7	5.4	12.1
Iraq	159.8	75.2	23.0	0.4	4.5	19.6	3.5	5.4	5.5	1.1	0.9	8.3
Jordan	28.8	23.0	6.4	0.7	1.0	4.6	1.0	1.6	2.3	0.9	0.4	2.8
Kuwait	160.6	44.6	6.9	0.1	3.5	10.4	5.4	3.5	3.3	1.5	1.5	4.3
Oman	70.0	25.2	4.9	0.1	1.4	4.6	1.0	1.5	4.0	1.2	0.9	2.8
Qatar	171.0	28.3	3.0	0.1	1.0	6.4	1.2	2.1	2.4	0.6	2.1	4.3
Saudi Arabia	669.5	245.9	39.0	0.8	11.8	51.0	16.2	20.3	16.7	10.3	7.5	42.2
Sudan[b]	70.0	49.1	25.4	0.3	2.2	7.2	3.2	0.6	4.0	0.8	1.1	1.6
United Arab Emirates	348.6	184.0	21.6	0.3	22.7	61.0	6.5	2.8	29.6	10.7	5.0	8.6
West Bank and Gaza	9.8	10.6	3.3	0.4	0.6	1.1	0.5	0.8	1.0	0.3	0.3	0.9
Yemen, Rep.	31.4	22.9	10.4	1.1	1.0	3.3	0.7	2.2	1.3	0.2	0.1	1.6
Total (12)	**1,978.3**	**904.3**	**222.2**	**10.4**	**61.5**	**195.6**	**48.9**	**58.4**	**82.2**	**32.9**	**26.0**	**91.1**

Restaurants and hotels	Miscellaneous goods and services	Net purchases abroad	Individual consumption expenditure by households	Individual consumption expenditure by government	Collective consumption expenditure by government	Gross fixed capital formation	Machinery and equipment	Construction	Other products	Changes in inventories and valuables	Balance of exports and imports	Domestic absorption	Individual consumption expenditure by households without housing
(13)	(14)	(15)	(16)	(17)	(18)	(19)	(20)	(21)	(22)	(23)	(24)	(25)	(26)
0.0	0.0	0.0	0.2	0.0	0.0	0.1	0.0	0.0	0.0	0.0	0.0	0.3	0.2
0.0	0.1	0.0	0.7	0.1	0.1	0.2	0.0	0.2	0.0	0.0	0.0	1.1	0.5
0.0	0.2	0.0	1.6	0.4	0.2	0.7	0.2	0.5	0.0	0.0	−0.4	3.0	1.2
0.3	0.9	0.0	5.6	0.5	0.7	2.1	1.0	1.1	0.0	0.1	−1.1	9.0	4.3
0.7	0.3	−0.9	3.6	0.3	0.5	0.7	0.3	0.3	0.0	0.0	−0.6	5.0	1.8
0.0	0.1	0.0	1.1	0.1	0.2	0.2	0.1	0.1	0.0	0.0	−0.1	1.5	0.8
0.5	0.6	0.0	3.7	0.6	0.5	1.1	0.6	0.5	0.0	0.1	−0.4	6.0	2.6
0.0	…	0.0	0.2	…	…	…	…	…	…	0.0	…	…	0.1
0.1	0.4	0.0	2.3	0.1	0.3	0.7	0.4	0.4	0.0	0.0	−0.2	3.4	1.6
0.1	0.5	−0.2	2.1	0.2	0.2	1.2	0.7	0.3	0.2	0.0	−0.8	3.8	1.7
0.0	0.0	0.0	0.4	0.0	0.1	0.1	0.1	0.1	0.0	−0.1	−0.1	0.6	0.3
0.0	0.1	0.0	0.7	0.1	0.1	0.2	0.1	0.1	0.0	0.0	−0.2	1.0	0.6
1.7	1.6	−1.8	12.4	1.1	1.2	3.0	1.5	1.5	0.1	0.1	−3.3	17.8	11.3
0.0	0.0	0.0	0.0	0.0	0.0	0.0	0.0	0.0	0.0	0.0	0.0	0.1	0.0
0.0	0.1	0.0	0.5	0.0	0.1	0.2	0.1	0.2	0.0	0.0	−0.1	0.8	0.4
0.0	0.1	0.0	0.9	0.1	0.1	0.4	0.1	0.2	0.0	0.0	−0.2	1.5	0.8
0.0	0.1	−0.1	0.6	0.1	0.1	0.2	0.0	0.1	0.0	0.0	−0.2	0.9	0.5
0.0	0.1	0.0	0.6	0.0	0.1	0.2	0.1	0.0	0.0	0.0	0.1	0.9	0.4
0.0	0.2	0.0	1.6	0.0	0.5	1.6	1.3	0.3	0.0	0.3	0.3	4.1	1.5
1.3	1.9	0.0	10.8	2.9	0.4	3.5	1.7	1.7	0.1	0.0	5.9	17.6	9.8
0.0	0.0	0.0	0.3	0.0	0.1	0.1	0.0	0.1	0.0	0.0	0.2	0.5	0.2
0.0	0.0	0.0	0.3	0.0	0.0	0.2	0.1	0.1	0.0	0.0	0.3	0.6	0.3
4.9	**7.2**	**−3.0**	**49.9**	**6.8**	**5.6**	**16.7**	**8.3**	**7.9**	**0.4**	**0.6**	**−1.0**	**79.5**	**40.8**
0.6	0.8	0.3	11.2	1.5	2.5	4.5	1.4	3.1	0.0	0.2	9.0	19.9	9.1
5.8	13.0	−11.9	173.7	9.1	17.2	38.4	17.9	19.5	1.0	0.9	−9.5	239.4	157.6
0.7	2.3	0.0	63.6	11.6	24.1	31.1	12.0	18.9	0.1	−0.7	30.2	129.6	49.7
0.5	0.7	0.1	20.6	2.4	3.2	6.2	1.6	4.2	0.4	0.5	−4.0	32.8	17.5
1.3	2.9	0.0	37.4	7.2	16.8	25.4	10.1	12.7	2.6	0.9	72.9	87.7	28.1
0.7	1.9	0.2	21.0	4.2	7.8	18.4	7.3	9.2	1.9	−2.2	20.7	49.3	17.5
0.6	4.0	0.6	21.8	6.5	14.9	50.1	24.5	7.8	17.7	0.0	77.7	93.3	16.0
9.3	12.0	8.8	181.8	64.1	66.0	151.7	58.5	75.2	17.9	27.6	178.2	491.3	146.0
1.1	1.3	0.3	48.7	0.4	4.4	15.6	8.2	7.4	0.0	1.8	−0.9	70.9	43.9
6.8	8.3	0.0	180.2	3.8	21.7	76.7	30.5	38.3	7.9	3.3	62.9	285.7	127.7
0.3	0.9	0.1	9.4	1.1	1.8	2.0	0.4	1.4	0.2	−0.3	−4.3	14.0	9.0
0.0	1.0	0.0	21.4	1.6	2.9	4.1	0.4	3.2	0.5	1.8	−0.3	31.7	19.7
27.5	**49.1**	**−1.4**	**790.9**	**113.5**	**183.3**	**424.2**	**172.7**	**201.1**	**50.5**	**33.9**	**432.6**	**1,545.7**	**642.0**

(continued)

Table 2.10 (Continued)

NOMINAL EXPENDITURES (US$, billions) Economy	Gross domestic product	Actual individual consumption	Food and nonalcoholic beverages	Alcoholic beverages, tobacco, and narcotics	Clothing and footwear	Housing, water, electricity, gas, and other fuels	Furnishings, household equipment and maintenance	Health	Transport	Commu- nication	Recreation and culture	Education
(00)	(01)	(02)	(03)	(04)	(05)	(06)	(07)	(08)	(09)	(10)	(11)	(12)
SINGLETONS												
Georgia	14.4	11.3	3.6	0.6	0.3	1.3	0.4	1.2	1.0	0.3	0.8	0.8
Iran, Islamic Rep.	576.3	255.9	62.1	1.2	11.0	73.7	9.5	20.8	18.7	8.0	6.2	8.1
Total (2)	**590.7**	**267.2**	**65.6**	**1.8**	**11.2**	**75.0**	**9.9**	**22.0**	**19.8**	**8.3**	**7.0**	**8.9**
WORLD[g] (179)	**70,294.6**	**46,714.2**	**6,138.8**	**1,148.3**	**1,926.1**	**8,093.2**	**2,046.6**	**6,037.4**	**4,648.4**	**1,166.5**	**3,314.5**	**3,494.2**

Source: ICP, http://icp.worldbank.org/.

Note: n.a. = not applicable; ... = data suppressed because of incompleteness.

a. The Arab Republic of Egypt participated in both the Africa and Western Asia regions. The regional results for Egypt were averaged by taking the geometric mean of the regional PPPs, allowing Egypt to have the same global results in each region.

b. Sudan participated in both the Africa and Western Asia regions. The regional results for Sudan were averaged by taking the geometric mean of the regional PPPs, allowing Sudan to have the same global results in each region.

c. The results presented in the tables are based on data supplied by all the participating economies and compiled in accordance with ICP principles and the procedures recommended by the 2011 ICP Technical Advisory Group. The results for China are estimated by the 2011 ICP Asia and the Pacific Regional Office and the Global Office. The National Bureau of Statistics of China does not recognize these results as official statistics.

d. The Russian Federation participated in both the CIS and Eurostat-OECD comparisons. The PPPs for Russia are based on the Eurostat-OECD comparison. They were the basis for linking the CIS comparison to the ICP.

e. The official GDP of Cuba for reference year 2011 is 68,990.15 million in national currency. However, this number and its breakdown into main aggregates are not shown in the tables because of methodological comparability issues. Therefore, Cuba's results are provided only for the PPP and price level index. In addition, Cuba's figures are not included in the Latin America and world totals.

f. Bonaire's results are provided only for the individual consumption expenditure by households. Therefore, to ensure consistency across the tables, Bonaire is not included in the Caribbean or the world total.

g. This table does not include the Pacific Islands and does not double count the dual participation economies: the Arab Republic of Egypt, Sudan, and the Russian Federation.

Restaurants and hotels	Miscella-neous goods and services	Net purchases abroad	Individual consumption expenditure by households	Individual consumption expenditure by government	Collective consumption expenditure by government	Gross fixed capital formation	Machinery and equipment	Construc-tion	Other products	Changes in inventories and valuables	Balance of exports and imports	Domestic absorption	Individual consumption expenditure by households without housing
(13)	(14)	(15)	(16)	(17)	(18)	(19)	(20)	(21)	(22)	(23)	(24)	(25)	(26)
0.4	0.7	0.0	10.7	0.6	2.0	3.2	1.2	1.6	0.5	0.6	−2.7	17.1	10.1
3.0	27.2	6.5	240.8	15.1	48.4	147.9	66.9	76.5	4.4	62.7	61.5	514.8	181.2
3.3	27.9	6.5	251.5	15.7	50.4	151.1	68.1	78.1	4.9	63.3	58.8	531.9	191.3
2,627.2	6,131.5	−58.5	40,330.5	6,383.7	5,978.4	16,193.5	5,579.5	8,826.1	1,787.9	832.6	575.9	69,718.8	34,383.8

Table 2.11 Nominal Expenditures Per Capita in U.S. Dollars, ICP 2011

NOMINAL EXPENDITURES PER CAPITA (US$) Economy	Gross domestic product	Actual individual consumption	Food and nonalcoholic beverages	Alcoholic beverages, tobacco, and narcotics	Clothing and footwear	Housing, water, electricity, gas, and other fuels	Furnishings, household equipment and maintenance	Health	Transport	Communication	Recreation and culture	Education
(00)	(01)	(02)	(03)	(04)	(05)	(06)	(07)	(08)	(09)	(10)	(11)	(12)
AFRICA												
Algeria	5,518	2,483	745	43	72	121	62	176	300	141	63	237
Angola	5,311	3,224	1,323	140	163	338	180	169	173	33	69	158
Benin	801	647	312	19	27	66	17	22	47	20	10	33
Botswana	7,381	4,033	719	305	248	449	239	207	647	99	109	513
Burkina Faso	608	411	211	26	9	45	18	15	27	14	10	12
Burundi	240	224	98	31	2	35	2	6	15	3	2	12
Cameroon	1,327	1,040	478	27	86	95	96	16	85	16	16	24
Cape Verde	3,773	2,667	926	126	73	526	190	145	185	91	25	217
Central African Republic	486	449	258	41	32	22	23	7	16	4	8	13
Chad	1,053	723	348	34	16	68	48	51	68	27	17	10
Comoros	358	353	181	1	11	110	14	3	7	2	4	9
Congo, Rep.	3,575	885	325	36	24	116	31	69	72	46	24	66
Congo, Dem. Rep.	372	239	131	7	11	29	8	11	6	3	3	10
Côte d'Ivoire	1,291	922	392	29	32	90	76	39	101	26	32	39
Djibouti	1,276	912	274	71	27	285	51	29	57	3	11	59
Egypt, Arab Rep.[a]	2,888	2,297	962	75	139	300	111	210	136	59	68	152
Equatorial Guinea	24,621	3,168	1,201	72	96	448	120	297	254	119	59	155
Ethiopia	353	286	106	7	15	47	27	23	5	1	1	10
Gabon	11,114	4,236	1,273	239	214	607	193	291	355	188	96	222
Gambia, The	508	405	172	11	29	28	10	61	11	10	13	35
Ghana	1,585	1,060	394	15	151	107	74	36	69	16	11	146
Guinea	490	276	160	4	19	22	11	20	15	0	2	9
Guinea-Bissau	637	436	222	7	35	60	31	11	31	2	19	8
Kenya	825	722	247	35	18	56	33	52	73	22	25	104
Lesotho	1,151	1,270	325	34	158	133	110	55	42	36	44	120
Liberia	278	314	84	11	40	71	17	6	8	12	5	37
Madagascar	470	426	186	13	28	26	57	8	55	4	18	15
Malawi	476	470	229	23	12	51	48	19	37	8	11	24
Mali	672	449	209	6	26	44	27	18	59	10	18	20
Mauritania	1,295	758	457	7	25	72	21	30	33	29	7	56
Mauritius	8,611	6,804	1,969	567	397	1,050	544	337	916	207	443	543
Morocco	3,074	2,055	701	65	83	284	94	127	183	126	90	235
Mozambique	524	450	232	20	22	33	13	13	38	6	12	31
Namibia	5,369	3,841	769	155	184	734	275	424	156	31	152	539
Niger	399	320	134	7	25	32	15	13	24	7	18	10
Nigeria	1,520	979	370	14	141	100	69	31	65	15	11	125
Rwanda	579	503	241	17	17	83	16	13	32	6	8	26

Restaurants and hotels	Miscellaneous goods and services	Net purchases abroad	Individual consumption expenditure by households	Individual consumption expenditure by government	Collective consumption expenditure by government	Gross fixed capital formation	Machinery and equipment	Construction	Other products	Changes in inventories and valuables	Balance of exports and imports	Domestic absorption	Individual consumption expenditure by households without housing
(13)	(14)	(15)	(16)	(17)	(18)	(19)	(20)	(21)	(22)	(23)	(24)	(25)	(26)
59	464	0	1,735	748	510	1,760	744	916	100	188	578	4,940	1,688
95	383	0	2,696	528	1,392	908	282	584	42	15	−227	5,538	2,618
60	20	−6	613	34	59	166	57	107	2	7	−78	879	571
160	337	0	3,502	531	866	2,423	999	1,394	29	494	−435	7,816	3,268
14	12	0	396	16	93	100	41	51	8	47	−43	651	373
9	5	4	208	17	31	46	20	23	3	2	−62	302	176
70	24	9	1,007	33	121	273	127	140	6	0	−107	1,435	948
327	167	−333	2,356	311	383	1,768	639	1,059	70	35	−1,079	4,853	2,055
9	17	0	437	12	22	75	21	40	13	0	−60	546	433
5	16	15	701	22	46	301	122	145	35	13	−30	1,082	650
0	11	1	351	2	82	48	21	24	2	13	−139	497	264
66	26	−17	795	90	172	1,232	200	1,020	11	0	1,286	2,289	740
14	6	0	230	9	43	88	32	52	3	0	1	370	215
13	42	10	872	50	102	144	51	86	7	−85	208	1,083	813
9	21	14	846	66	253	336	111	224	2	56	−281	1,557	686
72	163	−149	2,182	114	216	482	224	245	13	11	−119	3,006	1,980
108	173	65	2,956	213	448	8,136	4,167	2,657	1,313	0	12,869	11,752	2,715
13	30	0	278	8	22	91	34	41	16	7	−53	407	254
195	137	225	3,886	350	1,053	2,111	618	622	871	4	3,710	7,404	3,490
5	18	0	386	18	36	136	87	43	7	0	−69	577	376
0	40	0	974	87	177	406	230	151	25	30	−88	1,673	958
4	7	3	272	4	22	117	74	38	4	9	65	425	257
2	7	0	426	10	112	82	36	42	3	7	0	637	411
45	50	−38	624	99	69	165	91	74	0	4	−136	961	594
17	76	121	1,117	153	242	305	79	212	14	14	−680	1,831	1,024
2	22	0	313	2	34	36	31	4	0	18	−124	402	268
14	7	−4	413	13	34	82	36	42	4	0	−72	542	409
12	11	−14	443	27	33	79	59	16	5	−16	−90	566	411
8	11	−7	426	23	81	149	64	78	7	6	−12	684	396
5	14	0	671	87	197	744	366	312	66	−310	−94	1,389	627
234	427	−830	6,323	481	685	2,068	621	1,353	95	168	−1,113	9,724	5,861
119	134	−187	1,811	244	316	944	405	487	51	162	−403	3,477	1,638
4	23	5	418	32	38	93	32	62	0	11	−68	593	397
232	335	−146	3,313	528	831	1,143	419	685	39	−67	−379	5,748	2,834
16	19	0	309	11	40	148	65	79	3	0	−109	508	293
0	37	0	913	65	134	156	89	58	10	0	251	1,269	899
16	18	9	483	20	53	124	27	91	6	0	−101	680	429

(continued)

Table 2.11 *(Continued)*

NOMINAL EXPENDITURES PER CAPITA (US$) Economy	Gross domestic product	Actual individual consumption	Food and nonalcoholic beverages	Alcoholic beverages, tobacco, and narcotics	Clothing and footwear	Housing, water, electricity, gas, and other fuels	Furnishings, household equipment and maintenance	Health	Transport	Communication	Recreation and culture	Education
(00)	(01)	(02)	(03)	(04)	(05)	(06)	(07)	(08)	(09)	(10)	(11)	(12)
São Tomé and Príncipe	1,473	1,723	941	78	68	163	58	68	169	22	25	67
Senegal	1,123	930	456	12	32	179	52	27	46	45	12	49
Seychelles	12,196	7,400	2,939	204	316	1,318	315	488	447	140	181	775
Sierra Leone	490	440	174	14	35	33	12	70	14	12	15	34
South Africa	7,963	5,438	964	239	235	741	333	602	703	140	222	581
Sudan[b]	1,656	1,162	601	8	52	170	75	15	95	19	27	38
Swaziland	3,399	3,063	1,399	27	171	412	325	195	238	40	130	257
Tanzania	517	353	233	2	24	25	15	12	14	0	4	17
Togo	599	530	230	12	26	41	24	34	30	12	7	36
Tunisia	4,340	3,231	711	103	223	456	197	228	462	114	106	256
Uganda	528	478	159	28	14	86	27	13	28	9	29	51
Zambia	1,544	853	498	7	54	102	13	44	12	22	6	53
Zimbabwe	695	663	370	22	36	42	19	18	50	1	14	47
Total (50)	**1,838**	**1,230**	**429**	**39**	**76**	**146**	**70**	**83**	**108**	**32**	**35**	**107**
ASIA AND THE PACIFIC												
Bangladesh	874	658	335	14	39	113	21	24	28	3	5	36
Bhutan	2,600	1,343	393	34	99	236	24	150	128	33	83	118
Brunei Darussalam	42,432	10,124	1,838	53	442	1,219	438	559	1,512	548	771	1,668
Cambodia	902	760	348	29	15	113	14	54	57	2	21	51
China[c]	5,456	2,341	440	50	162	325	114	351	137	79	127	236
Fiji	4,393	3,369	995	112	82	828	295	173	261	14	162	197
Hong Kong SAR, China	35,173	23,433	2,540	248	1,024	4,448	1,297	1,967	1,638	504	2,624	824
India	1,533	907	255	27	64	117	34	42	136	9	14	41
Indonesia	3,511	2,044	773	35	76	416	55	68	140	39	40	151
Lao PDR	1,262	740	378	38	12	95	20	17	78	9	20	31
Macao SAR, China	66,063	15,444	1,476	106	951	2,357	310	1,101	1,338	433	1,590	1,120
Malaysia	9,979	5,354	911	79	98	790	235	315	705	322	211	562
Maldives	6,653	2,521	487	113	51	981	102	146	97	50	50	331
Mongolia	3,701	2,246	642	160	112	322	33	105	353	66	64	226
Myanmar	914	638	333	13	20	84	9	39	21	10	7	53
Nepal	739	594	333	19	15	77	11	25	19	8	15	34
Pakistan	1,255	1,066	471	10	50	207	35	66	68	18	12	51
Philippines	2,379	1,831	748	22	25	217	72	58	189	55	32	130
Singapore	51,242	21,960	1,369	401	582	4,007	1,108	1,852	2,748	411	2,377	2,039
Sri Lanka	2,836	2,178	922	162	65	296	53	113	169	41	30	120
Taiwan, China	20,030	12,910	1,520	257	549	2,135	572	1,231	1,342	459	1,230	1,123
Thailand	5,395	3,343	857	118	113	304	136	254	468	69	156	293

Restaurants and hotels	Miscel-laneous goods and services	Net purchases abroad	Individual consumption expenditure by households	Individual consumption expenditure by government	Collective consumption expenditure by government	Gross fixed capital formation	Machinery and equipment	Construction	Other products	Changes in inventories and valuables	Balance of exports and imports	Domestic absorption	Individual consumption expenditure by households without housing
(13)	(14)	(15)	(16)	(17)	(18)	(19)	(20)	(21)	(22)	(23)	(24)	(25)	(26)
22	32	12	1,657	66	113	290	218	52	21	2	–655	2,129	1,566
8	36	–25	882	48	111	267	102	163	2	16	–202	1,325	787
52	226	0	6,442	959	2,479	4,138	1,702	2,261	175	711	–2,532	14,728	5,606
5	21	0	429	11	39	204	145	57	2	2	–195	685	417
113	619	–54	4,726	712	1,022	1,510	718	723	69	42	–49	8,012	4,219
26	30	6	1,153	9	104	369	193	176	0	43	–22	1,678	1,040
19	49	–198	2,873	190	316	316	122	147	46	0	–295	3,694	2,548
0	7	0	342	11	73	186	80	102	4	3	–99	616	341
43	57	–22	508	22	49	106	32	69	5	11	–96	695	488
307	202	–134	2,849	382	417	940	307	597	35	76	–323	4,663	2,498
14	20	0	434	45	9	130	38	87	6	2	–91	619	396
2	42	0	801	52	241	334	101	218	15	22	93	1,451	751
4	33	5	608	55	61	77	26	51	0	32	–138	834	584
34	**96**	**–24**	**1,105**	**125**	**196**	**384**	**169**	**195**	**19**	**20**	**8**	**1,830**	**1,026**
15	25	0	644	13	32	248	59	186	3	5	–68	942	586
15	29	0	1,136	206	309	1,730	715	1,014	1	–10	–772	3,372	974
508	570	0	8,263	1,861	5,347	5,557	1,667	3,501	389	–284	21,688	20,744	7,342
36	21	0	718	42	33	105	51	52	1	5	–1	903	641
119	201	0	1,875	467	341	2,487	713	1,570	204	146	140	5,316	1,690
89	160	0	3,128	241	266	850	410	319	121	132	–224	4,617	2,470
2,355	3,962	0	22,251	1,181	1,879	8,267	3,644	3,887	735	213	1,380	33,792	18,483
23	146	0	857	50	127	474	181	275	18	112	–87	1,620	778
147	103	0	1,917	127	189	1,122	185	910	27	106	50	3,462	1,668
22	22	0	717	24	98	451	135	220	96	19	–46	1,308	676
2,923	1,739	0	13,547	1,897	2,779	8,198	1,900	6,222	75	951	38,690	27,372	11,687
442	685	0	4,719	635	663	2,225	804	1,110	311	98	1,639	8,340	4,278
45	68	0	2,145	376	1,190	3,350	1,293	2,057	0	0	–408	7,061	1,360
39	122	0	2,031	215	264	1,743	1,038	644	62	445	–998	4,698	1,755
29	19	0	582	55	38	244	119	106	19	0	–6	920	537
12	25	0	568	25	49	153	33	85	35	118	–175	914	507
11	68	0	1,027	38	89	162	52	78	33	20	–82	1,337	944
65	218	0	1,748	82	149	445	171	222	52	41	–87	2,466	1,599
2,272	2,793	0	19,964	1,996	3,310	12,178	4,535	7,167	477	–608	14,401	36,841	16,531
83	124	0	1,980	198	221	768	235	485	48	81	–413	3,248	1,796
692	1,800	0	12,033	877	1,602	4,187	1,949	1,896	343	–10	1,341	18,689	10,256
261	315	0	2,948	395	487	1,443	967	454	22	30	92	5,303	2,739

(continued)

Table 2.11 (Continued)

NOMINAL EXPENDITURES PER CAPITA (US$) Economy	Gross domestic product	Actual individual consumption	Food and nonalcoholic beverages	Alcoholic beverages, tobacco, and narcotics	Clothing and footwear	Housing, water, electricity, gas, and other fuels	Furnishings, household equipment and maintenance	Health	Transport	Communication	Recreation and culture	Education
(00)	(01)	(02)	(03)	(04)	(05)	(06)	(07)	(08)	(09)	(10)	(11)	(12)
Vietnam	1,543	978	253	27	40	224	56	71	98	7	39	84
Total (23)	**3,527**	**1,786**	**425**	**40**	**104**	**262**	**77**	**183**	**152**	**48**	**80**	**147**
COMMONWEALTH OF INDEPENDENT STATES												
Armenia	3,363	2,988	1,630	135	104	241	41	183	154	159	68	133
Azerbaijan	7,285	2,989	1,103	70	277	239	149	128	312	168	103	220
Belarus	5,596	3,174	1,004	193	201	246	144	285	264	136	169	270
Kazakhstan	11,358	5,491	1,119	122	324	1,189	217	430	589	215	270	461
Kyrgyz Republic	1,178	1,103	417	50	79	81	39	57	116	71	46	89
Moldova	1,971	2,215	622	129	128	285	157	78	222	81	71	184
Russian Federation[d]	13,298	7,670	1,943	527	581	747	315	609	792	295	419	427
Tajikistan	846	974	431	3	83	59	33	44	76	59	20	41
Ukraine	3,575	2,830	927	164	150	304	104	248	294	58	116	251
Total (9)	**9,870**	**5,772**	**1,525**	**364**	**417**	**606**	**235**	**455**	**592**	**217**	**300**	**356**
EUROSTAT-OECD												
Albania	4,467	3,812	1,441	102	146	466	253	217	194	76	90	125
Australia	65,464	42,056	3,643	1,293	1,181	8,267	1,619	5,333	3,679	876	4,217	3,466
Austria	49,590	32,703	2,748	942	1,635	5,858	1,781	3,441	3,650	542	3,169	2,611
Belgium	46,759	31,959	3,185	828	1,187	5,661	1,352	4,649	2,930	507	2,366	2,947
Bosnia and Herzegovina	4,957	4,631	1,337	295	183	586	242	395	392	129	226	262
Bulgaria	7,284	5,120	960	337	142	815	354	498	793	276	417	258
Canada	51,572	35,250	2,615	969	1,163	6,790	1,555	4,480	4,160	693	2,818	2,765
Chile	14,546	10,009	1,440	272	497	1,454	635	955	1,134	352	687	846
Croatia	14,429	10,199	1,940	650	440	1,797	536	1,206	985	333	1,032	811
Cyprus	29,208	22,349	2,725	946	1,264	3,927	1,060	1,923	2,402	708	1,804	2,199
Czech Republic	20,592	12,642	1,585	992	329	2,881	568	1,494	1,002	326	1,161	881
Denmark	60,030	41,430	3,269	1,017	1,331	8,354	1,438	5,392	3,520	491	3,592	3,809
Estonia	16,821	10,305	1,692	777	550	1,855	321	932	1,096	318	794	814
Finland	48,686	35,144	3,209	1,282	1,280	6,940	1,382	4,244	2,949	552	3,368	2,859
France	42,728	31,505	3,221	764	1,021	6,318	1,392	3,951	3,419	661	2,517	2,302
Germany	44,365	30,903	2,769	779	1,175	5,836	1,512	3,915	3,360	634	2,419	1,811
Greece	25,654	20,948	3,196	858	736	4,687	784	2,081	2,329	576	1,133	1,387
Hungary	13,790	8,841	1,289	559	215	1,644	325	1,004	974	281	677	609
Iceland	43,969	30,161	3,200	931	917	4,962	1,524	3,766	3,262	505	3,007	3,070
Ireland	49,383	30,131	2,295	1,256	943	5,608	982	4,444	2,956	671	1,780	2,349
Israel	33,259	23,118	3,041	480	556	4,618	1,157	1,982	2,976	742	1,461	2,388
Italy	36,180	26,467	3,191	606	1,676	4,949	1,590	3,168	2,815	534	1,792	1,571
Japan	46,131	33,421	3,768	746	868	6,953	1,378	3,539	2,957	943	2,509	1,688
Korea, Rep.	22,388	13,403	1,490	260	583	1,876	383	1,476	1,356	494	938	1,475

Restaurants and hotels	Miscel-laneous goods and services	Net purchases abroad	Individual consumption expenditure by households	Individual consumption expenditure by government	Collective consumption expenditure by government	Gross fixed capital formation	Machinery and equipment	Construction	Other products	Changes in inventories and valuables	Balance of exports and imports	Domestic absorption	Individual consumption expenditure by households without housing
(13)	(14)	(15)	(16)	(17)	(18)	(19)	(20)	(21)	(22)	(23)	(24)	(25)	(26)
43	36	0	909	69	91	459	119	313	27	78	−64	1,607	771
89	**180**	**0**	**1,552**	**234**	**234**	**1,334**	**411**	**826**	**97**	**107**	**67**	**3,460**	**1,390**
35	94	11	2,814	174	261	875	146	706	23	33	−794	4,157	2,716
95	125	0	2,714	275	463	1,470	761	644	65	7	2,356	4,929	2,635
92	131	40	2,667	507	273	2,115	922	1,175	18	95	−60	5,656	2,577
189	365	1	4,858	634	578	2,378	685	1,548	145	485	2,426	8,932	4,028
43	46	−31	983	121	94	279	125	146	9	21	−319	1,498	964
34	192	31	1,903	312	85	459	145	277	37	17	−805	2,776	1,800
214	655	147	6,529	1,141	1,252	2,763	992	1,546	225	474	1,138	12,159	6,202
11	49	64	905	69	44	274	121	125	29	31	−477	1,323	890
62	153	−3	2,404	426	226	664	255	394	15	78	−222	3,798	2,256
160	**455**	**90**	**4,936**	**835**	**853**	**2,080**	**752**	**1,178**	**150**	**332**	**834**	**9,036**	**4,650**
96	214	394	3,587	226	246	1,477	311	1,133	33	−38	−1,030	5,497	3,299
2,455	6,176	−149	35,097	6,959	4,597	17,642	4,269	10,140	3,232	317	852	64,612	28,697
3,283	4,082	−1,036	27,158	5,546	3,863	10,521	4,023	5,463	1,036	1,019	1,484	48,106	23,482
1,459	4,519	371	24,651	7,309	4,123	9,687	3,620	5,193	874	601	388	46,371	20,835
291	418	−126	4,108	523	583	889	375	483	30	11	−1,157	6,114	3,835
313	316	−358	4,545	575	569	1,569	675	834	61	27	−2	7,285	4,059
1,889	4,864	490	28,724	6,525	4,663	12,075	2,402	8,024	1,649	224	−641	52,213	23,149
420	1,343	−27	8,909	1,100	645	3,262	1,280	1,733	250	153	477	14,070	8,058
1,533	886	−1,950	8,646	1,553	1,301	2,766	896	1,656	214	173	−10	14,439	7,644
3,226	1,904	−1,739	19,782	2,568	3,290	4,860	1,412	3,228	220	−20	−1,272	30,479	17,233
830	1,079	−486	10,422	2,220	2,049	4,969	2,206	2,488	275	78	854	19,738	8,692
1,497	7,653	67	29,229	12,201	4,825	10,417	3,650	5,270	1,497	213	3,147	56,884	23,461
652	950	−444	8,503	1,802	1,432	3,968	1,834	2,004	130	496	620	16,201	7,272
1,654	5,499	−75	27,141	8,003	3,914	9,452	2,267	6,360	825	527	−350	49,036	22,321
1,688	4,409	−160	24,664	6,841	3,619	8,539	2,310	5,313	916	331	−1,266	43,994	20,306
1,405	4,682	607	25,470	5,433	3,059	8,043	3,080	4,476	487	54	2,306	42,059	21,460
2,307	1,887	−1,013	19,138	1,810	2,649	3,887	1,569	2,046	272	246	−2,076	27,729	15,990
500	1,133	−370	7,348	1,493	1,409	2,470	1,035	1,287	148	179	891	12,900	6,433
1,878	3,174	−35	22,806	7,355	3,808	6,195	2,356	3,367	473	125	3,680	40,289	18,878
2,881	3,400	565	23,746	6,384	2,694	5,251	1,982	2,817	452	639	10,668	38,715	19,706
1,279	2,709	−272	19,051	4,067	3,594	6,796	2,177	3,287	1,331	−83	−165	33,424	15,434
2,238	2,666	−330	22,158	4,309	3,064	6,898	2,761	3,288	849	257	−506	36,686	18,739
1,787	6,037	248	27,915	5,506	3,924	9,496	3,706	4,474	1,315	−289	−420	46,551	22,150
936	1,956	180	11,879	1,524	1,912	6,165	2,180	3,494	491	456	452	21,936	10,575

(continued)

Table 2.11 *(Continued)*

NOMINAL EXPENDITURES PER CAPITA (US$) Economy	Gross domestic product	Actual individual consumption	Food and nonalcoholic beverages	Alcoholic beverages, tobacco, and narcotics	Clothing and footwear	Housing, water, electricity, gas, and other fuels	Furnishings, household equipment and maintenance	Health	Transport	Communication	Recreation and culture	Education
(00)	(01)	(02)	(03)	(04)	(05)	(06)	(07)	(08)	(09)	(10)	(11)	(12)
Latvia	13,658	9,571	1,641	634	410	1,960	330	684	1,211	263	765	649
Lithuania	14,212	10,468	2,175	688	547	1,464	533	1,039	1,351	218	674	693
Luxembourg	111,689	46,959	3,533	3,634	1,981	10,446	2,723	5,075	8,175	718	3,639	4,897
Macedonia, FYR	5,050	4,181	1,284	127	187	731	155	264	376	222	132	222
Malta	22,201	15,901	2,367	465	633	1,888	1,063	1,890	1,971	586	1,685	1,135
Mexico	10,115	7,333	1,563	176	200	1,381	381	460	1,253	249	309	381
Montenegro	7,244	6,656	2,224	316	219	927	674	453	811	367	265	287
Netherlands	49,888	31,142	2,620	689	1,192	5,509	1,320	3,898	2,844	928	2,563	2,520
New Zealand	36,591	26,252	3,141	1,144	979	5,103	1,079	3,217	2,601	691	2,415	2,111
Norway	99,035	54,733	4,956	1,595	1,991	8,096	2,133	7,305	5,607	979	5,492	4,183
Poland	13,382	9,563	1,526	521	356	1,981	365	920	813	238	729	715
Portugal	22,396	17,213	2,536	510	840	2,442	833	2,100	2,003	445	1,255	1,331
Romania	8,549	6,175	1,456	266	201	1,175	261	686	584	263	380	295
Russian Federation[d]	13,298	7,670	1,943	527	581	740	315	605	792	295	410	424
Serbia	6,027	5,409	1,281	258	175	1,065	179	564	628	210	276	282
Slovak Republic	17,762	11,781	1,812	475	421	2,628	606	1,103	804	374	1,075	735
Slovenia	24,480	17,095	2,214	813	818	2,905	912	1,971	2,261	483	1,486	1,496
Spain	31,534	22,355	2,674	561	1,012	3,995	911	2,584	2,197	530	1,851	1,634
Sweden	56,704	38,081	3,237	962	1,284	7,202	1,339	4,585	3,534	881	3,477	3,730
Switzerland	83,854	53,258	4,231	1,697	1,588	11,376	1,970	7,159	4,283	1,135	4,281	4,232
Turkey	10,435	8,224	1,793	262	418	1,498	611	630	1,286	224	345	408
United Kingdom	39,241	30,769	2,211	863	1,410	6,122	1,205	3,417	3,272	521	3,431	2,442
United States	49,782	37,390	2,238	665	1,173	6,290	1,376	7,371	3,458	790	3,192	2,983
Total (47)	**34,067**	**24,366**	**2,395**	**617**	**887**	**4,421**	**1,023**	**3,425**	**2,451**	**570**	**1,956**	**1,752**
LATIN AMERICA												
Bolivia	2,360	1,478	499	23	32	157	105	128	253	16	15	90
Brazil	12,874	8,804	1,270	159	370	1,180	592	984	1,193	283	411	753
Colombia	7,142	4,860	807	135	284	697	185	361	538	193	229	420
Costa Rica	8,935	6,924	1,388	63	302	434	403	845	1,233	162	673	706
Cuba[e]	…	…	…	…	…	…	…	…	…	…	…	…
Dominican Republic	5,541	4,926	1,195	292	160	730	176	307	636	208	107	218
Ecuador	5,226	3,505	711	87	141	475	247	285	391	188	179	360
El Salvador	3,701	3,644	930	72	192	611	345	291	317	125	165	168
Guatemala	3,247	2,922	1,132	47	153	367	161	196	209	212	89	121
Haiti	734	832	486	19	57	94	28	28	43	3	20	36
Honduras	2,282	1,961	580	62	86	242	79	192	187	62	73	170
Nicaragua	1,635	1,372	358	38	40	183	76	147	168	47	53	97
Panama	8,411	5,554	942	31	342	1,092	405	399	724	195	298	317

Restaurants and hotels	Miscellaneous goods and services	Net purchases abroad	Individual consumption expenditure by households	Individual consumption expenditure by government	Collective consumption expenditure by government	Gross fixed capital formation	Machinery and equipment	Construction	Other products	Changes in inventories and valuables	Balance of exports and imports	Domestic absorption	Individual consumption expenditure by households without housing
(13)	(14)	(15)	(16)	(17)	(18)	(19)	(20)	(21)	(22)	(23)	(24)	(25)	(26)
397	629	–2	8,491	1,081	1,343	2,913	1,208	1,618	86	486	–655	14,313	7,353
257	915	–86	8,927	1,540	1,111	2,562	843	1,506	213	459	–387	14,599	8,341
2,840	8,174	–8,875	35,487	11,472	7,216	20,710	7,674	11,757	1,280	2,884	33,920	77,769	27,555
143	295	44	3,792	388	536	1,040	349	648	43	284	–991	6,041	3,351
2,579	2,038	–2,397	13,505	2,396	2,138	3,356	1,228	1,702	425	–51	857	21,344	12,255
274	740	–34	6,708	625	553	2,202	678	1,479	45	154	–127	10,242	5,595
983	452	–1,324	5,975	681	876	1,336	411	892	32	–18	–1,606	8,850	5,444
1,119	6,067	–127	22,632	8,510	5,425	8,900	2,746	5,034	1,120	139	4,283	45,605	19,035
1,545	2,758	–533	21,876	4,376	3,018	6,641	2,279	3,817	546	165	514	36,076	17,547
2,258	8,631	1,507	40,757	13,976	7,300	19,330	5,229	9,195	3,906	4,533	13,138	85,897	34,754
231	1,226	–57	8,178	1,386	1,020	2,703	1,016	1,519	168	249	–154	13,536	7,606
1,684	1,925	–691	14,786	2,426	2,034	4,028	1,199	2,474	355	100	–979	23,375	13,237
177	415	19	5,428	747	541	2,230	723	1,402	104	58	–455	9,004	4,692
214	676	147	6,529	1,141	1,252	2,763	992	1,546	225	474	1,138	12,159	6,209
107	454	–70	4,639	770	393	1,114	473	571	69	100	–989	7,016	4,010
509	1,233	6	10,233	1,548	1,652	4,109	1,362	1,855	892	123	97	17,665	9,297
994	1,706	–964	14,070	3,025	2,077	4,550	1,953	2,262	335	381	379	24,102	12,479
3,269	2,132	–994	18,470	3,886	2,827	6,531	1,898	3,346	1,287	153	–331	31,866	15,773
1,495	6,575	–221	27,228	10,854	4,202	10,602	3,930	5,162	1,510	658	3,161	53,543	21,976
3,199	8,107	0	48,070	5,188	4,050	17,244	7,560	7,816	1,868	600	8,704	75,150	38,542
483	603	–337	7,429	795	658	2,277	1,321	949	8	181	–905	11,340	6,323
2,028	3,687	160	25,337	5,433	3,176	5,636	1,146	3,225	1,265	254	–594	39,835	20,245
2,150	5,779	–76	34,329	3,061	5,034	9,064	3,252	4,150	1,662	117	–1,823	51,605	29,180
1,429	**3,474**	**–34**	**20,918**	**3,448**	**2,974**	**6,671**	**2,297**	**3,464**	**910**	**198**	**–142**	**34,209**	**17,566**
115	44	1	1,439	39	287	448	251	168	29	14	134	2,226	1,359
497	1,113	0	7,767	1,037	1,625	2,482	1,299	1,028	155	58	–94	12,968	6,961
508	501	1	4,381	479	648	1,684	583	1,037	63	13	–62	7,204	3,938
322	324	69	5,838	1,087	518	1,768	761	954	53	162	–438	9,373	5,650
...	...	...	...	...	...	...	...	...	...	...	...	...	...
401	522	–27	4,795	131	277	903	256	633	14	7	–572	6,113	4,309
141	320	–20	3,192	313	348	1,360	441	386	533	157	–144	5,370	2,834
246	204	–21	3,452	192	217	464	234	228	2	67	–691	4,392	3,083
169	120	–55	2,769	154	181	478	250	227	1	14	–348	3,595	2,485
2	17	0	823	9	1	213	5	207	0	0	–312	1,046	789
107	121	0	1,772	190	177	558	310	218	29	36	–450	2,732	1,644
83	104	–21	1,272	101	140	369	142	197	30	13	–259	1,894	1,154
289	520	0	5,066	488	549	2,197	996	1,200	1	91	21	8,390	4,259

(continued)

Table 2.11 *(Continued)*

NOMINAL EXPENDITURES PER CAPITA (US$) Economy	Gross domestic product	Actual individual consumption	Food and nonalcoholic beverages	Alcoholic beverages, tobacco, and narcotics	Clothing and footwear	Housing, water, electricity, gas, and other fuels	Furnishings, household equipment and maintenance	Health	Transport	Communication	Recreation and culture	Education
(00)	(01)	(02)	(03)	(04)	(05)	(06)	(07)	(08)	(09)	(10)	(11)	(12)
Paraguay	3,836	2,920	807	37	152	264	236	237	250	108	189	271
Peru	6,066	3,792	858	84	236	400	188	245	405	148	226	319
Uruguay	13,722	10,363	1,915	243	466	1,978	574	1,249	764	409	349	675
Venezuela, RB	10,731	6,513	1,402	192	298	319	373	587	864	365	414	551
Total (17)	**9,366**	**6,421**	**1,090**	**134**	**288**	**818**	**399**	**650**	**825**	**232**	**309**	**535**
CARIBBEAN												
Anguilla	20,982	18,380	2,278	416	545	3,754	718	448	3,342	1,427	770	762
Antigua and Barbuda	13,172	8,975	1,386	146	205	2,462	386	802	939	461	291	505
Aruba	25,355	19,816	1,482	116	632	6,599	817	2,366	2,366	719	1,358	1,226
Bahamas, The	21,490	16,496	1,564	187	539	5,060	710	1,407	1,278	664	689	1,075
Barbados	15,483	13,790	1,908	212	252	7,192	377	638	956	578	508	679
Belize	4,721	3,587	650	56	281	898	235	265	461	114	235	191
Bermuda	85,839	67,145	5,816	1,156	1,333	18,618	3,181	5,524	4,109	1,819	3,849	4,935
Bonaire[f]	...	...	1,222	67	522	...	658	...	1,935	584	...	...
Cayman Islands	56,883	42,553	2,590	489	1,258	14,655	1,994	1,930	3,977	1,824	2,063	2,121
Curaçao	20,055	15,378	1,624	187	1,166	4,905	463	1,173	1,448	589	682	634
Dominica	6,881	6,174	1,060	45	298	1,398	306	397	1,179	232	233	389
Grenada	7,410	7,204	1,419	127	315	1,394	295	290	1,306	699	192	446
Jamaica	5,248	4,883	1,370	66	88	662	272	295	695	132	433	361
Montserrat	11,343	10,808	1,700	223	133	2,025	448	1,093	2,886	696	322	640
St. Kitts and Nevis	13,744	10,290	1,695	283	439	2,700	650	600	929	532	363	556
St. Lucia	6,755	5,436	1,086	93	328	1,241	304	292	505	299	103	452
St. Vincent and the Grenadines	6,191	5,731	1,131	322	118	1,536	242	360	999	383	353	341
Sint Maarten	25,402	16,324	1,378	49	810	6,776	705	531	1,883	805	643	510
Suriname	8,082	3,098	1,155	83	109	528	149	152	237	112	111	40
Trinidad and Tobago	17,660	10,265	2,160	103	139	1,248	428	792	1,096	208	665	1,084
Turks and Caicos Islands	22,971	9,055	1,278	159	315	966	350	860	2,079	154	471	1,025
Virgin Islands, British	32,580	12,517	2,109	244	1,158	2,590	1,550	698	1,185	375	500	695
Total (22)	**11,732**	**8,472**	**1,564**	**115**	**223**	**1,914**	**390**	**590**	**916**	**276**	**511**	**616**
WESTERN ASIA												
Bahrain	24,200	10,580	1,421	39	603	2,158	751	768	1,103	492	679	1,174
Egypt, Arab Rep.[a]	2,888	2,297	962	75	139	300	111	210	136	59	68	152
Iraq	4,794	2,255	691	13	134	587	106	162	164	32	26	250
Jordan	4,615	3,681	1,027	117	161	738	157	257	372	144	60	452
Kuwait	52,379	14,541	2,236	33	1,126	3,393	1,776	1,145	1,068	484	506	1,407
Oman	21,234	7,647	1,490	19	431	1,394	295	446	1,220	362	262	852
Qatar	97,091	16,069	1,706	45	561	3,612	657	1,168	1,378	349	1,175	2,465
Saudi Arabia	23,594	8,667	1,374	30	417	1,798	571	717	587	362	264	1,489

Restaurants and hotels	Miscellaneous goods and services	Net purchases abroad	Individual consumption expenditure by households	Individual consumption expenditure by government	Collective consumption expenditure by government	Gross fixed capital formation	Machinery and equipment	Construction	Other products	Changes in inventories and valuables	Balance of exports and imports	Domestic absorption	Individual consumption expenditure by households without housing
(13)	(14)	(15)	(16)	(17)	(18)	(19)	(20)	(21)	(22)	(23)	(24)	(25)	(26)
140	230	0	2,689	231	176	628	267	311	50	15	98	3,739	2,617
337	345	0	3,606	185	373	1,576	567	959	50	64	261	5,805	3,334
718	822	201	9,321	1,042	767	2,607	830	1,614	163	52	−67	13,789	7,818
785	335	27	5,919	593	643	1,903	863	972	68	573	1,100	9,631	5,689
431	**707**	**1**	**5,743**	**678**	**1,004**	**1,869**	**886**	**866**	**117**	**89**	**−16**	**9,382**	**5,189**
719	3,202	0	17,674	707	2,629	3,677	957	2,651	69	−328	−3,376	24,358	15,447
288	1,105	0	7,910	1,066	1,360	2,757	577	2,129	52	81	−1	13,173	6,398
454	1,681	0	15,734	4,082	2,415	6,692	1,653	5,040	0	403	−3,972	29,327	11,287
874	2,450	0	15,248	1,248	1,941	5,671	2,776	2,880	16	360	−2,978	24,468	11,692
2,540	1,133	−3,183	12,611	1,179	1,647	2,409	1,183	1,225	1	−138	−2,225	17,708	6,327
24	176	0	3,381	206	535	714	302	399	13	65	−179	4,901	2,566
7,811	8,994	0	57,654	9,491	7,079	17,377	8,989	8,351	37	959	−6,721	92,560	40,832
789	...	0	11,141	...	...	...	...	...	...	...	...	...	9,389
2,051	7,599	0	40,002	2,551	5,061	12,756	6,294	6,431	31	0	−3,487	60,369	28,763
474	3,188	−1,153	13,856	1,522	1,459	7,987	4,328	2,273	1,386	302	−5,071	25,126	11,050
169	469	0	5,630	543	936	1,584	765	789	30	−769	−1,043	7,924	4,704
126	520	75	6,665	539	622	1,513	590	895	28	−7	−1,922	9,332	5,887
599	576	−666	4,495	388	450	1,090	527	543	20	25	−1,201	6,450	4,095
34	1,157	−550	9,161	1,647	3,742	3,258	948	2,249	61	0	−6,465	17,807	8,092
585	957	0	9,409	880	1,476	4,250	1,055	3,116	79	2	−2,274	16,018	7,520
93	641	0	4,990	446	676	2,026	623	1,365	38	0	−1,384	8,139	4,249
180	486	−718	5,081	650	635	1,479	452	999	28	93	−1,747	7,938	4,184
269	1,966	0	15,346	978	3,232	4,264	2,311	1,213	740	0	1,582	23,820	10,249
39	383	0	3,022	76	921	2,990	2,456	478	56	562	512	7,570	2,844
945	1,396	0	8,090	2,176	297	2,649	1,306	1,287	56	0	4,449	13,211	7,319
334	1,065	0	8,235	820	4,375	3,329	1,163	2,166	0	17	6,195	16,776	7,692
676	737	0	11,436	1,081	1,682	7,790	3,445	4,105	239	−628	11,219	21,361	9,715
730	**1,073**	**−445**	**7,460**	**1,012**	**833**	**2,495**	**1,248**	**1,180**	**67**	**86**	**−154**	**11,886**	**6,105**
465	662	264	9,366	1,214	2,112	3,781	1,163	2,606	13	177	7,550	16,650	7,605
72	163	−149	2,182	114	216	482	224	245	13	11	−119	3,006	1,980
22	70	0	1,907	347	722	932	360	568	4	−21	906	3,888	1,490
75	107	13	3,296	385	510	989	259	669	61	73	−637	5,252	2,806
418	949	0	12,194	2,346	5,485	8,272	3,286	4,129	856	309	23,772	28,607	9,171
217	590	70	6,374	1,273	2,379	5,590	2,221	2,790	578	−657	6,275	14,959	5,302
318	2,273	361	12,399	3,670	8,462	28,453	13,926	4,450	10,077	0	44,107	52,983	9,088
327	422	311	6,407	2,260	2,326	5,345	2,062	2,652	631	974	6,282	17,312	5,146

(continued)

Table 2.11 *(Continued)*

NOMINAL EXPENDITURES PER CAPITA (US$) Economy	Gross domestic product	Actual individual consumption	Food and nonalcoholic beverages	Alcoholic beverages, tobacco, and narcotics	Clothing and footwear	Housing, water, electricity, gas, and other fuels	Furnishings, household equipment and maintenance	Health	Transport	Communication	Recreation and culture	Education
(00)	(01)	(02)	(03)	(04)	(05)	(06)	(07)	(08)	(09)	(10)	(11)	(12)
Sudan[b]	1,656	1,162	601	8	52	170	75	15	95	19	27	38
United Arab Emirates	42,182	22,267	2,610	41	2,749	7,381	788	344	3,581	1,301	608	1,039
West Bank and Gaza	2,345	2,537	802	101	147	276	131	185	238	77	61	214
Yemen, Rep.	1,318	963	435	46	42	137	29	92	55	10	4	68
Total (12)	**8,403**	**3,841**	**944**	**44**	**261**	**831**	**208**	**248**	**349**	**140**	**110**	**387**
SINGLETONS												
Georgia	3,231	2,531	795	133	64	287	95	265	232	75	177	175
Iran, Islamic Rep.	7,669	3,405	826	16	146	980	126	277	249	106	82	108
Total (2)	**7,420**	**3,356**	**824**	**22**	**141**	**941**	**125**	**276**	**248**	**104**	**87**	**112**
WORLD[g] (179)	**10,438**	**6,937**	**912**	**171**	**286**	**1,202**	**304**	**897**	**690**	**173**	**492**	**519**

Source: http://icp.worldbank.org/.

Note: n.a. = not applicable; ... = data suppressed because of incompleteness.

a. The Arab Republic of Egypt participated in both the Africa and Western Asia regions. The regional results for Egypt were averaged by taking the geometric mean of the regional PPPs, allowing Egypt to have the same global results in each region.

b. Sudan participated in both the Africa and Western Asia regions. The regional results for Sudan were averaged by taking the geometric mean of the regional PPPs, allowing Sudan to have the same global results in each region.

c. The results presented in the tables are based on data supplied by all the participating economies and compiled in accordance with ICP principles and the procedures recommended by the 2011 ICP Technical Advisory Group. The results for China are estimated by the 2011 ICP Asia and the Pacific Regional Office and the Global Office. The National Bureau of Statistics of China does not recognize these results as official statistics.

d. The Russian Federation participated in both the CIS and Eurostat-OECD comparisons. The PPPs for Russia are based on the Eurostat-OECD comparison. They were the basis for linking the CIS comparison to the ICP.

e. The official GDP of Cuba for reference year 2011 is 68,990.15 million in national currency. However, this number and its breakdown into main aggregates are not shown in the tables because of methodological comparability issues. Therefore, Cuba's results are provided only for the PPP and price level index. In addition, Cuba's figures are not included in the Latin America and world totals.

f. Bonaire's results are provided only for the individual consumption expenditure by households. Therefore, to ensure consistency across the tables, Bonaire is not included in the Caribbean or the world total.

g. This table does not include the Pacific Islands and does not double count the dual participation economies: the Arab Republic of Egypt, Sudan, and the Russian Federation.

Restaurants and hotels	Miscel- laneous goods and services	Net purchases abroad	Individual consumption expenditure by households	Individual consumption expenditure by government	Collective consumption expenditure by government	Gross fixed capital formation	Machinery and equipment	Construction	Other products	Changes in inventories and valuables	Balance of exports and imports	Domestic absorption	Individual consumption expenditure by households without housing
(13)	(14)	(15)	(16)	(17)	(18)	(19)	(20)	(21)	(22)	(23)	(24)	(25)	(26)
26	30	6	1,153	9	104	369	193	176	0	43	−22	1,678	1,040
822	1,004	0	21,805	463	2,623	9,281	3,688	4,633	960	402	7,608	34,574	15,458
62	211	33	2,262	275	426	485	85	347	52	−80	−1,023	3,368	2,168
0	43	0	897	65	120	174	16	135	23	74	−14	1,331	825
117	**208**	**−6**	**3,359**	**482**	**778**	**1,802**	**734**	**854**	**214**	**144**	**1,838**	**6,566**	**2,727**
83	149	0	2,391	140	448	726	271	350	105	124	−599	3,829	2,250
39	362	87	3,204	201	643	1,968	890	1,018	59	835	818	6,851	2,411
42	**350**	**82**	**3,159**	**197**	**632**	**1,898**	**856**	**981**	**62**	**795**	**739**	**6,681**	**2,402**
390	**910**	**−9**	**5,989**	**948**	**888**	**2,405**	**829**	**1,311**	**265**	**124**	**86**	**10,353**	**5,106**

Supplementary Table 2.12 Main Results and Reference Data, Pacific Islands, ICP 2011

INDIVIDUAL CONSUMPTION EXPENDITURE BY HOUSEHOLD	Expenditure (US$, millions)		Expenditure per capita (US$)		Price level index	PPP	Reference data		
Economy	Based on PPPs	Based on XRs	Based on PPPs	Based on XRs	(world = 100.0)	(US$ = 1.000)	Exchange rate (US$ = 1.000)	Population (thousands)	Expenditure in national currency unit (millions)
(00)	(01)	(02)	(03)	(04)	(05)	(13)[a]	(14)[a]	(15)	(16)[b]
PACIFIC ISLANDS[c]									
American Samoa[d]	469.0	432.0	7,032	6,478	109.9	0.921	1.000	66.69	432.0
Cook Islands	93.3	116.0	6,228	7,747	148.4	1.564	1.257	14.97	145.8
French Polynesia	3,351.8	4,272.1	12,330	15,716	152.0	119.593	93.830	271.83	400,850.5
Guam[d]	2,697.2	2,926.0	16,900	18,333	129.4	1.085	1.000	159.60	2,926.0
Kiribati	158.3	173.7	1,541	1,692	130.9	1.066	0.971	102.70	168.7
Marshall Islands	156.1	169.1	2,937	3,182	129.2	1.083	1.000	53.16	169.1
Micronesia, Fed. States	229.8	229.4	2,245	2,241	119.1	0.998	1.000	102.36	229.4
Nauru	69.2	86.1	6,860	8,540	148.5	1.209	0.971	10.08	83.6
New Caledonia	3,976.2	5,514.8	15,758	21,855	165.4	130.139	93.830	252.33	517,453.9
Niue[e]	...	...	...	...	164.2	1.730	1.257	1.61	...
Northern Mariana Islands[d]	503.5	527.0	9,345	9,781	124.9	1.047	1.000	53.88	527.0
Palau	121.1	108.7	5,864	5,268	107.2	0.898	1.000	20.64	108.7
Papua New Guinea	7,284.5	7,325.3	1,032	1,038	120.0	2.138	2.126	7,059.65	15,573.5
Samoa	758.3	591.6	4,038	3,150	93.1	1.900	2.436	187.82	1,441.0
Solomon Islands	338.5	313.8	612	567	110.6	7.131	7.692	553.25	2,413.9
Tokelau[e]	...	...	...	...	115.6	1.218	1.257	1.21	...
Tonga	436.3	407.8	4,225	3,950	111.5	1.639	1.753	103.25	714.9
Tuvalu	7.2	8.8	686	829	144.1	1.173	0.971	10.56	8.5
Vanuatu	367.7	462.2	1,460	1,836	149.9	115.827	92.150	251.78	42,591.0
Wallis and Futuna[e]	...	...	...	...	180.5	141.986	93.830	13.19	...
Total (20)	**n.a.**	**n.a.**	**n.a.**	**n.a.**	**n.a.**	**n.a.**	**n.a.**	**9,332.71**	**n.a.**
ECONOMIES FOR REFERENCE[f]									
Australia	507.3	798.9	22,288	35,097	187.8	1.527	0.969	22.76	774.5
Fiji	3.9	2.7	4,611	3,128	80.9	1.217	1.793	0.85	4.8
New Zealand	76.9	96.6	17,425	21,876	149.8	1.589	1.266	4.41	122.2

Source: ICP, http://icp.worldbank.org/.

Note: n.a. = not applicable; PPP = purchasing power parity; XR = exchange rate; ... = data suppressed because of incompleteness.

a. All exchange rates (XRs) and PPPs are rounded to three decimal places.

b. Data source: World Development Indicators (World Bank) or National Accounts Main Aggregates (United Nations).

c. Results for the Pacific Islands are provided only for the individual consumption expenditure by households.

d. Therefore, to ensure consistency across the tables, the Pacific Islands are not included in the world totals in the main results tables.

e. Data source, expenditure: Bureau of Economic Analysis, U.S.Department of Commerce. No expenditure estimate is available for the economy.

f. Data for the three economies involved in the linking of the Pacific Islands are shown for reference purposes only. Figures shown are from the main results tables for the respective economies.

Supplementary Table 2.13 Estimated Results and Reference Data, Nonbenchmark Economies, ICP 2011

GROSS DOMESTIC PRODUCT	Expenditure (US$, billions)		Expenditure per capita (US$)		Price level index	PPP	Reference data		
Economy	Based on PPPs	Based on XRs	Based on PPPs	Based on XRs	(world = 100.0)	(US$ = 1.000)	Exchange rate (US$ = 1.000)	Population (thousands)	Expenditure in national currency unit (millions)
(00)	(01)	(02)	(03)	(04)	(05)	(13)[a]	(14)[a]	(15)[b]	(16)[b]
NONBENCHMARK ECONOMIES[c]									
Afghanistan	49.3	17.9	1,695	614	46.7	17.356	47.919	29.11	856.3
Argentina	691.2	446.0	16,972	10,952	83.2	2.665	4.130	40.73	1,842.0
Eritrea	6.8	2.6	1,139	440	49.8	5.932	15.375	5.93	40.1
Guyana	4.6	2.6	5,808	3,258	72.3	114.435	204.007	0.79	525.7
Kosovo	14.6	6.6	8,146	3,706	58.7	0.327	0.719	1.79	4.8
Lebanon	72.0	40.1	16,437	9,148	71.8	838.986	1,507.500	4.38	60,442.2
Libya[d]	69.3	34.7	11,358	5,687	64.6	0.613	1.224	6.10	42.5
Puerto Rico	123.8	98.8	33,512	26,734	102.9	0.798	1.000	3.69	98.8
San Marino[e]	2.1	2.0	66,240	65,462	127.4	0.710	0.719	0.03	1.5
Somalia[f]	3.0	…	301	…	…	11,427.680	…	9.91	34,047.0
South Sudan	37.0	19.1	3,563	1,844	66.7	1.465	2.830	10.38	54.2
Syrian Arab Republic[f]	142.9	…	6,505	…	…	21.325	…	21.96	3,046.3
Timor-Leste	2.2	1.1	1,857	960	66.6	0.517	1.000	1.18	1.1
Turkmenistan	58.0	29.2	11,361	5,725	65.0	1.436	2.850	5.11	83.3
Uzbekistan	129.5	45.3	4,412	1,545	45.1	600.579	1,715.428	29.34	77,750.6
Total (15)	**n.a.**	**n.a.**	**n.a.**	**n.a.**	**n.a.**	**n.a.**	**n.a.**	**170.43**	**n.a.**

Source: ICP, http://icp.worldbank.org/.

Note: n.a. = not applicable; PPP = purchasing power parity; XR = exchange rate; … = data suppressed because of incompleteness.

a. All exchange rates (XRs) and PPPs are rounded to three decimal places.

b. Data source: World Development Indicators (World Bank).

c. The results for the nonbenchmark economies are estimated only for reference purposes. Therefore, to ensure consistency across the tables, nonbenchmark economies are not included in the world totals in the main results tables.

d. Data sources, exchange rate and expenditure: World Economic Outlook (International Monetary Fund).

e. Data sources, exchange rate: World Economic Outlook (International Monetary Fund); expenditure: National Accounts Main Aggregates (United Nations).

f. Data source, expenditure: National Accounts Main Aggregates (United Nations). No exchange rate information is available for the economy.

ANALYSIS OF RESULTS

The tables described and presented in the previous section provide PPP-based estimates of expenditures and relative price levels for GDP and 25 major aggregates. In this section, these estimates are used to present analyses of the size of economies, measures of material well-being, price level indexes, and measures of equality for the 177 economies included in the tables. (All GDP expenditures unless otherwise noted—such as exchange rate–based or in a local currency unit—are PPP-based estimates.) By way of explanation, of the 199 economies that participated in ICP 2011, it was only possible to provide the full set of results for 177 economies.[1] Partial results are provided for the remaining economies. The Pacific Islands comparison, for example, covered only household consumption, and those results are given in supplementary table 2.12.

The analyses make only limited reference to ICP 2005.[2] The addition of 53 economies (ICP 2011 covered 199 economies compared with 146 by ICP 2005), the shifting of economies from one region to another, and improvements in the methodology limit the comparisons that can be made between the two benchmarks. Moreover, the world has changed since 2005, with some economies enjoying remarkable GDP growth rates even though they were buffeted by the global financial crisis at the midpoint of the 2005–11 period.

However, a major outcome of ICP 2011 is the finding that the world is more equal because consumption and GDP values in most poor economies are larger relative to those of the United States than previously thought. The following sections present the major outcomes by reviewing results for the size of economies, material well-being, price levels, and measures of inequality.

Size of economies

In 2011 the PPP-based world GDP as represented by the 177 economies was $90,647 billion compared with $70,295 billion measured by exchange rates (XRs). Figure 2.1 shows that this 29 percent increase was produced by the middle-income[3] economies, whose share of world GDP went from 32 percent using exchange rates to 48 percent using PPPs. In low-income economies, PPP world shares were more than twice as large as exchange rate shares in 2011, and yet accounted for only 1.5 percent of the global economy with nearly 11 percent of the world's population. High-income economies accounted for about half of world GDP. The figure also shows, for reference, the share of GDP by income group as it stood in 2005.[4]

Although high-income economies account for 50 percent of world GDP, they are home to only about 17 percent of the world's population. In 2005, 35 percent of the world's population was in low-income economies. This figure dropped to 11 percent in 2011 because the percentage of the world's population in middle-income economies rose from 48 percent to 72 percent.

Figure 2.2 shows the distribution of global GDP by ICP region, comparing PPP-based shares with exchange rate–based shares. According to the PPP-based distribution, the Asia and the

---

[3] The categorization of economies is based on the Atlas conversion factor, which is the average of an economy's exchange rate (or alternative conversion factor) for that year and its exchange rates for the two preceding years, adjusted for the difference between the rate of inflation in the economy and international inflation. International inflation is determined by inflation in a subset of economies. Since 2001, the subset has included the Euro Area, Japan, the United Kingdom, and the United States. The income categories for 2011 are as follows: low-income economies, gross national income (GNI) per capita of less than $1,025; middle-income economies, $1,026–$12,475; high-income economies, more than $12,475. Three Caribbean islands—Anguilla, Montserrat, and the British Virgin Islands—are not classified by income group. Thus they are not included in the analyses
and tables related to income groups. For detailed information on the classification, visit http://data.worldbank.org/about/country-classifications.
[4] For 2005, 142 economies for which both benchmark ICP data and 2005 income classification were available are included in figure 2.1. The income categories for 2005 are as follows: low-income economies, GNI per capita of less than $875; middle-income economies, $876 –$10,725; high-income economies, more than $10,725. The comparison between the two benchmarks is limited by the fact that 40 economies moved up in income classification between 2005 and 2011.

---

[1] The main tables cover 179 economies, but two of the economies—Cuba and Bonaire—do not have a full set of results and are not included in either the regional or world totals. Nor are they included in the analyses in this chapter.
[2] The 2005 data used in this section are based on the ICP 2005 global report (World Bank 2008). They differ from the revised 2005 data in appendix H of this report.

2011

2005

■ PPP-based ■ Exchange rate–based □ Population

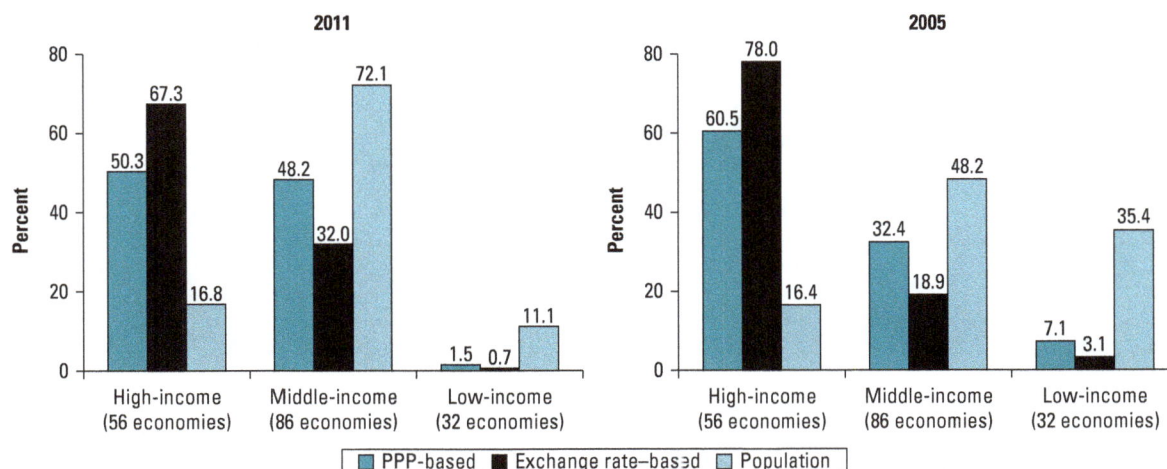

Source: ICP, http://icp.worldbank.org/.

Note: Figure based on unrevised 2005 data. Income categories for 2011: low-income economies, gross national income (GNI) per capita of less than $1,025; middle-income economies, $1,026–$12,475; high-income economies, more than $12,475. Income categories for 2005: low-income economies, GNI per capita of less than $875; middle-income economies, $876–$10,725; high-income economies, more than $10,725. GDP= gross domestic product; PPP = purchasing power parity.

Pacific region accounted for over 30 percent of world GDP in 2011. The Eurostat-OECD region becomes significantly smaller when PPP-based GDPs are used. The following sections will shed more light on these distributions. Chile and Mexico are not included in the Latin America and Caribbean regions; rather, they are in the Eurostat-OECD region, along with Japan and the Republic of Korea.

Table 2.14 shows the share of world GDP of the 12 largest economies. In 2011 six of the 12 largest economies (identified in the table by boldface) were in the middle-income category, but together with the other six economies they accounted for two-thirds of the world's economy and 59 percent of the world's population. Except for Brazil, the shares of world GDP of the middle-income economies increased when using PPPs instead of exchange rates to measure GDP. The United States remained the world's largest economy, but it was closely followed by China when measured using PPPs. India was now the world's third largest economy, moving ahead of Japan.

The largest economies were not the richest, as shown in the ranking of GDP per capita in table 2.14. The middle-income economies with large GDPs also had large populations, setting the stage for continued growth.

Figure 2.2 PPP-Based and Exchange Rate–Based GDP Regional Shares (World = 100), ICP 2011

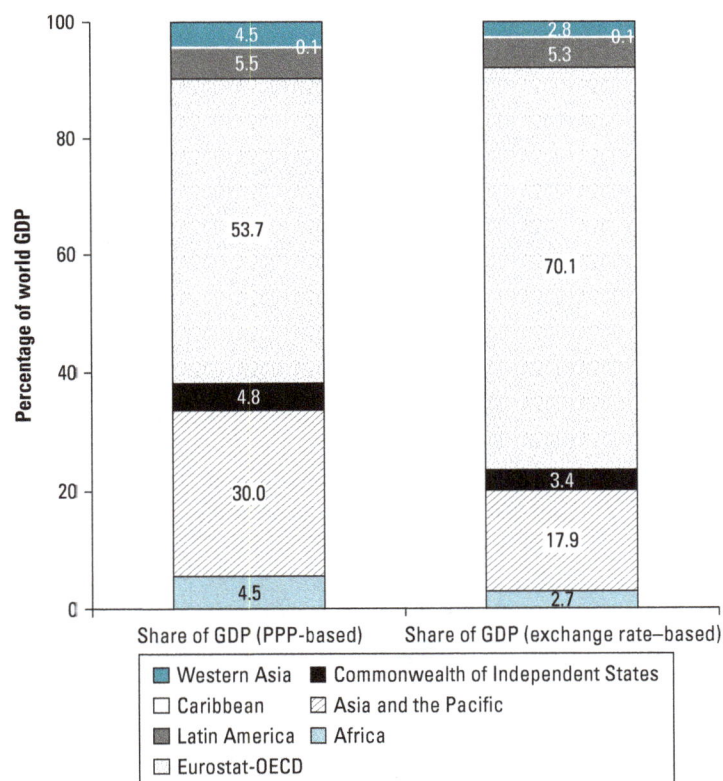

■ Western Asia   ■ Commonwealth of Independent States
□ Caribbean   ▨ Asia and the Pacific
■ Latin America   ■ Africa
□ Eurostat-OECD

Source: ICP, http://icp.worldbank.org/.

Note: Singleton economies account for 1.5 percent in PPP terms and 0.8 percent in exchange rate terms. The percentage shares add up to more than 100 because of dual participating economies that are counted in two regions.

Table 2.14 Twelve Largest Economies by Share of World GDP, ICP 2011

Ranking by GDP (PPP-based)	Economy	Share of world GDP (PPP-based, world = 100)	Share of world GDP (exchange rate-based, world = 100)	Ranking by GDP per capita (PPP-based)
1	United States	17.1	22.1	12
2	China	14.9	10.4	99
3	India	6.4	2.7	127
4	Japan	4.8	8.4	33
5	Germany	3.7	5.2	24
6	Russian Federation	3.5	2.7	55
7	Brazil	3.1	3.5	80
8	France	2.6	4.0	30
9	United Kingdom	2.4	3.5	32
10	Indonesia	2.3	1.2	107
11	Italy	2.3	3.1	34
12	Mexico	2.1	1.7	72

Source: ICP, http://icp.worldbank.org/.
Note: The six of the 12 largest economies that are in the middle-income category are in boldface.

Table 2.15 Percentage of GDP to U.S. GDP (PPP-Based) for 12 Largest Economies, ICP 2011 and ICP 2005

Economy	2011	2005
United States	100.0	100.0
China	86.9	43.1
India	37.1	18.9
Japan	28.2	31.3
Germany	21.6	20.3
Russian Federation	20.7	13.7
Brazil	18.1	12.8
France	15.3	15.0
United Kingdom	14.2	15.4
Indonesia	13.2	5.7
Italy	13.2	13.1
Mexico	12.2	9.5

Source: ICP, http://icp.worldbank.org/.

It is difficult to compare the results of the 2005 and 2011 rounds of the ICP because the number of economies compared was very different, as noted. Table 2.15 shows the relative size of the largest economies compared with the United States. India went from the 10th largest economy in 2005 to the third largest in 2011. Relative to the United States, Japan and the United Kingdom became smaller, while Germany increased slightly and France and Italy remained the same. The relative shares of the three Asian economies—China, India, and Indonesia—to the United States doubled, while Brazil, Mexico, and Russia increased by one-third or more. As discussed elsewhere in this report, some of the large differences in the Asian economies and developing economies in general can be attributed to the changes in the methodology used for the two benchmark comparisons.

Table 2.16 provides an example of how the GDP shares relate to world shares of major aggregates for the ICP regions. The regional GDP shares are the same as those shown in figure 2.2. The remaining columns of the table show the regional shares for selected aggregates. Note the variability in the aggregate shares for each region. In Africa, shares range from 3.7 percent of the world expenditures for health care to 8.2 percent for food and nonalcoholic beverages. The food and nonalcoholic beverage expenditure share exceeds those of the other aggregates shown for Africa, but it is the smallest shown for the Eurostat-OECD region, except for construction. The regional shares for construction in the Asia and the Pacific region far exceed the shares of the other aggregates shown.

The construction aggregate is examined in more detail in table 2.17, which shows shares of construction expenditures as a percentage of the total for the six economies with the largest values. China accounts for nearly 35 percent of the world's expenditures on construction. Together, these economies account for over 61 percent of the world's expenditure on construction and over 53 percent of the world's expenditure on machinery and equipment.

Table 2.6 shows the world shares for GDP and 25 major aggregates and provides more detail on the relative sizes of economies and how they are distributed by region.

Material well-being

An economy's GDP divided by its population provides a measure of its relative material well-being compared with that of other economies.

Table 2.16 Regional Shares of World GDP and Major Aggregates, ICP 2011

percent

Region	GDP	Food	Housing	Health	Education	Construction
Africa	4.5	8.2	4.7	3.7	7.4	4.0
Asia and the Pacific	30.0	35.2	25.3	27.3	30.5	55.2
Commonwealth of Independent States	4.8	6.8	6.4	3.8	7.2	2.1
Eurostat-OECD	53.7	44.3	56.7	59.7	46.2	30.7
Latin America	5.5	6.7	5.1	5.5	7.5	4.6
Caribbean	0.1	0.1	0.2	0.1	0.2	0.1
Western Asia	4.5	4.5	5.8	2.5	4.8	4.1

Source: ICP, http://icp.worldbank.org/.
Note: The percentage shares add up to more than 100 because of dual participating economies that are counted in two regions.

Table 2.17 Shares of World Expenditure on Construction and Machinery and Equipment of Economies with Largest Construction Shares, ICP 2011

percent

Economy	Construction	Machinery and equipment
China	34.6	16.7
India	9.0	4.5
United States	7.2	21.3
Indonesia	5.6	0.9
Brazil	2.5	3.1
Japan	2.4	6.9
Total	61.3	53.4

Source: ICP, http://icp.worldbank.org/.

The GDP per capita comparison between economies is best carried out using PPPs. Table 2.18 shows the PPP-based world shares and expenditures per capita for GDP, with the economies grouped into the high-, middle-, and low-income categories used in figure 2.1. Huge differences in the per capita levels are evident between income categories.

The PPP-based expenditures per capita average $40,282 over the 56 high-income economies. However, the 24 economies with GDP expenditures per capita above this average account for over 40 percent of world GDP. Further analysis shows that the distribution of expenditures per capita is highly skewed. Twenty-eight percent of the world's population lives in economies with GDP expenditures per capita above the $13,460 world average, and 72 percent live in economies

that are below that average. The approximate median expenditure per capita of $10,057 means that half of the world's population is experiencing expenditures per capita above that amount and half are experiencing those below. Although comparisons with the 2005 ICP results should be carried out with caution, 25 percent of the population lived in economies above the world average in 2005 compared with 28 percent in 2011. These differences are within the range of statistical variability.

As a group, the middle-income economy shares of world GDP are nearly as large as the high-income economy shares, and the middle-income economies have the largest shares of gross fixed capital formation (GFCF). However, the expenditures per capita of the middle-income economies are significantly lower than those of the high-income economies. Recall that 72 percent of the world population is in middle-income economies, led by China and India.

The world shares and expenditures per capita for the major aggregates are consistent with the measures for GDP. One exception is gross fixed capital formation for the middle-income economies, where the world share for GFCF at 55.4 percent greatly exceeds that for other aggregates. This is consistent with the expenditure shares shown in table 2.17 for construction and machinery and equipment for China, India, and Indonesia.

Figure 2.3 is a view of the regional per capita values as a ratio of the world average for GDP, actual individual consumption (AIC), collective government, and GFCF. AIC per capita provides a general measure of the material well-being of

Table 2.18 PPP-Based Shares of World GDP and Per Capita Measures: High-, Middle-, and Low-Income Economies, ICP 2011

	High-income economies (56)	Middle-income economies (86)	Low-income economies (32)	World (174)
EXPENDITURE SHARE (PPP-BASED, WORLD = 100)				
Gross domestic product	50.3	48.2	1.5	100.0
Actual individual consumption	53.6	44.5	1.9	100.0
Individual household consumption	54.5	43.5	2.0	100.0
Individual government consumption	49.0	49.8	1.2	100.0
Collective government consumption	50.6	48.1	1.3	100.0
Gross fixed capital formation	43.3	55.4	1.3	100.0
Domestic absorption	50.1	48.2	1.7	100.0
AVERAGE EXPENDITURES PER CAPITA (PPP-BASED, US$)				
Gross domestic product	40,282	9,004	1,839	13,460
Actual individual consumption	27,570	5,345	1,473	8,647
Individual household consumption	23,207	4,309	1,263	7,144
Individual government consumption	5,149	1,221	188	1,766
Collective government consumption	3,703	822	143	1,230
Gross fixed capital formation	8,083	2,414	370	3,139
Domestic absorption	39,535	8,872	2,004	13,258

Source: ICP, http://icp.worldbank.org/.
Note: See note to figure 2.1 for ICP 2011 income categories.

Figure 2.3 Index of Regional Average Real Expenditures Per Capita (World = 100) on Major Aggregates (PPP-Based), ICP 2011

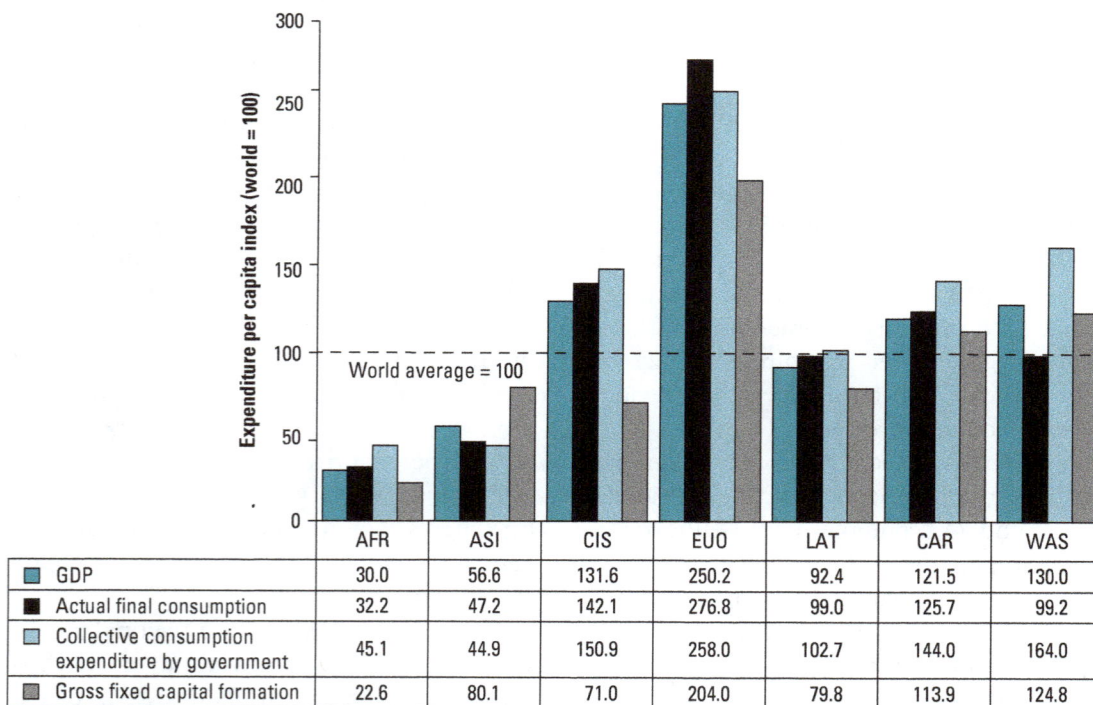

	AFR	ASI	CIS	EUO	LAT	CAR	WAS
GDP	30.0	56.6	131.6	250.2	92.4	121.5	130.0
Actual final consumption	32.2	47.2	142.1	276.8	99.0	125.7	99.2
Collective consumption expenditure by government	45.1	44.9	150.9	258.0	102.7	144.0	164.0
Gross fixed capital formation	22.6	80.1	71.0	204.0	79.8	113.9	124.8

Source: ICP, http://icp.worldbank.org/.
Note: AFR = Africa; ASI = Asia and the Pacific; CAR = Caribbean; CIS = Commonwealth of Independent States; EUO = Eurostat-OECD; LAT = Latin America; WAS = Western Asia.

each economy's population. AIC makes up the greatest share of GDP in the Eurostat-OECD region, but it is exceeded by collective government expenditures in every other region except Asia and the Pacific, where the two measures are about the same. GFCF shares exceed those of all other aggregates in the Asia-Pacific region, which is consistent with the large values observed when reviewing the relative sizes of economies in previous tables.

Table 2.19 shows the ranking by GDP per capita for the economies with the highest and lowest values. It reveals the extreme variability of relative well-being across the world. In two economies, GDP per capita is more than $100,000, and in 11 economies it is more than

$50,000. By contrast, eight economies have a GDP per capita of less than $1,000. The economies with the largest per capita values are small in terms of their GDP. Even though Ethiopia has one of the lowest per capita values in the world, its GDP is larger than the GDP of four of the economies with the largest per capita values. The last two columns of table 2.19 show the per capita values as a percentage of the U.S. values for 2011 and 2005. The non–Eurostat-OECD economies with the highest per capita values in 2011 exhibit the greatest increases from 2005 to 2011. The economies with the lowest per capita values also showed gains relative to 2005.

PPP-based per capita values exceed exchange rate values for all economies except Luxembourg,

Table 2.19 PPP-Based and Exchange Rate–Based GDP Per Capita Expenditures for the 10 Economies with the Largest and Smallest Values and Ratios Relative to the United States, ICP 2011

Ranking, GDP per capita (PPP-based)	Economy	GDP per capita (US$)		Ranking, GDP	Ratio of GDP per capita relative to United States (%)	
		PPP-based	Exchange rate–based	(PPP-based)	2011	2005
1	Qatar	146,521	97,091	52	294	165
2	Macao SAR, China	115,441	66,063	83	232	89
3	Luxembourg	88,670	111,689	95	178	168
4	Kuwait	84,058	52,379	53	169	108
5	Brunei Darussalam	74,397	42,432	106	149	114
6	Singapore	72,296	51,242	40	145	100
7	Norway	61,879	99,035	48	124	114
8	United Arab Emirates	60,886	42,182	31	122	—
9	Bermuda	54,899	85,839	156	110	—
10	Switzerland	51,582	83,854	37	104	85
168	Guinea	1,287	490	137	2.6	2.3
169	Ethiopia	1,214	353	73	2.4	1.4
170	Malawi	973	476	133	2.0	1.7
171	Mozambique	951	524	123	1.9	1.8
172	Central African Republic	897	486	153	1.8	1.6
173	Niger	852	399	136	1.7	1.5
174	Burundi	712	240	148	1.4	n.a.
175	Congo, Dem. Rep.	655	372	97	1.3	0.6
176	Comoros	610	358	175	1.2	2.6
177	Liberia	537	278	161	1.1	0.9

Source: ICP, http://icp.worldbank.org/.

Note: — = economy did not participate in ICP 2005; n.a. = not available.

Norway, Bermuda, and Switzerland. The analysis that follows shows that these economies have high price levels.

Figure 2.4 shows the distribution of global GDP; economies are arranged in order of GDP per capita along the horizontal axis and presented as rectangles. The horizontal scale corresponds to each economy's share of the world's population. GDP per capita is shown on the vertical axis. Each economy's size in terms of GDP is thus represented by the area of its rectangle, which is the product of GDP per capita and population. The United States, with the 12th largest GDP per capita, is placed at the right. The remaining 11 economies with the highest GDP per capita are not visible in this figure because together they account for less than 0.6 percent of the world's population. The intersection of the average line with the rectangles shows the disparity in GDP per capita across the world.

Table 2.20 shows the actual individual consumption per capita first for the 10 economies with the largest values and then for the 10 economies with the smallest values. Except for the United States and Germany, the economies with the largest per capita values are small. At the other end of the distribution are the 10 economies with per capita values below $1,000, and all are in the Africa region. The last two columns of table 2.20 show the ratio of AIC per capita relative to the United States in 2011 and 2005. It is important to note that the relative AIC ratios of the economies with the smallest values were in most cases greater in 2011 than they were in 2005.

In the economies with the largest per capita values, only Hong Kong SAR, China, has

Figure 2.4 Real GDP Per Capita and Shares of Global Population, ICP 2011

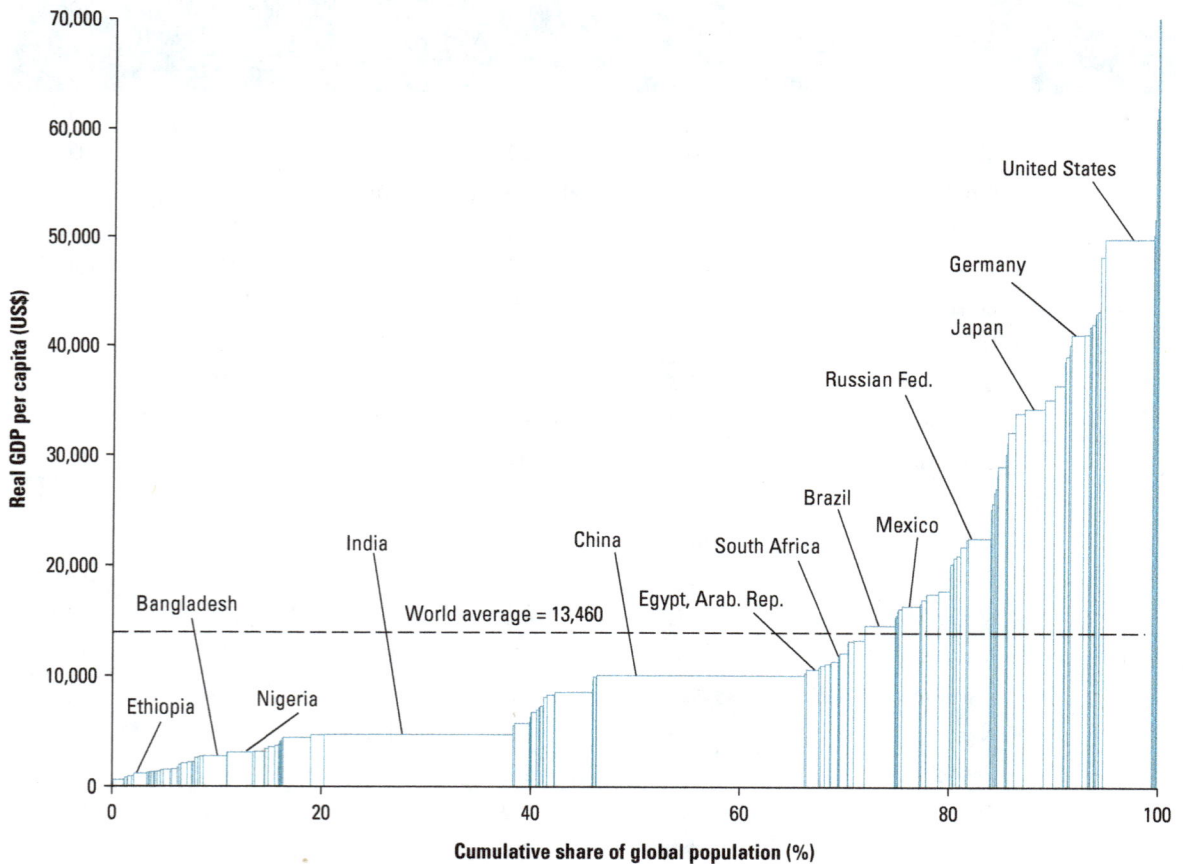

Source: ICP, http://icp.worldbank.org/.
Note: Economies are arranged in the order of increasing real GDP per capita. Each rectangle describes an economy: (1) width corresponds to its population share; (2) height corresponds to its real GDP per capita; and (3) area corresponds to its share of world total real GDP—(3) = (1) × (2).

Table 2.20 PPP-Based and Exchange Rate–Based Actual Individual Consumption (AIC) Per Capita and Ratios Relative to the United States, ICP 2011

| Ranking, AIC per capita (PPP-based) | Economy | AIC per capita | | Ranking, AIC (PPP-based) | Ratio of AIC per capita relative to United States (%) | |
		PPP-based	Exchange rate–based		2011	2005
1	Bermuda	37,924	67,145	155	101	—
2	United States	37,390	37,390	1	100	100
3	Cayman Islands	34,020	42,553	160	91	—
4	Hong Kong SAR, China	32,690	23,433	43	87	61
5	Luxembourg	32,000	46,959	120	86	105
6	Norway	31,014	54,733	51	83	77
7	Switzerland	29,465	53,258	42	79	72
8	United Arab Emirates	29,463	22,267	37	79	—
9	Germany	28,478	30,903	5	76	68
10	Austria	27,677	32,703	41	74	73
169	Guinea-Bissau	928	436	162	2.5	1.4
170	Mozambique	890	450	107	2.4	1.9
171	Central African Republic	869	449	148	2.3	2.0
172	Guinea	789	276	136	2.1	2.1
173	Niger	719	320	132	1.9	1.5
174	Burundi	648	224	145	1.7	n.a.
175	Comoros	621	353	173	1.7	2.8
176	Liberia	606	314	154	1.6	0.8
177	Congo, Dem. Rep.	447	239	96	1.2	0.5

Source: ICP, http://icp.worldbank.org/.
Note: — = economy did not participate in ICP 2005; n.a. = not available.

PPP-based values greater than the exchange rate numbers. The PPP-based per capita values exceed those from exchange rates for all of the economies with the smallest per capita values. These economies have low price levels compared with those with high per capita values. The section that follows examines price level indexes and their relationship to the per capita measures.

Price level indexes

The price level index (PLI), the ratio of a PPP to a corresponding exchange rate, is used to compare the price levels of economies. Figure 2.5 presents a multidimensional comparison of the GDP per capita of each economy relative to its price level index with the world equal to 100. In this figure, each economy is represented by a circle with an area proportional to its size. The economies are color-coded by region. As a general observation, PLIs at the GDP level tend to be generally lower in economies with lower GDP per capita. This observation is consistent with the fact that as an economy develops, consumers move from consuming basic goods that are also tradable to consuming more services that are not tradable. As wage rates increase, so do the costs of services. After a certain level of expenditure per capita is reached, there is a rapid rise in price levels rather than continued increases in the expenditure per capita. As the figure shows, for economies in the Eurostat-OECD comparison, the price levels increase very sharply with

Figure 2.5 GDP Price Level Index versus GDP Per Capita (and Size of GDP Expenditures), ICP 2011

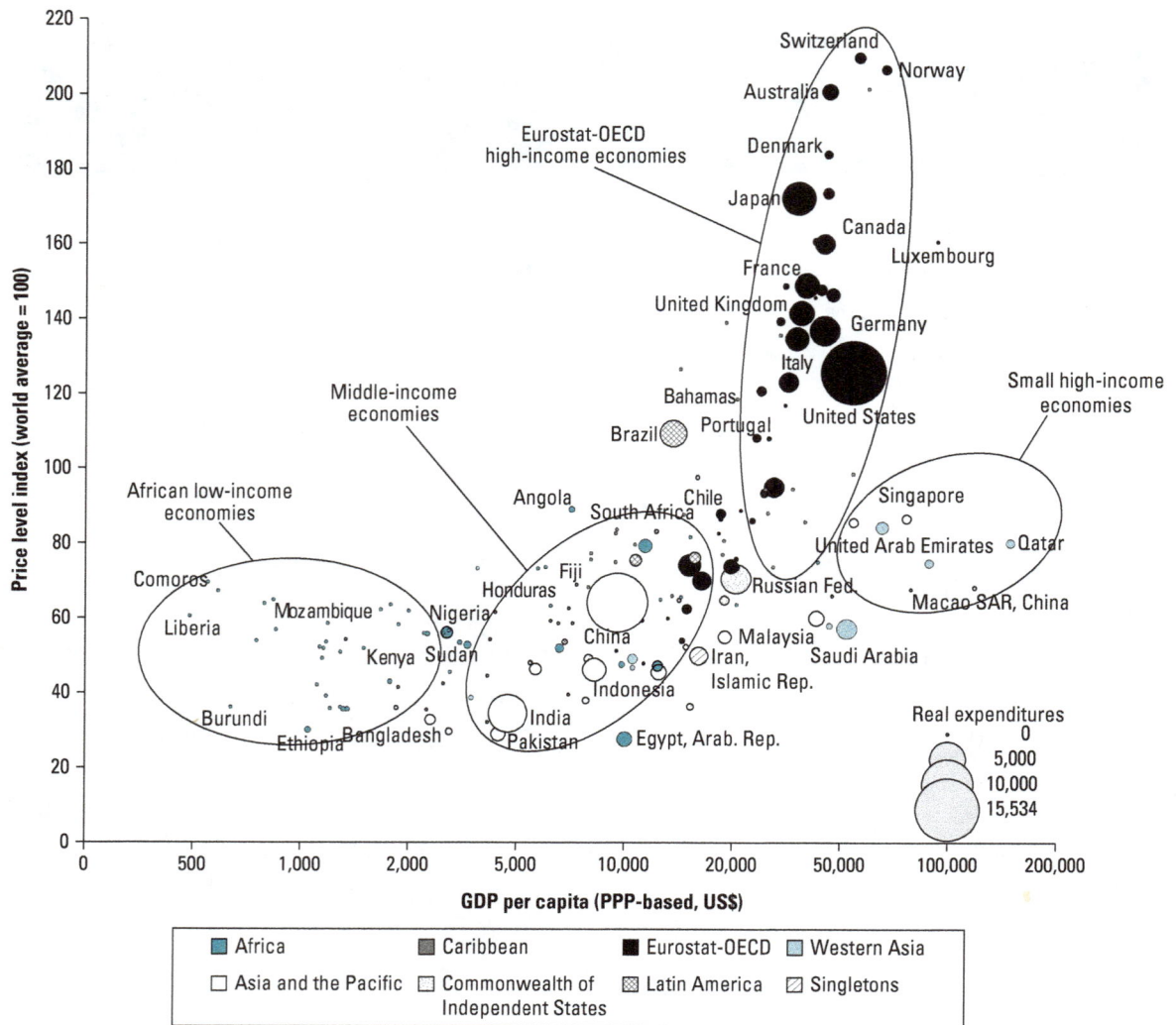

Source: ICP, http://icp.worldbank.org/.

relatively small changes in the expenditure per capita, whereas other regions follow somewhat different patterns.

It is useful to look at the Eurostat-OECD and non–Eurostat-OECD economies separately because Eurostat-OECD mainly represents high-income economies. Figure 2.6 shows the same distribution as figure 2.5, but the Eurostat-OECD economies are represented by dark grey squares and the rest of the world by blue squares for GDP and the three major aggregates (actual individual consumption, collective government, and gross fixed capital formation). The R² value between the PLI and per capita measures is the highest for GDP and actual individual consumption in the

Eurostat-OECD region at 0.84 and falls to 0.44 and 0.60, respectively, for collective government and GFCF. However, the R² value for non–Eurostat-OECD economies is relatively weak. The GDP and AIC per capita measures for the Eurostat-OECD economies are much less variable than shown for the rest of the world, whose economies cover the full range of per capita measures, but in a more narrow price band.

Table 2.21 shows the PLIs (world = 100) for the 10 most expensive and 10 least expensive economies in the world. With the exception of Bermuda, the most expensive economies are in the Eurostat-OECD region. The economies with the lowest prices are either in Africa or the Asia

Figure 2.6 GDP Price Level Index versus Expenditure Per Capita with Trend Lines, Eurostat-OECD and Non–Eurostat-OECD Economies, ICP 2011

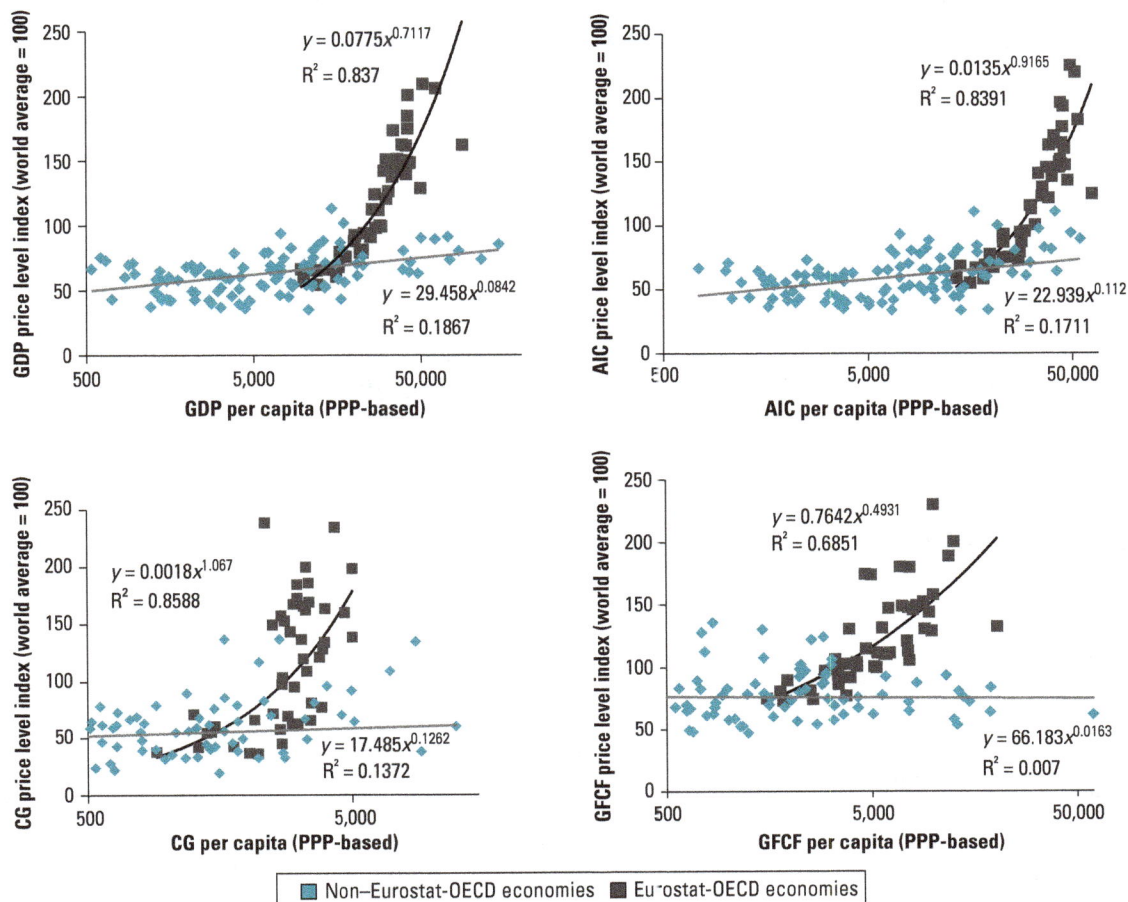

Source: ICP, http://icp.worldbank.org/.
Note: AIC = actual individual consumption; CG = collective government; GDP = gross domestic product; GFCF = gross fixed capital formation.

Table 2.21 Economies with Highest and Lowest Price Level Indexes (PLIs), ICP 2011

Ranking by GDP PLI	Economy	GDP PLI (world = 100)	GDP PLI (US = 100)	Ranking by GDP (PPP-based, per capita)
1	Switzerland	209.6	162.6	10
2	Norway	206.4	160.0	7
3	Bermuda	201.6	156.4	9
4	Australia	201.0	155.9	20
5	Denmark	185.0	143.5	21
6	Sweden	175.1	135.8	22
7	Japan	173.6	134.6	33
8	Finland	162.6	126.1	28
9	Luxembourg	162.4	126.0	3
10	Canada	161.9	125.6	23

(continued)

Table 2.21 *(Continued)*

Ranking by GDP PLI	Economy	GDP PLI (world = 100)	GDP PLI (US = 100)	Ranking by GDP (PPP-based, per capita)
168	Cambodia	42.8	33.2	146
169	Uganda	42.6	33.0	156
170	Vietnam	42.2	32.7	128
171	India	41.7	32.4	127
172	Bangladesh	40.3	31.2	144
173	Lao PDR	39.6	30.7	133
174	Ethiopia	37.5	29.1	169
175	Myanmar	37.0	28.7	139
176	Pakistan	36.4	28.2	129
177	Egypt, Arab Rep.	35.1	27.2	97

Source: ICP, http://icp.worldbank.org/.

Figure 2.7 Regional Average Price Level Indexes by GDP and Major Aggregates, ICP 2011

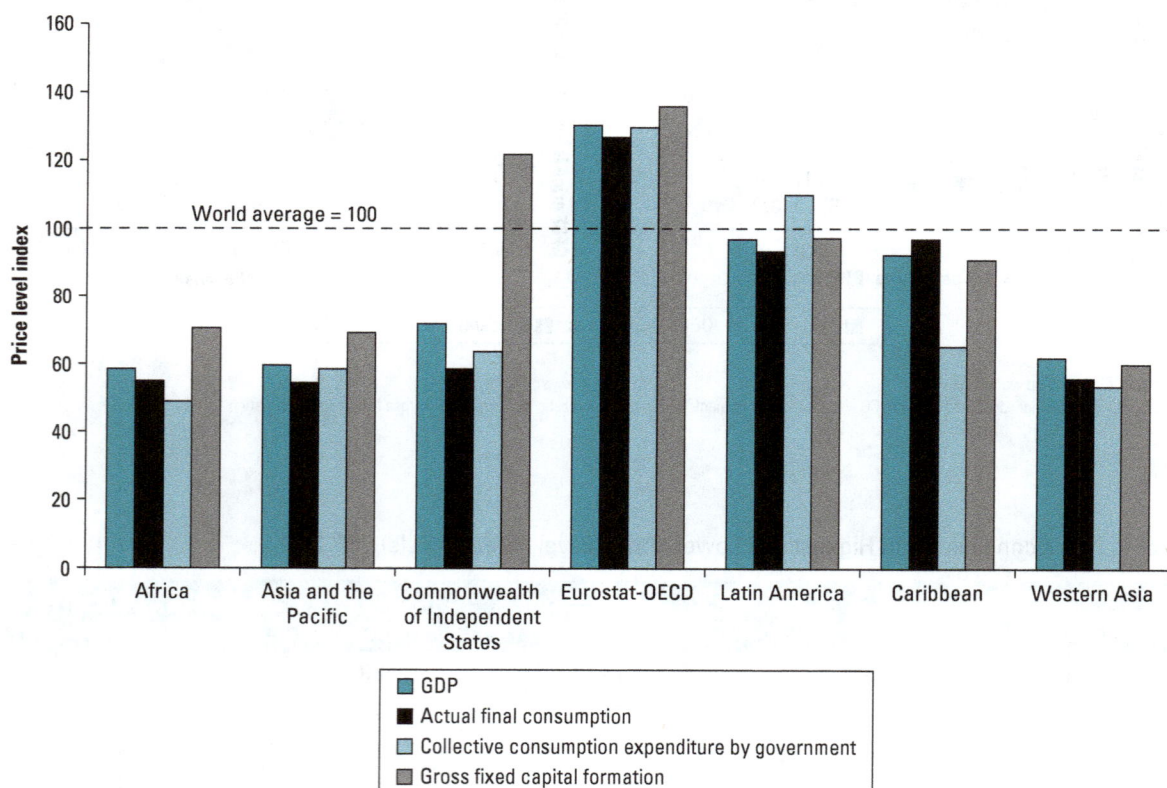

Source: ICP, http://icp.worldbank.org/.

and the Pacific region and include India, which has the third-largest economy. Economies with the lowest prices still have GDP per capita values among the smallest in the world even though the PPP-based real expenditures are more than double the exchange rate–based nominal expenditures.

Price level indexes can be computed for each aggregation level of GDP and by region. Figure 2.7 is a view of the regional price levels of three major aggregates of GDP. Actual individual consumption includes all household consumption expenditure, as well as general government and NPISH expenditures on individual goods and services such as health and education. Collective consumption expenditures by general government include expenditures on services such as defense, justice, general administration, and protection of the environment. Gross fixed capital formation measures investment expenditures, which mostly are on purchases of machinery and equipment and construction services.

All three aggregates in the Eurostat-OECD region have price levels above the world average. Only gross fixed capital formation in the CIS region and collective government in Latin America are at price levels above the world average for the remaining regions. The high price levels of gross fixed capital formation in the CIS region translate to the real expenditures per capita in figure 2.3 that are below those of all other regions except Africa.

Figure 2.8 presents the regional average PLIs for GDP and 15 aggregates with the world average equal to 100. The Eurostat-OECD area shows higher than average price levels across all categories, except for machinery and equipment, where the price index is near the world average. The Eurostat-OECD economies lead the world in price levels for construction, followed by various services: education, housing, and health.

At the same time, the Western Asia, Africa, and Asia and the Pacific regions all show significantly lower than average price levels in virtually all categories except machinery and equipment, again with service PLIs the lowest. For example, health services, at 40, are significantly below the world average in all these regions, and the housing and education price levels are quite low as well.

Price levels in Latin America are about average at the GDP level, but they exhibit significant variation at the component level. For example, clothing and footwear and machinery and equipment price levels exceed those of all other regions.

The Caribbean region, which is not much different from Latin America at the GDP level, is quite different from Latin America at the component level. For example, the clothing and footwear price level in the Caribbean is 111 compared with 178 in Latin America. Similar differences are shown for communication and machinery and equipment.

The CIS in general has lower than average prices, except for construction where the prices are significantly higher than the world average. At the same time, the prices for most services such as housing, health, and education are among the lowest in the world.

Variations in GDP per capita and PLI

The world economy is very complex, with extreme differences in the overall size of economies as measured by GDP and how it is distributed across the major aggregates. Per capita measures provide another view, as do the price level indexes. This section reviews the inherent variability across economies for the per capita and price level indexes.

Across the 177 economies analyzed here, GDP per capita ranges from $146,521 in Qatar to $655 in the Democratic Republic of Congo—a range of 223 based on the ratio of the maximum to minimum values. The price level index across the 177 economies varies from 209.6 in Switzerland to 35.1 in the Arab Republic of Egypt—a range of 6.0—suggesting there is much less variation in price levels than in per capita measures. The coefficient of variation (CV) provides a measure of the average variability. Figure 2.9 shows the coefficients of variation by major aggregates for the world and region for the GDP per capita and price level indexes.

The coefficient of variation for the GDP per capita index appears on the left-hand side of each graph and for the PLI on the right-hand side. With few exceptions, the variation in the GDP per capita measures is much greater than the variation in price levels. One exception is the variability in the education price levels, which is driven by the CV of 72 percent for the Eurostat-OECD, the largest of any aggregate at the regional level. The Eurostat-OECD used a different methodology to estimate PPPs for education than was used in the rest of the world (see appendix C).

Figure 2.9 also displays the homogeneity of economies within each region. The Asia and the Pacific region contains some of the world's largest economies, but with smaller per capita measures. The Africa region, with its 50 economies,

Figure 2.8 Regional Average Price Level Indexes (World = 100) for GDP and 15 Aggregates, ICP 2011

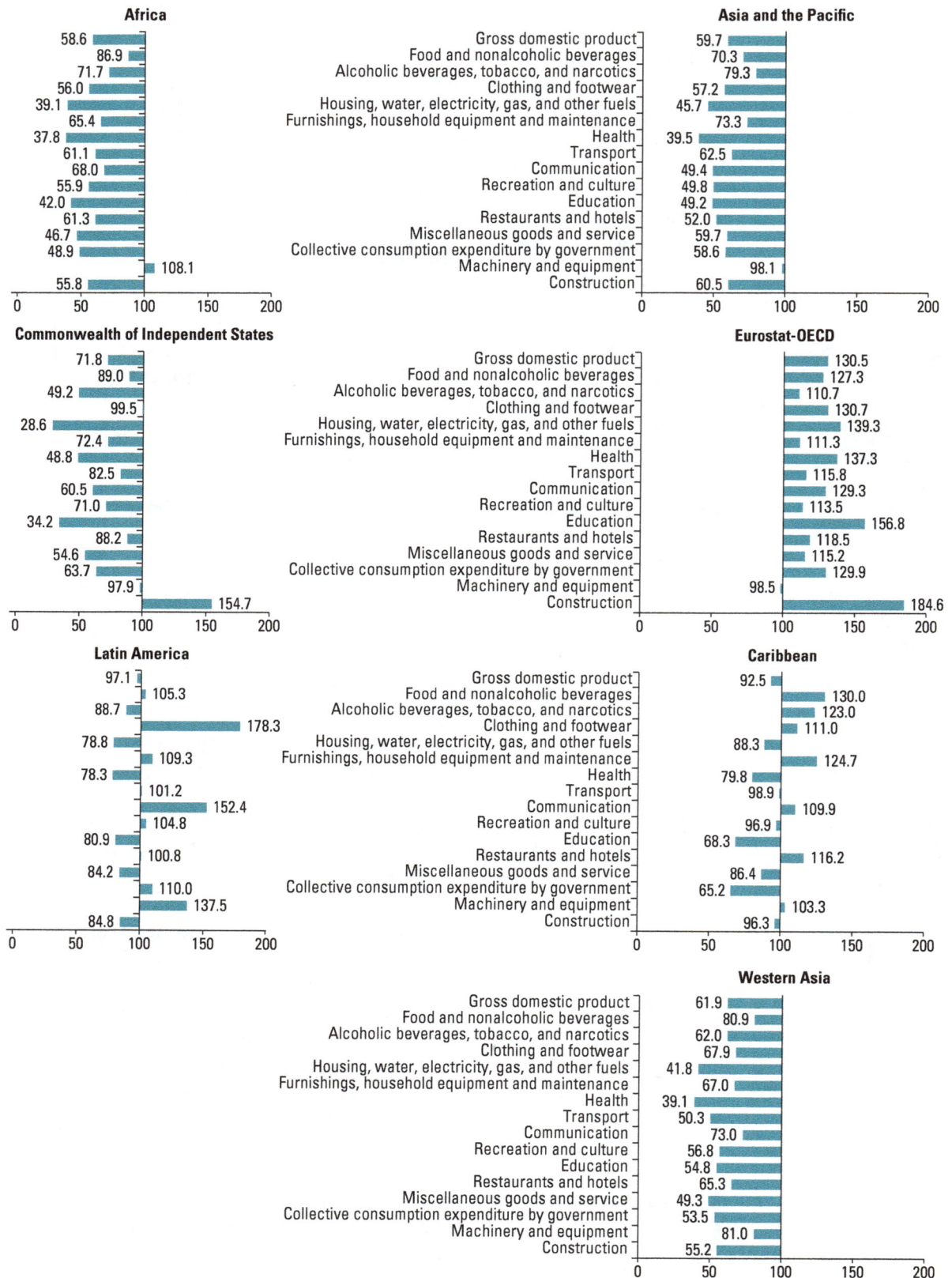

	Africa	Asia and the Pacific
Gross domestic product	58.6	59.7
Food and nonalcoholic beverages	86.9	70.3
Alcoholic beverages, tobacco, and narcotics	71.7	79.3
Clothing and footwear	56.0	57.2
Housing, water, electricity, gas, and other fuels	39.1	45.7
Furnishings, household equipment and maintenance	65.4	73.3
Health	37.8	39.5
Transport	61.1	62.5
Communication	68.0	49.4
Recreation and culture	55.9	49.8
Education	42.0	49.2
Restaurants and hotels	61.3	52.0
Miscellaneous goods and service	46.7	59.7
Collective consumption expenditure by government	48.9	58.6
Machinery and equipment	108.1	98.1
Construction	55.8	60.5

	Commonwealth of Independent States	Eurostat-OECD
Gross domestic product	71.8	130.5
Food and nonalcoholic beverages	89.0	127.3
Alcoholic beverages, tobacco, and narcotics	49.2	110.7
Clothing and footwear	99.5	130.7
Housing, water, electricity, gas, and other fuels	28.6	139.3
Furnishings, household equipment and maintenance	72.4	111.3
Health	48.8	137.3
Transport	82.5	115.8
Communication	60.5	129.3
Recreation and culture	71.0	113.5
Education	34.2	156.8
Restaurants and hotels	88.2	118.5
Miscellaneous goods and service	54.6	115.2
Collective consumption expenditure by government	63.7	129.9
Machinery and equipment	97.9	98.5
Construction	154.7	184.6

	Latin America	Caribbean
Gross domestic product	97.1	92.5
Food and nonalcoholic beverages	105.3	130.0
Alcoholic beverages, tobacco, and narcotics	88.7	123.0
Clothing and footwear	178.3	111.0
Housing, water, electricity, gas, and other fuels	78.8	88.3
Furnishings, household equipment and maintenance	109.3	124.7
Health	78.3	79.8
Transport	101.2	98.9
Communication	152.4	109.9
Recreation and culture	104.8	96.9
Education	80.9	68.3
Restaurants and hotels	100.8	116.2
Miscellaneous goods and service	84.2	86.4
Collective consumption expenditure by government	110.0	65.2
Machinery and equipment	137.5	103.3
Construction	84.8	96.3

	Western Asia
Gross domestic product	61.9
Food and nonalcoholic beverages	80.9
Alcoholic beverages, tobacco, and narcotics	62.0
Clothing and footwear	67.9
Housing, water, electricity, gas, and other fuels	41.8
Furnishings, household equipment and maintenance	67.0
Health	39.1
Transport	50.3
Communication	73.0
Recreation and culture	56.8
Education	54.8
Restaurants and hotels	65.3
Miscellaneous goods and service	49.3
Collective consumption expenditure by government	53.5
Machinery and equipment	81.0
Construction	55.2

Source: ICP, http://icp.worldbank.org/.

contains a large number of the world's poorest economies.

The lowest price level CVs are observed in the CIS data, even though real expenditures per capita vary significantly more.

The aggregate machinery and equipment exhibits the lowest price variation (10 percent) at both the regional and global levels, which is explained by its highly tradable character. However, the variability of the per capita index for machinery and equipment has the highest value at the world level and also in several regions.

Services such as health and education, as well as collective government consumption, show in general the largest price level variations across

Figure 2.9 Coefficients of Variation (CVs): GDP Per Capita Index and Price Level Indexes (PLIs) for GDP and Major Aggregates by Region, ICP 2011

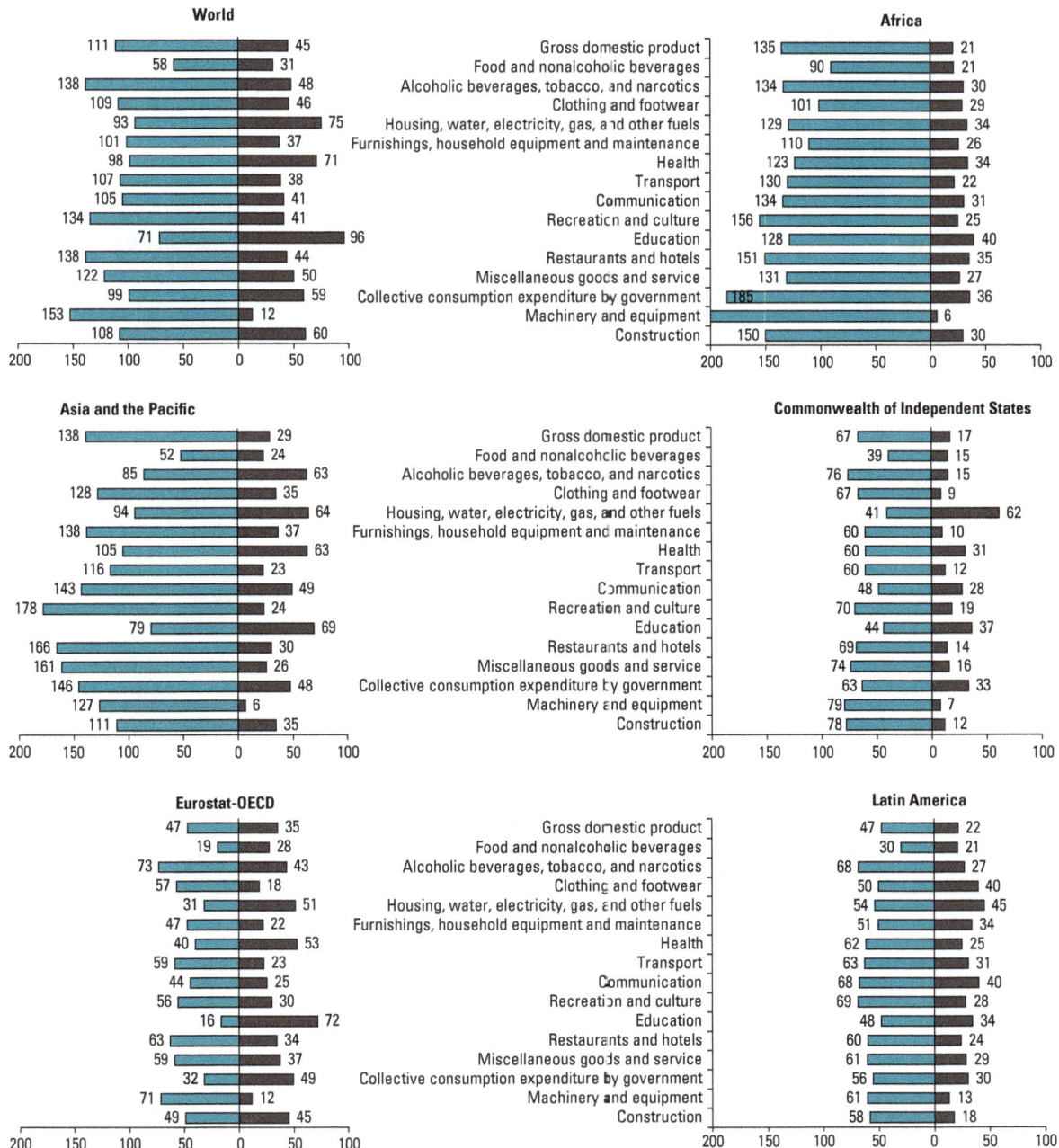

(continued)

Figure 2.9 *(Continued)*

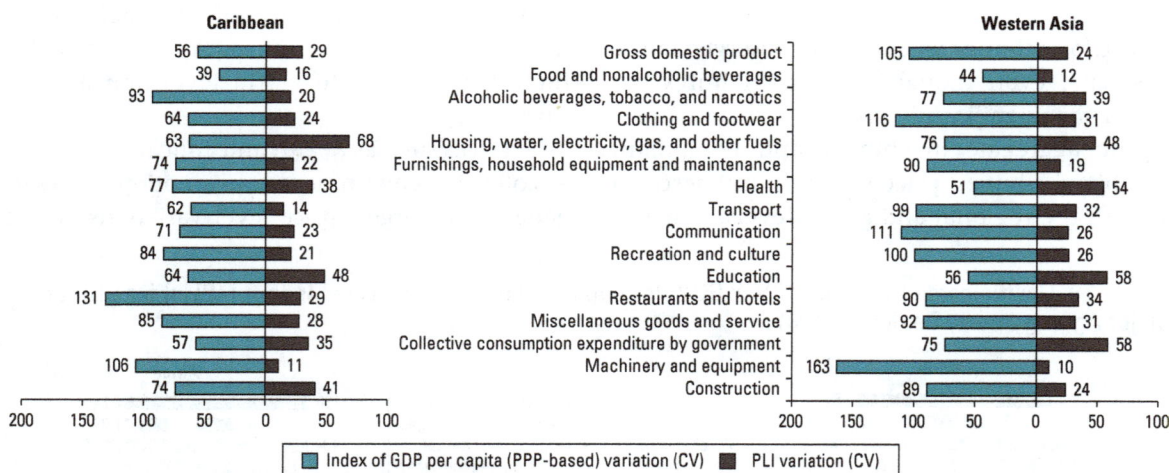

Category	Caribbean — Index of GDP per capita (PPP-based) variation (CV)	Caribbean — PLI variation (CV)	Western Asia — Index of GDP per capita (PPP-based) variation (CV)	Western Asia — PLI variation (CV)
Gross domestic product	56	29	105	24
Food and nonalcoholic beverages	39	16	44	12
Alcoholic beverages, tobacco, and narcotics	93	20	77	39
Clothing and footwear	64	24	116	31
Housing, water, electricity, gas, and other fuels	63	68	76	48
Furnishings, household equipment and maintenance	74	22	90	19
Health	77	38	51	54
Transport	62	14	99	32
Communication	71	23	111	26
Recreation and culture	84	21	100	26
Education	64	48	56	58
Restaurants and hotels	131	29	90	34
Miscellaneous goods and service	85	28	92	31
Collective consumption expenditure by government	57	35	75	58
Machinery and equipment	106	11	163	10
Construction	74	41	89	24

Legend: ■ Index of GDP per capita (PPP-based) variation (CV) ■ PLI variation (CV)

Source: ICP, http://icp.worldbank.org/.

all regions. Housing, too, has high PLI variances. These aggregates are also the most difficult to measure.

Inequality in incomes among economies

The Gini index measures the distribution of consumption expenditures across economies and the extent to which an economy deviates from the hypothetical l distribution if all economies had the same share of world GDP. A Lorenz curve plots the cumulative percentages of expenditures against the cumulative population starting with the poorest economy. The 45° line represents the plot of equality. The Gini index reflects the area between the Lorenz curve and the line of equality. A Gini index of zero represents perfect equality, and an index of 100 represents perfect inequality.

According to table 2.22, ICP 2011 revealed a population-weighted Gini measure of inequality among economies in real expenditures per capita in PPP terms of 0.49, which indicates a sharp drop from 0.57 in ICP 2005. Even though the economies participating in ICP 2005 and ICP 2011 were different, the general trend is a sharp fall in inequality, which would have significant implications for estimates of poverty incidence worldwide. Similar trends in inequality among economies are also evident when per capita household consumption or per capita actual individual consumption is used. Exchange

Table 2.22 Population-Weighted Gini Coefficient for ICP Economies, ICP 2011 and ICP 2005

	2011	2005
GDP, PPP-based	0.49	0.57
GDP, exchange rate–based	0.64	0.71
Actual individual consumption, PPP-based	0.51	0.60
Household consumption, PPP-based	0.52	0.62

Source: ICP, http://icp.worldbank.org/.

rate–based expenditures exhibit the same trend between the two benchmark years.

Figure 2.10, shows, using the Lorenz curve, the distribution of 2005 GDP per capita (dotted line) and 2011 GDP per capita. The area between the line of equality and the line showing the per capita distribution represents the inequality, which became smaller between 2005 and 2011.

Summary

This section has described the interaction between the real sizes of GDP for 177 economies with the relative price levels for major aggregates and expenditures per capita based on their population sizes. The results indicate that only a small number of economies have the greatest shares of world GDP. However, the shares of large economies such as China and India more than doubled relative to that of the United States between 2005 and 2011. The results also

Figure 2.10 Lorenz Curve for ICP 2011 and ICP 2005 GDP Per Capita Distribution

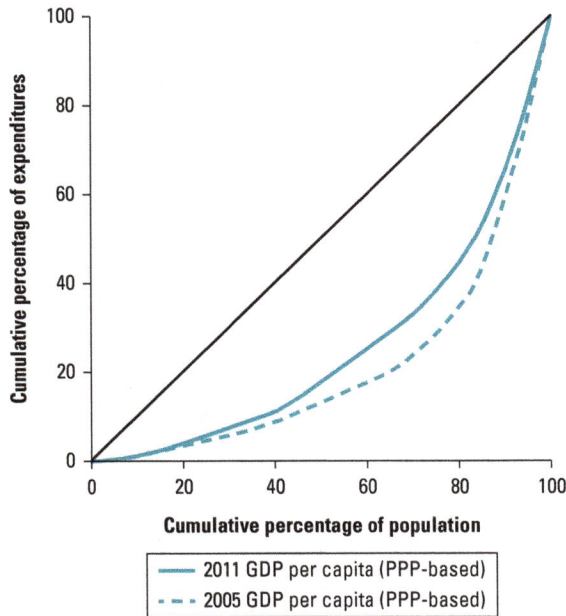

Source: ICP, http://icp.worldbank.org/.

reveal that PPP-based consumption and GDP expenditures in most poor economies are larger than previously thought, based on analysis of the ICP 2005 results.

Meanwhile, the spread of actual individual consumption per capita as a percentage of that of the United States has been greatly reduced, suggesting that the world has become more equal regarding the distribution of income. However, this reduction in the spread must be interpreted with caution because changes in the ICP methodology and economy coverage make it difficult to make direct comparisons with previous benchmark results. The sections on methodology in this report should be carefully considered when using the ICP 2011 results.

RELIABILITY AND LIMITATIONS OF PPPs AND REAL EXPENDITURES

Reliability of PPPs and real expenditures

PPPs are statistical constructs rather than precise measures—that is, they are point estimates that fall within some margin of error of the unknown true values. The error margins surrounding PPPs depend on the reliability of the expenditure weights and price data reported by the participating economies as well as the extent to which the goods and services priced reflect the consumption patterns and price levels of each participating economy. The margins of error around PPPs are the result of sampling and nonsampling errors plus the inherent variability in price and economic structures between economies.

Sampling errors emerge from several of the steps taken to collect prices and calculate basic heading PPPs. First, a sample of products is selected for pricing rather than pricing the universe of products. Second, a sample of outlets is selected rather than including every outlet in the economy in the price surveys. Third, prices from the sample of outlets are generally observed monthly, quarterly, or annually, depending on the seasonal variability in the prices. Although selection of the sample of products and outlets is a subjective process involving expert judgment, sampling theory can be used to determine the number of products to be priced, the number of outlets to be selected for the price surveys, and the number of times prices are observed for each selected product.

Chapter 7 of *Measuring the Real Size of the World Economy: The Framework, Methodology, and Results of the International Comparison Program (ICP)* (World Bank 2013) provides measures of the sources of sampling error. Table 7.3 shows that only 10–15 rice products need to be priced compared with 70–100 garments and 50+ pharmaceutical products to obtain about the same level of precision of the estimated basic heading PPPs. Products such as rice, milk, and eggs are very homogeneous, whereas the garment basic heading, which includes clothing for men, women, and children, is very heterogeneous. The desired degree of precision also depends on the relative expenditure shares of each basic heading. PPPs for basic headings with large shares of GDP must be measured with greater precision than those with small shares. In general, the sampling errors of the basic heading PPPs are mostly kept below 10 percent by increasing the number of products and prices where there is greater variability.

A nonsampling error is one that cannot be reduced by increasing the number of products surveyed or the number of prices observed. It also can be considered a source of bias.

The weights used to aggregate basic heading PPPs to GDP depend on the coverage and completeness of the national accounts. The per capita measures are dependent on the reliability of the population numbers, and the PLIs are dependent on the accuracy of the exchange rates as well as of the PPPs. The need for national average prices can be difficult to fulfill in large economies with large rural areas and populations. Product specifications can be vague, which means that economies may not price the same products. These nonsampling errors and sources of bias are minimized by the exhaustive data validation process described in chapter 9 of *Measuring the Real Size of the World Economy* (World Bank 2013) and in the chapters on data validation in *Operational Guidelines and Procedures for Measuring the Real Size of the World Economy: 2011 International Comparison Program* (World Bank forthcoming).

The reliability of the aggregated PPPs is affected not only by sampling and nonsampling errors, but also by the underlying variability inherent in each economy's price and economic structure. The relative price of rice as shown by the basic heading PPP for rice may be very cheap in an economy in which the relative prices for other basic headings are relatively expensive. The basic heading PPPs of an economy to the base will differ by factors of 20 for most basic headings and much more for those difficult to measure. This source of variability does not mean there are errors. Rather, it is an example of the variability of PPPs across economies with wide differences in economic and price structures. The variability of basic heading PPPs is less when comparing economies of similar price and economic structures, which is the main reason PPPs are first computed at the regional level.

Another source of variability in aggregated PPPs arises from the variation in the basic heading expenditures. The PPPs between any pair of economies are aggregated to GDP first using economy A's expenditures as weights (Laspeyres index) and then using economy B's weights (Paasche index). The Laspeyres and Paasche indexes will result in different estimates of the PPPs and real expenditures of each economy. The geometric mean is then taken, which is the Fisher index. The variability around the Fisher index is approximated by the Paasche-Laspeyres ratio or spread. Analysis by Deaton (2012) has shown that these standard errors for economies similar to the United States—Canada, for example—are about 2.5 percent. For less similar economies, such as China and India, they are about 7 percent, and over 10 percent for several CIS economies.

The Fisher indexes are not transitive or base economy–invariant. Therefore, the GEKS method is used for the final calculation. The aggregated PPP between France and Germany is the direct PPP between France and Germany times the geometric mean of the indirect PPPs through the $n - 2$ other economies in the comparison. Because of the transitivity requirement, the price level of the direct comparison between France and Germany must also be the same as the PPP for the entire chain of economies—that is, from the United States to India to Tajikistan and so forth, through all economies in the comparison. Although the GEKS method produces multilateral results satisfying transitivity and base economy invariance, the relative standard errors are increased for comparisons of similar economies such as the United States with its major trading partners. The relative standard error of the India and China to U.S. PPPs just described could increase to 15 percent from the multilateral comparison, although in practice this is likely to be somewhat lower because of fixity.

Limitations in the use of 2011 PPPs

Anyone comparing economies by the size of their real GDP or their real GDP per capita should do so with caution. Such comparisons require that all the economies employ the same definition of GDP and that their measurement of GDP be equally exhaustive. Although the first requirement is broadly met because the GDP estimates of most ICP participants are compiled more or less in line with the System of National Accounts 1993 (Commission of the European Communities et al. 1993), the measurement of GDP is not sufficiently uniform over all participants to satisfy the second requirement. In particular, the GDPs of participants with large nonobserved economies could be underestimated. Bearing in mind that there may be errors in the population data in addition to those in the price and expenditure data, one should not consider small differences between real GDP and real GDP per capita significant.

ICP 2011 includes economies ranging from city-states and small islands, such as Hong Kong SAR, China and Qatar, to large and diverse economies, such as Brazil, China, India, Russia, South Africa, and the United States. Because of the wide differences in the price and economic structures of economies and the inherent statistical variability in the methods used to calculate PPPs, the following guidelines are recommended for those using the 2011 PPPs and real expenditures:

- Comparisons between economies that are similar are more precise than comparisons between economies that are dissimilar. For example, the PPP between Nigeria and South Africa is more precise than the PPP of either to Liberia or Zimbabwe. Comparisons between economies in the same region will be more precise than between economies in other regions. For example, the China-India comparison will be more precise than the comparison of either to the United States.

- PPPs based on the prices of goods are more precise than PPPs for services. Areas such as housing and health will have wider measures of error than those for food products.

- PPPs provide the overall price level of an economy, but do not capture price differences within an economy.

Because of the sampling errors and statistical errors arising from the calculation methods, differences in real GDP of less than 5 percent should not be considered significant. This margin of error can rise to plus or minus 15 percent for economies that differ widely in their price and economic structures. This should be kept in mind when using, for example, the PPPs of the United States, China, India, and Brazil to compare the economies not only with each other but also with more disparate economies such as most of those in the Africa region.

Correct usage of 2011 PPPs

Linked to reliability is correct usage. PPPs appear in international trade theory in the context of equilibrium exchange rates (the underlying rates of exchange to which actual exchange rates are assumed to converge in the long term). But ICP PPPs should not be interpreted as equilibrium exchange rates. They have been calculated specifically to enable international comparisons of prices and real expenditures for GDP. They refer to the entire range of goods and services that make up GDP and include many items that are not traded internationally. Moreover, except for exports and imports, they are valued at domestic market prices, and PPPs for GDP are calculated using expenditure weights that reflect domestic demand. For the same reason, ICP PPPs do not indicate whether a currency is undervalued or overvalued and should not be used for this purpose.

ICP comparisons are designed to compare the volumes of goods and services that enter GDP at specific points in time. They are not designed to measure the relative rates of growth in GDP between these points. Each ICP comparison produces indexes of real GDP that show the relative volume levels of GDP among participating economies for the reference year. When the indexes for consecutive reference years are placed side by side, they appear to provide points in a time series of relative GDP volume levels over the intervening years. This apparent time series of volume measures is actually a time series of value indexes because the volume indexes for each reference year are calculated using the prices and expenditures for that year. Changes in the volume indexes between reference years are thus due to changes in the relative price levels as well as changes in the relative volume levels. As a result, the rates of relative growth derived from the indexes are not consistent with those obtained from times series of GDP volumes estimated by the economies themselves. The rates of growth estimated by the economies should be used to determine relative rates of growth in GDP.

The PLIs for the household final consumption expenditure provide a measure of the differences in the cost of living between economies—that is, they indicate whether the overall price level for consumer goods and services faced by the average household in one economy is higher or lower than that faced by the average household in another economy. Even so, people considering moving from one economy to another should not use these PLIs to infer how the change of economy will affect their cost of living. For one thing, PLIs reflect the expenditure pattern of the average household, which in all likelihood is different from that of the person contemplating the move. For another, PLIs are national averages and do not reflect differences in the cost of living between specific locations.

Reliability of PPPs for poverty analysis

Global poverty numbers require a large and varied set of data collected from different places, time periods, and sources. Five unique data sources are required for the World Bank's calculation of global poverty numbers and global poverty lines: household surveys, population censuses, national accounts, consumer price indexes, and PPPs from the ICP. Each new round of the ICP brings revisions of the PPPs, and these revisions, like revisions of the other data sources, can have large effects on global, regional, and national poverty counts. The global poverty line itself is calculated as an average of the PPP equivalents of the poverty lines of the world's poorest economies. In general, therefore, the global line will also change with new PPPs, even if the underlying national poverty lines remain unchanged.

The PPPs for individual consumption expenditures by households generated by ICP 2011 are designed to match the national accounts estimates of consumption, and the weights used to construct them are the shares of each good or service in the aggregate individual consumption expenditures by households. The use of those PPPs for poverty measurement has sometimes been criticized on the grounds that people who live at or below the global poverty line have different patterns of consumption than the aggregates in the national accounts. In particular, they spend a much larger share of their budgets on food, and they spend very little on housing and essentially nothing at all on air travel or on financial services indirectly measured, just to take one example.

PPPs offer comparisons across economies, not across the rich and poor within economies. As a consequence, in comparisons of any two economies the shift from aggregate to "poor" weights should have roughly the same effect in both economies so that, if the prices are the same in the aggregate and "poor" comparisons, the PPPs are not much affected. There are some exceptions, however, such as in economies that have extensive food subsidies so that the poor pay lower prices. There would be more exceptions if the prices paid by the poor were systematically different from the average prices in a way that differed from one economy to another. Some attempts have been made to measure such price differences, but there is no general agreement on how to do so, or on whether such differences are important. Thus additional research will be needed before international poverty rates can be estimated using ICP PPPs.

DIFFERENCES BETWEEN THE 2005 AND 2011 COMPARISONS

The ICP is designed to compare levels of economic activity across economies, expressed in a common currency, in a particular benchmark year. The ICP should not be used to compare changes in an economy's GDP volume over time: the national accounts volume estimates of each individual economy are the best data source for this purpose. The 2005 and 2011 global comparisons are the first two that include comparable real expenditures for such a large number of economies. With the release of ICP 2011 results, it is inevitable that many analysts will attempt to compare the positions of economies in 2011 with those in 2005 by simultaneously studying changes over time and across economies. However, many of the comparisons will be problematical because they will be based on two different price levels, and so real expenditures and PLIs will not be directly comparable between 2005 and 2011. In addition, some of the economies participating in one comparison were not in the other comparison, a small number of economies moved from one region to another, and, most important, some significant changes in methodology were implemented in ICP 2011. Both the changes in the composition of regions between 2005 and 2011 and the methodological changes introduced in 2011 will affect any comparisons between ICP 2005 and ICP 2011.

ICP 2005 estimated the real expenditure on GDP for 146 economies, ICP 2011 for

199 economies. The greater part of this increase can be explained by the inclusion of 22 Caribbean islands and 21 Pacific islands in ICP 2011. Other newcomers to ICP 2011 were Algeria and the Seychelles in Africa; Myanmar in the Asia and the Pacific region; Costa Rica, Cuba, Dominican Republic, El Salvador, Guatemala, Haiti, Honduras, Nicaragua, and Panama in the Latin America region; and the United Arab Emirates and West Bank and Gaza in the Western Asia region. Economies that participated in ICP 2005 but not in ICP 2011 included Argentina in the Latin America region and Lebanon and the Syrian Arab Republic in the Western Asia region. Other changes in the composition of regions were the result of Chile leaving the Latin America region to join the OECD and the Islamic Republic of Iran leaving the Asia and the Pacific region and Georgia leaving the CIS to become singletons.

The major methodological changes in ICP 2011 were as follows:

- *Global linking and aggregation.* The 2011 linking procedures differ from those used in 2005 in two important respects:
  - *At the basic heading level.* In 2005 only 18 economies participated in the Ring, a special group of representative economies from ICP regions that priced a common list of products (the Ring list) to be used in linking regions, whereas in 2011 almost all participating economies contributed to the interregional linking by pricing products in the global core list, the worldwide list of products designed to provide links between regions.
  - *At the aggregate levels above the basic heading.* In 2011 a new procedure, the country aggregation with redistribution (CAR), replaced the 2005 super-region method in which linking factors were computed for regional aggregates.

  The change in methods was based on the outcomes of an analysis of the 2005 results that showed that the linking factors were overly sensitive to pricing problems in the Ring economies. The 2011 methodology is considered a significant improvement over the 2005 linking method at both the basic heading level and above.

- *Calculating basic heading PPPs.* In 2005 basic heading PPPs were calculated using the country dummy product (CPD) method without assigning any weight at the product level. In 2011 it was decided that products would be classified as important or less important and that weights of 3:1 would be used in computing basic heading PPPs at the intraregion level and also in estimating linking factors. Thus basic heading PPPs were calculated using the weighted country product dummy (CPD-W) method. The classification and weighting of products by their relative importance affected the 2011 PPPs.

- *Dwellings.* In ICP 2005, Africa and the CIS used the dwelling stock approach, Latin America the rental approach, and Asia and the Pacific the reference volume approach, whereas Eurostat-OECD and Western Asia used a combination of rental and dwelling stock data. The regional results were linked using dwelling stock data. In ICP 2011, Africa, Latin America, the Caribbean, and Western Asia calculated PPPs using rental data collected for the global list of dwelling types; Asia and the Pacific used the reference volume approach; the CIS used dwelling stock data; and the Eurostat-OECD used a combination of rental and dwelling stock data. Linking was carried out in stages. The Africa, Latin America, Caribbean, and Western Asia regions were linked using the same rental data that went into the estimation of their intraregion PPPs. For Asia and the Pacific, the CIS, and Eurostat-OECD, dwelling stock data were used to link them to each other and then to the rest of the world.

- *Government.* In 2005 government consumption estimates were adjusted for productivity differences between economies in three of the six regions—Africa, Asia and the Pacific, and Western Asia—but the regional linking factors were computed without any productivity adjustments. In 2011 the Africa, Asia and the Pacific, Latin America, and Caribbean regions used productivity adjustments when computing their regional results, but no productivity adjustments were applied within the Eurostat-OECD, CIS, and Western Asia regions. The linking factors for all regions were computed with productivity adjustments to produce the global results.

- *Construction.* The method used to estimate construction PPPs changed completely in ICP 2011 and is not comparable with that used in 2005. In ICP 2005, construction PPPs were estimated using a hybrid approach that combined prices for some construction outputs with those for some inputs. Because of the difficulties encountered in implementing this approach, a simplified input method based on the prices of basic materials, labor, and machinery was adopted for ICP 2011.

Aside from the methodological changes, directly comparing the ICP estimates of real expenditures for 2011 with those for 2005 is not a valid exercise. Not only did price levels change between 2005 and 2011, but they also changed to a different extent across economies. Even comparing the relative positions of economies can be misleading when world or regional averages are used as the basis for comparison. For example, in the Asia and the Pacific region, whose economic activity is dominated by China, the relationship between the real expenditure for one of the high-income economies such as Hong Kong SAR, China, and the regional average will decline between 2005 and 2011, even though the real GDP of that economy rose appreciably between these two years. The reason is that the regional average real expenditure on GDP increased even more than the real GDP of Hong Kong SAR, China, because of the dominance in the region of the rapidly growing Chinese economy.

COMPARING 2011 PPPs EXTRAPOLATED FROM ICP 2005 AND ICP 2011 BENCHMARK PPPs

Purchasing power parities can be extrapolated at any level, ranging from the most detailed, the basic heading level, up to total GDP. Extrapolating at the more detailed levels is likely to produce better results when compared with successive benchmarks, but it is more likely that an approach based on extrapolating at fairly broad levels will generally be used in practice because of a lack of detailed price deflators that are consistent across economies. The methods used to produce the national accounts estimates that provide the basis for extrapolating PPPs can differ significantly from one economy to another, thereby affecting the reliability of extrapolations. For example, economies differ in the ways in which they treat productivity changes over time, in how they update their national accounts to take into consideration revised data or the introduction of new methodology, and in the methods they use to adjust price deflators for quality change.

The most common method used to interpolate PPPs and real expenditures between ICP benchmarks and to extrapolate from the most recent one the latest set of benchmark PPPs for each economy is a time series of price deflators at a broad level (typically GDP but sometimes a handful of major components of GDP). The process involves comparing changes in national accounts deflators for an economy with those in a base economy and using these comparative movements to extrapolate from the latest ICP benchmark. Some very restrictive assumptions underlie this method, the most important of which is that the economies have similar economic structures and are evolving in a similar way. Clearly, this is not the case when developing economies are compared with the United States, which is regularly used as the base economy. Changes in an economy's terms of trade also can have a significant effect on the consistency of extrapolated PPPs and real expenditures. In addition, the global financial crisis of 2008–09 affected economies very differently, with some economies, mainly high-income ones, falling into recession for a year or more, while others continued to grow despite the financial crisis.

Several assumptions relate to the consistency of the methods used to estimate an economy's national accounts with those used by the ICP. For example, the products priced by the ICP are carefully defined to ensure comparability between economies, but the products priced in the time series used in estimating the volumes in an economy's national accounts are selected to ensure that they are the most representative products available in the economy. In addition, the weighting patterns used in an economy's price indexes are specific to that economy, whereas those underlying the ICP results are an amalgam of those for the economies participating in the ICP. Finally, the prices in an economy's price indexes, such as the consumer price index, are adjusted for quality changes over time, and economies do not use common methods to adjust for these changes. For example, hedonic methods are used to a different extent in different economies, or not at all in many economies, with the result that the quality-adjusted time series are not consistent across economies.

Many economies use chain-linked volumes in their time series because of the distortions introduced by using a fixed base year for volume estimates for a lengthy period of time. As a result, the GDP deflators derived from chain-linked volumes behave differently from those for economies that use the more traditional fixed-base methods to estimate their GDP volumes. In practice, fixed-base volumes tend to be biased upward for the most recent years, which means that any deflators derived from them are biased downward.

Experience has shown that sizable discrepancies can arise between extrapolated estimates and a new benchmark, even when they are only a couple of years apart. The gap between the latest ICP rounds was six years, which resulted in some very large differences for many economies between the extrapolated real expenditures for 2011 and the benchmark real expenditures that have become available from ICP 2011. It is not possible to quantify separately the various factors underlying these differences.

A detailed explanation of the issues underlying extrapolation is available in chapter 18 of *Measuring the Real Size of the World Economy* (World Bank 2013).

Chapter 3

Data Requirements

The International Comparison Program (ICP) compares the gross domestic products (GDPs) of participating economies in real terms by removing the differences in GDPs that are attributable to differences in price levels and expressing the GDPs in a common currency. The conceptual framework of an ICP comparison is determined by the definition of GDP, which for the 2005 and 2011 rounds of the ICP was the internationally agreed-on definition of GDP in the System of National Accounts 1993 or SNA93 (Commission of the European Communities et al. 1993).

CONCEPTUAL FRAMEWORK

General approach

ICP comparisons of price and real expenditure levels of GDP are based on the expenditure aggregates of the national accounts using spatial price deflators or purchasing power parities (PPPs) as the measure of the price component. In these cases, the prices of products constituting final demand are collected and compared across economies to produce the price relatives, PPPs, with which the GDPs and component expenditures being compared are deflated to obtain the real expenditure relatives. In other words, the price measures are derived directly and the real expenditure measures indirectly. This is called the price approach.

The price approach is usually applied in ICP comparisons because prices are generally easier to observe directly than quantities, which are required to directly estimate real expenditures. In addition, direct measures of relative prices normally have a smaller variability than direct measures of relative quantities. Even so, the price approach is not applied in every instance. Of the exceptions, the most notable are the real expenditures for housing services, which are measured directly via the quantity approach in many economies. In such cases, PPPs are derived indirectly by dividing the real expenditures into the nominal values for the relevant aggregate(s). The direct measurement of real expenditures and the indirect measurement of PPPs are known as the quantity approach.

Each ICP comparison has a reference year, and the most recent one is 2011. The basic data that an economy participating in the comparison provides for the reference year are as follows: a set of prices for a selection of products chosen from a common basket of precisely defined goods and services, a detailed breakdown of the national expenditure according to a common classification, the economy's exchange rates, and its resident population. The prices and expenditures are used to calculate PPPs and real expenditures (or volumes); the exchange rates and PPPs are used to calculate price level indexes; and the population totals and real expenditures are used to calculate real expenditures per capita. Prices and expenditures are reported in national currencies. Both cover the whole range of final goods and services comprising GDP as defined in the ICP expenditure classification in appendix D of this volume.

The ICP expenditure classification adheres to the concepts, definitions, classifications, and accounting rules of SNA93. It gives the comparison structure. Economies are expected to estimate their national expenditure for the reference year broadly in line with SNA93 and to break down their GDP estimate into the component expenditures identified in the classification. The component expenditures comprise different levels of aggregation. At the lowest level of aggregation, they are called basic headings. The classification breaks down the expenditure on final goods and services into 155 basic headings that comply with the functional and product classifications of SNA93.

Basic headings are the building blocks of the comparison. They are the level at which expenditures are defined and estimated, products are selected for pricing, prices are collected and validated, and PPPs are first calculated and averaged. In theory, basic headings should be homogeneous, each covering a group of similar well-defined goods or services, but in practice they often are not. Basic headings are determined by the lowest level of final expenditure for which economies in the comparison can be expected to estimate explicit expenditures. As a result, basic headings can cover a broader range of products than is theoretically desirable, and they can include both goods and services.

For each basic heading, economies report prices for a subset of products covered by the basic heading and their expenditure on the basic heading. The prices are used to calculate PPPs for the basic heading, and the PPPs are used to deflate the expenditures on the basic heading, which are at national price levels, to real expenditures at a uniform price level. The basic heading PPPs are subsequently aggregated, using the expenditures on the basic headings as weights, to provide PPPs for each level of aggregation up to the level of GDP. Real expenditures for an aggregation level are obtained by deflating the expenditures on the aggregation level with the PPPs for the aggregation level.

Expenditure approach

SNA93 defines GDP from the expenditure side as the sum of the expenditures on final consumption, gross capital formation, and net exports. Final consumption is the total expenditure on the goods and services consumed by individual households or the community to satisfy their individual or collective needs. Gross capital formation is the total expenditure on gross fixed capital formation, changes in inventories, and acquisitions less disposals of valuables. Net exports are the difference between the value of goods and services exported and the value of goods and services imported. ICP comparisons are based largely on PPPs calculated using prices collected for the component expenditures of final consumption and gross fixed capital formation. Prices are not collected for changes in inventories, the acquisition and disposal of valuables, and net exports; they are deflated with reference PPPs. Reference PPPs are described in appendix G.

Expenditures on final consumption are incurred by three of the five institutional sectors recognized by SNA93—households, nonprofit institutions serving households (NPISHs), and general government—but not by financial corporations or nonfinancial corporations. Expenditures on gross fixed capital formation are incurred by resident producers of goods and services irrespective of institutional sector and include households when engaged in own-account production (e.g., subsistence production by a farmer). In the ICP classification, expenditures on final consumption are classified by the institutional sector making the purchase, with the final consumption expenditures of households, NPISHs, and general government identified and treated separately. No such distinction is made for expenditures on gross fixed capital formation.

Actual Individual Consumption

SNA93 classifies the expenditure on final consumption as either an individual consumption expenditure or a collective consumption expenditure. The individual consumption expenditure comprises the expenditures made by households, NPISHs, and general government on individual goods and services—that is, they benefit households individually. The collective consumption expenditure comprises the expenditures made by general government on collective services—that is, they benefit households collectively. Health, education, and social protection are examples of individual services. Defense, public order and safety, and environmental protection are examples of collective services.

In the ICP classification, the expenditure on final consumption is broken down into four aggregates: (1) individual consumption expenditure by households, (2) individual consumption expenditure by NPISHs, (3) individual consumption expenditure by government, and (4) collective consumption expenditure by government. Each aggregate clearly indicates who benefits from the expenditure—households either individually or collectively—and who makes the expenditure—households, NPISHs, or general government. SNA93 uses the distinction between who consumes and who pays to derive an additional aggregate: actual individual consumption.

Actual individual consumption is the sum of the individual consumption expenditures of households, NPISHs, and general government. It is a measure of the individual goods and services consumed by households. It is particularly pertinent to comparisons of material well-being when well-being is measured in terms of the individual goods and services that households consume. The alternative, the consumption expenditure by households on goods and services, is a measure of the expenditure incurred by households rather than a measure of their total consumption. It covers only the individual goods and services that households themselves purchase and does not take into account the individual services that NPISHs and general government supply households as social transfers in kind (e.g., subsidized medical services).

The financing and provision of individual services, especially health and education, can vary considerably from economy to economy. If only the individual consumption expenditure by households is compared, economies in which households themselves purchase health care and education will appear to consume more than households in economies in which these services are provided (or subsidized) by NPISHs

or general government, and thus misleading conclusions about the relative material well-being of economies can result. Comparing the actual individual consumption of economies, which covers the individual goods and services that households receive from NPISHs and general government as well as their own purchases of individual goods and services, avoids such conclusions.

Derivation of Actual Individual Consumption

The ICP classification is primarily an expenditure classification in which the final consumption expenditure is structured by who pays. However, because one of the principal aims of ICP comparisons is to compare actual individual consumption at various levels of aggregation, the results of comparisons are presented by who consumes. The classification is designed to allow the final consumption expenditures of households, NPISHs, and general government to be reclassified and combined according to whether they benefit households individually or collectively. This is achieved by applying two classifications from SNA93: the Classification of Individual Consumption According to Purpose (COICOP) and the Classification of the Functions of Government (COFOG)—see United Nations Statistics Division (1999a, 1999b).

COICOP classifies the individual consumption expenditures of households, NPISHs, and general government by purpose. It ensures that the treatment of the three expenditures is consistent and harmonized. In principle, the three expenditures should be broken down so that they can be compared and summed at the lowest level of aggregation, the basic heading level. In practice, this is feasible only for the individual consumption expenditures of households and general government because most economies cannot provide the required level of detail for the individual consumption expenditure of NPISHs. (In recognition of this constraint, the ICP classification requires economies to report a single figure for the NPISH consumption expenditure. Prior to the calculation of PPPs for actual individual consumption, the NPISH consumption expenditures reported by economies are distributed across the relevant basic headings in the same proportions in which their household consumption expenditures are distributed.)

COFOG classifies the outlays of general government by function. As for the outlays on final consumption, it distinguishes between the individual consumption expenditure and collective consumption expenditure, defining the former in line with COICOP.

Imputed Expenditures

Expenditures on final consumption and gross fixed capital formation include the actual expenditures covering monetary transactions and the imputed expenditures covering nonmonetary transactions. Expenditures on monetary transactions can be measured directly because a price is stated in monetary units for each transaction. Expenditures on nonmonetary transactions cannot be measured directly because there is either no price or, in the case of barter, there is no price stated in monetary units. Expenditures on nonmonetary transactions are obtained by imputing a value to them. The values to be imputed are defined by the national accounting conventions adopted by SNA93. The general rule is that the goods and services in a nonmonetary transaction should be valued at the basic prices at which they would be sold if offered for sale on the market or, in the absence of basic prices, as the sum of their costs of production.

The imputations of particular relevance to ICP comparisons are those made for goods that households produce and consume themselves; gross fixed capital formation carried out by producers on their own account, such as the construction of dwellings by households; housing services that owner-occupiers are said to purchase from themselves; financial intermediation services indirectly measured (FISIM); unfunded social insurance schemes operated by general government for its employees; and consumption of fixed capital by NPISHs and general government.

The consumption of own-account production of agricultural produce, preserved foodstuffs, and wine and spirits is significant in many economies. For ICP purposes, not only must the imputed expenditure be included in the estimate of GDP so it will not be underestimated, but the basic prices used to impute the expenditure must be weighted and averaged with the purchasers' prices collected from outlets for the same goods

and the PPPs calculated with the average of the two prices. If the basic prices are not taken into account, the PPPs will be overestimated and the real expenditures underestimated.

The imputed rents of owner-occupiers are also important, but many economies have difficulty estimating them to international standards. This problem usually arises because they do not have a large representative rental market that would allow them to use actual rents for rented houses and apartments to estimate imputed rents for equivalent owner-occupied houses and apartments as recommended by SNA93. For such economies, volumes are estimated directly using a quality-adjusted quantity approach based on housing stock numbers broken down by size of dwelling and the percentage of dwellings having facilities such as electricity, running water, a private toilet, a private kitchen, and central heating or air-conditioning.

Nonmarket Services

SNA93 distinguishes between market services and nonmarket services. Market services are sold at economically significant prices; nonmarket services are supplied free or at prices that are not economically significant. The individual services that general government purchases for households from market producers are bought at economically significant prices and are market services. The individual services and the collective services that general government itself produces for households and that it provides free or at noneconomically significant prices are nonmarket services.

Economically significant prices are prices that have a significant influence on the amounts producers are willing to supply and on the amounts purchasers wish to buy, and so they influence the amounts producers supply and purchasers buy. By multiplying the quantities sold by the prices at which they are sold, one could determine the expenditure on market services, although the values for most market services in the national accounts are based on directly collecting the values (e.g., from a household survey). These are the same prices required to calculate the PPPs for market services. Because nonmarket services have no economically significant prices, their expenditures and their PPPs cannot be derived in the same way that they are for market services. Instead, following the convention adopted by national accountants, expenditures on nonmarket services are estimated by summing the costs to produce them, and their PPPs are calculated using the prices of inputs. This is known as the input price approach.

To implement the input price approach, one must break down the expenditures on nonmarket services by cost components. The cost components identified in the ICP classification for government-produced health, education, and collective services are compensation of employees, intermediate consumption, gross operating surplus, net taxes on production, and receipts from sales (which are deducted from the value of output to derive the final consumption expenditure). Of these cost components, compensation of employees is by far the largest and most important. It is the only cost component for which the ICP collects prices. Reference PPPs are used for the other cost components.

Productivity adjustments

The disadvantage of the input price approach is that differences in productivity between economies are not reflected in the real expenditures. It is assumed that producers of nonmarket services are equally efficient and that the same level of input will yield the same volume of output regardless of the economy in which the producer is operating. However, this assumption is difficult to defend because of the degree to which levels of economic development vary among the economies participating in ICP comparisons. If productivity differences are not taken into account when calculating the real expenditures, they will be disguised as price differences. In economies in which input costs are relatively low, the real expenditures on nonmarket output would be overestimated, and in economies in which input costs are relatively high, the real expenditures on nonmarket output would be underestimated.

Failure to take into account productivity differences between the producers of nonmarket services in different economies affects not only the PPPs and real expenditures for nonmarket services, but also the PPPs and real expenditures for GDP. In some cases, not adjusting for

productivity differences can even have a significant effect on the real expenditures for GDP. In ICP 2011, adjustments for differences in productivity were made to the real expenditure estimates for government-produced nonmarket services in the regional comparisons for Africa, Asia and the Pacific, Latin America, and the Caribbean. Productivity adjustments were not made in the regional comparisons for the Commonwealth of Independent States (CIS) and Western Asia, nor were they made in the comparison conducted by Eurostat and the Organisation for Economic Co-operation and Development (OECD). The reason was that differences in labor productivity between economies in each of these regions were considered to be relatively small. Productivity adjustments were made to all regions when they were combined in the global comparison.

Price approach

The real expenditures of economies participating in an ICP comparison are generally obtained by deflating their national expenditures for the reference year with PPPs for the reference year. To ensure that the deflation of national expenditures produces unbiased real expenditures, the PPPs used as deflators have to be based on prices that meet three conditions. First, they should be consistent with the prices underlying the national expenditure estimates of the economies. Second, they should be for products that are comparable across the economies. And, third, the products priced should be important items of expenditure within the economies. Deflating with PPPs based on prices that do not satisfy these three requirements can result in PPPs that are either too high or too low and a corresponding underestimation or overestimation of real expenditures.

Comparability and importance are not necessarily complementary. Consumption patterns can vary from economy to economy because of differences in taste, culture, climate, price structures, product availability, and income levels. Products that are important in one economy are not necessarily important in other economies, and products that are strictly comparable across economies are unlikely to have equal importance in all of them. At times, a choice has to be made between pricing a comparable but less important product and pricing an important product that is not comparable. When such a choice has to be made, comparability has priority over importance. If products are not comparable, there can be no valid comparison because like is not being compared with like. If products are comparable but not equally important, a comparison can be made, although the result may be biased.

Consistency

ICP comparisons are based on an identity: value = price × volume. If volumes are to be derived correctly, then the prices that economies provide for the comparison should be consistent with the valuation methods used to estimate their national expenditures. In principle, the national expenditures reported for the reference year are compiled according to SNA93, which calls for expenditures to be estimated using the purchasers' prices for actual transactions. To be consistent with SNA93, economies have to collect the prices that purchasers actually pay sellers to acquire a particular good or service. Transaction prices paid by purchasers include the supplier's retail and wholesale margins, transport and insurance charges, and any nondeductible value added tax on products. They should also be net prices that include all discounts, surcharges, rebates, and, for certain services, invoiced service charges and voluntary gratuities. Moreover, because the national expenditures cover the whole economic territory of an economy, the prices should be national averages that take into account regional variations in prices within the economic territory. They should also be annual averages that take into account seasonal variations in prices, general inflation, and changes in price structures during the reference year.

Ideally, economies would collect national annual purchasers' prices for actual transactions from purchasers, but, because it is neither practical nor cost-effective to do so, the prices are collected from sellers instead. Most sellers display the prices at which they are prepared to sell their products, but the prices at which products are offered for sale are not necessarily the prices at which they are actually sold. Unless price collectors have access to data on actual transactions such as scanner data, they cannot collect actual transaction prices. Rather, they have to collect the prices that purchasers would have to pay if they were to purchase the goods and services specified at the time of the price collection. In other words, in practice the prices at which goods and services are offered, and not actual transaction prices, should be observed. However, before recording an offer price as the purchaser's price, the price collector must first establish whether the price includes nondeductible value added taxes, discounts, and, if relevant, delivery and installation costs, invoiced service charges, and voluntary gratuities. If not, the price collector must adjust the offer price accordingly.

Total Price

For most products, collecting the purchaser's price is relatively straightforward because a purchase normally involves a transaction between a seller and a single buyer. But this is not always the case. Certain products purchased from market producers can entail a transaction involving a seller and two independent buyers. Such transactions are particularly prevalent in health services where the provider of the service can be paid in part by households and in part by a second party (government, NPISH, or private health insurer). When there are two purchasers, there are two prices and two expenditures. What is consistent in these circumstances? Should PPPs be calculated separately for each buyer based on the prices each pays and their expenditures deflated accordingly? Or should the PPPs used to deflate the expenditures be based on the total price—that is, the sum of the price paid by the household and the price paid by the second party? With the first option, the PPPs used to deflate the two expenditures will be based on prices that are consistent with the prices underlying the expenditures, but the real expenditure on health services will be twice what it should be. With the second option, the PPPs used to deflate the two expenditures will not be based on prices that are consistent with the prices underlying the expenditures, but the real expenditure on health services will be correct, which is the primary objective of consistency. For ICP comparisons, PPPs for the expenditure on health services are calculated using the total price, which is consistent with the expenditures when combined.

Comparability

The national annual purchasers' prices that economies supply for the comparison should be for products that are comparable between them. Products are said to be comparable if they have identical or equivalent physical and economic characteristics. Equivalent means the products meet the same needs with equal efficiency so that purchasers are indifferent between them and are not prepared to pay more for one product than for the other. The pricing of comparable products ensures that the differences in prices between economies for a product reflect actual price differences and are not influenced by differences in quality. If differences in quality are not avoided or corrected, they can be mistaken for apparent price differences, leading to the underestimation or overestimation of price levels.

Comparability is obtained in ICP comparisons by economies using product specifications in their pricing that fully define the products in terms of the principal characteristics that influence their transaction prices. Product specifications can be brand- and model-specific (that is, a particular brand and model are stipulated), or they can be generic (that is, only the relevant technical parameters and other price-determining characteristics are specified, and no brand is designated). Ideally, all product specifications would be brand- and model-specific so that economies would price products of identical quality. In practice, however, this is not possible in many cases because the brand or the model is not generally available or, if available, is not an important item of expenditure, and so generic specifications have to be employed. Generic specifications are typically looser than brand and model specifications, and some variability in quality between the products priced by economies can occur. Differences in quality can arise because economies price products that do not match exactly the product specifications, or because the products priced appear to match the product specifications exactly but the product specifications are too loose or too open-ended to ensure that economies price products of the same quality. Differences in quality are usually identified and corrected when the price data are validated.

Product specifications for ICP comparisons are defined using the structured product descriptions (SPDs) introduced during ICP 2005. They standardize the product specifications for different types of products so that all specifications for a specific product type are uniformly defined and list the same technical and transactional characteristics that price collectors have to match. The purpose of SPDs is to improve the precision of the specifications and to simplify price collection. The more precise a specification the easier it is for price collectors to determine whether the product in an outlet matches the product specified. SPDs identify those characteristics that are price-determining because only characteristics that have an impact on the price of the product should be included in the product specification. Characteristics that do not have an effect on price do not need to be specified. They do not affect comparability, and their inclusion only increases the number of characteristics to be matched. This can make it more difficult for a price collector to find the product in an outlet, and fewer prices will be collected as a result. By focusing on the characteristics that influence price, SPDs strike a balance between the need for precision and the need for a sufficient number of price observations.

Importance

In addition to being comparable across economies, the products that economies price for the comparison should be products that reflect, or are characteristic of, their final expenditures. In other words, the products should be important items of expenditure. Usually, such products are volume sellers. Products that are important generally have a lower price level than products that are less important, and this factor has to be taken into account when choosing products for the product list and when calculating the PPPs for a basic heading; otherwise, the PPPs can be biased. Either they will be either too high and yield real expenditures that are too low, or they will be too low and yield real expenditures that are too high. To avoid such a situation, economies are expected to (1) ensure that a sufficient number of their important products are included in the regional product list when drawing up the product list prior to price collection (at least one important product per basic heading); (2) price the important products of other economies as well as their own important products during price collection (otherwise, the number of over-laps between economies will be insufficient and no comparison can be made); and (3) indicate which of the products they priced are important and which are less important when reporting prices after price collection so that the product's importance can be taken into account during the validation of prices and the calculation of basic heading PPPs.

The importance of a product is determined by its share of expenditure in its basic heading. The decision about whether a product is important is made in the context of its basic heading and is independent of the relative importance of the basic heading with respect to other basic head-ings. Whether its basic heading has a high or low share of GDP expenditure is not a consideration when deciding a product's importance. Defining importance by reference to expenditure shares is problematic because usually there are no explicit expenditure details below the basic heading level. The relative importance of the various products within a basic heading has to be deter-mined by other means, using alternative sources of information. Examples of such sources for consumer products are the consumer price index, retail price index, household budget surveys, and retail trade surveys. More generally, information can be obtained by consulting marketing experts, producers, importers, distributors, sales managers, shop buyers, and the Internet.

Ideally, the product list would be balanced. For each basic heading, the number of impor-tant products to be priced and the number of less important products to be priced would be the same for each economy. The number would not be the same for all basic headings; it would vary with the importance and homoge-neity of the basic heading. A comparison based on a list of products that is not balanced may result in biased price relatives. There is a risk that price levels for economies pricing a smaller number of important products will be overesti-mated and that price levels for economies pricing a larger number of important products will be underestimated. In practice, though, the product list will not be balanced. Each economy will not have the same number of important and less important products for each basic heading. However, the methods used to calculate PPPs for a basic heading in ICP comparisons ensure that any imbalance between economies in the number of impor-tant and less important products priced does not produce biased PPPs. The methods give greater weight to important products.

SURVEYS AND DATA COLLECTION

Coverage of surveys

Economies participating in ICP 2011 collected prices for a selection of the goods and services that make up the final consumption expendi-ture and gross fixed capital formation. The four principal price surveys that economies conducted covered (1) consumer goods and services (also known as the main price sur-vey), (2) compensation of employees paid by general government to employees producing individual and collective services, (3) machin-ery and equipment, and (4) construction and civil engineering (all described in the separate sections that follow). Because the household consumption expenditure accounts for over 60 percent of GDP in the majority of econo-mies, the most important of the four price surveys was the survey of consumer goods and services. It included a wide assortment of products, ranging from food, beverages, clothing, footwear, electricity, furniture, and household appliances to motor vehicles, transport services, audiovisual and informa-tion processing equipment, restaurants, hotels, and hairdressers.

Pricing of most of these consumer products was relatively straightforward. Price collectors visited a sample of outlets, identifying products in the outlets that matched the product specifi-cations on the product list and recording their prices. But some consumer goods and services required a different or more focused treatment, and these were surveyed separately from other consumer products. Separate surveys were orga-nized for housing services, private health services, private education, water supply, and fast-evolving technology products. These five surveys and the price surveys for compensation of employees, machinery and equipment, and construction and civil engineering men-tioned earlier were referred to collectively as the special price surveys, thereby emphasizing their specificity as well as distinguishing them from the main price survey covering consumer goods and services.

Global core products

The 2011 global comparison combined seven regional comparisons—six ICP regional comparisons (Africa, Asia and the Pacific, CIS, Latin America, the Caribbean, and Western Asia) and the Eurostat-OECD comparison—in a single comparison. The Pacific Islands priced a separate product list that did not include the global core products. Linking the seven regions into a global comparison was achieved by using global core products—that is, products that had been selected for the specific purpose of providing links or overlaps between the regional comparisons in which they were priced. For the main price survey and for each of the special price surveys, the Global Office compiled a list of global core products in consultation with regional and national coordinators and, in the case of the special price surveys, with subject matter experts. SPDs were used to define the price-determining characteristics of the products. Table 3.1 presents the number of priced global core products per region and survey and the total number of global core products for each survey.

Particular care was taken with the global core product list for the main price survey. Consultation was an iterative process, with the list evolving in line with the comments and proposals of those consulted. Considerable effort was made to ensure that the list was not dominated by the products of any one region and that the products were global so that they could be priced across most if not all regions. The final version of the list specified 618 core consumer products.

For the main price survey, regions developed their own regional product list by revising their regional product list from ICP 2005. Products no longer available or problematic were dropped; products still available were retained and their specifications updated; and new products, fully specified, were added to replace deleted products and to stay abreast of market trends. The global core products were combined with those on the revised regional lists, and care was taken to avoid duplication. Regional products that matched a global core product exactly or were comparable to a global core product were removed from the regional list and replaced by the global core product.

The economies in a region were asked to review the global and regional products on the regional list and indicate the availability and

Table 3.1 Number of Priced Global Core Products per Region and Survey, ICP 2011

	Household consumption[a]	Housing rentals	Private education	Government compensation[b]	Machinery and equipment	Construction
Africa	610	64	7	209	176	137
Asia and the Pacific	412	64	6	41	160	124
Commonwealth of Independent States	560	n.a.[c]	3	25	132	114
Eurostat-OECD	394	n.a.[c]	n.a.[d]	19[d]	131	135
Latin America	489	51	7	31	175	144
Caribbean	446	8	5	42	75	157
Western Asia	606	64	7	210	174	156
Total number of global products	**618**	**64**	**7**	**210**	**177**	**165**

Source: ICP, http://icp.worldbank.org/.

Note: n.a. = not applicable. An item is counted as priced if at least one country within a region priced it. In addition to the priced global core products, economies also priced regional products for regional comparisons.

a. Excluding housing and private education, which are counted separately in this table.

b. Two regions—Africa and Western Asia—provided remunerations for all four levels of experience, in addition to average remunerations, and the remaining regions provided average remunerations only. See the section on compensation of government employees later in this chapter for more information on government remunerations.

c. The quantity data for housing were used for linking the CIS and Eurostat-OECD.

d. The Eurostat-OECD implements a different approach for education, and thus it does not provide data on private education or on the compensation for education-related occupations.

importance of each product specified. Inclusion in the final regional list depended on a product's availability within the region (the number of economies in the region that could price it) and on its importance within the region (the number of economies in the region that could price it and for which it was important). When finalizing its lists, a region endeavored to ensure that, as a minimum, each economy in the region could price at least one global core product and three regional products for a basic heading. Global core products selected for the final regional list were treated as regional products meeting the same validation criteria and included in the calculation of regional PPPs.

With the exception of the CIS and Eurostat-OECD, the regions did not draw up their own product lists for the special price surveys. Instead, as in ICP 2005, the global core product lists for the special price surveys doubled as the regional product lists for the surveys. The CIS and Eurostat-OECD identified products on their lists that matched those on the global lists.

Survey frameworks

The objective of the main price survey and the special price surveys was to collect prices that were consistent with the prices underlying the national expenditures that economies had estimated for 2011. Because their estimates covered the whole of their economic territory throughout 2011, the prices collected had to be the national annual averages for 2011. Moreover, because economies compiled their estimates broadly in line with SNA93, the prices had to be those that purchasers actually paid to sellers, although, for practical reasons, they had to be collected from sellers rather than purchasers. The fact that the average prices had to be national averages and the averages had to be derived from the prices observed at sales outlets had implications for the survey framework, particularly that for the main price survey.

When drawing up the survey framework for the main price survey, economies were required to ensure that their economic territories were stratified so that all parts of the territory were represented. Balanced coverage of both urban and rural areas is important because the two frequently exhibit different pricing patterns and diverging price levels. Underrepresentation of rural areas, for example, could result in overestimation of the national price level for those items such as food products whose price levels are generally lower in rural areas than in urban areas. However, not all types of products are available in rural areas, and when this occurs the urban price level is also the national price level.

Prior to selecting outlets, economies were required to classify the outlets in each geographical stratum by type. For ICP purposes, nine categories of outlets were identified: supermarkets and department stores; kiosks, neighborhood shops, grocery stores, and the like; open and closed markets; mobile shops and street vendors; wholesale stores and discount shops; specialized shops; private service providers; public service providers; and Internet shopping sites. Later, when selecting outlets, the national coordinators were expected to ensure that each outlet type was adequately represented in order to accommodate the different distribution profiles of different product types during price collection. In other words, the mix of outlet types selected would allow for the possibility that the mix of outlet types visited to price foodstuffs would not necessarily be the same as the mix visited to price clothing or the mix visited to price household appliances. In making the selection, the national coordinators had to take into account the sales volumes of both individual outlets and outlet types, the variability in prices both within and between outlet types, the location and distribution of outlets, and the number of outlets per outlet type.

A similar approach was adopted for the special price surveys, although the selection of outlets was more focused: real estate agents (plus newspapers and the Internet) for the rental part of the housing survey; pharmacies and private providers of health services for the private health survey; private schools and colleges engaged in primary, secondary, or tertiary education for the private education survey; shops and specialist stores selling audiovisual, photographic, and information processing equipment for the survey of fast-evolving technology products; central, state, and local government units for the survey of the compensation of general government employees;

producers, importers, and distributors of equipment goods for the survey of machinery and equipment; and construction contractors for the construction and civil engineering survey.

The selection of products to be priced was made by basic heading. Economies based their selection on the availability of the product in the economic territory and the importance of the product relative to other products in the basic heading. For the main price survey, economies were required to select at least one global core product and three regional products from the combined global-regional product list for each basic heading. The heterogeneity and importance of the basic heading were deciding factors in the number of products that were selected for the product list for the basic heading. They were also factors influencing the number of products that economies selected to price for the basic heading.

Consumer goods and services (main survey)

As noted, the main survey covered all consumer goods and services except housing services, private health, private education, and fast-evolving technology products; special surveys were organized for these areas (these surveys are described in the sections that follow). Prices for the main survey were collected from a sample of outlets in rural and urban areas. Most economies collected prices quarterly throughout 2011. The main exceptions were the Eurostat-OECD economies, which surveyed prices over three years: 2010, 2011, and 2012, and adjusted the prices to averages for 2011 using detailed times series price indexes. In addition, the majority of Eurostat-OECD economies collected prices only in their capital cities. (How these prices were converted to national average prices for 2011 is explained in appendix C.) Some African economies began by collecting prices monthly, but later changed to quarterly price collection.

When selecting products to price from the regional product list, economies were asked to take into account the importance of the products listed by classifying those products that were available in their economic territory as either important (it would account for a significant share of the basic heading expenditure in

their economy) or less important (it would account for a relatively small share). Economies were expected to price important products and a selection of less important products in order to provide the links with prices collected by other economies. When reporting prices, economies were required to indicate which of the products priced were important and which were less important. Important products were given a bigger weight than less important products when calculating an economy's PPP for a basic heading.

Housing Services

The household expenditure on housing services constitutes a single basic heading in the ICP classification and covers actual rents and imputed rents. Actual rents are the rents that tenants pay to the owner of the dwelling they are leasing. Imputed rents are estimates of the rents that owner-occupiers would have to pay for their dwelling if they rented it instead of owning it. SNA93 recommends that imputed rents be estimated using the actual rents paid for equivalent dwellings. An equivalent dwelling is one that is the same type and size, has the same facilities, and is in the same location with the same neighborhood amenities. For economies applying the rental equivalence method, the price approach can be used to compute the PPPs directly for both actual and imputed rents.

Implementation of the rental equivalence method requires a well-organized and representative rent market. Economies in which such a market does not exist cannot use rental equivalents to estimate imputed rents, and so another method has to be employed. SNA93 recommends summing the costs of production of the housing service, but in ICP 2011 this was not the alternative followed by the majority of economies not using the rental equivalence method. Instead, a variety of approaches that did not conform to international standards were used—such as not making an imputation, making an imputation only for urban areas, or asking owner-occupiers what rent they would pay if they rented their dwelling—and the expenditure estimates that resulted were of poor quality. In economies that did not apply the rental equivalence method, the PPPs for housing services were obtained indirectly using the quantity approach.

The special survey for housing services was designed to collect data for both the price approach and the quantity approach. For the price approach, the global core product list specified 54 dwellings of which 12 were traditional dwellings and 42 were modern dwellings. Traditional dwellings were specified by their size, facilities, and age. The facilities identified were electricity, inside water, private toilet, and private kitchen. Some of the traditional dwellings had all the facilities, some had none, and the others had various combinations. Modern dwellings were broken down by type—individual single-family house or villa, detached or row house, studio apartment, one-bedroom apartment, and two-bedroom apartment—and then by size and age. All modern dwellings were specified as having electricity, inside water, private toilet, and private kitchen, and about half were specified as also having either central heating or air-conditioning. For both traditional and modern dwellings, age was defined as less than five years or more than five years (although regions could change this parameter if they wished).

Regions were expected to select from the global core product list those specifications that were relevant to the region. When pricing the specifications selected, economies were required to collect annual rents for 2011 in both urban and rural areas and to report national annual average rents. The PPPs for actual and imputed rents were calculated using the national annual average rents that economies reported.

Estimating the volume of housing services directly by the quantity approach involves first calculating a measure of relative quantity and a measure of relative quality between economies. Subsequently, the quality measure is used to convert the quantity measure into a real expenditure (volume) measure. Therefore, for the quantity approach the special survey on housing services collected data on the quantity and quality of the housing stock. The reporting form had three sections: the first covered all dwellings irrespective of type and location; the second covered dwellings by type of construction—modern houses, modern apartments, and traditional dwellings; and the third covered dwellings

by location—large urban areas, small urban areas, and rural areas.

For each section, economies were expected to report the number of dwellings, the number of rooms, the usable surface area, the number of occupants, and the land area occupied by the dwellings—these were the indicators for the quantity measure. Economies were also expected to report the number of dwellings with electricity, inside water, private toilet, central heating, and air-conditioning—these were the indicators for the quality measure—as well as the percentage of dwellings rented and the percentage owner-occupied. All economies, including those pricing the rental specifications for the price approach, were required to complete the reporting form for the quantity approach. The data supplied by economies were to refer either to 2011 or to a year close to 2011.

The Eurostat-OECD comparison employed the same dual approach as the ICP regions—that is, PPPs and real expenditures were based on a mix of rental data and housing stock data. The rental specifications used for the comparison differed from the global core specifications, but the quantity and quality data collected were similar.

Private Health

For ICP 2011, the health expenditure was broken down into the expenditure by households and the expenditure by general government. Subsequently, the household expenditure was broken down into the expenditure on medical products (which included pharmaceuticals), outpatient services, and hospital services, and the government expenditure was broken down into the expenditure on health benefits and reimbursements and the expenditure on the production of health services. Prices were collected from market producers for medical products and outpatient services, but not for hospital services (except in the Eurostat-OECD comparison, as explained in appendix C). The PPPs calculated using prices collected from market producers for medical products and outpatient services were used to deflate both the household expenditure and the government expenditure (under health benefits and reimbursements) on these goods and services. The

PPP for outpatient services was also used as the reference PPP for the household expenditure on hospital services.

PPPs for government-produced hospital services, which are supplied free or at prices that are not economically significant, were obtained using the input price approach. For this approach, the compensation that government paid to employees in a selection of occupations supplying medical, technical, administrative, and support services in government hospitals was collected as described shortly. The PPPs were used to deflate the expenditure on government-produced hospital services as well as the government expenditure on hospital services under health benefits and reimbursements.

The special survey for health collected prices for pharmaceutical products; other medical products; therapeutic appliances and equipment; and medical, dental, and paramedical outpatient services. Prices were collected from market producers, generally quarterly. The prices collected were total prices—that is, the total amount paid for the good or service to its provider—which is not necessarily straightforward in the case of medical products. Although the sale of most consumer products involves a transaction between a seller and a single buyer, the sale of medical products can entail a transaction involving a seller and two independent buyers. The seller is paid in part by a household and in part by a second party (such as government, NPISH, or private health insurer). For such transactions, price collectors were required to establish the total price by consulting either the seller or the second party because both would be aware of what the household pays.

Pricing pharmaceutical products posed additional problems. First, the same product can be sold under different names in different economies. For this reason, the identification of pharmaceutical products has to be based on the active substance or active ingredient and its strength. This requires specialist knowledge, which is usually not available in statistical offices. Thus price collection forms had to be completed either by the pharmacist or by the price collector in consultation with the pharmacist. Second, pharmaceuticals may be available as brand-name products or as generic products. Brand-name products are medicines produced and sold by their innovative pharmaceutical companies. A generic product is identical (bioequivalent) to an existing brand-name medicine in dosage form, safety, strength, route of administration, quality, performance, and intended use. Although chemically identical to its branded counterpart, a generic medicine is typically sold at a lower price than the branded product because the drug has already been tested and approved. In general, the only differences between the brand-name product and the generic product are the price and the trade name. To compare the prices of the two directly would lead to biased PPPs. This bias was avoided by comparing the prices of brand-name products with brand-name products and the prices of generic products with generic products. Finally, drugs may be sold in different quantities in different economies. This problem was overcome by converting the price for the quantity observed and reported by the price collector to a price for the quantity specified. When the product was available in a range of quantities other than the specified quantity, the price collector was required to collect prices for the range. These prices were subsequently rebased to the specified quantity and averaged.

Other medical products are sold not only over the Internet and in pharmacies, but also in supermarkets, petrol stations, and low-cost optician chains, whereas therapeutic appliances and equipment are sold by the suppliers of medical equipment. Economies were required to include such outlets in their sample of outlets in proportion to their share of total sales when pricing other medical products and therapeutic appliances and equipment. As with pharmaceutical products, the total price had to be collected.

Total prices were to be collected for outpatient health services as well, but this was not always possible, and the prices had to be estimated. In some economies, households do not pay anything to the private service provider for the outpatient service received because the private service provider is reimbursed by the social security system under a general agreement between the government and private health service providers. In other words, no actual price may exist for a particular service—the government simply pays the private service provider a lump sum payment. This sum may be based on the total number of visits to a given clinic, the size of the population living in a given area, the number of persons registered with the private service provider, and so forth. If the second party is a NPISH or a private health insurer, the situation might be similar— that is, it may not be possible to obtain directly the prices related to a certain individual service. Economies were required to consult with health service experts to identify the best way of establishing reliable estimates of the total prices paid for the outpatient health services specified.

Private Education

The ICP expenditure classification distinguishes between the expenditure on education by households and the expenditure on education by general government. The expenditure on education by NPISHs is not identified separately, although it is included in the total individual consumption expenditure reported for NPISHs. PPPs for government expenditure on education were obtained using the input price approach. For this, the compensation that government paid to employees in a selection of occupations supplying educational, administrative, and support services in government schools and colleges was collected as described shortly. PPPs for household expenditure were calculated using the tuitions collected by the special survey for private education.

The special survey collected tuitions from private schools and colleges for seven global core products: primary education; lower secondary education; upper secondary education; tertiary education: a degree in computer science; tertiary education: a degree in the humanities or social sciences; a foreign language course; and a private lesson in mathematics outside school hours. For primary, secondary, and tertiary education, economies collected annual tuition fees. For the language course and the private lesson, economies collected hourly fees. Both the tuition fees and the hourly fees were to cover only the cost of education. Expenditures on educational materials

(textbooks and stationery) and on educational support services (health transport, catering, and accommodation) were not to be included. Schools and colleges often reported fees that covered the cost of educational materials and support services as well as the cost of tuition. When this happened, economies were required to estimate the cost of the materials and support services and subtract it from the total reported to obtain the cost of education.

The tuition fees supplied by economies were the annual averages for 2011. However, the academic and school years do not necessarily coincide with the calendar year, and economies were expected to adjust fees to a calendar year basis if the academic or school year extended over two years. For example, if the academic or school year ran from the beginning of September to the end of June, economies were required to add six-tenths of the fees for the school year that began in September 2010 to four-tenths of the fees for the school year that began in September 2011.

The tuition fees and hourly fees that economies reported were supposed to be national averages as well as annual averages. Fees were collected directly from a selection of private schools and colleges. The selection reflected the distribution of all types of private schools and colleges operating in the capital city, in urban areas other than the capital city, and in rural areas.

Economies in the Eurostat-OECD comparison did not follow the price approach just described. They did not collect tuitions from private schools and colleges, nor did they collect the compensation of employees from government schools and colleges. Instead, the quantity approach was applied, with a quality adjustment based on country scores from the Programme for International Student Assessment (PISA). Real expenditures were estimated directly, and PPPs were estimated indirectly, as explained in appendix C.

Fast-Evolving Technology Products

Products based on fast-evolving technology tend to have short life cycles, making it difficult for economies to price the same product throughout the reference year. A further complication is that new models are not necessarily introduced in all economies at the same time, or they are introduced with minor variations between economies. To deal with this problem, the following approach was adopted. It involved pricing two sets of products: one in the first half of the year and the other in the second half of the year. The approach was limited to audiovisual equipment, photographic equipment, and information processing equipment for which the problem is especially acute. Together, the three types of equipment constitute a single basic heading.

Prior to price collection, a set of products was selected for the basic heading and included in the global core product list. The selection focused on products that were widely available and had a small number of alternative models and that had a relatively long life span with clearly identified replacement models. Particular care was taken to ensure that all the key price-determining parameters of the selected products were included in their specification. Rather than specifying a brand and a specific model, the product list specified a brand and a series. Price collectors were expected to price the cheapest model available in the series specified. If models in the series were not available, price collectors had to price a model from another series whose parameters were the closest to those specified and note the model number and differences in parameters. Economies priced this set of products during the first and second quarters of 2011. Meanwhile, a second set of products was selected and specified for the global core product list. Economies priced this second set in the third and fourth quarters of 2011. PPPs were calculated using products from both sets.

Compensation of government employees

Government provides households with both collective and individual services. Collective services are produced by government, whereas individual services can be produced by government, or they can be purchased by government from market producers. The individual services that government purchases from market producers are called market services. Their outputs can be valued and their PPPs calculated using the economically significant prices at which they are sold. The collective and individual services that government produces itself are nonmarket services. They are not sold at economically significant prices, and, in the absence of such prices, their outputs are valued by summing the costs of their production, and their PPPs are calculated using the prices of inputs. In practice, prices are collected only for the most important input, compensation of employees. Reference PPPs are used for the other inputs.

ICP comparisons used the input price approach to compute PPPs for collective services and for the two most important individual services produced by government: health and education. Reference PPPs were used for the other individual services produced by government—housing, recreation and culture, and social protection.

The special survey of the compensation of government employees for ICP 2011 covered a selection of occupations in collective services, public health services, and public education services. This selection was made so that they represent the various education and skill levels that are commonly found among employees working in these three government services. Thirty-seven occupations were included in the selection. The civilian occupations were defined using job descriptions taken from the International Standard Classification of Occupations 2008 (International Labor Office). These descriptions specified the occupations in terms of the kind of work done.

Of the 37 occupations, 23 were for collective services, 10 for public health services, and 9 for public education services. Thirty-four of the occupations were specific to only one service, one was common for two services, and two were common to all three services. Because work such as cleaning and catering were outsourced to private companies on contract to the government, some occupations were no longer relevant in some economies and could not be priced by them.

The national coordinators were expected to provide the compensation of employees for as many of the selected occupations as possible. Compensation of employees as defined in SNA93 comprised the basic salary or wage, allowances and cash payments over and above the basic salary or wage, income in kind, and the employer's social security contribution.

When the government did not place social security payments in a separate fund for its employees, economies were required to report the imputed contribution calculated in the same way as in their national accounts. For each occupation, economies were expected to supply compensation data for an employee at four stages of his or her career: starting level, after 5 years, after 10 years, and after 20 years.

The national coordinators were required to use official government pay scales to determine the compensation of employees in the selected occupations. The basic salaries and wages laid down in government pay scales were the basis for the compensation of employees by government. Once the basic salary or wage was established for an occupation, computing the compensation of employees was relatively straightforward because the other components of compensation of employees are normally related to the salary scale by being defined as percentage additions to the basic salary or wage.

Pay scales are typically made up of grades. Each grade has a number of levels, and each level has a number of steps. Grades usually reflect education and skill requirements; levels, experience and responsibility; and steps, years of service. Each step is generally 12 months, although steps of 18 or 24 months are not uncommon. To derive the compensation of employees for the selected occupations and career stages, the national coordinators had to first locate the grade, level, and step for each selected occupation and career stage in the government pay scale. This provided the basic salary or wage for the selected occupation and career stage, which could then be augmented as appropriate to arrive at the compensation of employees for the occupation and career stage.

The compensation of employees reported for each selected occupation and career stage had to be annual. When there were revisions of the salary or wage scales during the reference year, a weighted average was calculated based on the number of months the original scale and the revised scale were operational. The compensation of employees also had to be the national average, taking into account the discrepancies in compensation that may arise between the several levels of government—that is, between central, regional, state, and local governments—and within the same level of government—that is, between different ministries and departments of central government or between different regional governments, state governments, or local governments. The national coordinators were advised to calculate weighted averages based on the number of employees.

For each occupation and career stage, the national coordinators also had to supply information on the official and actual hours worked per week, the number of workdays per week, the number of days of paid annual leave, and the number of public holidays falling on working days during the reference year. These data were needed to compute compensation per hour. PPPs were calculated using the compensation per hour for the 37 occupations, each with four career stages, and also for the average remuneration for each occupation.

Economies in the Eurostat-OECD comparison reported the compensation paid to government employees working in selected occupations in collective services and public health services. For the ICP 2011 global comparison, they also reported the compensation paid to government employees working in selected occupations in public education services. There was a good overlap between occupations selected for the global list and those selected for the Eurostat-OECD list. However, the compensation of employees reported for an occupation was the average compensation paid for the occupation for a standardized number of working hours and did not take into account career stages. Moreover, it was extracted from the government payroll and not from government pay scales.

Machinery and equipment

To determine the availability of the products initially selected as core products for the special survey of machinery and equipment prices, the Global Office carried out a pilot study in nine economies. The list of core products priced during the special survey was based on the findings of the pilot study. In line with the ICP expenditure classification, the list covered eight basic headings as shown in table 3.2. For each basic heading, a number of products were chosen, and for each product a number of items were specified. Item specifications were either

Table 3.2 Machinery and Equipment Core Product List, ICP 2011

Basic heading		Item			
Code	Title	Product	Brand-specific	Generic (no brand)	Total
150111.1	Fabricated metal products except machinery and equipment	5	3	6	9
150112.1	General-purpose machinery	9	14	6	20
150113.1	Special-purpose machinery	24	33	17	50
150114.1	Electrical and optical equipment	25	41	15	56
150115.1	Other manufactured goods not elsewhere classified (n.e.c.)	4	5	3	8
150121.1	Motor vehicles, trailers, and semitrailers	5	13	4	17
150121.2	Other road transport	1	2	1	3
150311.1	Other products	4	14	0	14
Total		**77**	**125**	**52**	**177**

Source: ICP, http://icp.worldbank.org/.

brand-specific, with the SPD specifying a brand and model as well as the item's technical parameters, or generic, with the SPD specifying the item's technical parameters only; no brand and model was specified. Seventy percent of the item specifications on the list were brand-specific.

When pricing items, economies were expected to match the brand, model, and technical parameters of the brand-specific specifications and the technical parameters of the generic specifications, but this was not always possible. With brand-specific specifications, the brand may have been available in the economy's market but not the model; with generic specifications, the technical parameters of the items in the economy's market may not have matched exactly the technical parameters of the specified item. In such circumstances, economies were expected to price items that were comparable—that is, items in the economy's market with technical parameters that came closest to the technical parameters of the brand and model specification or the generic specification. To help economies identify comparable items, item specifications listed up to 12 key parameters in approximate order of importance. Matching was not just a question of counting the number of parameters that did or did not match, but also one of taking into account the degree to which the parameters differed. Items with near misses on most parameters could still be an acceptable substitute for the item specified.

Economies collected prices only for new products, even though in some economies a significant proportion of the capital formation in machinery and equipment consists of imported second-hand products. So far it has proven impossible to collect prices for comparable second-hand machines and equipment. Experimental pricing of such goods has revealed that there is considerable variation in the quality of the second-hand items priced by different economies and that substantial quality adjustments would be needed to make the prices comparable. Such quality adjustments are not feasible in practice. The PPPs calculated for new products would be appropriate only for deflating the expenditures on machinery and equipment recorded in the national accounts (which include expenditures on both new and second-hand products) if the relative prices of new products are similar to the relative prices of second-hand products. This is probably a reasonable assumption, but because of the lack of comparability between second-hand equipment goods, it is difficult to establish empirically.

In ICP 2011, economies were expected to report national average prices. In some small economies, it was sufficient to collect prices in only a single location, such as the capital city or the largest industrial or commercial urban area, but in larger economies prices had to be collected in several urban areas. In economies in which a single dealer had exclusive rights to sell the type of equipment specified, a single price observation was sufficient, but in economies in which there were several distributors of the specified equipment, several price observations were needed to establish the national average price. The national average prices reported were also to be the average prices for the reference year—that is, the average of prices collected at regular intervals throughout the year. However, experience suggests that if all economies price equipment goods during the same period, there is no need to collect prices throughout the year. Economies were asked to collect midyear prices for 2011.

Economies obtained prices for the specified items of machinery and equipment either directly from producers, importers, and distributors, or from their catalogues and websites. Some economies were able to use prices from their producer price index or their import price index. Economies had to ensure that the prices collected were purchasers' prices and included import duties and other product taxes actually paid by the purchaser, the costs of transporting the good to the place it would be used, any charges for installing the good so that it was ready for production, and the discounts generally available to most purchasers for most of the year. Economies adjusted the prices when they did not meet these requirements.

Experience from previous rounds of the ICP has shown that national statistics institutes generally lack the specialized knowledge required to collect prices for most types of machinery and equipment. Economies were encouraged to hire outside experts to carry out the special survey.

Construction

Gross fixed capital formation in construction is broken down into three basic headings in the ICP expenditure classification. Each basic heading covers a specific type of structure: residential buildings, nonresidential buildings, and civil engineering works. PPPs are calculated for each of these basic headings separately, and they are then aggregated to provide the PPPs for construction as a whole. The usual procedure in ICP comparisons is to calculate PPPs directly using the prices of products that are comparable across the participating economies. In principle, the PPPs for construction should be obtained in a

similar manner. In practice, however, the complexity and the country specificity of the products of the construction industry mean that the products are basically unique. For example, no two economies build exactly the same kind of house or power station. It is therefore difficult to price construction products that are comparable between economies.

One way of getting around this difficulty is for economies to price a common set of standard construction projects covering different types of buildings and civil engineering works. The projects are fictitious in that they are not actually built, but they are based on actual structures and on the materials and methods commonly used in their construction. For each project, the components required for its construction are itemized and defined in a product specification called a bill of quantities. A quantity is specific for each component. Multiplying the quantity by the unit price of a component yields a total price for the component. Summing the total prices of all components itemized in the bill yields the overall price for the project. Because all economies pricing a specific project price the same bill of quantities, their overall prices for the project are the prices of a comparable product. PPPs for construction are calculated using the overall prices of the projects.

The bill of quantities approach was used in the Eurostat-OECD comparison. Of the 11 standard construction projects specified, economies were expected to price seven of them. The unit prices used to price the projects were based on the prices of successful tenders submitted during the reference year. Strictly speaking, tender prices are price forecasts for construction activity that will take place after the reference year. However, the overall price derived using tender prices is considered an acceptable proxy for the purchaser's price of a project in the reference year because it includes the contractor's markups for general site costs, head office overheads, and profit, as well as the percentage addition for the professional fees of architects and engineers.

A modified version of the bill of quantities approach was applied in the CIS comparison. CIS economies were required to provide unit prices for 66 inputs covering materials and labor. The unit prices were used by the regional coordinating agency to price a variety of model structures. The PPPs for construction were calculated using the overall prices for the model structures. The bills of quantities for the models were simpler and less complete than those in the Eurostat-OECD comparison, but the range of structures specified was more extensive.

The other ICP regions did not use the bill of quantities approach in their comparisons, chiefly because of the cost of hiring construction experts to price the bills of quantities for the economies. Instead, they followed the approach developed by the Global Office for ICP 2011. Rather than trying to collect prices for comparable products, economies were required to collect unit prices for a common set of inputs. The unit prices were to be those paid by construction contractors to their suppliers—that is, the purchasers' prices complete with nondeductible taxes and discounts. The inputs did not include the contractors' markups or professional fees, and so these were assumed to be proportional to the overall costs. The unit prices had to be national averages, and they had to be collected in a number of different locations in line with the size of the economy's economic territory and the price variation within it. They also had to be annual averages or midyear prices.

More specifically, economies were expected to report unit prices for 38 kinds of basic building materials, the hourly cost of hiring five types of building equipment with and without an operator, and the hourly rate of compensation paid to construction workers in seven occupations. The 55 inputs constituted the global core product list for the special survey of construction prices. The same 55 inputs were listed for each of the three basic headings. In addition to providing unit prices for the inputs that were available, the national coordinators had to indicate the types of structures for which each of the inputs was commonly used: residential buildings, nonresidential buildings, or civil engineering works. In other words, the national coordinators had to identify the basic headings for which inputs were available and important and the basic headings for which they were relevant (e.g., roofing tiles in civil engineering projects).

In addition to unit prices, economies were required to provide information on the average resource mix for each basic heading—that is, the percentages of total expenditure on the basic heading that were spent on materials, equipment hire, and labor. The percentage shares were used to derive expenditure weights for three subheadings—materials, equipment hire, and labor—within the basic heading. PPPs were calculated separately for each subheading using the unit prices of the relevant inputs. PPPs for the basic heading were obtained by aggregating the PPPs of its subheadings with subheading expenditure weights.

No adjustments were made for differences in productivity across the participating economies because the weights supplied for each economy to combine labor, materials, and equipment hire would differ according to the productivity level in each economy. In effect, the underlying assumption was that total factor productivity was identical across participating economies.

DATA VALIDATION

Prices

Before the PPPs for the basic headings were calculated, the prices on which they were to be based were checked and corrected for any nonsampling error. The process of checking and correcting the prices is called validation, and a nonsampling error is the error that occurs during the collection and processing of price data. The objective of the validation process was to minimize the incidence of nonsampling error through editing and verification. Editing is the process of checking the prices for possible errors. Verification is the process of either confirming prices or correcting those prices identified as possibly wrong.

In ICP 2011, validation had three distinct stages. The first was the intra-economy or national validation stage during which the prices collected by a single economy were edited and verified. The second was the intereconomy or regional validation stage during which the prices collected by all economies participating in a regional comparison were edited and verified. And the third was the interregional or global validation stage during which the prices collected for global core products—prices that had already been edited and verified within regions during the intereconomy validation—were edited and verified across all economies and all regions. The Global Office supplied custom-built software for each stage of validation.

Intra-economy validation was directed at an economy's individual price observations and the average prices to which they gave rise. The objective was to verify that price collectors within an economy had priced comparable products and had priced them correctly. It was carried out by the economy's national coordinating agency (NCA). Intereconomy validation and interregional global validation were directed at the average prices reported by participating economies and the price ratios that the average prices generated between the economies. The objective was to verify that price collectors in different economies had priced products that were comparable across the economies and had priced them correctly. Intereconomy validation, which was conducted after intra-economy validation, was carried out jointly by the regional coordinating agency (RCA) and the NCAs. Interregional validation followed intereconomy validation and involved the NCAs, RCAs, and Global Office. It was overseen by the ICP's Validation Expert Group.

Validation was an iterative process requiring a number of rounds of editing and verification. Possible errors were found by identifying prices that diverged significantly from the other prices in the series. They were detected by having a measure of divergence that was greater than a given critical value or a value that fell outside a given range of acceptable values. The divergence measures were generally defined by the parameters of the series being edited—parameters such as the average and the standard deviation. Thus if some of the possible errors identified in the initial edit were found to be actual errors and were corrected, the parameters of the price series changed and the divergence measures of each price remaining in the series also changed. A second edit would then uncover new possible errors that needed to be verified. When those that were actual errors were corrected, the parameters of the price series would change again, which could lead to more possible errors being detected if a third edit was conducted. Usually, the number of new possible errors fell as validation progressed, until the return on further rounds was considered marginal and not worth pursuing. Time was also a consideration. The longer the delay between price collection and verification the more difficult it became to correct prices that were wrong.

Intra-economy validation generally consisted of two rounds of editing and verification and took from two to two and a half months to complete. By contrast, intereconomy validation required an average of four rounds of editing and verification and three to four months to complete. This validation took longer because of the interactions that arose during validation between the data sets of different economies. Revisions introduced by one economy could alter the outcome of the edits made on the prices of other economies. The interactions were compounded because not all economies participating in the comparison were covered in the early rounds of intereconomy validation and were introduced in later rounds as their average prices become available. Interregional validation required about the same length of time as intereconomy validation.

Validation focused on two types of nonsampling error: price error and product error. Price error occurs when price collectors price products that match the product specification but they record the price incorrectly, or they record the price correctly and an error is introduced afterward in the process of reporting and transmitting the price. Associated with each price are two quantities: the specified quantity (the quantity to be priced) and the reference quantity (the quantity to which the price collected is to be adjusted). A price error can also arise when, even though the price is correctly recorded, the quantity priced is recorded incorrectly (or it is recorded correctly and an error is introduced later during processing). Thus the adjusted price for the reference quantity (the price that is validated) will be wrong as well.

Product error occurs when price collectors price products that do not match the product specification and they neglect to report having done so. They may not be aware of the mismatch, such as when the product specification is too loose, or they may price a substitute product as required by the pricing guidelines but do not mention this on the price reporting form. ICP price collectors were instructed to collect the price of a substitute product if they were unable to find the product specified. They were further instructed to flag the substitution and to note the differences between the substitute product and the specified product. Flagging would bring the substitution to the attention of the NCA, which, together with the RCA, would then decide what to do with the price collected. It might be possible to adjust the price for quality differences between the product priced and the product specified. Or, if other economies reported prices for the same substitute product, price comparisons could be made for the substitute product as well as for the product originally specified. If neither of these options was feasible, the price would have to be discarded.

Editing for price and product errors involved identifying extreme price observations or outliers—that is, prices found to be either too high or too low vis-à-vis the average according to given criteria. The prices identified as outliers were not necessarily wrong, but the fact that they were considered extreme suggested that they could be wrong—that is, they were possible errors. As possible errors, they needed to be investigated to ascertain whether they were accurate observations. Once this was determined, it could be decided how to deal with them. Outliers found to be wrong were either corrected or dropped, whereas outliers shown to be valid observations were retained, at least in principle. In practice, it was not unusual for valid outliers to be replaced by an imputed value or discarded during intereconomy validation in order to remove the noise they introduced in the data set.

Intra-economy Validation

To establish that price collectors within the same economy had priced products that matched the product specifications and that they had reported prices correctly, intra-economy editing searched for outliers first among the individual prices that an economy had collected for each product it had chosen to survey and then among the average prices of these products. Outliers were defined as price observations or average prices that scored a value for a given test that fell outside a critical value.

Outliers among price observations were identified by two tests: the ratio-to-average price test and the t-value test. The ratio-to-average price test is the ratio of the reference quantity price for a price observation to the average reference quantity price for the product. To pass the test, the price observation's ratio had to be within the 0.5–1.5 range. In other words, an individual price was expected to be no less than half the average price or no more than double the average price. Price observations with ratios that fell outside the range failed the test and were flagged as outliers. The t-value test is the ratio of the deviation of the reference quantity price for a price observation from the average reference quantity price for the product to the standard deviation of the product. To pass the test, the price observation's ratio had to be 2.0 or less. (A value greater than 2.0 was suspect because it generally fell outside the 95 percent confidence limit.) Price observations with ratios greater than 2.0 failed the test and were flagged as outliers.

Outliers among average prices were also identified by two tests: the max-min ratio test and the coefficient of variation test. The max-min ratio is the ratio of the maximum reference quantity price observed for a product to the minimum reference quantity price observed for a product. Average prices with ratios greater than 2.0 failed the test and were flagged as outliers. (A ratio of 2.0 implied a coefficient of variation of between 20 and 30 percent at the 95 percent confidence limit.) The coefficient of variation is the standard deviation for the product expressed as a percentage of the average price of the product. For an average price to pass the test, its coefficient of variation had to fall below 40 percent. Average prices with coefficients of variation of 40 or above failed the test and were flagged as outliers.

The intra-economy validation software developed by the Global Office screened the price observations and average prices for outliers and generated two diagnostic tables: one for price observations and one for average prices. The tables revealed which of the price observations and which of the average prices were outliers to be verified. Verification determined the reliability of the flagged price observations and the flagged average prices or, more precisely, the reliability of the flagged price observations and the price observations underlying the flagged average prices.

This entailed revisiting the outlets where the prices were collected to ascertain whether the products priced matched the product specifications and whether the prices reported were correct. If the product matched the product specification and the correct price had been reported, verification was complete. The outlier was found to be an accurate observation. If the product priced did not match the product specification or if the price had been incorrectly reported, it was necessary to rectify the situation by finding a product in the outlet that did match the product specification and pricing it or establishing the correct price for the product originally priced if it was still available.

After verification, the price observations that were flagged as outliers and found to be incorrect were either replaced by the correct observation or suppressed. Price observations that were flagged as failing the ratio-to-average price test—but not the t-value test—and that were found to be correct were retained, providing that they were part of the population as defined by the rest of the price observations for the product. This was established by recalculating the average price and the standard deviation without including the outlier and using them to derive a t-value for the outlier. If the t-value was greater than 2.0, the outlier, although accurate, was considered invalid and discarded. If the t-value still did not fall outside the critical value, it was considered a valid observation and retained, at least initially. (Later, during intereconomy validation, it was decided whether to keep the observation, to replace it by an imputation, or to suppress it.) Price observations that were flagged as failing the t-value test and found to be correct were removed because they clearly were not part of the same population as the other price observations even when included in the calculation of the average price and standard deviation.

Once intra-economy validation was completed, the economy's NCA provided the RCA with validated average prices for the products the economy had priced, plus the coefficient of variation, the max-min ratio, and the number of price observations for each of the average prices reported. These were reviewed by the RCA before starting intereconomy validation. In some instances, the review prompted the RCA to send the average prices back to the NCA after highlighting the anomalies among them that needed further explanation. The average prices were returned to the RCA after the NCA answered the questions posed by the RCA and corrected the prices as required.

Intereconomy Validation

Intereconomy validation involved editing the average prices reported by the economies for possible errors by assessing the reliability of the PPPs they provided. The objective was to verify that the average prices were for comparable products and that the products had been correctly priced—that is, to ascertain that the economies had interpreted the product specifications in the same way and that they had also priced the products accurately. This was done by comparing the prices for the same product in different economies and by analyzing the dispersion of the price ratios that the average prices generated between economies. In short, intereconomy editing entailed detecting outliers among the average prices through their price ratios. It was during this process that the final selection of products to be included in the final computation of regional PPPs was made.

Because economies reported their average prices in national currencies, the prices could be compared only if they were expressed in a common currency. Once converted to a common currency, the average prices of different economies for the same product could be compared and outliers identified according to predetermined criteria. But prices, even when expressed in the same currency, could not be compared across products directly. Even so, the price ratios of economies pricing a product could be compared with the equivalent price ratios for other products, providing that they had first been standardized. Standardized price ratios for a product are the ratios between the individual average prices of the economies pricing the product and the geometric mean of the average prices of all the economies pricing the product when the average prices are expressed in a common currency (see box 3.1).

Both exchange rates and PPPs were employed to convert the average prices to a common currency; both the exchange rate–converted average prices and the PPP-converted average prices were used to derive standardized price ratios;

BOX **3.1**

Standardized Price Ratios

A standardized price ratio equals $(\text{CC-price}_{1A}/[\text{CC-price}_{1A} \times \text{CC-price}_{1B} \times \ldots \text{CC-price}_{1N}]^{1/N})\, 100$, where CC-price_{1A} is the average price for product 1 in economy A in the common currency. CC-price_{1A} is itself equal to $\text{NC-price}_{1A}/\text{CC}_{1A}$, where NC-price_{1A} is the average price for product 1 in economy A in national currency and CC_{1A} is the currency conversion rate between the national currency of economy A and the common currency. The currency conversion rate is either the exchange rate or the PPP: $\text{CC}_{1A} = \text{XR}_{1A}$ or PPP_{1A}.

---

and both sets of standardized price ratios were edited and verified. The reason for this approach was that the PPPs used to convert the average prices to a common currency were calculated from the average prices that were being validated. This meant that editing began with PPPs calculated from prices that still had to be verified. These opening PPPs were likely to be unreliable, and the flagging of outliers among the standardized price ratios based on PPP-converted prices (PPP-ratios) was likely to be unreliable as well. Exchange rates, however, are not determined by the average prices and remain unaffected by them. It is for this reason that standardized price ratios based on exchange rate–converted prices (XR-ratios) were used in the initial stages of editing and verification. Experience has shown that XR-ratios provide a better feel for the reliability of the average prices reported at the beginning of the validation process. Experience has also shown that many of the ratios initially identified as outliers among the XR-ratios are found to be incorrect.

Intereconomy validation involved several iterations or rounds. After each round, as incorrect prices were corrected or removed, the PPPs became more reliable and so too did the flagging of outliers among the PPP-ratios. As validation progressed, the focus on outliers shifted from those among the XR-ratios to those among the PPP-ratios—the purpose of the exercise was to remove, or at least reduce, the outliers among the PPP-ratios. Thus in later rounds, as the PPP-ratios became more reliable, the outliers remaining among the XR-ratios could be ignored. XR-ratios and PPP-ratios that fell outside the 80–125 range were flagged as outliers requiring verification.

The PPPs used to obtain the PPP-ratios can be calculated using the average prices of products covered by a basic heading or the average prices of products covered by an aggregate. Intereconomy editing is carried out first at the basic heading level and subsequently at the various aggregation levels of the ICP expenditure classification. Validation at the aggregate level places the editing and verification of average prices in a broader context. Are the average prices consistent, not just within the basic heading but also within a larger set of products? Editing at the aggregate level enables inconsistencies to be identified that would not be found by editing solely at the basic heading level. For example, if for the basic heading for alcoholic beverages an economy had priced all its beverages in quarts instead of liters as specified, its price ratios would be consistent within the basic heading, but they would not be consistent with the economy's price ratios in other basic headings. Such errors are identified by editing across basic headings. In this respect, it is useful to validate at different levels of aggregation progressively—for example, checking the basic headings for food products using first the PPPs for the basic heading, then the PPPs for food and nonalcoholic beverages, and finally the PPPs for the household final consumption expenditure.

In addition to flagging outliers among the PPP-ratios, intereconomy validation involved analyzing their dispersion. For this purpose, three coefficients of variation were calculated during the validation process: the product coefficient of variation, the economy coefficient of variation, and the overall coefficient of variation.

The product coefficient of variation measures dispersion among PPP-ratios for a product. It is an indicator of comparability and accuracy and addresses the question of whether the economies pricing the product priced the same product (or an equivalent product) and whether they priced it correctly. The higher the product's value the less likely it is that economies priced a comparable product or, if they did, that they all priced it accurately. The economy coefficient of variation measures dispersion among the PPP-ratios for an economy either at the basic heading level or at the level of an aggregate. It is an indicator of the reliability of the economy's PPPs for the basic heading or the aggregate. The higher the coefficient's value the less uniform are the economy's price levels and the less reliable are the economy's PPPs. Finally, the overall coefficient of variation measures dispersion among all the PPP-ratios for a basic heading or an aggregate. It is an indicator of the homogeneity of the price structures of the economies covered by the basic heading or aggregate. The higher the value of the coefficient the less homogeneous are the price structures and the less reliable are the PPPs for the basic heading or aggregate.

In ICP 2011, the critical value for all three coefficients of variation was 39 percent. Products, economies, and basic headings with coefficients of variation of 40 percent and above were considered to be outliers that warranted investigation. During verification, priority was given to basic headings with a coefficient of variation over the critical value and with a large expenditure weight because they would have a greater influence on the overall PPPs than basic headings with a small expenditure weight.

In addition to their role as editing tools, the coefficients provided the means to monitor progress during validation and, at its conclusion, to assess how effective the whole process of editing and verification had been in reducing the incidence of nonsampling error among the price data. Coefficients should be significantly smaller at the end of validation than they were at the beginning.

The intereconomy validation software developed by the Global Office generated two diagnostic tables: the Quaranta table and the Dikhanov table. Both tables flagged outliers among the PPP-ratios and provided similar measures of price variation for products and economies employing either basic heading PPPs for editing basic headings individually or PPPs for an aggregate for editing across the products and basic headings constituting the aggregate.[1] During intereconomy validation, Quaranta tables were employed to edit average prices within a basic heading and Dikhanov tables were used to edit average prices within an aggregate.

The Quaranta table was originally designed to edit prices within a basic heading. It provides a large amount of information about product prices, but its presentation becomes unwieldy when applied to a large number of products such as those priced for an aggregate. A Dikhanov table contains much of the same information, but it is programmed to hide certain items (which can be called up as required) so that only key series are displayed. The more compact format of the Dikhanov table makes it better suited to editing prices across the basic headings and products comprising an aggregate. Moreover, to assist in the identification of outliers, the Dikhanov table uses different colors to indicate different ranges of extreme values. The coding helps to identify those products having average prices that need verification. But, more important, it makes identification of possible problem economies easier because such economies will have columns with a significant amount of coloring.

Editing a basic heading with a Quaranta table or an aggregate with a Dikhanov table entailed identifying average prices that were outliers or, more precisely, the PPP-ratios that were outliers. The average prices underlying the PPP-ratios flagged as outliers were only possible errors. They were not errors by definition and could not be removed automatically; they had to be referred back to the economy reporting them for verification. NCAs were required to investigate the average prices returned to them as possible

---

[1] The layout of the tables, their differences, and how to read them are described in chapter 9 of *Measuring the Real Size of the World Economy: The Framework, Methodology, and Results of the International Comparison Program (ICP)* (World Bank 2013) and in the chapter on validation tables in *Operational Guidelines and Procedures for Measuring the Real Size of the World Economy: 2011 International Comparison Program* (World Bank forthcoming) and so are not repeated here.

errors and to confirm whether they were correct or incorrect. When prices were found to be incorrect, NCAs were expected to correct them; otherwise, they were suppressed. But if they were found to be correct, a decision had to be made on whether to keep them, to replace them with an imputed value, or to drop them—not necessarily an easy decision. Some of the deviations, even large ones, were legitimate. For example, the prices of economies with particular pricing policies, such as low fuel prices in some of the oil-producing economies, were likely to be flagged as outliers, but they were not incorrect; they were a reality. It would have been wrong to remove them, and, despite the noise they introduced into the data set, they were retained.

If, however, there were no extenuating circumstances, the disturbance created by an outlier could affect not only the PPP of the economy reporting the outlier but also the PPPs of other economies in the regional comparison. In such cases, replacing the outlier with an imputed value or suppressing it were options to be considered. If, within the context of a basic heading, the outlying average price referred to a product that was important to the reporting economy, removing it might not be justified, although imputing a value might be. But if the average price referred to a less important product, removing it was probably warranted. Whatever the action taken, it was decided jointly by the economy's NCA and the RCA on a case-by-case basis.

The mechanics of the intereconomy validation process were straightforward. Validation usually started before all economies participating in the regional comparison had supplied their average prices. The RCA prepared Quaranta and Dikhanov tables for the economies whose average prices were available and sent them to the NCAs for verification. After each round of verification, the RCA changed the regional price database in line with the findings reported by the economies covered in the round, added the prices of economies joining the validation process to the database, and produced new Quaranta and Dikhanov tables. These tables identified new outliers as a result of the changes introduced by the RCA, and these had to be investigated by the NCAs. Gradually, after a number of rounds of verification and after the prices of all

economies participating in the comparison had been included in the database, there was convergence, and the return on further rounds of verification was deemed marginal by the NCAs and the RCA and not worth pursuing. Intereconomy validation was considered to be complete.

Interregional Validation

Intereconomy validation was followed by interregional validation. The process consisted of three steps. The first step was to assess how well the price level indexes (PLIs) and PPPs of the global core products priced in the region reflected regional PLIs and PPPs. This was carried out by comparing the PLIs and PPPs calculated for the complete set of regional products (which included global core products) with the PLIs and PPPs calculated only for global core products and with the PLIs and PPPs calculated for regional products other than global core products.

The second step was to validate the prices of global core products across regions in order to establish whether the global core products priced by the regions were comparable. The large number of economies made it difficult to apply the conventional bottom-up approach of the Quaranta and Dikhanov tables. Instead, a top-down approach was followed. Validation began at the class level (the aggregation level above the basic heading level) and the basic heading level, only descending to the product level when problem cases were encountered. It consisted of the following tasks: (1) calculating PPPs and PLIs for all economies based on global core products; (2) compiling two matrixes showing, respectively, the PLIs and the economy coefficients of variation for all aggregation levels (basic headings and above); (3) flagging basic heading PLIs in the PLI matrix that had a large discrepancy vis-à-vis the PLI for its class; (4) flagging basic headings in the coefficient of variation matrix that had a coefficient of variation of 40 percent or more; and (5) analyzing the flagged outliers using economy diagnostic reports (a summary report containing all information related to a single economy that is provided by a Quaranta table).

Outliers identified in the first and second steps were reviewed by the RCAs and NCAs concerned. Outliers that could not be verified were removed from the global calculation by the Global Office after consultation with the RCAs.

The third step was validating the global PPPs. Validation took place at each level of aggregation, starting at the basic heading level. It entailed looking first at the spread between the Paasche-type indexes and Laspeyres-type indexes generated by the Gini-Éltetö-Köves-Szulc (GEKS) aggregation method between each pair of economies and then at the variability of the indirect PPPs that the GEKS generated to make the bilateral Fisher-type PPPs multilateral and transitive. Paasche-Laspeyres spreads (the ratio of the Paasche indexes to the Laspeyres indexes) with small values indicated that two economies had similar price and expenditure structures; large values indicated that they did not. When pairs of economies had a value greater than 2, their distributions of basic heading PPPs and expenditure shares were reviewed in case one or both were outliers requiring additional investigation. Variability between the indirect PPPs for each economy was measured by the relative standard deviation of the indirect PPPs. When economies had large deviations, their PPPs were reappraised to determine whether they should be excluded from the global GEKS (any such economies were still included in the final results, but they did not contribute to the linking of their region to other regions).

National accounts

The national expenditures that economies supply for an ICP comparison are essential to the comparison, first, because they are the expenditures that are to be deflated and expressed as real expenditures, and, second, because they are the weights used to aggregate basic heading PPPs through the various levels of aggregation up to GDP. Neither the real expenditures nor the aggregated PPPs will be reliable unless the national expenditures provided by economies are comparable—that is, they are compiled using the same definitions of GDP and its component expenditures and are equally exhaustive in their measurement of economic activity. For ICP 2011, the common national accounts framework was that of SNA93. Economies were required to report their national expenditures broken down into 155 basic headings, as defined in the ICP

expenditure classification in appendix D. The classification adheres to the concepts, definitions, classifications, and accounting rules of SNA93.

The same expenditure classification was employed in ICP 2005, and many of the economies participating experienced difficulties breaking down their GDP expenditures into the 155 basic headings. To help economies overcome these difficulties in ICP 2011, the Global Office drew up the Model Report on Expenditure Statistics, or MORES (described in appendix E). It was designed so that economies could estimate the expenditure on each basic heading and, at the same time, document how the expenditure was estimated. The detailed metadata provided by MORES were referred to throughout the validation of national accounts data. In addition to MORES, the Global Office prepared the National Accounts Quality Assurance Questionnaire and GDP Exhaustiveness Questionnaire (both described in appendix E). The former focused on the extent to which an economy's GDP estimate complied with SNA93 and the latter on the degree of exhaustiveness of an economy's GDP estimates. Both were consulted during the validation process.

As for the process itself, it had the same three stages as price validation: intra-economy validation carried out by the NCAs individually, intereconomy validation carried out by the RCAs in consultation with their NCAs, and interregional validation carried out by the Global Office in consultation with the RCAs and the NCAs. Intra-economy validation and intereconomy validation were facilitated by the national accounts workshops that each RCA organized for its region. The workshops gave ICP staff in the region an opportunity to exchange information on how their basic heading expenditures were estimated and to compare the distribution of the expenditures. This promoted comparability. Economies could adopt what they considered to be the better practices of others, and economies having difficulty in breaking down expenditure on a specific aggregate by basic heading could borrow the breakdowns of other economies.

Intra-economy Validation
Before sending its national accounts data to the RCA, the NCA was expected to carry out a

number of basic checks on the data. These included verifying that there was a non-zero value recorded for every basic heading; that negative values were clearly marked as negative; that the value of each aggregate was the sum of its constituent subaggregates; that FISIM was allocated across institutional sectors; and that the values at the level of GDP and main aggregates corresponded to the latest official estimates disseminated by the economy. Basic headings with zero values had to be flagged and justified. For example, an economy that based its estimate of the household final consumption expenditure on a household budget survey would not provide a value for net purchases abroad because the estimate was already on a national basis, but this had to be explained and reported.

In addition to the basic checks, an NCA was expected to check the basic heading expenditure shares for 2011 against the basic heading expenditure shares for ICP 2005 to ensure that they were coherent over time. Large differences had to be flagged and justified. For the same reason, an economy was also required to calculate and compare basic heading notional real expenditures per capita for 2005 and 2011. Large variations had to be flagged and justified. (The notional real expenditure for a basic heading is the estimated expenditure on the basic heading divided by the geometric average of the prices collected for the basic heading. Variations over time can be explained by changes in expenditure, changes in prices, or both.) Having completed these various checks, the NCA submitted the edited data and relevant metadata to the RCA.

Intereconomy Validation

Upon receipt of an economy's national accounts data, the RCA repeated the basic checks just described. In addition to checking that the values at the level of GDP and main aggregates corresponded to the latest official estimates disseminated by the economy, the RCA verified that they were the same as those in the UNSD database. The RCA also compared the basic heading expenditure shares reported for 2011 with those reported for 2005.

After the basic checks, the RCA reviewed the plausibility of the economy's data within the region. This review was carried out by grouping the economies in the region into clusters of similar economies using indicators such as GDP per capita and comparing their basic heading shares of GDP. The comparison was repeated using first basic heading shares based on notional real expenditures and then basic heading notional real expenditures per capita. Finally, the RCA checked for consistency between an economy's national accounts data and price data by looking at the economy's comparison of basic heading notional real expenditures per capita for 2005 and 2011 and analyzing the differences to see from which of the two data sets—prices or expenditures—they arose. Basic headings identified as problematic during these checks were flagged. The RCA then returned to each NCA its national accounts data with the problem basic headings flagged, requesting either justification or correction. After justifying or correcting the problem basic headings, the NCA returned the verified national accounts data to the RCA, which repeated all the checks. This process continued until the data were considered final and included in the regional database.

Interregional Validation

Upon completion of the intereconomy validation, the economy's edited and verified national accounts data were sent to the Global Office. There, they were given a final review before being combined with the national accounts data of other economies in the global database that covered all regions. The review carried out by the Global Office simply repeated the checks already undertaken by the economy's RCA. The difference was that the review took place in the context of all economies and all regions. The Global Office was then able to compare the results of each regional review with the results of the other regional reviews. Problem basic headings identified in this global overview were sent back to the RCA and the NCA concerned for justification or correction. After justifying or correcting the problem basic headings, the verified national accounts data were returned to the Global Office, which repeated the checks. The process was repeated until the data were considered final and ready for inclusion in the global database.

Chapter 4

Methodologies Used to Calculate Regional and Global PPPs

The International Comparison Program (ICP) has three major components. The first component is the conceptual framework, which is determined by the final expenditures making up the gross domestic product (GDP). The second component is the basket of goods and services from which products are selected for pricing: the products are comparable across economies and are an important part of each economy's final purchases. The national annual average prices or quantity data collected for these goods and services must be consistent with the underlying values in the national accounts. The third component is the methodology used to compute purchasing power parities (PPPs), first within regions for the regional comparisons and then across regions for the global comparison.

The PPPs provided by the ICP are based on a large body of statistical and economic theory fully documented in *Measuring the Real Size of the World Economy: The Framework, Methodology, and Results of the International Comparison Program (ICP)* (World Bank 2013). This volume describes the many methods available for ICP 2005, the choices made, and the lessons learned that were applied to ICP 2011.

As described in earlier chapters, the estimation of PPPs begins by breaking down GDP into 155 basic headings. Basic headings, the lowest level at which expenditure estimates are required, are the product groups into which individual goods or services are placed for

pricing purposes. Basic headings fall into three categories. The first consists of the products consumers purchase in various markets. Prices are obtained by means of market surveys. This category is the basis for nearly all basic headings under the aggregate household final consumption expenditure. The second category is housing rents, health, education, government services, machinery and equipment, and construction. These goods and services are difficult to compare and require data beyond what can be collected in market surveys. The third category is those basic headings for which price or value data are either not available, such as narcotics, or too difficult or too expensive to obtain.

PPPs are first computed at the individual product level within each basic heading for each pair of economies being compared. Suppose three economies—A, B, and C—price three kinds of rice for the basic heading rice. For each kind of rice, there are three PPPs: P_B/P_A, P_C/P_A, and P_C/P_B. The basic heading PPP for each pair of economies can be computed directly by taking the geometric mean of the PPPs between them for the three kinds of rice. This is a bilateral comparison. The PPP between economies B and A can be computed indirectly: $PPP_{C/A} \times PPP_{B/C} = PPP_{B/A}$. The use of both direct and indirect PPPs is a multilateral comparison. This means that the PPPs between any two economies are affected by their respective PPPs with each other economy. A change in the mix of economies included in the comparison will also change the PPPs between any two economies.

Different methods can be used to compute multilateral PPPs. The choice of method is based on two basic properties: transitivity and base country invariance. PPPs are transitive when the PPP between any two economies is the same whether it is computed directly or indirectly through a third economy. PPPs are base country–invariant if the PPP between any two economies is the same regardless of the choice of base country. These properties apply for every computational step: computing basic heading PPPs between economies, aggregating basic heading PPPs to the within-region GDP, linking basic heading PPPs across regions, and then computing global PPPs.

Another property underlying the computational steps to obtain PPPs for ICP 2011 (and ICP 2005) is that economies are treated equally regardless of the size of their GDP. Weights based on basic heading expenditures are used in the methodology to weight a group of basic headings to an aggregate level. Therefore, PPPs are first weighted using economy A's weights (Laspeyres index), and then weighted again using economy B's weights (Paasche index). Each index provides a weighted average of the PPP between economy A and economy B. To maintain symmetry, the geometric mean is taken of the two aggregated PPPs for every pair of economies in the comparison. The result is a Fisher index. For each pair of economies, the multilateral PPP is the geometric mean of the direct and indirect Fisher indexes.

This method, however, does not satisfy the additivity requirement. Additivity occurs when the sum of the real expenditures of the basic headings constituting an aggregate equals the real expenditures based on the PPPs for the aggregate. Additive methods have the disadvantage of giving more weight to the relative prices of the larger, more developed economies. As a result, the real expenditures of poor economies become artificially larger and move closer to the real expenditures of rich economies. This is known as the Gerschenkron effect. For uses of ICP PPPs such as poverty analysis, nonadditive methods that avoid the Gerschenkron bias are preferred.

Fixity is yet another concept that determines the methods used. The fixity concept means that the relative volume—the ratio of real expenditures—between any pair of economies in a region remains the same after the region has been combined with economies in other regions.

The following sections are an overview of the methodologies used to obtain regional and global PPPs for household consumption, housing, government compensation, machinery and equipment, and construction.

HOUSEHOLD CONSUMPTION

Statistical theory suggests that a master frame should list every possible product purchased by consumers and the annual expenditures associated with each product for every economy. A random sample of products would be selected for which national annual average prices would be determined. The expenditure on each product would be used to weight product PPPs to basic heading PPPs. The reality, however, is that there is no such list. Although statistical theory can be used to determine the number of products to be priced, it is left to the regional and national coordinators using their expert judgment to select the actual products out of the thousands of possibilities. *Measuring the Real Size of the World Economy* (World Bank 2013) provides guidelines on the number of products to be priced. For example, it recommends that 10–15 products be priced for the rice basic heading compared with 70–100 for the garment basic heading. Rice is a relatively homogeneous product, although it is necessary to specify the different varieties to be priced. Garments are much more heterogeneous.

Comparability of the products being priced is an essential principle underlying the estimation of PPPs. A dilemma facing the ICP is that, although a product may be available in several economies, it may be a significant part of consumption in only a few. Because no data are available on expenditures for individual products, the relative prices or product PPPs would have to be averaged with equal weights to obtain the basic heading PPP. To overcome this problem, the Eurostat–Organisation for Economic Co-operation and Development (OECD) and Commonwealth of Independent States (CIS) regions adopted the concept of representativity to induce a form of weighting. A representative product is one that is purchased frequently by households and has a price level consistent with the majority of products in the basic heading. Because representative products are those most frequently purchased, it is likely that they have lower price levels in economies where they are representative compared with the price levels in economies where the product is available but not representative. This factor can lead to bias if not taken into account when computing basic heading PPPs.

A simpler method was used in the remaining regions. Economies other than those in the Eurostat-OECD and CIS regions were asked to classify all goods and services for household consumption as either important or less important. Importance is defined by reference to the notional expenditure share of a product within its basic heading. The importance classification is a subjective process, as is the assignment of representativeness, but it is easier to apply. If the expenditure share is thought to be large, the product is classified as important; if the expenditure share is thought to be small, the product is classified as less important.

The steps taken to arrive at PPPs for household consumption within regions took into account the methods used to calibrate within-region PPPs to global PPPs:

- The Global Office developed a list of global core products that would be priced by all economies. These prices would be used to compute between-region PPPs for each basic heading.

- Each region developed its own list of products for its comparison and incorporated as many of the global core list products as possible.

- Each economy within a region classified the products they priced from the regional product list and the global core product list as important or less important.

Chapters 4 and 5 of *Measuring the Real Size of the World Economy* (World Bank 2013) describe the different properties of the various indexes that can be used to compute basic heading PPPs and aggregate them to GDP. The basic methodology used in 2011 was as follows:

- Within-region basic heading PPPs were based on regional product prices and global core

product prices. Product PPPs were averaged to the basic heading using the weighted country product dummy (CPD-W) method, with weights of 3:1 for important versus less important products. The Jevons–Gini-Èltetö-Köves-Szulc* (Jevons-GEKS*) method was used in the Eurostat-OECD and CIS regions to compute basic heading PPPs. This method used the representative classification by giving a weight of 1 to the prices of representative products and a weight of 0 to unrepresentative products.

- All regions used the GEKS method to aggregate the basic headings to higher level aggregates. These multilateral PPPs are transitive and base country–invariant.

At this stage, within-region PPPs are aggregated to the level of household consumption. Chapter 6 in *Measuring the Real Size of the World Economy* (World Bank 2013) reviews the properties of the various methods to link the within-region PPPs. The steps used in ICP 2011 to link basic heading PPPs for household consumption across regions were the following:

- Global core product prices provided by all economies were deflated to a regional currency using within-region basic heading PPPs. The result was five sets of regional prices treated as "super economies."

- The CPD-W over these five sets of regional prices provided between-region basic heading PPPs linking each region to a base region.

- Multiplying the within-region basic heading PPPs by the between-region basic heading PPPs converted them to a global currency. Multiplying the same regional scalar by each economy's within-region PPP converted it to a global PPP. This method preserved within-region fixity, which means the relative rankings between economies in the same region remained the same after linking.

The steps just described were applied only to the Africa, Asia and the Pacific, Eurostat-OECD, Latin America, and Western Asia regions. The CIS region was linked to the Eurostat-OECD region through the Russian Federation and through the Eurostat-OECD region to the other regions, and the Caribbean region was linked through Latin America. These methods are described later in this chapter in the section on special situations.

The concepts and methodology just described were essentially the same for the remaining aggregates, which are described in the rest of this chapter.

COMPARISON-RESISTANT COMPONENTS

Some components of expenditure on GDP have a long history of being difficult to estimate—in ICP parlance, they are known as "comparison-resistant" goods and services. They are found mainly in the basic headings for housing, health, education, collective government, and investment in equipment and construction.

In ICP 2011, different approaches were used to obtain prices and PPPs for these activities. The Global Office consulted closely with experts in the relevant organizations or employed experts on investment in equipment and construction to assist in setting up special pricing lists for the products involved. The requirements for the prices recorded were similar to those for the household final consumption products—that is, they had to be national annual average prices consistent with the expenditures recorded in an economy's national accounts.

Housing

All economies participating in the ICP were asked to collect average annual rents for a global list of dwelling types and dwelling stock data: number of dwellings, usable surface area in square meters, and information on three quality indicators. In addition, national accounts expenditure data on actual and imputed rentals were collected.

Not all economies were able to report rents and dwelling stock data, and some were only able to provide rents for a subset of dwelling types or limited dwelling stock data. Each regional coordinator then decided on the best way to use the collected data for his or her region:

- The Africa, Latin America, Caribbean, and Western Asia regions calculated their regional PPPs on the basis of the rents collected for the global list of dwelling types, relying on the same country product dummy (CPD) method

used for the rest of household consumption but without importance indicators.

- The Asia and the Pacific region, after in-depth analysis of the available data, resorted to using a reference volume approach. This implies that the relative volumes of housing services between economies are equal to the relative volumes of household expenditure, excluding rents.

- The Eurostat-OECD region used a mix of rents and dwelling stock data. Generally, for economies that have a well-developed rental market, PPPs were determined on the basis of the rental data, whereas for other economies dwelling stock data were used to obtain estimates of PPPs indirectly. Indirect PPPs are based on the relationship price × quantity = expenditure. An indirect PPP can be derived by dividing the expenditure on rents from an economy's national accounts by the real expenditure on rents estimated using dwelling stock data adjusted for quality. This is known as the quantity method of estimating real expenditures and the indirect method of estimating PPPs.

- The quantity method was used in the CIS region, which was then linked to other regions using Russia as the bridge country.

The rental data used to link the Africa, Latin America, Caribbean, and Western Asia regions were the same as those that entered the calculation of their regional PPPs. The linking factors for these four regions were calculated by means of the same CPD method used to link the rest of household expenditures. For the Asia and the Pacific and Eurostat-OECD regions, the method chosen was to link them to each other and to the rest of the world through use of the dwelling stock data.

The dwelling stock data provided by the economies were carefully analyzed. The preferred measure of housing quantity—usable surface area in square meters—could not be utilized because too few economies had reliable data. Thus the basic quantity information used was number of dwellings, for which a sufficient number of economies within each region provided an estimate. It was not possible to make further distinctions within total dwellings, which would have enriched the estimations.

The plausibility of each economy's estimate of number of dwellings was evaluated by calculating the ratio of the number of dwellings to the total population. Economies with very high or very low ratios were not included in the linking process. For each economy with a plausible estimate of number of dwellings, the data on housing quality were reviewed. Three quality indicators were available: share of dwellings with electricity, share of dwellings with inside water, and share of dwellings with a private toilet. Only economies for which a plausible estimate for all three indicators was available or could be imputed were included in the linking process.

Government compensation

The main components of the government final consumption expenditure are health, education, and collective services such as general administration, defense, police, fire fighting, and environmental protection. The health and education services provided by government are classified as individual services because they are offered to individuals rather than collectively to an economy's residents. The individual services provided by government are combined with similar services purchased by residents (and nonprofit institutions serving households, NPISHs) as part of the household final consumption expenditure to form actual final consumption. Actual final consumption covers all expenditures on individual services. It is an important aggregate because it enables comparisons of economies that have markedly different institutional arrangements for providing services such as health and education. For example, in some economies these types of services are supplied (sold) largely by the private sector, while in others government agencies provide virtually all of these services. Most economies fall somewhere between these two extremes, and estimating real expenditures for actual final consumption provides a means of comparing economies that are not affected by the extent to which these services are provided (or financed) by either the government or the private sector.

Government-produced services are considered to be nonmarket services because they are provided free or sold at prices that are not economically significant and therefore have no observable value of output. The System of National Accounts 1993 or SNA93 (Commission of the European Communities et al. 1993) recommends that nonmarket services be measured using the input cost approach. In other words, the value of their output is recorded as the sum of the costs of production—that is, the sum of compensation of employees, intermediate consumption, and consumption of fixed capital. In ICP 2011, basic headings were specified for each of these inputs in the ICP expenditure classification, but prices were collected only for the compensation of a range of employees engaged in producing government health, education, and collective services. The compensation collected covered a number of carefully selected and well-defined occupations that are typical of government expenditures around the world.[1]

Measuring the compensation of government employees is a difficult area for the ICP because labor productivity in government varies markedly between economies. Detailed specifications were provided for each occupation, including required level of skill and experience. Because factors such as workers' levels of skill and experience and the availability of equipment such as computers are key elements of such differences in productivity, it was essential to adjust for productivity differences between economies. In some regions, not adjusting for them would have significantly distorted the estimates of real expenditures for government. In some cases, the distortions would have been so large that they would have affected comparisons of real expenditures on GDP. For example, in the Asia and the Pacific region average compensation (based on exchange rates) in the government sector of Hong Kong SAR, China, was about 100 times higher than in the poorest economies in the region. If no productivity adjustments

---

[1] For education, the Eurostat-OECD region used an output approach for the first time. PPPs were based on numbers of students and average student scores from the Programme for International Student Assessment (PISA). These within-region PPPs were linked to the rest of the world using five Latin American economies that have data for both the input approach used by ICP regions and the Eurostat-OECD output approach.

were made, economies in which government salaries were very low would have had very high real consumption of government services compared with the high-income economies in the region in which government salaries were relatively much higher.

Productivity Adjustment for Government Compensation

Productivity adjustments were calculated using capital-labor estimates for each economy.[2] It was not possible to estimate productivity adjustments directly for the government sector, and so they were based on comparisons of economy-wide capital-labor estimates. Productivity estimates were imputed for economies that had insufficient data to calculate such estimates. They were based on the productivity estimates for similar types of economies in their region.

The capital/worker adjustment is straightforward conceptually because it answers the question of how much higher labor productivity would be if workers in the economy of concern had the same level of capital as the base country. The production function framework that was used in ICP 2005 was applied, assuming that output is produced by means of two inputs: labor and capital (World Bank 2008; Heston 2013). It is assumed that output of government services Y is produced using capital K and labor L with efficiency level A:

$$Y = f(K, L, A). \qquad (4.1)$$

Assuming the production function has constant returns to scale and exhibits Hicks-neutral efficiency, (4.1) can be rewritten as

$$\frac{Y}{L} = A\left(\frac{K}{L}\right)^{\alpha} \Leftrightarrow y = Ak^{\alpha} \qquad (4.2)$$

where α is the output elasticity of capital.

The aim is to compare labor productivity y between any given pair of countries i and j (multilateral comparisons). Each country could be at a different point on the production function and thus could have a different

output elasticity of capital. The standard approach to this problem is to define a hypothetical "average" country, with variables denoted by an upper bar, and compare each country to this average. This procedure is akin to the GEKS index number approach, but is based on the Törnqvist index instead of the Fisher index. Relative labor productivity between country i and the average country is then equal to

$$\ln\left(\frac{y_i}{\bar{y}}\right) = \ln\left(\frac{A_i}{\bar{A}}\right) + \frac{1}{2}(\alpha_i + \bar{\alpha})\ln\left(\frac{k_i}{\bar{k}}\right). \qquad (4.3)$$

Following the earlier work on this approach, it is assumed that efficiency in the use of inputs is the same across countries. Once the necessary data are available, adjustment factors for the relative wages (F) can be computed. These are based on capital input (relative to the average country) for country i compared with capital input for base country b in each region:

$$F_{i,b} = 1/e^{(P_i - P_b)} \qquad (4.4)$$

where $P_i = \frac{1}{2}(\alpha + \bar{\alpha})\ln\left(\frac{k_i}{\bar{k}}\right)$ and similarly for base country b.

The adjustment factors, as defined in equation (4.4), are used to adjust the PPP for wages in country i relative to base country b for productivity differences:

$$\widetilde{PPP}_{i,b}^w = PPP_{i,b}^w \times F_{i,b}. \qquad (4.5)$$

Because this model implies that a government worker is less productive in a country with less capital per worker, that worker's productivity-adjusted wage should be higher, which leads to higher input PPPs and thus lower relative output volumes. Another element that would normally lead to cross-country differences in labor productivity, and thus wages, are differences in levels of schooling. Because the ICP wages are collected for precisely specified categories of workers, also distinguished by their educational qualifications, it is assumed that no further adjustments are required. The productivity adjustment would be applied across all categories of workers.

The key input in implementing a capital-based productivity adjustment is an estimate of

---

[2] This section is based an unpublished working paper, "Productivity Adjustment for Government Services PPPs: Alternatives and Proposal for ICP 2011," by Inklaar and Timmer (2013).

capital stocks at current national prices. Capital stocks are estimated using the perpetual inventory method (PIM) and data on investment by asset. In contrast to the approach followed in the 2005 ICP round, in the 2011 round capital-labor ratios were calculated based on country-specific data on capital stocks and capital elasticities. For some economies time series of investment by assets were readily available from national accounts sources. For economies in which this was not the case, the starting point was the ICP investment by asset data. For economies that participated in an ICP comparison before 2011, the benchmark investment shares were used in combination with the commodity flow method (CFM) to estimate the share of each asset in total investment over time. The CFM uses changes in the total supply (imports + production – exports) of a commodity to approximate the change in investment. For economies that were newcomers in ICP 2011, it was assumed that their 2011 asset investment pattern was constant over time.

The investment PPPs from ICP 2011 were available at a more detailed level than was required for the productivity adjustment. As a first step, they were aggregated to six assets using a within-region GEKS procedure and investment shares as weights. As long as the depreciation rates within each of the six assets are approximately the same, this simplification does not lead to a bias in the final PPP. In the second step, the six asset PPPs were combined into an overall capital stock PPP using a within-region GEKS procedure and the capital stocks at current national prices as weights.

The second type of national data needed for a capital-based productivity adjustment is the marginal productivity of capital as reflected in the output elasticity of capital. This is not directly observable, but a common approach is to assume perfect competition in the labor and product markets so that the revenue share of capital can be used instead. In ICP 2011, no information about the revenue share of capital for government services was available, and so the capital share in overall GDP was used instead. It also allowed consistency with the capital stock measures.

Implementing equation (4.4) also requires data on employment. Employment data were taken from the Conference Board's Total Economy Database, supplemented by data from the International Labour Organization (ILO) and the World Bank's World Development Indicators. For economies for which these sources did not provide enough information—in particular in the Caribbean region—the average employment-to-population ratio of the region was used. Adjustments for productivity differences were made to the real expenditure estimates for government in the Africa, Asia and the Pacific, Latin America, and Caribbean regions. No productivity adjustments were applied within the Eurostat-OECD, CIS, and Western Asia regions because differences in labor productivity within each of those regions were considered to be relatively small. However, productivity adjustments were made to all regions when the interregional linking factors were estimated to maintain consistency in the global comparison.

Machinery and equipment

In the ICP 2011 expenditure classification, the category machinery and equipment was broken down into two groups, metal products and equipment and transport equipment, which were further disaggregated into eight basic headings. Economies collected the prices of several specified items within most of these basic headings. The prices included import duties, other product taxes actually paid by the purchaser, the costs of transporting the asset to the place where it would be used, and any charges for installing the asset so that it was ready for use in production. Any discount generally available to most producers was deducted from the price. Only new equipment goods were priced in all economies in one or two quarters, depending on the region.

The procedures followed for collecting prices for machinery and equipment were similar to those followed for household consumption. Detailed product specifications were prepared for a global list that was generally used by all ICP regions for their regional comparisons and again by the Global Office to link the regions. For consistency with SNA93, pricing rules were defined for transport and installation costs, nondeductible taxes, and discounts. Basic heading PPPs were computed using the CPD method—the importance classification was not applied.

Construction

Construction is a comparison-resistant component of the ICP because it is not possible to compare actual construction projects from one economy to another. Historically, the ICP used an output method to price construction. It involved specifying models in bills of quantities for various construction projects such as a dwelling, a factory, or a bridge. For its 2005 round, the ICP changed its approach and introduced the basket of construction components (BOCC) method, mainly because of the greater number of participating economies and the high cost of collecting price data in all those economies for the various models specified in previous rounds. However, problems were encountered in data collection and validation, and so yet another approach was adopted for ICP 2011. Meanwhile, the Eurostat-OECD PPP Programme continues to use the bills of quantities approach, and the CIS economies use a hybrid method that embodies some characteristics of both the input approach and the output approach.

The 2011 ICP construction and civil engineering survey was based on an input approach in which economies priced 50 basic and common resources for construction work that were selected to correspond with the main inputs to national construction output. In addition, information was collected on product relevance, resource mixes (the weights needed to combine prices for labor, materials, and equipment hire), typical markups (overheads, profits, etc.), and professional fees.

The initial proposal included adjustments to the input prices for markups and professional fees, but the data collected on these elements turned out to be patchy and incomplete. Many economies did not provide these estimates, and the data that were supplied proved to be so inconsistent that they could not be used. Therefore, the 2011 construction PPPs for each of the regions coordinated by the Global Office were based on input prices for the three categories weighted together. More than 80 percent of economies reported details of the resource mixes, and weights were imputed for the remaining economies, based mainly on those of similar economies. The PPPs were not adjusted for productivity differences across economies because it was assumed that the different weights used took into account differences in the combined labor and capital productivity—that is, total factor productivity—between economies. In other words, the underlying assumption was that total factor productivity was constant across economies.

The construction PPPs were estimated in four separate but consecutive steps: (1) input prices collected for materials, labor, and equipment were allocated to the three construction category basic headings (residential buildings, nonresidential buildings, and civil engineering works) using product relevance information; (2) PPPs for the input groups (materials, labor, and equipment), or subheadings under the three basic headings, were calculated using the CPD, resulting in nine sets of subheading PPPs; (3) the subheading PPPs were aggregated using resource mixes as weights, resulting in three sets of basic heading PPPs; and (4) PPPs for the three basic headings were aggregated using national accounts expenditure data as weights, resulting in PPPs for the construction category.

Construction PPPs for the CIS economies were linked to the Eurostat-OECD economies using Russia as a bridge (Russia priced construction using both the bills of quantities approach and the CIS hybrid approach). Several economies involved in the Eurostat-OECD comparison also priced the inputs specified for the other regions, which provided a link for construction between the Eurostat-OECD economies and the rest of the world.

REFERENCE PPPs

For basic headings for which no price or other data were collected, PPPs were imputed in three different ways. In the first approach, most missing PPPs were imputed using price-based reference PPPs. This simply means that the PPPs from a similar basic heading or headings became the PPP for the missing value. The second approach was the reference volume method used for housing and described earlier. Finally, exchange rates were used for the two basic headings exports of goods and services and imports of goods and services and the two basic headings expenditures of residents abroad and expenditures of nonresidents on the economic territory. Appendix G provides a complete listing of the reference PPPs and the basic headings for which they were used.

AGGREGATING LINKED BASIC HEADING PPPs TO GDP

At this stage, there was a matrix of 148 economies[3] (Africa, 50; Asia and the Pacific, 23; Eurostat-OECD, 47; Latin America, 16; and Western Asia, 12) times 155 basic heading PPPs. Another matrix of the same size contained 155 basic heading expenditures. A final computational step was to link regions at higher-level aggregates and GDP. The country aggregation with redistribution (CAR) procedure was used for the global aggregation, and it included the following steps:

- A global aggregation that included all 148 economies and 155 basic headings in a GEKS computation provided PPPs calibrated to a global currency.

- To preserve within-region fixity, real expenditures expressed in the global currency were summed to regional totals, which were then distributed within each region according to the distribution from the within-region computations. These results were base country–invariant and transitive, and they preserved fixity.

SPECIAL SITUATIONS

The methods just described were used in the main ICP regions: Africa, Asia and the Pacific, Eurostat-OECD, and Western Asia. This section is an overview of the special actions taken to increase the number of economies included in the global comparison. Those actions included the following:

- The CIS region was linked to the global comparison via Russia, which participated in both

---

[3] The CIS region, Cuba, the Caribbean region, and the singleton economies were linked in a second stage after the 148 economies were linked.

the CIS and Eurostat-OECD comparisons. Because Russia was included in the Eurostat-OECD comparison, its basic heading PPPs were linked to the rest of the world and aggregated to world GDP using the CAR procedure. Global PPPs for the CIS economies were their PPPs from the CIS comparison (Russia = 1), multiplied by Russia's global PPP in the global comparison.

- The Caribbean was linked to the global comparison via the Latin America economies. As an initial step, the 22 Caribbean economies were linked to the 16 Latin America economies, first at the basic heading level and then at aggregated levels. Linking at the basic heading level was carried out by calculating separate sets of CPD-W PPPs for Latin America and the Caribbean, by subsequently calculating a combined set of respective PPPs, and finally by re-indexing the combined set of PPPs in accordance with the intraregional results in order to maintain fixity of both the Latin America and Caribbean basic heading PPPs. Linking at the aggregated level was carried out using the CAR procedure. The GEKS aggregation was carried out first for Latin America and the Caribbean separately and then for the combined set of data. Finally, subregional totals of real expenditures were redistributed in accordance with the economy's real expenditure shares from separate Latin America and Caribbean aggregations in order to maintain fixity of both the Latin America and Caribbean results at all aggregated levels. As in the case of the standard ICP regions, the aggregated PPPs were calculated indirectly by dividing the nominal expenditures by the real expenditures. This approach enabled regional linking of the Caribbean economies, using the Latin America economies as a base, while maintaining base economy invariance and fixity of results for both subregions. As a second step, the Caribbean results were linked to the global comparison using Latin America's global results as a bridge.

- Cuba was linked to the Latin America comparison via Peru for household consumption, government compensation, machinery and equipment, and construction. For housing, Cuba was linked via República Bolivariana de Venezuela, which had a typical housing volume index per capita for the Latin America comparison as well as the dwelling stock quantity and quality data needed for the bilateral comparison. The price and expenditure data used for Cuba in the calculations were expressed in convertible pesos.

- The global results contain two singleton economies that were not part of a regional comparison. Georgia was linked to the CIS comparison through a bilateral comparison with Armenia, and the Islamic Republic of Iran was linked to the Eurostat-OECD comparison through a bilateral comparison with Turkey. The global PPP for Georgia is a bilateral PPP (Armenia = 1), multiplied by Armenia's global PPP in the global comparison. Similarly, the global PPP for Iran is a bilateral PPP (Turkey = 1), multiplied by Turkey's global PPP in the global comparison.

- The Pacific Islands comparison covered only the individual consumption expenditures by households. The islands were linked to the rest of the world through economies in other regional comparisons: Fiji from the Asia and the Pacific comparison and Australia and New Zealand from the Eurostat-OECD comparison.

The PPPs for the CIS, the Caribbean, Cuba, the Pacific Islands, and the singletons were not directly included in the global aggregations as described in previous sections. Instead, they were linked to the global aggregation in a way that had no impact on the comparisons of the other economies.

The results for the CIS, the Caribbean, Cuba, and the singletons are included in the main tables. The results for the Pacific Islands appear in supplementary table 2.12.

IMPUTING PPPs FOR NONPARTICIPATING ECONOMIES

The 2011 round of the ICP attracted the participation of 199 economies. Even so, coverage of the world economy was not exhaustive. Some economies did not participate in the comparison for a variety of reasons, including civil unrest, lack of resources, or no national interest. Although these nonparticipating economies account for a small share of the world economy and world population, it is still important that they be included in any comprehensive measurement of the world's economic size or of world poverty. Thus to provide a more complete set of PPPs for the world economy, the ICP imputed PPPs for 15 of the economies that did not participate in ICP 2011.

For its 2005 round, the ICP imputed PPPs for 42 nonparticipating economies. The drop in the number of nonparticipants in ICP 2011 was the result of the improved coverage in the Latin America region and the introduction of two new regions, the Caribbean region and the Pacific Islands region. Four of the nonparticipants in ICP 2011 participated in ICP 2005: Argentina, Lebanon, South Sudan (as part of Sudan), and the Syrian Arab Republic. Eight of the nonparticipants in ICP 2011 were also nonparticipants in ICP 2005: Afghanistan, Eritrea, Guyana, Libya, San Marino, Timor-Leste, Turkmenistan, and Uzbekistan.

ICP 2005

The regression model used for ICP 2011 was not the same as that used for ICP 2005. The 2005 model is described in the report *Global Purchasing Power Parities and Real Expenditures: 2005 International Comparison Program* (World Bank 2008) as

ln(GDP per capita)
= $a + b \times$ ln(GNI per capita) $+ c \times$ ln(SGER)

where GDP per capita is the ICP estimate based on 2005 PPPs; GNI per capita is gross national income per capita in U.S. dollars estimated by the World Bank Atlas method; and SGER is the secondary (school) gross enrollment rate. The model was originally used to impute GDP per capita for economies missing from the 1993–96 ICP round.

The 2008 World Bank report pointed out that the fit of the model could probably be improved by including additional independent variables, but that a full exploration of various model specifications would have to wait until after the report's publication. Subsequently, the search for a better regression model was carried out, and the alternative model found yielded better estimates.

ICP 2011

The improved method was used to impute PPPs for nonbenchmark economies for ICP 2011. The regression model uses the price level index (PLI) for participating economies as the dependent variable (the PLI is the ratio of a PPP to a corresponding market exchange rate). The PLI with the United States equal to 100 is modeled as

$$PLI_i = a + b \times X_i + e_i. \qquad (4.6)$$

The explanatory variables, X_i, are GDP per capita at market prices in U.S. dollars (based on exchange rates), imports as a share of GDP, exports as a share of GDP, and the age dependency ratio. Dummy variables are included for each of the groups—Sub-Saharan Africa economies, OECD economies, island economies, and landlocked developing economies— and finally the interaction terms of GDP per capita and the dummy variables.

Because the United States is the base economy in the global multilateral comparison, its PPPs are always 1 and its PLIs are always 100. This requires a constraint on equation (4.6) to force those values. The constraint can be written as

$$PLI_{usa} = a + b \times X_{usa}. \qquad (4.7)$$

If (4.7) is substituted into (4.6), the equation becomes

$$PLI_i - PLI_{usa} = b \times (X_i - X_{usa}) + e_c. \qquad (4.8)$$

Both the dependent variable and explanatory variables are normalized by the corresponding values of the United States. In the regression, all continuous variables are in natural log. In fact, there are two regressions, one for the PLI at the level of GDP, the other for the PLI at the level of private consumption. The two regressions are run together using Zellner's Seemingly Unrelated Regression method.

Supplemental table 2.13 in chapter 2 presents the regression results for the 15 economies that did not participate in ICP 2011 for which estimates were imputed using this approach. It shows the regression PLI rebased on the world (world = 100); the PPP based on the United States (US\$ = 1.000)—obtained by dividing the economy's regression PLI based on the United States by its exchange rate; the real GDP (and real GDP per capita) in U.S. dollars—obtained by dividing the economy's expenditure in national currency by its PPP (and its population); and the nominal GDP (and nominal GDP per capita) in U.S. dollars—obtained by dividing the economy's expenditure in national currency by its exchange rate (and its population).

Appendix **A**

History of the
International Comparison Program (ICP)

Statisticians have long recognized that using exchange rates to compare economies' levels of economic activity can lead to misleading results. In particular, the differences in the size of high-income economies with high price levels and low-income economies with low price levels will appear larger than they actually are. This distortion can be avoided by using purchasing power parities (PPPs) instead of exchange rates to undertake such comparisons.

In his study, *The Conditions of Economic Progress*, British economist Colin Clark was the first to use PPPs to estimate levels of real income. The first edition of his study was published in 1940, followed by second and third editions in 1951 and 1957 (all published by Macmillan, London). The first edition covered the United States and 52 other economies. Other economies were linked through a series of bilateral comparisons with the United States. The results were then used to quantify the intereconomy spread in real income per capita and to provide an estimate of world income. Income was defined as consumer expenditure and did not include government expenditure or capital expenditure. For income per capita, total persons employed rather than total population was the denominator. The PPPs were calculated using Fisher's ideal index formula. Referred to as international units, they measured the purchasing power of national currencies over the period 1925–34 based on average prices for the period. In the

second and third editions of his study, Clark increased the number of economies covered and refined the methodology applied.

Clark's pioneering stimulated further research. In the 1950s, the Organisation for European Economic Cooperation used purchasing power equivalents to compare the national products of France, Germany, Italy, the United Kingdom, and the United States. The comparison was subsequently enlarged to include Belgium, Denmark, the Netherlands, and Norway. All final expenditures, including government and capital expenditures, were covered in the comparison. In the 1960s, the Economic Commission for Latin America carried out PPP-based comparisons of real product in 19 Latin American economies; the Council for Mutual Economic Assistance (COMECON) conducted PPP-based comparisons of national income between several central and eastern European centrally planned economies; and the Conference of European Statisticians approved a project to undertake PPP-based comparisons of consumption levels among a small group of market economies and centrally planned economies.

In 1965 the United Nations Statistical Commission (UNSC) discussed the problems inherent in exchange rate–based comparisons and agreed that the United Nations Statistical Office (UNSO)[1] should develop a more suitable

---
[1] Now called the United Nations Statistics Division (UNSD).

215

methodology for making international comparisons of gross domestic product (GDP). In 1968 the UNSC considered a report that outlined a research project to be run from 1968 to 1971 aimed at developing PPP-based comparisons. The report proposed using a small group of economies representative of different income levels, social systems, and geographical areas to test and assess methodology. The UNSC agreed that the project should proceed, and, because the UNSO had only limited resources, asked other international organizations and UN member economies to assist in the project. At this stage, the research endorsed by the UNSC was to cover GDP measured from both the expenditure and production sides of the national accounts. Even so, it was understood that the initial efforts would concentrate on the expenditure side—it was less difficult to implement in practice because a single set of expenditures was involved rather than both outputs and inputs, which gave rise to the added complexity of double deflation.

The International Comparison Project was launched in 1968 as a joint undertaking between the UNSO and the University of Pennsylvania, which established a special unit funded by a grant from the Ford Foundation. The World Bank became involved, providing financial assistance directly and also through a grant from the Scandinavian economies that was channeled through the Bank. The U.S. Agency for International Development and the U.S. Social Science Research Council assisted with monetary contributions. The United Kingdom offered in-kind statistical support for the participating economies. The director of UNSO was responsible for supervising the project. The advisory board set up to provide technical advice considered detailed proposals for the project at a meeting held in October 1969.

One of the proposals discussed by the advisory board resulted in the ICP adopting a concept of consumption that summed the individual consumption expenditures of households and government to obtain an aggregate of total individual consumption called the consumption expenditure of the population (CEP). The objective in measuring the CEP was to minimize the effect on the volume comparisons of differences in institutional arrangements, particularly

regarding the extent to which the government and private sectors provided health and education services in different economies. In this respect, the ICP was more than two decades ahead of the System of National Accounts 1993 (SNA93), which set out the concept of actual individual consumption (defined almost identically to the CEP) as an official national accounts measure (Commission of the European Communities et al. 1993).

Until 1993, the ICP was conducted in phases; after 1993 it was organized by rounds. Phase I had two stages. The first stage was a pilot study based on data collected for 1967 for six economies (Hungary, India, Japan, Kenya, the United Kingdom, and the United States). The second stage was run for 1970 and included four additional economies (Colombia, France, Germany, and Italy) that had not been able to report the necessary data for 1967. The outcome consisted of different sets of estimates, including multilateral comparisons between all 10 economies for GDP and a range of expenditure components for 1970. The results of Phase I were published in 1975 in *A System of International Comparisons of Gross Product and Purchasing Power* (Kravis et al. 1975). The details presented in this publication include the overall results of the multilateral comparison for 1970, a variety of bilateral comparisons for both 1967 and 1970, and the outcomes of various experiments on important issues such as rents, motor vehicle prices, and the consistency of different quantity comparisons.

Phase II included six more economies (Belgium, the Islamic Republic of Iran, the Republic of Korea, Malaysia, the Netherlands, and the Philippines), initially to enable a broader comparison for 1970, but mainly to update the PPPs and associated price and volume measures to 1973. Results for the 16 economies were published in 1978 in *International Comparisons of Real Product and Purchasing Power* (Kravis, Heston, and Summers 1978).

Thirty-four economies participated in Phase III for reference year 1975. In the earlier phases, the detailed characteristics of products in the U.S. consumer price index were used as the starting point for developing the ICP product lists. Later, they were modified in consultation with some of the participating economies, including India and the COMECON group, to make the ICP product specifications more generally applicable—for example, by removing characteristics such as brand name that were specific to the United States. The greater diversity of economies in Phase III meant that the range of products to be priced had to be further expanded so that all participating economies could price a sufficient number of products representative of their expenditures. At this point, the ICP considered the pros and cons of continuing with a single global comparison or moving to regional comparisons that would be linked to produce worldwide results. The trade-off involved in regionalizing the project was improved comparisons between economies within a region but at the expense of the comparisons between economies in different regions because of the difficulties inherent in linking results between regions. In the end, however, Phase III went ahead as a single global comparison, although some regional results were presented as having been calculated for the relevant economies from the globally based results. The results of this phase were published in 1982 in *World Product and Income: International Comparisons of Real Gross Product* (Kravis, Heston, and Summers 1982).

Phase IV saw some major developments in the program. The first was that the number of participating economies almost doubled, from 34 to 60. The second was that the ICP shifted from being a research project to being a regular operational part of the UNSO work program. With this development, the University of Pennsylvania's participation in the day-to-day running of the project ended, although it continued to advise on methodological issues. The third significant change was the regionalization of the ICP. The principal reason for regionalization was the large number of economies now involved worldwide, making it no longer feasible to organize comparisons centrally. Another factor was the decision by the Organisation for Economic Co-operation and Development (OECD) to set up a PPP program for its member economies in conjunction with the PPP program being run by Eurostat for economies in what is now the European Union. In addition to the Eurostat-OECD region, Africa, Asia, and Latin America participated in Phase IV as regions. The regions were linked using the bridge economy

approach in which selected economies priced a range of product specifications from another region to provide a bridge or link between their region and the other region. The reference year for Phase IV was 1980.

The reference year for Phase V was 1985. It saw only a small increase in the number of participating economies, from 60 to 64, with some new economies replacing some that had been in Phase IV but then dropped out of Phase V. Once again, a regional approach was adopted. The regions were Africa, Asia, the Caribbean, and Eurostat-OECD. In addition, three central and eastern European economies were added to the Eurostat-OECD region using Austria as a bridge. The bridge economy approach was again used to link the regions, but some of the links were problematic because of the difficulties several bridge economies encountered in collecting prices for a sufficiently broad range of products from the other region.

Phase VI, conducted with 1993 as the reference year, was the most ambitious phase yet, seeking to produce PPP-based comparisons for 118 economies. In the end, however, only 83 were covered. From the outset, this phase was beset by difficulties. Lack of funding was the major problem, although the lack of overall coordination also led to some major deficiencies in the final outcome. Regional comparisons were undertaken for Africa, Asia, Eurostat-OECD, and Western Asia, but not for Latin America. Moreover, there was no global comparison because it proved virtually impossible to link the regions. In response to these problems, in 1997 the UNSC commissioned a major review of the ICP before further phases were attempted.

The report on the review was presented to the UNSC in 1999. It concluded that PPPs and PPP-related statistics were needed, but that the ICP was not producing these data on a timely and regular basis for a sufficient number of economies as required by potential users. Poor management and insufficient resources at all levels—central, regional, and national—were identified as the principal reasons for the difficulties. Other important contributory factors were inadequate documentation, heavy data requirements that did not take into account the circumstances of individual economies, lack of uniformity in the execution of activities across regions, lack of confidence among economies that others were following guidelines and standards consistently, and failure to involve economies in the editing and calculation stages of the exercise. The report recommended that the UNSC not sanction a new round until at least the management and resource issues had been resolved.

The UNSC's response was to ask the World Bank to consult with other interested parties and propose a strategy to address the deficiencies identified by the review and to draw up an implementation plan for a new round of the ICP. The plan involved mobilizing funds from a variety of sources and establishing a governance infrastructure to provide effective management and coordination between the center and the regions and between the regions and the participating economies. It also involved providing complete and clearly written documentation on the ICP's technical and procedural guidelines and standards. Such guidelines would allow economies to participate in a full comparison covering GDP or in a partial comparison covering actual final consumption, using, as far as possible, regular national statistical programs to obtain price and national accounts data for the ICP and linking participation in the ICP to national statistical capacity building.

The UNSC considered the implementation plan in 2000 and again in 2001. It was reluctant to start another round of the ICP before adequate funding had been secured. However, after the World Bank embarked on a successful major fund-raising exercise, the UNSC agreed to a new round in 2002.

The new round was launched in 2003 and ended in 2008. The reference year was 2005. Regional comparisons were organized by the ICP regional coordinating agencies—the African Development Bank, the Asian Development Bank (assisted by the Australian Bureau of Statistics), the Interstate Statistical Committee of the Commonwealth of Independent States (CIS) with the State Statistical Service of the Russian Federation, the United Nations Economic Commission for Latin America and the Caribbean with Statistics Canada, and the United Nations Economic and Social Commission for Western Asia—and by Eurostat and the OECD. The ICP Global Office was established at the World Bank to provide overall coordination and to ensure technical and procedural uniformity across the regions. The Global Office was also responsible for organizing the Ring comparison that, by comparing a small number of economies from each region across regions, provided the means to link the regional comparisons in one global or worldwide comparison. The final results of the regional and global comparisons were published at the end of 2007 and the beginning of 2008.

ICP 2005 was generally considered to be a success. It covered 146 economies, including the major emerging ones such as Brazil, China, India, Indonesia, the Russian Federation, and South Africa, and its results were published on a timely basis in 2008 in *Global Purchasing Power Parities and Real Expenditures: 2005 International Comparison Program* (World Bank 2008). An important contributory factor was the governance structure that the World Bank had put in place prior to the start of the exercise to ensure that the ICP regional coordinating agencies would deliver within a common time frame regional results that would be consistent across regions and that could be combined in a global comparison. The governance structure was retained after ICP 2005 to commence preparations for the next round of the ICP proposed for 2011. The proposal was approved by the UNSC in 2009. Appendix B describes the governance structure of the ICP.

Governance of ICP 2011

As described in appendix A, the regional comparisons of the 1993 round of the International Comparison Program (ICP) could not be combined in a global comparison. In response to this problem, in 1997 the United Nations Statistical Commission (UNSC) called for a major review of the ICP before it would agree to another round of comparisons. The findings of the review were reported to the UNSC in 1999. Among the principal shortcomings identified were the lack of a formally defined governance structure and the consequent poor coordination between regions. Methods, processes, and timetables were not uniform across regions; results were not consistent between regions; and there was no blueprint for linking the regional comparisons.

One major result of the review was that in 2002 the World Bank put in place a governance structure to ensure that each region produced results consistent with the results of other regions and that each region's results could be combined with the results of other regions in a global comparison. This goal was to be achieved by coordinating the work globally, establishing a single set of standards, providing centralized technical and practical guidance, and ruling on issues that had the potential to be interpreted in different ways in the regions. The structure had several tiers: the UNSC; the ICP Executive Board; the Global Office and global manager; the Technical Advisory Group and affiliate task

forces; the regional coordinating agencies and regional coordinators; and the national coordinating agencies and national coordinators. It contributed significantly to the successful conclusion of ICP 2005 and the timely publication of the results of the global comparison covering 146 economies. The governance structure was retained for ICP 2011.

The *UNSC* was the governing body at the top of the structure. Because it included the national statistics institutes of UN members, the majority of which were participating in ICP 2011, as well as the World Bank and other international organizations, it was well placed to provide overall supervision of ICP 2011 and to review and act on issues raised by the Executive Board in its annual progress reports.

The *Executive Board* was made up of eminent economists and statisticians and experienced statistical managers. Many were heads of national statistics institutes or the statistics departments in international organizations. Others were managers of economic statistics divisions and so were well versed in national accounts and price statistics. The board provided strategic leadership and made decisions about ICP priorities, standards, the overall work program, and the budget. It had a key role in providing oversight of the activities of the Global Office and ensuring that the ICP was completed on time and within budget and that it produced and disseminated high-quality purchasing power parities (PPPs) and real expenditures. The board met twice a year. Usually the first meeting of the year was held back to back with the annual meeting of the UNSC. Between meetings, the board was kept informed about program implementation by means of a midyear progress report prepared by the Global Office. In 2013, the final year of ICP 2011, the Global Office provided the board with a status report every two months in addition to the midyear report.

The *Global Office* was situated in the headquarters of the World Bank in Washington, DC. It was subject to the World Bank's administrative and fiduciary rules and regulations, and on routine matters it reported to the director of the World Bank's Development Data Group. The Global Office carried out the day-to-day work required to implement ICP 2011 worldwide. The *global manager* was responsible for the operations of the Global Office, supported by a team of professional statisticians and administrative staff. The Global Office reported regularly to the Executive Board and, through the board, to the UNSC. Its annual work program and budget required the approval of the board.

The principal activities carried out by the Global Office during ICP 2011 included developing ICP methodologies and standards; preparing *Measuring the Real Size of the World Economy: The Framework, Methodology, and Results of the International Comparison Program (ICP)* (World Bank 2013) and the *Operational Guidelines and Procedures for Measuring the Real Size of the World Economy: 2011 International Comparison Program* (World Bank forthcoming); updating and maintaining the ICP website; drawing up the product specifications for the global core product lists for consumer goods and services, dwelling services, government services, and capital goods; coordinating data collection and data validation across regions; integrating economies not participating in a regional comparison in the global comparison; producing software for data validation and for the calculation of PPPs and related price and real expenditure measures; providing the regions with technical assistance as required; calculating and publishing the global PPPs and real expenditures; and, with the Executive Board, formulating policies such as those on data access and revisions. Particular attention was paid to improving the estimation of GDP and basic head-

ing expenditures, the reporting of metadata, and the establishment of a quality assurance framework. The Global Office also imputed the real GDP per capita of economies that did not participate in ICP 2011.

Helping the Global Office to resolve conceptual, methodological, and technical issues was the *Technical Advisory Group* (TAG). Its members, who were international experts in the fields of index numbers, prices, or national accounts, were appointed by the Executive Board. TAG met twice a year, usually in tandem with the spring and fall meetings of the regional coordinating agencies organized by the Global Office. Working with TAG and the Global Office were three task forces: the *Validation Expert Group,* the *PPP Computation Task Force,* and the *Results Review Group.* The Validation Expert Group was concerned primarily with the interregional validation of the price, expenditure, and other data that regions provided for the global comparison, ensuring that it was carried out correctly following the agreed-on approach and processes. The PPP Computation Task Force focused on calculating the results for the global comparison. It consisted of a group of computation experts who calculated the global results independently of each other to ensure that they converged and were computed in full accordance with TAG recommendations. Finally, the Results Review Group reviewed the plausibility of the global results and their compliance with approved methods and procedures.

The regional coordinating agencies, working with the *regional coordinators,* oversaw the regional comparisons for ICP 2011. They were responsible for developing the regional product lists and selecting the global core products to be included in them; coordinating price data collection, expenditure data validation, and data validation within their region; and compiling and disseminating the regional PPPs and real expenditures. The regional coordinators met regularly at meetings convened by the Global Office to discuss methodology, implementation, timetable, and progress.

In ICP 2011, there were eight regions, of which seven (all geographical) were overseen by the Global Office: Africa, Asia and the Pacific, Commonwealth of Independent States (CIS), Latin America, the Caribbean, Western

Asia, and the Pacific Islands. The eighth region comprised the group of economies participating in the 2011 comparison under way within the PPP program being run by Eurostat, the statistical arm of the European Union, and the Organisation for Economic Co-operation and Development (OECD)—see appendix C. The group consisted mainly of European economies, but also included economies from regions outside Europe. The economies were treated as an autonomous region for the purposes of incorporating them in the global comparison. The regional coordinating agencies for the seven ICP regions were the African Development Bank, Asian Development Bank, Interstate Statistical Committee of the Commonwealth of Independent States, United Nations Economic Commission for Latin America and the Caribbean, United Nations Economic and Social Commission for Western Asia, and Australian Bureau of Statistics. Comparisons in the eighth region were organized by Eurostat and the OECD. The methodology employed was, with some exceptions, basically the same as that used in the seven ICP regions. The Global Office, Eurostat, and the OECD worked closely together during all phases of ICP 2011 to ensure that the economies in the eighth region could be included in the global comparison.

In most economies, different units within their statistical offices and sometimes different agencies were involved in providing the various data sets required for ICP 2011. In such cases, one unit or agency was nominated as the *national coordinating agency* and within that unit or agency a *national coordinator* was appointed. The national coordinator was responsible for assembling the economy's ICP data (national final expenditures; prices for consumer products, equipment goods, and construction; compensation of employees for selected occupations in government; actual and imputed rents; quantitative and qualitative data on the dwelling stock; population; and exchange rates) and transmitting them to the regional coordinating agency. This responsibility entailed ensuring that the economy's data were correctly estimated and complied with ICP requirements; that statistical staff, particularly price collectors, were trained in the concepts underlying the ICP and the practical implications for collecting prices; that data were edited and entered into the ICP database; and that editing queries from the regional coordinator were handled promptly. The national coordinators also attended the data validation workshops held in each of the regions to check the consistency of the data supplied within each region.

Not all economies participated in the framework of the governance structure. Georgia and the Islamic Republic of Iran did not participate in any of the regional comparisons. Their link to the global comparison was established through a bilateral comparison with an economy participating in a regional comparison. Georgia was linked to the CIS comparison through a bilateral comparison with Armenia, and the Islamic Republic of Iran was linked to the Eurostat-OECD comparison through a bilateral comparison with Turkey. The bilateral comparisons were organized and coordinated by the Global Office. By contrast, the Arab Republic of Egypt, Fiji, the Russian Federation, and Sudan participated in two regional comparisons. Egypt and Sudan participated in the Africa comparison and the Western Asia comparison; Russia participated in the CIS comparison and the Eurostat-OECD comparison; and Fiji participated in the Asia and the Pacific comparison and the Pacific Islands comparison. The dual participation was coordinated by the regional agencies responsible for the regional comparisons involved and the Global Office.

Eurostat-OECD PPP Programme

The output of the purchasing power parity (PPP) program jointly managed by Eurostat (the statistical arm of the European Union) and the Organisation for Economic Co-operation and Development (OECD) is PPP-based comparisons of the gross domestic product (GDP) and its component expenditures of economies that are members, or candidates for membership, or associates of either the European Union or the OECD. The program was established in the early 1980s, but its origins can be traced back to 1975 when, as part of Phase II of the International Comparison Program (ICP), Eurostat conducted the first official comparison for the European Community (see appendix A). The comparison covered the nine economies that were members of the European Community at the time: Belgium, Denmark, France, Germany, Ireland, Italy, Luxembourg, the Netherlands, and the United Kingdom.

In the beginning, Eurostat-OECD comparisons were conducted every five years: 1980, 1985, and 1990. After the 1990 comparison, Eurostat adopted the rolling survey approach and began making annual comparisons—see chapter 18 of *Measuring the Real Size of the World Economy: The Framework, Methodology, and Results of the International Comparison Program (ICP)* (World Bank 2013). This approach entails collecting prices for consumer goods and services over three years and pricing roughly one-third of the product list for the household

expenditure each year. Annual comparisons of the household expenditure are made with the prices of products priced in the reference year and with the extrapolated or retropolated prices of products priced in adjacent years. Annual comparisons of other components of GDP—government expenditure and capital formation—are made with the prices collected each year for government services and capital goods.

The OECD also adopted the rolling survey approach and the collection of consumer prices over three years, but it did not adopt the yearly pricing of government services and capital goods that annual comparisons of GDP require. Instead, because of the cost involved in pricing capital goods and the resource constraints of the economies participating in OECD comparisons, it was decided to price government services and capital goods every third year. Thus since 1990, Eurostat-OECD comparisons have been carried out every three years; the comparison for 2011 is the latest. The next joint comparison will be conducted in 2014, with preliminary results becoming available toward the end of 2015.

EUROSTAT-OECD COMPARISONS

Eurostat-OECD comparisons, like ICP comparisons, are made from the expenditure side. Each economy participating in the comparison supplies a set of national annual purchasers' prices for a selection of goods and services chosen from a common list of precisely defined products and a detailed breakdown of the national expenditure according to a common classification. Prices and expenditures refer to the year of the comparison and cover the entire range of final goods and services comprising GDP: consumer goods and services, government services, capital goods, inventories, valuables, imports, and exports. In practice, economies report detailed expenditure data for the complete range of final goods and services, but they report only prices for consumer goods and services, government services, and capital goods because they are not required to price inventories, valuables, imports, and exports. For the most part, the price approach is followed. PPPs are calculated directly, with the prices provided by the participating economies, and volumes are obtained indirectly by deflating the national expenditures with the PPPs. The two exceptions to this are housing and education, for which volumes are calculated directly.

Consumer goods and services are priced over three years in line with the rolling survey approach. Not all household expenditures are covered by the surveys that make up the approach. Housing, hospital services, and education have their own surveys. Housing is surveyed separately because the data sources are different from those for other consumer services. The economies have to supply quantity and quality data on the housing stock in addition to prices. Hospital services and education are surveyed separately because of the overlap between consumer services and government services. Both are purchased by households and are provided as well by government. Moreover, an output-based approach, and not the input-price approach used previously, is employed for both of them. The approach requires economically significant quasi prices for hospital outputs and quantity and quality data for education outputs. The three surveys are conducted every year by Eurostat economies and every three years by OECD economies.

Government services, or more precisely collective services, are priced annually by Eurostat economies and every three years by OECD economies. The input-price approach is still used for collective services. As for capital goods, Eurostat economies price construction every year and machinery and equipment every two years. OECD economies price capital goods every three years.

Both the Eurostat and OECD economies provide a breakdown of their national expenditure for the reference year t in $t + 1$, $t + 2$, and, in the case of Eurostat economies, $t + 3$. OECD comparisons are considered final two years after the reference year, whereas Eurostat comparisons are considered final three years after the reference year. The global results for the Eurostat and OECD economies included in this report are based on the breakdowns of national expenditure that they reported in 2013 for 2011.

ORGANIZATION OF THE 2011 COMPARISON

Forty-seven economies participated in the 2011 Eurostat-OECD comparison: 37 European economies and 10 non-European economies (Australia, Canada, Chile, Israel, Japan, the Republic of Korea, Mexico, New Zealand, the Russian Federation, and the United States). Eurostat was responsible for the European economies and the OECD for the non-European economies. The large number of economies made it difficult for Eurostat and the OECD to manage centrally the six price surveys that constitute the three-year survey cycle of the rolling survey approach. The organization of the effort was therefore decentralized for operational reasons.

The 37 European economies were divided into four groups; the 10 non-European economies were treated as one group. Each group was headed by a group leader. The group leader's principal responsibilities were coordinating the establishment of a product list for the group for each survey and overseeing validation of the prices collected by the group during each survey. Comparisons between groups were made by means of overlap products—that is, products included in two or more group product lists. When drawing up the product lists, group leaders were required to ensure that there was a sufficient number of overlap products to combine all five groups in a single comparison. Eurostat and the OECD supervised the coordination of group leaders and ensured a harmonized approach to the surveys.

Economies were divided into groups solely to facilitate implementation of the rolling survey approach. All other surveys, such as those covering housing, hospital services, education, collective services, capital goods, and GDP expenditures, were organized and coordinated centrally by Eurostat and the OECD.

DATA COLLECTION FOR THE 2011 COMPARISON

The prices for *consumer goods and services* were collected over three years: 2010, 2011, and 2012. Economies reported purchasers' prices for all items except motor vehicles, for which they reported list prices because of the difficulty in establishing discounts for individual transactions. The majority of economies collected prices from a variety of outlets—convenience stores, corner and neighborhood shops, department stores, discount stores, kiosks, markets, supermarkets, specialist shops and shop chains, service establishments, etc.—located in the capital city. Some economies did not limit their price collections to capital cities and collected prices in other cities as well. When averaged, these prices were considered to be national prices. In most cases, however, the prices were not national because they referred to the capital city. In all cases, the prices were not annual because they referred to the month in which they were collected (usually May or November of the survey year).

Economies that collected prices in their capital city provided spatial adjustment factors with which to convert their capital city prices to national prices. All economies provided monthly temporal adjustment factors with which to convert their survey prices to annual prices. Spatial adjustment factors and temporal adjustment factors were supplied for basic headings. Spatial adjustment factors that were relevant to the basic headings covered by a particular price survey were reported one month after reporting the prices for the survey. The temporal adjustment factors, which were monthly and which economies extracted from their consumer price index database, were reported at the end of each year. They covered all basic headings comprising the household expenditure because they were also used to extrapolate and retropolate prices from years adjacent to the reference year.

For the services of cafés, restaurants, and hairdressers, economies reported the prices that purchasers paid for the service specified before allowing for tips. They also provided the global tipping rates that their national accountants use to estimate the total expenditures on these services. The rates were used to adjust the PPPs calculated using the prices originally reported for these services. (Formerly, economies were also required to report a global rate for discounts on motor vehicles and a global rate for tips to taxi drivers. However, this practice was discontinued. Economies found it difficult to supply global rates for discounts on motor vehicles, and, because PPPs are not calculated specifically for taxis but for passenger transport by road in general, an adjustment could not be made.)

The data that an economy provided for *housing* depended on its rental market and how it estimated imputed rents in its national accounts. Economies with a large, representative, well-organized rental market typically estimated imputed rents by the stratification method, whereby the housing stock was broken down by type, size, quality, and location into strata and combined with information on actual rents paid in each stratum. Economies with small, unrepresentative, informally organized rental markets tended to estimate imputed rents by the user cost method, which entails summing all the costs that owner-occupiers incur in owning their dwellings. Economies employing the stratification method reported actual rents and imputed rents for a selection of apartments and houses. The rents reported were the national annual averages for 2011. Economies employing the user cost method provided details on their housing stock. The data on the quantity and quality of the housing stock were used to estimate volumes for housing directly. The link between the two groups of economies was provided by a small subset of economies supplying both sets of data.

For *hospital services*, economies reported economically significant quasi prices for a common set of tightly defined treatments or case types typically offered in general and specialist hospitals. The quasi prices were economically significant in that they reflected the direct, capital, and overhead costs of the case types and influenced decisions on the allocation of hospital resources. They were extracted from databases that health administrations and national insurance funds maintain for the purposes of health financing and reimbursement. Case types referred to groups of treatments that were similar from a clinical perspective and in terms of their consumption of resources. Two kinds of case types were specified: medical, which referred only to inpatients, and surgical, which were divided between those that applied only to inpatients and those that were performed on both inpatients and outpatients (day patients). The specification for each case type included the relevant codes from the *International Classification of Diseases, 10th Revision* (World Health Organization 2008) to help economies locate the case type within national classification and coding systems.

Economies did not collect prices for *education* because volumes are estimated directly in Eurostat-OECD comparisons. In the volumes for 2011, student numbers were measured in full-time equivalents that Eurostat and the OECD extracted from the Eurostat-OECD-UNESCO education database for each of the following six levels of education: pre-primary, primary, lower secondary, upper secondary, postsecondary nontertiary, and tertiary. Results from the OECD's Programme for International Student Assessment (PISA) were used to make quality adjustments at the primary and lower secondary levels. No quality adjustments were made at other levels.

The *collective services* produced by government are nonmarket services that have no economically significant market price. Because there are no market prices with which to value output, nonmarket services are valued in the national accounts at cost. To preserve consistency with the prices underlying the estimates, the current practice in Eurostat-OECD comparisons is to calculate PPPs for nonmarket services using input prices. Not all inputs are priced, only the most important, labor. Thus for the 2011 comparison, economies reported the annual compensation that government paid to a cross

section of occupations in collective services in 2011. The compensation of employees collected for an occupation was the average compensation paid for the occupation for a standardized number of working hours. It was extracted from the government payroll.

For *capital goods* in Eurostat-OECD comparisons, Eurostat economies collect national purchasers' prices without the value added tax (VAT). Later, after the prices have been collected, economies report the global rate of the VAT actually paid on capital goods during the year to which the prices refer. The global rate is taken from their national accounts. The rates are used to adjust the PPPs calculated using the national purchasers' prices originally reported for individual capital items. OECD economies also collect national purchasers' prices but with nondeductible taxes. No global rate is subsequently reported. There are two price surveys for capital goods: one for equipment goods, the other for construction.

For the 2011 comparison, economies collected prices for *equipment goods* between April and July of 2011. The prices were obtained from producers, importers, distributors, or actual purchasers. The prices collected were either purchasers' prices for actual market transactions or purchasers' prices for hypothetical market transactions—that is, what purchasers would pay if they made a purchase.

For *construction* in Eurostat-OECD comparisons, economies price eight standard construction projects covering different types of buildings and structures. Each project is defined by a bill of quantities, and each bill of quantities has two versions: a complete version specifying all the components making up the project and a reduced version specifying only the key components. Each year, four projects are priced using the complete version of their bill of quantities, and four projects are priced using the reduced version of their bill of quantities. There is a two-year pricing cycle, and the version priced for a project alternates from year to year. Prices for the projects have to be at the level of the prevailing tender prices—that is, the prices of tenders that have been accepted by purchasers.

For the 2011 comparison, the four complete bills of quantities and the four reduced bills of quantities were priced by construction experts in the economies between May and July of 2011.

In addition to the prices, quantities, and adjustment factors just enumerated, participating economies reported detailed *basic heading expenditures* for the 2011 comparison, first in 2012 and then again in 2013. The GDP expenditure was broken down into 206 basic headings in line with the definitions, concepts, classifications, and accounting rules of the System of National Accounts 1993 (Commission of the European Communities et al. 1993) and the *European System of Accounts 1995* (Eurostat 1996). The 206 basic headings summed exactly to the 155 basic headings of the ICP expenditure classification (see appendix D).

Also required for the 2011 comparison were each economy's annual average *exchange rates* and annual average resident *population*. These data were extracted by Eurostat or the OECD from in-house databases. The exchange rates were the annual averages of daily market or central rates compiled by the European Central Bank or the International Monetary Fund. Average annual resident population referred to the economic territories covered by the GDPs of participating economies.

CALCULATION AND AGGREGATION OF PPPs

In the Eurostat-OECD comparisons, the Gini-Éltetö-Köves-Szulc (GEKS) method is used to compute the multilateral PPPs that are transitive and base country–invariant at both the basic heading and aggregate levels.

For the 2011 comparison, PPPs for basic headings covering consumer goods and services and equipment goods were calculated using quasi expenditure weights that take the representativity (importance) of the products priced into account: a weight of 1 if the product is representative (important) for an economy and a weight of 0 if it is not. PPPs for the basic headings for housing, hospital services, education, and collective services were calculated using the expenditure shares of products within the basic heading as weights. Basic heading PPPs for construction were calculated without weights.

PPPs for aggregates were obtained by weighting and summing the PPPs of their component basic headings. GDP expenditures on the basic headings were used as weights. The results of the joint comparison for 2011 respect fixity—that is, the relativities established between economies in the Eurostat comparison remain unchanged when the economies are included in the comparison with OECD economies. This ensures that there is only one set of results for the European Union, an important consideration because of the administrative uses to which PPPs are put by the European Commission.

ADDITIONAL INFORMATION

Further details about the Eurostat-OECD PPP Programme can be found in the 2012 edition of the *Eurostat-OECD Methodological Manual on Purchasing Power Parities* (OECD and Eurostat 2012). The manual explains the theory and practice underlying the program and describes the methods, organization, and information technology tools employed by Eurostat and the OECD in making their comparisons.

ICP Expenditure Classification

The classification of gross domestic product (GDP) expenditures used by the International Comparison Program (ICP) adheres to the internationally agreed-on concepts, definitions, classifications, and accounting rules of the System of National Accounts 1993 (Commission of the European Communities et al. 1993). It is structured first by type of final expenditure—individual consumption expenditure, collective consumption expenditure, or capital expenditure—and then, in the case of individual consumption expenditure, by purchaser—households, nonprofit institutions serving households (NPISHs), and general government. The individual consumption expenditure and collective consumption expenditure are classified by purpose or function following the Classification of Individual Consumption According to Purpose (COICOP) and the Classification of the Functions of Government (COFOG)—see United Nations Statistics Division (1999a, 1999b). Capital expenditure is classified by type of product broadly in line with the Central Product Classification (CPC)—see United Nations Statistics Division (1998).

GDP comprises seven main aggregates, and in the classification these are broken down into 26 expenditure categories, 61 expenditure groups, 126 expenditure classes, and 155 basic headings, as shown in table D.1.

In the outline of the expenditure classification that appears in table D.2, main aggregates are identified by a two-digit code, categories by a four-digit code, groups by a five-digit code, and classes by a six-digit code. Basic headings have a seven-digit code. Thus

110000 INDIVIDUAL CONSUMPTION EXPENDITURE BY HOUSEHOLDS
(main aggregate)
110100 FOOD AND NONALCOHOLIC BEVERAGES (category)
110110 Food (group)
110111 *Bread and cereals* (class)
110111.1 Rice (basic heading).

Of these aggregation levels, the basic heading level is particularly important. It is at this level that expenditures are defined and estimated, products are selected for pricing, prices are collected and validated, and purchasing power parities (PPPs) are first calculated and averaged. In principle, a basic heading consists of a group of similar well-defined goods or services. In practice, a basic heading is defined by the lowest level of final expenditure for which explicit expenditures can be estimated by the participating economies. Consequently, basic headings can cover a broader range of goods or services than is theoretically desirable.

DERIVING ACTUAL INDIVIDUAL CONSUMPTION

ICP comparisons of material well-being compare the actual individual consumption of households

Table D.1 Structure of the ICP Expenditure Classification, ICP 2011

Main aggregates with code description	Categories	Groups	Classes	Basic headings
11. Individual consumption expenditure by households	13	43	90	110
12. Individual consumption expenditure by nonprofit institutions serving households (NPISHs)	1	1	1	1
13. Individual consumption expenditure by government	5	7	16	21
14. Collective consumption expenditure by government	1	1	5	5
15. Gross fixed capital formation	3	6	11	12
16. Changes in inventories and valuables	2	2	2	4
17. Balance of exports and imports	1	1	1	2
Gross domestic product	26	61	126	155

Source: ICP, http://icp.worldbank.org/.

and not the individual consumption expenditure of households. Actual individual consumption is obtained by summing the individual consumption expenditures of households, NPISHs, and general government. The individual consumption expenditures of NPISHs and general government cover their expenditures on the services they provide individual households as social transfers in kind—that is, services related to housing, health, recreation and culture, education, and social protection. Combining these expenditures is necessary because of the various ways in which individual services are financed in different economies. If the expenditures are not combined and only the individual consumption expenditures of households are compared, households in economies in which NPISHs or general government provide individual services will appear to consume a smaller volume of goods and services than households in economies in which households themselves pay directly for these services.

In order to combine the individual consumption expenditures of households and general government, the classification breaks down the individual consumption expenditures of government so that they can be added to their counterpart expenditures under the household expenditure. The breakdowns are structured so that the summation is at the lowest level of aggregation feasible, which is generally at the level of the basic heading. In the outline of the classification shown in table D.2, the combinations are indicated in italics. For example, under household expenditure

the outline shows that basic heading 110631.1, hospital services, is combined with basic heading 130212.4, hospital services, under (government) health benefits and reimbursements, and with group 130220 (government), production of health services, which is assumed to be predominantly the provision of hospital services.

The individual consumption expenditures of NPISHs should also be broken down, but they are not because most economies are unable to provide the required level of detail. Instead, the expenditures of NPISHs are reported in total. Subsequently, this total is distributed over the 13 basic headings covering individual services under the household expenditure in the same proportions that the household expenditure on individual services is distributed across the 13 basic headings. Thus if households spend a total of $100,000 on the 13 basic headings, of which $10,000 is spent on the basic heading 110411.1, actual and imputed rentals, and if the total individual consumption expenditure by NPISHs is $50,000, then $5,000 of the NPISH expenditure will be allocated to the basic heading for actual and imputed rents.

FACILITATING THE INPUT PRICE APPROACH

The collective and individual services produced by general government are nonmarket services because they are either provided free or sold at prices that are not economically significant. In the absence of economically significant prices, national accountants obtain the expenditure on nonmarket services by summing the costs of the inputs required to produce them. To maintain consistency with the prices underlying the estimated expenditure on nonmarket services in the national accounts, the PPPs for nonmarket services are based on input prices. To enable application of the input price approach, the classification breaks down the final consumption expenditure by government on the production of collective services and the principal individual services—education and health—into the following components: compensation of employees, intermediate consumption, gross operating surplus, and net taxes on production (the sum of these four components is a measure of government output). Receipts from sales (such as those from statistical publications) are deducted from output to provide the estimate of the government final consumption expenditure.

A distinction is made between the government expenditure on the health and education services that a government produces and a government's expenditure on the health and education services that it purchases from market producers in the private sector under benefits and reimbursements. This approach ensures that the input price approach is applied only to the government expenditure on government-produced services.

ADJUSTING THE HOUSEHOLD EXPENDITURE TO THE NATIONAL CONCEPT

Expenditures on the basic headings constituting the individual consumption expenditure by households are defined according to the national concept—that is, they cover only expenditures by resident households, including their expenditures abroad, and exclude the expenditures of nonresident households within the economic territory. Many economies, however, estimate the expenditures on these basic headings according to the domestic concept—that is, irrespective of whether the household making the purchase is resident or not. For these economies, the classification contains a global adjustment to rectify this difference. The adjustment is defined as the balance of the expenditures of residents abroad less the expenditures of nonresidents within the economic territory or as net purchases abroad. It is important to note that many economies base their estimates of the household final consumption expenditure on household budget surveys, and so the estimates are automatically on a national basis. For these economies, the global adjustment is not required.

Table D.2 Expenditure Classification, ICP 2011

Code	Description	
100000	**GROSS DOMESTIC PRODUCT**	
110000	**INDIVIDUAL CONSUMPTION EXPENDITURE BY HOUSEHOLDS**	
110100	**FOOD AND NONALCOHOLIC BEVERAGES**	
110110	**Food**	
110111	***Bread and cereals***	
110111.1	Rice	
110111.2	Other cereals, flour, and other cereal products	
110111.3	Bread	
110111.4	Other bakery products	
110111.5	Pasta products	
110112	***Meat***	
110112.1	Beef and veal	
110112.2	Pork	

(continued)

Code	Description
110112.3	Lamb, mutton, and goat
110112.4	Poultry
110112.5	Other meats and meat preparations
110113	*Fish*
110113.1	Fresh, chilled, or frozen fish and seafood
110113.2	Preserved or processed fish and seafood
110114	*Milk, cheese, and eggs*
110114.1	Fresh milk
110114.2	Preserved milk and other milk products
110114.3	Cheese
110114.4	Eggs and egg-based products
110115	*Oils and fats*
110115.1	Butter and margarine
110115.3	Other edible oils and fats
110116	*Fruit*
110116.1	Fresh or chilled fruit
110116.2	Frozen, preserved, or processed fruit and fruit-based products
110117	*Vegetables*
110117.1	Fresh or chilled vegetables other than potatoes
110117.2	Fresh or chilled potatoes
110117.3	Frozen, preserved, or processed vegetables and vegetable-based products
110118	*Sugar, jam, honey, chocolate, and confectionery*
110118.1	Sugar
110118.2	Jams, marmalades, and honey
110118.3	Confectionery, chocolate, and ice cream
110119	*Food products n.e.c.*
110119.1	Food products n.e.c.
110120	**Nonalcoholic beverages**
110121	*Coffee, tea, and cocoa*
110121.1	Coffee, tea, and cocoa
110122	*Mineral waters, soft drinks, fruit and vegetable juices*
110122.1	Mineral waters, soft drinks, fruit and vegetable juices
110200	**ALCOHOLIC BEVERAGES, TOBACCO, AND NARCOTICS**
110210	**Alcoholic beverages**
110211	*Spirits*
110211.1	Spirits
110212	*Wine*
110212.1	Wine
110213	*Beer*
110213.1	Beer
110220	**Tobacco**
110221	*Tobacco*
110221.1	Tobacco

Code	Description
110230	**Narcotics**
110231	***Narcotics***
110231.1	Narcotics
110300	**CLOTHING AND FOOTWEAR**
110310	**Clothing**
110311	***Clothing materials, other articles of clothing, and clothing accessories***
110311.1	Clothing materials, other articles of clothing, and clothing accessories
110312	***Garments***
110312.1	Garments
110314	***Cleaning, repair, and hire of clothing***
110314.1	Cleaning, repair, and hire of clothing
110320	**Footwear**
110321	***Shoes and other footwear***
110321.1	Shoes and other footwear
110322	***Repair and hire of footwear***
110322.1	Repair and hire of footwear
110400	**HOUSING, WATER, ELECTRICITY, GAS, AND OTHER FUELS**
110410	**Actual and imputed rentals for housing**
110411	***Actual and imputed rentals for housing***
110411.1	Actual and imputed rentals for housing *(combines with 130111.1)*
110430	**Maintenance and repair of the dwelling**
110431	***Maintenance and repair of the dwelling***
110431.1	Maintenance and repair of the dwelling
110440	**Water supply and miscellaneous services relating to the dwelling**
110441	***Water supply***
110441.1	Water supply
110442	***Miscellaneous services relating to the dwelling***
110442.1	Miscellaneous services relating to the dwelling
110450	**Electricity, gas, and other fuels**
110451	***Electricity***
110451.1	Electricity
110452	***Gas***
110452.1	Gas
110453	***Other fuels***
110453.1	Other fuels
110500	**FURNISHINGS, HOUSEHOLD EQUIPMENT, AND ROUTINE MAINTENANCE OF THE HOUSE**
110510	**Furniture and furnishings, carpets, and other floor coverings**
110511	***Furniture and furnishings***
110511.1	Furniture and furnishings
110512	***Carpets and other floor coverings***
110512.1	Carpets and other floor coverings

(continued)

Code	Description
110513	***Repair of furniture, furnishings, and floor coverings***
110513.1	Repair of furniture, furnishings, and floor coverings
110520	**Household textiles**
110521	***Household textiles***
110521.1	Household textiles
110530	**Household appliances**
110531	***Major household appliances whether electric or not***
110531.1	Major household appliances whether electric or not
110532	***Small electric household appliances***
110532.1	Small electric household appliances
110533	***Repair of household appliances***
110533.1	Repair of household appliances
110540	**Glassware, tableware, and household utensils**
110541	***Glassware, tableware, and household utensils***
110541.1	Glassware, tableware, and household utensils
110550	**Tools and equipment for house and garden**
110551	***Major tools and equipment***
110551.1	Major tools and equipment
110552	***Small tools and miscellaneous accessories***
110552.1	Small tools and miscellaneous accessories
110560	**Goods and services for routine household maintenance**
110561	***Nondurable household goods***
110561.1	Nondurable household goods
110562	***Domestic services and household services***
110562.1	Domestic services
110562.2	Household services
110600	**HEALTH**
110610	**Medical products, appliances, and equipment**
110611	***Pharmaceutical products***
110611.1	Pharmaceutical products *(combines with 130211.1)*
110612	***Other medical products***
110612.1	Other medical products *(combines with 130211.2)*
110613	***Therapeutic appliances and equipment***
110613.1	Therapeutic appliances and equipment *(combines with 130211.3)*
110620	**Outpatient services**
110621	***Medical Services***
110621.1	Medical services *(combines with 130212.1)*
110622	***Dental services***
110622.1	Services of dentists *(combines with 130212.2)*
110623	***Paramedical services***
110623.1	Paramedical services *(combines with 130212.3)*
110630	**Hospital services**

Code	Description
110631	***Hospital services***
110631.1	Hospital services *(combines with 130212.4 ana 130220)*
110700	**TRANSPORT**
110710	**Purchase of vehicles**
110711	***Motor cars***
110711.1	Motor cars
110712	***Motorcycles***
110712.1	Motorcycles
110713	***Bicycles***
110713.1	Bicycles
110714	***Animal-drawn vehicles***
110714.1	Animal-drawn vehicles
110720	**Operation of personal transport equipment**
110722	***Fuels and lubricants for personal transport equipment***
110722.1	Fuels and lubricants for personal transport equipment
110723	***Maintenance and repair of personal transport equipment***
110723.1	Maintenance and repair of personal transport equipment
110724	***Other services in respect of personal transport equipment***
110724.1	Other services in respect of personal transport equipment
110730	**Transport services**
110731	***Passenger transport by railway***
110731.1	Passenger transport by railway
110732	***Passenger transport by road***
110732.1	Passenger transport by road
110733	***Passenger transport by air***
110733.1	Passenger transport by air
110734	***Passenger transport by sea and inland waterway***
110734.1	Passenger transport by sea and inland waterway
110735	***Combined passenger transport***
110735.1	Combined passenger transport
110736	***Other purchased transport services***
110736.1	Other purchased transport services
110800	**COMMUNICATION**
110810	**Postal services**
110811	***Postal services***
110811.1	Postal services
110820	**Telephone and telefax equipment**
110821	***Telephone and telefax equipment***
110821.1	Telephone and telefax equipment
110830	**Telephone and telefax services**
110831	***Telephone and telefax services***
110831.1	Telephone and telefax services

(continued)

Code	Description
110900	**RECREATION AND CULTURE**
110910	**Audiovisual, photographic, and information processing equipment**
110911	***Audiovisual, photographic, and information processing equipment***
110911.1	Audiovisual, photographic, and information processing equipment
110914	***Recording media***
110914.1	Recording media
110915	***Repair of audiovisual, photographic, and information processing equipment***
110915.1	Repair of audiovisual, photographic, and information processing equipment
110920	**Other major durables for recreation and culture**
110921	***Major durables for outdoor and indoor recreation***
110921.1	Major durables for outdoor and indoor recreation
110923	***Maintenance and repair of other major durables for recreation and culture***
110923.1	Maintenance and repair of other major durables for recreation and culture
110930	**Other recreational items and equipment, gardens and pets**
110931	***Other recreational items and equipment***
110931.1	Other recreational items and equipment
110933	***Gardens and pets***
110933.1	Gardens and pets
110935	***Veterinary and other services for pets***
110935.1	Veterinary and other services for pets
110940	**Recreational and cultural services** *(combines with 130311.1)*
110941	***Recreational and sporting services***
110941.1	Recreational and sporting services
110942	***Cultural services***
110942.1	Cultural services
110943	***Games of chance***
110943.1	Games of chance
110950	**Newspapers, books, and stationery**
110951	***Newspapers, books, and stationery***
110951.1	Newspapers, books, and stationery
110960	**Package holidays**
110961	***Package holidays***
110961.1	Package holidays
111000	**EDUCATION**
111010	**Education**
111011	***Education***
111011.1	Education *(combines with 130400)*
111100	**RESTAURANTS AND HOTELS**
111110	**Catering services**
111111	***Catering services***
111111.1	Catering services

Code	Description
111120	**Accommodation services**
111121	***Accommodation services***
111121.1	Accommodation services
111200	**MISCELLANEOUS GOODS AND SERVICES**
111210	**Personal care**
111211	***Hairdressing salons and personal grooming establishments***
111211.1	Hairdressing salons and personal grooming establishments
111212	***Appliances, articles, and products for personal care***
111212.1	Appliances, articles, and products for personal care
111220	**Prostitution**
111221	***Prostitution***
111221.1	Prostitution
111230	**Personal effects n.e.c.**
111231	***Jewelry, clocks, and watches***
111231.1	Jewelry, clocks, and watches
111232	***Other personal effects***
111232.1	Other personal effects
111240	**Social protection**
111241	***Social protection***
111241.1	Social protection *(combines with 130511.1)*
111250	**Insurance**
111251	***Insurance***
111251.1	Insurance
111260	**Financial services n.e.c.**
111261	***Financial intermediation services indirectly measured (FISIM)***
111261.1	Financial intermediation services indirectly measured (FISIM)
111262	***Other financial services n.e.c***
111262.1	Other financial services n.e.c.
111270	**Other services n.e.c.**
111271	***Other services n.e.c.***
111271.1	Other services n.e.c.
111300	**BALANCE OF EXPENDITURES OF RESIDENTS ABROAD AND EXPENDITURES OF NONRESIDENTS ON THE ECONOMIC TERRITORY**
111310	**Balance of expenditures of residents abroad and expenditures of nonresidents on the economic territory**
111311	**Balance of expenditures of residents abroad and expenditures of nonresidents on the economic territory**
111311.1	Individual consumption expenditure by resident households in the rest of the world
111311.2	Individual consumption expenditure by nonresident households on the economic territory
120000	**INDIVIDUAL CONSUMPTION EXPENDITURE BY NPISHs**
120100	**INDIVIDUAL CONSUMPTION EXPENDITURE BY NPISHs**
120110	**Individual consumption expenditure by NPISHs**
120111	**Individual consumption expenditure by NPISHs**

(continued)

Table D.2 *(Continued)*

Code	Description
120111.1	Individual consumption expenditure by NPISHs *(distributed over 110411.1, 110611.1 to 110631.1, 110941.1 to 110943.1, 111011.1, and 111241.1 in line with the distribution of household expenditure on these basic headings)*
130000	**INDIVIDUAL CONSUMPTION EXPENDITURE BY GOVERNMENT**
130100	**HOUSING**
130110	**Housing**
130111	***Housing***
130111.1	Housing *(combines with 110411.1)*
130200	**HEALTH**
130210	**Health benefits and reimbursements**
130211	***Medical products, appliances, and equipment***
130211.1	Pharmaceutical products *(combines with 110611.1)*
130211.2	Other medical products *(combines with 110612.1)*
130211.3	Therapeutic appliances and equipment *(combines with 110613.1)*
130212	***Health services***
130212.1	Outpatient medical services *(combines with 110621.1)*
130212.2	Outpatient dental services *(combines with 110622.1)*
130212.3	Outpatient paramedical services *(combines with 110623.1)*
130212.4	Hospital services *(combines with 110631.1)*
130220	**Production of health services** *(combines with 110631.1)*
130221	***Compensation of employees***
130221.1	Compensation of employees
130222	***Intermediate consumption***
130222.1	Intermediate consumption
130223	***Gross operating surplus***
130223.1	Gross operating surplus
130224	***Net taxes on production***
130224.1	Net taxes on production
130225	***Receipts from sales***
130225.1	Receipts from sales
130300	**RECREATION AND CULTURE**
130310	**Recreation and culture**
130311	***Recreation and culture***
130311.1	Recreation and culture *(combines with 110940)*
130400	**EDUCATION** *(combines with 111011.1)*
130410	**Education benefits and reimbursements**
130411	***Education benefits and reimbursements***
130411.1	Education benefits and reimbursements
130420	**Production of education services**
130421	***Compensation of employees***
130421.1	Compensation of employees
130422	***Intermediate consumption***
130422.1	Intermediate consumption

Code	Description
130423	***Gross operating surplus***
130423.1	Gross operating surplus
130424	***Net taxes on production***
130424.1	Net taxes on production
130425	***Receipts from sales***
130425.1	Receipts from sales
130500	**SOCIAL PROTECTION**
130510	**Social protection**
130511	*Social protection*
130511.1	Social protection (*combines with 111241.1*)
140000	**COLLECTIVE CONSUMPTION EXPENDITURE BY GOVERNMENT**
140100	**COLLECTIVE SERVICES**
140110	**Collective services**
140111	***Compensation of employees***
140111.1	Compensation of employees
140112	***Intermediate consumption***
140112.1	Intermediate consumption
140113	***Gross operating surplus***
140113.1	Gross operating surplus
140114	***Net taxes on production***
140114.1	Net taxes on production
140115	***Receipts from sales***
140115.1	Receipts from sales
150000	**EXPENDITURE ON GROSS FIXED CAPITAL FORMATION**
150100	**MACHINERY AND EQUIPMENT**
150110	**Metal products and equipment**
150111	***Fabricated metal products, except machinery and equipment***
150111.1	Fabricated metal products, except machinery and equipment
150112	***General-purpose machinery***
150112.1	General-purpose machinery
150113	***Special-purpose machinery***
150113.1	Special-purpose machinery
150114	***Electrical and optical equipment***
150114.1	Electrical and optical equipment
150115	***Other manufactured goods n.e.c.***
150115.1	Other manufactured goods n.e.c.
150120	**Transport equipment**
150121	***Road transport equipment***
150121.1	Motor vehicles, trailers, and semitrailers
150121.2	Other road transport
150122	***Other transport equipment***
150122.1	Other transport equipment

(continued)

Table D.2 (Continued)

Code	Description
150200	**CONSTRUCTION**
150210	**Residential buildings**
150211	***Residential buildings***
150211.1	Residential buildings
150220	**Nonresidential buildings**
150221	***Nonresidential buildings***
150221.1	Nonresidential buildings
150230	**Civil engineering works**
150231	***Civil engineering works***
150231.1	Civil engineering works
150300	**OTHER PRODUCTS**
150310	**Other products**
150311	***Other products***
150311.1	Other products
160000	**CHANGES IN INVENTORIES AND VALUABLES**
160100	**CHANGES IN INVENTORIES**
160110	**Changes in inventories**
160111	***Changes in inventories***
160111.1	Opening value of inventories
160111.2	Closing value of inventories
160200	**CHANGE IN VALUABLES**
160210	**Change in valuables**
160211	***Change in valuables***
160211.1	Acquisitions of valuables
160211.2	Disposals of valuables
170000	**BALANCE OF EXPORTS AND IMPORTS**
170100	**BALANCE OF EXPORTS AND IMPORTS**
170110	**Balance of exports and imports**
170111	***Balance of exports and imports***
170111.1	Exports of goods and services
170111.2	Imports of goods and services

Source: ICP, http://icp.worldbank.org/.
Note: n.e.c. = not elsewhere classified.

National Accounts: Estimation, Compliance, and Exhaustiveness

Economies participating in the International Comparison Program (ICP) are required to provide a detailed breakdown of their national expenditure for the reference year according to a common classification. The breakdown is used first in the regional comparison in which the reporting economy is engaged and then in the global comparison. An outline of the classification used for ICP 2011 appears in appendix D; it consists of 155 basic headings. Expenditures on the basic headings are used as weights when basic heading purchasing power parities (PPPs) are weighted together to obtain PPPs for aggregation levels above the basic heading level. The PPPs so obtained are used to convert the nominal expenditures (in an economy's national currency) for each of the aggregation levels, including the gross domestic product (GDP) itself, to real expenditures. It is therefore essential that each participating economy supply a complete set of basic heading expenditures.

ESTIMATION

Many economies experience difficulties in breaking down their expenditure on GDP to the basic heading level. To help economies overcome these difficulties during ICP 2011, the Global Office developed the Model Report on Expenditure Statistics, or MORES. It was designed so that economies could estimate the expenditure on each basic heading and, at the same time, document how the expenditure was estimated. The documentation aspect of MORES was important because it allowed the estimation to be repeated if data were revised or if basic heading expenditures had to be estimated for another reference year. It was also in keeping with the emphasis placed on metadata and quality assessment during ICP 2011.

MORES worksheets

The MORES reporting form covered two years: a recent year prior to 2011 and 2011. It was to be completed in two stages: first for the recent year before national accounts data for 2011 became available and then for 2011 when data for 2011 became available. The two-stage approach was adopted because it would allow national accountants to address problems well beforehand. Moreover, in the absence of data for a basic heading in 2011, the estimate for the recent year could be extrapolated to 2011.

There were three worksheets for each year (see the examples in box E.1). On worksheet 1, economies recorded the initial expenditure values that were available for the year in question. These initial values could be just for GDP and the main aggregates, or the values for the main aggregates could be broken down further by category or even by group and class. If broken down further, not all main aggregates would necessarily be broken down with the same degree of detail. The initial expenditure values provided the control totals. Values estimated for the basic headings on worksheet 2 and recorded under estimated expenditure values on worksheet 1 had to sum to these totals. Discrepancies between initial values and estimated values had to be resolved before the estimated values could be considered final and recorded on worksheet 3.

Data sources, extrapolators, and estimation methods

To support MORES, the Global Office compiled for each basic heading a list of potential data sources and a list of possible indicators with which to extrapolate or adjust data. For example, for the basic heading rice, the list of sources included household expenditure surveys, retail trade surveys, agricultural surveys, Food and Agriculture Organization (FAO) food balances, sales tax data, and the consumer price index. The list of indicators covered measures of domestic production, imports, population growth, and consumer price inflation.

The Global Office also identified five approaches to estimating basic heading expenditures. These approaches were not linked to specific basic headings because the choice of approach depended on the availability of data. The five approaches were as follows:

1. Estimating expenditure on the basic heading using data for the year for which the estimate was being made.
2. Extrapolating the expenditure on the basic heading in a recent year or the previous comparison (ICP 2005).
3. Borrowing from another economy in the region a per capita quantity or volume related to the basic heading.
4. Borrowing from another economy in the region the structure of the class, group, or category that includes the basic heading.
5. Breaking down the quantity or volume of a class, group, or category into its constituent basic headings in line with expert opinion.

BOX **E.1**

MORES Worksheets, ICP 2011

Worksheet 1

ICP Code	Heading	Initial Expenditure Value	Estimated Expenditure Values	Discrepancies
100000	GROSS DOMESTIC PRODUCT	168,527.54	168,527.54	0
110000	INDIVIDUAL CONSUMPTION EXPENDITURE BY HOUSEHOLDS	117,081.29	117,081.29	0
110100	FOOD AND NON-ALCOHOLIC BEVERAGES	59,812.66	59,812.66	0
110110	FOOD	0.00	51,634.63	
110111	Bread and cereals	0.00	19,335.26	
110111.1	Rice		6,370.77	
110111.2	Other cereals, flour and other products		3,874.10	
110111.3	Bread		3,435.03	
110111.4	Other bakery products		1,907.83	
110111.5	Pasta products		3,747.53	

MORES Worksheets, ICP 2011

Worksheet 2

Code	Name	#	Indicator name	Source name	Year	Value	Unit
1101111	Rice	1	Sales of Rice	Retail Census	2007	5,364	
	Splitting Approach	2	Population increase from 2007 to 2011	Population Census	2011	5.30%	
	Please indicate all the approaches used in calculation of expenditure for this basic heading	3	CPI price increase	CPI	2011	12.1%	
		4	Adjusted expenditure for rice [5364 × 1.053 × 1.121]		2011	6,331.74	
	2	Extrapolation	5	Summation of adjusted basic heading values under "bread and cereals"		2011	19,216.79	
		6	Expenditure for "bread and cereals" subgroup	Household Expenditure Survey	2009	17,965.00	
		7	Population increase from 2009 to 2011	Population Census	2011	2.60%	
		8	CPI increase for this subgroup	CPI	2011	4.90%	
		9	Adjusted expenditure for "bread and cereals" [17965 × 1.026 × 1.049]		2011	19,335.26	
		10					
			Estimated 2011 expenditure for 1101111 Rice [6331.74/19216,79] × 19335.26			6,370.77	

Worksheet 3

ICP Code	Heading	Expenditure Value
100000	**GROSS DOMESTIC PRODUCT**	168,527.54
110000	**INDIVIDUAL CONSUMPTION EXPENDITURE BY HOUSEHOLDS**	117,081.29
110100	FOOD AND NON-ALCOHOLIC BEVERAGES	59,812.66
110110	FOOD	51,634.63
110111	Bread and cereals	19,335.26
110111.1	Rice	6,370.77
110111.2	Other cereals, flour and other products	3,874.10
110111.3	Bread	3,435.03
110111.4	Other bakery products	1,907.83
110111.5	Pasta products	3,747.53

Of these approaches, the first, in which the expenditure on the basic heading is estimated directly with data for the reference year, was the recommended method. Because the four other approaches estimate expenditure indirectly using data other than that for the reference year, they were considered second-best methods. Even so, they were better than allocating expenditure on a class evenly across all basic headings in the class. Of the four, extrapolation was the preferred method. The third and fourth approaches, which involved borrowing from another economy in the region, required the advice and assistance of the regional coordinator. Exchanges between economies were facilitated by the national accounts workshops that regional coordinators organized for the economies in their region.

COMPLIANCE AND EXHAUSTIVENESS

Volume comparisons of GDP and its component expenditures require that all economies in a comparison employ the same definitions of GDP and its component expenditures and that their measurement of GDP and its component expenditures be exhaustive.

ICP participants compile, or attempt to compile, their national accounts estimates in line with the System of National Accounts 1993 or SNA93 (Commission of the European Communities et al. 1993), but compliance is not necessarily complete. For example, many economies do not follow the SNA93 recommendation that imputed bank services charges—otherwise known as financial intermediation services indirectly measured (FISIM) in SNA93—be allocated to households, general government, and the rest of the world, where they would be shown as final consumption, which increases GDP. Instead, the economies retain the SNA68 practice of allocating all the imputed bank service charges to producers, where they are treated as intermediate consumption, which offsets the value of the charges and so they have no impact on GDP. Thus the levels of GDP of economies that allocate FISIM and the levels of GDPs of economies that do not allocate FISIM are not strictly comparable.

FISIM is only one of the imputations required by SNA93 that economies have problems implementing. Many economies have difficulty estimating the imputed rents of owner-occupiers by the stratification approach or by the user cost approach as advocated by SNA93. They either use an alternative approach, such as asking owner-occupiers how much rent their dwelling would warrant, or limit the imputation to urban areas, or make no imputation at all. When properly measured, total rents for dwellings (that is, both actual and imputed rents together) account for at least 5 percent of GDP in low-income economies, and that percentage is nearly twice as much in high-income economies. Thus the GDP of economies that do not follow the SNA rules on estimation of imputed rents are likely to be underestimated when compared with the GDP of economies that do.

Even when economies adhere strictly to the definitions and accounting rules of SNA93, their measurement of GDP and its component expenditures will not necessarily be exhaustive. If they have a large nonobserved economy, their GDPs could be underestimated. Nonobserved refers to economic activities that are hidden because they are illegal, or are legal but carried out clandestinely, or are undertaken by households for their own use. The term also refers to activities that are missed because of deficiencies in the statistical system. Such deficiencies include out-of-date survey registers, surveys that have reporting thresholds that are too high or that have high rates of nonresponse, poor survey editing procedures, and no surveys of informal activities such as street trading. Adjustments for the nonobserved economy can be significant. For example, the 10 eastern and central European countries that joined the European Union in 2004 adjusted their GDP at that time by an average of 12 percent.

To ascertain the degree to which the GDPs of economies participating in ICP 2011 were comparable, the Global Office prepared two questionnaires for the economies to complete: the National Accounts Quality Assurance Questionnaire, which focused on compliance with SNA93 and ICP requirements, and the GDP Exhaustiveness Questionnaire, which focused on quantifying the adjustments to be made to an economy's estimates of GDP to compensate for various types of nonexhaustiveness.

National accounts quality assurance questionnaire

This questionnaire was made up of 30 questions that required a yes or no answer. There were also boxes for comments if respondents wished to elaborate on their answers. The questions are listed in box E.2.

GDP exhaustiveness questionnaire

Exhaustiveness is the extent to which an economy's national accounts cover all the economic activities that are supposed to be included in GDP according to SNA93. The questionnaire drawn up by the Global Office to determine the exhaustiveness of the national accounts of participants in ICP 2011 was based on the tabular approach to exhaustiveness developed by Eurostat in the 1990s. The Eurostat approach focused primarily on the exhaustiveness of estimates from the production side. It took the form

---

ICP National Accounts Quality Assurance Questionnaire, ICP 2011

01. Do you implement SNA93?
02. Does your estimate of GDP cover the full range of economic activities and transactions that are included in the production boundary of SNA93?
03. Do your estimates of final expenditures on GDP cover all basic headings as defined in the ICP classification of expenditure and in line with SNA93?
04. Does the price survey framework provide national annual average prices for the basic headings defined in the ICP classification of expenditure that are consistent with the prices underlying the expenditures on the basic headings?
05. Do you classify institutional sectors in line with SNA93?
06. In general, are transactions valued at the actual prices agreed by the transactors—that is, at purchasers' prices?
07. Are imputed rentals valued in accordance with the guidelines given in the ICP operational material?
08. Are goods produced on own account for consumption by the household valued at basic prices?
09. Is income in kind valued at purchasers' prices if the employer has purchased the goods or services and at producers' prices if the goods or services have been produced by the enterprise itself?
10. Is the individual consumption expenditure of nonprofit institutions serving households valued as the sum of the costs of production, including the consumption of fixed capital?
11. Is the production of individual services by government valued as the sum of the costs of production, including the consumption of fixed capital?
12. Are the purchases of goods and services by government that are passed on to households without any further processing by government valued at purchasers' prices?
13. Is the collective consumption expenditure by government valued as the sum of the costs of production, including the consumption of fixed capital?
14. Is gross fixed capital formation valued at purchasers' prices?
15. Is own-account production of fixed capital assets valued at basic prices?

(continued)

ICP National Accounts Quality Assurance Questionnaire, ICP 2011

16. Is change in inventories valued as the change in the physical quantities at the beginning and end of the year using either the average of prices over the year or the prices prevailing at the middle of the year?

17. Are total imports and exports valued on an f.o.b. (free-on-board) basis?

18. Are transactions in foreign currency converted using the midpoint exchange rate prevailing in the market at the moment they take place?

19. Are the prices used in your national accounts national annual average prices, or, if they are not, are they adjusted to national annual average prices by accepted procedures?

20. Are transactions and flows recorded on an accrual basis?

21. Is work in progress recorded in the period it is produced?

22. Are government-related transactions recorded on an accrual basis, in particular taxes and subsidies on products and expenditures?

23. Does gross fixed capital formation consist of net acquisitions (acquisitions less disposals) of fixed assets?

24. Are valuables measured as acquisitions less disposals?

25. Are transaction prices measured net of discounts or rebates?

26. Do statistical procedures used by your office to adjust country final expenditure data to meet ICP requirements follow a detailed, case-by-case approach using specific sources that are most closely related to the estimated variables and pertinent to the reference period?

27. Do you maintain and disseminate detailed methodological notes about your national accounts compilation process?

28. Has your country compiled supply and use tables (SUTs)?

29. If yes, please indicate the reference year of the latest SUT, as well as the number of products (rows) in the SUT.

30. Please indicate the reference year of the most recent household expenditure survey.

of a matrix in which types of nonexhaustiveness were columns and economic activities were rows. Definitions of the types of nonexhaustiveness, together with the compilation methods that could be employed to measure them, are given in box E.3. Of the seven types of nonexhaustiveness identified, all but the last, N7, are defined in terms of producers. The economic activities covered are listed in the first column of table E.1. Economies were expected to complete the matrix by indicating in the relevant cells the adjustments needed for the various types of nonexhaustiveness to render the initial estimate for an economic activity exhaustive.

The Global Office extended the Eurostat approach to include estimates made from the expenditure side and from the income side. The expenditure categories and the income transactions considered are listed in the second and third columns of table E.1. The types of nonexhaustiveness remained unchanged. The questionnaire consisted of five matrixes: three for the production account covering gross output, intermediate consumption, and gross value added; one for the expenditure account; and one for the income account. In addition, the Global Office prepared two simplified versions of the questionnaire. The first was limited to gross value added by economic activity and

Types of Nonexhaustiveness Identified in GDP Exhaustiveness Questionnaire, ICP 2011

N1—Producer deliberately does not register (underground activity) in order to avoid tax and social security obligations or to avoid losing some social benefits. Typically, this category includes small producers with income above the threshold set for registration. Producers who do not register because they are engaged in illegal activities should be classified as N2, while producers who deliberately misreport their activities should be classified as N6. The methods that can be used to estimate the adjustments required include labor inputs (from household-based labor force surveys), commodity flow, and supply and use tables.

N2—Producer deliberately does not register (illegal activity) because the producer is involved in illegal activities such as prostitution, sale of stolen goods, drug dealing, smuggling, or illegal gambling. This category excludes any illegal production not reported by registered producers, which should be classified as N6, and illegal production by units not required to register, which should be classified as N3. The methods that can be used to estimate the adjustments are the quantity price method, unit per input or use, and expert judgment.

N3—Producer not required to register because the producer does not have any market output or the producer's market output is below a set threshold. Activities include production for own final consumption or own fixed capital formation, including construction of own dwellings and repairs to dwellings. Also includes market output of households that is below the level at which the producer is obliged to register as a business: paid domestic services, etc. No adjustment is necessary if the estimation method for a particular activity (or survey) implicitly takes into account the nonregistered activity. The methods that can be used to estimate adjustments are household expenditure surveys, building permits, commodity flow, administrative data, and time use surveys.

N4—Legal producer not surveyed because, although registered, the producer is excluded from statistical surveys. For example, the producer may be newly registered and not yet recorded in the business register because the register updating procedures are slow or inadequate. On the other hand, a producer may be recorded in the business register but excluded from survey frames because the classification data used in developing the survey frames (such as activity code, size of business, geographic location) may be wrong, or there may be a size cutoff that precludes the producer from being selected to participate in a particular survey. The methods that can be used to estimate adjustments are surveying the quality of the business register, reviewing the lags involved in update procedures and whether they change over time, or cross-checking the business register against other administrative sources covering businesses.

N5—Registered entrepreneurs not surveyed. Registered entrepreneurs such as consultants, private writers, and freelance journalists may not be recorded in the business register, either deliberately or because the register updating sources do not include the details on such persons. Even if their details are recorded in the business register, they may be excluded from statistical surveys either because of errors in the details recorded or because of the small size of their individual activities. The methods that can be used to estimate adjustments are conducting surveys of the quality of the register, cross-checking against other administrative sources (such as income tax statements), or carrying out specialized surveys.

(continued)

| BOX **E.3** | *(Continued)* |

Types of Nonexhaustiveness Identified in GDP Exhaustiveness Questionnaire, ICP 2011

N6—Misreporting by producers. Misreporting involves underreporting gross output (and therefore revenues) or overreporting intermediate consumption (and therefore the costs of production) in order to avoid paying income tax, other taxes such as value added tax, or social security contributions. The methods that can be used to estimate adjustments are consulting the data from tax audits, comparing average salaries and profits with similar businesses, comparing input-output ratios with those of similar businesses, conducting special surveys, or relying on expert judgment on the accounting relationships expected to be observed in such businesses.

N7—Other statistical deficiencies. This category can be divided into two parts: data that are incomplete or cannot be directly collected from surveys and data that are incorrectly compiled during survey processing. The items that should be considered in determining the adjustments to be made include how nonresponse was taken into account, the extent to which wages and salaries were paid in kind, production for own final use by market producers, tips, valuation techniques, and adjustments for accruals.

Table E.1 Economic Activities, Expenditure Categories, and Income Transactions Identified in Exhaustiveness Questionnaire, ICP 2011

Production approach	Expenditure approach	Income approach
Gross value added (basic prices):	Household final consumption:	Compensation of employees
A. Agriculture, hunting, and forestry	01. Food and nonalcoholic beverages	Gross operating surplus and mixed income
B. Fishing	02. Alcoholic beverages, tobacco, and narcotics	Taxes on production and imports
C. Mining and quarrying	03. Clothing and footwear	Subsidies
D. Manufacturing	04. Housing, water, electricity, gas, and other fuels	Statistical discrepancy
E. Electricity, gas, and water supply		Gross domestic product
F. Construction	05. Furnishings, household equipment, and routine household maintenance	
G. Wholesale and retail trade; repair of motor vehicles, motorcycles, and personal and household goods	06. Health	
H. Hotels and restaurants	07. Transport	
I. Transport, storage, and communications	08. Communication	
J. Financial intermediation	09. Recreation and culture	
K. Real estate, renting, and business activities	10. Education	
L. Public administration and defense; compulsory social security	11. Restaurants and hotels	
M. Education	12. Miscellaneous goods and services	
N. Health and social work		
O. Other community, social, and personal service activities		
P. Private households with employed persons		
Q. Extraterritorial organizations and bodies		

Table E.1 *(Continued)*

Production approach	Expenditure approach	Income approach
Taxes on products	NPISH final consumption	Compensation of employees received from rest of world
Value added type taxes	Government final consumption	
Other taxes on products	Gross capital formation	Compensation of employees paid to rest of world
Subsidies on products	Gross fixed capital formation	
Statistical discrepancy	Change in inventories	Property income received from rest of world
	Acquisition less disposals of valuables	
	Exports of goods and services	Property income paid to rest of world
	Goods	
	Services	Taxes on production and imports subsidies
	Imports of goods and services	
	Goods	
	Services	
	Statistical discrepancy	
Gross domestic product	Gross domestic product	Gross national income

Source: ICP, http://icp.worldbank.org/.

expenditures by category and the second to expenditures by category.

For each account, economies were asked to report the adjustments required to make the initial estimates for the economic activities, the expenditure categories, and the income transactions exhaustive. The adjustments were to be given as a percentage of the initial estimate. Economies were advised that the distinction between the seven types of nonexhaustiveness was not hard and fast because some adjustments could just as easily be classified under one type of nonexhaustiveness as another. What was important was that all omissions from the accounts be identified and included under one of the seven types of nonexhaustiveness and that there be no double counting. Not all economies could quantify the adjustments to improve exhaustiveness. Economies that could not provide an actual adjustment were asked to indicate in the matrixes the estimates that were not exhaustive (or considered to be not exhaustive) and the reason they were not exhaustive (the type of nonexhaustiveness).

Changes in Methodology between the 2005 and 2011 ICP Rounds

Measuring the Real Size of the World Economy: The Framework, Methodology, and Results of the International Comparison Program (ICP) (World Bank 2013) is a comprehensive review of the statistical and economic theory underlying the estimation of purchasing power parities (PPPs). Even though the PPPs provided by the ICP rest on a large body of statistical and economic theory, many decisions based on expert judgment have to be made.[1] In fact, because the decisions to be made require expertise ranging from survey design to price and index number theory, the system of national accounts, and methods of aggregating PPPs to the gross domestic product (GDP), the ICP formed a Technical Advisory Group (TAG) composed of internationally known experts in each of these areas as well as those who use the ICP results for research, especially on poverty.

Indeed, the outcome of each ICP comparison is a function of the choices made, starting by determining what products to price and how to price them, choosing the index number formula to turn prices into basic heading PPPs, and then determining the multilateral formula needed to aggregate the PPPs to GDP. Decisions about these different methods are made first at the regional level, and then again on the process

needed to link every economy in every region to a common numéraire currency.

The choices do not make much difference when the economies being compared have similar expenditure patterns and relative prices. However, when computing PPPs across economies such as Tajikistan and the United States or Chad and the United States, the choices affect the results to a greater degree. And, finally, some aggregates of GDP are difficult to compare, such as housing rents, government expenditures, and construction, thereby adding another dimension of decisions to be made.

Lessons learned from previous ICP comparisons led to the development of several significantly new and improved methods for ICP 2005. Subsequent analysis of the 2005 data set the stage for making additional improvements in ICP 2011.

The dilemma facing the ICP is that the continual improvement of methods is limiting the comparison of PPPs over time. Although each benchmark may be based on the best methods available at the time, their comparability may be limited. The purpose of this appendix is to describe the new methods implemented in ICP 2011, explain why they were chosen, and provide a subjective assessment of the potential impact of the changes. The following sections go into more detail about the choices made for ICP 2011 and how they affect comparability with ICP 2005.

---

[1] This appendix is based on the paper "Understanding Changes in Methodology between the 2005 and 2011 International Comparison Programs" by Paul McCarthy and Frederic A. Vogel, co-chairs of the ICP Technical Advisory Group (see McCarthy and Vogel 2014).

HOUSEHOLD CONSUMPTION: PRODUCT SELECTION AND IMPORTANT PRODUCTS

Statistical theory suggests that a master frame should list every possible product purchased by consumers and the annual expenditures associated with each product for every economy. A random sample of products would then be selected and the national annual average prices for them would be determined. The expenditure on each product would be used to weight product PPPs to basic heading PPPs. The reality, however, is that there is no such list. Although statistical theory can be used to determine the number of products to be priced, it is left to the regional and national coordinators using their expert judgment to select the actual products out of the thousands of possibilities. The ICP's *Measuring the Real Size of the World Economy* (World Bank 2013) provides guidelines on the number of products to be priced. For example, it recommends that six products be priced for the rice basic heading but about 70–100 for the garment basic heading. The reason is that rice is a relatively homogeneous product (although it is necessary to specify different varieties to be priced), whereas garments are much more heterogeneous.

The comparability of the products being priced is an essential principle underlying the estimation of PPPs. A dilemma facing the ICP is that, although a product may be available in several economies, it may be a significant part of consumption in only a few of them. Because there are no data on expenditures for individual products, the relative prices or product PPPs are averaged with equal weights to obtain the basic heading PPP. To overcome this problem, two regions—the Eurostat–Organisation for Economic Co-operation and Development (OECD) region and Commonwealth of Independent States (CIS) region—have adopted the concept of representativity to induce a form of weighting. A representative product is one that is purchased frequently by households and has a price level consistent with all products in the basic heading. Because representative products are those most frequently purchased, it is likely that they have lower price levels in economies in which they are representative compared with the price levels in the economies in which they are

available but not representative. Economies in the ICP regions attempted to use the representative classification in 2005 but were unable to apply the notion of a representative price level consistently. As a result, the concept was not used in 2005 in the ICP regions or for estimating interregional linking factors.

TAG proposed a simpler method for ICP 2011. Economies other than those in the Eurostat-OECD and CIS regions were asked to classify all goods and services for household consumption as either important or less important. Importance was defined by reference to the notional expenditure share of the product within a basic heading. The importance classification was a subjective process, as was the assignment of representative status, but simpler. If it was thought that the expenditure share would probably be large, the product was classified as important; if small, it was classified as less important.

The procedure to determine the products to be priced for household consumption in 2005 differed from that for 2011:

- In 2005 each regional coordinator, in collaboration with the national coordinators, used structured product descriptions (SPDs) furnished by the Global Office to create product specifications. Each region did so independently of other regions.

- After data collection and several iterations of data validation were completed, all regions submitted their final set of priced products.

- The Global Office harmonized definitions and collapsed the combined lists from the regions into a list of about 1,000 products called the Ring list. This list was the basis for a separate data collection by a subset of economies in each region—the Ring economies—that was then used to link PPPs across regions.

- The resulting price levels from the Ring data collection were not consistent with those for the corresponding economies within each of the regions. For example, some Ring economies priced products that were not representative of their consumption patterns, but those products received equal weight in the computation of linking factors. To the degree this took place, it points to an overestimate of price levels and an underestimate of real expenditures in the Africa and the Asia and the Pacific regions compared with the other regions.

Subsequent analysis of the Ring list, prices, PPPs, and linking factors produced several lessons learned. First, the selected Ring economies did not always turn out to be representative of the other economies in the region. Analysis showed that between-economy variability was greater than the variability in relative prices within basic headings. Based on this analysis, TAG recommended the following steps:

- Develop a set of global core products that would be priced by all economies for linking purposes. The final 2005 Ring list became the starting point for determining the set of global core products for 2011.

- Include the global core products in the regional lists as well. The starting point in each region to develop the list for 2011 was the 2005 regional product list and the set of global core products.

- Classify products as important or less important. Although economies were expected to be able to price a large number of global core products, not all would have the same price levels or relative expenditures. Products common in some economies may be more difficult to find in other economies, with the likelihood of higher prices. Therefore, the importance classification is needed to prevent an upward bias in the price levels used to estimate the between-region PPPs.

- Aggregate product PPPs to the basic heading level using the weighted country product dummy (CPD-W) method, with a weight of 3 for important products and a weight of 1 for less important products.

Because the representative classification was used only in the Eurostat-OECD and CIS regions in ICP 2005, the likely result was an upward bias in PPPs (that is, smaller real expenditures) in the remaining ICP regions. If the use of the importance classification were successful in 2011, the result would be lower relative prices and larger real expenditures in the remaining regions. These price level differences

would be difficult to quantify because one would assume that the regional and national coordinators, because of their previous experience, would be able to better validate prices for the 2011 comparison.

HOUSING RENTS

Housing rents have proven to be one of the most problematic components of each ICP comparison, in part because the values are estimated so poorly in many economies' national accounts and in part because the prices provided for the ICP are often not consistent with the national accounts values. It is difficult to estimate PPPs for housing rents because of the varying mix of rental versus owner-occupied housing. PPPs for dwellings were computed in three different ways in 2005. Rental rates were used where there was a large rental market. Where the rental market was not large enough, PPPs were computed indirectly using the quantity approach. Because the rental markets in the Africa and the Asia and the Pacific regions were not large enough to use market rents to estimate PPPs, the regions attempted to use the quantity method. However, this approach produced implausible results, and so PPPs were imputed for those regions using the reference volume method. Even though there were insufficient data to use the quantity method within those regions, there was enough to compute between-region linking factors.

In view of the importance of housing PPPs, it was agreed by TAG and the regions to place greater emphasis on obtaining rental data. TAG recommended that all economies provide two sets of data. First, all economies were to redouble efforts to provide rental prices. Second, all economies were to provide data on quantities (ideally, square meters of dwellings but at least numbers of dwellings, classified by type) and quality (indoor plumbing, etc.) of the entire housing stock even where there was a large rental market. Global specifications were prepared to collect data on rents and quantities, which meant that the within-region PPPs were based on the same data used to compute the between-region PPPs or linking factors.

The dilemma was that economies without rental markets also had difficulty providing consistent and comparable quantity and quality data. For that reason, the Asia and the Pacific region imputed PPPs for dwellings in the same way it did in 2005, relying on the reference volume method. Rental data were used to estimate dwelling PPPs in the Africa, Latin America, Caribbean, and Western Asia regions; quantity data in the CIS region; and a combination of both in the Eurostat-OECD region. Regions were linked using a combination of rental and quantity data for the subset of economies able to provide them.

Although the PPPs for dwellings are not optimal, the results between 2005 and 2011 are mostly comparable.

GOVERNMENT COMPENSATION

For ICP 2005, the Global Office prepared a global list of over 40 government occupations for which economies provided annual salaries. Government salaries were adjusted for productivity in the Africa, Asia and the Pacific, and Western Asia regions because of the huge differences in the salaries paid in the economies in those regions. (Not adjusting for productivity differences would have resulted in some implausibly large estimates of the government final consumption expenditure in lower-income economies.) The annual salaries from the same list of occupations were used to compute between-region linking factors. However, they were not adjusted for productivity.

For ICP 2011, the list of global occupations remained about the same as those used in 2005. A major change was that the Eurostat-OECD region was now using output indicators to estimate real expenditures on education, whereas the other regions were continuing to use input indicators (salaries). Therefore, it was necessary to develop some special procedures to link the Eurostat-OECD region to the other regions for the education PPPs.

Productivity adjustments were made to the real expenditure estimates for government in the Africa, Asia and the Pacific, Latin America, and Caribbean regions. No productivity adjustments were applied within the Eurostat-OECD, CIS, and Western Asia regions because differences in labor productivity within each of those regions were considered to be relatively small. However, productivity adjustments were made to all regions when the interregional linking factors were estimated, thereby improving the quality of the resulting PPPs and real expenditures.

CONSTRUCTION

Prior to ICP 2005, PPPs for construction were based on an output (model-based) approach. The pricing methods for construction were changed in ICP 2005, in part for cost reasons (pricing models required specialists such as quantity surveyors) and in part for methodological reasons (it had proven to be virtually impossible to specify a small number of models that were relevant to all economies in a region). The method adopted in ICP 2005 was known as the basket of construction components (BOCC) approach.

The BOCC approach involved collecting prices for a range of major construction components and basic inputs that were common across economies. The term *construction components* was used to describe specific physical outputs that were produced as intermediate steps in construction projects. A key element in this process was that the overall price estimated for each composite component related to an installed component, including the costs of materials, labor, and equipment—that is, the price was more related to an output price than to an input price.

The objective of the BOCC approach was to provide simple and affordable price comparisons for construction. An important goal was to develop a technique that would enable construction to be priced in major locations within each economy. Such a technique would result in comparable prices for similar components across economies that had different labor-to-equipment mixes because of their different levels of economic development.

In practice, the BOCC method did not prove to be satisfactory. The main problems were the difficulty in pricing the composite components (they required construction specialists) and overlaps between the composite and the basic materials that also had to be priced to ensure adequate coverage of products.

The approach initially proposed for ICP 2011 was based on pricing inputs (basic materials and equipment hire) and using them to approximate an output price on the basis of the relationships between the outputs and inputs for each economy, as estimated in each economy's input-output tables. However, investigations showed that up-to-date input-output tables were not available in enough economies for the approach to be viable.

In April 2011, TAG endorsed the proposal to use an input-price approach and recommended the following:

- Basic heading PPPs for construction would be based on a simple combination of three groups of inputs (materials, labor, and equipment) rather than allocating each input to model projects, or weighting each input in any other way.

- An unweighted country product dummy (CPD) regression would be used to estimate PPPs within each of the three product groups for each basic heading: residential buildings, nonresidential buildings, and civil engineering works. Each basic heading would then have three PPPs—one for materials, one for labor, and one for equipment. These would be combined using their respective weights.

- Basic headings PPPs would be computed as weighted averages of the PPPs for materials, labor, and equipment. The weights would be centrally determined for five clusters of economies in each region (although economies could provide their own specific weights, if available, rather than having a cluster-based weight applied). This was later changed to three clusters (high, middle, and low income).

- Prices would be collected for 38 material inputs and seven categories of labor, and hire rates would be collected for five types of equipment.

- Economies would be asked to confirm which resources were relevant to each basic heading.

- Information on markups (profits, value added tax, project overheads, etc.) would be collected from construction experts, thereby enabling the PPPs for each basic heading to be adjusted to account for markups. Ideally, markups would be specific to each economy, but it might be necessary in some cases to estimate markups for a group of similar economies.

Later, in October 2011, TAG discussed whether labor productivity adjustments should be applied. It concluded that there was no need to adjust for labor productivity differences between economies because each economy had to provide weights for materials, labor, and equipment hire for each basic heading. However, an assumption underlying not making this adjustment was that total factor productivity (TFP) was equal across economies.

In May 2013, TAG examined the construction data collected. It found that the data quality was poor in a number of areas, particularly that related to the relevance indicators (the types of materials being used in different types of construction) and the overheads for markups and professional fees. In many cases, economies did not provide any estimates of these markups. As a result, TAG recommended the following:

- A single set of relevance indicators should be used within each region rather than those provided by individual economies. Each region would use a construction expert to provide advice on the relevance of the various components to the different types of construction activity.

- Resource weights provided by the Global Office should be used to average PPPs for materials, labor, and equipment for economies not able to provide the data.

- Construction prices should not be adjusted for markups and professional fees because of the poor quality of the data collected on these aspects.

- The prices for equipment hire should be split into those including an operator and those excluding an operator and treated as separate product specifications.

Finally, in September 2013 TAG reconsidered its earlier recommendation that no productivity adjustment be applied to construction labor, which implied that the TFP in construction would be identical across economies. TAG considered the possibilities for specific adjustments for labor productivity or for TFP, and the eventual consensus was that no adjustment should be applied for labor productivity but that an adjustment for TFP should be considered. Thus a set of TFP adjustment factors was produced, but it became clear that they added noise to the construction price estimates rather than improving them. As a result, TAG reaffirmed its earlier decision that no adjustments should be applied to construction prices for either labor productivity or TFP differences across economies.

Fully implementing TAG's recommendations regarding adjustments to prices for construction markups proved problematic because of the poor quality (or nonprovision) of data by the participating economies. Data were available for some economies, but they had not been properly validated because of the regional coordinators' views that an insufficient number of economies had provided data on markups, and there was a large degree of variability in the data that were available. At this late stage, it was not possible to ask economies to collect new markup data for 2011.

Because of problems in 2005 pricing the composite components, the construction PPPs were essentially based on the basic components, which meant that the resulting PPPs mostly reflected an input approach. The basic components priced in 2011 were about the same as those priced in 2005. The net result was that neither the 2005 PPPs nor the 2011 PPPs were based on output prices. Although this was not the desired method, the construction results for 2005 and 2011 were considered to be broadly comparable.

ESTIMATING WITHIN-REGION PPPs

Chapters 4 and 5 of *Measuring the Real Size of the World Economy* (World Bank 2013) describe the different properties of the various indexes that can be used to compute basic heading PPPs and aggregate them to GDP. These chapters are also the basis for the choices made for ICP 2011.

The basic methodology used in ICP 2005 was as follows:

- The CPD method was used in the ICP regions coordinated by the Global Office and the Jevons-GEKS* (Gini-Éltetö-Köves-Szulc) method in the Eurostat-OECD and CIS regions to compute basic heading PPPs. The Jevons-GEKS* method used the representative classification; the CPD method did not.

- The GEKS method was used in the final stage of estimation to ensure that the PPPs were transitive and base country–invariant. In 2005 Africa used the Iklé method, which produces additive results but also is subject to the Gerschenkron effect. Both approaches provide results that are transitive and base country–invariant. The base country–invariant property ensures that the PPPs between any two economies are the same no matter which economy is the base. The transitive property simply means that the price level—for example, of the United Kingdom relative to the United States—is the same whether it is calculated directly or through any possible chain of economies such as the United States to Nepal to Nigeria, etc. If one imposes the transitive property, the PPPs between any two economies can change if the mix of the remaining economies changes. When a region is homogeneous, the direct and indirect PPPs remain similar. However, the process induces more variability when indirect PPPs enter from economies with widely different price and expenditure structures. This effect has implications for the linking methods discussed in the next section.

- Housing rent PPPs in the Africa and the Asia and the Pacific regions were imputed, with the other regions using either rental prices or quantities adjusted for quality. Government salaries were adjusted for productivity in the Africa, Asia and the Pacific, and Western Asia regions. Although these steps improved the results within the Africa and Asia and the Pacific regions, they affected their comparability with economies in other regions. This especially applied to government compensation because the between-region PPPs were not adjusted for productivity.

- Prices for each product were to represent national annual average prices. Where this was not possible, economies were to use the consumer price index and other information to calibrate the prices to national annual averages. There was much debate about China, which submitted prices that mostly represented urban areas and so were potentially overstating national average prices. Experts such as Deaton and Heston (2008) estimated that adjustments based on the distribution of consumption between urban and rural areas would raise the estimates of the real expenditure on Chinese GDP by about 10 percent in 2005.

The methodology for ICP 2011, adhering to the TAG recommendations, was the following:

- The CPD-W for household consumption was used in ICP regions, with weights of 3:1 for important versus less important products. The Jevons-GEKS* method used in the Eurostat-OECD and CIS regions in 2005 remained in effect.

- The GEKS method was used in the final stage of estimation to ensure that the PPPs were transitive and base country–invariant.

The issue now is whether the relative rankings within each region are comparable between 2011 and 2005. The within-region 2011 results will not be exactly comparable with those for 2005 if the methods used to estimate housing rents and the application of productivity adjustments differ between the two periods. The set of economies changed between some regions—for example, Chile became part of the OECD, major economies such as Argentina did not take part, and others such as the Islamic Republic of Iran were treated separately. In other words, changes in the relative rankings of economies within regions can be the result of changes in methodology or because of the different composition of economies within a region.

LINKING THE REGIONS

The methodology to link the regions remained about the same between 2005 and 2011 at the basic heading level except that all economies provided prices for a set of global core products instead of 18 economies providing prices for a separate Ring list. However, a significant change was made in how the linking took place for higher aggregates up to GDP. The linking method at the basic heading level was as follows:

- Core product prices provided by all economies (18 Ring economies in 2005) were deflated to a regional currency using within-region basic heading PPPs.

- The result was five sets of regional prices treated as super economies. The CPD-W (CPD in 2005) regression over these five sets of regional prices provided between-region basic heading PPPs. These between-region PPPs, when multiplied by within-region basic heading PPPs, were converted to a global currency. The same regional scalar, say for rice, times each economy's within-region PPP converted it to a global PPP.

- This method preserved within-region fixity, which means the relative rankings between economies in the same region remained the same after linking.

- In 2005 this computation step included only the 18 Ring economies and the Ring prices, whereas in 2011 the between-region PPPs were based on core prices provided by every economy. Because these core prices were also included in the estimation of within-region PPPs, the between-region results were more consistent with the within-region results.

- The CIS region in both 2005 and 2011 was linked to the Eurostat-OECD region using the Russian Federation as a bridge economy. Two new 2011 regions, the Caribbean and Pacific Islands, were linked similarly using the bridge approach. The Caribbean economies were linked through Latin America, and the Pacific Islands were linked through Australia, Fiji, and New Zealand as bridge economies.

Between-region linking factors for 2011 were based on all economies instead of a subset of subjectively selected economies. Thus the factors were more statistically robust. The final computational step was to link regions at the higher-level aggregates and GDP. In 2005 the between-region PPPs (linking factors) were aggregated to GDP using the GEKS method. In a separate computation, within-region PPPs were aggregated to GDP as described in the previous section. Again, the aggregated between-region PPPs times the aggregated within-region PPPs calibrated the results to the global currency.[2]

After considering several alternatives, TAG proposed that a procedure called the country aggregation with redistribution (CAR) be used:

- A global aggregation that includes all 177 economies and 155 basic headings in a GEKS aggregation would provide PPPs calibrated to a global currency. To preserve within-region fixity, real expenditures would be summed to regional totals, which would then be distributed within each region according to the distribution from the within-region computations. These results would be base country–invariant and transitive, and they would preserve fixity.

- The global PPP between any two economies would be the geometric mean of the direct comparison and the $n - 2$ indirect comparisons with every other economy. The range of the direct and indirect comparisons would be small for economies with similar price and expenditure structures, but could become large where economies differed significantly.

- Simulations show that real expenditures were increased in Asia and the Pacific by 9 percent and 6 percent, respectively, for 2005 and 2011. This simulation did not include the impact of using global core prices from all economies versus Ring prices from 18 economies.

---

[2] Chapter 6 in *Measuring the Real Size of the World Economy* (World Bank 2013) reviews the properties of this method, which reveals that the computations are dependent on the choice of base economy.

SUMMARY

The ICP includes economies ranging from city-states and small islands to large and diverse economies such as Brazil, China, India, and Russia. Like all statistical endeavors, PPPs are statistical estimates that fall within some margin of error of the unknown true values. The ICP 2005 final report suggested using caution when comparing economies by the size of their GDP or expenditures per capita because there could be errors in the calculation of GDP and population sizes in addition to the statistical variability inherent in the PPPs (World Bank 2008). The report indicated that differences in GDP of less than 5 percent lie within the margin of error of the PPP estimation. Deaton (2013) has suggested a method to measure statistical variability in the estimation of PPPs that stems from the choice of products, the range of PPP product prices, and differences in basic heading expenditures. He shows that standard errors of PPPs become larger for economies with different price and expenditure structures. Approximations revealed that the standard errors of Indian or Chinese prices to U.S. 2005 prices were between 10 and 15 percent.

The range suggested by the standard errors reflects the variability resulting from the choice of methods. This analysis has pointed out that a possible adjustment for urban/rural prices in China would have raised its real expenditures by about 10 percent in 2005. The CAR procedure would have raised real expenditures for all Asia and the Pacific economies in 2005 by about 9 percent compared with the other regions. Therefore, adopting the CAR approach for 2011 rather than the Ring approach would have raised the real expenditures of all Asia and the Pacific economies in 2011 compared with those of the Eurostat-OECD economies. Table H.2 in appendix H presents the analytical 2005 results calculated using the CAR procedure.

Reference PPPs Used in ICP 2011

Reference PPPs Used in ICP 2011

The gross domestic product (GDP) expenditures used for the 2011 round of the International Comparison Program (ICP) were classified into 155 basic headings. However, prices for 42 basic headings were not collected. For some of these basic headings it was too difficult to specify comparable products that could be priced across economies; for others it was too expensive and time-consuming to collect prices. The basic headings for which prices were not collected are listed in table G.1. Some obvious examples are narcotics, prostitution, financial intermediation services indirectly measured (FISIM), gross operating surplus, inventories, exports, and imports.

Without prices for those basic headings, aggregation at higher aggregate levels is clearly not possible because it is necessary to have a complete matrix of basic heading PPPs. For that reason, reference PPPs were used in ICP 2011 as proxies for the basic headings for which no prices were collected. This is standard practice in all ICP comparisons.

Reference PPPs fall into three categories: price-based, volume-based, and exchange rate–based. Two types of price-based reference PPPs can be distinguished: those that are specific and those that are neutral. Specific price-based reference PPPs are based on the PPPs of basic headings considered similar to the basic headings for which no prices were collected. An example of a specific price-based reference PPP is that for package holidays, which is the weighted average

of the PPP for transport services and the PPP for restaurants and hotels where the weights are the expenditures on the constituent basic headings. Neutral price-based reference PPPs are based on the PPPs of a large group of basic headings. For example, one could use the PPP for the individual consumption expenditure by households as the reference PPP for FISIM and intermediate consumption. The objective is to ensure that the use of a reference PPP does not change the PPP of the larger group to which the basic heading with missing PPPs belongs.

The reference PPPs used for ICP 2011 and the basic headings to which they apply are detailed in table G.1. They were either price-based reference PPPs or exchange rate–based reference PPPs. A volume-based reference PPP was employed in the Asia and the Pacific comparison for the basic heading actual and imputed rentals. Exchange rate–based reference PPPs were used for four basic headings: purchases by resident households in the rest of the world, purchases by nonresident households in the economic territory, exports of goods and services, and imports of goods and services.

In calculating reference PPPs, with the exception of narcotics, weighted Gini-Éltető-Köves-Szulc (GEKS) indexes were used. The weights were the expenditures on the basic headings whose PPPs were being averaged. Basic headings with reference PPPs were not used to generate reference PPPs for other basic headings for which no prices were collected.

Table G.1 Reference PPPs, ICP 2011

Basic heading		Reference PPP
Individual consumption expenditure by households and nonprofit institutions serving households (NPISHs)		
110231.1	Narcotics	Unweighted geometric average of the PPP for tobacco (110221.1) and the PPP for pharmaceutical products (110611.1)
110442.1	Miscellaneous dwelling services	Weighted Gini-Éltetö-Köves-Szulc (GEKS) of the PPP for maintenance and repair of the dwelling (110431.1) and the PPP for water supply (110441.1)
110631.1	Hospital services	PPP for outpatient health services (110620)
110714.1	Animal-drawn vehicles	PPP for bicycles (110713.1)
110734.1	Passenger transport by sea	PPP for transport services (110730), excluding basic headings (BHs) with reference PPPs
110735.1	Combined passenger transport	Weighted GEKS of the PPP for passenger transport by railway (110731.1) and the PPP for passenger transport by road (110732.1)
110736.1	Other transport services	Weighted GEKS of the PPP for passenger transport by railway (110731.1) and the PPP for passenger transport by road (110732.1)
110923.1	Maintenance of other major durables	Weighted GEKS of the PPP for maintenance and repair of personal transport equipment (110723.1) and the PPP for repair of audiovisual, photographic, and information processing equipment (110915.1)
110943.1	Games of chance	PPP for recreational and sporting services (110941.1)
110961.1	Package holidays	Weighted GEKS of the PPP for transport services (110730) and the PPP for restaurants and hotels (111100), excluding BHs with reference PPPs
111221.1	Prostitution	PPP for individual consumption expenditure by households (110000), excluding health and education BHs and BHs with reference PPPs
111241.1	Social protection	PPP for collective consumption expenditure by government (140000), excluding BHs with reference PPPs
111251.1	Insurance	PPP for individual consumption expenditure by households (110000), excluding health and education BHs and BHs with reference PPPs
111261.1	Financial intermediation services indirectly measured (FISIM)	PPP for individual consumption expenditure by households (110000), excluding health and education BHs and BHs with reference PPPs
111311.1	Purchases by resident households in the rest of the world	Exchange rate
111311.2	Purchases by nonresident households in the economic territory	Exchange rate
120111.1	NPISHs	PPP for individual consumption expenditure by government (130000), excluding BHs with reference PPPs
Individual and collective consumption expenditure by government		
130111.1	Housing	PPP for actual and imputed rentals (110411.1)
130212.4	Hospital services	PPP for production of health services by government (130220), excluding BHs with reference PPPs
130222.1	Intermediate consumption (health)	PPP for individual consumption expenditure by households (110000), excluding health and education BHs and BHs with reference PPPs
130223.1	Gross operating surplus (health)	PPP for gross fixed capital formation (150000), excluding BHs with reference PPPs
130224.1	Net taxes on production (health)	PPP for production of health services by government (130220), excluding BHs with reference PPPs
130225.1	Receipts from sales (health)	PPP for production of health services by government (130220), excluding BHs with reference PPPs
130311.1	Recreation and culture	Weighted GEKS of the PPP for recreational and sporting services (110941.1) and the PPP for cultural services (110942.1)

Table G.1 (Continued)

Basic heading		Reference PPP
130411.1	Education benefits and reimbursements	PPP for production of education services by government (130420), excluding BHs with reference PPPs
130422.1	Intermediate consumption (education)	PPP for individual consumption expenditures by households (110000), excluding health and education BHs and BHs with reference PPPs
130423.1	Gross operating surplus (education)	PPP for gross fixed capital formation (150000), excluding BHs with reference PPPs
130424.1	Net taxes on production (education)	PPP for production of education services by government (130420), excluding BHs with reference PPPs
130425.1	Receipt from sales (education)	PPP for production of education services by government (130420), excluding BHs with reference PPPs
130511.1	Social protection	PPP for collective consumption expenditure by government (140000), excluding BHs with reference PPPs
140112.1	Intermediate consumption (collective services)	PPP for individual consumption expenditures by households (110000), excluding health and education BHs and BHs with reference PPPs
140113.1	Gross operating surplus (collective services)	PPP for gross fixed capital formation (150000), excluding BHs with reference PPPs
140114.1	Net taxes on production (collective services)	PPP for collective consumption expenditure by government (140000), excluding BHs with reference PPPs
140115.1	Receipts from sales (collective services)	PPP for collective consumption expenditure by government (140000), excluding BHs with reference PPPs
Gross fixed capital formation		
150121.2	Other road transport	PPP for motor vehicles, trailers, and semitrailers (150121.1)
150122.1	Other transport equipment	PPP for machinery and equipment (150100), excluding BHs with reference PPPs
Other expenditures		
160111.1	Opening value of inventories	Weighted GEKS of the PPPs of BHs classified as containing predominantly goods, excluding BHs with reference PPPs
160111.2	Closing value of inventories	Weighted GEKS of the PPPs of BHs classified as containing predominantly goods, excluding BHs with reference PPPs
160211.1	Acquisitions of valuables	Exchange rate
160211.2	Disposals of valuables	Exchange rate
170111.1	Exports of goods and services	Exchange rate
170111.2	Imports of goods and services	Exchange rate

Source: ICP, http://icp.worldbank.org/.

Updated ICP 2005 Results

This appendix provides updated results for the 2005 International Comparison Program (ICP). Table H.1 presents revised ICP 2005 results using updated 2005 expenditure, population, and exchange rate data. Subsequently, all related indicators were revised. In addition, purchasing power parities (PPPs) for the Eurostat— Organisation for Economic Co-operation and Development (OECD) comparison were updated as per their published revised 2005 results. Table H.2 presents the revised ICP 2005 results, calculated using the ICP 2011 aggregation procedure, the country aggregation with redistribution (CAR).

In tables H.1 and H.2, the updated ICP 2005 summary results are broken down into the following indicators:

- Column (01): Gross domestic product (GDP) based on PPPs in U.S. dollars
- Column (02): GDP based on exchange rates in U.S. dollars
- Column (03): GDP per capita based on PPPs in U.S. dollars
- Column (04): GDP per capita based on exchange rates in U.S. dollars
- Column (05): Price level index for GDP with the world equal to 100
- Column (06): GDP per capita index based on PPPs with the world equal to 100
- Column (07): GDP per capita index based on exchange rates with the world equal to 100

- Column (08): GDP per capita index based on PPPs with the United States equal to 100
- Column (09): GDP per capita index based on exchange rates with the United States equal to 100
- Column (10): Share of PPP-based world GDP
- Column (11): Share of exchange rate–based world GDP
- Column (12): Share of world population
- Column (13): PPP for GDP with the U.S. dollar equal to 1.000
- Column (14): Exchange rate with the U.S. dollar equal to 1.000
- Column (15): Resident population
- Column (16): Nominal GDP in national currency unit

Column (01) shows the real expenditures of economies and regions on GDP in U.S. dollars. The expenditures reflect only volume differences between economies and regions. They were obtained by dividing the nominal expenditures for GDP in column (16) by the PPPs for GDP in column (13). The GDP per capita in column (03), the GDP per capita indexes in columns (06) and (08), and the shares of world GDP in column (10) are all based on the real expenditures in column (01).

Column (02) shows the nominal expenditures of economies and regions on GDP in U.S. dollars. The expenditures reflect both price differences and volume differences between economies and regions (see box 2.1 in chapter 2). They were derived by dividing the nominal expenditures on GDP in column (16) by the exchange rates in column (14). The GDP per capita in column (04), the GDP per capita indexes in columns (07) and (09), and the shares of world GDP in column (11) are all based on the nominal expenditures in column (02).

Users are reminded that, as explained in chapter 1, exchange rate–converted GDPs are not reliable measures of either the size of economies or the material well-being of their populations. They are included in the summary table and in the supplementary tables for reference only.

Table H.1 Revised ICP 2005 Summary Results: GDP

GROSS DOMESTIC PRODUCT	Expenditure (US$, billions)		Expenditure per capita (US$)		Price level index	Expenditure per capita index				Share (world = 100.0)			PPP	Reference data		
						World = 100.0		US = 100.0		Expenditure		Popula-tion		Exchange rate	Popula-tion	Expenditure in national currency unit
Economy	Based on PPPs	Based on XRs	Based on PPPs	Based on XRs	(world = 100.0)	Based on PPPs	Based on XRs	Based on PPPs	Based on XRs	Based on PPPs	Based on XRs		(US$ = 1.000)	(US$ = 1.000)	(millions)	(billions)
(00)	(01)	(02)	(03)	(04)	(05)	(06)	(07)	(08)	(09)	(10)ᵃ	(11)ᵃ	(12)ᵃ	(13)ᵇ	(14)ᵇ	(15)	(16)
AFRICA																
Angola	60.0	30.6	3,627	1,851	63.6	39.3	25.0	8.2	4.2	0.1	0.1	0.3	44.488	87.159	16.54	2,669.6
Benin	10.5	4.4	1,279	533	51.9	13.9	7.2	2.9	1.2	0.0	0.0	0.1	219.585	527.468	8.18	2,298.7
Botswana	20.5	9.7	10,927	5,176	59.0	118.4	69.8	24.7	11.7	0.0	0.0	0.0	2.421	5.110	1.88	49.6
Burkina Faso	14.4	5.5	1,072	407	47.3	11.6	5.5	2.4	0.9	0.0	0.0	0.2	200.227	527.468	13.42	2,881.4
Burundiᶜ	...	...	...	...	39.5	...	...	...	...	...	...	0.1	342.964	1,081.577	7.77	...
Cameroon	35.0	16.6	1,929	918	59.3	20.9	12.4	4.4	2.1	0.1	0.0	0.3	251.015	527.468	18.14	8,781.0
Cape Verde	1.4	1.1	2,912	2,278	97.4	31.5	30.7	6.6	5.1	0.0	0.0	0.0	69.360	88.670	0.48	96.7
Central African Republic	2.7	1.4	682	341	62.3	7.4	4.6	1.5	0.8	0.0	0.0	0.1	263.740	527.468	3.96	712.1
Chad	16.8	6.6	1,680	662	49.1	18.2	8.9	3.8	1.5	0.0	0.0	0.2	208.000	527.468	10.01	3,499.3
Comoros	0.6	0.4	1,076	615	71.2	11.7	8.3	2.4	1.4	0.0	0.0	0.0	226.195	395.601	0.60	146.2
Congo, Dem. Rep.	22.9	10.3	424	191	56.3	4.6	2.6	1.0	0.4	0.0	0.0	0.9	214.267	473.908	54.03	4,903.0
Congo, Rep.	12.0	6.1	3,395	1,730	63.5	36.8	23.3	7.7	3.9	0.0	0.0	0.1	268.760	527.468	3.54	3,232.7
Côte d'Ivoire	31.3	17.1	1,802	982	67.9	19.5	13.3	4.1	2.2	0.1	0.0	0.3	287.485	527.468	17.39	9,011.8
Djibouti	1.5	0.7	1,916	913	59.3	20.7	12.3	4.3	2.1	0.0	0.0	0.0	84.685	177.721	0.78	126.0
Egypt, Arab Rep.ᵈ	351.6	98.2	5,023	1,402	34.8	54.4	18.9	11.4	3.2	0.6	0.2	1.1	1.616	5.789	70.00	568.2
Equatorial Guinea	13.2	7.2	21,904	11,936	67.9	237.3	161.0	49.5	27.0	0.0	0.0	0.0	287.423	527.468	0.60	3,800.5
Ethiopia	42.5	11.1	559	145	32.4	6.1	2.0	1.3	0.3	0.1	0.0	1.2	2.254	8.666	76.17	95.9
Gabon	19.5	9.5	14,116	6,857	60.5	152.9	92.5	31.9	15.5	0.0	0.0	0.0	256.230	527.468	1.38	4,989.3
Gambia, The	2.4	0.6	1,642	434	33.0	17.8	5.9	3.7	1.0	0.0	0.0	0.0	7.560	28.575	1.44	17.8
Ghanaᵉ	41.9	17.2	1,961	805	51.1	21.2	10.9	4.4	1.8	0.1	0.0	0.3	0.372	0.906	21.38	15.6
Guinea	8.8	2.9	917	307	41.7	9.9	4.1	2.1	0.7	0.0	0.0	0.2	1,219.348	3,644.333	9.58	10,703.7
Guinea-Bissau	1.9	0.8	1,344	554	51.3	14.6	7.5	3.0	1.3	0.0	0.0	0.0	217.300	527.468	1.42	415.3
Kenya	48.0	18.7	1,340	524	48.7	14.5	7.1	3.0	1.2	0.1	0.0	0.6	29.524	75.554	35.79	1,415.8
Lesotho	2.5	1.4	1,295	711	68.4	14.0	9.6	2.9	1.6	0.0	0.0	0.0	3.490	6.359	1.93	8.7
Liberia	1.2	0.6	378	186	61.3	4.1	2.5	0.9	0.4	0.0	0.0	0.1	0.493	1.000	3.27	0.6
Madagascar	15.7	5.1	857	278	40.4	9.3	3.8	1.9	0.6	0.0	0.0	0.3	649.568	2,003.026	18.29	10,186.7
Malawi	10.1	3.4	779	259	41.5	8.4	3.5	1.8	0.6	0.0	0.0	0.2	39.457	118.420	12.92	397.1
Mali	20.9	9.5	1,752	798	56.7	19.0	10.8	4.0	1.8	0.0	0.0	0.2	240.092	527.468	11.94	5,024.2
Mauritania	5.9	2.2	1,865	694	46.4	20.2	9.4	4.2	1.6	0.0	0.0	0.1	98.840	265.528	3.15	580.0

Table H.1 *(Continued)*

GROSS DOMESTIC PRODUCT	Expenditure (US$, billions)		Expenditure per capita (US$)		Price level index	Expenditure per capita index				Share (world = 100.0)			PPP	Reference data		
						World = 100.0		US = 100.0		Expenditure		Popula-tion		Exchange rate	Popula-tion	Expenditure in national currency unit
Economy	Based on PPPs	Based on XRs	Based on PPPs	Based on XRs	(world = 100.0)	Based on PPPs	Based on XRs	Based on PPPs	Based on XRs	Based on PPPs	Based on XRs		(US$ = 1.000)	(US$ = 1.000)	(millions)	(billions)
(00)	(01)	(02)	(03)	(04)	(05)	(06)	(07)	(08)	(09)	(10)ᵃ	(11)ᵃ	(12)ᵃ	(13)ᵇ	(14)ᵇ	(15)	(16)
Mauritius	12.5	6.2	10,014	4,983	62.0	108.5	67.2	22.6	11.3	0.0	0.0	0.0	14.677	29.496	1.24	182.7
Morocco	107.1	59.0	3,556	1,957	68.5	38.5	26.4	8.0	4.4	0.2	0.1	0.5	4.878	8.865	30.13	522.6
Mozambiqueᵉ	13.9	6.6	662	313	58.9	7.2	4.2	1.5	0.7	0.0	0.0	0.3	10.909	23.061	21.01	151.7
Namibia	10.8	7.3	5,341	3,582	83.5	57.9	48.3	12.1	8.1	0.0	0.0	0.0	4.265	6.359	2.03	46.2
Niger	7.8	3.4	595	256	53.5	6.4	3.4	1.3	0.6	0.0	0.0	0.2	226.661	527.468	13.18	1,777.0
Nigeria	247.3	113.5	1,772	813	57.1	19.2	11.0	4.0	1.8	0.4	0.2	2.3	60.232	131.274	139.59	14,894.5
Rwanda	7.7	2.6	820	274	41.6	8.9	3.7	1.9	0.6	0.0	0.0	0.2	186.182	557.823	9.43	1,439.8
São Tomé and Príncipe	0.2	0.1	1,514	797	65.6	16.4	10.8	3.4	1.8	0.0	0.0	0.0	5,558.089	10,557.970	0.15	1,301.3
Senegal	18.3	8.7	1,619	773	59.4	17.5	10.4	3.7	1.7	0.0	0.0	0.2	251.668	527.468	11.27	4,593.1
Sierra Leone	4.4	1.7	867	322	46.3	9.4	4.3	2.0	0.7	0.0	0.0	0.1	1,074.122	2,889.588	5.12	4,769.8
South Africa	405.8	247.1	8,517	5,186	75.8	92.3	70.0	19.3	11.7	0.7	0.5	0.8	3.872	6.359	47.64	1,571.1
Sudanᵉ	79.6	35.3	2,199	974	55.2	23.8	13.1	5.0	2.2	0.1	0.1	0.6	1.077	2.430	36.20	85.7
Swaziland	5.0	2.6	4,517	2,339	64.5	48.9	31.6	10.2	5.3	0.0	0.0	0.0	3.293	6.359	1.10	16.4
Tanzania	35.9	12.6	926	324	43.6	10.0	4.4	2.1	0.7	0.1	0.0	0.6	395.627	1,128.934	38.82	14,219.1
Togo	4.6	2.1	836	381	56.8	9.1	5.1	1.9	0.9	0.0	0.0	0.1	240.381	527.468	5.54	1,113.1
Tunisia	72.0	32.3	7,182	3,218	55.8	77.8	43.4	16.2	7.3	0.1	0.1	0.2	0.581	1.297	10.03	41.9
Uganda	28.9	10.0	1,004	350	43.3	10.9	4.7	2.3	0.8	0.1	0.0	0.5	619.640	1,780.666	28.72	17,877.9
Zambiaᵉ	13.9	7.5	1,214	657	67.4	13.2	8.9	2.7	1.5	0.0	0.0	0.2	2.415	4.464	11.47	33.6
Zimbabweᶠ	3.6	...	287	...	184.2	3.1	...	0.6	1.0	0.0	...	0.2	1.479	...	12.71	5.4
Total (48)	**1,898.7**	**863.7**	**2,230**	**1,014**	**56.7**	**24.2**	**13.7**	**5.0**	**2.3**	**3.3**	**1.9**	**13.8**	**n.a.**	**n.a.**	**851.4**	**n.a.**
ASIA AND THE PACIFIC																
Bangladesh	191.3	67.3	1,381	486	43.8	15.0	6.6	3.1	1.1	0.3	0.1	2.3	22.642	64.327	138.60	4,332.3
Bhutan	2.3	0.8	3,639	1,299	44.5	39.4	17.5	8.2	2.9	0.0	0.0	0.0	15.739	44.100	0.63	36.4
Brunei Darussalam	17.6	9.5	49,001	26,587	67.6	530.7	358.7	110.8	60.1	0.0	0.0	0.0	0.903	1.664	0.36	15.9
Cambodia	20.1	6.3	1,558	487	38.9	16.9	6.6	3.5	1.1	0.0	0.0	0.2	1,278.552	4,092.500	12.93	25,754.3
Chinaᵍ	5,364.3	2,256.9	4,123	1,735	52.4	44.7	23.4	9.3	3.9	9.4	4.9	21.1	3.448	8.194	1,301.16	18,493.7
Hong Kong SAR, China	248.3	181.6	36,440	26,650	91.1	394.7	359.5	82.4	60.2	0.4	0.4	0.1	5.688	7.777	6.81	1,412.1
Macao SAR, China	17.9	11.8	37,041	24,365	81.9	401.2	328.7	83.7	55.1	0.0	0.0	0.0	5.270	8.011	0.48	94.5
Taiwan, China	607.0	365.0	26,659	16,029	74.9	288.7	216.2	60.3	36.2	1.1	0.8	0.4	19.341	32.167	22.77	11,740.3
Fiji	3.6	3.0	4,300	3,636	105.3	46.6	49.0	9.7	8.2	0.0	0.0	0.0	1.430	1.691	0.83	5.1
India	2,425.5	806.8	2,202	733	41.4	23.9	9.9	5.0	1.7	4.3	1.8	17.9	14.669	44.100	1,101.32	35,579.1
Indonesia	705.2	285.9	3,192	1,294	50.5	34.6	17.5	7.2	2.9	1.2	0.6	3.6	3,934.264	9,704.742	220.93	27,74,281.1
Iran, Islamic Rep.	725.7	216.6	10,345	3,087	37.2	112.1	41.6	23.4	7.0	1.3	0.5	1.1	2,674.755	8,963.959	70.15	19,41,187.6
Lao PDR	9.7	2.7	1,723	483	34.9	18.7	6.5	3.9	1.1	0.0	0.0	0.1	2,988.385	10,655.167	5.62	28,947.8
Malaysia	313.5	143.5	12,036	5,511	57.0	130.4	74.3	27.2	12.5	0.6	0.3	0.4	1.734	3.787	26.05	543.6
Maldives	1.7	1.1	5,070	3,222	79.1	54.9	43.5	11.5	7.3	0.0	0.0	0.0	8.134	12.800	0.34	14.0
Mongolia	7.3	2.5	2,845	985	43.1	30.8	13.3	6.4	2.2	0.0	0.0	0.0	417.222	1,205.247	2.56	3,041.4
Nepal	27.3	8.7	1,119	355	39.5	12.1	4.8	2.5	0.8	0.0	0.0	0.4	22.651	71.368	24.44	619.4
Pakistan	398.4	127.9	2,588	831	40.0	28.0	11.2	5.8	1.9	0.7	0.3	2.5	19.102	59.514	153.96	7,610.8

(continued)

Table H.1 (Continued)

GROSS DOMESTIC PRODUCT	Expenditure (US$, billions) Based on PPPs	Based on XRs	Expenditure per capita (US$) Based on PPPs	Based on XRs	Price level index (world = 100.0)	Expenditure per capita index World = 100.0 Based on PPPs	Based on XRs	US = 100.0 Based on PPPs	Based on XRs	Share (world = 100.0) Expenditure Based on PPPs	Based on XRs	Population	PPP (US$ = 1.000)	Exchange rate (US$ = 1.000)	Population (millions)	Expenditure in national currency unit (billions)
Economy (00)	(01)	(02)	(03)	(04)	(05)	(06)	(07)	(08)	(09)	(10)[a]	(11)[a]	(12)[a]	(13)[b]	(14)[b]	(15)	(16)
Philippines	261.0	103.1	3,061	1,209	49.2	33.2	16.3	6.9	2.7	0.5	0.2	1.4	21.755	55.085	85.26	5,677.7
Singapore	193.6	125.4	45,374	29,403	80.7	491.5	396.7	102.6	66.5	0.3	0.3	0.1	1.079	1.664	4.27	208.8
Sri Lanka	69.7	24.4	3,546	1,241	43.6	38.4	16.7	8.0	2.8	0.1	0.1	0.3	35.170	100.498	19.67	2,452.8
Thailand	476.2	188.6	7,314	2,897	49.3	79.2	39.1	16.5	6.5	0.8	0.4	1.1	15.932	40.220	65.10	7,586.3
Vietnam	193.9	57.6	2,368	704	37.0	25.6	9.5	5.4	1.6	0.3	0.1	1.3	4,712.688	15,858.917	81.91	9,14,000.8
Total (23)	**12,281.2**	**4,997.0**	**3,670**	**1,493**	**50.7**	**39.8**	**20.1**	**8.3**	**3.4**	**21.6**	**11.0**	**54.4**	**n.a.**	**n.a.**	**3,346.1**	**n.a.**
COMMONWEALTH OF INDEPENDENT STATES																
Armenia	12.6	4.9	4,008	1,564	48.6	43.4	21.1	9.1	3.5	0.0	0.0	0.1	178.580	457.688	3.13	2,242.9
Azerbaijan[e]	38.4	13.2	4,579	1,580	43.0	49.6	21.3	10.4	3.6	0.1	0.0	0.1	0.326	0.946	8.38	12.5
Belarus	83.5	30.2	8,639	3,126	45.1	93.6	42.2	19.5	7.1	0.1	0.1	0.2	779.330	2,153.800	9.66	65,067.1
Georgia	15.3	6.2	3,505	1,427	50.7	38.0	19.3	7.9	3.2	0.0	0.0	0.1	0.738	1.813	4.36	11.3
Kazakhstan	131.8	57.1	8,699	3,771	54.0	94.2	50.9	19.7	8.5	0.2	0.1	0.2	57.610	132.880	15.15	7,590.6
Kyrgyz Republic	8.9	2.5	1,776	491	34.5	19.2	6.6	4.0	1.1	0.0	0.0	0.1	11.350	41.012	5.01	100.9
Moldova	8.5	3.0	2,364	831	43.8	25.6	11.2	5.3	1.9	0.0	0.0	0.1	4.430	12.600	3.60	37.7
Russian Federation[h]	1,696.7	764.1	11,822	5,324	56.1	128.1	71.8	26.7	12.0	3.0	1.7	2.3	12.736	28.280	143.52	21,609.8
Tajikistan	9.7	2.3	1,436	341	29.6	15.6	4.6	3.2	0.8	0.0	0.0	0.1	0.740	3.118	6.78	7.2
Ukraine	262.8	86.1	5,578	1,829	40.8	60.4	24.7	12.6	4.1	0.5	0.2	0.8	1.680	5.125	47.11	441.5
Total (10)	**2,268.1**	**969.7**	**9,194**	**3,931**	**53.3**	**99.6**	**53.0**	**20.8**	**8.9**	**4.0**	**2.1**	**4.0**	**n.a.**	**n.a.**	**246.7**	**n.a.**
EUROSTAT-OECD																
Albania	18.7	8.1	5,942	2,574	54.0	64.4	34.7	13.4	5.8	0.0	0.0	0.1	43.640	100.739	3.14	814.8
Australia	693.4	735.2	33,755	35,789	132.1	365.6	482.8	76.3	80.9	1.2	1.6	0.3	1.388	1.309	20.54	962.7
Austria	276.7	305.1	33,638	37,095	137.4	364.3	500.4	76.0	83.8	0.5	0.7	0.1	0.886	0.804	8.23	245.2
Belgium	337.3	377.5	32,204	36,042	139.4	348.8	486.2	72.8	81.5	0.6	0.8	0.2	0.900	0.804	10.47	303.4
Bosnia and Herzegovina	25.4	11.6	6,608	3,019	56.9	71.6	40.7	14.9	6.8	0.0	0.0	0.1	0.718	1.572	3.84	18.2
Bulgaria	75.9	28.9	9,835	3,748	47.5	106.5	50.6	22.2	8.5	0.1	0.1	0.1	0.599	1.572	7.72	45.5
Canada	1,132.0	1,133.8	35,106	35,161	124.7	380.2	474.3	79.3	79.5	2.0	2.5	0.5	1.214	1.212	32.25	1,373.8
Croatia	68.1	44.8	15,329	10,089	82.0	166.0	136.1	34.6	22.8	0.1	0.1	0.1	3.915	5.949	4.44	266.7
Cyprus	18.4	16.9	24,917	22,893	114.4	269.9	308.8	56.3	51.7	0.0	0.0	0.0	0.426	0.464	0.74	7.8
Czech Republic	217.7	130.2	21,268	12,719	74.5	230.3	171.6	48.1	28.7	0.4	0.3	0.2	14.316	23.939	10.23	3,116.1
Denmark	179.9	258.0	33,196	47,608	178.6	359.6	642.3	75.0	107.6	0.3	0.6	0.1	8.590	5.990	5.42	1,545.3
Estonia	22.3	13.9	16,525	10,320	77.8	179.0	139.2	37.4	23.3	0.0	0.0	0.0	7.854	12.577	1.35	175.0
Finland	161.1	195.9	30,709	37,335	151.4	332.6	503.7	69.4	84.4	0.3	0.4	0.1	0.977	0.804	5.25	157.4
France	1,860.7	2,137.4	29,555	33,950	143.1	320.1	458.0	66.8	76.7	3.3	4.7	1.0	0.923	0.804	62.96	1,718.0
Germany	2,566.0	2,767.4	31,117	33,559	134.3	337.0	452.7	70.3	75.9	4.5	6.1	1.3	0.867	0.804	82.46	2,224.4
Greece	270.4	240.2	24,348	21,629	110.6	263.7	291.8	55.0	48.9	0.5	0.5	0.2	0.714	0.804	11.10	193.0
Hungary	171.2	110.4	16,975	10,948	80.3	183.9	147.7	38.4	24.7	0.3	0.2	0.2	128.593	199.381	10.09	22,018.3
Iceland	10.4	16.3	34,976	55,110	196.2	378.8	743.5	79.1	124.6	0.0	0.0	0.0	99.078	62.881	0.30	1,025.7
Ireland	161.4	202.8	38,795	48,758	156.5	420.2	657.8	87.7	110.2	0.3	0.4	0.1	1.010	0.804	4.16	163.0
Israel	161.4	133.7	23,210	19,223	103.2	251.4	259.3	52.5	43.5	0.3	0.3	0.1	3.717	4.488	6.96	600.0

Table H.1 (Continued)

GROSS DOMESTIC PRODUCT	Expenditure (US$, billions)		Expenditure per capita (US$)		Price level index	Expenditure per capita index				Share (world = 100.0)			PPP	Reference data		
						World = 100.0		US = 100.0		Expenditure		Popula-tion		Exchange rate	Popula-tion	Expenditure in national currency unit
Economy	Based on PPPs	Based on XRs	Based on PPPs	Based on XRs	(world = 100.0)	Based on PPPs	Based on XRs	Based on PPPs	Based on XRs	Based on PPPs	Based on XRs		(US$ = 1.000)	(US$ = 1.000)	(millions)	(billions)
(00)	(01)	(02)	(03)	(04)	(05)	(06)	(07)	(08)	(09)	(10)a	(11)a	(12)a	(13)b	(14)b	(15)	(16)
Italy	1,657.4	1,787.0	28,280	30,491	134.3	306.3	411.3	63.9	68.9	2.9	3.9	1.0	0.867	0.804	58.61	1,436.4
Japan	3,889.6	4,571.9	30,446	35,786	146.4	329.8	482.8	68.8	80.9	6.8	10.0	2.1	129.552	110.218	127.76	5,03,903.0
Korea, Rep.	1,096.7	844.9	22,783	17,551	95.9	246.8	236.8	51.5	39.7	1.9	1.9	0.8	788.920	1,024.120	48.14	8,65,240.9
Latvia	29.8	16.1	13,312	7,183	67.2	144.2	96.9	30.1	16.2	0.1	0.0	0.0	0.302	0.560	2.24	9.0
Lithuania	48.7	26.1	14,657	7,851	66.7	158.8	105.9	33.1	17.7	0.1	0.1	0.1	1.487	2.775	3.32	72.4
Luxembourg	31.8	37.7	68,167	80,812	147.7	738.3	1090.2	154.1	182.7	0.1	0.1	0.0	0.953	0.804	0.47	30.3
Macedonia, FYR	16.0	6.0	7,877	2,939	46.5	85.3	39.7	17.8	6.6	0.0	0.0	0.0	18.389	49.280	2.04	295.1
Malta	8.7	6.1	21,590	15,222	87.8	233.8	205.4	48.8	34.4	0.0	0.0	0.0	0.244	0.346	0.40	2.1
Mexico	1,293.8	846.1	12,461	8,149	81.5	135.0	109.9	28.2	18.4	2.3	1.9	1.7	7.127	10.898	103.83	9,220.7
Montenegro	5.2	2.3	8,288	3,624	54.5	89.8	48.9	18.7	8.2	0.0	0.0	0.0	0.352	0.804	0.62	1.8
Netherlands	572.9	638.7	35,111	39,145	138.9	380.3	528.1	79.4	88.5	1.0	1.4	0.3	0.896	0.804	16.32	513.4
New Zealand	103.9	112.3	25,046	27,069	134.6	271.3	365.2	56.6	61.2	0.2	0.2	0.1	1.535	1.420	4.15	159.5
Norway	220.2	304.3	47,640	65,834	172.1	516.0	888.1	107.7	148.8	0.4	0.7	0.1	8.896	6.438	4.62	1,958.9
Poland	526.1	304.1	13,786	7,968	72.0	149.3	107.5	31.2	18.0	0.9	0.7	0.6	1.869	3.234	38.16	983.3
Portugal	225.4	191.9	21,370	18,194	106.0	231.5	245.4	48.3	41.1	0.4	0.4	0.2	0.684	0.804	10.55	154.3
Romania	203.1	99.3	9,390	4,591	60.9	101.7	61.9	21.2	10.4	0.4	0.2	0.4	1.423	2.910	21.62	289.0
Russian Federationh	1,696.7	764.1	11,822	5,324	56.1	128.1	71.8	26.7	12.0	3.0	1.7	2.3	12.736	28.280	143.52	21,609.8
Serbia	63.4	25.2	8,515	3,391	49.6	92.2	45.7	19.2	7.7	0.1	0.1	0.1	26.564	66.707	7.44	1,683.2
Slovak Republic	87.1	47.9	16,175	8,889	68.4	175.2	119.9	36.6	20.1	0.2	0.1	0.1	17.050	31.026	5.39	1,485.6
Slovenia	47.0	35.7	23,470	17,863	94.8	254.2	241.0	53.0	40.4	0.1	0.1	0.0	146.564	192.563	2.00	6,883.0
Spain	1,188.8	1,131.3	27,392	26,067	118.5	296.7	351.7	61.9	58.9	2.1	2.5	0.7	0.765	0.804	43.40	909.3
Sweden	295.3	371.2	32,702	41,105	156.6	354.2	554.5	73.9	92.9	0.5	0.8	0.1	9.378	7.461	9.03	2,769.4
Switzerland	274.9	385.0	36,649	51,321	174.4	397.0	692.3	82.8	116.0	0.5	0.8	0.1	1.743	1.245	7.50	479.1
Turkey	781.2	481.4	11,394	7,021	76.7	123.4	94.7	25.8	15.9	1.4	1.1	1.1	0.831	1.348	68.57	648.9
United Kingdom	1,984.9	2,297.4	32,952	38,140	144.2	356.9	514.5	74.5	86.2	3.5	5.0	1.0	0.636	0.550	60.24	1,262.7
United States	13,095.5	13,095.5	44,243	44,243	124.6	479.2	596.9	100.0	100.0	23.0	28.7	4.8	1.000	1.000	295.99	13,095.5
Total (46)	**37,872.3**	**37,297.3**	**27,492**	**27,075**	**122.7**	**297.8**	**365.3**	**62.1**	**61.2**	**66.7**	**81.8**	**22.4**	**n.a.**	**n.a.**	**1,377.6**	**n.a.**
LATIN AMERICA																
Argentina	419.0	183.2	10,843	4,740	54.5	117.4	63.9	24.5	10.7	0.7	0.4	0.6	1.269	2.904	38.65	531.9
Bolivia	34.5	9.5	3,747	1,037	34.5	40.6	14.0	8.5	2.3	0.1	0.0	0.1	2.232	8.066	9.21	77.0
Brazil	1,582.6	882.0	8,502	4,738	69.4	92.1	63.9	19.2	10.7	2.8	1.9	3.0	1.357	2.434	186.15	2,147.2
Chile	206.4	123.1	12,690	7,565	74.2	137.4	102.1	29.7	17.1	0.4	0.3	0.3	333.690	559.768	16.27	68,882.8
Colombia	314.4	146.6	7,280	3,394	58.1	78.9	45.8	16.5	7.7	0.6	0.3	0.7	1,081.948	2,320.830	43.19	3,40,156.0
Ecuador	98.2	41.5	7,116	3,007	52.6	77.1	40.6	15.1	6.8	0.2	0.1	0.2	0.423	1.000	13.80	41.5
Paraguay	26.9	8.7	4,554	1,479	40.5	49.3	20.0	10.3	3.3	0.0	0.0	0.1	2,006.827	6,177.960	5.90	53,962.3
Peru	176.0	79.4	6,348	2,863	56.2	68.8	38.6	14.3	6.5	0.3	0.2	0.5	1.487	3.296	27.73	261.7
Uruguay	32.0	17.4	9,626	5,221	67.6	104.3	70.4	21.8	11.8	0.1	0.0	0.1	13.278	24.479	3.33	425.0
Venezuela, RBe	263.8	145.5	9,869	5,445	68.7	106.9	73.5	22.3	12.3	0.5	0.3	0.4	1.153	2.090	26.73	304.1
Total (10)	**3,153.9**	**1,636.9**	**8,502**	**4,413**	**64.6**	**92.1**	**59.5**	**19.2**	**10.0**	**5.6**	**3.6**	**6.0**	**n.a.**	**n.a.**	**370.9**	**n.a.**

(continued)

GROSS DOMESTIC PRODUCT	Expenditure (US$, billions)		Expenditure per capita (US$)		Price level index	Expenditure per capita index				Share (world = 100.0)			PPP	Reference data		
						World = 100.0		US = 100.0		Expenditure		Popula-tion		Exchange rate	Popula-tion	Expenditure in national currency unit
Economy	Based on PPPs	Based on XRs	Based on PPPs	Based on XRs	(world = 100.0)	Based on PPPs	Based on XRs	Based on PPPs	Based on XRs	Based on PPPs	Based on XRs		(US$ = 1.000)	(US$ = 1.000)	(millions)	(billions)
(00)	(01)	(02)	(03)	(04)	(05)	(06)	(07)	(08)	(09)	(10)[a]	(11)[a]	(12)[a]	(13)[b]	(14)[b]	(15)	(16)
WESTERN ASIA																
Bahrain	24.2	15.9	27,173	17,901	82.1	294.3	241.5	61.4	40.5	0.0	0.0	0.0	0.249	0.378	0.89	6.0
Egypt, Arab Rep.[d]	351.6	98.2	5,023	1,402	34.8	54.4	18.9	11.4	3.2	0.6	0.2	1.1	1.616	5.789	70.00	568.2
Iraq	95.6	36.2	3,417	1,296	47.2	37.0	17.5	7.7	2.9	0.2	0.1	0.5	558.701	1,473.000	27.96	53,386.4
Jordan	23.5	12.6	4,485	2,406	66.8	48.6	32.5	10.1	5.4	0.0	0.0	0.1	0.381	0.709	5.23	8.9
Kuwait	110.4	80.8	49,899	36,504	91.1	540.5	492.5	112.8	82.5	0.2	0.2	0.0	0.214	0.292	2.21	23.6
Lebanon	38.9	21.9	9,750	5,481	70.0	105.6	73.9	22.0	12.4	0.1	0.0	0.1	847.518	1,507.500	3.99	32,944.0
Oman	51.1	30.9	20,381	12,318	75.3	220.7	166.2	46.1	27.8	0.1	0.1	0.1	0.232	0.385	2.51	11.9
Qatar	59.0	44.4	69,612	52,357	93.7	754.0	706.3	157.3	118.3	0.1	0.1	0.0	2.745	3.650	0.85	162.1
Saudi Arabia	510.6	328.2	21,886	14,068	80.1	237.1	189.8	49.5	31.8	0.9	0.7	0.4	2.410	3.750	23.33	1,230.8
Syrian Arab Rep.	76.4	28.9	4,206	1,590	47.1	45.6	21.5	9.5	3.6	0.1	0.1	0.3	19.717	52.140	18.17	1,506.4
Yemen, Rep.	52.5	19.1	2,626	953	45.2	28.4	12.9	5.9	2.2	0.1	0.0	0.3	69.490	191.400	19.98	3,646.6
Total (11)	**1,393.7**	**717.0**	**7,959**	**4,094**	**64.1**	**86.2**	**55.2**	**18.0**	**9.3**	**2.5**	**1.6**	**2.8**	**n.a.**	**n.a.**	**175.1**	**n.a.**
WORLD[i] (146)	**56,819.6**	**45,619.4**	**9,232**	**7,413**	**100.0**	**100.0**	**100.0**	**20.9**	**16.8**	**100.0**	**100.0**	**100.0**	**n.a.**	**n.a.**	**6,154.30**	**n.a.**

Source: ICP, http://icp.worldbank.org/.

Note: n.a. = not applicable; XR = exchange rate; ... = data suppressed because of incompleteness.

a. All shares are rounded to one decimal place. More precision can be found in the Excel version of the table, which can be downloaded from the ICP website.

b. All exchange rates (XRs) and PPPs are rounded to three decimal places. More precision can be found in the Excel version of the table, which can be downloaded from the ICP website.

c. Burundi submitted prices, but it did not provide official national accounts data.

d. The Arab Republic of Egypt participated in both the Africa and Western Asia regions. The results for Egypt from each region were averaged by taking the geometric mean of the PPPs, allowing Egypt to be shown in each region with the same ranking in the world comparison.

e. Currency adjusted to reflect 2011 currency.

f. Zimbabwe's exchange rate–related data were suppressed because of extreme volatility in the official exchange rate. PPP adjusted to reflect 2011 currency.

g. Results for China were based on the national average prices extrapolated by the World Bank and Asian Development Bank using price data for 11 cities submitted by the National Bureau of Statistics of China. The data for China do not include Hong Kong SAR, China; Macao SAR, China; and Taiwan, China.

h. The Russian Federation participated in both the Commonwealth of Independent States (CIS) and Eurostat-Organisation for Economic Co-operation and Development (OECD) comparisons. The PPPs for Russia are based on the Eurostat-OECD comparison. They were the basis for linking the CIS comparison to the ICP.

i. Does not double count the dual participation economies: the Arab Republic of Egypt and the Russian Federation.

Table H.2 Analytical ICP 2005 Summary Results Using the Country Aggregation with Redistribution (CAR) Method: GDP

GROSS DOMESTIC PRODUCT	Expenditure (US$, billions)		Expenditure per capita (US$)		Price level index	Expenditure per capita index				Share (world = 100.0)			PPP	Reference data		
						World = 100.0		US = 100.0		Expenditure		Popula-tion		Exchange rate	Popula-tion	Expenditure in national currency unit
Economy	Based on PPPs	Based on XRs	Based on PPPs	Based on XRs	(world = 100.0)	Based on PPPs	Based on XRs	Based on PPPs	Based on XRs	Based on PPPs	Based on XRs		(US$ = 1.000)	(US$ = 1.000)	(millions)	(billions)
(00)	(01)	(02)	(03)	(04)	(05)	(06)	(07)	(08)	(09)	(10)[a]	(11)[a]	(12)[a]	(13)[b]	(14)[b]	(15)	(16)
AFRICA																
Angola	59.2	30.6	3,577	1,851	65.8	38.0	25.0	8.1	4.2	0.1	0.1	0.3	45.117	87.159	16.54	2,669.6
Benin	10.3	4.4	1,262	533	53.7	13.4	7.2	2.9	1.2	0.0	0.0	0.1	222.691	527.468	8.18	2,298.7
Botswana	20.2	9.7	10,775	5,176	61.1	114.3	69.8	24.4	11.7	0.0	0.0	0.0	2.455	5.110	1.88	49.6
Burkina Faso	14.2	5.5	1,057	407	48.9	11.2	5.5	2.4	0.9	0.0	0.0	0.2	203.059	527.468	13.42	2,881.4
Burundi[c]	…	…	…	…	40.9	…	…	…	…	…	…	0.1	347.817	1,081.577	7.77	…
Cameroon	34.5	16.6	1,902	918	61.4	20.2	12.4	4.3	2.1	0.1	0.0	0.3	254.567	527.468	18.14	8,781.0
Cape Verde	1.4	1.1	2,872	2,278	100.9	30.5	30.7	6.5	5.1	0.0	0.0	0.0	70.342	88.670	0.48	96.7
Central African Republic	2.7	1.4	672	341	64.5	7.1	4.6	1.5	0.8	0.0	0.0	0.1	267.472	527.468	3.96	712.1
Chad	16.6	6.6	1,657	662	50.8	17.6	8.9	3.7	1.5	0.0	0.0	0.2	210.943	527.468	10.01	3,499.3
Comoros	0.6	0.4	1,061	615	73.7	11.3	8.3	2.4	1.4	0.0	0.0	0.0	229.395	395.601	0.60	146.2
Congo, Dem. Rep.	22.6	10.3	418	191	58.3	4.4	2.6	0.9	0.4	0.0	0.0	0.9	217.298	473.908	54.03	4,903.0
Congo, Rep.	11.9	6.1	3,348	1,730	65.7	35.5	23.3	7.6	3.9	0.0	0.0	0.1	272.563	527.468	3.54	3,232.7
Côte d'Ivoire	30.9	17.1	1,777	982	70.3	18.9	13.3	4.0	2.2	0.1	0.0	0.3	291.553	527.468	17.39	9,011.8
Djibouti	1.5	0.7	1,889	913	61.4	20.0	12.3	4.3	2.1	0.0	0.0	0.0	85.883	177.721	0.78	126.0
Egypt, Arab Rep.[d]	346.7	98.2	4,953	1,402	36.0	52.6	18.9	11.2	3.2	0.6	0.2	1.1	1.639	5.789	70.00	568.2
Equatorial Guinea	13.0	7.2	21,599	11,936	70.3	229.2	161.0	48.8	27.0	0.0	0.0	0.0	291.489	527.468	0.60	3,800.5
Ethiopia	42.0	11.1	551	145	33.5	5.8	2.0	1.2	0.3	0.1	0.0	1.2	2.286	8.666	76.17	95.9
Gabon	19.2	9.5	13,919	6,857	62.6	147.7	92.5	31.5	15.5	0.0	0.0	0.0	259.855	527.468	1.38	4,989.3
Gambia, The	2.3	0.6	1,619	434	34.1	17.2	5.9	3.7	1.0	0.0	0.0	0.0	7.667	28.575	1.44	17.8
Ghana[e]	41.3	17.2	1,934	805	52.9	20.5	10.9	4.4	1.8	0.1	0.0	0.3	0.377	0.906	21.38	15.6
Guinea	8.7	2.9	904	307	43.1	9.6	4.1	2.0	0.7	0.0	0.0	0.2	1,236.599	3,644.333	9.58	10,703.7
Guinea-Bissau	1.9	0.8	1,326	554	53.1	14.1	7.5	3.0	1.3	0.0	0.0	0.0	220.375	527.468	1.42	415.3
Kenya	47.3	18.7	1,321	524	50.4	14.0	7.1	3.0	1.2	0.1	0.0	0.6	29.942	75.554	35.79	1,415.8
Lesotho	2.5	1.4	1,277	711	70.8	13.5	9.6	2.9	1.6	0.0	0.0	0.0	3.539	6.359	1.93	8.7
Liberia	1.2	0.6	372	186	63.5	4.0	2.5	0.8	0.4	0.0	0.0	0.1	0.500	1.000	3.27	0.6
Madagascar	15.5	5.1	845	278	41.8	9.0	3.8	1.9	0.6	0.0	0.0	0.3	658.758	2,003.026	18.29	10,186.7
Malawi	9.9	3.4	768	259	43.0	8.1	3.5	1.7	0.6	0.0	0.0	0.2	40.015	118.420	12.92	397.1
Mali	20.6	9.5	1,728	798	58.7	18.3	10.8	3.9	1.8	0.0	0.0	0.2	243.489	527.468	11.94	5,024.2
Mauritania	5.8	2.2	1,839	694	48.0	19.5	9.4	4.2	1.6	0.0	0.0	0.1	100.238	265.528	3.15	580.0
Mauritius	12.3	6.2	9,875	4,983	64.2	104.8	67.2	22.3	11.3	0.0	0.0	0.0	14.885	29.496	1.24	182.7
Morocco	105.6	59.0	3,507	1,957	70.3	37.2	26.4	7.9	4.4	0.2	0.1	0.5	4.947	8.865	30.13	522.6
Mozambique[e]	13.7	6.6	653	313	61.0	6.9	4.2	1.5	0.7	0.0	0.0	0.3	11.064	23.061	21.01	151.7
Namibia	10.7	7.3	5,267	3,582	86.5	55.9	48.3	11.9	8.1	0.0	0.0	0.0	4.325	6.359	2.03	46.2
Niger	7.7	3.4	586	256	55.4	6.2	3.4	1.3	0.6	0.0	0.0	0.2	229.868	527.468	13.18	1,777.0
Nigeria	243.8	113.5	1,747	813	59.2	18.5	11.0	3.9	1.8	0.4	0.2	2.3	61.084	131.274	139.59	14,894.5
Rwanda	7.6	2.6	809	274	43.0	8.6	3.7	1.8	0.6	0.0	0.0	0.2	188.816	557.823	9.43	1,439.8
São Tomé and Príncipe	0.2	0.1	1,493	797	67.9	15.8	10.8	3.4	1.8	0.0	0.0	0.0	5,636.722	10,557.970	0.15	1,301.3

(continued)

Table H.2 *(Continued)*

GROSS DOMESTIC PRODUCT	Expenditure (US$, billions)		Expenditure per capita (US$)		Price level index	Expenditure per capita index				Share (world = 100.0)			PPP	Reference data		
						World = 100.0		US = 100.0		Expenditure		Popula-tion		Exchange rate	Popula-tion	Expenditure in national currency unit
Economy	Based on PPPs	Based on XRs	Based on PPPs	Based on XRs	(world = 100.0)	Based on PPPs	Based on XRs	Based on PPPs	Based on XRs	Based on PPPs	Based on XRs		(US$ = 1.000)	(US$ = 1.000)	(millions)	(billions)
(00)	(01)	(02)	(03)	(04)	(05)	(06)	(07)	(08)	(09)	(10)[a]	(11)[a]	(12)[a]	(13)[b]	(14)[b]	(15)	(16)
Senegal	18.0	8.7	1,597	773	61.5	16.9	10.4	3.6	1.7	0.0	0.0	0.2	255.228	527.468	11.27	4,593.1
Sierra Leone	4.4	1.7	855	322	47.9	9.1	4.3	1.9	0.7	0.0	0.0	0.1	1,089.318	2,889.588	5.12	4,769.8
South Africa	400.1	247.1	8,398	5,186	78.5	89.1	70.0	19.0	11.7	0.7	0.5	0.8	3.927	6.359	47.64	1,571.1
Sudan[e]	78.5	35.3	2,168	974	57.1	23.0	13.1	4.9	2.2	0.1	0.1	0.6	1.092	2.430	36.20	85.7
Swaziland	4.9	2.6	4,454	2,339	66.8	47.3	31.6	10.1	5.3	0.0	0.0	0.0	3.340	6.359	1.10	16.4
Tanzania	35.4	12.6	913	324	45.2	9.7	4.4	2.1	0.7	0.1	0.0	0.6	401.224	1,128.934	38.82	14,219.1
Togo	4.6	2.1	824	381	58.8	8.7	5.1	1.9	0.9	0.0	0.0	0.1	243.782	527.468	5.54	1,113.1
Tunisia	71.0	32.3	7,082	3,218	57.8	75.2	43.4	16.0	7.3	0.1	0.1	0.1	0.590	1.297	10.03	41.9
Uganda	28.4	10.0	990	350	44.9	10.5	4.7	2.2	0.8	0.0	0.0	0.5	628.407	1,780.666	28.72	17,877.9
Zambia[e]	13.7	7.5	1,198	657	69.8	12.7	8.9	2.7	1.5	0.0	0.0	0.2	2.449	4.464	11.47	33.6
Zimbabwe[f]	3.6	...	283	...	190.6	3.0	...	0.6	...	0.0	...	0.2	1.500	...	12.71	5.4
Total (48)	**1,872.2**	**863.7**	**2,199**	**1,014**	**58.6**	**23.3**	**13.7**	**5.0**	**2.3**	**3.2**	**1.9**	**13.8**	**n.a.**	**n.a.**	**851.4**	**n.a.**
ASIA AND THE PACIFIC																
Bangladesh	209.7	67.3	1,513	486	40.8	16.1	6.6	3.4	1.1	0.4	0.1	2.3	20.658	64.327	138.60	4,332.3
Bhutan	2.5	0.8	3,988	1,299	41.4	42.3	17.5	9.0	2.9	0.0	0.0	0.0	14.360	44.100	0.63	36.4
Brunei Darussalam	19.3	9.5	53,706	26,587	62.9	569.9	358.7	121.4	60.1	0.0	0.0	0.0	0.824	1.664	0.36	15.9
Cambodia	22.1	6.3	1,708	487	36.2	18.1	6.6	3.9	1.1	0.0	0.0	0.2	1,166.549	4,092.500	12.93	25,754.3
China[a]	5,879.3	2,256.9	4,519	1,735	48.8	47.9	23.4	10.2	3.9	10.1	4.9	21.1	3.146	8.194	1,301.16	18,493.7
Hong Kong SAR, China	272.1	181.6	39,939	26,650	84.8	423.8	359.5	90.3	60.2	0.5	0.4	0.1	5.190	7.777	6.81	1,412.1
Macao SAR, China	19.6	11.8	40,597	24,365	76.3	430.8	328.7	91.8	55.1	0.0	0.0	0.0	4.808	8.011	0.48	94.5
Taiwan, China	665.3	365.0	29,218	16,029	69.7	310.1	216.2	66.0	36.2	1.1	0.8	0.4	17.646	32.167	22.77	11,740.3
Fiji	3.9	3.0	4,713	3,636	98.1	50.0	49.0	10.7	8.2	0.0	0.0	0.0	1.304	1.691	0.83	5.1
India	2,658.4	806.8	2,414	733	38.6	25.6	9.9	5.5	1.7	4.6	1.8	17.9	13.384	44.100	1,101.32	35,579.1
Indonesia	772.9	285.9	3,498	1,294	47.0	37.1	17.5	7.9	2.9	1.3	· 0.6	3.6	3,589.617	9,704.742	220.93	27,74,281.1
Iran, Islamic Rep.	795.4	216.6	11,339	3,087	34.6	120.3	41.6	25.6	7.0	1.4	0.5	1.1	2,440.443	8,963.959	70.15	19,41,187.6
Lao PDR	10.6	2.7	1,888	483	32.5	20.0	6.5	4.3	1.1	0.0	0.0	0.1	2,726.598	10,655.167	5.62	28,947.8
Malaysia	343.6	143.5	13,192	5,511	53.1	140.0	74.3	29.8	12.5	0.6	0.3	0.4	1.582	3.787	26.05	543.6
Maldives	1.9	1.1	5,556	3,222	73.7	59.0	43.5	12.6	7.3	0.0	0.0	0.0	7.421	12.800	0.34	14.0
Mongolia	8.0	2.5	3,118	985	40.2	33.1	13.3	7.0	2.2	0.0	0.0	0.0	380.672	1,205.247	2.56	3,041.4
Nepal	30.0	8.7	1,226	355	36.8	13.0	4.8	2.8	0.8	0.1	0.0	0.4	20.666	71.368	24.44	619.4
Pakistan	436.7	127.9	2,836	831	37.2	30.1	11.2	6.4	1.9	0.8	0.3	2.5	17.429	59.514	153.96	7,610.8
Philippines	286.0	103.1	3,355	1,209	45.8	35.6	16.3	7.6	2.7	0.5	0.2	1.4	19.849	55.085	85.26	5,677.7
Singapore	212.1	125.4	49,731	29,403	75.2	527.7	396.7	112.4	66.5	0.4	0.3	0.1	0.984	1.664	4.27	208.8
Sri Lanka	76.4	24.4	3,886	1,241	40.6	41.2	16.7	8.8	2.8	0.1	0.1	0.3	32.089	100.498	19.67	2,452.8
Thailand	521.9	188.6	8,017	2,897	45.9	85.1	39.1	18.1	6.5	0.9	0.4	1.1	14.536	40.220	65.10	7,586.3
Vietnam	212.6	57.6	2,595	704	34.5	27.5	9.5	5.9	1.6	0.4	0.1	1.3	4,299.850	15,858.917	81.91	9,14,000.8
Total (23)	**13,460.3**	**4,997.0**	**4,023**	**1,493**	**47.2**	**42.7**	**20.1**	**9.1**	**3.4**	**23.2**	**11.0**	**54.4**	**n.a.**	**n.a.**	**3,346.1**	**n.a.**

Table H.2 *(Continued)*

GROSS DOMESTIC PRODUCT / Economy	Expenditure (US$, billions)		Expenditure per capita (US$)		Price level index	Expenditure per capita index				Share (world = 100.0)			PPP	Reference data		
						World = 100.0		US = 100.0		Expenditure		Popula-tion		Exchange rate	Popula-tion	Expenditure in national currency unit
	Based on PPPs	Based on XRs	Based on PPPs	Based on XRs	(world = 100.0)	Based on PPPs	Based on XRs	Based on PPPs	Based on XRs	Based on PPPs	Based on XRs		(US$ = 1.000)	(US$ = 1.000)	(millions)	(billions)
(00)	(01)	(02)	(03)	(04)	(05)	(06)	(07)	(03)	(09)	(10)a	(11)a	(12)a	(13)b	(14)b	(15)	(16)
COMMONWEALTH OF INDEPENDENT STATES																
Armenia	12.6	4.9	4,008	1,564	49.6	42.5	21.1	9.1	3.5	0.0	0.0	0.1	178.580	457.688	3.13	2,242.9
Azerbaijan e	38.4	13.2	4,579	1,580	43.9	48.6	21.3	10.4	3.6	0.1	0.0	0.1	0.326	0.946	8.38	12.5
Belarus	83.5	30.2	8,639	3,126	46.0	91.7	42.2	19.5	7.1	0.1	0.1	0.2	779.330	2,153.800	9.66	65,067.1
Georgia	15.3	6.2	3,505	1,427	51.8	37.2	19.3	7.9	3.2	0.0	0.0	0.1	0.738	1.813	4.36	11.3
Kazakhstan	131.8	57.1	8,699	3,771	55.1	92.3	50.9	19.7	8.5	0.2	0.1	0.2	57.610	132.880	15.15	7,590.6
Kyrgyz Republic	8.9	2.5	1,776	491	35.2	18.8	6.6	4.0	1.1	0.0	0.0	0.1	11.350	41.012	5.01	100.9
Moldova	8.5	3.0	2,364	831	44.7	25.1	11.2	5.3	1.9	0.0	0.0	0.1	4.430	12.600	3.60	37.7
Russian Federation h	1,696.7	764.1	11,822	5,324	57.3	125.5	71.8	26.7	12.0	2.9	1.7	2.3	12.736	28.280	143.52	21,609.8
Tajikistan	9.7	2.3	1,436	341	30.2	15.2	4.6	3.2	0.8	0.0	0.0	0.1	0.740	3.118	6.78	7.2
Ukraine	262.8	86.1	5,578	1,829	41.7	59.2	24.7	12.6	4.1	0.5	0.2	0.8	1.680	5.125	47.11	441.5
Total (10)	**2,268.1**	**969.7**	**9,194**	**3,931**	**54.4**	**97.6**	**53.0**	**20.8**	**8.9**	**3.9**	**2.1**	**4.0**	**n.a.**	**n.a.**	**246.7**	**n.a.**
EUROSTAT-OECD																
Albania	18.7	8.1	5,942	2,574	55.1	63.1	34.7	13.4	5.8	0.0	0.0	0.1	43.640	100.739	3.14	814.8
Australia	693.4	735.2	33,755	35,789	134.8	358.2	482.8	76.3	80.9	1.2	1.6	0.3	1.388	1.309	20.54	962.7
Austria	276.7	305.1	33,638	37,095	140.2	357.0	500.4	76.0	83.8	0.5	0.7	0.1	0.886	0.804	8.23	245.2
Belgium	337.3	377.5	32,204	36,042	142.3	341.7	486.2	72.8	81.5	0.6	0.8	0.2	0.900	0.804	10.47	303.4
Bosnia and Herzegovina	25.4	11.6	6,608	3,019	58.1	70.1	40.7	14.9	6.8	0.0	0.0	0.1	0.718	1.572	3.84	18.2
Bulgaria	75.9	28.9	9,835	3,748	48.4	104.4	50.6	22.2	8.5	0.1	0.1	0.1	0.599	1.572	7.72	45.5
Canada	1,132.0	1,133.8	35,106	35,161	127.3	372.5	474.3	73.3	79.5	2.0	2.5	0.5	1.214	1.212	32.25	1,373.8
Croatia	68.1	44.8	15,329	10,089	83.7	162.7	136.1	34.6	22.8	0.1	0.1	0.1	3.915	5.949	4.44	266.7
Cyprus	18.4	16.9	24,917	22,893	116.8	264.4	308.8	53.3	51.7	0.0	0.0	0.0	0.426	0.464	0.74	7.8
Czech Republic	217.7	130.2	21,268	12,719	76.0	225.7	171.6	43.1	28.7	0.4	0.3	0.2	14.316	23.939	10.23	3,116.1
Denmark	179.9	258.0	33,196	47,608	182.3	352.3	642.3	75.0	107.6	0.3	0.6	0.1	8.590	5.990	5.42	1,545.3
Estonia	22.3	13.9	16,525	10,320	79.4	175.4	139.2	37.4	23.3	0.0	0.0	0.0	7.854	12.577	1.35	175.0
Finland	161.1	195.9	30,709	37,335	154.6	325.9	503.7	69.4	84.4	0.3	0.4	0.1	0.977	0.804	5.25	157.4
France	1,860.7	2,137.4	29,555	33,950	146.0	313.6	458.0	66.8	76.7	3.2	4.7	1.0	0.923	0.804	62.96	1,718.0
Germany	2,566.0	2,767.4	31,117	33,559	137.1	330.2	452.7	70.3	75.9	4.4	6.1	1.3	0.867	0.804	82.46	2,224.4
Greece	270.4	240.2	24,348	21,629	112.9	258.4	291.8	55.0	48.9	0.5	0.5	0.2	0.714	0.804	11.10	193.0
Hungary	171.2	110.4	16,975	10,948	82.0	180.1	147.7	38.4	24.7	0.3	0.2	0.2	128.593	199.381	10.09	22,018.3
Iceland	10.4	16.3	34,976	55,110	200.3	371.2	743.5	79.1	124.6	0.0	0.0	0.0	99.078	62.881	0.30	1,025.7
Ireland	161.4	202.8	38,795	48,758	159.8	411.7	657.8	87.7	110.2	0.3	0.4	0.1	1.010	0.804	4.16	163.0
Israel	161.4	133.7	23,210	19,223	105.3	246.3	259.3	52.5	43.5	0.3	0.3	0.1	3.717	4.488	6.96	600.0
Italy	1,657.4	1,787.0	28,280	30,491	137.1	300.1	411.3	63.9	68.9	2.9	3.9	1.0	0.867	0.804	58.61	1,436.4
Japan	3,889.6	4,571.9	30,446	35,786	149.4	323.1	482.8	68.8	80.9	6.7	10.0	2.1	129.552	110.218	127.76	5,03,903.0
Korea, Rep.	1,096.7	844.9	22,783	17,551	97.9	241.8	236.8	51.5	39.7	1.9	1.9	0.8	788.920	1,024.120	48.14	8,65,240.9
Latvia	29.8	16.1	13,312	7,183	68.6	141.3	96.9	30.1	16.2	0.1	0.0	0.0	0.302	0.560	2.24	9.0

(continued)

Table H.2 *(Continued)*

GROSS DOMESTIC PRODUCT / Economy	Expenditure (US$, billions) Based on PPPs	Expenditure (US$, billions) Based on XRs	Expenditure per capita (US$) Based on PPPs	Expenditure per capita (US$) Based on XRs	Price level index (world = 100.0)	Expenditure per capita index World = 100.0 Based on PPPs	Expenditure per capita index World = 100.0 Based on XRs	Expenditure per capita index US = 100.0 Based on PPPs	Expenditure per capita index US = 100.0 Based on XRs	Share (world = 100.0) Expenditure Based on PPPs	Share (world = 100.0) Expenditure Based on XRs	Share (world = 100.0) Population	PPP (US$ = 1.000)	Reference data Exchange rate (US$ = 1.000)	Reference data Population (millions)	Reference data Expenditure in national currency unit (billions)
(00)	(01)	(02)	(03)	(04)	(05)	(06)	(07)	(08)	(09)	(10)[a]	(11)[a]	(12)[a]	(13)[b]	(14)[b]	(15)	(16)
Lithuania	48.7	26.1	14,657	7,851	68.1	155.5	105.9	33.1	17.7	0.1	0.1	0.1	1.487	2.775	3.32	72.4
Luxembourg	31.8	37.7	68,167	80,812	150.7	723.4	1090.2	154.1	182.7	0.1	0.1	0.0	0.953	0.804	0.47	30.3
Macedonia, FYR	16.0	6.0	7,877	2,939	47.4	83.6	39.7	17.8	6.6	0.0	0.0	0.0	18.389	49.280	2.04	295.1
Malta	8.7	6.1	21,590	15,222	89.6	229.1	205.4	48.8	34.4	0.0	0.0	0.0	0.244	0.346	0.40	2.1
Mexico	1,293.8	846.1	12,461	8,149	83.1	132.2	109.9	28.2	18.4	2.2	1.9	1.7	7.127	10.898	103.83	9,220.7
Montenegro	5.2	2.3	8,288	3,624	55.6	87.9	48.9	18.7	8.2	0.0	0.0	0.0	0.352	0.804	0.62	1.8
Netherlands	572.9	638.7	35,111	39,145	141.7	372.6	528.1	79.4	88.5	1.0	1.4	0.3	0.896	0.804	16.32	513.4
New Zealand	103.9	112.3	25,046	27,069	137.4	265.8	365.2	56.6	61.2	0.2	0.2	0.1	1.535	1.420	4.15	159.5
Norway	220.2	304.3	47,640	65,834	175.7	505.5	888.1	107.7	148.8	0.4	0.7	0.1	8.896	6.438	4.62	1,958.9
Poland	526.1	304.1	13,786	7,968	73.5	146.3	107.5	31.2	18.0	0.9	0.7	0.6	1.869	3.234	38.16	983.3
Portugal	225.4	191.9	21,370	18,194	108.2	226.8	245.4	48.3	41.1	0.4	0.4	0.2	0.684	0.804	10.55	154.3
Romania	203.1	99.3	9,390	4,591	62.2	99.6	61.9	21.2	10.4	0.4	0.2	0.4	1.423	2.910	21.62	289.0
Russian Federation[h]	1,696.7	764.1	11,822	5,324	57.3	125.5	71.8	26.7	12.0	2.9	1.7	2.3	12.736	28.280	143.52	21,609.8
Serbia	63.4	25.2	8,515	3,391	50.6	90.4	45.7	19.2	7.7	0.1	0.1	0.1	26.564	66.707	7.44	1,683.2
Slovak Republic	87.1	47.9	16,175	8,889	69.9	171.6	119.9	36.6	20.1	0.2	0.1	0.1	17.050	31.026	5.39	1,485.6
Slovenia	47.0	35.7	23,470	17,863	96.8	249.1	241.0	53.0	40.4	0.1	0.1	0.0	146.564	192.563	2.00	6,883.0
Spain	1,188.8	1,131.3	27,392	26,067	121.0	290.7	351.7	61.9	58.9	2.0	2.5	0.7	0.765	0.804	43.40	909.3
Sweden	295.3	371.2	32,702	41,105	159.8	347.0	554.5	73.9	92.9	0.5	0.8	0.1	9.378	7.461	9.03	2,769.4
Switzerland	274.9	385.0	36,649	51,321	178.0	388.9	692.3	82.8	116.0	0.5	0.8	0.1	1.743	1.245	7.50	479.1
Turkey	781.2	481.4	11,394	7,021	78.3	120.9	94.7	25.8	15.9	1.3	1.1	1.1	0.831	1.348	68.57	648.9
United Kingdom	1,984.9	2,297.4	32,952	38,140	147.1	349.7	514.5	74.5	86.2	3.4	5.0	1.0	0.636	0.550	60.24	1,262.7
United States	13,095.5	13,095.5	44,243	44,243	127.1	469.5	596.9	100.0	100.0	22.6	28.7	4.8	1.000	1.000	295.99	13,095.5
Total (46)	**37,872.3**	**37,297.3**	**27,492**	**27,075**	**125.2**	**291.7**	**365.3**	**62.1**	**61.2**	**65.3**	**81.8**	**22.4**	**n.a.**	**n.a.**	**1,377.6**	**n.a.**
LATIN AMERICA																
Argentina	413.5	183.2	10,698	4,740	56.3	113.5	63.9	24.2	10.7	0.7	0.4	0.6	1.287	2.904	38.65	531.9
Bolivia	34.0	9.5	3,697	1,037	35.7	39.2	14.0	8.4	2.3	0.1	0.0	0.1	2.263	8.066	9.21	77.0
Brazil	1,561.6	882.0	8,389	4,738	71.8	89.0	63.9	19.0	10.7	2.7	1.9	3.0	1.375	2.434	186.15	2,147.2
Chile	203.7	123.1	12,521	7,565	76.8	132.9	102.1	28.3	17.1	0.4	0.3	0.3	338.197	559.768	16.27	68,882.8
Colombia	310.2	146.6	7,183	3,394	60.1	76.2	45.8	16.2	7.7	0.5	0.3	0.7	1,096.560	2,320.830	43.19	3,40,156.0
Ecuador	96.9	41.5	7,021	3,007	54.5	74.5	40.6	15.9	6.8	0.2	0.1	0.2	0.428	1.000	13.80	41.5
Paraguay	26.5	8.7	4,494	1,479	41.9	47.7	20.0	10.2	3.3	0.0	0.0	0.1	2,033.929	6,177.960	5.90	53,962.3
Peru	173.7	79.4	6,263	2,863	58.1	66.5	38.6	14.2	6.5	0.3	0.2	0.5	1.507	3.296	27.73	261.7
Uruguay	31.6	17.4	9,497	5,221	69.9	100.8	70.4	21.5	11.8	0.1	0.0	0.1	13.458	24.479	3.33	425.0
Venezuela, RB[e]	260.2	145.5	9,738	5,445	71.1	103.3	73.5	22.0	12.3	0.4	0.3	0.4	1.168	2.090	26.73	304.1
Total (10)	**3,111.9**	**1,636.9**	**8,389**	**4,413**	**66.9**	**89.0**	**59.5**	**19.0**	**10.0**	**5.4**	**3.6**	**6.0**	**n.a.**	**n.a.**	**370.9**	**n.a.**
WESTERN ASIA																
Bahrain	25.7	15.9	28,874	17,901	78.8	306.4	241.5	65.3	40.5	0.0	0.0	0.0	0.234	0.378	0.89	6.0
Egypt, Arab Rep.[d]	373.6	98.2	5,337	1,402	33.4	56.6	18.9	12.1	3.2	0.6	0.2	1.1	1.521	5.789	70.00	568.2
Iraq	101.5	36.2	3,631	1,296	45.4	38.5	17.5	8.2	2.9	0.2	0.1	0.5	525.779	1,473.000	27.96	53,386.4

Table H.2 *(Continued)*

GROSS DOMESTIC PRODUCT	Expenditure (US$, billions)		Expenditure per capita (US$)		Price level index	Expenditure per capita index				Share (world = 100.0)			PPP	Reference data		
						World = 100.0		US = 100.0		Expenditure		Popula-tion		Exchange rate	Popula-tion	Expenditure in national currency unit
Economy	Based on PPPs	Based on XRs	Based on PPPs	Based on XRs	(world = 100.0)	Based on PPPs	Based on XRs	Based on PPPs	Based on XRs	Based on PPPs	Based on XRs		(US$ = 1.000)	(US$ = 1.000)	(millions)	(billions)
(00)	(01)	(02)	(03)	(04)	(05)	(06)	(07)	(08)	(09)	(10)ᵃ	(11)ᵃ	(12)ᵃ	(13)ᵇ	(14)ᵇ	(15)	(16)
Jordan	24.9	12.6	4,766	2,406	64.2	50.6	32.5	10.8	5.4	0.0	0.0	0.1	0.358	0.709	5.23	8.9
Kuwait	117.4	80.8	53,023	36,504	87.5	562.7	492.5	119.8	82.5	0.2	0.2	0.0	0.201	0.292	2.21	23.6
Lebanon	41.3	21.9	10,360	5,481	67.3	109.9	73.9	23.4	12.4	0.1	0.0	0.1	797.578	1,507.500	3.99	32,944.0
Oman	54.3	30.9	21,657	12,318	72.3	229.8	166.2	48.9	27.8	0.1	0.1	0.0	0.219	0.385	2.51	11.9
Qatar	62.7	44.4	73,971	52,357	90.0	785.0	706.3	167.2	118.3	0.1	0.1	0.0	2.583	3.650	0.85	162.1
Saudi Arabia	542.6	328.2	23,257	14,068	76.9	246.8	189.8	52.6	31.8	0.9	0.7	0.4	2.268	3.750	23.33	1,230.8
Syria, Arab Rep.	81.2	28.9	4,469	1,590	45.2	47.4	21.5	10.1	3.6	0.1	0.1	0.3	18.555	52.140	18.17	1,506.4
Yemen, Rep.	55.8	19.1	2,790	953	43.4	29.6	12.9	6.3	2.2	0.1	0.0	0.3	65.395	191.400	19.98	3,646.6
Total (11)	**1,481.0**	**717.0**	**8,457**	**4,094**	**61.5**	**89.7**	**55.2**	**19.1**	**9.3**	**2.6**	**1.6**	**2.8**	**n.a.**	**n.a.**	**175.1**	**n.a.**
WORLDⁱ (146)	**57,995.4**	**45,619.4**	**9,424**	**7,413**	**100.0**	**100.0**	**100.0**	**21.3**	**16.8**	**100.0**	**100.0**	**100.0**	**n.a.**	**n.a.**	**6,154.30**	**n.a.**

Source: ICP, http://icp.worldbank.org/.

Note: n.a. = not applicable; XR = exchange rate; … = data suppressed because of incompleteness.

a. All shares are rounded to one decimal place. More precision can be found in the Excel version of the table, which can be downloaded from the ICP website.

b. All exchange rates (XRs) and PPPs are rounded to three decimal places. More precision can be found in the Excel version of the table, which can be downloaded from the ICP website.

c. Burundi submitted prices, but it did not provide official national accounts data.

d. The Arab Republic of Egypt participated in both the Africa and Western Asia regions. The results for Egypt from each region were averaged by taking the geometric mean of the PPPs, allowing Egypt to be shown in each region with the same ranking in the world comparison.

e. Currency adjusted to reflect 2011 currency.

f. Zimbabwe's exchange rate-related data were suppressed because of extreme volatility in the official exchange rate. PPP adjusted to reflect 2011 currency.

g. Results for China were based on the national average prices extrapolated by the World Bank and Asian Development Bank using price data for 11 cities submitted by the National Bureau of Statistics of China. The data for China do not include Hong Kong SAR, China; Macao SAR, China; and Taiwan, China.

h. The Russian Federation participated in both the Commonwealth of Independent States (CIS) and Eurostat-Organisation for Economic Co-operation and Development (OECD) comparisons. The PPPs for Russia are based on the Eurostat-OECD comparison. They were the basis for linking the CIS comparison to the ICP.

i. Does not double count the dual participation economies: the Arab Republic of Egypt and the Russian Federation.

Comparison of ICP 2011 Results with 2011 Results Extrapolated from ICP 2005

This appendix presents the difference between the new benchmark results of the 2011 round of the International Comparison Program (ICP) and the previous estimates for the year 2011 based on extrapolations from the 2005 benchmark data. The extrapolations were published in the World Bank's World Development Indicators (WDI) database released in April 2014, before the 2005-based purchasing power parities (PPPs) were replaced with the figures based on the 2011 results.

Table I.1 compares the PPPs arising from the ICP 2011 benchmark data and from the ICP 2005 results extrapolated to 2011, as well as the gross domestic product (GDP) expenditures in current local currency units between ICP 2011 and WDI for the year 2011. The table provides the following indicators:

- Column (01): GDP PPPs with the U.S. dollar equal to 1.00 based on ICP 2011
- Column (02): GDP PPPs with the U.S. dollar equal to 1.00 based on World Bank's WDI 2011 PPPs, extrapolated from ICP 2005 benchmark PPPs
- Column (03): Percentage difference between columns (01) and (02)
- Column (04): GDP expenditure in national currency units based on ICP 2011
- Column (05): GDP expenditure in national currency units based on WDI

- Column (06): Percentage difference between columns (04) and (05)
- Column (07): Status of participation in ICP 2005 benchmark survey

Column (01) shows the GDP PPPs for 2011 from ICP 2011, and column (02) shows the GDP PPPs for 2011 from WDI, which is based on extrapolations from the 2005 benchmark data.

Column (03) shows the percentage difference between the two sets of GDP PPPs for 2011 by subtracting the ICP 2011 GDP PPP in column (01) from the WDI GDP in column (02) and then dividing it by the WDI GDP PPP in column (02).

Column (04) shows the GDP expenditure from ICP 2011, and column (05) shows the GDP expenditure from the WDI data published in April 2014.

Column (06) shows the percentage difference between the two sets of GDP PPPs for 2011 by subtracting the ICP 2011 GDP PPP in column (04) from the WDI GDP in column (05) and then dividing it by the WDI GDP PPP in column (05).

Column (07) indicates whether the economy participated in the benchmark survey in ICP 2005. If an economy did participate in the benchmark survey, its PPPs were calculated from the benchmark 2005 data and then extrapolated to 2011. If an economy is labeled non-benchmark, its PPPs were estimated using the regression model described in chapter 4 and then extrapolated to 2011.

Table I.1 Comparison of ICP 2011 Global Results with Data in World Development Indicators (Extrapolation from ICP 2005)

| Economy | PPP (US$ = 1.000) | | | Expenditure in national currency unit (billions) | | | ICP 2005 benchmark or nonbenchmark |
	ICP 2011	WDI	Percentage difference	ICP 2011	WDI	Percentage difference	
(00)	(01)	(02)ᵃ	(03)	(04)	(05)ᵃ	(06)	(07)
AFRICA							
Algeria	30.502	46.952	−35	14,481.0	14,519.8	0	Nonbenchmark
Angola	68.315	85.009	−20	9,767.6	9,780.1	0	Benchmark
Benin	214.035	235.872	−9	3,439.8	3,442.2	0	Benchmark
Botswana	3.764	3.435	10	102.5	104.6	−2	Benchmark
Burkina Faso	213.659	224.166	−5	4,868.5	4,905.4	−1	Benchmark
Burundi	425.768	579.047	−26	2,599.9	2,970.7	−12	Benchmark
Cameroon	227.212	255.110	−11	12,545.7	12,026.4	4	Benchmark
Cape Verde	48.592	64.393	−25	149.0	147.9	1	Benchmark
Central African Republic	255.862	233.100	10	1,029.7	1,044.1	−1	Benchmark
Chad	250.443	239.124	5	5,725.3	5,736.2	0	Benchmark
Comoros	207.584	260.700	−20	95.4	216.0	−56	Benchmark
Congo, Dem. Rep.	521.870	576.744	−10	23,146.1	14,436.4	60	Benchmark
Congo, Rep.	289.299	380.687	−24	6,982.5	6,807.0	3	Benchmark
Côte d'Ivoire	228.228	317.985	−28	12,275.5	11,359.6	8	Benchmark
Djibouti	94.003	...	...	205.3	...	...	Benchmark
Egypt, Arab Rep.ᵇ	1.625	2.671	−39	1,371.1	1,371.1	0	Benchmark
Equatorial Guinea	294.572	377.683	−22	8,367.3	7,930.6	6	Benchmark
Ethiopia	4.919	5.491	−10	506.1	506.1	0	Benchmark
Gabon	318.156	369.552	−14	8,046.1	8,852.0	−9	Benchmark
Gambia, The	9.939	8.315	20	26.6	26.5	0	Benchmark
Ghana	0.699	1.286	−46	59.8	59.8	0	Benchmark
Guinea	2,518.386	2,963.644	−15	33,128.3	33,738.6	−2	Benchmark
Guinea–Bissau	220.085	236.595	−7	464.7	456.7	2	Benchmark
Kenya	34.298	42.373	−19	3,048.9	2,985.9	2	Benchmark
Lesotho	3.923	4.894	−20	18.3	18.3	0	Benchmark
Liberiaᶜ	0.517	0.644	−20	1.1	1.5	−25	Benchmark
Madagascar	673.730	981.330	−31	20,276.4	20,072.5	1	Benchmark
Malawi	76.259	76.107	0	1,140.8	879.8	30	Benchmark
Mali	210.193	285.393	−26	5,024.5	5,037.6	0	Benchmark
Mauritania	115.855	135.243	−14	1,309.4	1,201.3	9	Benchmark
Mauritius	15.941	17.625	−10	323.0	323.0	0	Benchmark
Morocco	3.677	4.930	−25	802.6	802.6	0	Benchmark
Mozambique	16.030	15.727	2	364.7	365.3	0	Benchmark
Namibia	4.663	5.824	−20	90.6	91.7	−1	Benchmark
Niger	221.087	258.520	−14	3,025.5	3,025.5	0	Benchmark
Nigeria	74.378	93.161	−20	38,017.0	38,017.0	0	Benchmark
Rwanda	260.751	274.541	−5	3,814.4	3,814.4	0	Benchmark
São Tomé and Príncipe	8,527.157	13,508.864	−37	4,375.5	4,375.5	0	Benchmark

Table I.1 *(Continued)*

Economy	PPP (US$ = 1.000)			Expenditure in national currency unit (billions)			ICP 2005 benchmark or nonbenchmark
	ICP 2011	WDI	Percentage difference	ICP 2011	WDI	Percentage difference	
(00)	(01)	(02)[a]	(03)	(04)	(05)[a]	(06)	(07)
Senegal	236.287	273.913	−14	6,766.8	6,814.1	−1	Benchmark
Seychelles	6.690	5.931	13	13.1	13.3	−1	Nonbenchmark
Sierra Leone	1,553.139	1,874.545	−17	12,754.9	12,781.1	0	Benchmark
South Africa	4.774	5.284	−10	2,917.5	2,917.5	0	Benchmark
Sudan[d]	1.224	1.941	−37	186.6	170.7	9	Benchmark
Swaziland	3.900	4.546	−14	29.7	28.8	3	Benchmark
Tanzania	522.483	558.527	−6	37,533.0	37,533.0	0	Benchmark
Togo	215.060	272.137	−21	1,739.2	1,739.2	0	Benchmark
Tunisia	0.592	0.664	−11	64.7	65.4	−1	Benchmark
Uganda	833.540	851.008	−2	45,944.1	39,085.7	18	Benchmark
Zambia[c]	2,378.380	4,299.701	−45	101,104.8	93,344.4	8	Benchmark
Zimbabwe	0.504	...	...	8.9	8.9	0	Benchmark.
Total (50)	**n.a.**	**n.a.**	**n.a.**	**n.a.**	**n.a.**	**n.a.**	**n.a.**
ASIA AND THE PACIFIC							
Bangladesh	23.145	30.074	−23	9,702.9	7,967.0	22	Benchmark
Bhutan	16.856	19.492	−14	85.9	85.6	0	Benchmark
Brunei Darussalam	0.717	0.989	−27	21.0	20.6	2	Benchmark
Cambodia	1,347.115	1,557.872	−14	52,068.7	52,068.7	0	Benchmark
China[e]	3.506	4.230	−17	47,310.4	47,310.4	0	Benchmark
Fiji	1.042	1.642	−37	6.7	6.7	0	Benchmark
Hong Kong SAR, China	5.462	5.469	0	1,936.1	1,936.1	0	Benchmark
India	15.109	20.063	−25	86,993.1	90,097.2	−3	Benchmark
Indonesia	3,606.566	6,665.474	−46	7,422,781.2	7,422,781.2	0	Benchmark
Lao PDR	2,467.753	3,827.025	−36	64,727.1	66,514.7	−3	Benchmark
Macao SAR, China	4.589	6.866	−33	295.0	295.0	0	Benchmark
Malaysia	1.459	1.922	−24	884.5	884.5	0	Benchmark
Maldives	8.527	10.956	−22	31.6	31.4	0	Benchmark
Mongolia	537.127	842.962	−36	12,546.8	11,087.7	13	Benchmark
Myanmar	234.974	...	...	45,128.0	...	...	Nonbenchmark
Nepal	24.628	36.648	−33	1,449.5	1,375.0	5	Benchmark
Pakistan	24.346	39.401	−38	19,187.9	18,284.9	5	Benchmark
Philippines	17.854	25.142	−29	9,706.3	9,706.3	0	Benchmark
Singapore	0.891	1.066	−16	334.1	334.1	0	Benchmark
Sri Lanka	38.654	56.712	−32	6,542.7	6,544.0	0	Benchmark
Taiwan, China	15.112	...	...	13,709.1	...	...	Benchmark
Thailand	12.370	17.701	−30	11,120.5	10,540.1	6	Benchmark
Vietnam	6,709.192	8,854.016	−24	2,779,880.2	2,779,881.0	0	Benchmark

(continued)

Table I.1 (Continued)

| Economy | PPP (US$ = 1.000) | | | Expenditure in national currency unit (billions) | | | ICP 2005 benchmark or nonbenchmark |
	ICP 2011	WDI	Percentage difference	ICP 2011	WDI	Percentage difference	
(00)	(01)	(02)[a]	(03)	(04)	(05)[a]	(06)	(07)
Total (23)	n.a.	n.a.	n.a.	n.a.	n.a.	n.a.	n.a.
COMMONWEALTH OF INDEPENDENT STATES							
Armenia	187.095	212.057	−12	3,777.9	3,777.9	0	Benchmark
Azerbaijan	0.360	0.575	−37	52.1	52.1	0	Benchmark
Belarus	1,889.308	2,115.740	−11	297,157.7	297,157.7	0	Benchmark
Kazakhstan	80.171	128.313	−38	27,571.9	27,571.9	0	Benchmark
Kyrgyz Republic	17.757	21.794	−19	286.0	286.0	0	Benchmark
Moldova	5.535	6.933	−20	82.3	82.3	0	Benchmark
Russian Federation[f]	17.346	17.346	0	55,799.6	55,799.6	0	Benchmark
Tajikistan	1.740	1.874	−7	30.1	30.1	0	Benchmark
Ukraine	3.434	3.990	−14	1,302.1	1,302.1	0	Benchmark
Total (9)	n.a.	n.a.	n.a.	n.a.	n.a.	n.a.	n.a.
EUROSTAT–OECD[g]							
Albania	45.452	45.452	0	1,282.3	1,307.6	−2	Benchmark
Australia	1.511	1.511	0	1,444.5	1,403.9	3	Benchmark
Austria	0.830	0.830	0	299.2	299.2	0	Benchmark
Belgium	0.839	0.839	0	369.3	369.3	0	Benchmark
Bosnia and Herzegovina	0.724	0.724	0	26.8	25.7	4	Benchmark
Bulgaria	0.660	0.660	0	75.3	75.3	0	Benchmark
Canada	1.243	1.240	0	1,759.7	1,719.6	2	Benchmark
Chile	348.017	348.017	0	121,492.7	121,492.7	0	Benchmark
Croatia	3.802	3.802	0	330.2	330.2	0	Benchmark
Cyprus	0.673	0.673	0	17.9	17.9	0	Benchmark
Czech Republic	13.468	13.468	0	3,823.4	3,823.4	0	Benchmark
Denmark	7.689	7.689	0	1,791.8	1,791.8	0	Benchmark
Estonia	0.524	0.524	0	16.2	16.2	0	Benchmark
Finland	0.907	0.907	0	188.7	188.7	0	Benchmark
France	0.845	0.845	0	2,001.4	2,001.4	0	Benchmark
Germany	0.779	0.779	0	2,609.9	2,609.9	0	Benchmark
Greece	0.693	0.693	0	208.5	208.5	0	Benchmark
Hungary	123.650	123.650	0	27,635.4	27,635.4	0	Benchmark
Iceland	133.563	133.563	0	1,628.7	1,628.7	0	Benchmark
Ireland	0.827	0.827	0	162.6	162.6	0	Benchmark
Israel	3.945	3.945	0	923.9	923.9	0	Benchmark
Italy	0.768	0.768	0	1,580.4	1,580.4	0	Benchmark
Japan	107.454	107.454	0	470,623.2	470,623.2	0	Benchmark
Korea, Rep.	854.586	854.586	0	1,235,160.5	1,235,160.5	0	Benchmark
Latvia	0.347	0.347	0	14.3	14.3	0	Benchmark
Lithuania	1.567	1.567	0	106.9	106.4	0	Benchmark

Table I.1 *(Continued)*

Economy	PPP (US$ = 1.000)			Expenditure in national currency unit (billions)			ICP 2005 benchmark or nonbenchmark
	ICP 2011	WDI	Percentage difference	ICP 2011	WDI	Percentage difference	
(00)	(01)	(02)ª	(03)	(04)	(05)ª	(06)	(07)
Luxembourg	0.906	0.906	0	41.7	41.7	0	Benchmark
Macedonia, FYR	18.680	18.680	0	459.8	461.7	0	Benchmark
Malta	0.558	0.558	0	6.6	6.6	1	Benchmark
Mexico	7.673	7.673	0	14,536.9	14,423.7	1	Benchmark
Montenegro	0.369	0.369	0	3.2	3.2	0	Benchmark
Netherlands	0.832	0.832	0	599.0	599.0	0	Benchmark
New Zealand	1.486	1.486	0	204.5	206.5	−1	Benchmark
Norway	8.973	8.973	0	2,750.0	2,750.8	0	Benchmark
Poland	1.823	1.823	0	1,528.1	1,528.1	0	Benchmark
Portugal	0.628	0.628	0	171.1	171.1	0	Benchmark
Romania	1.615	1.615	0	556.7	556.7	0	Benchmark
Russian Federation[f]	17.346	17.346	0	55,799.6	55,799.6	0	Benchmark
Serbia	37.288	37.288	0	3,208.6	3,175.0	1	Benchmark
Slovak Republic	0.508	0.508	0	69.0	69.0	0	Benchmark
Slovenia	0.625	0.625	0	36.1	36.2	0	Benchmark
Spain	0.705	0.705	0	1,046.3	1,046.3	0	Benchmark
Sweden	8.820	8.820	0	3,480.5	3,480.5	0	Benchmark
Switzerland	1.441	1.441	0	585.1	585.1	0	Benchmark
Turkey	0.987	0.987	0	1,297.7	1,297.7	0	Benchmark
United Kingdom	0.698	0.698	0	1,536.9	1,536.9	0	Benchmark
United States	1.000	1.000	0	15,533.8	15,533.8	0	Benchmark
Total (47)	**n.a.**	**n.a.**	**n.a.**	**n.a.**	**n.a.**	**n.a.**	**n.a.**
LATIN AMERICA							
Bolivia	2.946	3.260	−10	166.1	166.1	0	Benchmark
Brazil	1.471	1.827	−19	4,143.0	4,143.0	0	Benchmark
Colombia	1,161.910	1,323.970	−12	621,615.0	621,615.0	0	Benchmark
Costa Rica	346.738	362.710	−4	20,748.0	20,748.0	0	Nonbenchmark
Cuba[h]	0.322	...	...	...	68.2	...	Nonbenchmark
Dominican Republic	19.449	21.716	−10	2,119.3	2,119.3	0	Nonbenchmark
Ecuador	0.526	0.550	−4	79.8	76.8	4	Benchmark
El Salvador	0.503	0.545	−8	23.1	23.1	0	Nonbenchmark
Guatemala	3.626	5.138	−29	371.3	371.3	0	Nonbenchmark
Haiti	19.108	25.340	−25	297.7	297.7	0	Nonbenchmark
Honduras	9.915	10.688	−7	335.0	335.0	0	Nonbenchmark
Nicaragua	8.919	9.637	−7	216.1	216.1	0	Nonbenchmark
Panama	0.547	0.567	−4	31.3	31.3	0	Nonbenchmark
Paraguay	2,227.340	2,708.237	−18	105,203.2	108,794.6	−3	Benchmark
Peru	1.521	1.668	−9	497.8	497.8	0	Benchmark

(continued)

Table I.1 *(Continued)*

Economy	PPP (US$ = 1.000)			Expenditure in national currency unit (billions)			ICP 2005 benchmark or nonbenchmark
	ICP 2011	WDI	Percentage difference	ICP 2011	WDI	Percentage difference	
(00)	(01)	(02)[a]	(03)	(04)	(05)[a]	(06)	(07)
Uruguay	15.282	17.706	−14	896.8	896.8	0	Benchmark
Venezuela, RB	2.713	3.671	−26	1,357.5	1,357.5	0	Benchmark
Total (17)	**n.a.**	**n.a.**	**n.a.**	**n.a.**	**n.a.**	**n.a.**	**n.a.**
CARIBBEAN							
Anguilla	2.077	...	...	0.8	...	...	Nonbenchmark
Antigua and Barbuda	1.731	1.768	−2	3.0	3.0	3	Nonbenchmark
Aruba	1.260	...	...	4.6	4.6	0	Nonbenchmark
Bahamas, The	0.949	0.705	35	7.9	7.9	0	Nonbenchmark
Barbados	2.017	1.185	70	8.7	8.7	0	Nonbenchmark
Belize	1.150	1.244	−8	3.0	3.0	0	Nonbenchmark
Bermuda	1.564	...	...	5.6	5.6	0	Nonbenchmark
Bonaire[i]	...	...	...	0.2	...	...	Nonbenchmark
Cayman Islands	0.959	...	...	2.7	...	...	Nonbenchmark
Curaçao	1.292	...	...	5.4	...	...	Nonbenchmark
Dominica	1.861	1.467	27	1.3	1.3	1	Nonbenchmark
Grenada	1.783	1.957	−9	2.1	2.2	−5	Nonbenchmark
Jamaica	54.122	...	...	1,241.8	1,239.8	0	Nonbenchmark
Montserrat	1.943	...	...	0.2	...	...	Nonbenchmark
St. Kitts and Nevis	1.803	2.085	−14	2.0	1.9	4	Nonbenchmark
St. Lucia	1.844	1.681	10	3.3	3.4	−4	Nonbenchmark
St. Vincent and the Grenadines	1.691	1.600	6	1.8	1.9	−2	Nonbenchmark
Sint Maarten	1.379	...	...	1.7	...	...	Nonbenchmark
Suriname	1.826	3.233	−44	14.3	14.3	0	Nonbenchmark
Trinidad and Tobago	3.938	4.389	−10	150.9	150.9	0	Nonbenchmark
Turks and Caicos Islands	1.100	...	...	0.7	...	...	Nonbenchmark
Virgin Islands, British	1.076	...	...	0.9	...	...	Nonbenchmark
Total (22)	**n.a.**	**n.a.**	**n.a.**	**n.a.**	**n.a.**	**n.a.**	**n.a.**
WESTERN ASIA							
Bahrain	0.211	0.301	−30	10.9	10.9	0	Benchmark
Egypt, Arab Rep.[c]	1.625	2.671	−39	1,371.1	1,371.1	0	Benchmark
Iraq	516.521	1,026.903	−50	191,652.9	223,677.0	−14	Benchmark
Jordan	0.293	0.561	−48	20.5	20.5	0	Benchmark
Kuwait	0.172	0.318	−46	44.3	44.3	0	Benchmark
Oman	0.192	0.331	−42	26.9	26.9	0	Benchmark
Qatar	2.419	3.650	−34	624.2	624.2	0	Benchmark
Saudi Arabia	1.837	3.041	−40	2,510.6	2,510.7	0	Benchmark
Sudan[d]	1.224	1.941	−37	186.6	170.7	9	Benchmark

Table I.1 *(Continued)*

| Economy | PPP (US$ = 1.000) | | | Expenditure in national currency unit (billions) | | | ICP 2005 benchmark or nonbenchmark |
	ICP 2011	WDI	Percentage difference	ICP 2011	WDI	Percentage difference	
(00)	(01)	(02)[a]	(03)	(04)	(05)[a]	(06)	(07)
United Arab Emirates	2.544	3.567	−29	1,280.2	1,280.2	0	Nonbenchmark
West Bank and Gaza	2.189	...	...	35.0	...	...	Nonbenchmark
Yemen, Rep.	75.818	125.914	−40	6,714.9	7,217.4	−7	Benchmark
Total (12)	**n.a.**	**n.a.**	**n.a.**	**n.a.**	**n.a.**	**n.a.**	**n.a.**
SINGLETONS							
Georgia	0.859	1.002	−14	24.3	24.3	0	Benchmark
Iran, Islamic Rep.	4,657.463	5,968.997	−22	6,121,004.0	5,609,930.0	9	Benchmark
Total (2)	**n.a.**	**n.a.**	**n.a.**	**n.a.**	**n.a.**	**n.a.**	**n.a.**
WORLD[j] (179)	**n.a.**	**n.a.**	**n.a.**	**n.a.**	**n.a.**	**n.a.**	**n.a.**

Source: ICP, http://icp.worldbank.org/.

Note: n.a. = not applicable; ... data suppressed because of incompleteness.

a. Data source: World Development Indicators (WDI), World Bank; data as of April 2014.

b. The Arab Republic of Egypt participated in both the Africa and Western Asia regions. The results for Egypt from each region were averaged by taking the geometric mean of the PPPs, allowing Egypt to be shown in each region with the same ranking in the world comparison.

c. WDI data were released in a different currency unit, and they were converted to the same currency as ICP 2011 for comparison purposes.

d. Sudan participated in both the Africa and Western Asia regions. The results for Sudan from each region were averaged by taking the geometric mean of the PPPs, allowing Sudan to be shown in each region with the same ranking in the world comparison.

e. The results presented in the table are based on data supplied by all the participating economies and compiled in accordance with ICP principles and the procedures recommended by the 2011 ICP Technical Advisory Group. The results for China are estimated by the 2011 ICP Asia and the Pacific Regional Office and the Global Office. The National Bureau of Statistics of China does not recognize these results as official statistics.

f. The Russian Federation participated in both the Commonwealth of Independent States (CIS) and Eurostat-Organisation for Economic Co-operation and Development (OECD) comparisons. The PPPs for Russia are based on the Eurostat-OECD comparison. They were the basis for linking the CIS comparison to the ICP.

g. Eurostat-OECD provides data directly to WDI from their PPP program. Thus the figures for Eurostat-OECD economies are not based on the WDI extrapolation method.

h. The official GDP of Cuba for the reference year 2011 is 68,990.15 million in national currency. However, this number and its breakdown into main aggregates are not shown in the table because of methodological comparability issues. Therefore, Cuba's results are provided only for the PPP and price level index. In addition, Cuba's figures are not included in the Latin America and world totals.

i. Bonaire's results are provided only for the individual consumption expenditure by households. Therefore, to ensure consistency across the tables, Bonaire is not included in the Caribbean total or the world total.

j. This table does not include the Pacific Islands and does not double count the dual participation economies: the Arab Republic of Egypt, Sudan, and the Russian Federation.

ICP 2011 Data Access and Archiving Policy

This appendix outlines the elements of the data access and archiving policy of the 2011 International Comparison Program (ICP), as approved by the 2011 ICP Executive Board. These elements include the objectives, guiding principles, and procedures for data access and archiving.

CONTEXT

The ICP compiles the large amounts of price data and detailed national accounts expenditure data submitted by its participating economies. The resulting ICP databases are put to various statistical and analytical uses by policy makers and researchers at international, regional, and national agencies and ministries, as well as at universities and research centers. This rich data set is an important contributor to the value of the ICP.

In the 2005 ICP round, the data access and archiving policy strongly limited access to detailed ICP data (that is, data below the basic heading level for each economy). For example, to access price data at the product level, users could only gain access in regions where memoranda of understanding between regional coordinating agencies and economies preventing data sharing had not been drafted. By the end of the 2005 round, it was clear that the user community would press for greater access to more detailed data in subsequent ICP rounds.

In the face of the mounting demands for more detailed data, the ICP Executive Board agreed that ICP 2011 should provide access to such data while respecting confidentiality constraints and data quality limitations. To increase the quality and utility of the data collected, the 2011 ICP round should also focus on collecting, archiving, and providing access to metadata.

DATA ACCESS OBJECTIVES

The overall objective of ICP's data access policy is that *data derived from the ICP be utilized to the maximum extent possible for statistical and analytical purposes.* Specifically, the objective is to provide users with access to detailed data beyond what was accessible through ICP 2005 as follows:

1. Purchasing power parities (PPPs), price level indexes (PLIs), and expenditure data for all economies are being published at the analytical level, with the supporting metadata. For ICP 2011 data, the analytical level is the level of detail (that is, aggregates, categories, groups, and classes) that the Global Office, Organisation for Economic Co-operation and Development (OECD), Eurostat, and regional coordinating agencies agree to publish.

2. PPPs, PLIs, and expenditure data for all economies at various levels of detail below the published level (that is, categories, groups, and classes not included above as well as basic headings) are available to data users, with the supporting metadata.

3. National average price data for all economies at the product level for items on the global core list, with the supporting metadata and measures of quality, are available to data users, except when the confidentiality of respondents is jeopardized.

4. National average price data for all economies at the product level for regional items not on the global core list, with the supporting metadata and measures of quality, are available to data users, except when the confidentiality of respondents is jeopardized.

5. Subnational data and individual price observations, with the supporting metadata, are available where permitted by the laws of individual economies, as long as the confidentiality of respondents is protected.

The availability of individual economy data must respect legislation and policies that protect respondent confidentiality. Such protections may place restrictions on public access to data, especially at the finer levels of detail.

GUIDING PRINCIPLES

The following guiding principles support the objective of greater data access:

1. *Appropriate use.* Data should be made available for analytical, research, and statistical purposes. Users should not misuse data by attempting to deduce the underlying confidential data.

2. *Equality of access.* ICP data are a public good and thus should be made available on an equal basis to anyone who wants to use them, in the same way that most national statistical offices make data available to users.

3. *Preservation of microdata confidentiality.* Provision of data should be consistent with legal and other arrangements that ensure the confidentiality of respondents.

4. *Transparency.* The principles and procedures for access to detailed ICP data, as well as the uses of these data, should be transparent and publicly available.

5. *Consistency.* The principles and procedures for data access should strive to be consistent across all regions and economies, with a view toward promoting equality in the treatment of all economies.

6. *Reciprocity.* Reciprocity between participating economies should be established to the maximum extent possible. All participating economies are automatically considered to be approved users of ICP data. Nonparticipating economies are not considered to be approved users of ICP data, but they may apply for access to these data following the procedures highlighted shortly.

7. *Reliability.* Releases of ICP data should be accompanied by the appropriate metadata, including metadata that describe the quality limitations of the data.

8. *Quality limitations.* Users of ICP data should be informed of the quality limitations, and they should agree that the data are still useful for their purposes.

9. *Serviceability.* ICP data should be archived to ensure that they can be used to service future approved requests for access to data, that they are available for possible use in future ICP rounds, and that they are available as backup in case these data are lost through a disaster or other reasons by a region or an economy.

10. *Disclosure limitations.* Users accessing detailed ICP data should publish the detailed data only when the data are accompanied by a statement of the data's quality.

11. *Promotion of uses.* To promote the use of ICP data, users are encouraged to share their feedback and research findings with all stakeholders, consistent with the disclosure limitations in this policy.

12. *Limitations on users' findings.* Indicators computed by users based on ICP data are not considered part of the official publications program of the ICP.

13. *Ease of access.* Data access procedures should ensure a simple and expedited process for access to ICP data.

PROCEDURES FOR DATA ARCHIVING

The procedures for archiving data for the ICP 2011–related variables are as follows:

1. PPPs, PLIs, and expenditure data for all economies are published at the analytical level (that is, aggregates, categories, groups, and classes), with the supporting metadata. They are archived by the World Bank Development Economics Data Group (DECDG) and also by the regional coordinating agencies.

2. PPPs, PLIs, and expenditure data at various levels of detail below the published level (that is, categories, groups, and classes not included in procedure 1, as well as basic headings) for all economies, with the supporting metadata, are archived by DECDG and also by the relevant regional coordinating agencies.

3. National average price data at the product level for items on the global core list for all economies, with the supporting metadata and measures of quality, are archived by DECDG and also by the relevant regional coordinating agencies.

4. National average price data at the product level for regional items not on the global core list for all economies, with the supporting metadata and measures of quality, are archived by DECDG and also by the relevant regional coordinating agencies.

5. Participating economies are responsible for archiving their subnational data and individual price observations, with the supporting metadata. However, some economies may ask DECDG or the relevant regional coordinating agency to archive these data and observations because they do not have their own facilities for archiving them. If an economy asks DECDG or the relevant regional coordinating agency to archive these data, the data should be encrypted and the economy in question should hold the encryption key.

The data to be archived by DECDG will be treated with confidentiality. The data will be archived in a secure database with limited access rights and administered by a designated data custodian. Access to the data (or any portions of the data) will be subject to the procedures highlighted in the next section.

PROCEDURES FOR DATA ACCESS

The procedures for accessing data for the ICP 2011–related variables are as follows:

1. PPPs, PLIs, and expenditure data for all economies at the analytical level, with the supporting metadata, will be published in ICP reports electronically and in paper format. They will also be available for downloading from an online database.

2. PPPs, PLIs, and expenditure data at various levels of detail below the published level for all economies, with the supporting metadata, can be accessed by users through an application process administered by DECDG.

3. National average price data at the product level for items on the global core list for all economies, with the supporting metadata and measures of quality, can be accessed by users through an application process administered by DECDG, consistent with the participating economy's confidentiality laws and processes. An economy should inform the relevant regional coordinator which average prices are considered confidential and thus cannot be released. The regional coordinator will in turn inform the Global Office. Product names and descriptions will be rendered anonymous before sharing them with users—that is, brand names will be suppressed.

4. National average price data at the product level for regional items not on the global core list for all economies, with the supporting metadata and measures of quality, can be accessed by users through an application process administered by DECDG, consistent with the participating economy's confidentiality laws and processes. An economy should inform the relevant regional coordinator

which average prices are considered confidential and thus cannot be released. The regional coordinator will in turn inform the Global Office. Product names and descriptions will be rendered anonymous before sharing them with users—that is, brand names will be suppressed.

5. Access to subnational data and individual price observations, with the supporting metadata, is restricted in general. However, users may address applications of access to these data directly to the economies in question.

Applying for access to the ICP 2011–related variables listed in procedures 2, 3, and 4 is initiated by the user with a written and signed application addressed to the director of the Development Data Group at the World Bank.

An outline of the information required by this application is available on the ICP website.[1]

The director of DECDG decides whether to approve requests, in line with the access policy agreed on by the ICP Executive Board. The director may also seek other expert advice before making a final decision on applications.

Alternatively, users may approach the regional coordinating agencies for access to the regional data (regional PPPs, expenditure data, and average prices). In this case, the regional coordinating agencies follow the access policy agreed on by the Executive Board. The release of regional data does not require clearance from DECDG.

---

[1] http://siteresources.worldbank.org/ICPINT/Resources/270056-1255977254560/121120_ICPDataAccessPrinciples&Procedures.pdf.

ICP Revision Policy

The motivation for developing a revision policy for the International Comparison Program (ICP) is user interest in comparing the latest ICP results with those from subsequent benchmark rounds.

For its benchmark rounds, the ICP publishes indicators for all participating economies that include: (1) real expenditures and real expenditures per capita; (2) purchasing power parities (PPPs) and price level indexes (PLIs); and (3) nominal expenditures and nominal expenditures per capita. Indicators are published at the analytical level—that is, the level of detail (gross domestic product [GDP] and major components and categories) at which the Global Office, Organisation for Economic Co-operation and Development (OECD), Eurostat, and regional coordinating agencies agree to publish data from the ICP benchmark rounds. Results at various levels of detail below the published level—down to the basic heading level—for all economies are available to researchers through the data access process stipulated in the ICP data access and archiving policy (see appendix J).

Comparing results from ICP benchmarks is complicated by three significant factors. First, ICP benchmark rounds are designed to provide a onetime "snapshot" of ICP indicators. Second, the collection and estimation methodologies for some components are improved between

rounds. And, third, for each benchmark round some economies are added and others may drop out or shift from one region to another. Such changes affect comparisons between economies because the multilateral results will differ, depending on the economies included and their ICP grouping. In addition, the national accounts in virtually all economies are revised over time as additional data become available. For example, the 2005 estimates of the expenditures related to the GDP and its major components have been revised in most economies since the ICP 2005 results were released in December 2007. Indeed, in 22 economies these revisions were in excess of 10 percent. Analogous problems arise with revisions to population estimates.

The ICP benchmarks produce a onetime snapshot of ICP indicators, whereas the World Bank's World Development Indicators database produces a time series of ICP indicators on an annual basis for nonbenchmark years, beginning with 1980. These interim estimates are computed on the basis of an extrapolation method.

This appendix summarizes the ICP policy that defines how ICP indicators are revised. It describes the triggers and guidelines for revising ICP indicators, as well as the timing of revisions and the steps to be taken to communicate these revisions to users.

TRIGGERS FOR REVISING ICP INDICATORS

Revisions in input data

- *Revisions in aggregate GDP estimates* trigger a revision of real expenditures and real expenditures per capita and nominal expenditures and nominal expenditures per capita.

- *Revisions in major components of GDP* trigger a revision of real expenditures and real expenditures per capita and nominal expenditures and nominal expenditures per capita. It may also trigger a revision of PPPs and PLIs.

- *Revisions in population figures* trigger a revision of real expenditures per capita and nominal expenditures per capita.

- *Changes in economies' currency units* trigger a revision of real expenditures and real expenditures per capita, PPPs, PLIs, and nominal expenditures and nominal expenditures per capita.

- *Release of new results from regional nonbenchmark exercises* may trigger a revision of global-level results related to real expenditures and real expenditures per capita, PPPs, and PLIs for nonbenchmark years.

- *Correction of errors in source data or results* may trigger a revision of real expenditures and real expenditures per capita, PPPs, PLIs, and nominal expenditures and nominal expenditures per capita.

New methodology

- *Materially improved PPP computation and aggregation methods* trigger a revision of real expenditures and real expenditures per capita, PPPs, and PLIs.

- *Materially improved global linking approach* triggers a revision of real expenditures and real expenditures per capita, PPPs, and PLIs.

- *Materially improved extrapolation method* triggers a revision of real expenditures and real expenditures per capita, PPPs, and PLIs for nonbenchmark years.

GUIDELINES FOR REVISING ICP INDICATORS

Historical revisions

- The World Bank assumes that historical estimates of country prices and exchange rates used in the ICP benchmarks will remain unchanged.

- Revisions triggered by changes in an economy's national accounts estimates may require a revision of the time series of ICP indicators—including benchmark data—going back historically as far as necessary to incorporate the changes in the economy's national accounts time series. For example, revisions in a country's GDP from 2004 to 2011 would trigger a revision in the real expenditures and real expenditures per capita of the ICP 2005 benchmark. However, if the revisions spanned 2006 through 2011, the ICP 2005 benchmark data would not be revised.

- Revisions triggered by a new benchmark ICP methodology should not go beyond the last benchmark. For example, ICP 2011 uses an improved global linking method, so revisions could be carried out for the last benchmark indicators (2005) but not for the previous benchmark indicators (1993–96).

Geographical scope

- It is desirable to introduce revisions first to regional benchmark indicators' and then to global benchmark indicators in order to preserve the consistency between the regional and global data sets. Revised within-region PPPs will be the input to estimation of the between-region linking factors needed to determine global-level PPPs.

- The World Bank is responsible for revising benchmark indicators at the global level (that is, denominated in the global numéraire currency).

- If a particular region does not revise its regional benchmark indicators, the World Bank will revise and publish global benchmark indicators to take into account any revision in other regions.

- Results of regional interim exercises may be incorporated in the time series of ICP indicators if the results are deemed of sufficient quality by the World Development Indicators team.

Fixity

- Revised global benchmark results should respect, to the extent possible, regional price fixity—the convention whereby the price relativities established between economies in a regional comparison are retained when the economies are included in the global comparison.

Classification level

- PPPs could be revised at various classification levels (GDP, major components, categories, groups, or classes), depending on the level of detail of the national accounts expenditure revisions. For example, revised expenditures at the class level would result in revisions to higher-level PPP aggregates (GDP, major components, categories, and groups) through the aggregation process.

Categories of indicators

- *Real expenditures* and *real expenditures per capita* will be revised when the national accounts expenditure data or population data are revised.

- *PPPs and PLIs* may be revised, depending on the level of detail of the national accounts expenditure revisions. When economies revise their expenditure data for major components, categories, groups, classes, or basic headings, then PPPs (and the resulting PLIs) may be revised at levels above the lowest level for which expenditures were revised.

- *Nominal expenditures and nominal expenditures per capita* will be revised when the national accounts expenditure data or population data are revised.

Quality review

- Revised ICP indicators should go through an expert review before they are published to ensure data quality.

- The World Bank will maintain a database containing the various vintages of data for quality purposes.

Publication of revised results

- Revised ICP indicators should be published once they have been compiled and have undergone the quality review process.

- Revised ICP indicators should be released at the analytical level of the benchmark results, as established in the ICP data access and archiving policy (see appendix J).

Consistency between published and unpublished data sets

- The World Bank provides researchers with a detailed data set from benchmark ICP exercises, as stipulated in the ICP data access and archiving policy. This data set includes real expenditures and real expenditures per capita, PPPs, PLIs, and nominal expenditures and nominal expenditures per capita at all levels, down to the basic heading level. When revising ICP indicators, the ICP may need to revise this unpublished detailed data set in order to maintain the consistency between the published and the unpublished data sets. For example, if a revision of nominal expenditures and nominal expenditures per capita is triggered, it may be desirable to reflect it at all levels—down to that of the basic heading—depending on the World Bank's assessment of the need to do so.

TIMING AND COMMUNICATION OF REVISIONS

- The time series of ICP indicators will be revised by the World Bank on an annual basis as part of the World Development Indicators April update.

- The schedule of revisions will be announced to stakeholders and users well in advance.

- When a methodology is improved, the new method will be communicated to users well in advance.

- Results will be made publicly available on the Internet, ICP portal, and all other relevant sites.

Glossary

accounting period. The period to which estimates of GDP refer, usually a calendar year or a quarter. For ICP comparisons of GDP, the accounting period is a calendar year.

actual individual consumption. The total value of the individual consumption expenditures of households, nonprofit institutions serving households, and general government. It is a measure of the individual goods and services that households actually consume as opposed to what they actually purchase.

additive. An aggregation method is additive if, for each economy being compared, it provides real expenditures for aggregates that are equal to the sum of the real expenditures of their constituent basic headings. An additive aggregation method provides real expenditures that satisfy the average test for volumes but are subject to the Gerschenkron effect.

aggregate. A set of transactions related to a specified flow of goods and services in a given accounting period, such as the total purchases of consumer goods and services by resident households or the total expenditure on collective services by government or the total value of gross fixed capital formation.

aggregation. The process of weighting and averaging basic heading PPPs to obtain PPPs for each level of aggregation up to GDP.

analytical categories. GDP, main aggregates, expenditure categories, expenditure groups, and expenditure classes for which the results of a comparison are published.

average test for volumes. A test that requires the volume index for an aggregate to lie between the smallest and the largest of its component volume indexes.

base country invariance. The property whereby the relativities between the PPPs, price level indexes, and volume indexes of economies are not affected by either the choice of national currency as numéraire or the choice of reference economy.

basic heading. The lowest aggregation level in the ICP expenditure classification. In theory, a basic heading is defined as a group of similar well-defined goods or services. In practice, it is defined by the lowest level of final expenditure for which explicit expenditure weights can be estimated. Thus an actual basic heading can cover a broader range of products than is theoretically desirable and include both goods and services. It is at the level of the basic heading that expenditures are defined and estimated, products are selected for pricing, prices are collected and validated, and PPPs are first calculated and averaged.

basic price. The amount received by the producer from the purchaser for a unit of good or service produced as output. It includes subsidies on products and other taxes on production. It excludes taxes on products, other subsidies on production, the supplier's retail and wholesale margins, and separately invoiced transport and insurance charges. Basic prices are the prices most relevant for decision making by suppliers (producers).

bias. A systematic error in a PPP or volume index. Bias can arise for a number of reasons, including failure to respect importance, comparability, or consistency; the price collection and measurement procedures followed; and the calculation and aggregation formula employed.

bilateral or binary comparison. A price or volume comparison between two economies that draws on data only for those two economies.

bilateral or binary PPP. A PPP between two economies calculated using only the prices and weights for those two economies.

bridge economy. An economy that provides the link or bridge between two or more separate comparisons involving different groups of economies. The bridge economy participates in all comparisons and by doing so enables the economies in one comparison to be compared with the economies in the other comparisons. An alternative to linking groups of economies through bridge economies is to combine them using core products.

change in inventories. The acquisition less disposals of stocks of raw materials, semifinished goods, and finished goods that are held by producer units prior to being further processed or sold or otherwise used. Semifinished goods cover work in progress (partially completed products whose production process will be continued by the same producer in a subsequent accounting period), including the natural growth of agricultural crops prior to harvest and the natural growth in livestock raised for slaughter. Inventories also cover all raw materials and goods stored by government as strategic reserves.

change in valuables. The acquisition less disposals of valuables. Valuables are defined as produced assets such as nonmonetary gold, precious stones, antiques, paintings, sculptures, and other art objects that are not used primarily for production or consumption,

that are expected to appreciate or at least not decline in real value, that do not deteriorate over time in normal conditions, and that are acquired and held primarily as stores of value.

characteristics. The technical parameters and price-determining properties of a product listed in a product specification.

Classification of the Functions of Government (COFOG). Classification of transactions by general government, including outlays on the final consumption expenditure, intermediate consumption, gross fixed capital formation, and capital and current transfers, by function or purpose. A major use of COFOG is to identify which final consumption expenditures of general government benefit households individually and which benefit households collectively.

Classification of Individual Consumption According to Purpose (COICOP). Classification of the individual consumption expenditures of three institutional sectors—households, nonprofit institutions serving households (NPISHs), and general government—by the ends that they wish to achieve through these expenditures. Individual consumption expenditures are those that are made for the benefit of individual households. All final consumption expenditures by households and NPISHs are defined as individual, but only the final consumption expenditures by general government on individual services are treated as individual.

collective consumption expenditure by government. The final consumption expenditure of general government on collective services. It is a measure of the services that general government provides to the community as a whole and that households consume collectively. Also called actual collective consumption.

collective services. Services provided by general government that benefit the community as a whole: general public services, defense, public order and safety, economic affairs, environmental protection, and housing and community amenities. They also include the overall policy-making, planning, budgetary, and coordinating responsibilities of government ministries overseeing individual services and government research and development for individual services. These activities cannot be identified with specific individual households and are considered to benefit households collectively.

comparability. The requirement that economies price products that are identical or, if not identical, equivalent. Products are said to be comparable if they have identical or equivalent technical parameters and price-determining properties. Equivalent means that they meet the same needs with equal efficiency so that purchasers are indifferent between them and are not prepared to pay more for one than for the other. The pricing of comparable products ensures that the differences in prices between economies for a product reflect actual price differences and are not affected by differences in quality. If differences in quality are not avoided or corrected, they can be mistaken for apparent price differences leading to an underestimation or overestimation of price levels and an overestimation or underestimation of volume levels.

comparison-resistant. A term first used to describe nonmarket services that are difficult to compare across economies because they have no economically significant prices with which to value outputs, their units of output cannot be otherwise defined and measured, the institutional arrangements for their provision and the conditions of payment differ from economy to economy, and their quality varies between economies but the differences cannot be identified and quantified. Increasingly, the term is being used to describe construction and market services such as telecommunications, whose complexity, variation, and economy specificity make it difficult to price them comparably across economies.

compensation of employees. All payments in cash and in kind made by employers to employees in return for work carried out during the accounting period. These payments comprise gross wages and salaries in cash and in kind, employers' actual social contributions, and imputed social contributions.

component. A subset of goods or services or both that make up some defined aggregate.

consistency. The requirement that the prices collected by economies be consistent with the prices underlying their estimates of GDP and its component expenditures. In most cases, this means that they should be national annual purchasers' prices for actual market transactions. The basis of a comparison is an identity, expenditure = price × volume, and volumes are obtained by dividing expenditures by prices. Using prices that do not correspond to those used to derive the expenditures would result in volumes that are either underestimated or overestimated.

consumption of fixed capital. The reduction in the value of the fixed assets used in production during the accounting period resulting from physical deterioration, normal obsolescence, or normal accidental damage.

core product. A product that appears on the product lists of two or more separate groups of economies for the purpose of combining the groups in a single multilateral comparison. The use of core products is an alternative to linking groups of economies through bridge economies.

country aggregation with redistribution (CAR) procedure. A means of obtaining for a specified aggregate global volumes and PPPs for economies within each region that retain the relativities established between the economies in the regional comparison. In other words, each region's results for the aggregate remain fixed when linked with the results of other regions. The procedure is as follows. The global basic heading PPPs for all economies in the comparison are aggregated to the level of the aggregate. The global PPPs for the aggregate are used to calculate global real expenditures for each economy, with which the total global real expenditure on the aggregate for each region can be determined. The total global real expenditure of each region is redistributed across the economies in the region in line with the distribution of the real expenditures in the regional comparison. Global PPPs for economies are calculated indirectly with the redistributed global real expenditure.

country product dummy (CPD) method. The multilateral method used to obtain transitive PPPs at the basic heading level through regression analysis. It treats the calculation of PPPs as a matter of statistical inference—that is, an estimation problem rather than an index number problem. The underlying hypothesis is that, apart from random disturbance, the PPPs for individual products within a basic heading are all constant between any given pair of economies. In other words, it is assumed that the pattern of the relative prices of the different products within a given basic heading is the same in all economies. It is also assumed that each economy has its own overall price level for the basic heading, and that this overall price level fixes the levels of absolute prices of the products in the basic heading for the economy. By treating the prices observed in the economies for the basic heading as random samples, the PPPs between each pair of economies and the common pattern of relative prices can be estimated using classical least square methods. The method allows the estimation of sampling errors for the PPPs.

country product dummy-weighted (CPD-W) method. A variant of the country product dummy method in which important products receive a higher weight in the calculation than less important products. For example, important products could have a weight of 2 or 3 and less important products a weight of 1. The choice of weights is arbitrary as it is in the Gini-Élteto-Köves-Szulc* (GEKS*) method. However, the weight of 1 for an important product and 0 for a less important product used in the GEKS* method cannot be used in a weighted CPD because the assignment of 0 to prices of less important products will remove them from the calculation. In ICP 2011, important products were given a weight of 3 and less important products a weight of 1.

country product representativity dummy (CPRD) method. A variant of the country product dummy (CPD) method that has an additional dummy variable to denote whether or not the product is important. The assumption is that the ratio of price levels for important and less important products is the same for all products within a basic heading. In theory, the ratio should be less than 1 because less important products are expected to be more expensive than important products.

deflation. The division of the current value of an aggregate by a price index—the deflator—in order to value its volumes at the prices of the price reference period.

Dikhanov editing procedure. The iterative intereconomy validation procedure developed by Yuri Dikhanov to edit the average survey prices reported by economies. It can be viewed as an alternative or as a complement to the Quaranta editing procedure. Both procedures provide similar measures of price variation for products and economies employing either basic heading PPPs for editing basic headings individually or PPPs for an aggregate for editing across the basic headings constituting the aggregate. In practice, the Quaranta procedure is employed to edit prices within basic headings, and the Dikhanov procedure is used to edit prices within aggregates. The Dikhanov procedure is specific to the country product dummy (CPD)–based methods of calculating PPPs, whereas the Quaranta table has a broader application that includes Gini-Èlteto-Köves-Szulc (GEKS)–based methods as well as CPD-based methods.

Dikhanov table. The intereconomy validation table generated by the Dikhanov editing procedure.

economically significant price. A price that has a significant influence on the amounts producers are willing to supply and on the amounts purchasers wish to buy. This is the basic price for producers and the purchasers' price for purchasers.

economic territory. The geographical territory of an economy plus any territorial enclaves in the rest of the world. By convention, it includes embassies, military bases, and ships and aircraft abroad. The economic territory does not include extraterritorial enclaves—that is, the parts of the economy's own geographical territory used by government agencies of other economies or by international organizations under international treaties or agreements between states.

editing. The first step of validation, which entails scrutinizing data for errors. It is the process of checking survey prices for nonsampling errors by identifying those prices that have extreme values—that is, prices whose value is determined to be either too high or too low vis-à-vis the average according to certain criteria. The price may score a value for a given test that exceeds a predetermined critical value, or its value may fall outside some prespecified range of acceptable values. Both are standard ways of detecting errors in survey data, and both are employed by the ICP. Prices with extreme values are not necessarily wrong. But the fact that their values are considered extreme suggests that they could be wrong. They are possible errors, and as such they need to be investigated to establish whether they are actual errors.

employers' actual social contributions. Payments actually made by employers to social security funds, insurance enterprises, or autonomous pension funds for the benefit of their employees.

error. The difference between the observed value of a PPP or volume index and its correct value. Errors may be random or systematic. Random errors are generally called errors; systematic errors are called biases.

exhaustiveness. The extent to which an economy's estimate of GDP covers all economic activity in its economic territory.

expenditure weight. The share of the expenditure on a basic heading in nominal GDP.

final consumption expenditure. The expenditure on goods and services consumed by individual households or the community to satisfy their individual or collective needs or wants.

financial intermediation services indirectly measured (FISIM). An indirect measure of the value of the financial intermediation services that financial institutions provide clients but for which they do not charge explicitly.

Fisher-type PPP. The PPP for a basic heading or an aggregate between two economies that is defined as the geometric mean of the Laspeyres-type PPP and the Paasche-type PPP for the basic heading or the aggregate. See Laspeyres-type PPP and Paasche-type PPP (their formulation depends on whether they are being used to calculate basic heading PPPs or to aggregate basic heading PPPs).

fixity. The convention whereby the relativities between a group of economies that were established in a comparison covering just that group of economies remain unchanged, or fixed, when the economies of the group are included in comparisons with a wider group of economies. For example, the price and volume relativities of the ICP regions and Eurostat-OECD remain unchanged in the global comparison. If fixity were not observed, there would be two sets of relativities for the participating economies that would not necessarily be in agreement because the relativities and ranking of economies can change as the composition of the group of economies being compared changes. Fixity ensures that participating economies have only one set of results to explain to users.

free on board (f.o.b.) value. The price of a good delivered at the customs frontier of the exporting economy. It includes the freight and insurance charges incurred to that point and any export duties or other taxes on exports levied by the exporting economy.

Geary-Khamis (GK) method. An average price aggregation method for computing PPPs and real expenditures above the basic heading level. It entails valuing a matrix of quantities using a vector of international prices. The vector is obtained by averaging national prices across participating economies after they have been converted to a common currency with PPPs and weighted by economy quantity shares. The economy PPPs are obtained by averaging the ratios of national and international prices weighted by economy expenditure shares. The international prices and the PPPs are defined by a system of interrelated linear equations that must be solved simultaneously. The GK method produces PPPs that are transitive and real expenditures that are additive. One of its disadvantages is that a change in the composition of the group can alter significantly the international prices as well as the relationships between economies. Another is that the real expenditures are subject to the Gerschenkron effect, which can be large. GK results are considered better suited to the analysis of price and volume structures across economies.

general government. The institutional sector that consists of federal, central, regional, state, and local government units together with the social security funds imposed and controlled by those units. It includes non-profit institutions engaged in nonmarket production that are controlled and mainly financed by government units or social security funds.

Gerschenkron effect. An effect applicable only to aggregation methods that use either a reference price structure, whereby each economy's quantities are valued by a uniform set of prices to obtain volumes, or a reference volume structure, whereby each economy's prices are used to value a uniform set of quantities to obtain PPPs. For methods employing a reference price structure, an economy's share of total GDP—that is, the total for the group of economies being compared—will rise as the reference price structure becomes less characteristic of its own price structure. For methods employing a reference volume structure, an economy's share of total GDP will fall as the reference volume structure becomes less characteristic of its own volume structure. The Gerschenkron effect arises because of the negative correlation between prices and volumes.

Gini-Èltetö-Köves-Szulc (GEKS) method. A method to calculate PPPs for basic headings or to aggregate basic heading PPPs to obtain PPPs for each level of aggregation up to GDP. There are two versions of the GEKS at the basic heading level: one that takes account of the importance of the products priced and one that does not. The version that takes the importance of products into consideration is referred to as GEKS* in the literature.

Strictly speaking, the GEKS is a procedure whereby any set of intransitive binary index numbers are made transitive and multilateral while respecting characteristicity (the property in which the resulting multilateral indexes differ as little as possible from the original binary indexes). The procedure is independent of the method used to calculate the intransitive binary indexes. But as used in the current literature, GEKS covers both the way in which the intransitive binary PPPs are calculated and the procedure used to make them transitive and multilateral.

The intransitive binary PPPs for a basic heading or an aggregate are obtained by calculating first a matrix of Laspeyres-type PPPs and then a matrix of Paasche-type PPPs, and finally by taking the geometric mean of the two, a matrix of Fisher-type PPPs. The Fisher-type PPPs are made transitive and multilateral by applying the GEKS procedure, which involves replacing the Fisher-type PPP between each pair of economies with the geometric mean of itself squared and all the corresponding indirect Fisher-type PPPs between the pair obtained using the other economies as bridges. The resulting GEKS PPPs provide real expenditures that are not subject to the Gerschenkron effect and that are not additive. GEKS results are considered better suited to comparisons across economies of the price and volume levels of individual basic headings or aggregates. See Laspeyres-type PPP and Paasche-type PPP (their formulation depends on whether they are being used to calculate basic heading PPPs or to aggregate basic heading PPPs).

global core product. A product priced for the specific purpose of providing a link or overlap between regional comparisons at the basic heading level in order to combine them in a single world comparison. For ICP 2011, lists of global core products were compiled for consumer goods and services, government services, and capital goods by the Global Office in consultation with the regions, participating economies, and subject matter experts. Regions selected products from the global core product lists and added them to their regional product lists in line with product availability and importance in their region. The global core products priced by the regions were included in the regional comparisons as well as the world comparison.

goods. Physical objects for which a demand exists, over which ownership rights can be established, and whose ownership can be transferred from one institutional unit to another by engaging in transactions on the market. They are in demand because they may be used to satisfy the needs or wants of households or the community or used to produce other goods or services.

government final consumption expenditure. The actual and imputed final consumption expenditure incurred by general government on individual goods and services and collective services. It is the total value of the individual consumption expenditure and collective consumption expenditure by general government.

gross capital formation. The total value of gross fixed capital formation, changes in inventories, and acquisitions less disposals of valuables.

gross domestic product (GDP). When estimated from the expenditure side, GDP is defined as the total value of the final consumption expenditures of households, nonprofit institutions serving households, and general government plus gross capital formation plus the balance of exports and imports.

gross fixed capital formation. The total value of acquisitions less disposals of fixed assets by resident institutional units during the accounting period, plus the additions to the value of nonproduced assets realized by the productive activity of resident institutional units.

gross operating surplus. The surplus or deficit accruing from production before taking into account (1) consumption of fixed capital by the enterprise; (2) any interest, rent, or similar charges payable on financial or tangible nonproduced assets borrowed or rented by the enterprise; or (3) any interest, rent, or similar charges receivable on financial or tangible nonproduced assets owned by the enterprise.

gross wages and salaries. The wages and salaries in cash and in kind paid by enterprises to employees before the deduction of taxes and social contributions payable by employees.

household. A small group of persons who share the same living accommodation, who pool some or all of their income and wealth, and who consume certain types of goods and services collectively, mainly food and housing. A household can consist of only one person.

Iklé method. An average price aggregation method similar to the Geary-Khamis (GK) method. It was used in the 2005 ICP regional comparison for Africa. Like the GK method, it derives a vector of international prices by averaging national prices across participating economies after the prices have been converted to a common currency with PPPs and weighted. The GK method uses quantity shares as weights, whereas the Iklé method uses expenditure shares as weights. In addition, GK international prices are arithmetic means, while Iklé international prices are harmonic means. The Iklé method is designed to prevent prices in economies with large expenditures from dominating the average prices. Because the sum of expenditure shares in each economy is equal to one, the Iklé method can be regarded as equi-representative of all economies. The Iklé method produces PPPs that are transitive and real expenditures that are additive. Compared with the GK method, the Iklé method minimizes the Gerschenkron effect.

importance. A concept that is defined in terms of a specific economy within a basic heading. A product is either important or less important in the economy for the given basic heading. An important product is one that accounts for a significant share of the expenditure on the basic heading in the economy in question. Formerly, important products were called representative products.

imputed expenditure. Some transactions that are desirable to include in GDP do not take place in money terms and so cannot be measured directly. Expenditures on these nonmonetary transactions are obtained by imputing a value to them. The values to be imputed are defined by national accounting conventions. These vary from case to case and are described in the System of National Accounts (SNA).

imputed rent. Owner-occupiers use the dwelling they own and occupy to produce housing services for themselves. Thus they are in effect renting the dwelling to themselves and the value of the rent has to be imputed. The imputed rent should be valued at the estimated rent a tenant pays for a dwelling of the same size and quality in a comparable location with similar neighborhood amenities. When markets for rented accommodation are virtually nonexistent or unrepresentative, the value of the imputed rent has to be derived by some other objective procedure such as the user cost method.

imputed social contributions. The imputations that have to be made when employers provide social benefits directly to their employees, former employees, or dependents out of their own resources without involving an insurance enterprise or autonomous pension fund and without creating a special fund or segregated reserve for the purpose.

indirect binary comparison. A price or volume comparison between two economies made through a third economy. For example, for economies A, B, and C, the PPP between A and C is obtained by dividing the PPP between A and B by the PPP between C and B so that $PPP_{A/C} = PPP_{A/B}/PPP_{C/B}$.

individual consumption expenditure by government. The actual and imputed final consumption expenditure incurred by general government on individual goods and services.

individual consumption expenditure by households. The actual and imputed final consumption expenditure incurred by resident households on individual goods and services. Includes expenditures on individual goods and services sold at prices that are not economically significant. By definition, all final consumption expenditures of households are for the benefit of individual households and are individual.

individual consumption expenditure by nonprofit institutions serving households (NPISHs). The actual and imputed final consumption expenditure incurred by NPISHs on individual goods and services.

Because most final consumption expenditures of NPISHs are individual, all final consumption expenditures of NPISHs are treated by convention as individual.

individual good or service. A consumption good or service acquired by a household and used to satisfy the needs and wants of members of that household.

individual services. A term used to describe the services (and goods) provided to individual households by nonprofit institutions serving households and by general government. Such services include housing, health, recreation and culture, education, and social protection. They do not include the overall policy-making, planning, budgetary, and coordinating responsibilities of the government ministries overseeing individual services. Nor do they include government research and development for individual services. These activities are considered to benefit households collectively and are therefore classified under collective services.

input price approach. The approach used to obtain PPPs for nonmarket services. Because there are no economically significant prices with which to value the outputs of these services, national accountants follow the convention of estimating the expenditures on nonmarket services by summing the costs of the inputs required to produce them. PPPs for nonmarket services are calculated using input prices because these are the prices that are consistent with the prices underlying the estimated expenditures. In practice, prices are only collected for labor, which is by far the largest and most important input.

institutional sector. The System of National Accounts identifies five institutional sectors: nonfinancial corporations, financial corporations, general government, households, and nonprofit institutions serving households.

intereconomy validation. The validation that takes place after participating economies have completed their intra-economy validation and submitted their survey prices to the regional coordinator. It is an iterative process consisting of several rounds of questions and answers between the regional coordinator and participating economies. It involves editing and verifying the average survey prices reported by participating economies for a basic heading and assessing the reliability of the PPPs they produce for the basic heading. The objective is to establish that the average survey prices are for comparable products, that the products have been accurately priced, and that the allocation of importance indicators is correct. In other words, it seeks to ascertain whether economies have interpreted the product specifications in the same way and whether their price collectors have priced them without error. The Quaranta and Dikhanov editing procedures are employed for this purpose. Both procedures entail detecting outliers among the average survey prices by identifying outliers among the corresponding price ratios. Economies verify the outliers found in order to ascertain whether they are valid observations. If they are not, the economy either corrects or suppresses them.

intermediate consumption. The value of the goods and services, other than fixed assets, that are used or consumed as inputs by a process of production.

intra-economy validation. The validation that precedes intereconomy validation. It is undertaken by participating economies prior to submitting their survey prices to the regional coordinator. Each economy edits and verifies its own prices without reference to the price data of other economies. Validation is carried out at the product level. The objective is to establish that price collectors within the economy have priced items that match the product specifications and that the prices they have reported are accurate. This entails an economy searching for outliers first among the individual prices that have been collected for each product it has chosen to survey and then among the average prices for these products. Subsequently, the economy verifies the outliers found in order to ascertain whether they are valid observations. If they are not, the economy either corrects or suppresses them.

Laspeyres-type PPP. A PPP for a basic heading or an aggregate between two economies, economy B and economy A, where the reference economy is economy A and the weights are those of economy A. At the basic heading level, the PPP is defined as a quasi-weighted geometric average of the price relatives between economy B and economy A for the important products of economy A. At the aggregate level, the PPP is defined as the weighted arithmetic average of the PPPs between economy B and economy A for the basic headings covered by the aggregate. The expenditure shares of economy A are used as weights.

market price. The amount of money a willing buyer pays to acquire a good or service from a willing seller—that is, the actual price for a transaction agreed to by the transactors. It is the net price inclusive of all discounts, surcharges, and rebates applied to the transaction. Also called the transaction price.

material well-being. The volume of goods and services that households consume to satisfy their individual needs.

Model Report on Expenditure Statistics (MORES). A set of worksheets designed to help economies participating in a comparison break down their expenditure on GDP for the reference year to the basic heading level and, at the same time, document how each basic heading expenditure was estimated.

multilateral comparison. A price or volume comparison of more than two economies simultaneously that is made with price and expenditure data from all economies covered and that produces consistent relations among all pairs of participating economies—that is, one that satisfies the transitivity requirement, among other requirements.

national annual price. A price that has been averaged both over all localities of an economy in order to take into account the regional variations in prices and over the whole of the reference year in order to allow for seasonal variations in prices as well as general inflation and changes in price structures.

net taxes on production. Taxes less subsidies on production.

nominal expenditure. An expenditure that is valued at national price levels. It can be expressed in national currencies or in a common currency to which it has been converted with exchange rates. It reflects both volume and price differences between economies.

nonmarket service. A service that is provided to households free or at a price that is not economically significant by nonprofit institutions serving households or by general government.

nonobserved economy. Activities that are hidden because they are illegal or because they are legal but carried out clandestinely or because they are undertaken by households for their own use. These activities also include those that are missed because of deficiencies in the statistical system. Such deficiencies include out-of-date survey registers, surveys whose reporting thresholds are too high or that have high rates of nonresponse, poor survey editing procedures, and lack of surveys of informal activities such as street trading.

nonprofit institution serving households (NPISH). A nonprofit institution that is not predominantly financed and controlled by government, that provides goods or services to households free or at prices that are not economically significant, and whose main resources are voluntary contributions by households.

numéraire currency. The currency unit selected to be the common currency in which PPPs and real and nominal expenditures are expressed.

observation. An individual price, or one of a number of individual prices, collected for an item at an outlet.

outlet. A shop, market, service establishment, internet site, mail order service, or other place from where goods or services can be purchased and from where the purchasers' or list prices of the products sold can be obtained.

outlier. A term generally used to describe any extreme value in a set of survey data. Can also mean an extreme value that has been verified as being correct.

Paasche-Laspeyres spread. The ratio of the Paasche-type index to the Laspeyres-type index in a binary comparison.

Paasche-type PPP. A PPP for a basic heading or an aggregate between two economies, economy B and economy A, where the reference economy is economy A and the weights are those of economy B. At the basic heading level, the PPP is defined as a quasi-weighted geometric average of the price relatives between economy B and economy A for the important products of economy B. At the aggregate level, the PPP is defined as the weighted harmonic average of the PPPs between economy B and economy A for the basic headings covered by the aggregate. The expenditure shares of economy B are used as weights.

Penn effect. The overstatement of the economic size of high-income economies with high price levels and the understatement of the economic size of low-income economies with low price levels that result when exchange rate–converted GDPs are used to establish the relative sizes of economies. It arises because exchange rates do not take into account price level differences between economies when used to convert their GDPs to a common currency.

price approach. The approach whereby the price comparison between two or more economies is made by comparing the prices for a representative sample of comparable products. PPPs are generally derived using the price approach.

price error. An error that arises when price collectors price products that match the product specification, but record the price incorrectly or record the price correctly and error is introduced afterward in the process of reporting and transmitting the price. A price error can also arise because the quantity priced is recorded incorrectly (or error is introduced later during processing). Thus when the price collected is standardized and adjusted to a reference quantity, it will not be correct.

price level index (PLI). PLIs are the ratios of PPPs to exchange rates. They provide a measure of the differences in price levels between economies by indicating for a given aggregation level the number of units of the common currency needed to buy the same volume of the aggregation level in each economy.

At the level of GDP, they provide a measure of the differences in the general price levels of economies.

price measure. Price measures are the PPPs and the price level indexes to which they give rise.

price relative. The ratio of the price of an individual product in one economy to the price of the same product in some other economy. It shows how many units of currency A must be spent in economy A to obtain the same quantity and quality—that is, the same volume—of the product that X units of currency B purchase in economy B.

product. A good or service that is the result of production. Products are exchanged and used for various purposes—as inputs in the production of other goods and services, for final consumption, or for investment.

product error. An error that occurs when price collectors price products that do not match the product specification and neglect to report having done so. They may not have been aware of the mismatch, such as when the product specification is too loose, or they may have priced a substitute product as required by the pricing guidelines but failed to mention that they had done so on the price reporting form.

productivity adjustment. An adjustment made to the prices paid by nonmarket producers for labor, capital, and intermediate inputs so that they correspond to a common level of multifactor productivity. In practice, it is an adjustment made to the prices (compensation of employees) paid by nonmarket producers for labor so that they represent the same level of labor productivity.

product list. The common list of well-defined goods and services from which economies participating in a comparison make a selection of products to price for the purpose of compiling PPPs.

product specification. A list of the physical and economic characteristics that can be used to identify a product selected for pricing, thereby ensuring that economies price comparable items. A product specification can be either brand- and model-specific—that is, a specification in which a particular brand and model is stipulated—or generic—that is, a specification in which only the relevant price-determining and technical characteristics are given and no brand is designated.

purchaser's price. The amount paid by the purchaser in order to take delivery of a unit of a good or service at the time and place required by the purchaser. It excludes any value added tax (or similar deductible tax on products) that purchasers can deduct from their own VAT liability with respect to the VAT invoiced to their customers. It includes suppliers' retail and wholesale margins, separately invoiced transport and insurance charges, and any VAT (or similar deductible tax on products) that purchasers cannot deduct from their own VAT liability. For equipment goods, it would also include the installation costs if applicable. The purchaser's price is the price most relevant for decision making by buyers.

purchasing power parity (PPP). Spatial deflator and currency converter that eliminates the effects of the differences in price levels between economies, thereby allowing volume comparisons of GDP and GDP component expenditures.

PPPs are calculated in three stages: (1) for individual products, (2) for groups of products or basic headings, and (3) for groups of basic headings or aggregates. The PPPs for individual products are the ratios of national prices in national currencies for the same good or service. The PPPs for basic headings are the unweighted averages of the PPPs for individual products. And the PPPs for aggregates are the weighted averages of the PPPs for basic headings. The weights used are the expenditures on the basic headings.

At all stages, PPPs are price relatives. They show how many units of currency A need to be spent in economy A to obtain the same volume of a product or a basic heading or an aggregate that X units of currency B purchases in economy B. In the case of a single product, the same volume means an identical volume. But in the case of the complex assortment of goods and services that make up an aggregate such as GDP, the same volume does not mean an identical basket of goods and services. The composition of the basket will vary among economies according to their economic, social, and cultural differences, but each basket will provide equivalent satisfaction or utility.

quality adjustment. An adjustment to the prices of a product whose characteristics are broadly similar but not the same in all economies pricing it. The aim of the adjustment is to remove from the price differences observed between economies that part of the difference due to the difference in the characteristics of the product priced. The adjustment is made so that the price differences between economies reflect only pure price differences.

quantity approach. The approach whereby a volume comparison between two or more economies is made by comparing the volumes of a representative sample of comparable products. Volume comparisons are not usually made directly, but indirectly by dividing the expenditure ratios between economies by their corresponding price ratios.

Quaranta editing procedure. The iterative intereconomy validation procedure proposed by Vincenzo Quaranta that is used to edit the average survey prices reported by economies for a basic heading. For each basic heading covered by a price survey, the procedure screens the average survey prices for possible errors and evaluates the reliability of the price ratios they provide. It does this by comparing the average survey prices for the same product across economies (the average survey prices are expressed in the same currency unit for this purpose) and by analyzing the dispersion of the price ratios across economies and across products (the price ratios are standardized for this purpose). It is thus both an editing tool and an analytical tool. As an editing tool, it identifies among the average survey prices outliers that have to be returned to the participating economies for verification. As an analytical tool, it provides a range of variation coefficients—at the product, economy, and basic heading levels—that can be used to assess the reliability of completed price surveys and assist the planning of future price surveys.

Quaranta table. The intereconomy validation table generated by the Quaranta editing procedure.

real expenditure. An expenditure that has been converted to a common currency and valued at a uniform price level with PPPs. It reflects only volume differences between economies.

reference economy. The economy, or group of economies, for which the value of the PPP is set at 1.00 and the value of the price level index and of the volume index is set at 100.

reference PPP. The PPP used for a basic heading for which no prices are collected and no PPP is calculated. It is based on prices collected for other basic headings and serves as a proxy for the missing PPP.

reference quantity. The quantity to which the prices collected for a product must be rebased to ensure that they refer to the same quantity when being compared.

reference year. The calendar year to which the results of the comparison refer.

resident population. The average number of people present in the economic territory of an economy during the reference year.

seasonal product. A product for which both prices and the quantities sold vary significantly throughout the year. Typically, the pattern of variation is repeated from one year to the next. Seasonal products vary from economy to economy.

services. Outputs produced to order and that cannot be traded separately from their production. Ownership rights cannot be established over services, and by the time their production is completed they must have been provided to the consumers. An exception to this rule is a group of industries, generally classified as service industries, some of whose outputs have the characteristics of goods. These industries are those concerned with the provision, storage, communication, and dissemination of information, advice, and entertainment in the broadest sense of those terms. The products of these industries, where ownership rights can be established, may be classified as either goods or services, depending on the medium by which these outputs are supplied.

social transfers in kind. Individual goods and services provided as transfers in kind to individual households by government units (including social security funds) and nonprofit institutions serving households (NPISHs). The goods and services can be purchased on the market or produced as nonmarket output by government units or NPISHs.

structured product description (SPD). A tool designed to standardize the product specifications for different types of products so that all product specifications for a particular type of product are defined in the same way and specify the same parameters. Standardizing product specifications helps to improve their precision, making it easier for price collectors to determine whether a product in an outlet matches the product specified. Also, by identifying the parameters that need to be specified for different products, SPDs provide a framework within which economies can present their proposals for new products.

subsidies on production. Subsidies on goods and services produced as outputs by resident enterprises that become payable as a result of the production of these goods or services (that is, subsidies payable per unit of good or service produced) as well as subsidies that resident enterprises may receive as a consequence of engaging in production (e.g., subsidies to reduce pollution or to increase employment). The former are called subsidies on products; the latter are called other subsidies on production.

symmetric index. An index that treats the two economies being compared symmetrically by giving equal importance to the price and expenditure data of both economies. The price and expenditure data for both economies enter into the index number formula in a balanced or symmetric way.

taxes on production. Taxes on the goods and services produced as outputs by resident enterprises that become payable as a result of the production of these goods or services (that is, taxes payable per unit of good or service produced, such as excise duties and a nondeductible value added tax) as well as taxes that resident enterprises may pay as a consequence of engaging in production (such as, payroll taxes and taxes on motor vehicles). The former are called taxes on products; the latter are called other taxes on production.

transitivity. The property whereby the direct PPP between any two economies yields the same result as an indirect comparison via any other economy. For example, for economies A, B, and C, the ratio of the PPP between A and B and the PPP between C and B is equal to the PPP between A and C so that $PPP_{A/C} = PPP_{A/B}/PPP_{C/B}$.

user cost method. The method of estimating the value of imputed rentals for owner-occupiers by summing the relevant cost items: intermediate consumption (current maintenance and repairs, insurance), consumption of fixed capital, other taxes on production, and net operating surplus (nominal rate of return on the capital invested in the dwelling and land).

value added tax (VAT). A tax on products collected in stages by enterprises. This wide-ranging tax is usually designed to cover most or all goods and services. Producers are obliged to pay the government only the difference between the VAT on their sales and the VAT on their purchases for intermediate consumption or capital formation. The VAT is not usually levied on exports.

verification. The second step of validation, which entails investigating the possible errors detected during the editing of survey prices to establish whether they are actual errors and, if they are actual errors, correcting or suppressing them. In many cases, verification will require revisiting the outlets where the prices were collected to determine whether what was priced matches the product description and whether the correct price and quantity were recorded. Price observations found to be incorrect should be either eliminated or replaced by the correct observation.

volume index. A weighted average of the relative levels in the quantities of a specified set of goods and services between two economies. The quantities have to be homogeneous, and the relative levels for the different goods and services must be weighted by their economic importance as measured by their values in one or both economies.

volume measure. Volume measures are the real expenditures, the real expenditures per capita, and the volume indexes to which they give rise.

References

Commission of the European Communities, International Monetary Fund, Organisation for Economic Co-operation and Development, United Nations, and World Bank. 1993. *System of National Accounts 1993.* https://unstats.un.org/unsd/nationalaccount/sna1993.asp.

Deaton, Angus. 2013. "Calibrating Measurement Uncertainty in Purchasing Power Exchange Rates." Paper presented at seventh meeting of the ICP Technical Advisory Group, Washington, DC, September 17–18.

Deaton, A., and A. H. Heston. 2008. "Understanding PPPs and PPP-based National Accounts." NBER Working Paper No. 14499, National Bureau of Economic Research, Cambridge, MA.

Eurostat. 1996. *European System of Accounts 1995.* Luxembourg: Publications Office of the European Union.

Heston, Alan. 2013. "Government Services: Productivity Adjustments." In *Measuring the Real Size of the World Economy: The Framework, Methodology, and Results of the International Comparison Program (ICP).* Washington, DC: World Bank.

Inklaar, Robert, and Marcel P. Timmer. 2013. "Productivity Adjustment for Government Services PPPs: Alternatives and Proposal for ICP 2011." Groningen Growth and Development Centre, University of Groningen, September.

Kravis, Irving B., Alan Heston, and Robert Summers. 1978. *International Comparisons of Real Product and Purchasing Power.* Baltimore: Johns Hopkins University Press.

———. 1982. *World Product and Income: International Comparisons of Real Gross Product.* Baltimore: Johns Hopkins University Press.

Kravis, Irving B., Zoltan Kenessey, Alan Heston, and Robert Summers. 1975. *A System of International Comparisons of Gross Product and Purchasing Power.* Washington, DC: World Bank.

McCarthy, Paul, and Fred Vogel. 2014. "Understanding Changes in Methodology between the 2005 and 2011 International Comparison Programs." Paper presented at 10th meeting of the ICP Executive Board, Washington, DC, January 24.

OECD (Organisation for Economic Co-operation and Development) and Eurostat. 2012. *Eurostat-OECD Methodological Manual on Purchasing Power Parities.* Luxembourg: Publications Office of the European Union.

United Nations Statistics Division. 1998. *Central Product Classification, Version 1.0.* New York: United Nations.

———. 1999a. "Classification of Individual Consumption According to Purpose (COICOP)." *Classification of Expenditure According to Purpose.* New York: United Nations.

———. 1999b. "Classification of the Functions of Government (COFOG)." *Classification of Expenditure According to Purpose.* New York: United Nations.

World Bank. 2008. *Global Purchasing Power Parities and Real Expenditures: 2005 International Comparison Program.* http://siteresources.worldbank.org/ICPINT/Resources/icp-final.pdf.

———. 2013. *Measuring the Real Size of the World Economy: The Framework, Methodology, and Results of the International Comparison Program (ICP).* Washington, DC: World Bank.

———. Forthcoming. *Operational Guidelines and Procedures for Measuring the Real Size of the World Economy: 2011 International Comparison Program.* Washington, DC: World Bank.

World Health Organization. 2008. *International Classification of Diseases, 10th Revision.* http://www.who.int/classifications/icd/en/.